LANDMARK CASES IN PRIVACY LAW

This new addition to Hart's acclaimed Landmark Cases series is a diverse and engaging edited collection bringing together eminent commentators from the United Kingdom, the United States, Australia, Canada, and New Zealand, to analyse cases of enduring significance to privacy law.

The book tackles the conceptual nature of privacy in its various guises, from data protection, to misuse of private information, and intrusion into seclusion. It explores the practical issues arising from questions about the threshold of actionability, the function of remedies, and the nature of damages.

The cases selected are predominantly English but include cases from the United States (because of the formative influence of United States' privacy jurisprudence on the development of privacy law), Australia, Canada, the Court of Justice of the European Union, and the European Court of Human Rights. Each chapter considers the reception and application (and, in some instances, rejection) outside of the jurisdiction where the case was decided.

Landmark Cases in Privacy Law

Edited by
Paul Wragg
and
Peter Coe

•HART•
OXFORD • LONDON • NEW YORK • NEW DELHI • SYDNEY

HART PUBLISHING

Bloomsbury Publishing Plc

Kemp House, Chawley Park, Cumnor Hill, Oxford, OX2 9PH, UK

1385 Broadway, New York, NY 10018, USA

29 Earlsfort Terrace, Dublin 2, Ireland

HART PUBLISHING, the Hart/Stag logo, BLOOMSBURY and the Diana logo are trademarks of Bloomsbury Publishing Plc

First published in Great Britain 2023

A catalogue record for this book is available from the British Library.

A catalogue record for this book is available from the Library of Congress.

Library of Congress Control Number: 2022948634

ISBN: HB: 978-1-50994-076-9
ePDF: 978-1-50994-078-3
ePub: 978-1-50994-077-6

Typeset by Compuscript Ltd, Shannon

Preface

THE 'PRIVACY LAW' canon is not a simple one. In fact, whether a 'law of privacy' even exists is, depending on the jurisdiction, a contentious topic. In England and Wales for instance, the House of Lords was clear in *Wainwright v Home Office*[1] that the then recently enacted Human Rights Act 1998 demanded no general 'blockbuster' tortious right to privacy to be created through the common law. Whereas this did not prevent the later creation, in *Campbell v MGN Ltd*, of the tortious cause of action misuse of private information (from the equitable cause of action breach of confidence), the question remains as to whether Article 8 is fully realised in England and Wales. This common law tort and the statutory protections afforded by the data protection regime, are not the totality of domestic privacy rights for we can see other context-specific rights in, say, property law and constitutional law. Moreover, we see elements of, and interesting questions about the scope of, a privacy right in cases decided long before the introduction of the Human Rights Act 1998.

Undoubtedly, these English and Welsh developments have been influenced by not only the Strasbourg jurisprudence (decisions of the European Court of Human Rights) but also the common law of the United States, Australia, Canada, New Zealand, and the Court of Justice of the European Union. Indeed, when we read across these different legal systems, we find a multi-jurisdictional stable of laws that protect individual privacy in different ways, and which, over time, have resulted in the privacy jurisprudence within these jurisdictions becoming, if not quite inter-dependent, then certainly dialectical; as is often the case, when an apex court from one of these jurisdictions hands down a judgment relating to its domestic privacy laws, it tends to influence how one or more of the other jurisdictions deals with similar issues.

What this means is that in the history of privacy 'law', many cases could claim, rightly, to be of 'landmark' status. Similarly, the landmark status of others may be, of itself, a deeply contested proposition. As editors of this collection, then, it has been our privilege and our lot to make some difficult choices in selecting the cases that appear in this volume. We know that our selections will not please everyone. Nevertheless, we can say with the utmost confidence that we have been fortunate in persuading some of the leading experts from around the world to contribute to this book. As a result, this book provides an exceptional level of expert insight from commentators based in the United Kingdom,

[1] [2003] UKHL 53.

the United States, Australia, Canada, and New Zealand which promises to be of enduring significance to privacy law scholarship. Specifically, it not only tackles the conceptual nature of privacy in its various forms, from misuse of private information, and intrusion into seclusion, to data protection, but it also explores the practical issues that arise from questions about evolving technology and its use, the threshold of actionability, the function of remedies and the nature of damages, with each chapter considering the reception and application (and, in some instances, rejection) outside of the jurisdiction where the case was decided.

As a consequence, this collection will, we hope, take you on a journey concerning privacy. It considers how the parameters of privacy have, throughout history, been constantly tested by the evolution of technology (for example, from the advent of the camera to the internet, and the ubiquitous use of smartphones and social media), and how the advancement of technology has led to the exploitation of individuals, and their expectation of privacy, for commercial gain. Thus, it tells the tale of the protection that privacy has, and in some cases, has not, been afforded by the law.

Professor Paul Wragg and Dr Peter Coe
September 2022
Leeds and Birmingham

Table of Contents

Preface .... *v*
List of Contributors .... *ix*
Table of Cases .... *xi*
Table of Legislation .... *xxvii*

1. *Pollard v Photographic Company* (1888) *1*
   Megan Richardson

2. *Roberson v Rochester Folding Box* (1900) *19*
   Amy Gajda

3. *Pavesich v New England Insurance Co* (1905) *39*
   Rebecca Moosavian

4. *Whalen v Roe* (1977) *65*
   Ronald J Krotoszynski, Jr.

5. *Kaye v Robertson* (1990) *85*
   Jacob Rowbottom

6. *Australian Broadcasting Corporation v Lenah Game Meats Pty Ltd* (2001) *107*
   David Rolph

7. *A v B & C* (2002) *137*
   N A Moreham

8. *Campbell v Mirror Group Newspapers* (2004) *159*
   Gavin Phillipson

9. *Von Hannover v Germany* (2004) *187*
   Kirsty Hughes

10. *Douglas v Hello! Ltd* (2005) *207*
    Tanya Aplin and Judith Skillen

11. *Jones v Tsige* (2012) *237*
    David Mangan

12. *Google Spain, Google Inc. v Agencia Española de Protección de Datos* (2014) *261*
    David Erdos

13. *Gulati v Mirror Group Newspapers* (2015) 281
John Hartshorne

14. *PJS v News Group Newspapers Ltd* (2016) 301
Thomas DC Bennett

Index 327

List of Contributors

Tanya Aplin is Professor of Intellectual Property Law at The Dickson Poon School of Law, King's College London.

Thomas Bennett is a Senior Lecturer in Law at City Law School, City, University of London.

Peter Coe is an Associate Professor in Law at Birmingham Law School, University of Birmingham, a Visiting Senior Research Fellow at the School of Law, University of Reading, and an Associate Research Fellow at the Institute of Advanced Legal Studies and the Information Law and Policy Centre, University of London.

David Erdos is Professor in Law and the Open Society, Co-Director of the Centre for Intellectual Property and Information Law, and WYNG Fellow in Law at Trinity Hall, University of Cambridge.

Amy Gajda is the Class of 1937 Professor of Law at Tulane University Law School.

John Hartshorne is an Associate Professor at Leicester Law School, University of Leicester.

Kirsty Hughes is a University Senior Lecturer in Public Law, and Fellow of Clare College, University of Cambridge.

Ronald Krotoszynski is the John S. Stone Professor of Law, and Director of Faculty Research, at Alabama Law, University of Alabama.

David Mangan is an Assistant Professor in the Department of Law, Maynooth University, and is an Adjunct Professor at Osgoode Hall Law School, York University.

Rebecca Moosavian is an Associate Professor at the School of Law, University of Leeds.

N A Moreham is Professor of Law in the Faculty of Law, Victoria University of Wellington.

Gavin Phillipson is Professor of Law at the University of Bristol Law School, University of Bristol.

Megan Richardson is Professor of Law at the Melbourne Law School, The University of Melbourne, and a Chief Investigator in the ARC Centre for Excellence for Automated Decision-Making and Society.

David Rolph is a Professor of Law at the University of Sydney Law School, University of Sydney, and a Fellow of the Australian Academy of Law.

Jacob Rowbottom is a Fellow of University College, Oxford, and Professor of Law in the Faculty of Law, University of Oxford.

Judith Skillen is an Assistant Professor at the School of Law, University of Nottingham.

Paul Wragg is Professor of Media Law at the School of Law, University of Leeds.

Table of Cases

A v B & C v MGN Ltd (aka Flitcroft v MGN Ltd) [2002] EWCA Civ 337, [2003] QB 195, [2002] 3 WLR 542, [2002] 2 All ER 545 ... 128, 131, 137–43, 145, 147, 148–56, 169, 177–8, 179, 211

AAA v Associated Newspapers Ltd [2012] EWHC 2103 (QB), [2013] EMLR 2, [2012] HRLR 31 ... 141, 142, 153, 217–8, 219, 226, 283, 284, 288, 292, 296, 312

AAA v Associated Newspapers Ltd [2013] EWCA Civ 554, [2013] WLR (D) 189, [2013] 5 WLUK 507 ... 218, 315

ABC and others v Telegraph Media Group Ltd [2018] EWCA Civ 2329, [2019] 2 All ER 684, [2019] EMLR 5 ... 150

Abernethy v Hutchinson (1824-25) 1 H & Tw 28, 47 ER 1313 ... 4, 10

Al-Ghamdi v Alberta 2017 ABQB 684, aff'd 2020 ABCA 81 ... 253

Ali v Channel 5 Broadcasting Ltd [2018] EWHC 298 (Ch), [2018] EMLR 17 ... 226–7, 292

Ali and Aslam v Channel 5 Broadcasting Ltd [2019] EWCA Civ 677, [2019] 4 WLUK 255 ... 150, 292

Ambrosiadou v Coward [2010] EWHC 1794 (QB), [2010] 2 FLR 1775, [2010] Fam Law 1176 ... 306, 309, 312

AMC and KLJ v News Group Newspapers Ltd [2015] EWHC 2361 (QB), [2015] 8 WLUK 48 ... 142, 151, 154

American Cyanamid v Ethicon Ltd [1975] AC 396, [1975] 2 WLR 316, [1975] 1 All ER 504, HL ... 232–3

Andrew v Television New Zealand Ltd [2009] 1 NZLR 220, HC ... 127

Angela Roddy (a minor), Re [2003] EWHC 2927 (Fam), [2004] 1 FCR 481, [2004] EMLR 127 ... 146

AP v Secretary of State for the Home Department [2010] UKSC 24, [2011] 2 AC 1, [2010] 3 WLR 51 ... 307, 308, 309

Applause Store Productions Ltd v Raphael [2008] EWHC 1781 (QB), [2008] Info TLR 318 ... 224

Archer (Lady) v Williams [2003] EWHC 1670 (QB), [2003] EMLR 869 (38), [2003] FSR 869 ... 224

Argyll (Duchess) v Argyll (Duke) [1967] Ch 302, [1965] 2 WLR 790, [1965] 1 All ER 611, ChD ... 15, 120, 140

Ari v Insurance Corporation of British Columbia 2013 BCSC 1308 ... 253

Armonienė v Lithuania (36919/02) (2009) 48 EHRR 53, [2009] EMLR 7, 27 BHRC 389, ECtHR.......288
Armory v Delamirie (1722) 1 Strange 505, 93 ER 664, Ct of KB.......287
ASG v GSA [2009] EWCA Civ 1574, [2009] 8 WLUK 221.......143, 144
Ashley v Chief Constable of Sussex [2008] UKHL 25, [2008] AC 962, [2008] 2 WLR 975.......225
Associated Newspapers Ltd v HRH Prince of Wales [2006] EWCA Civ 1776, [2008] Ch 57, [2007] 3 WLR 222.......149
Athans v Canadian Adventure Camps Ltd (1977), 17 O.R. (2d) 425 (H.C.J.).......259
Atkinson v John E Doherty & Co (1899) 121 Mich 372, 80 NW 285.......41, 42, 48
Attorney-General v Guardian Newspapers Ltd (No 2), ('Spycatcher' case) [1990] 1 AC 109, [1988] 3 WLR 776, [1988] 3 All ER 545, HL.......15–17, 99–100, 124, 168, 184, 211, 282
Aubry v Éditions Vice-Versa Inc [1998] 1 SCR 591, 157 DLR (4th) 577.......242
Australian Broadcasting Corporation v Lenah Game Meats Pty Ltd [2001] HCA 63, (2001) 208 CLR 199, 185 ALR 1, HCA.......16, 17, 107–8, 110–17, 118, 119, 120, 121, 122, 123, 124, 125, 126, 127, 128, 131, 133, 136, 163, 171
Australian Consolidated Press Ltd v Ettingshausen (unreported) 13 October 1993, CA(NSW).......108, 133
Australian Football League v The Age Co Ltd [2006] VSC 308, (2006) 15 VR 419.......124
Axel Springer v Germany (39954/08) [2012] ECHR 227, (2012) 55 EHRR 6, ECtHR.......150, 188, 200
Baldwin v Morningstar 2019 ONSC 1276.......252
Batistatos v Roads and Traffic Authority of New South Wales [2006] HCA 27, (2006) 226 CLR 256.......124
Bauer Media Pty Ltd v Wilson (No 2) [2018] VSCA 154, (2018) 56 VR 674.......132
Behar and Gutman v Bulgaria (App no 29335/13), [2021] ECHR 134, 16 February 2021.......196, 204
Beloff (Nora) v Pressdram Ltd [1973] 1 All ER 241, [1973] FSR 33, [1973] RPC 765, ChD.......124
Bennett v Lenovo 2017 ONSC 1082.......251
Beoku-Betts v Secretary of State for the Home Department [2008] UKHL 39, [2009] AC 115, [2008] 3 WLR 166.......309–10
BH v Lord Advocate; sub nom H v Lord Advocate [2012] UKSC 24, 2012 SC (UKSC) 308, [2012] 3 WLR 151.......312

Bingo Enterprises Ltd v Plaxton (1986) 26 DLR (4th) 604 (Man. C.A.) 248
Bivens v Six Unknown Named Agents of the Federal Bureau of Narcotics, 403 U.S. 388 (1971) 67
Bloch v Ribar, 156 F. 3d 673 (6th Cir. 1998) 77
Bloomberg LP v ZXC [2022] UKSC 5, [2022] AC 1158, [2022] 2 WLR 424 .... 149, 150, 160, 293
Bodil Lindqvist, Criminal Proceedings against C-101/01, EU:C:2003:596, [2003] ECR I-12971, [2004] QB 1014, CJEU 266
Bogomolova v Russia (App no 13812/09) [2017] ECHR 571, 20 June 2017, ECtHR 202
Boyd v United States, 116 U.S. 616 (1886) 20
Bradley v Wingnut Films [1993] 1 NZLR 415 127
Brake v Guy [2021] EWHC 671 (Ch), [2021] 3 WLUK 423 ....128, 226
Broutzas v Rouge Valley Health System 2018 ONSC 6315 252
Brown, ex parte 7 Mo. App. 484 (Mo. Ct. App. 1879) 20, 24
Browne of Madingley (Lord) v Associated Newspapers Ltd [2007] EWCA Civ 295, [2008] QB 103, [2007] 3 WLR 289 ....131, 149, 153
Bull v Desporte [2019] EWHC 1650 (QB), [2019] 6 WLUK 541 ....292, 309
Burrell v Clifford [2016] EWHC 578 (Ch), [2016] 3 WLUK 860 291
C v Holland [2012] NZHC 2155, [2012] 3 NZLR 672 ....123, 260, 299
Campbell v MGN Ltd [2002] EWCA Civ 1373, [2003] QB 633, [2003] 2 WLR 80 .... 128, 152, 161, 162, 163–9, 178, 179, 284
Campbell v MGN Ltd [2002] EWHC 499 (QB), [2002] EMLR 617 (30), [2002] HRLR 28 .... 128, 224, 283, 284
Campbell v Mirror Group Newspapers Ltd [2004] UKHL 22, [2004] 2 AC 457, [2004] 2 WLR 1232 .... v, 16, 17, 99, 100, 118, 121, 126, 127, 128, 131, 139, 141, 149, 150, 153, 159–85, 197, 209, 210–11, 212, 215, 216, 231, 238, 284, 287, 294, 297, 299, 304, 318, 319
Canada v John Doe 2016 FCA 191, 486 NR 223 (FCA) 238, 251, 256
Candelora v Fraser 2020 NSSC 177, aff'd 2021 NSCA 49 258
Capital District Health Authority v Murray 2017 NSCA 28 251
CC v AB [2006] EWHC 3083 (QB), [2007] 2 FLR 301, [2007] EMLR 312 145
CDE v Mirror Group Newspapers Ltd [2010] EWHC 3308 (QB), [2011] 1 FLR 1524, [2011] Fam Law 360 .... 306, 307, 308, 309, 310, 311, 312, 316
Chan v Sellwood [2009] NSWSC 1335 ....119, 136
Chandler v Thompson (1811) 3 Camp 80, (1811) 170 ER 1312 109
Chandra v CBC 2015 ONSC 5303 ....245, 249, 259
Chapman v Western Union Telegraph Co (1891) 88 Ga. 763 42

Chasensky v Walker, 740 F. 3d 1088 (7th Cir, 2014) 77
Chester v Afshar [2004] UKHL 41, [2005] 1 AC 134, [2004] 3 WLR 927.......225
Church of Scientology Inc v Woodward [1982] HCA 78, (1982) 154 CLR 25, 43 ALR 587...136
Coco v AN Clark (Engineers) Ltd [1969] RPC 41, [1968] FSR 415, ChD 15, 16, 168, 169, 302
Cooper v Turrell [2011] EWHC 3269 (QB), [2011] 12 WLUK 330.........153, 284
Corliss v E W Walker Co (1894) 64 F. 280... 48, 51
Corliss v E.W.Walker Co., 57 F. 434 (C.C.D. Mass. 1893)..............................24
Cornelius v De Taranto [2001] EMLR 12, [2000] MHLR 145, QBD 121, 223, 224, 282–3
Corrs Pavey Whiting & Byrne v Collector of Customs (Vic) [1987] FCA 266, (1987) 14 FCR 434..124
Couderc and Hachette Filipacchi Associés v France (App no 40454/07) [2016] EMLR 19, 40 BHRC 436, ECtHR (Grand Chamber) 146–7, 150, 196, 202
Coulson (William) and Sons v James Coulson & Co (1887) 3 TLR 846, CA 94
Cox Broadcasting Corporation v Cohn 420 U.S. 469 (1975) 61
Cream Holdings Ltd v Banerjee [2004] UKHL 44, [2005] 1 AC 253, [2004] 3 WLR 918 233–4
Creation Records Ltd v News Group Newspapers Ltd [1997] EMLR 444, (1997) 16 Tr LR 544, (1997) 20(7) IPD 20070, ChD 15, 16, 170
Cruise (Tom) and Nicole Kidman v Southdown Press Pty Ltd (1993) 26 IPR 125, FCA.. 108
Cruzan v Director, Mo.Dept.of Health, 497 U.S. 261 (1990) 67
CTB v News Group Newspapers Ltd [2011] EWHC 1232 (QB), [2011] 5 WLUK 383 131
CTB v News Group Newspapers Ltd (No 3) [2011] EWHC 1334 (QB), [2011] 5 WLUK 620...141
D v L [2003] EWCA Civ 1169, [2004] EMLR 1.......................................179
Del Giudice v Thompson 2021 ONSC 5379 255
Delfi AS v Estonia (64669/09), [2015] EMLR 26, (2016) 62 EHRR 6, 39 BHRC 151, ECtHR (Grand Chamber) 279
Demme v Healthcare Insurance Reciprocal of Canada, 2022 ONCA 503.....249
Denisov v Ukraine (App no 76639/11) [2018] ECHR 1061, 25 September 2018 196
Digital Rights Ireland Ltd v Minister for Communications, Marine, and Natural Resources, joined Cases C-293/12 and C-594/12 EU:C:2014:238, [2015] QB 127, [2014] 3 CMLR 44, CJEU.........69
Dillard v O'Kelley, 961 F. 3d 1048 (8th Cir. 2020)...77
Dobbs v Jackson Women's Health Organization 142 S Ct 2228, 597 US ____ (2022) 242

Dobson v Thames Water Utilities Ltd [2009] EWCA Civ 28, [2009] 3 All ER 319, [2009] HRLR 19 315
Doe v Australian Broadcasting Corporation [2007] VCC 281 .... 118–9, 134
Doe v N.D., 2016 ONSC 4920 256
Dorset Yacht Club v Home Office [1970] AC 1004, [1970] 2 WLR 1140, [1970] 2 All ER 294, HL 247
Doucette v Nova Scotia 2016 NSSC 25 251
Douez v Facebook, Inc 2017 SCC 33, [2017] 1 SCR 751 .... 243, 244, 259
Douez v Facebook 2018 BCCA 186 259
Douez v Facebook Inc 2019 BCSC 715 .... 245, 259
Douez v Facebook 2022 BCSC 914 .... 244, 245
Douglas v Hello! Ltd (No 1) [2000] EWCA Civ 353, [2001] QB 967, [2001] 2 WLR 992, [2001] 2 All ER 289, CA 16, 17, 98, 99, 131, 137, 163, 170, 208, 210, 219, 222, 231, 232, 233
Douglas v Hello! Ltd [2003] EWHC 786 (Ch), [2003] 3 All ER 996, [2003] 3 EMLR 31 .... 128, 170, 208, 209, 210, 227
Douglas v Hello! ('Douglas quantum') [2003] EWHC 2629 (Ch), [2004] EMLR 2 .... 223, 228
Douglas v Hello! Ltd (No 3) [2005] EWCA Civ 595, [2006] QB 125, [2005] EMLR 609 .... 16, 17, 100, 121, 170, 207–223, 225, 227, 228–9, 230, 231, 233, 234–5, 238
Dowd v Skip the Dishes Restaurant Services Inc 2019 MBQB 63, aff'd (on other grounds) 2020 MBQB 155 244
Driver v Radio New Zealand Ltd [2019] NZHC 3275 127
Duchess of Sussex v Associated Newspapers Ltd [2021] EWHC 273 (Ch), [2021] 4 WLR 35, [2021] 3 All ER 1163 .... 131, 207, 214, 220
Duchess of Sussex v Associated Newspapers Ltd [2021] EWCA Civ 1810, [2022] 4 WLR 81, [2022] 3 All ER 539 .... 207, 214, 220
Dudgeon v United Kingdom (Series A no 45) (1982) 4 EHRR 149, ECtHR 141
Dupate v Latvia (App no 18068/11) (2021) 72 EHRR 34, ECtHR 188, 197, 198, 202
Dyne Holdings Ltd v Royal Insurance Co.of Canada (1996) 135 DLR (4th) 142 (P.E.I.C.A.), leave to appeal to the Supreme Court of Canada refused, [1996] SCCA No 344 248
Earl v Nationwide News Pty Ltd [2013] NSWSC 839 123
EF v AB [2015] IRLR 619, EAT 309, 316
Emcorp Pty Ltd v Australian Broadcasting Corporation [1988] 2 Qd R 169 111
ES v Shillington 2021 ABQB 739 .... 256, 257

ETK v News Group Newspapers Ltd. See K v News Group Newspapers Ltd
Euteneier v Lee (2005) 77 OR (3d) 61 (CA), leave to appeal to Sup Ct of Canada refused, [2005] SCCA No 516 239
Faesenkloet v Jenkin [2014] NZHC 1637 127
Facilities Subsector Bargaining Assn.v B.C.N.U. 2009 BCSC 1562 253
Farah Constructions Pty Ltd v Say-Dee Pty Ltd [2007] HCA 22, (2007) 230 CLR 89, HCA 134
FDIC v Meyer, 510 U.S. 471 (1994) 67
Ferdinand v MGN Ltd [2011] EWHC 2454 (QB), [2011] 9 WLUK 621 .... 131, 154, 155
Ferguson v City of Charleston, 532 U.S 67 (2001) 77
Flitcroft v MGN Ltd. See A v B & C
Foster v Svenson (2013) 41 Media Law Report 2564 (N.Y. Sup. Ct. 2013) 34–6
Foster v Svenson, 7 N.Y.S.3d 96 (N.Y. App. Div. 2015) 35–7
Francome v Mirror Group Newspapers Ltd [1984] 1 WLR 892, [1984] 2 All ER 408, (1984) 81 LSG 2225, CA 15, 16, 100
Fraser v Evans [1969] 1 QB 349, [1968] 3 WLR 1172, [1969] 1 All ER 8, CA 124
Fressoz v France (29183/95) (2001) 31 EHRR 2, 5 BHRC 654, ECtHR 163, 178
Friedl v Austria (15225/89) 19 May 1994, ECommHR 195, 197
GC v Commission Nationale de l'Informatique et des Libertés (C-136/17), EU:C:2019:773, [2020] 1 WLR 1949, [2020] 1 CMLR 26 (Grand Chamber), CJEU 262, 270, 272, 273, 274
Gee v Burger [2009] NSWSC 149 119
Gee v Pritchard (1818) 2 Swanst 402, 36 ER 670, Ct of Chancery 4
Giller v Procopets [2008] VSCA 236, (2008) 24 VR 1 .... 120–21, 122, 123
Giller v Procopets [2004] VSC 113 120
Glencore International AG v Commissioner of Taxation (Cth) [2019] HCA 26, (2019) 265 CLR 646 124–5
Goldman v United States 316 U.S. 129 (1942) 61
Goodwin v NGN Ltd and VBN [2011] EWHC 1437 (QB), [2011] EMLR 27, [2011] HRLR 31 153–4
Google Inc v Vidal-Hall [2015] EWCA Civ 311, [2016] QB 1003, [2015] 3 WLR 409 .... 124, 213, 214, 223, 298, 304, 305, 318, 319
Google LLC v Commission Nationale de l'Informatique et des Libertés, Case C-507/17, EU:C:2019:772, [2020] 1 WLR 1993, [2020] 1 CMLR 24 (Grand Chamber), CJEU 82, 262, 278
Google Spain, Google Inc.v Agencia Española de Protección de Datos (AEPD), Mario Costeja González, C-131/12, EU:C:2013:424, Opinion of AG Jääkinen 262–6, 267, 277

Google Spain, Google Inc v Agencia Española de Protección de Datos (AEPD), Mario Costeja González, C-131/12, EU:C:2014:317, [2014] QB 1022, [2014] 3 WLR 659 .... 261–6, 268, 270, 271–80
Gould Estate v Stoddart Publishing Co (1996), 30 O.R. (3d) 520 (Gen.Div.), aff'd (1998), 39 O.R. (3d) 545 (C.A.), leave to appeal to the SCC refused [1998] SCCA 373 259
Grant v Winnipeg Regional Health Authority 2015 MBCA 44, (2015) 319 Man.R.(2d) 67 (CA) 252
Griswold v Connecticut 381 U.S. 479, 85 S. Ct. 1678 (1965) 61, 66, 71, 78, 242
Grosse v Purvis [2003] QDC 151, (2003) Aust Torts Reports ¶81–706 117–8
GS v News Ltd (1998) Aust Torts Reports ¶81–466, 64, 913–64, 15 108
Guardian News and Media Ltd, Re [2010] UKSC 1, [2010] 2 AC 697, [2010] 2 WLR 325 .... 307, 309
Gulati v MGN Ltd [2013] EWHC 3392 (Ch), [2013] 11 WLUK 89 285
Gulati v MGN Ltd [2015] EWHC 1482 (Ch), [2016] FSR 12 ....156, 225, 226, 227, 229, 230, 240, 281–2, 284–300
Gulati v MGN Ltd [2015] EWCA Civ 1291, [2017] QB 149, [2016] 2 WLR 1217; permission to appeal refused UKSC 2016/0016 (23 March 2016) 225, 226, 281, 285, 290–91, 295–6, 298
H v Lord Advocate. See BH v Lord Advocate
H (H) v Deputy Prosecutor of the Italian Republic (Genoa) [2012] UKSC 25, [2013] 1 AC 338, [2012] 3 WLR 90 312
Hajovsky v Slovakia (App no 7796/16) [2021] ECHR 591, 1 July 2021 .... 198, 202, 203
Halford v United Kingdom (20605/92) (1997) 24 EHRR 523, 3 BHRC 31, ECtHR 288
Harris v Digital Pulse Pty Ltd [2003] NSWCA 10, (2003) 56 NSWLR 298 121
Hegglin v Persons Unknown and Google [2014] EWHC 2808 (QB), [2014] 7 WLUK 1187 277
Hellewell v Chief Constable of Derbyshire [1995] 1 WLR 804, [1995] 4 All ER 473, (1995) 139 SJLB 49, QBD 16, 17, 98, 113
Henderson v Walker [2019] NZHC 2184 127
Henry v Cherry & Webb (1909) 30 R.I. 13 .... 41, 55, 61
Hill v Church of Scientology of Toronto [1995] 2 SCR 1130, 126 DLR (4th) 129 .... 242, 243
Holloway v State of Tasmania [2005] TASSC 90, (2005) 15 Tas R 127 136
Hopkins v Kay 2015 ONCA 112 .... 245, 249
Hosking v Runting [2005] 1 NZLR 1 .... 123, 126, 127

HRH Prince of Wales v Associated Newspapers Ltd [2006] EWCA Civ 1776, [2008] Ch 57, [2007] 3 WLR 222 131
Hung v Gardiner 2003 BCCA 257 253
Hunter v Southam Inc [1984] 2 SCR 145, 11 DLR (4th) 641 242
Hutchens v City of Holdfast Bay [2007] SASC 238, (2007) 98 SASR 412 136
Hutcheson v News Group Newspapers Ltd [2011] EWCA Civ 808, [2012] EMLR 2, [2011] UKHRR 1329 .... 141, 143, 147, 150, 151
Hutcheson (formerly 'KGM') v News Group Newspapers Ltd MGN Ltd and Associated Newspapers Ltd [2010] EWHC 3145 (QB), [2010] 12 WLUK 35 .... 142, 143
Hyndman v Walker [2019] NZHC 2188 127
Hyndman v Walker [2021] NZCA 25 127
Hynes v Western Regional Integrated Health Authority 2014 NLTD(G) 13 251
Imerman v Tchenguiz. See Tchenguiz v Imerman
Initial Services Ltd v Putterill [1968] 1 QB 396, [1967] 3 WLR 1032, [1967] 3 All ER 145, CA 124
IVT v Romania (App no 35582/15) 1 March 2022, ECtHR 202, 203
Jane Doe 464533 v N.D. 2016 ONSC 541 .... 256, 257
Jane Doe 464533 v N.D., 2017 ONSC 127 256
Jane Doe 72511 v M.(N.) 2018 ONSC 6607 .... 256, 257, 258
Jersild v Denmark (A/298) (1994) 19 EHRR 1, ECtHR 178, 179
John v Associated Newspapers Ltd [2006] EWHC 1611 (QB), [2006] EMLR 27 216
John Fairfax Publications Pty Ltd v Hitchcock [2007] NSWCA 364, (2007) 70 NSWLR 484 .... 119, 133, 136
Johnson v Cline 2017 ONSC 3916, aff'd sub nom Cline v Drummond 2019 ONCA 188, leave to appeal to the Supreme Court of Canada refused (25 July 2019) 248
Jones v Tsige 2011 ONSC 1475 .... 239, 240
Jones v Tsige 2012 ONCA 32, (2012) 108 OR (3d) 241, Ontario CA 123, 237–241, 243–55, 257–60, 299
JQL v NTP [2020] EWHC 1349 (QB), [2020] 5 WLUK 408 291
JR38 (application for Judicial Review), Re [2015] UKSC 42, [2016] AC 1131, [2015] 3 WLR 155 .... 139, 217
K v News Group Newspapers Ltd [2011] EWCA Civ 439, [2011] 1 WLR 1827, [2011] EMLR 22 .... 141, 149, 151, 306, 309, 310, 311, 312, 314, 316, 322
Kalaba v Commonwealth of Australia [2004] FCA 763 199
Kalaba v Commonwealth of Australia [2004] FCAFC 326 119
Kaye v Robertson & Sport Newspapers Ltd [1991] FSR 62, CA 15, 16, 85–8, 90, 92–105, 169

Khorasandjian v Bush [1993] QB 727, [1993] 3 WLR 476, [1993] 3 All ER 669, CA 98
Khuja v Times Newspapers Ltd [2017] UKSC 49, [2019] AC 161, [2017] 3 WLR 351 128
Kitechnology BV v Unicor GmbH Plastmaschinen [1995] FSR 765, [1994] IL Pr 568, CA 211, 213
Kostov v Nationwide News Pty Ltd (No 1) [2018] NSWSC 1822 120
Krouse v Chrysler Canada Ltd (1970), 1 O.R. (2d) 225, 40 DLR (3d) 15, ON CA 259
Lamb v Evans (1893) 1 Ch 218 14
Larizza v Royal Bank of Canada 2017 ONSC 6140, aff'd 2018 ONCA 632 252
Lavigne v Canada (Office of the Commissioner of Official Languages) 2002 SCC 53, [2002] 2 SCR 773 244
Lawrence v Texas, 539 U.S. 558 (2003) 71
Lee v City of Columbus, Ohio, 636 F. 3d 245 (6th Cir. 2011) 77
Leiser v Moore, 903 F. 3d 1137 (10th Cir. 2018) 77
Lenah Game Meats Pty Ltd v Australian Broadcasting Corporation (1999) 9 Tas R 355 111–12
Leung v Shanks 2013 ONSC 4943 251
Li Yau-wai v Genesis Films Ltd [1987] HKLR 711 168
Lillo-Stenberg v Norway (13258/09), [2014] ECHR 59 201
Lincoln Hunt Australia Pty Ltd v Willesee (1986) 4 NSWLR 457 111
Lion Laboratories Ltd v Evans [1985] QB 526, [1984] 3 WLR 539, [1984] 2 All ER 417, CA 124
Lloyd v Google LLC [2018] EWHC 2599 (QB), [2019] 1 WLR 1265, [2019] EMLR 4 ....228, 294, 296
Lloyd v Google LLC [2019] EWCA Civ 1599, [2020] QB 747, [2020] 2 WLR 484 294
Lloyd v Google LLC [2021] UKSC 50, [2022] AC 1217, [2021] 3 WLR 1268 ....229, 294, 297
Lord Ashburton v Pape [1913] 2 Ch 469, CA 14
Lumba v Secretary of State for the Home Department [2011] UKSC 12, [2012] 1 AC 245, [2011] 2 WLR 671 ....226, 281, 283, 288, 289, 295
Mackenzie v Soden Mineral Springs Co., 27 Abb. N. Cas. 402, 408 (N.Y. Sup. Ct. 1891) 24–5, 28, 30
Mafart v Television New Zealand Ltd [2006] 3 NZLR 534 127
Mahmood v Galloway [2006] EWHC 1286 (QB), [2006] EMLR 26 216
Malone v Metropolitan Police Commissioner (No 2) [1979] Ch 344, [1979] 2 WLR 700, [1979] 2 All ER 620, ChD 15
Malone v United Kingdom (A/82), (8691/79) (1984) 7 EHRR 14, ECtHR 15
Manola v Stevens (1890) (unreported) 48, 56

Marathon Asset Management LLP v Seddon [2017] EWHC 300 (Comm), [2017] FSR 36, [2017] ICR 791, [2017] 2 CLC 182 228
Marbury v Madison, 5 U.S. (1 Cranch) 137 (1803).................................79–80
Marks v Jaffa 6 Misc 290 (1893) 48
Mathews v Eldridge, 424 U.S. 319 (1976)...81
Maynes v Casey [2011] NSWCA 156 119
McIntosh v Legal Aid Ontario 2014 ONSC 6136 250
McKennitt v Ash [2005] EWHC 3003 (QB), [2006] EMLR 10......................224
McKennitt v Ash [2006] EWCA Civ 1714, [2008] QB 73, [2007] 3 WLR 194 ....131, 143, 151, 152, 171, 212, 297
McLaren v News Group Newspapers Ltd [2012] EWHC 2466 (QB), [2012] EMLR 33, (2012) 162 NLJ 1156..154
Merrifield v Canada (Attorney General) 2019 ONCA 205, leave to appeal to Sup Ct of Canada refused (19 September 2019)......................247
Merryweather v Moore (1892) 2 Ch 518 14
Messenger v Jahr Printing and Publishing, 727 N.E.2d 549 (N.Y. 2000) 34
Mills v News Group Newspapers [2001] EMLR 41, ChD 85
Missoulian v Bd. of Regents, 207 Mont. 513, 675 P. 2d 962 (1984) 65
Mohl v University of British Columbia 2009 BCCA 249, leave to appeal to Sup Ct of Canada refused [2009] SCCA No 340......................253
Moohan v Lord Advocate (Advocate General for Scotland intervening) [2014] UKSC 67, [2015] AC 901, [2015] 2 WLR 141 159
Moore-McQuillan v Work Cover Corporation [2005] SASC 13 136
Moorgate Tobacco Co Ltd v Philip Morris Ltd [1984] HCA 85, (1984) 154 CLR 414..16
Morison v Moat (1851) 9 Hare 241, 68 ER 492 .... 9, 10, 12, 14
Morris-Garner v One Step (Support) Ltd [2018] UKSC 20, [2019] AC 649, [2018] 2 WLR 1353 ....227, 228
Mosley v News Group Newspapers Ltd [2008] EWHC 1777 (QB), [2008] EMLR 20.. 141, 156, 212, 225, 226, 281, 282, 283, 284, 288, 291, 295, 298, 318
Mosley v United Kingdom (App no 48009/08), [2012] EMLR 1, [2012] 1 FCR 99, ECtHR 152, 225
Motherwell v Motherwell (1976), 73 DLR (3d) 62, Alta. S.C. (A.D.) 247–8
Munden v Harris (1911) 153 Mo. App. 652 .... 41, 55
Murray v Big Pictures (UK) Ltd. See Murray v Express Newspapers plc
Murray v Capital District Health Authority 2015 NSSC 61, aff'd 2017 NSCA 28 242
Murray v Express Newspapers plc; sub nom Murray v Big Pictures (UK) Ltd [2008] EWCA Civ 446, [2009] Ch 481, [2008] 3 WLR 1360 .... 101, 139, 141, 160, 171, 197, 217, 218, 312, 315, 318, 325

Murray v Express Newspapers Ltd [2007] EWHC 1908 (Ch), [2007] EMLR 583, [2007] 3 FCR 331 131
Murray v Gast Lithographic & Engraving Co (1894) 8 Misc. 36 .... 42, 48
Mustapha v Culligan of Canada Ltd 2008 SCC 27, [2008] 2 SCR 114 255
NASA v Nelson, 562 U.S. 134 (2011) 67, 68, 74–83
Nationwide News Pty Ltd v Rush [2020] FCAFC 115, (2020) 380 ALR 432 132
Ndidi v United Kingdom (41215/14) (2017) *The Times*, October 9, [2017] 9 WLUK 231, ECtHR, 14 September 2017 201
Nelson v NASA, 506 F.3d 713, 715 (9th Cir. 2007) 75
Nelson v NASA, 512 F.3d 1134 (9th Cir. 2008), rev'd, 562 U.S. 134 (2011) 75
Neulinger v Switzerland (41615/07) (2012) 54 EHRR 31, (2010) 28 BHRC 706, [2011] 1 FLR 122, ECtHR 310
Nevsun Resources Ltd v Araya 2020 SCC 5, [2020] 4 WWR 1 241
Nitsopoulos v Wong (2008), 298 DLR (4th) 265 (Ont.S.C.) 248
Nixon v Administrator of General Servs., 433 U.S. 425, 97 S Ct 2777 (1977) 68, 77
Northern Security Company v United States, 193 US 197 (1903) 17
NPV v QEL and ZED [2018] EWHC 703 (QB), [2018] EMLR 20 .... 142, 143
NT1 and NT2 v Google llc [2018] EWHC 799 (QB), [2019] QB 344, [2018] 3 WLR 1165 293–4
Ntuli v Donald [2010] EWCA Civ 1276, [2011] 1 WLR 294, [2011] EMLR 10 .... 131, 141, 143, 145, 307, 308, 309
O v A; sub nom OPO (A Child by BHM his litigation friend) v MLA [2014] EWHC 2468 (QB), [2015] All ER (D) 23 (Jun) 321
O v A [2014] EWCA Civ 1277, [2015] EMLR 4, [2014] HRLR 31 .... 315, 319, 321
O v A [2015] UKSC 32, [2016] AC 219, [2015] 2 WLR 1373 .... 315, 324
OBG Ltd v Allan (Douglas v Hello! Ltd (HL)) [2007] UKHL 21, [2008] 1 AC 1, [2007] 2 WLR 920 .... 208, 212–3, 222
Obodo v Trans Union of Canada, Inc 2021 ONSC 7297 255
Ogbonna v Qantas Airways Ltd [2019] WASCA 146 122
Ontario (Attorney General) v Dieleman (1994), 117 DLR (4th) 449 (Ont. Gen. Div.) 250
O'Rourke et al v Schacht [1976] 1 SCR 53, 55 DLR (3d) 96 247
Owsianik v Equifax Canada Co 2021 ONSC 4112 (Div Ct) 238, 254–5
P v D [2000] 2 NZLR 591 127
Parasiuk v Canadian Newspapers Co Ltd [1998] 2 WWR 737 (Man. Q.B.), ... 257
Pavesich v New England Life Insurance Company (1905) 122 Ga. 190 .... 38, 39, 40, 42, 44–62

Pavesich v New England Life Insurance Company (May 1904) Atlanta City Ct 45, 46
Peck v United Kingdom 44647/98, (2003) 36 EHRR 41, [2003] EMLR 287, ECtHR 192, 195, 215–6
Pell Frischmann Engineering Ltd v Bow Valley Iran Ltd [2009] UKPC 45, [2011] 1 WLR 2370, [2010] BLR 73 228
People v Schade NY Suppl 612, 615 (1937) 11
Perry & Anor v Harris (A Minor) [2008] EWCA Civ 907, [2009] 1 WLR 19 315
Peters v Attorney-General [2021] NZCA 355, [2021] 3 NZLR 191 144
Peters v Bennett [2020] NZHC 761 127
Pinder v Canada (Minister of the Environment) 2015 FC 1376, aff'd on other grounds, 2016 FCA 317 253
PJS v News Group Newspapers [2016] UKSC 26, [2016] AC 1081, [2016] 2 WLR 1253, [2016] 4 All ER 554 .... 103, 141, 142, 152, 182, 183, 214, 219, 230, 301–3, 305–6, 311–14, 322, 324, 325–6
Planned Parenthood of Southeastern Pennsylvania v Casey, 505 U.S. 833 (1992) 71
Plessy v Ferguson 163 US 537 (1896) 58, 59
Poirier v Wal-Mart Canada Corp 2006 BCSC 1138 259
Pollard v Photographic Company (1888) 40 Ch D 345, ChD 1–2, 5, 7–17, 23, 24, 25, 28, 39, 48, 56
Powell v Shirley 2016 ONSC 3577 252
Pretty v United Kingdom (2346/02) [2002] ECHR 427, (2002) 35 EHRR 1, 12 BHRC 149, ECtHR 145
Prince Albert v Strange (1849) 2 De G & Sm 652, 64 ER 293; 1 Mac & G 25, 45 ER 1171; 1 H & Tw 1, 47 ER 1302 (Lord Chancellor) 2, 4, 9, 10, 11, 12, 14
R v Dyment, [1988] 2 SCR 417, (1988) 89 NR 249 .... 237, 242
R v Jarvis 2019 SCC 10, [2019] 1 SCR 488 243
R v Khan (Sultan) [1997] AC 558, [1996] 3 WLR 162, [1996] 3 All ER 289, HL 98
R v O'Connor [1995] 4 SCR 411, 130 DLR (4th) 235 244
R v Tessling 2004 SCC 67, [2004] 3 SCR 432 242
R (AB) v Secretary of State for Justice [2021] UKSC 28, [2022] AC 487, [2021] 3 WLR 494 159
R (Ullah) v Special Adjudicator [2004] UKHL 26, [2004] 2 AC 323, [2004] 3 WLR 23 159
Racing Partnership Ltd v Sports Information Services Ltd [2020] EWCA Civ 1300, [2021] Ch 233, [2021] 2 WLR 469 215
Racki v Racki 2021 NSSC 46 257

Reid v Price [2020] EWHC 594 (QB), [2020] 3 WLUK 240 ....226, 291, 296
Reklos and Davourlis v Greece (1234/05) [2009] ECHR 200, [2009] EMLR 16, 27 BHRC 420, ECtHR 188, 203, 218, 298, 312
Retail, Wholesale & Department Store Union, Local 580 v Dolphin Delivery (1987) 33 DLR (4th) 174, Can Sup Ct 242
Rhodes v OPO and others [2015] UKSC 32, [2016] AC 219, [2015] 2 WLR 1373 146
Richard v BBC [2018] EWHC 1837 (Ch), [2019] Ch 169, [2018] 3 WLR 1715 ....226, 293
Rinsale Pty Ltd v Australian Broadcasting Corporation (1991) Aust Torts Reports ¶81–231 111
Roberson v Rochester Folding Box Co (1901) 64 A.D. 30 41
Roberson v Rochester Folding Box Co, 71 N.Y.S. 876 (N.Y. App. Div. 1901) 27–8, 33, 36, 37, 38
Roberson v Rochester Folding Box Co., 64 N.E. 442, 442 (N.Y. 1902) 28–32, 33, 34, 36, 37, 38
Roberson v Rochester Folding Box Co., 72 N.Y.S. 1125 (N.Y. App. Div. 1901) 28, 33, 36, 37, 38
Roberson v Rochester Folding-Box Co 171 N.Y. 538 (1902)..... 39, 41, 42, 47, 48, 52, 55, 56, 57, 60, 61
Roberson v Rochester Folding-Box Co., 65 N.Y.S. 1109 (N.Y. Sup. Ct. 1900) 19–20, 23–7, 33, 36, 37, 38
Rocknroll v News Group Newspapers Ltd [2013] EWHC 24 (Ch), [2013] 1 WLUK 209..309, 322
Roe v Wade, 410 U.S. 113, 93 S Ct 705, 35 L Ed 2d 147 (1973) 68, 71
Roth v Roth (1991) 4 O.R. (3d) 740 (Gen. Div.)..248
Ruusunen v Finland Application (73579/10), [2014] ECHR 35, ECtHR...201
S (A Child) (Identification: Restrictions on Publication), Re [2004] UKHL 47, [2005] 1 AC 593, [2004] 3 WLR 1129 ....101, 173, 318
Saltman Engineering Co Ltd v Campbell Engineering Co Ltd (1948) 65 RPC 203, [1963] 3 All ER 413 (note) 14
Sands v State of South Australia [2013] SASC 44...119
Schuyler v Curtis (1895) 147 N.Y. 434 48
Schuyler v Curtis, 15 N.Y.S. 787 (N.Y. Sup. Ct. 1891) 24
Seven Network (Operations) Ltd v Australian Broadcasting Corporation [2007] NSWSC 1289 122
Severs v Hyp3R Inc 2021 BCSC 226 244
Shaw v Kovac [2017] EWCA Civ 1028, [2017] 1 WLR 4773, [2018] 2 All ER 71 297
Shelley Films Ltd v Rex Features Ltd [1994] EMLR 134, ChD............ 15, 16, 98, 168, 170

Sicri v Associated Newspapers Ltd [2020] EWHC 3541 (QB), [2021] 4 WLR 9, [2021] EMLR 10 .... 223, 293
Singh-Boutilier v Ontario College of Social Workers and Social Service Workers 2015 ONSC 5297 252
SKA and PLM v CRH and persons unknown who have threatened to reveal private information about the claimants [2012] EWHC 766 (QB), [2012] 3 WLUK 855 .... 143, 144, 147
SKA, PLM and CRH v Persons Unknown [2012] EWHC 2236 (QB), [2012] 7 WLUK 972 144
Smethurst v Commissioner of Police (Cth) [2020] HCA 14, (2020) 376 ALR 575 125
Smith Kline & French Laboratories (Aust) Ltd v Department of Community Services and Health [1989] FCA 556, (1990) 22 FCR 73 124
SOJ v JAO [2019] EWHC 2569 (QB), [2019] 10 WLUK 63 .... 143, 154
Somwar v McDonald's Restaurants of Canada Ltd (2005) 79 O.R. (3d) 172 (S.C.) 248
Spelman v Express Newspapers Ltd [2012] EWHC 355 (QB), [2012] 2 WLUK 711 .... 154, 224–5, 284
Spencer v United Kingdom (App no 28851/95 28852/95) 25 EHRR CD 105, ECommHR 192
'Spycatcher' case. See Attorney-General v Guardian Newspapers Ltd (No 2)
ST (A Child) v L Primary School [2020] EWHC 1046 (QB), [2020] ELR 555 227
State v Mann 13 N. C. 263 (1829) 57
Stephens v Avery [1988] Ch 449, [1988] 2 WLR 1280, [1988] 2 All ER 477, ChD 120
Stevens v Walsh 2016 ONSC 2418 251
Stewart v Demme 2020 ONSC 83 .... 252, 255
Stewart v Demme 2022 ONSC 1790 (Div. Ct.) 252
Sullivan v Sclanders [2000] SASC 273, (2000) 77 SASR 419 124
Tapling v Jones (1865) 11 HLC 290, (1865) 11 ER 1344 109
Target Holdings Ltd v Redferns [1996] AC 421, [1995] 3 WLR 352, [1995] 3 All ER 785, HL 223
Tchenguiz v Imerman [2010] EWCA Civ 908, [2011] Fam 116, [2011] 2 WLR 592 .... 212–3, 298
Television New Zealand Ltd v Rogers [2007] NZSC 91, [2008] 2 NZLR 277 127
Terry (formerly LNS) v Persons Unknown [2010] EWHC 119 (QB), [2010] EMLR 16 .... 131, 154, 155, 252, 316
Theakston v MGN Ltd [2002] EWHC 137 (QB), [2002] EMLR 22 .... 131, 140, 151, 179, 215
TLT v Secretary of State for the Home Department [2016] EWHC 2217 (QB), [2016] Info TLR 373 .... 226, 291

TSE v News Group Newspapers Ltd [2011] EWHC 1308 (QB), [2011] 5 WLUK 602 306
TVK and BVP v ICM [2016] EWHC 2810 (QB), [2016] 11 WLUK 179 144
Tolley v JS Fry Ltd [1931] AC 333, [1931] All ER 131, HL 94
Tran v Financial Debt Recovery Ltd (2000) 193 DLR (4th) 168 (S.C.J.) (reversed on other grounds, [2001] OJ No 4103 (Div. Ct.)) 247
Trout Point Lodge Ltd v Handshoe 2012 NSSC 245 251
Tucci v Peoples Trust Company 2017 BCSC 1525 253
Tucci v Peoples Trust Company 2020 BCCA 246 .... 245, 253
Turner v Spooner (1861) 30 LJ Ch 301 109
T.W.v Seo, [2003] OTC 940 (S.C.J.), (varied on other grounds at (2005), 256 DLR (4th) 1 (C.A.) 248
Unuane v United Kingdom (App no 80343/17) [2020] ECHR 832, 24 November 2020 201
US Office of Personnel Management Data Security Breach Litigation, Re 928 F. 3d 42 (D.C. Cir. 2019) 82
Vachon v Canada Revenue Agency 2015 ONSC 6096 252
Vercoe v Rutland Fund Management Ltd [2010] EWHC 424 (Ch), [2010] Bus LR D141 228
Victoria Park Racing & Recreation Grounds Co Ltd v Taylor (1936) 37 SR(NSW) 322 108
Victoria Park Racing and Recreation Grounds Co Ltd v Taylor [1937] HCA 45, (1937) 58 CLR 479, [1937] ALR 597 .... 14, 15, 107, 108–10, 113, 114–5, 116, 136
Vidal-Hall v Google Inc [2014] EWHC 13 (QB), [2014] WLR 4155, [2014] EMLR 14 .... 304, 305, 318, 319
Vidal-Hall v Google Inc. See Google Inc v Vidal-Hall
Volkszählungsurteil (Census Act Case), 65 BverfGE 1, 68–69 (15 December 1983) (German Federal Constitutional Ct) 66, 69
Von Hannover v Germany (No 1) (59320/00) (2005) 40 EHRR 1, [2004] EMLR 21, ECtHR 172, 187–9, 191–205, 215, 216, 231
Von Hannover v Germany (No 2) (40660/08 and 60641/08) (2012) 55 EHRR 15, [2012] EMLR 16, ECtHR Grand Chamber 188, 189, 199–202
Von Maltzahn v Koopernaes 2018 NSSC 192 250
Vucina v Croatia (App no 58955/13) 24 September 2019, ECtHR 196
Wainwright v Home Office [2001] EWCA Civ 2081, [2002] QB 1334, [2002] 3 WLR 405 .... 98, 99
Wainwright v Home Office [2003] UKHL 53, [2004] 2 AC 406, [2003] 3 WLR 1137 .... v, 98, 99, 211, 253, 300, 302, 319
Wakeling v Desjardins General Insurance 2021 ONCA 672 255
Washington v Glucksberg, 521 U.S. 702 (1997) 67

Weller v Associated Newspapers Ltd [2014] EWHC 1163 (QB), [2014] EMLR 24 ......226, 283, 288, 296, 315, 325
Weller v Associated Newspapers Ltd [2015] EWCA Civ 1176, [2016] 1 WLR 1541, [2016] 3 All ER 357 ......131, 217, 218–9, 315
Whalen v Roe 429 U.S. 589, 97 S Ct 869 (1977) 65–83
Wilkinson v Downton [1897] 2 QB 57, QBD 117, 120, 121, 315
Wilson v Ferguson [2015] WASC 15 ...... 121–2, 123
Winder v Marriott International, Inc 2022 ONSC 390 255
Windridge Farm Pty Ltd v Grassi [2011] NSWSC 196, (2011) 254 FLR 87 114
Winer v the United Kingdom (App no 10871/84) Commission Dec. 10 July 1986, DR 48, 154 191–2
Wolfe v Schaefer, 619 F.3d 782 (7th Cir. 2010) 77
Woodward v Hutchins [1977] 1 WLR 760, [1977] 2 All ER 751, (1977) 121 SJ 409, CA 124
Wrotham Park Estate Co Ltd v Parkside Homes Ltd [1974] 1 WLR 798, [1974] 2 All ER 321, (1974) 27 P & CR 296, ChD 227
X v Iceland (App no 2525/65) [1967] ECHR 24, (1967) 18 CD 33 (06 February 1967), ECtHR 191
X Health Authority v Y [1988] 2 All ER 648, [1988] RPC 379, (1987) 137 NLJ 1062, QBD 124
YXB v TNO [2015] EWHC 826 (QB), [2015] 3 WLUK 701 142
Yenovkian v Gulian 2019 ONSC 7279 257–8
ZH (Tanzania) v Secretary of State for the Home Department [2011] UKSC 4, [2011] 2 AC 166, [2011] 2 WLR 148 ......310, 312
Zoumbas v Secretary of State for the Home Department [2013] UKSC 74, [2013] 1 WLR 3690, [2014] 1 All ER 638 312
ZXC v Bloomberg [2019] EWHC 970 (QB), [2019] EMLR 20 293
ZXC v Bloomberg [2020] EWCA Civ 611, [2021] QB 28, [2020] 3 WLR 838 ......149, 150, 293
ZXC v Bloomberg [2022] UKSC 5, [2022] AC 1158, [2022] 2 WLR 424 ...... 149, 150, 160, 293

Table of Legislation

Statutes

Canada Act 1982, 1982, c. 11
 Sch B 241
Chancery Amendment Act 1858 (Lord Cairns' Act) 121, 282
Children Act 1989 .... 309, 315
Constitution Act 1867, 30 & 31 Victoria, c. 3
 s 91 240
Criminal Justice Act 1988,
 s 158 91
Data Protection Act 1998 .... 161, 223, 227, 229, 230, 294
 s 13 .... 227, 230, 294
Fair Trading Act 1973
 s 57(4) 88
Fine Arts Copyright Act 1862, 25 & 26 Vict c 6-8 7
 s 1 7
Human Rights Act 1998 .... v, 16, 99, 124, 133, 137, 159, 162, 163, 169, 172, 184, 185, 187, 210, 211, 212, 214, 281, 306, 307, 308, 317
 s 2 172
 s 6 .... 138, 169, 172, 307, 310
 s 6(1) 169, 297
 s 6(3) 169, 297
 s 12 .... 148, 231, 234, 318
 s 12(1) 148, 231
 s 12(3) 148, 231, 232, 233, 234
 s 12(4) 148, 149, 231, 232, 233
 s 12(4)(b) 312, 313, 314
Judicature Acts of 1873–1875 8
Sexual Offences (Amendment) Act 1976 91
 s 4(6) 91

Statutory Instruments and Codes of Practice

Independent Press Standards Organisation (IPSO) Editors' Code of Practice (IPSO 2016) 313, 314
Newspaper Publishers' Association Code of Practice November 1989......92
Trade Secrets (Enforcement, etc) Regulations 2018, SI 2018/597......222

EU and International Material

Article 29 Working Party, *Opinion 1/2008 on Data Protection Issues Related to Search Engines* (2008) 14......263–4, 267, 268
Article 29 Working Party, *Guidelines* (2014) 279
Pt 2......275
6, 7......269
8......271, 277
9......277–8
Council of Europe Parliamentary Assembly Resolution 1165 (1998) – Right to Privacy, 26 June 1998......192
Directive 95/46/EC of the European Parliament and of the Council of 24 October 1995 on the protection of individuals with regard to the processing of personal data and on the free movement of such data (DPD)......261, 262, 266, 268, 272, 278, 279
recital 2......277
Art 2(d)......266
Art 2(e)......271
Art 8......267
Art 8(1)–(3)......273
Art 8(4), (5)......274
Art 9......266, 271
Art 13......274
Directive 2000/31/EC of the European Parliament and of the Council of 8 June 2000 on certain legal aspects of information society services, in particular electronic commerce, in the Internal Market ('Directive on electronic commerce')......266, 268
Arts 12–15......266
Art 21(2)......266
Directive (EU) 2016/943 of the European Parliament and of the Council of 8 June 2016 on the protection of undisclosed know-how and business information (trade secrets) against their unlawful acquisition, use and disclosure [2016] OJ L157/1......222
EU European Charter of Fundamental Rights......65, 82
Art 7......272

Art 8 .... 272, 277
Art 8(1) 65
Art 11 274
Art 24 310
European Convention on Human Rights 1950 .... 15, 16, 33, 148, 162, 163, 165, 169, 171, 176, 187, 189, 194, 209, 231, 233, 307, 308, 311, 317
Art 8 .... v, 15, 99, 137, 138, 146, 148, 149, 150, 160, 163, 165, 166, 169, 171, 172, 173, 175, 176, 178, 179, 182, 187, 188, 189, 191, 192, 194, 195, 196, 197, 198, 201, 202, 203, 204, 205, 209, 211, 212, 213, 216, 218, 222, 232, 242, 288, 296, 297, 306, 307, 312, 316
Art 8(1) 137, 191
Art 8(2) 137
Art 10 .... 137, 138, 146, 148, 149, 150, 152, 160, 162, 163, 165, 166, 169, 172, 173, 175, 176, 178, 180, 181, 182, 184, 189, 191, 194, 196, 198, 202, 204, 211, 222, 232, 297
Art 10(1) 138
Art 10(2) 138, 149
Art 17 204
European Data Protection Board, *Guidelines 5/2019 on the Criteria of the Right to be Forgotten in the search engine cases under the GDPR (part 1) – version adopted after public consultation* (2020) 265
European Data Protection Board, *Guidelines 5/2019 (Part 1) Version 2.0* (2020) 275
5 270
Regulation (EU) 2016/679 of the European Parliament and of the Council of 27 April 2016 on the protection of natural persons with regard to the processing of personal data and on the free movement of such data, and repealing Directive 95/46/EC (General Data Protection Regulation / GDPR) 82, 262, 264, 265, 270, 271, 272, 274, 275, 276, 278
recital 2 277
recital 153 272
Art 2(4) 266
Art 4(7) 266
Art 4(8) 271
Art 9 273

Art 9(2)(g) 274
Art 10 274
Art 23 274
Art 70(1)(d) 271
Art 85(1) 275
Art 85(2) 272
United Nations Convention of the Rights of the Child 1989 (UNCRC)
Art 3 .... 314, 315, 316
Art 3(1) 310
United Nations Declaration of the Rights of the Child 1959
second principle 310
Universal Declaration of Human Rights 33

National Materials

AUSTRALIA

Charter of Human Rights and Responsibilities Act 2006 (Vic)
s 13 133
Civil Law (Wrongs) Act 2002 (ACT)
s 127 (repealed) 133
Commonwealth Constitution 116
Copyright Act 1968 (Cth)
s 90 114
s 98 114
Crimes Act 1914 (Cth) 125
Defamation Act 1889 (Qld)
s 15 (repealed) 133
Defamation Act 1957 (Tas)
s 15 (repealed) 133
Defamation Act 1974 (NSW)
s 15(2)(b) (repealed) 133
Human Rights Act 2004 (ACT)
s 12 133
Human Rights Act 2019 (Qld)
s 25 133
Judicial Proceedings Reports Act 1958 (Vic)
s 4(1A) 118
Privacy Act 1988 (Cth) 130
Slander and Libel Act 1847 (NSW)
s 4 (repealed) 133
Supreme Court Act 1970 (NSW) 123

CANADA

Canadian Charter of Rights and Freedoms 73, 239, 242, 243, 246
s 2 242
s 2(b) 242
ss 7–15 242
s 8 .... 241, 242, 243
s 26 242
s 32 243
Consumer Privacy Protection Act (Draft) 246
Criminal Code R.S.C. 1985, c.C-46
s 162.1 246
Digital Charter Implementation Act 2022 (Draft) 246
Electronic Documents Act (Draft) 246
Intimate Image Protection Act CCSM c. I87 246
Intimate Images and Cyber-protection Act, S.N.S. 2017, c. 7 246
Protecting Victims of Non-Consensual Distribution of Intimate Images Act, S.A. 2017, C.P-26.9 246
Personal Information and Data Protection Tribunal Act (Draft) 246
Personal Information Protection and Electronic Documents Act SC 2000, c.5 .... 240, 244, 245, 246
Privacy Act, R.S.C. 1985, c.P-21 244
Protecting Canadians from Online Crime Act S.C. 2014, c.31 246

Alberta

Alberta Government Telephones Act 1958 c.85 247

British Columbia

Privacy Act, R.S.B.C. 1996 c.373
s 1 252
s 1(1) 244
s 3(2) 259
s 4 244

Manitoba

Privacy Act, C.C.S.M. c.P125 245
s 2 244
s 4(2) 250

Newfoundland and Labrador

Privacy Act, R.S.N.L. 1990, c.P-22
s 3 244
s 3(2) 245

Nova Scotia

Intimate Images and Cyber-Protection Act S.N.S. 2017, c.7
ss 5, 8 258

Ontario

Personal Health Information Protection Act 2004, S.O. 2004, c. 3 245
Sch A 245

Québec

Québec Charter of Human Rights and Freedoms, c.C-12
ss 4, 5 242

Saskatchewan

Privacy Act, R.S.S. 1978, c.P-24
s 2 244

GERMANY

Basic Law
Art 1 66
Art 2(1) 66

RUSSIA

Federal Law of 13 July 2015 N 264-FZ 'On Amendments to the Federal Law "On Information, Information Technologies and Information Protection"' 279

SOUTH AFRICA

Constitution
s 14 242

TURKEY

Kişisel Verileri Koruma Kurumu, Kişilerin Ad ve Soyadı ile Arama Motorları Üzerinden Yapılan Aramalarda Çıkan Sonuçların İndeksten Çıkarılmasına Yönelik Talepler ile ilgili olarak Kişisel Verileri Koruma Kurulunun 23/06/2020 Tarihli ve 2020/481 Sayılı Kararı (2020) 279

UNITED STATES

Administrative Procedure Act 5 U.S.C. §§ 554, 556 and 557 (2018) 81
Constitution 49, 61, 65, 66, 67, 68, 70, 71, 72, 76, 79, 80, 81, 83, 242

1st Amendment 12, 181
5th Amendment 68, 71, 81
13th Amendment (1865) 56
14th Amendment 50, 68, 71, 77
§ 1 71
Declaration of Independence (4 July 1776) 51
Fair Credit Report Act 1970, Pub. L. 91–508, 84 Stat. 1114 (codified at 15 U.S.C. §§ 1681–1681x (2018) 81, 82
Family Educational Rights and Privacy Act 1974, Pub. L. 93–380, 88 Stat. 571 (codified at 20 U.S.C. § 1232g (2018) 81
Health Insurance Portability and Accountability Act of 1996, Pub. L. 104–191, 110 Stat. 1936 (codified as amended in ss of 18, 26, 29, and 42 U.S.C. (2018) 81
Privacy Act 1974, Pub. L. 93–579, 88 Stat. 1896 as amended, codified at 5 U.S.C. § 552a (2018) 76, 80, 81, 82, 83
§ 552a(b) 75, 80
§ 552a(d)(1) 80
§ 552a(e)(10) 81
§ 552a(f) 81
§ 552a(g) 81
Restatement (First) of Torts, § 867 (Am. L. Inst. 1939) 32
Restatement (Second) of Torts, (Am. L. Inst. 1977, updated 2010) 241, 249, 255, 256, 257, 258, 259, 260
§ 652B (Am. L. Inst. 1977) 127
§ 652C (Am. L. Inst. 1977) 33
§§ 652 B, D, E (Am. L. Inst. 1977) 33

Florida

Const. Art. I, § 23 (1968) 65

Georgia

Constitution 49

Montana

Constitution 65
Const. Art II, § 10 (1972) 65

New York

Act to prevent the unauthorized use of the name or picture of any person for the purposes of trade – 1903 N.Y. Laws 308 32
Chapter 132 of the Laws of 1903 39

N.Y. Pub. Health Law 70
§ 3306 70
§§ 3331-3334 70
§§ 3338-3339 70
§§ 3370-3371 70
N.Y. Civ. Rights Law, § 50 (McKinney 2003) 33
N.Y. Civ. Rights Law, §§ 50-51 (McKinney 2003) 39
N.Y. Civ. Rights Law, §§ 52 A-B (McKinney 2003) 34
New York State Controlled Substances Act of 1972
1970 N.Y. Laws, c. 474 .... 70, 71, 72

Pennsylvania

Constitution 74

1

Pollard v Photographic Company (1888)

MEGAN RICHARDSON*

I. INTRODUCTION

Sandwiched between George Eastman's release of his Kodak 'detective camera'[1] and Samuel Warren and Louis Brandeis's anxieties about the future of privacy in the face of the threats posed by 'instantaneous photographs' (along with 'newspaper enterprise' and a public propensity for 'gossip'),[2] one might have expected more from the judgment of North J in *Pollard v Photographic Company* than a passing comment that 'if the negative likeness were taken on the sly the person who took it might exhibit or sell copies'.[3] So why is this case which seems to have so little to say about the law's feasible protection of privacy in the face of a novel technology of intrusion in the late 1880s included in a book of landmark cases on privacy law? I would say that it is precisely *because* of what it tells us about the restricted state of privacy law at the *fin de siècle* – at least in the British common law world. And, further, because of its remarkable influence across much of that world, albeit more a product of the prominence accorded by those coming after than any apparent design of its author.

Earlier in the nineteenth century, one could give a story of the flexibility of equity in the face of a revived technology of domestic etching, tabloid media, and public curiosity about the private affairs of celebrities focused on the

* With grateful thanks to Michael Bryan and Thomas Vranken for invaluable advice.

[1] Patented synchronously in the US and UK (US 388,850/1988, GB6950/1888), the Kodak 'detective camera' was launched with much fanfare in September 1888. It was not the first detective camera (even for Eastman) but its unique patented design, relative in-expense (although not as cheap as later models) and mass-marketing under the banner 'you press the button, we do the rest' ensured its success: see J Lake, 'Kodak Camera' in C Op den Kamp and D Hunter, A *History of Intellectual Property in 50 Objects* (Cambridge UK, Cambridge University Press, 2019) ch 14, 123.

[2] SD Warren and LD Brandeis, 'The Right of Privacy' (1890) 4 *Harvard Law Review* 193, 195–196.

[3] *Pollard v Photographic Company* (1888) 40 Ch D 345, North J at 346 (asking the plaintiffs' lawyers whether they disputed the proposition: they did not).

mid-century case of *Prince Albert v Strange* where the judges at first instance and on appeal drew on a variety of doctrines to protect the right to privacy.[4] But by November 1888, when *Pollard* came to be decided, all that seemed to be forgotten, with the only reference to *Prince Albert v Strange* in North J's judgment in *Pollard* made on the question of the availability of an injunction in the absence of a property right.[5] The question is how a judge in the Chancery Division (and not an especially adventurous judge by most accounts)[6] could pay so little regard to the authority of the Vice-Chancellor and Lord Chancellor just 40 years earlier, while purporting to interpret and apply the relevant 'principles'.[7] One answer offered by Lionel Bently in his study of the shifting 'landmark' status of *Prince Albert v Strange* is that 'the case was [by the time of *Pollard*] thought of neither as a key "first" in the development of the law, nor as a particularly clear enunciation of a legal "principle"'.[8] Another answer which I offer in this chapter is that *Pollard* is a particular example of a late-Victorian mechanistic technique of interpretation of authority employed to mask a judicial ideology of non-regulation of new technologies – an ideology which would ultimately need to be revisited.

II. VICTORIAN TECHNOLOGY AND THE SCIENCE OF 'INTERPRETATION'

By the last decades of the nineteenth century, technological change seemed to be an ever-present feature of everyday life for many of the British Empire's citizens. Nor was it just about photography, although its dramatic recording of visual experience, its constant stream of improvements, and its incorporation into all 'the principal fields of human activity' ensured it a central role in the discourse of progress.[9] Inter alia, the telephone, the telegraph, the typewriter, the phonograph, the wireless, and cinema, along with the lightbulb, the train, the electric tram, and the motor car served to reconfigure the human experience in the Victorian century. And people were becoming acclimatised to the changing world around them. As Eric Hobsbawm says, already by the late 1870s 'serious lay observers' would have predicted 'important developments in electricity,

[4] *Prince Albert v Strange* (1849) 2 De G & Sm 652, 64 ER 293 (Knight Bruce V-C); 1 Mac & G 25, 45 ER 1171; 1 H & Tw 1, 47 ER 1302 (Lord Chancellor).

[5] *Pollard* (n 3) 354.

[6] See RE Megarry, *Miscellany-at-Law: A Diversion for Lawyers and Others* (London, Stevens & Sons, 1955) 10 (Sir Ford North considered 'want[ing in] worldly knowledge', 'sound', but 'painfully slow').

[7] *Pollard* (n 3) 349.

[8] L Bently, '*Prince Albert v Strange* (1849)' in C Mitchell and P Mitchell (eds), *Landmark Cases in Equity* (Oxford, Hart Publishing, 2012) ch 8, 255.

[9] See Q Bajac, *The Invention of Photography: The First Fifty Years* (trans from the French by R Taylor, London, Thames and Hudson, 2002) 127.

photography and chemical synthesis', and would not have been surprised that technology would succeed in solving 'so obvious and urgent a problem as the invention of a mobile engine to mechanise road transport'; as to the broader population, '[they] were certainly hungry for new inventions, the more dramatic the better'.[10]

Inevitably, there would be more pervasive effects for human behaviours and practices, including the self-reflexive practices of reading and writing. As Clare Pettitt puts it, throughout the nineteenth century, technology reordered the narrative 'from the inside as the outside', becoming 'part of the politics of form of the wider work in which they [were] embedded'.[11] This shift towards the mechanisation of reading and writing only became more pronounced as the century wore on. The English utilitarians with their reasoned arguments for more systematic scientific approaches to law were prominent in the political environment that brought the change on the legal side.[12] But there were broader influences as well. Thus, John Austin's exposition in his *Lectures on Jurisprudence* of close reading of judicial precedents to determine their 'principle' based not just on 'what the judge says' but 'what his decision implies', in order that the judge's arguments can 'serve as a guide of conduct, or … [be] applied to the solution of subsequent cases',[13] finds a parallel in John Ruskin's championing of close 'seeing' in *Modern Painters*.[14] For Ruskin's seeing could be neatly summed up as the act of 'reading deeply into the object, recognizing the comprehensiveness of its self-expression, as it demonstrates its energies, displays the formal laws of its being, and sums up its past and its potential simply by the impact of its visual presence'.[15] Pettitt observes that '[i]t is 'no accident' that Ruskin was formulating his theory of seeing 'just as the technology of microscopy was becoming available to more and more people at mid-century'.[16] The same might be said of Austin's theory of close reading reflecting a microscopic-like attention

[10] EJ Hobsbawm, *The Age of Empire 1875–1914* (London, Weidenfeld and Nicolson, 1987) ch 1, 28.

[11] C Pettitt, '"The Annihilation of Space and Time": Literature and Technology' in K Flint (ed), *The Cambridge History of Victorian Literature* (Cambridge, Cambridge University Press, 2012) ch 26, 565–566.

[12] See GJ Postema, 'The British Tradition of Legal Positivism' in T Spaak and P Mindus (eds), *A Companion to Legal Positivism* (Cambridge, Cambridge University Press, 2021) ch 8. It might be more precise to call this an 'invented tradition', albeit not in the sense of one 'actually invented, constructed and formally instituted' but rather 'emerging in a less easily traceable manner within a brief and dateable period': see E Hobsbawm, 'Introduction: Inventing Traditions' in E Hobsbawm and T Ranger (eds), *The Invention of Tradition* (Cambridge, Cambridge University Press 2012) 1–2.

[13] J Austin, *Lectures on Jurisprudence or the Philosophy of Positive Law*, 3rd edn (R Campbell, ed, London, John Murray, 1869) vol 2, 643. As Postema points out (n 12) 192, Austin's reputation only really became established after his death in 1859, when his works were reissued in expanded form.

[14] J Ruskin, *Modern Painters* (London, Smith, Elder, 1856–1860) Vol 3, 268 ('the greatest thing a human soul ever does in this world is to *see* something, and to tell what it *saw* in a plain way').

[15] PM Ball, *The Science of Aspects: The Changing Role of Fact in the work of Coleridge, Ruskin and Hopkins* (London, Athlone Press, 1971) 69.

[16] Pettit (n 11) 568.

to detail. More generally, these Victorians' expositions of a scientific process where readers draw out a meaning that is already there rather than working creatively to fashion a meaning of their own seems designed to encourage a machine-like process of reading over one infused with human character – or at least in a time where it was difficult to conceive of machines as engaging in creative activity,[17] involving (in Ruskin's words) 'active intellect in choice and arrangement'.[18]

Nevertheless, some degree of active intellect in choice and arrangement in reading might be tempting, no matter what the rules say – even the rules that were themselves a product of earlier invention. As Suzy Anger explains, over time

> Victorian [legal] commentators became more conscious not only of the problems involved in discovering intention but also of the ways in which historical distance exacerbates those problems, particularly in the case of the law, where the judge seeks not only to interpret the law, but to apply it in the present.[19]

A particular example is the interpretation and application of the law with respect to photography – 'the most marvellous invention of the century', according to Ruskin[20] – which by the 1880s succeeded in 'managing only in a very loose manner the prolific spread of the photographic image',[21] and was now confronted with demands to provide an effective solution to proliferating incursions on privacy relying on traditional doctrines shaped in terms of earlier technologies and practices.[22] While Frederick Pollock, as the leading English jurist of the late-nineteenth century,[23] accepted that '[i]nasmuch as no general rule can anticipate all possible questions … [of future application], … interpretation makes it a living body',[24] this was only under limited conditions. Thus Pollock added, 'the law, when once defined by authority on any point, is or ought to be … certain', the difficulty being 'when case-law has taken a

[17] See JS Mill, *On Liberty* (London, JW Parker and Son, 1859) 107 ('[h]uman nature is not a machine to be built after a model, and set to do exactly the work prescribed for it, but a tree, which requires to grow and develop itself on all sides, according to the tendency of the inward forces which make it a living thing').

[18] J Ruskin, *Lectures on Art Delivered Before the University of Oxford in Hilary Term 1870* (Maynard, Merrill, & Company, 1893) 215 (here comparing photography with 'fine art').

[19] S Anger, *Victorian Interpretation* (Ithaca, Cornell University Press, 2005) 58.

[20] J Ruskin, letter to WH Harrison (12 August 1846): see Bajac (n 9) 146.

[21] Bajac (n 9) 126–127.

[22] For instance, *Gee v Pritchard* (1818) 2 Swanst. 402 (book publishing); *Abernethy v Hutchinson* (1825) 1 H & Tw 28 (journal publishing), *Prince Albert v Strange* (n 4) (exhibition of etchings with printed catalogue). See generally M Richardson, M Bryan, M Vranken and K Barnett, *Breach of Confidence: Social Origins and Modern Developments* (Cheltenham, Edward Elgar, 2012) chs 2 and 3.

[23] N Duxbury, *Frederick Pollock and the English Juristic Tradition* (Oxford, Oxford University Press, 2004).

[24] F Pollock, *First Book of Jurisprudence for Students of the Common Law* (London, Macmillan, 1889) 226.

wrong turn'.[25] Or as New Zealander John Salmond put it, '[i]n any system in which precedents are authoritative the courts are engaged in forging fetters for their own feet'.[26] It is especially in such cases that we find, to paraphrase Austin, a reversion to older practices of 'judicial interpretation ... establishing new law, under guise of expounding the old'.[27]

Indeed, it is ironic, given the mechanical approach to precedents they expounded, that late-nineteenth century judges sought to limit their operation in cases involving new technologies. Was it because of their fascination with the technologies, their laissez faire ideology, or both? Certainly, it seemed to be widely thought by this point that the possibilities of new technologies were wonderfully fluid when joined with human imagination and enterprise and subjected to minimal legal restriction.[28] In the next part of this chapter I explore the implications of such ways of thinking in the 1888 case of *Pollard v Photographic Company*, concluding that the implications for privacy might be subtle but they were highly significant.

III. THE DECISION IN POLLARD V PHOTOGRAPHIC COMPANY

In November 1888 the case of *Pollard v Photographic Company* came before North J, a judge known for his interest in science and shortly to become a fellow of the Royal Microscopic Society followed later by the Royal Society, positions he held until his death in 1913.[29] We can imagine him reading the account of the Royal Photographic Society's annual exhibition in *The Times* a month earlier, and perhaps even attending the exhibition which still, at the height of photography's popularity, included 'the best photographic work of the year, both professional and amateur'.[30] The review contained a full discussion of the exhibition's displays, with some portraits deemed to be of sufficient quality and finish to make them 'excellently suited for book illustration' (the use of photographs in more ephemeral media still rare in the late 1880s).[31] It concluded with a description of the latest technological innovations, noting that among the

[25] ibid 231–232.

[26] J Salmond, *Jurisprudence or the Theory of the Law* (London, Stevens and Haynes, 1902) 174–175.

[27] J Austin, *The Province of Jurisprudence Determined*, 2nd edn (S Austin, ed, London, John Murray, 1861) 19.

[28] See R Friedel, *Culture of Improvement: Technology and the Western Millennium* (Cambridge, MA, MIT Press, 2007) 305 ('new technologies, especially when they were recognized as socially important and the potential sources of great profit, could be the object of enormous experimentation and variation').

[29] See 'Sir Ford North' (Obituary, *The Times*, 14 October 1913) 11; [1913] *Journal of the Royal Microscopical Society* 646 (fellow from 1894); The Royal Society (Past Fellows): catalogues.royalsociety.org/CalmView/ (fellow from 1900).

[30] 'The Photographic Exhibition' (*The Times*, 1 October 1888) 4.

[31] Bajac (n 9) 118.

most curious were 'the "detective" cameras' coming in several types and forms. For instance, there was one invented by Dr Rudolf Krügener of Germany and shown by Marion and Co made up in the form of a book and taking pictures 'about an inch and a quarter square' including an ingenious device for shifting the tiny plates used as each exposure was made with the result that 24 pictures could be taken at a time.[32] Another was 'the very clever little instrument shown by the American Eastman Company, and named, doubtless for some good reason, the "Kodak"':[33]

> In this the sensitive film is mounted on paper instead of glass, so that the apparatus is much lighter and more compact. The camera is about six inches long by three broad and high, but it contains in this small space material for taking no less than 100 pictures, each a circle of two inches and a half in diameter. The shutter is of very novel construction, so contrived that in setting it the lens is not uncovered, as is the case with most, if not all, ordinary spring shutters. The paper is wound in a continuous roll, as in the now well-known 'roller slides,' so that a fresh surface is exposed each time by the turn of a key.

The Times deemed this altogether 'the neatest and most complete apparatus of the sort yet brought out', already anticipating the Kodak's success in the market for detective cameras.[34] It was only as the cameras began to be used that their ability to effect a social transformation would become fully apparent. As Lynda Nead observes, by the 1890s, '[m]etaphorically, at least, it seemed that the new hand cameras had broken down the tacit distance and norms of social interaction that had evolved among individuals in social space. Their speed and intrusion into new areas of representation transgressed and subjected to scrutiny an assumed sense of decorum that had come to define the conduct of social relations in the mid-Victorian period' – and 'nowhere was this confrontation between modern technology and social behavior keener than on the city streets … Instant photography exposed the ethical dimension of image making and disturbed the hitherto neglected question of individual rights to privacy in the public urban sphere'.[35] Nor were the breaches confined to social spaces (*viz* public streets and parks and squares) – even what might be considered 'private' places (*viz* private buildings and gardens, and the like) were not immune from the intrusions of the modern 'snap-shot fiend' armed with 'the hand-camera'.[36]

[32] 'Marion and Company was the largest and most important supplier of photographic equipment and material in Europe during the second half of the nineteenth century': J Hannavy (ed), *Encyclopedia of Nineteenth-Century Photography* (New York, Taylor and Francis, 2007) 892.

[33] 'The Photographic Exhibition' (n 30) 4.

[34] ibid. As to camera's well-calculated success in the hands of Eastman Photographic, see Lake (n 1).

[35] L Nead, 'Animating the Everyday: London on Camera circa 1900' (2004) 43 *Journal of British Studies* 65, 70–72.

[36] The idea of hidden cameras, of unobserved observation, of secret photography caught the imagination. In 1895, *The Amateur Photographer* magazine (founded in 1884 and a manifestation of

Coming on the cusp of this change it is unsurprising that the question of use of detective cameras would feature in discussion in *Pollard v Photographic Company*.[37] Almost immediately after Cozens-Hardy QC and Silvester opened argument for the plaintiffs, North J put the question directly: 'Do you dispute that if the negative likeness were taken on the sly the person who took it might exhibit or sell copies?'[38] Their answer was definite: 'In that case there would be no contract or consideration to support a contract.'[39] Thereafter the discussion proceeded on the basis that breach of a contract was the straightforward basis of liability. Nor was it difficult to construct one. In August 1888, Mrs Pollard and other members of her family attended the studio of the Photographic Company and posed for their photographs, for which she paid a sum of £7 10s; the complaint was raised in November 1888 after it was found that one of the photographs taken of Mrs Pollard had been made up in the popular form of a Christmas card featuring a vignette with scrolls and leaves and exposed for sale in the window of the defendant's shop.[40] This was not the case where the fee was waived in exchange for the photographer's right to use the photograph for advertising purposes, in line with a common practice.[41] Nor could the defendant claim copyright, even apart from the point that copyright was not registered, as any copyright subsisting in the photograph would have been for the Pollards to claim under the terms of the Fine Arts Copyright Act 1862 as the parties commissioning the portrait (their contract not expressly stating to the contrary in writing).[42] Thus any putative property right in the photographs belonged to the plaintiffs in this case rather than

the rapid growth of photography as a hobby) complained that: 'We are gradually beginning to think that when a man gets hold of a hand-camera he loses some of his moral balance, and he does things which otherwise he would not think of doing; and unless he recognises this and pulls himself up short, he degenerates into that worst of all types – the snap-shot fiend' (*The Amateur Photographer*, 19 July 1895, 34): see Hannavy (n 32) 1277.

[37] *Pollard v Photographic Company* (n 3).

[38] ibid 346.

[39] ibid.

[40] ibid 347. The 1880s were within '[t]he Victorian heyday for Christmas cards (1860–1890)', following the practice initiated by George Cole, first director of the Victoria and Albert Museum (whose Christmas card also featured a vignette of his family in a scene circled with branches and leaves), bolstered by 'the new printing processes and techniques such as chromolithography, metallic inks, fabric appliqué and die-cutting to make elaborately shaped cards': see 'The First Christmas Card', Victoria and Albert Museum www.vam.ac.uk/articles/the-first-christmas-card. Cards that made space for a personal photograph to be inserted were also in use. See G Buday, *The History of the Christmas Card* (London, Spring Books, 1954) 202.

[41] As North J pointed out, 'a photographer is frequently allowed, on his own request, to take a photograph of a person under circumstances in which a subsequent sale by him must have been in the contemplation of both parties, though not actually mentioned': *Pollard v Photographic Company* (n 3) 349.

[42] ibid 353 (noting that the Act of 25 & 26 Vict c 6-8, s 1 provides that 'when the negative of any photograph is made or executed for or on behalf of another person for a good or valuable consideration, the person making or executing the same shall not retain the copyright thereof, unless it is expressly reserved to him by agreement in writing signed by the person for or on whose behalf the same is so made or executed').

the defendant.[43] Further, the contract contained 'no special terms or conditions of any sort'.[44] In the circumstances, North J had the fairly simple task of explaining why the defendant's action might be considered a breach of an implied term of the contract between the plaintiffs and the defendant, where '[the] lady's feelings are shocked by finding that the photographer she has employed to take her likeness for her own use is publicly exhibiting and selling copies thereof'.[45] (It was a conclusion that the self-appointed opinion leader *The Times* approved, holding that this was not a case of someone lending themself to a photographic exploit then complaining about their notoriety, but of a portrait commissioned for private use by a 'private sitter', who is 'clearly entitled' to be protected from undesired publicity, especially where 'the sitter is a lady'.)[46]

However, North J did not stop there, noting also the prospect of breach of an equitable obligation arising out of the defendant's 'confidential employment'.[47] It was an appropriate function of a respectable judge of the Court of Chancery in the 1880s to insist that not just the contract should be treated as governing but also the equitable doctrine of breach of confidence, reasserting the continuing relevance of equity after the fusion of common law and equity with the passing of the Judicature Acts of 1873–1875.[48] And North J insisted that '[t]he principles upon which I rest my judgment are well known, and of familiar application'.[49] But it was a minor point as the equitable doctrine was closely assimilated to contract in North J's statement that:

> The question, therefore, is whether a photographer who has been employed by a customer to take his or her portrait is justified in striking off copies of such photograph for his own use, and selling and disposing of them, or publicly exhibiting them

[43] Mr Pollard, a shadowy figure in this case, was presumably joined in the claim with Mrs Pollard as the only one of the two entitled to hold property under the current state of Victorian law.

[44] *Pollard v Photographic Company* (n 3) 347.

[45] ibid 352.

[46] 'The Judgment Delivered Yesterday by Mr Justice North', *The Times* (21 December 1888) 9.

[47] Like the 'restrain[ing of] a clerk from disclosing his master's accounts, or an attorney from making known his client's affairs, learned in the course of such employment': *Pollard v Photographic Company* (n 3) 349.

[48] See 'Sir Ford North' (Obituary) (n 29), describing Ford North (barrister, Inner Temple, before becoming a judge), as 'an admirable specimen of the old-fashioned Chancery lawyer'. Some scholars have suggested that he was a champion of equity appointed with the project of ensuring the project of fusing law and equity would continue to appropriately reflect equity principles: see P Polden, 'Mingling the Waters. Personalities, Politics and the Making of the Supreme Court of Judicature' (2002) 61 *Cambridge Law Journal* 575, 591. If so, he was not a particularly successful choice. As his *Times* Obituary goes on to state he was not a forceful character: '[s]ensible, painstaking, somewhat narrow and timid, without a spark of brilliancy, he never decided too much, but sometimes decided too little – he clung to the letter of the authorities when an abler judge would have grasped their true spirit'. Although, I would add, his citing of authorities in *Pollard* seems less than supportive of the more expansive framings of breach of confidence in the older Chancery decisions in this time of post-Judicature Act fusion.

[49] *Pollard v Photographic Company* (n 3) 350.

> by way of advertisement or otherwise, without the authority of such customer … To the question thus put, my answer is in the negative … The object for which he is employed and paid is to supply his customer with the required number of printed photographs of a given subject. For this purpose, the negative is taken by the photographer on glass; and from this negative copies can be printed in much larger numbers than are generally required by the customer. The customer who sits for the negative thus puts the power of reproducing the object in the hands of the photographer: and in my opinion the photographer who uses the negative to produce other copies for his own use, without authority, is abusing the power confidentially placed in his hands merely for the purpose of supplying the customer; and further, I hold that the bargain between the customer and the photographer includes, by implication, an agreement that the prints taken from the negative are to be appropriated to the use of the customer only.[50]

One might be forgiven for thinking that, in North J's statement of the relevant principles, breach of contract and breach of confidence were being fused into a single principle of mechanical application (effectively framed in terms of 'an agreement that the prints taken from the negative are to be appropriated to the use of the customer only'), responding in kind to the practice of portrait photography conceived as a form of mechanical reproduction enabling copies to be printed in much larger numbers than 'generally required by the customer'. Nevertheless, other references in the judgment to liability resting on 'breach of contract and breach of faith',[51] citing *Morison v Moat*,[52] and to 'breach of contract or confidence' as warranting an injunction,[53] in line with the practice of the Court of Chancery, citing Lord Cottenham in *Prince Albert v Strange*[54] seem designed to reinforce (albeit in cautious and timid terms) the perception of these as still distinct doctrines shaped by distinct lines of authority.

Even so, there is a difference between the doctrine of breach of confidence as initially framed in those earlier cases and as interpreted in *Pollard*. For instance, Lord Cottenham in *Prince Albert v Strange* speaks of liability for 'a breach of trust, confidence, or contract' resting in that case on 'the private character' of the plaintiff's etchings, the absence of any licence or authority to publish, and the plaintiff's belief that 'the [defendant's] catalogue and the descriptive and other remarks therein contained, could not have been compiled or made, except by means of the possession of the several impressions of the said etchings surreptitiously and improperly obtained' (the defendant offering no answer as to how they could have been properly obtained).[55] This seems to extend well beyond situations of 'confidential employment' talked of by North J in *Pollard*.

[50] ibid 349–350.
[51] ibid 353.
[52] *Morison v Moat* (1851) 9 Hare 241, 68 ER 492.
[53] *Pollard v Photographic Company* (n 3) 354.
[54] *Prince Albert v Strange* (n 4).
[55] ibid, 1 Mac & G 25, 44; 45 ER 1171, 1178; 1 H & Tw 1, 23; 47 ER 1302, 1311.

Perhaps, Turner V-C was more ambiguous in *Morison v Moat*, suggesting that the principle of 'trust or confidence' might be aligned to 'breach of faith', in the sense that 'the Court fastens the obligation on the conscience of the party, and enforces it against him in the same manner as it enforces against a party to whom a benefit is given the obligation of performing a promise on the faith of which the benefit has been conferred'.[56] But in *Abernethy v Hutchinson*, cited as an authority in both of these earlier cases, Lord Eldon LC intimated that publication in *The Lancet* newspaper of the renowned Mr Abernethy's lectures on surgery could be the subject of an injunction whether the lectures were 'derived from a student [lawfully permitted access to the lecture room] or not', for 'I think it very difficult to tell me that that should not be restrained which is stolen, if you would restrain that which is a breach of contract or, of trust'[57] – noting that the lectures might have come into the defendant's hands by a variety of means:

> [for if they] have been published from shorthand writer's notes, they have been published from shorthand writer's notes taken by some student, or from shorthand writer's notes taken by some intruder into the lecture room; for I do not see how it is possible that-they could have been taken otherwise.[58]

Yet, in North J's account in *Pollard* the case of *Abernethy v Hutchinson* stood merely for the 'well known' principle that 'a student may not publish a lecture to which he has been admitted, even though by his own skill he has taken a copy of it in shorthand'.[59]

Why was it that North J so narrowly 'read' these older authorities in *Pollard v Photographic Company*, while proclaiming his allegiance to their 'principles'? One answer, offered by Bently in his thoughtful discussion of the changing 'landmark' status of *Prince Albert v Strange*, is that by the late-nineteenth century Lord Cottenham LC's reference to 'a breach of confidence arising out of the possession of etchings 'surreptitiously and improperly obtained' in Prince Albert's case was viewed as not 'a particularly clear enunciation of a legal "principle"' – and it was only in more recent years that the case came to be seen as a leading authority on the broad and flexible scope of breach of confidence regarding the protection of privacy.[60] I have suggested that the reasons were also social and cultural. In particular, the choice made by North J in *Pollard* to offer a confined scope of protection, geared to assuaging a lady's feelings which 'are shocked by finding that the photographer she has employed to take her likeness for her own use', but excluding photographs 'taken on the sly' (and without referencing 'the right to privacy' talked about

[56] *Morison v Moat* (n 52) (1851) 9 Hare 241, 255; 68 ER 492, 498.
[57] *Abernethy v Hutchinson* (1824–25) 1 H & Tw 28, 37–38; 47 ER 1313, 1316–1317.
[58] ibid, 1 H & Tw 28, 37; 47 ER 1313, 1316.
[59] *Pollard v Photographic Company* (n 3) 352.
[60] Bently (n 8) 255.

in *Prince Albert v Strange* 40 years earlier),[61] was a choice made by a fairly conventional judge faced with a remarkable modern invention of unknown potential in a time when respect for invention and enterprise was a prevailing ethos of the late-Victorian age – all under the guise of following older principles that were 'well-known, and of familiar application'.

IV. THE ACCIDENTAL LANDMARK

Most likely, North J would not have seen *Pollard* as a 'landmark' case, especially if this is taken to mean 'an event, action, statement, etc: historically significant as marking a period or turning-point; epoch-making; spec in Law, of a legal case or decision', which the *Oxford English Dictionary* traces back to the 1937 New York case *of People v Schade*.[62] After all, the late nineteenth century was not a time when English cases were especially celebrated as marking turning points in history.[63] They might be considered 'landmarks' in a more stable and enduring sense of milestones marking an established road or path that Victorian collators of 'leading cases' were fond of cataloguing.[64] Even then, there were plenty of influential figures who were arguing for a narrow reading of the mid-century breach of confidence cases when North J came to give judgment – most notably the authors of several of the popular late-Victorian legal treatises, typically barristers working in the Inns of Court in London (like North J in earlier life),[65] who provided a steady stream of cautious advice

[61] *Prince Albert v Strange* (n 4), 1 Mac & G 25, 47; 45 ER 1171, 1179; 1 H & Tw 1, 26; 47 ER 1302, 1312.

[62] *Oxford English Dictionary* (Oxford, Oxford University Press, 2000-), draft addition 1997. And see *People v Schade* NY Suppl 612, 615 (1937) per Judge Colden ('all of the cases subsequent to that landmark decision by Chief Justice Marshall [in the 1807 trial of Colonel Aaron Burr … lean heavily thereon').

[63] Although this meaning of 'landmark' in the history of philosophical thought was well understood: *cf* the OED's 'modern' definition of a 'landmark' as '[a]n object which marks or is associated with some event or stage in a process; esp. a characteristic, a modification, etc., or an event, which marks a period or turning-point in the history of a thing', citing inter alia JS Mill, *Utilitarianism* (1861) (London, Parker, Son and Bourn, 1863), referencing Kant's *Metaphysics of Ethics*, adding 'This remarkable man, whose system of thought will long remain one of the landmarks in the history of philosophical speculation': ibid 5.

[64] For instance, per W Shirley (Barrister, Inner Temple) in the Preface to the first edition of his *Leading Cases Made Easy: Selection of Leading Cases in the Common Law* (London, Stevens and Sons, 1880), repeated in later editions, distinguishing his work from other collections of leading cases inter alia on the basis of the sheer number of leading cases included in the work and quoting Samuel Warren (Barrister, Inner Temple): '"Fifty or sixty leading cases", says the late Mr Samuel Warren [*A Popular and Practical Introduction to Law Studies and to Every Department of the Legal Profession*, 2nd edn (London, A Maxwell & Son, 1845] 834, 'thoroughly understood and distinctly recollected, will be found of incalculable value in practice; serving as so many sure landmarks placed upon the trackless wilds of law. And why should not the number be doubled? or even trebled? What pains can be too great to secure such a result?': ibid v. Why not indeed!

[65] See 'Sir Ford North' (Obituary) (n 29).

for students of the law and lawyers already engaged in the practice of law,[66] probably agreed with their fellow-Victorians that the new technologies of the day reflected natural progress,[67] and implicitly held to the prevailing idea of 'the spirit of freedom' as guiding the development of 'the common law' with equity allowed at most a minor supplementary role.[68] Thus we can imagine North J seeing himself as merely solidifying rather than representing an important milestone of the law. Yet events coming after marked this apparently modest decision rendered by a modest judge as a significant moment in the history of breach of confidence.

First, there was the extended treatment of *Pollard* in Warren and Brandeis's article on 'The Right to Privacy' in the 1890 *Harvard Law Review*,[69] concluding that given the limited scope allowed for arguing breach of confidence as determined in this case, 'the next step which must be taken for the protection of the person, and for securing … the right "to be let alone"', in an age marked by the invention of 'instantaneous photographs' and 'other modern device[s] for recording or reproducing scenes or sounds',[70] the yellow press, and a public desire for gossip, was a new tort framed with 'the object' of the protection of 'the privacy of private life'.[71] The article, 'perhaps the most famous and certainly the most influential law review article ever written',[72] ushered in a wave of privacy tort law reform in the US, partly offset by the Supreme Court's broad reading of the Constitution's First Amendment right of free speech.[73] And its fame spread, receiving even an early endorsement from Pollock in England as making a 'suggestion … supported with great ability and ingenuity

[66] For instance, William Kerr (Barrister, Lincoln's Inn), offering the following summary of the 'principle' of *Morison v Moat* (n 52) in the first of many editions of his popular *Treatise on the Law and Practice of Injunctions in Equity* (London, William Maxwell & Son, 1867): 'In all cases where a confidential relationship can be shown to exist, the Court fastens an obligation on the conscience of the party who has derived any confidential communication through that relationship, and will enforce it against him in the same manner as it enforces against a party, to whom a benefit is given, the obligation of performing a promise on the faith of which the benefit has been conferred': ibid 177. Contrast the actual language of *Morison v Moat* (at n 56). Further, under Kerr's analysis of *Prince Albert v Strange* (n 4), this was simply concerned with liability of 'persons who have acquired their information at second hand': *Treatise*, ibid 177. Contrast Lord Cottenham LC's actual language of 'surreptitious or improper obtaining' (at n 55). Pollock (also a Barrister at Lincoln's Inn), treated breach of confidence as a branch of contractual confidence, in the first edition his *Principles of Contract at Law and in Equity* (London, Stevens and Sons, 1876) 384 ('rights arising out of a contract cannot be transferred if they … involve a relation of personal confidence such that the party whose agreement conferred those rights must have intended them to be exercised only by him in whose he actually confided'), a statement repeated in several later editions.

[67] See Hobsbawm (n 10).

[68] Sir F Pollock, *The Genius of the Common Law* (New York, Columbia University Press, 1912) 124.

[69] Warren and Brandeis (n 2).

[70] ibid 206.

[71] ibid 195–196, 214–215.

[72] MB Nimmer, 'The Right of Publicity' (1954) 19 *Law and Contemporary Problems* 203.

[73] See M Richardson, *The Right to Privacy: Origins and Influence of a Nineteenth-Century Idea* (Cambridge, Cambridge University Press, 2017) ch 4.

by its authors'.[74] In the passages dealing with *Pollard*, we see an evisceration of any idea that the doctrine of breach of confidence framed by North J to offer protection of privacy under past conditions of photographic portraiture could be suited to the technologies and practices of modern 'instantaneous photography':

> This process of implying a term in a contract, or of implying a trust ..., is nothing more nor less than a judicial declaration that public morality, private justice, and general convenience demand the recognition of such a rule, and that the publication under similar circumstances would be considered an intolerable abuse. So long as these circumstances happen to present a contract upon which such a term can be engrafted by the judicial mind, or to supply relations upon which a trust or confidence can be erected, there may be no objection to working out the desired protection through the doctrines of contract or of trust. But the court can hardly stop there. The narrower doctrine may have satisfied the demands of society at a time when the abuse to be guarded against could rarely have arisen without violating a contract or a special confidence; but now that modern devices afford abundant opportunities for the perpetration of such wrongs without any participation by the injured party, the protection granted by the law must be placed upon a broader foundation. While, for instance, the state of the photographic art was such that one's picture could seldom be taken without his consciously 'sitting' for the purpose, the law of contract or of trust might afford the prudent man sufficient safeguards against the improper circulation of his portrait; but since the latest advances in photographic art have rendered it possible to take pictures surreptitiously, the doctrines of contract and of trust are inadequate to support the required protection, and the law of tort must be resorted to.[75]

Indeed, Warren and Brandeis's challenge was not just to the breach of confidence's limited 'support [of] the required protection' of privacy but to the orthodoxy of the English judicial method, reflecting the influence of the idea put forward recently by Oliver Wendell Holmes Jr in his Lowell Institute Lectures in Boston that the life of the common law was not the 'logic' of the 'syllogism' but 'experience'.[76] This comes through most clearly in the statement that 'implying a trust' was nothing more or less than 'a judicial declaration that public morality, private justice, and general convenience demand the

[74] F Pollock, *A First Book of Jurisprudence for Students of the Common Law* (London, Macmillan, 1896) 190.

[75] Warren and Brandeis (n 2) 210–211. See also at 213: 'We must therefore conclude that the rights, so protected, whatever their exact nature, are not rights arising from contract or from special trust, but are rights as against the world; and ... the principle which has been applied to protect these rights is in reality not a principle of private property, unless that word is used in an extended and unusual sense. The principle which protects personal writings and any other productions of the intellect or of the emotions is the right to privacy, and the law has no new principle to formulate when it extends this protection to the personal appearance, sayings, acts, and to personal relation, domestic or otherwise.'

[76] OW Holmes Jr, *The Common Law* (Boston, Little, Brown, and Co, 1881) 1.

recognition of such a rule, and that the publication under similar circumstances would be considered an intolerable abuse'. But it is also implicit in the argument that, if judges, when they consider it necessary, engage in policymaking in response to modern exigencies, they should do so now in response to the 'intolerable abuse' of surreptitious photographs, using the affordance of the new detective camera. The reasoning, designed to free judges from fictional adherence to precedent in addressing novel situations – and at the same time expose their policy instincts to proper scrutiny, helped to pave the way for the American legal realist movement of the twentieth century,[77] while leaving British lawyers and judges – and indeed those of the rest of the British common law world – in the uncomfortable position of continuing to adhere to the strict 'authority' of *Pollard v Photographic Company* including its subtle jettisoning of the notion from older cases such as *Prince Albert v Strange* that breach of confidence could extend to surreptitious obtaining in favour of a more lenient treatment of 'instantaneous photography' and like technologies in a world that increasingly could see the implications for privacy of failing to regulate these novel technologies and practices.

Second, there was the initial reliance on the authority of *Pollard* in the British common law world, followed by its eventual reconsideration in much of that world. The precise shifts are difficult to pinpoint, as in the British fashion they were not openly announced – amounting rather to what Hobsbawm might call the framing of 'invented tradition' (rather like the decision of North J in *Pollard* itself).[78] Nevertheless, it took a while for British lawyers and judges to admit that a doctrine which after *Pollard* was construed to require a confidential relationship so closely aligned to a contractual relationship as to be the same or at least substantially akin in many respects,[79] imposed an unacceptable restraint on the protection of privacy in a time when technologies were becoming thoroughly imbricated with everyday life.[80] So in 1967

[77] See generally WW Fisher III, MJ Horwitz and T Reed (eds), *American Legal Realism* (New York, Oxford University Press, 1993).

[78] See Hobsbawm (n 10).

[79] For instance, *Merryweather v Moore* [1892] 2 Ch 518; *Lamb v Evans* [1892] 2 Ch 518; and (as to the textbooks) Kerr, *Treatise on the Law and Practice of Injunctions*, 3rd American edn (Philadelphia, Blackstone Pub Co, 1889) 420; Pollock, *Principle of Contract*, 5th edn (1889) 453. See generally Richardson et al (n 22) ch 4.

[80] Occasionally, courts would espouse a broader reading: see *Lord Ashburton v Pape* [1913] 2 Ch 469, 475 (Swinfen-Eady LJ): 'The principle upon which the Court of Chancery has acted for many years has been to restrain the publication of confidential information improperly or surreptitiously obtained or of information imparted in confidence which ought not to be divulged'; *Saltman Engineering Co Ltd v Campbell Engineering Co Ltd* (1948) 65 RPC 203, 213 (Lord Greene MR): 'If a defendant is proved to have used confidential information, directly or indirectly obtained from a plaintiff, without the consent, express or implied, of the plaintiff, he win be guilty of an infringement of the plaintiff's rights' (citing *Morison v Moat* (n 52)). But these cases were rare. Contrast, for instance, *Victoria Park Racing and Recreation Grounds Co Ltd v Taylor* (1937) 58 CLR 479 in Australia where it seemed to be assumed that breach of confidence could not be argued in a surreptitious obtaining case of overlooking a neighbouring race-ground and broadcasting the results on radio (passing references made to privacy in some judgments notwithstanding): see M Richardson

still Ungoed-Thomas J in *Argyll v Argyll* sought to reconcile the nineteenth-century authorities up to and including *Pollard* in his statement that 'a breach of confidence or trust or faith can arise independently of any right of property or contract other, of course, than any contract which the imparting of the confidence in the relevant circumstances may itself create',[81] as if 'imparting of the confidence' must be taken as given.[82] (Or, as Megarry J put it *Coco v AN Clark (Engineers) Ltd* two years later, the test was confidential information 'imparted in circumstances importing an obligation of confidence' then breached – or at least 'these three elements are normally required'.)[83] We may wonder whether Ungoed-Thomas J, in his former life as a member of the British delegation one of the architects of the European Convention on Human Rights 1950, considered this an appropriate response to the Convention's Article 8 right to private life – or perhaps he thought no response was necessary as the Convention was not yet incorporated into UK law.[84] In any event, the narrow framing in *Argyll* (following *Pollard*) offered enough protection of privacy in that case, concerning a proposed publication in the tabloid press of marital confidences between (then) husband and wife, the Duke and Duchess of Argyll. It was really in the next decade that the reconsideration would begin. And, as Warren and Brandeis foreshadowed in 1890, it would be photography, along with 'other modern devices for recording or reproducing scenes or sounds', that would prompt the change, especially where combined with tabloid press practices. By the 1980s and 90s, cases involving telephone tapping,[85] surreptitious photographs,[86] as well as photographs openly taken without the subject's consent,[87] were becoming prevalent – and judges struggled to bring their scenarios within the parameters of the doctrine of breach of confidence if understood merely in terms of confidential information imparted (and received) then breached. Ultimately, it was Lord Goff's restatement of the doctrine in the notorious '*Spycatcher*' case,

and M Trabsky, 'Radio and the Technology of the Common Law in 1930s Australia: *Victoria Park Racing v Taylor* Revisited' (2011) 20 *Griffith Law Review* 1020. In fact, there were few cases altogether in the first half of the twentieth century: See Richardson et al (n 22) ch 5.

[81] *Argyll (Duchess) v Argyll (Duke)* [1967] Ch 302, 322.

[82] Although Bently (n 8) 261 suggests that Ungoed-Thomas J effected a milestone in 'referr[ing] to Prince Albert in holding that personal information was … protectable through the action for breach of confidence'.

[83] *Coco v AN Clark (Engineers) Ltd* [1969] RPC 41, 44.

[84] As Noel Malcolm points out, he did seem to have a restricted view of the function of the Convention rights, declaring in the General Assembly debate of September 1949 'What we are concerned with is not every case of injustice which happens in a particular country, but with the question whether a country is ceasing to be democratic': 'The Nature of Human Rights: A New Approach' (2020) 62 *Critical Quarterly* 5, 36.

[85] *Francome v Mirror Group Newspapers Ltd* [1984] 1 WLR 892. Contrast *Malone v Metropolitan Police Commissioner* [1979] Ch 344 regarding a police tap (but see *Malone v United Kingdom* (1984) 7 EHRR 14).

[86] *Shelley Films Ltd v Rex Features Ltd* [1994] EMLR 134; *Creation Records Ltd v News Group Newspapers Ltd* [1997] EMLR 444.

[87] *Kaye v Robertson & Sport Newspapers Ltd* [1991] FSR 62.

Attorney-General v Guardian Newspapers Ltd (No 2),[88] as covering confidential information 'com[ing] to the knowledge of a person … [who] has notice, or is held to have agreed, that the information is confidential' with the effect that 'it would be just in all the circumstances' that 'disclosure should be precluded', subject to limiting principles of confidentiality, non-triviality and balance with other public interests such as free speech,[89] that would provide a new beginning[90] – especially after it was construed by Laws J in *Hellewell v Chief Constable*[91] to mean:

> If someone with a telephoto lens were to take from a distance and with no authority a picture of another engaged in some private act, his subsequent disclosure of the photograph would as surely amount to a breach of confidence as if he had found or stolen a letter or diary in which the act was recounted and proceeded to publish it. In such a case, of course, a defence based on the public interest would be available.[92]

Even then it took a further series of surreptitious photography and film cases,[93] some decided as the UK Human Rights Act 1998 was just coming into force, for the new position to become cemented, and then quite soon afterwards supplemented in the UK by the development of a misuse of private information tort.[94] No doubt the advent of the Human Rights Act, bringing the European Convention into UK law, was instrumental. But credit also needs to be given to Lord Goff in *Spycatcher*, who, ten years earlier, put paid to the suggestion from North J in *Pollard* that photographs 'taken on the sly' could not be the subject of protection. As to the judicial method, apparently less had changed since the late-nineteenth century. In the time-honoured British fashion (even in an era

[88] *Attorney-General v Guardian Newspapers (No 2)* [1990] 1 AC 109, 281–282.

[89] ibid 281–282, citing inter alia *Coco v AN Clark* (n 83), *Francome v Mirror Group* (n 85) and Deane J in the Australian case of *Moorgate Tobacco Co Ltd v Philip Morris Ltd* (1984) 154 CLR 414, 438 ('an obligation of conscience arising from the circumstances in or through which the information was communicated or obtained'), as well as 'Dr Francis Gurry's valuable monograph on *Breach of Confidence* (1984)' and 'Professors Birks' *An Introduction to the Law of Restitution*'. And, in the background, there was also the European Convention with its rights inter alia to private life and freedom of expression (although still not yet formally incorporated into UK law). See Richardson et al (n 22) ch 7.

[90] For instance, see *Shelley Films* (n 86); *Creation Records* (n 86). Contrast *Kaye v Robertson* (n 87), where breach of confidence was not argued but relief was given on another ground.

[91] *Hellewell v Chief Constable of Derbyshire* [1995] 1 WLR 804, 807.

[92] Although Laws J was thinking primarily of Lord Goff's statement in Spycatcher (a letter or diary found or stolen being examples offered by Lord Goff) he also cites *Pollard* as a case showing that 'disclosure of a photograph may, in some circumstances, be actionable as a breach of confidence': ibid.

[93] Most notably *Douglas v Hello! Ltd* [2001] QB 967 and [2006] QB 125 (surreptitious photography); *Australian Broadcasting Corporation v Lenah Game Meats Pty Ltd* (2001) 208 CLR 199 (surreptitious filming); *Campbell v Mirror Group Newspapers Ltd* [2004] 2 AC 457 (surreptitious photography).

[94] See the chapters on these cases later in this book.

where the declaratory theory of common law was supposedly on the wane),[95] Lord Goff insisted that 'I realise that, in the vast majority of cases, in particular those concerned with trade secrets, the duty of confidence will arise from the transaction or relationship between the parties … But it is well settled that a duty of confidence may arise in equity independently of such cases.'[96] Except, of course, that it was not well settled until Lord Goff's restatement planted the seeds of the new tradition, superseding the tradition set in train by in *Pollard* a century earlier. Thus, *Spycatcher* presents us with another example of an older authority judged out of step with modern times neatly sidestepped through a process of 'interpretation', following the path of changing the law under guise of keeping it the same. By then, or soon after, the end of *Pollard*'s status as a landmark case had finally arrived.[97]

V. CONCLUSION

Holmes complained that 'great cases … make bad law', offering more a response to 'some accident of immediate overwhelming interest which appeals to the feelings and distorts the judgment', exercising 'a kind of hydraulic pressure which makes what previously was clear seem doubtful, and before which even well settled principles of law will bend', than anything of 'real importance in shaping the law of the future'.[98] Although I would not call it a 'great case', this insight helps us make sense of *Pollard* which in response to an exciting new photographic technology bent the principles of breach of confidence to ensure minimal regulation in line with a late-nineteenth century laissez faire ideology, only to find the principles bent again a century later as the implications for privacy were worked out. While some might say the mistake was corrected, the case illustrates two other problems with a system of precedent (for all its strengths in fostering consistency) – first, the labyrinthine processes of correction, second, the time taken to effect it.[99] Better not to make the mistake to begin with.

[95] See R Goff, 'The Search for Principle' (Maccabaean Lecture on Jurisprudence, 5 May 1983) (1983) 69 Proceedings British Academy 169, 184 ('there is now a readiness among judges, not of course to disregard or ignore precedents by which they are bound, but, where they are at liberty to do so, to adapt or qualify them … to ensure that principles are so stated as to embrace the legally just result on facts possibly not foreseen by those who had previously formulated them'); and N Duxbury, *Jurists and Judges: An Essay on Influence* (Oxford, Hart Publishing, 2010) 66.

[96] *Attorney-General v Guardian Newspapers* (n 88) 281.

[97] *Pollard* does not figure in Lord Goff's 'interpretation' of authorities – and although cited by Laws J in *Hellewell* (n 87 and n 92) and Brooke LJ in *Douglas v Hello!* (2001) (n 93) [67] this is by way of example of the doctrine not as an authority on the scope of the doctrine; even such references were found unnecessary in the later cases of *Lenah* (n 93), *Douglas v Hello!* (2006) (n 93) and *Campbell v MGN* (n 93).

[98] *Northern Security Company v United States*, 193 US 197, 400–401 (1903).

[99] And see F Schauer, 'Do Cases Make Bad Law?' (2006) 73 *University of Chicago Law Review* 883.

2

Roberson v Rochester Folding Box (1900)

AMY GAJDA

IN THE EARLY 1900s, back in the days when the right to privacy was still finding its way into the jurisprudence of the US, Rochester Folding Box Company of Rochester, New York, had already become relatively famous for its paper boxes that packed flat but folded like origami into handy containers for everything from little pills to big skirts.[1] The company's lithography division designed 'advertising novelties'[2] for clients too, marketing materials that encouraged those walking past shop windows to buy certain products. That meant that when Franklin Mills Company of nearby Batavia wanted a poster that would draw the eyes of flour buyers, who better to hire than Rochester Folding Box?

It was a decision that would hasten the adoption of the right to privacy, not only in New York, but ultimately worldwide.

Without the back story, the poster created by Rochester Folding Box lithographers appears unremarkable.[3] It features a hazy cameo-like, head-and-shoulders image of a young woman looking off into the distance, her hair in a chignon, her ruffled blouse pulled down just low enough to reveal her clavicle. The wordplay 'Flour of the Family' is at the top of the poster and, at the bottom, just below the young woman's ruffles, it reads 'Franklin Mills Flour.' The product itself – a bag, a barrel, and a box of flour – is tucked into the poster's lower left corner, images that nearly disappear next to the striking ingénue.

Trouble was that the young woman pictured, 17-year-old Abigail Roberson of Rochester, had not agreed to pose for a Franklin Mills poster.[4] She was 'shocked', she said, when she walked by a Rochester store window one day in 1900[5] and saw her far-off gaze and her striking nape beckoning buyers.[6] Abby had seen the

[1] Advertisement, Rochester Folding Box Co., *Democrat and Chronicle* (N.Y.) 14 May 1900, 8.

[2] Advertisement, Rochester Folding Box Co., 1902, on file with author.

[3] Digital copy of poster, available at harvardpress.typepad.com/hup_publicity/2011/08/who-owns-your-face.html.

[4] D Concannon, 'It Was a Day to Remember', *Democrat and Chronicle* (N.Y.) 15 January 1967, 1.

[5] ibid.

[6] ibid.

original photograph itself before, of course; she had agreed to pose for it for a boyfriend and it was meant for his eyes alone. But, somehow, in a vignette that parallels modern stories about private social media posts that go public, it found its way to designers at Rochester Folding Box and thereafter to 25,000 posters scattered throughout not only Rochester but across the US. Some of them had even been pasted up onto the walls of saloons.[7]

So Abby Roberson sued Rochester Folding Box in New York State courts, arguing that her 'right of privacy' had been invaded.[8] An argument based on privacy rights was a bold one at the time; Abby's own lawyer, for one, initially suggested that privacy was 'a point which [had] never before been brought into court'.[9] That was not precisely accurate because, by then, the United States Supreme Court had written that the 'privacies of life' deserved protection[10] and lower courts had for some years endorsed certain aspects of privacy by sensibility if not by name.[11] 'The right of privacy with respect to one's personal affairs is, in many cases, as dear and as inseparable from the enjoyment of good government and free institutions as any right of property or of personal security', one judge had written in a Missouri case in 1879, for instance.[12] 'A system of laws which should treat with entire indifference such momentous interests–not to say rights–of the citizen, would disgrace any civilized people.'[13] Sure, that came in a dissenting opinion and was therefore far from precedential, but Abby's lawyer was emboldened nonetheless, and put her damages at $15,000.[14]

A man named Elbridge L Adams represented Rochester Folding Box in opposition to Abby's claim.[15] Adams was the company's president and, handily enough, a lawyer too.[16] That meant that he also readily understood the newness of privacy and what that might mean and, in a clever turnabout that used Abby's lawyer's own words against his teenaged client, he argued that because the right to privacy did not yet exist in an official sense, Abby could not prevail. No right of privacy? No liability for Rochester Folding Box's non-permissioned use of Abby's image on a poster.

What both attorneys, so focused on privacy at the turn of the twentieth century, surely knew was that two of their brethren 400 miles to the east in Boston, Massachusetts – Samuel Warren and Louis Brandeis of the Warren & Brandeis law firm – had been working behind the scenes through scholarship to

[7] 'Fate of the Roberson Case', *Buffalo Review*, 5 May 1902, 6.
[8] 'Girl's Portrait Her Exclusive Property', *Democrat and Chronicle*, 31 July 1900, 9.
[9] ibid.
[10] *Boyd v United States*, 116 U.S. 616, 630 (1886).
[11] For a more detailed story of the history of the right to privacy in the US, see A Gajda, *Seek and Hide: The Tangled History of the Right to Privacy*, a book published by Viking in 2022.
[12] *Ex parte Brown*, 7 Mo. App. 484, 495 (Mo. Ct. App. 1879) (Lewis, J, dissenting).
[13] ibid.
[14] 'Girl's Portrait Her Exclusive Property', *Democrat and Chronicle* (N.Y.) 31 July 1900, 9.
[15] 'Girl Fighting for Right of Privacy', *Democrat and Chronicle* (N.Y.) 26 June 1900, 11.
[16] JE Homans et al., *The Cyclopaedia of American Biography* 271 (New York, Press Association Compilers, 1924) 271.

have the right to privacy accepted by name more generally in US courts. Warren and Brandeis were former law partners who had met as students at Harvard Law School and, in 1890, had published a law review article in the *Harvard Law Review* entitled 'The Right to Privacy.'[17] Their interests diverged in a sense from Abby Roberson's, however: they argued chiefly that the gossipy privacy invasions published in the day's scandalous newspapers had to stop because otherwise family happiness and American cultural norms would be forever harmed. 'Each crop of unseemly gossip', they wrote, 'becomes the seed of more, and, in direct proportion to its circulation, results in a lowering of social standards and of morality.'[18]

Today, the law in most states reflects in some part those concerns and today, more than 130 years later, many say that The Right to Privacy law review article remains the most famous law review article ever written.

I. THE RIGHT TO PRIVACY IN THE HARVARD LAW REVIEW

Before a fuller discussion of what Samuel Warren and Louis Brandeis argued in The Right to Privacy, it is important to note that there is a backstory to the article too. Initially, it might appear that the two law partners were mostly concerned about others, that their forward-thinking concern was for society's greater good, and that their writing sprang from their belief that the implementation of higher social standards and morals through a right to privacy would help everyone live happier lives. Surely that sort of altruism was one of their motivations. Like many elites in Victorian times in the US, they believed strongly that the sort of scandal journalism produced by editors like Joseph Pulitzer in newspapers like the New York City-based daily *The World* would sink American culture but also its cultural norms, especially those norms that shielded high society from the prying eyes of the working class. Pulitzer, for one, had decided early on that the former would very much like to know more about the latter – and he encouraged his stable of journalists to write related articles and include detailed drawings about the rich and powerful designed to expose their secret lives. The elites argued in response that such coverage brought them great pain by detailing personal follies and embarrassing indiscretions once known only to family and that the law needed to put a stop to it.[19] The Right to Privacy reflects those concerns in large part.

But the two law partners' desire for privacy was decidedly a personal thing too. Samuel Warren, the millionaire son of millionaires, had been both directly

[17] SD Warren and LD Brandeis, 'The Right to Privacy' (1890) 4 *Harvard Law Review* 193.
[18] ibid 196.
[19] EL Godkin, 'The Rights of the Citizen: To His Own Reputation', *Scribner's Magazine*, July 1890, 58.

and indirectly affected by newspapers like Pulitzer's: not only was Warren friends with Grover Cleveland, the privacy-begging former President of the US known in part for his scandalous-for-the-day out-of-wedlock child (stories about whom were covered in great detail by the day's partisan press), Warren's wife Mabel Bayard had come from a political family and reporting on the Bayard family's woes, including its tragic deaths, seemed particularly invasive at times.[20] It is surely no coincidence that the Warrens, their social gatherings, and their extravagant expenditures routinely received mention in the *Boston Globe* newspaper column titled Table Gossip – and that The Right to Privacy slams gossip by name repeatedly, five times in one single paragraph.[21] Such '[t]riviality' as gossip 'destroys at once robustness of thought and delicacy of feeling', they wrote to conclude that part.[22] 'No enthusiasm can flourish, no generous impulse can survive under its blighting influence.'[23]

It was not just Pulitzer and Table Gossip that Samuel Warren and Louis Brandeis took to task. There is ample language in The Right to Privacy that directly targets newspapers more broadly – and also criticises the technical advancements that could be used to further scandalmongering. 'Instantaneous photographs and newspaper enterprise have invaded the sacred precincts of private and domestic life',[24] Warren and Brandeis wrote to link worries about advances in technology with an increasingly emboldened press, and had created an environment in which '[t]he press is overstepping in every direction the obvious bounds of propriety and of decency.'[25] '[N]umerous mechanical devices', they warned 'threaten to make good the prediction that "what is whispered in the closet shall be proclaimed from the house-tops"'[26] long before technology allowed it quite literally and then, in an internet age, far beyond.

Given such a world, Warren and Brandeis wrote, and given those who 'under the refining influence of culture, [had] become more sensitive to publicity'[27] and deserved the solitude that so many found essential,[28] there was need for a new tort, a new civil wrong. They called it the right to privacy, a right that would give people 'the right to enjoy life', the 'right to be let alone', and the right to sue those who revealed private information.[29] 'The design of the law', the law partners wrote, 'must be to protect those persons with whose affairs the community has no legitimate concern, from being dragged into an undesirable

[20] For the complete story, see A Gajda, 'What if Samuel D. Warren Hadn't Married a Senator's Daughter' [2008] *Michigan State Law Review* 35.

[21] SD Warren and LD Brandeis, 'The Right to Privacy' (1890) 4 *Harvard Law Review* 193, 196.

[22] ibid.

[23] ibid.

[24] ibid 195.

[25] ibid 196.

[26] ibid 195.

[27] ibid 196.

[28] ibid.

[29] ibid 193.

and undesired publicity and to protect all persons, whatsoever [] their position or station, from having matters which they may properly prefer to keep private, made public against their will'.[30]

But while most of The Right to Privacy focused on that sort of anti-newspaper sentiment, there is a notable part relevant to this story of the Rochester Folding Box case too because Warren and Brandeis also believed – and wrote – that people deserved the right to keep their images private and out of the hands of others who would use them for nefarious purposes. Sure, they likely were not thinking of the Abbys of the world as much as they were people like Mrs Grover Cleveland whose image by that time had been used without her permission in advertisements for everything from coffee[31] to bitters,[32] from thread[33] to sewing machines.[34] The Clevelands would routinely complain about such uses[35] and it is nearly certain that their friend Samuel Warren heard from them directly about it, given their collective broader interests in privacy and all.

And so there is this language in The Right to Privacy: methods that allow for reproduction of images of women's faces and forms, especially those 'colored to suit a gross and depraved imagination', deserved particular condemnation and warranted their own change in the law.[36] Notably, such a change would not only protect the famous like Mrs Cleveland. 'The right of one who has remained a private individual, to prevent his public portraiture, presents the simplest case for such extension' of a right to privacy, a sentence in the law review article reads.[37]

There, but also at a number of other times throughout The Right to Privacy, the two authors looked to England for support, specifically, given Mrs Cleveland's sort of trouble with advertisers, *Pollard v Photographic Co.*,[38] and its suggestion that an injunction would be necessary to prevent harm to a lady's feelings should she learn that a portrait photographer had planned to publicly exhibit and sell copies of her image to the general public.[39] If liability based on that sort of behaviour was good enough for England, Warren and Brandeis seemed to be saying, and if France also respected privacy, it was good enough precedent to support a right to privacy of a similar sort in the US.

But the two authors did not need to reach over the Atlantic to find such supportive case law; there were other decisions from courts in the US that had

[30] ibid 214–15.
[31] Copy of advertisement on file with author.
[32] Copy of advertisement on file with author.
[33] Copy of advertisement on file with author.
[34] Copies of advertisements on file with author.
[35] See, eg, Letter from Grover Cleveland to Joseph Clarke (15 March 1890), published in Allan Nevins, Letters From Grover Cleveland 220 (1933), complaining that a newspaper had named her the most popular woman in New York.
[36] SD Warren and LD Brandeis, 'The Right to Privacy' (1890) 4 *Harvard Law Review* 193, 214.
[37] ibid 213.
[38] This case is discussed in ch 1 of this volume.
[39] ibid 208–209.

similarly decided that privacy prevailed under such circumstances, just like the dissenting Missouri judge had suggested in 1879,[40] and, therefore, privacy seemed to be growing somewhat organically in the US even before The Right to Privacy was written. By the turn of the twentieth century, in fact, at just about the time that Rochester Folding Box chose Abby's portrait to adorn the lithograph that it had designed for Franklin Mills, an admittedly small number of courts had already started to use the phrases 'the right *to* privacy' or 'the right *of* privacy' or related language in their published decisions – and only some officially acknowledged the Warren and Brandeis article itself.[41]

Consider as a prime example of the latter a case involving an advertisement published in newspapers in March of 1891, just three months after The Right to Privacy appeared in the *Harvard Law Review*. 'We Grow Simpler as We Grow Older' that ad read in a bolded headline.[42] It thereafter quoted medical doctor Sir Morrell Mackenzie, 'the famous English Throat Specialist',[43] who confirmed that Soden's Mineral Pastilles had the power to cure 'obstinate catarrhal affections of the throat' and noted that these throat lozenges made from the evaporated waters of a German spring also prevented The Grippe and other infectious diseases.[44] Dr Mackenzie's endorsement was so powerful that Soden had placed his 'testimonial and signature' around each box of its pastilles.[45]

But in a twist that presaged Abby's, Dr Mackenzie had not offered his endorsement of Soden's Mineral Pastilles at all and, therefore, had not given permission for his name to be used in an ad or as an adornment on lozenge packages. And, just like Abby would about a decade later, Mackenzie sued the wrongdoer, Soden Mineral Spring Company, the maker of the pastilles, for the misuse of his identity. His very first claim, his attorney explained, was that the company had invaded his privacy.[46]

That attorney filed Mackenzie's claim to privacy in the New York State courts but, since there did not appear much in the lawbooks in New York that would serve as perfect precedent, Mackenzie's attorney looked instead to *Pollard v Photographic Co.* as support.[47] But he also relied on the newly published Right of Privacy article in a stateside bid to win over judicial sentiments[48] – perhaps he had read about *Pollard* there – and that meant that it would be the very first time that such a citation to the Warren and Brandeis work appeared in a judicial

[40] *Ex parte Brown*, 7 Mo. App. at 495 (Lewis, J, dissenting).

[41] See, eg, *Schuyler v Curtis*, 15 N.Y.S. 787 (N.Y. Sup. Ct. 1891) and *Corliss v E. W. Walker Co.*, 57 F. 434 (C.C.D. Mass. 1893).

[42] Advertisement, *St. Louis Globe-Democrat*, 18 March 1891, 12.

[43] ibid.

[44] ibid.

[45] ibid.

[46] *Mackenzie v Soden Mineral Springs Co.*, 27 Abb. N. Cas. 402, 408 (N.Y. Sup. Ct. 1891).

[47] ibid.

[48] ibid.

opinion. (('Citing, Article in Harvard Law Review, December, 1890, on the Right of Privacy)', is the way the court noted the plaintiff's reliance on the article.)[49] In short, Dr Mackenzie's attorney argued, *Pollard* and The Right to Privacy both helped prove that Soden Mineral Pastilles had made 'an unwarranted invasion of [his client's] reasonable right of privacy'[50] and therefore must stop its misuse of his name and identity.

Just a few weeks after the Soden Mineral Pastilles ad had graced newspapers, Dr Morrell Mackenzie won his lawsuit. A judge sitting on the Supreme Court of New York's First District trial court bench ordered that Soden Mineral Springs stop using advertising material that featured Dr Mackenzie without his permission.[51] Not only had the doctor suffered damage to his 'professional standing and income as a physician', the judge wrote, such a use was 'misleading and prejudicial to the public interest'.[52] That judge did not mention the right to privacy by phrase in his actual court order, but he did not need to because Mackenzie's attorney already had and that argument had apparently won the day.

What the outcome in *Mackenzie v Soden Mineral Springs Company* confirmed was that the right to privacy was a growing concept in courts in the US – and especially, it seemed, in the State of New York. It also confirmed that the truth was therefore somewhere in between what the two lawyers in *Roberson v Rochester Folding Box* would argue in the trial court nine years later: Abby's claim for a right to privacy was not the first ever, but it seemed that the best support for it in the US was grounded particularly in a work of scholarship.

Even so, things looked good for Abby, at least to start.

II. ROBERSON V ROCHESTER FOLDING BOX: ABBY'S VICTORIES

Despite clear support in both The Right to Privacy and the court's decision in *Mackenzie v Soden Mineral Springs Company*, the concept of the right to privacy in New York was still so new when Abby Roberson brought her claim that her extraordinary beauty almost scuttled it all. Courts back then were very much focused on *libel* as a cause of action in these sorts of cases – litigation that centred on published information that could harm the public perception of a person – and, while Abby herself argued that 'her good name ha[d] been attacked'[53] in a way that seemed similar to a libel claim, the striking image used on the lithograph of 'one of the most beautiful young women in Rochester'[54] didn't seem all that harmful, really. She looked lovely.

[49] ibid.
[50] ibid.
[51] ibid 410.
[52] ibid.
[53] *Roberson v Rochester Folding-Box Co.*, 65 N.Y.S. 1109, 1109 (N.Y. Sup. Ct. 1900).
[54] Untitled news story, *St. Albans Daily Messenger*, 29 June 1900.

Elbridge Adams knew that such an argument that focused on how good Abby appeared might well resonate with any libel-focused judge. He understood the far-reaching consequences of such an argument too; if the court saw it his way, his lithography department could keep right on using Abby's and others' images as they saw fit and the courts would have no power to stop them.[55] Therefore, he argued that without a cause of action for libel, Abby could not prevail.

At first Judge John Davy seemed persuaded. 'If the picture tended to bring ridicule on the lady', the judge told those gathered in the courtroom the day of oral argument, 'then it would be termed libelous'.[56] But this use was of a decidedly different sort, he acknowledged, one that seemed to glorify her beauty, and, therefore, had led to a legal quandary of sorts for him.[57] Abby's attorney quickly refocused the court: '[H]ere is a modest young girl of this city', he told the judge.[58] 'Certainly she has the right to protest against this promiscuous use of her picture.'[59] Maybe the right to privacy by name wasn't all that common in New York or other states as yet, but this seemed a perfect case for it.

The argument for a right to privacy ultimately won. Just as important, the outcome that Adams had suggested – that creators be allowed to use others' images as they saw fit – would be 'a blot upon our [impressive] system of jurisprudence', Judge Davy decided; it would be a horrible wrong for Abby and others like her should the courts be powerless to stop 'the doing of a wrongful act which would wound in the most cruel manner the feelings of a sensitive person'.[60] The judge equated Abby's emotional harm arising from the 'Flour of the Family' poster with the 'mental pain and distress', the societal disgrace and humiliation in those lawsuits brought by a woman for the breach of a contract of marriage.[61] The shame seemed similar and, therefore, Abby's mental suffering needed the same sort of monetary salve because 'the mind is no less a part of the person than the body', the judge wrote, 'and the sufferings of the former are sometimes more acute and lasting than those of the latter'.[62]

What all this meant was that Abby would indeed have 'the protection of her right of privacy',[63] Judge Davy wrote, a right that extended out from what he called the sacred privacy of the home to embrace individuals, human beings like Abby who needed protection because, when their privacy was invaded, it 'tend[ed] to destroy domestic and individual happiness'.[64]

[55] *Roberson*, 65 N.Y.S. at 1110.
[56] 'Girl Fighting for Right of Privacy', *Democrat and Chronicle* (N.Y.) 26 June 1900, 11.
[57] ibid.
[58] ibid.
[59] ibid.
[60] *Roberson*, 65 N.Y.S. at 1110.
[61] ibid.
[62] ibid.
[63] ibid.
[64] ibid at 1111.

'[I]f she desires a life of privacy', he noted in a bit of a rhetorical flourish because he knew that she did and he had just decided that it was her right, 'she has a right to enjoy'.[65]

The outcome made headlines across the US; 'Girl's Portrait Her Exclusive Property' Rochester's newspaper read.[66] *The Paper Box Maker*, a national trade publication for the owners of businesses such as Rochester Folding Box, suggested that it had received word from an unnamed correspondent about the outcome of *Roberson v Rochester Folding Box* and reported that the case stood for the notion that 'personal beauty may be a property right'.[67] *The Fourth Estate*, a trade publication for the makers of newspapers, spun the case a different way. 'Everybody who respects the rights of others will applaud [the] decision', it wrote, given that the 'unauthorized circulation of the portraits of pretty girls or well-known men for advertising purposes has grown to be an evil that ought to be suppressed.'[68] That publication called the judge's description of Abby's victory a 'right of privacy'.[69]

The trial court judge's decision in *Roberson v Rochester Folding Box* did not end the dispute, however. Elbridge Adams next took his argument that privacy did not exist and that, therefore, Abby had no claim, to the intermediate level appellate court for the State of New York. By that time, given the increasing national interest in the case through industry publications and otherwise, Abby had become a bit of a proxy for others who had been similarly wronged; newspapers had started to spin her case as 'a very important one', eagerly awaited by those 'public officials and others' frustrated by the misappropriation of their images for advertising purposes.[70] By the day of the oral argument at the intermediate level appeals court, so important was the hearing in Abby's case that the judges chose to wear their now-familiar black silk robes for the very first time in the court's history.[71]

William H Adams, the chief judge of New York's intermediate level appellate court, would not be one of those sitting on the bench in new judicial garb, however. He had recused himself from the case because Elbridge Adams was his son.[72] That left only four judges to decide this claim springing from the right to privacy[73] and, eventually, all four of the judges voted in favour of Abby.[74]

This time, the language that the court used seemed even stronger than that from the trial court judge. First, the fact that privacy did not previously exist

[65] ibid.
[66] 'Girl's Portrait Her Exclusive Property', *Democrat and Chronicle* (N.Y.) 31 July 1900, 9.
[67] 'Personal Beauty is a Property Right', *The Paper Box Maker* (N.Y.) 25 August 1900.
[68] 'The Right to Privacy', *The Fourth Estate* (N.Y.), 11 August 1900.
[69] ibid.
[70] 'Famous Picture Case Was Argued', *Democrat and Chronicle* (N.Y.) 2 April 1901, 9.
[71] 'Roberson Case Will Be Heard', *Democrat and Chronicle* (N.Y.) 14 May 1901, 11.
[72] See ibid 11; 'Elbridge L. Adams Dies in New York', *North Adams Transcript* (Massachusetts) 15 January 1934, 3.
[73] 'Fate of the Roberson Case' [1902] *Buffalo Review* 6.
[74] *Roberson v Rochester Folding Box*, 71 N.Y.S. 876 (N.Y. App. Div. 1901).

much at all in past jurisprudence made little difference to these appellate court judges: 'it is not the rule that the want of a precedent is a sufficient reason for turning the plaintiff out of court', the judges wrote.[75] This was especially true and important in Abby's case because it was 'an established principle of the common law' that people and property should not be interfered with.[76] Moreover, it was clear that the right to privacy had been otherwise acknowledged by New York courts in key cases,[77] and it remained the law of the land that, as Justice Thomas Cooley of Michigan's high court had written decades earlier, everyone 'has the absolute right to be let alone'.[78]

This time, the judges again cited *Pollard* but, perhaps because it was merely a work of scholarship, not The Right to Privacy – and, this time, they also gave a nod to the Soden Mineral Pastilles decision in favour of Dr Mackenzie ('an injunction was granted' and 'the action of the court was in consonance with well-established principles' in that case, they wrote).[79] It all made for a conclusive win for Abby Roberson.

But the case did not end there either. By this time, many '[l]aw journals, magazines and newspapers' around the world had written about the *Rochester Folding Box* case and what its lithographers had done to Abby and, despite the fact that only *one* of those publications was said to have agreed with him,[80] Elbridge Adams continued on his quest for victory: he asked the appellate court for leave to appeal the questions in the case to New York's highest court, the Court of Appeals, and the judges agreed.[81] '[W]e are to inquire', New York's high court judges would describe their work with regard to the case, 'whether the complaint … can be said to show any right to relief in either law or in equity'.[82]

At first, it all seemed a procedural repeat of what had happened in the lower courts. During oral argument before the Court of Appeals judges in Albany, Adams continued his mantra that the right to privacy did not exist, that '"feelings" were not actionable' through the right to privacy or otherwise, and that because no *libel* claim was possible springing from the publication of such a strikingly lovely image, Abby could not recover.[83] 'The complaint states no cause of action known to the common law', is how Adams' argument is paraphrased in the court's syllabus.[84]

[75] ibid at 877.
[76] ibid at 878.
[77] ibid at 883.
[78] ibid at 878.
[79] ibid at 882.
[80] 'Fate of the Roberson Case' [1902] *Buffalo Review* 6.
[81] *Roberson v Rochester Folding Box Co.*, 72 N.Y.S. 1125 (N.Y. App. Div. 1901).
[82] *Roberson v Rochester Folding Box Co.*, 64 N.E. 442, 442 (N.Y. 1902).
[83] 'Fate of the Roberson Case' [1902] *Buffalo Review* 6.
[84] *Roberson v Rochester Folding Box Co.*, 64 N.E. 442, 442 (N.Y. 1902).

In response, Abby's lawyer gave the same forceful argument in favour of privacy and protection for emotions that had worked so well below and, in doing so, he incorporated the same highly persuasive facts:

> They stole this picture. They defiled this girl. They hung her picture in saloons and on billboards; they might next tack it on the bunghole of a beer .... If a woman cannot own her face then any thief can steal it to use as he wishes. I do not think that Mr. Adams would tolerate seeing the picture of his wife painted on every billboard in the city or on beer kegs or cigar boxes. Neither does this poor young girl.[85]

The syllabus paraphrased the plaintiff's argument this way: 'Defendants' use of plaintiff's portrait for advertising purposes, without her consent, constitutes an unwarrantable invasion of her right of privacy for which an action lies.'[86]

It is not clear when things went wrong for Abby. Perhaps her attorney's plea built at least in some part on emotion simply backfired with these particular judges. Or maybe Elbridge Adams had finally found a clearer voice against the existence of the right to privacy and that voice suddenly resonated. In any case, for the first time in three tries, at New York's highest and, therefore, its most important court, Rochester Folding Box won the right to use Abby's image without her permission.

The Rochester newspaper's headline put the outcome simply: 'Miss Roberson Loses.'[87] Joseph Pulitzer's *World* saw the potential for an impact beyond Abby; its headline read 'Anybody May Use Your Picture for an "Ad."'[88] The *Boston Globe*, the newspaper that carried the Table Gossip column that so annoyed Samuel Warren in the 1880s, wrote an article about the high court's decision too. 'Has Not Right to Her Own Face' was its headline – and its editors had cheekily placed that language atop a two-column drawing of the winsome Abby and her clavicle just as she had appeared on the poster for Franklin Mills Flour itself.[89]

III. ROBERSON V ROCHESTER FOLDING BOX: ABBY'S DEFEAT

It is hard not to read the final, powerful decision from New York's Court of Appeals as a slam against The Right to Privacy by Samuel Warren and Louis Brandeis. In short, those on New York's highest court wrote, just because two lawyers at a law firm in another state had suggested in 1890 that the right to privacy needed to spring into existence to protect society did not make it so. While Abby Roberson argued that Rochester Folding Box 'had invaded what

[85] 'Fate of the Roberson Case' [1902] *Buffalo Review* 6.
[86] *Roberson*, 64 N.E. at 442.
[87] 'Miss Roberson Loses', *Democrat and Chronicle* (N.Y.) 29 June 1902, 19.
[88] 'Anybody May Use Your Picture for an "Ad"', *The World* (N.Y.) 2 July 1902, 1.
[89] 'Has Not Right to Her Own Face', *Boston Globe*, 7 July 1902, 6.

is called a "right of privacy" – in other words, [her] right to be let alone', the judges wrote, such a right could not be found in the much more significant writings of Blackstone or Kent or 'any other of the great commentators upon the law'.[90] Instead, it had been born merely a decade earlier 'when it was presented with attractiveness and no inconsiderable ability in the Harvard Law Review [] in an article entitled, "The Right to Privacy."'[91] Sure, the article was 'clever', those judges wrote, but it mostly referred to decisions from England[92] and, therefore, did not seem worthy ground for a sudden shift in the law of New York that would create a right that none of the learned of the past had embraced. The legal rule *against* notions of privacy as some sort of right of an 'inviolate personality' was, in turn, one that 'had been enforced for generations'.[93] As for those decisions from England that The Right to Privacy had relied upon as precedents, they 'rested either upon the ground of breach of trust or that [the] plaintiff had a *property* right in the subject of litigation which the court could protect'.[94] And those from the US that Abby's lawyer had argued were precedential – Dr Mackenzie's case was apparently not among them – mostly *refused* to find a privacy right under the presented circumstances and proved only that privacy 'ha[d] not as yet found an abiding place' in American jurisprudence.[95] Therefore, a decision from the New York Court of Appeals that embraced such a right would 'do[] violence to settled principles of law by which the profession and the public ha[d] long been guided'.[96]

The Abby-appears-beautiful-so-there-is-no-harm argument by Elbridge Adams also worked quite well with these judges. Judge Alton Parker, the chief judge of the Court of Appeals and the one who wrote for the four-to-three majority, seemingly could not understand why someone would want to sue if they ended up looking good in an advertisement, unauthorised or not. 'The likeness [of Abby] is said to be a very good one', he wrote, and 'others would have appreciated the compliment to their beauty implied in the selection of the picture for such purposes.'[97] It would be downright ludicrous to say that another's portrait, 'even if obtained upon the street by an impertinent individual with a camera', could be restrained by law when they appeared lovely in the use that resulted.[98]

All that was enough to decimate Abby's claim, of course, but the court noted in addition that it was worried about the potential for a never-ending series

[90] *Roberson*, 64 N.E. at 443.
[91] ibid.
[92] ibid at 444.
[93] ibid.
[94] ibid at 445 (emphasis added).
[95] ibid at 447.
[96] ibid.
[97] ibid at 442–43.
[98] ibid at 443.

of what it considered similarly silly claims: This 'so-called right of privacy',[99] New York's high court judges wrote, was a right that bordered 'upon the absurd' because if it came to exist in the law, the floodgates would open and thereafter include liability for things like 'the publication of a word-picture, a comment upon one's looks, conduct, domestic relations or habits.'[100] A 'vast field of litigation' would be created, the court predicted, 'should this court hold that privacy exist[ed] as a legal right'.[101]

So here, Judge Parker explained for the court, the outcome would be a different one. He was 'required to decide cases upon principle',[102] he wrote, and, here, the principle was clear: no right of privacy existed in New York jurisprudence or seemingly anywhere else and, therefore, Abby had no right to prevent Rochester Folding Box from doing what it did.

That holding may have sounded correct to him at the time, but Judge Parker would soon come to regret his strong words against a right to privacy. Just a few months later he would announce a bid to become President of the US and, soon after, began to complain about how his family's privacy had been invaded by 'camera fiends' and the constant 'surveillance of surreptitious snapshotters.'[103] 'I reserve the right to put my hands in my pockets and assume comfortable attitudes', he had said in frustrated response, 'without being everlastingly afraid that I shall be snapped by some fellow with a camera.'[104] Abby Roberson noted the shift in Judge Parker's feelings about the right to privacy and wrote a letter to him that ultimately found its way into the nation's newspapers. 'Naturally the camera fiends feel licenses to annoy yourself and family', she told him, since it was he himself who had 'contended that the rights of one who obtains a likeness surreptitiously are superior' to the rights of others.[105] Turnabout is fair play.

Eventually, those like Abby whose images had been used in advertising would prevail in the courts of the State of New York and elsewhere and it would indeed become a violation of the right to privacy to do what Rochester Folding Box had done to Abby in all states. But in what might be considered karma, Judge Parker not only lost the presidency to the wildly popular incumbent Theodore Roosevelt, he also effectively lost the right to prevent the camera fiends he found so annoying from continuing their intrusive behaviour.

It is a story that ends in more modern times, but it starts with Judge Parker's decision itself.

[99] ibid.
[100] ibid.
[101] ibid.
[102] ibid.
[103] 'The Right of Privacy', *Democrat and Chronicle* (N.Y.) 26 July 1904, 6.
[104] 'Girl Scores on Judge Parker', *Buffalo Morning Express*, 27 July 1904, 6.
[105] 'Parker's Decision Came Home to Roost', *The Gazette* (Iowa) 27 July 1904, 8.

IV. ROBERSON V ROCHESTER FOLDING BOX: THE FALLOUT

There is a line in the New York Court of Appeals' decision that foreshadows what happened next in the saga of *Roberson v. Rochester Folding Box*. 'The legislative body could very well interfere and arbitrarily provide that no one should be permitted for his own selfish purpose to use the picture or the name of another for advertising purposes without his consent', Judge Parker had written, suggesting that maybe, if people wanted a change in the law so badly, New York lawmakers might take up the matter that he and his colleagues had found inappropriate for the courts.[106]

And that is precisely what happened. Within ten months after the New York Court of Appeals had decided that privacy did not exist in New York and that Abby would not prevail, the New York legislature passed a statute that it titled 'An Act to prevent the unauthorized use of the name or picture of any person for the purposes of trade.'[107] The law was clearly meant to cover Abby's type of situation:

> A person, firm or corporation that uses for advertising purposes, or for the purposes of trade, the name, portrait or picture of any living person without having first obtained the written consent of such person, or if a minor of his or her parent or guardian, is guilty of a misdemeanor.[108]

The statute also gave those individuals who had been featured against their will in advertising the right to sue in 'an equitable action' and gave juries permission to award punitive damages in appropriate cases.[109]

Today, that right is called appropriation or misappropriation and it has become the law throughout the US. Its nationwide acceptance was helped along when, in 1939, the authoritative American Law Institute authored the first Restatement of the Law of Torts and included within it the misappropriation type of privacy: 'A person who unreasonably and seriously interferes with another's interest in not having his affairs known to others' is liable for invasion of privacy, the relevant section read, but so does a person who exhibits a likeness to the public against the other's wishes.[110] And just to be clear where they stood with regard to Abby's plight in particular, the authors added it an example of an appropriate claim, using A and B as characters: 'A surreptitiously takes a photograph of B, a young woman, and publishes it as an advertisement for flour under the caption: "The Flower of the Family." B has a cause of action against A.'[111]

[106] *Roberson*, 64 N.E. at 443.
[107] 1903 N.Y. Laws 308.
[108] ibid.
[109] ibid.
[110] Restatement (First) of Torts, § 867 (Am. L. Inst. 1939).
[111] ibid.

In 1977, the Second Restatement included in its definitions for privacy a parallel tort that it called 'Appropriation of Name or Likeness.'[112] 'One who appropriates to his own use or benefit the name or likeness of another', the modern Restatement reads, 'is subject to liability to the other for invasion of his privacy.'[113] This second Restatement of the Law did not use the fact pattern from Abby's case specifically, but suggested that '[t]he interest protected by the rule stated in this Section is the interest of the individual in the exclusive use of his own identity, in so far as it is represented by his name or likeness, and in so far as the use may be of benefit to him or to others' and it used advertisements as an example of a sort of misuse.[114]

In modern times, therefore, it is the law across the US that someone like Abby will win a claim against an entity like Rochester Folding Box, if that entity has used her image or name or identity without permission in advertising. Moreover, the Second Restatement has expanded to protect other parts of privacy in addition to misappropriation: 'Intrusion upon Seclusion', the tort that makes it a civil wrong to peer in on someone who is in a private place; 'Publicity Given to Private Life', one that holds liable a person who reveals another's embarrassing secrets; and 'Publicity Placing Person in False Light', a tort most similar to defamation but one that finds liability even if the false information is merely highly offensive and not necessarily reputation-harming.[115] Most states have accepted all four of those torts and, therefore, privacy is protected in multiple ways throughout the US well more than a century after *Roberson v Rochester Folding Box*. Those interests have impacted the law of privacy worldwide because it was ultimately *American* privacy interests that drafters relied on in significant part to create the Universal Declaration of Human Rights and, thereafter, the European Convention on Human Rights.[116]

But in New York, a state that was ultimately among the first to accept privacy, albeit as a legislative enactment after its high court refused to do so through the common law, things are a bit different. Sure, laws remain on the books in that state that protect the Abbys of the world: New York's Civil Rights law titled 'Right of privacy' continues to promise that 'A person, firm or corporation that uses for advertising purposes, or for the purposes of trade, the name, portrait or picture of any living person without having first obtained the written consent of such person, or if a minor of his or her parent or guardian, is guilty of a misdemeanor' and a separate section offers a private right of action, meaning that plaintiffs can sue for the wrong too.[117] In addition, there are specific

[112] Restatement (Second) of Torts, § 652C (Am. L. Inst. 1977).
[113] ibid.
[114] ibid.
[115] Restatement (Second) of Torts, §§ 652 B, D, E (Am. L. Inst. 1977).
[116] M Traynor, 'The Statement of Essential Human Rights – A Groundbreaking Venture', *ALI Reporter*, Winter 2007.
[117] N.Y. Civ. Rights Law, § 50 (McKinney 2003).

but limited 'rights of action' today for those whose privacy has been invaded in certain ways relating to 'unwarranted video imaging' of residential properties ('taking moving digital images of the recreational activities which occur in the backyard of the residential real property' is unlawful) and unlawful dissemination of intimate or sexually explicit images of individuals without their permission (if 'taken when such person had a reasonable expectation that the image would remain private').[118]

But unlike in a majority of states in the US, New York has never accepted the far broader privacy torts laid out in the Restatement. In fact, courts there have flatly rejected them, finding that privacy became statutory-only in the Empire State when the legislature responded to Judge Parker's decision in *Roberson v Rochester Folding Box* all the way back in the early 1900s. Moreover, since then, New York's high court has suggested that the state's statutory privacy law be 'narrowly construed' in order to protect conflicting constitutional principles such as free expression.[119]

That means that, today, the surreptitious snapshotters of the Big Apple and Albany and beyond have very nearly the same free reign that they did in Judge Parker's time. But if that is indeed some sort of karma that came back to bite Judge Parker, it has taken the much more innocent right down along with him.

V. FOSTER V SVENSON: THE NEIGHBORS

There is a photograph taken by famous art photographer Arne Svenson that makes up part of his series entitled The Neighbors.[120] It features a man who appears to be in his early thirties lying on a daybed; his back is to the camera, his blue jeans are pulled down just enough and his darker blue t-shirt is pulled up just enough to expose his lower back and maybe the black band of his underwear. Standing off to the right is a young woman of similar age who is handing him a glass of water. She is wearing a long grey sweater with thick blue stripes and a grey scoop-necked shirt; she has placed her left hand just above her distended belly and she looks as if she may be pregnant. (A different photograph in the series, one that appears to be of the same woman perhaps doing yoga, sitting cross-legged, hands clasped behind her back, seemingly confirms as much). A stuffed giraffe is barely visible in the background of the first photograph, so it appears as if the room where the two people are interacting is some type of nursery. Meantime, the man seems not to be looking at the glass in the woman's hand but down at something in his own hands, perhaps a cell phone.

[118] N.Y. Civ. Rights Law, §§ 52 A-B (McKinney 2003).

[119] *Messenger v Jahr Printing and Publishing*, 727 N.E.2d 549 (N.Y. 2000).

[120] A description of how Svenson captured these images and several of the photographs themselves were available in 2021 at arnesvenson.com/the-neighbors.html.

There are additional photographs that form The Neighbors. A dog peering out a window. The half face of a woman behind a drape. A robed woman, apparently fresh from the shower, sitting on a bed. Robed people, or, better put, the bottom halves of robed people, eating breakfast. A child alone. Young children together, one grabbing another in some sort of play.[121]

Svenson shot the photographs from the outside of the New York City apartment building, through its windows. You can tell this because the panes of glass often formed what he called a Mondrian-like foreground,[122] framing those pictured twice in a sense.

But we also know that Svenson shot his images from the outside through windows because those people captured in the photos were shocked when they saw them.[123] It had all happened in a way that paralleled Abby Roberson's story more than a century before; Svenson's neighbours first learned of his series when they saw in the newspaper that images of themselves taken through their apartment windows would be on display at a local art gallery selling for $7,500 each.[124]

The Neighbors had been captured the previous year when Svenson had set up shop inside his own Manhattan apartment across the street from his neighbours' glass-windowed building, carefully shooting from the shadows of his darkened home into theirs in night and day.[125] Because Svenson's neighbours were so far away, he necessarily used a telephoto camera lens, one specially designed to capture birds in trees. His goal, he said, was to show images of greater humanity by focusing on those across the street: 'I only reveal the turn of the head, the back against a window, the legs under a table', he wrote in explanation on his website, 'those tiny, private, scenarios and actions that portray a humanness that is unconsciously truthful and tender'.[126]

But those tender images of truth were sometimes hard to come by. A magazine reporter who followed Svenson as he photographed The Neighbors reported that Svenson would, in effect, lie in wait for people to appear and would yell 'Come to the window!' if they did not, as if they might hear him and respond.[127] Once, this reporter explained, Svenson snapped a photograph of a little girl inside her apartment. 'I don't like it when little girls are running around

[121] 'Foster v Svenson' (2013) 41 *Media Law Report* 2564 (N.Y. Sup. Ct. 2013).

[122] A Svenson, *The Neighbors*, Arne Svenson, arnesvenson.com/the-neighbors.html (last accessed 20 February 2021).

[123] Many of these facts are taken from the two reported decisions in the case: 'Foster v Svenson' (2013) 41 *Media Law Report* 2564 (N.Y. Sup. Ct. 2013) and *Foster v Svenson*, 7 N.Y.S.3d 96 (N.Y. App. Div. 2015).

[124] 'I Spy: Photographer Who Secretly Snapped Neighbors Goes to Court', *Reuters*, 8 June 2013.

[125] 'Foster v Svenson' (2013) 41 *Media Law Report* 2564 (N.Y. Sup. Ct. 2013).

[126] A Svenson, *The Neighbors*, Arne Svenson, arnesvenson.com/the-neighbors.html (last accessed 20 February 2021).

[127] *Foster*, 7 N.Y.S.3d at 98.

without their tops', the reporter said that Svenson said, 'but this is a beautiful image'.[128]

His neighbours, especially angry that their young children had been photographed in such a way without permission, sued. Svenson, for his part, maintained that he had the right to do what he did. 'Defending myself against these charges was one of the greatest challenges of my life', he would later say about the *Foster v Svenson* lawsuit, 'but given censorship as the alternative, I had no choice.'[129] In defence, he argued that his neighbours were but players 'performing behind a transparent scrim on a stage of their own creation with the curtain raised high' and that, therefore, they had no privacy.[130] His lawyers argued more pragmatically and less poetically that New York's privacy statute protected Svenson because it did not apply to The Neighbors' privacy claims.

At the trial court, the judge agreed with Svenson. 'While it makes Plaintiffs cringe to think their private lives and images of their small children can find their way into the public forum of an art exhibition', that judge wrote, 'there is no redress under the current laws of the State of New York.'[131] In short, it was an easy legal decision because the privacy-based relief that the plaintiffs sought was unavailable to them by statute.

Svenson's neighbours, thereafter, appealed to New York's intermediate level court.

At first, things looked good for the neighbours there; in the very first paragraph of the opinion the court highlighted the universal and long-standing need for a right to privacy. 'Concerns over privacy and the loss thereof have plagued the public for over a hundred years', the judges wrote, and thereafter cited specifically to Warren and Brandeis and The Right to Privacy.[132] Moreover, concerns about the loss of privacy had only intensified over the years, the court explained, with '[n]ew technologies [that] can track thought, movement, and intimacies, and expose them to the general public, often in an instant'.[133] The Neighbors was not a Facebook post, to be sure, but the court seemingly recognised the strong privacy implications in both.

But things thereafter took a sharp turn away from such worries. First, the court reiterated the history of *Roberson v Rochester Folding Box* and explained that lawmakers had acted rapidly back then in the face of '[p]ublic outcry over the perceived unfairness' of the decision to draft and pass a privacy statute.[134]

[128] ibid.

[129] A Svenson, *The Neighbors*, Arne Svenson, arnesvenson.com/theneighbors.html (last accessed 20 February 2021).

[130] *Foster*, 7 N.Y.S.3d at 98.

[131] 'Foster v Svenson' (2013) 41 *Media Law Report* 2564 (N.Y. Sup. Ct. 2013).

[132] *Foster v Svenson*, 7 N.Y.S.3d 96, 97 (N.Y. App. Div. 2015).

[133] ibid at 98.

[134] ibid at 100.

Second, the judges explained how, given that history – specifically, the New York Court of Appeals' rejection of privacy in the common law and its creation and existence, thereafter, solely through statute – its own decision was necessarily constrained. Finally, it wrote, that, under the statute, The Neighbors photographs would be considered works of art and, therefore, protected in the State of New York 'however disturbing it may be'.[135] This was not a 'trade' use as in the *Roberson* 'Flour of the Family' case; this was art. And so, the court decided, Svenson won and his neighbours lost.

There was one more important parallel with Abby's claim in the court's decision. Toward the end of the opinion, the judges looked toward the legislature for change, just as New York's high court had more than a century before. But here, it seemed clear that the judges *wanted* change. '[W]e do not, in any way, mean to give short shrift to plaintiffs' concerns', the court wrote, because 'many people would be rightfully offended by the intrusive manner in which the photographs were taken'.[136] And then a sort of lobbying began: 'Needless to say, as illustrated by the troubling facts here', the appellate judges wrote, 'in these times of heightened threats to privacy posed by new and ever more invasive technologies, we call upon the legislature to revisit this important issue.'[137]

VI. THE LEGACY

Two things happened in the 2010s to solidify the surprisingly strong legacy of *Roberson v Rochester Folding Box* and its legislative aftermath in New York. First, New York's high court refused to hear an appeal by Svenson's neighbours. Perhaps it was too difficult a case, given the conflict between privacy interests and free expression. Or maybe it was too easy, given that the statute appeared to apply, just like the intermediate appellate court had decided.

That left the New York legislature as the last and best driver for potential change once again. But, second, despite the surprising outcome in *Foster v Svenson* and its judicial pleas for legislative change, lawmakers showed little interest in amending New York's law. And thereafter the language of New York's privacy statute remained the same, the same as it had been when Arne Svenson began to take photographs of the families across the street, and the same as it was a century earlier when lawmakers took action directly in response to *Roberson v Rochester Folding Box*.

Since then, New York has taken steps to beef up data privacy and it has enacted those newer provisions that protect backyards from voyeurism and to punish what is colloquially known as 'revenge porn' (nude photographs of

[135] ibid at 105.
[136] ibid.
[137] ibid at 105–06.

people, usually taken with consent for personal use, subsequently posted online without consent, usually as revenge for a breakup). But the language of the so-called 'Right of Privacy' law in New York remains the same, despite society's growing privacy concerns and the 'troubling' images in The Neighbors.

That is not the case elsewhere in the US, however. And, as the history of the Right to Privacy shows, much of it had to do with that collective backlash against the outcome in *Roberson v Rochester Folding Box*, a cascade of cases in which judges in other states ruled the opposite, criticising New York's high court decision that failed to recognise the importance of the right to privacy. The first and, therefore, the best example comes from the State of Georgia, *Pavesich v New England Life Insurance Company*, the focus of the following chapter.

3

Pavesich v New England Insurance Co (1905)

REBECCA MOOSAVIAN

I. INTRODUCTION

IT IS NO coincidence that the first three landmark privacy cases in this volume concern photography, a cutting-edge technology that emerged in the mid-nineteenth century and raised profound questions about image, identity and how the law should respond. Like *Pollard v Photographic Company* (1889)[1] and *Roberson v Rochester Folding-Box Co* (1902),[2] *Pavesich v New England* entailed the judiciary dealing with what Barbas has termed 'the crisis of the circulating portrait',[3] ie unauthorised use of an individual's image in ways very much against their wishes. And in a pleasingly ironic narrative flourish, the privacy action was brought by an artist – a painter in the tradition that new photographic technology was rapidly replacing.

Despite *Pavesich's* legal influence and a reasonable body of American academic literature discussing the case, as Kent claims, it 'has not always received the attention it deserves'.[4] The reasons for this are unclear, though *Pavesich* does tend to be overshadowed by *Roberson*.[5] *Roberson*'s reputation is perhaps sealed by its distinctive facts; a sympathetic plaintiff who found herself co-opted into 'Flour of the Family' adverts and whose case instigated America's first privacy statute.[6] Yet, ultimately, the *Roberson* court controversially denied

[1] 40 Ch D 345.

[2] 171 N.Y. 538 (1902).

[3] S Barbas, *Laws of Image, Privacy & Publicity in America* (Palo Alto, Stanford University Press, 2015) ch 3.

[4] MB Kent Jr, 'Pavesich, Property & Privacy: The Common Origins of Property Rights & Privacy Rights in Georgia' (2009) 2(1) *John Marshall Law Journal* 1–22, 5.

[5] (n 2).

[6] Chapter 132 of the Laws of 1903 ('An act to prevent the unauthorised use of the name or picture of any person for the purposes of trade'). This later became the New York Civil Rights Law, ss 50–51. For a discussion of this, see: R Moosavian, 'Public Image (Un)Limited: Privacy Rights of the Photographic Subject in England and New York Compared' in A Koltay and P Wragg (eds) *Comparative Privacy & Defamation* (Cheltenham, Edward Elgar, 2020) ch 9.

a privacy right whereas the *Pavesich* court took the bold, activist step of upholding one.

As this chapter argues, *Pavesich* is a fascinating and intriguing landmark judgment, and not only because it was the first case where a US state Supreme Court upheld a common law privacy right (though this is surely sufficient to seal its landmark status). *Pavesich*'s significance also lies in two related points. First, by articulating in detail the founding political philosophy for privacy – Lockean natural rights – the *Pavesich* court made its own intellectual contribution to the development of the doctrine; in particular, the great influence of Lockean notions of 'property' and individual self-ownership are revealed. Second, by articulating these Lockean roots the *Pavesich* judgment aptly reveals the culturally – and historically-specific nature of the privacy right that emerged. Despite its noble, rhetorically-appealing universalist natural law claims, this was a privacy that primarily respected, protected and reflected white, middle-class men; men like artist Paolo Pavesich. This chapter discusses these points in detail, as well as providing new information about the hitherto elusive plaintiff himself. But let us commence with an overview of the background events that preceded the case.

II. HISTORIC AND LEGAL BACKGROUND

The emergence of photographic technology in the mid-nineteenth century spurred the popularisation of professional photographic studios where individuals could pay to get their portraits taken. Portraits became a popular middle-class activity, forming a means to express one's identity and social standing.[7] From the 1880s the reach of photography extended further as the practice came to be undertaken by amateur photographers using the new Kodak camera (which proudly claimed '*you press the button, we do the rest*'). But with these developments, some individuals' portraits came to be used without their knowledge or consent – the 'crisis of the circulating portrait' – prompting widespread public anxieties about this new technology.[8] Such unauthorised uses of image, particularly for commercial purposes like advertising, offended traditional elite Victorian sensibilities.[9]

It was against this background that in 1905 Justice Cobb delivered the judgment of the Georgia Supreme Court in *Pavesich*. Up to this point there had

[7] P Hamilton and R Hargreaves, *The Beautiful & The Damned, The Creation of Identity in Nineteenth Century Photography* (London, Lund Humphries Publishers, 2001) 20, 29–43.

[8] R Mensel, 'Kodakers Lying in Wait: Amateur Photography & the Right to Privacy in New York 1885–1915' (1991) 43(1) *American Quarterly* 24–45, 29–30, 32.

[9] Barbas (n 3) 56–57. For an account of Warren & Brandeis's patrician sensibilities, see: J Barron, 'Warren & Brandeis, The Right to Privacy', (1890) 4 *Harvard Law Review* 193: 'Demystifying a Landmark Citation' (1979) 13 *Suffolk University Law Review* 875, 904, 913–916.

been nascent calls for privacy rights to be respected, but legal precedent was mixed and, arguably tilted against a privacy right. Even following Warren and Brandeis's seminal 1890 article calling for a privacy right,[10] claims brought by the subjects of photographs were commonly rejected by the courts for two reasons. First, courts routinely held that a privacy right did not exist at common law. In *Atkinson v Doherty* (1899) a plaintiff failed in her action to prevent her deceased husband's name and image being used on a brand of cigars. Hooker J admitted that taking a photograph may be 'impertinent', but this was one of the ills law could not redress as the claimed right in one's image was not proprietary or contractual and lacked legal authority.[11] The New York Court of Appeals put forward similar reasoning in its controversial *Roberson* majority ruling, denying relief for the young plaintiff whose image had been used without her consent in the defendant's advertising campaign. In the majority judgment, Chief Judge Parker held there was no previous case where a plaintiff's privacy right had been explicitly recognised. He claimed that 'the so-called "right of privacy" has not yet found an abiding place in our jurisprudence' and incorporating such a right into common law would 'do violence to settled principles of law'. Instead, it was for the state legislature to enact such a right.[12]

The second reason for the failure of many privacy claims was that the law did not provide redress for free-standing emotional harms. Though the motives driving plaintiffs' claims were not always articulated in these early judgments, it is evident that most (if not all) were brought for dignitary harms caused by the use of their image, including distress and humiliation etc.[13] As Barbas claims, such feelings of violation were driven by an emerging 'sense of image consciousness' and the increasing social and personal importance attached to public image.[14] In particular, the notion that one might sell one's likeness to make money offended prevailing cultural sensibilities of the day.[15] Despite a shift away from this attitude by the first decades of the twentieth century,[16]

[10] S Warren and L Brandeis, 'The Right to Privacy' (1890) 4(5) *Harvard Law Review* 193.

[11] *Atkinson v John E Doherty & Co* (1899) 121 Mich 372, 375, 382.

[12] *Roberson* (n 2) 545, 556.

[13] For example: *Roberson v Rochester Folding Box Co* (1901) 64 A.D. 30 (plaintiff suffered great humiliation, scoffs and jeers of others, her good name was attacked and she suffered a severe nervous shock); *Munden v Harris* (1911) 153 Mo. App. 652 (plaintiff suffered humiliation, annoyance and disgrace); *Henry v Cherry & Webb* (1909) 30 R.I. 13 (plaintiff suffered great humiliation, public ridicule and mental anguish).

[14] S Barbas, 'The Laws of Image' (2012) 47 *New England Law Review* 23, 27.

[15] Barbas (n 3) 56.

[16] Numerous authors have noted that by the earliest decades of the 20th century fewer plaintiffs were claiming embarrassment and humiliation due to unauthorised use of their image and more were simply seeking recompense for appropriation. G Armstrong, 'The Reification of Celebrity Persona as Property' (1991) 51 *Louisiana Law Review* 443, 459, 461. See also: J Lake, *The Face That Launched a Thousand Lawsuits, The American Women Who Forged a Right to Privacy* (Yale University Press, 2016) 151–3.

early image cases, including *Atkinson* and *Roberson*,[17] did deal with claims for emotional harm caused by publication, quoting an influential passage by Lumpkin J which confirmed that the law would not permit damages for such injuries:

> The law protects the person and the purse. The person includes the reputation. The body, reputation and property of the citizen are not to be invaded without responsibility in damages to the sufferer. But outside these protected spheres, the law does not attempt to guard the peace of mind, the feelings or the happiness of everyone, by giving recovery of damages for mental anguish ... There is no right, capable of enforcement by process of law, to possess or maintain without disturbance any particular condition of feeling.[18]

Yet, despite the prevailing legal consensus around this time being generally unreceptive to image-based privacy claims, there were some notable isolated instances of judicial support for privacy in the form of sporadic plaintiff successes and dissenting judgments. As section V explains, the *Pavesich* court skilfully built a legal argument for a privacy right from these strands and took care to minimise the not-insubstantial body of contrary precedents.

III. WHO WAS PAOLO PAVESICH?

It was against this backdrop that Paolo Pavesich brought his privacy action. Yet one knowledge gap in the *Pavesich* case has been the plaintiff himself. The court judgment informs us that Paolo Pavesich was an artist, but provides scant detail beyond this intriguing fact. Numerous academics, including Davis in his excellent historic account of the case, have deemed Paolo Pavesich 'lost to history'[19] or merely recounted the bare known facts about him. But this chapter reveals that Pavesich is not 'lost to history' and a fuller account of the colourful plaintiff can be pieced together from local newspapers of the day.[20] Nevertheless, one must take account of the likelihood that certain reported biographical facts evidently came directly from Pavesich himself and so the possibility of some self-mythologising or reinvention cannot be discounted.

[17] *Atkinson v Doherty* (n 11) 380–381; *Roberson* (n 2) 552–553. Also quoted in *Murray v Gast Lithographic & Engraving Co* (1894) 8 Misc. 36, 37.

[18] *Chapman v Western Union Telegraph Co* (1891) 88 Ga. 763, 772–773. NB: this was a negligence case.

[19] JJ Davis, 'An Enforceable Right of Privacy: Enduring Legacy of the Georgia Supreme Court' (1994) 3 *Journal of Southern Legal History* 97, 98–99; A Allen, 'The Natural Law Origins of the American Right to Privacy: Natural Law, Slavery & the Right to Privacy Tort' (2012) 81 *Fordham Law Review* 1187–1216, 1194.

[20] All US newspapers cited are accessible via newspapers.com. Thanks to an anonymous user with the handle 'jdelombard' who had already identified many of the clippings referenced here and did not respond to the author's request to establish contact. 'jdelombard' undoubtedly saved the author some search time.

Paolo Pavesich was born in Trieste, Austria.[21] He claimed to have trained in the best European art schools in Florence and Milan, later undertaking work for the Czar in St Petersburg, before coming to the US around 1878.[22] He became a US citizen and lived there until his death in April 1920 in Kentucky, leaving a wife, one son and two daughters.[23] Pavesich was an itinerant and successful fresco artist who travelled the country undertaking commissions to decorate the large mansions of wealthy, high society families and public buildings (including numerous churches, the Grand Theatre in Atlanta, the state capitol in Lincoln, Nebraska and Pensacola City Hall).[24] In the early 1880s Pavesich travelled to various cities including Los Angeles, Denver and Dallas, advertising his services in local newspapers upon arrival.[25] Between 1888–1889 he stayed in St Joseph, Missouri, again advertising his services in local papers[26] and undertaking fresco work in private homes. The local newspaper noted 'The gentleman will remain in the city for a short time if sufficient work is furnished him';[27] such work must have been forthcoming because two months later he had opened an office in the city centre of St Joseph.[28] But by 1892 he was based in Chicago.[29]

Barbas writes that Pavesich 'was not famous by any means' and that his picture was probably used in the New England advert 'because it suggested health, wisdom, and respectability; the robust, bespectacled Pavesich bore a resemblance to Theodore Roosevelt, who was president at the time'.[30] Yet newspapers of the day do indeed suggest that Pavesich was an artist of some renown at the time of his privacy suit. In 1904 the Florida-based *Tampa Tribune* referred to him as 'the famous fresco artist' and 'one of the greatest artists of the country in his line',[31] and this renown continued in the years that followed.[32] Pavesich's

[21] *The Atlanta Constitution* (Atlanta, Georgia) 11 April 1920, 17.

[22] *St Joseph Gazette-Herald* (St Joseph, Missouri) 8 April 1888, 4; *The Tampa Tribune* (Tampa, Florida) 1 April 1915, 5. See also: *The Orlando Sentinel* (Orlando, Florida) 7 March 1917, 8. In 1917 *The Orlando Sentinel* reported that Pavesich had lived in America for 37 years (1880).

[23] *Atlanta Constitution* (n 21) 17.

[24] ibid; *The Pensacola News Journal* (Pensacola, Florida) 11 July 1909, 2; 14 July 1909, 7.

[25] *The Los Angeles Herald* (Los Angeles, California) 2 March 1881, 3; *The Dallas Daily Herald* (Dallas, Texas) 30 July 1884, 5.

[26] *St Joseph Gazette-Herald* (St Joseph, Missouri) 10 July 1888, 3.

[27] ibid, 11 March 1888, 5; 10 July 1888, 3; 28 January 1891, 3.

[28] ibid, 7 May 1888, 5.

[29] *The Lincoln Journal Star* (Lincoln, Nebraska) 27 June 1892, 5. See also: *St Joseph Gazette-Herald* (n 22) 4 ('His home is in Chicago, but he is called to every portion of the United States, and there is scarcely a large city but contains some samples of his skill, so that a permanent residence at any point is entirely out of the question with him.').

[30] Barbas (n 3) 60.

[31] *The Tampa Tribune* (Tampa, Florida) 23 October 1904, 1.

[32] He was described as a 'well-known mural decorator … who has decorated some of the handsomest residences in America': *The Tampa Tribune* (Tampa, Florida) 8 December 1907, 3. Elsewhere Pavesich was referred to as 'a mural artist of considerable renown': *The Pensacola News Journal* (Pensacola, Florida) 19 July 1909, 2.

reputation was founded on his artistic skill; his work was highly regarded and he was described 'as an artist of such rare merit'[33] and, elsewhere 'a master' whose work was 'simply beautiful'.[34] His commissions involved flowers, roses, cherubs and sky scenes in the style of Louis XIV and *The Tampa Tribune* heaped lavish praise upon his designs for the exclusive Rey and Clewis family residences.[35] So Pavesich was clearly no 'civilian' and enjoyed some cross-state renown for his work. But this is not to suggest that the defendants used his image because the plaintiff was well-known; the advert did not name Pavesich or refer in any way to his artistry. But this new information does shed light on Pavesich's motives for bringing the privacy action which, to date, have been shrouded in some uncertainty.[36] The judgment indicates that Pavesich claimed use of his image was 'peculiarly offensive to him'.[37] Furthermore, according to Davis, Pavesich's petition document stated that the advert brought him 'into ridicule before the world and especially with his friends and acquaintances'.[38] Yet despite this explicit emphasis on emotional damage, Pavesich claimed $25,000 in damages, 'a tremendous sum' for the time according to Barbas.[39] Pavesich's motive for bringing the action is thus ambiguous; Davis has suggested that it was perhaps a mix of principle and avarice.[40] Yet the newspaper reports above support the proposition that embarrassment or humiliation would have been a concern. The reports depict Pavesich as an 'Old World' gentleman artist, undertaking tasteful, exquisite work for high society clients with genteel sensibilities. His kudos and future commissions would arguably depend on maintaining this reputation, and thus appearing in a 'vulgar' advert would not have accorded with the bourgeois cultural sensibilities of his client base.

Newspapers of day shed new light on a further interesting fact about Paolo Pavesich; they indicate that he was engaged with another legal dispute at the same time as his privacy action. In October 1904, *The Tampa Tribune* reported that Pavesich was 'in the city on business of a legal nature' and he had filed suit for $1,100 for fresco work done for one John A Graham.[41] However, the outcome of this dispute was less successful than his privacy case; a couple of years later the same newspaper briefly noted that Pavesich 'reports having lost

[33] *St Joseph Gazette-Herald* (St Joseph, Missouri) 14 July 1888, 5.

[34] *St Joseph Gazette-Herald* (n 27) 11 March 1888, 5.

[35] *The Tampa Tribune* (Tampa, Florida) 21 April 1909, 3; (n 22) 5.

[36] It does also render curious some comments in Justice Cobb's judgment about public character, eg: 'The mere fact that he is an artist does not of itself establish a waiver of this [privacy] right. If he displayed in public his works as an artist, he would of course subject his works and his character as an artist, and possibly his conduct as a man, to such scrutiny and criticism as would be legitimate and proper … The plaintiff was in no sense a public character'. *Pavesich v New England Insurance Co* (1905) 122 Ga. 190, 217.

[37] ibid (head notes).

[38] Official record, quoted by Davis (n 19) 103.

[39] Barbas (n 3), 60; Davis (n 19) 99.

[40] Davis (n 19) 103.

[41] *The Tampa Tribune* (n 31) 1.

his suit against John A Graham'.[42] So Pavesich was of a class that could afford to hire lawyers to protect his legal interests where necessary, and he was by no means shy to do so. His decision to litigate in 1903 led to the landmark case that has etched his name into privacy law history, despite its fade into obscurity in the world of art.

IV. THE CASE

The facts of Pavesich's famous case are only preserved in outline. The dispute arose when Paolo Pavesich posed for a portrait in the studio of commercial photographer J Quinton Adams in Atlanta (this remained a popular activity of the day, despite the emergence of the Kodak camera). Adams passed the negative to Thomas Lumpkin, an agent of New England Insurance. It was made into an advert for New England Insurance (see Figure A) and published in *The Atlanta Constitution* newspaper on 15 November 1903.[43] *The Atlanta Constitution* was Georgia's leading newspaper that 'promoted economic revitalisation of Atlanta and the South'. It competed for readers and all-important advertising revenue against its rival, *The Atlanta Journal*. Pavesich saw his photograph published in *The Atlanta Constitution* and brought an action for libel and privacy against the insurance company, Adams and Lumpkin. He filed his petition with the City Court of Atlanta on 15 December 1903, one month after the advert's publication. The defendants filed a response rejecting both claims on the basis that libel was not made out and there existed no legally enforceable privacy right.[44]

At first instance the case was decided by Justice Harry Reid at the City Court of Atlanta in May 1904. Though this initial judgment was unreported, Davis uncovered the court records and notes that:

> [Reid] apparently made quick work of Pavesich's novel theory; he ruled simply, 'After hearing argument the general demurrers are sustained and the petition is dismissed.'[45]

Pavesich appealed Justice Reid's decision to the Georgia Supreme Court. The Supreme Court heard legal argument on 3 February 1905 and delivered its judgment one month later on 3 March. The Court bench was comprised of six justices: Chief Justice Thomas J Simmons, Presiding Justice William H Fish, Associate Justice John S Candler, Beverly D Adams, Joseph R Lamar and finally Associate Justice Andrew Jackson Cobb who delivered the unanimous judgment of the Court. This bench, unsurprisingly, was a remarkably homogenous group; all the justices were Georgian-born white men and all were Democrats.

[42] *The Tampa Tribune* (Tampa, Florida) 24 November 1906, 7.
[43] Davis (n 19) 99.
[44] ibid 105.
[45] ibid 106.

All had qualified for the bar via legal practice, except for Justice Cobb who had completed a law degree.[46] Yet Davis identifies one 'unusual' feature of the Pavesich bench that may have 'unconsciously influenced the innovative result'; the bench was a relatively young one. Davis writes:

> The average age of the justices was fifty, with Chief Justice Simmons at sixty-seven the only one in his sixties. The reason for this youth was probably the Civil War, which had decimated Simmons's generation.[47]

Justice Andrew Jackson Cobb, then aged 47, wrote the Court's judgment. Cobb came from a prominent and politically active slave-owning family.[48] Both his father and uncle had been leading Confederates, supporting the collective of southern states that resisted the union of all American states and sought to maintain the institution of slavery.[49] His father, Howell Cobb, had served as a Confederate General in the American Civil War (1861–1865) and his uncle, Thomas Cobb, had drafted the Confederate Constitution.[50] Justice Andrew Cobb's politics were thankfully more moderate than his elders; he did not share their views on slavery[51] and strongly criticised Georgia's failure to properly investigate and punish lynching.[52] But he was, nevertheless, 'a moderate social conservative' and a strict Baptist who supported alcohol prohibition laws.[53] Cobb had joined the Georgia Supreme Court bench in 1896 aged 39, one of its youngest ever appointments. Before this he had been a practising lawyer. He had had also run for office (as a Representative in General Assembly of Georgia) and in the 1890s taught at local law schools including the University of Georgia and Atlanta Law School, becoming Dean of the latter.[54]

The Georgia Supreme Court upheld Pavesich's libel and privacy claims; it found that Justice Reid had erred in dismissing Pavesich's claim and reversed his judgment. The Court held that the defendant's actions amounted to libel. Pavesich did not have an insurance policy so the advert would lead people to assume he had been paid to lie and he would thus 'become odious to every decent individual'. But even if Pavesich had not been paid for the lie, 'he would receive and merit the contempt of all persons having a correct conception of moral principles'.[55] Consistent with the wider culture outlined in section II, this finding

[46] ibid 106.
[47] ibid 107.
[48] Allen (n 19) 1204.
[49] Davis (n 19) 106; Allen (n 19) 1204–1206.
[50] Davis (n 19) 106.
[51] Allen (n 19) 1206.
[52] AJ Cobb, 'The Right to Live: Will the State Protect It or Must We Rely on Federal Authority?' (1922) 6(3) *Georgia Historical Quarterly* 189–196.
[53] TW Reed, *Men of Mark in Georgia*, Vol 5 (ed: William Northern) (Caldwell, 1910) 5–9. Accessible via: srvg.org/Members-Only/Library/Publications/Men-of-mark-in-Georgia---Volume-5--1912-.pdf (last accessed 21 April 2021).
[54] ibid.
[55] *Pavesich* (n 36) 221–222.

reveals judicial distaste for activities such as advertising; it was looked down upon by decent 'right-thinking' people to such an extent that involvement in it could be deemed reputationally-damaging. In holding the defendant's actions libellous, the Georgia Court did not have to uphold a privacy right to enable Pavesich to succeed … and yet it did. The Court boldly claimed 'The liberty of privacy exists, has been recognized by the law, and is entitled to continual recognition.'[56] Justice Cobb employed some bold and creative reasoning to enable him to confirm the existence of a privacy right and tort; it is to this reasoning that discussion now turns.

V. THE JUDGMENT

In a rich and wide-ranging judgment, Justice Cobb put forward numerous layers of inventive argument to justify the Court's conclusion. This part undertakes a close reading of the judgment. It shows how Justice Cobb wove natural law rights into the *Pavesich* judgment and the great influence of John Locke's work upon the structure and content of the natural right of privacy. This section also highlights three crucial features of Locke's work that found their way into the privacy right, in particular: the self-possessive individual, a shifting and ambiguous use of the term 'property' and claims of universal equal right.

Pavesich was a creative judgment that was not weighed down by the dearth of earlier supporting cases. Justice Cobb's approach shunned the legal formalism that had dominated American adjudication since the 1860s. In broad terms, such formalism entailed: a narrow deductive interpretive approach; autonomous, logical legal reasoning without recourse to matters 'outside' of law; explicit avoidance of generalised policy-making; and strict adherence to *stare decisis*.[57] By the turn of the twentieth century, such formalist reasoning was coming to be denounced as 'mechanical' and insufficiently responsive to the needs of a rapidly changing industrial society.[58] In keeping with this emerging anti-formalism, Justice Cobb was critical of excessive judicial conservatism, in particular a preoccupation with precedent as epitomised by the *Roberson* majority's earlier approach. Though he accepted such judicial conservatism

[56] ibid 201.

[57] N Duxbury, *Patterns of American Jurisprudence* (Oxford, Oxford University Press, 1997) ch 1; B Leiter, 'Legal Formalism and Legal Realism: What is the Issue?' (University of Chicago Public Law & Legal Theory Working Paper No 320, 2010).

[58] R Pound, 'Mechanical Jurisprudence' (1908) 8 *Columbia Law Review* 605–623; OW Holmes, 'The Path of The Law' (1897) 10(8) *Harvard Law Review* 457–478; Holmes, 'The Common Law' in W Fisher, M Horwitz and T Reed (eds), *American Legal Realism* (Oxford, Oxford University press, 1993) 9.

could be 'valuable', in this context it had resulted in undue caution and failure to recognise a privacy right.[59]

Cobb took a less slavish approach to prior privacy case law. He drew upon a slender cluster of favourable precedents[60] and took great care to limit the relevance of unfavourable authorities, skilfully distinguishing them on facts or *ratios*.[61] But the *Roberson* decision was more difficult to marginalise; Cobb therefore simply claimed 'we are utterly at variance with' the majority's conclusion and instead endorsed Justice Gray's dissenting opinion as the correct approach, before quoting a lengthy passage from it.[62] In short, Cobb constructed an approximate legal justification that was broadly defensible, though evidently a reasonable conclusion in the opposite direction could also have been extrapolated from these mixed authorities. Cobb's legal argument, expressed in modest terms as a double-negative, was that 'nothing in judicial decision … can be called to demonstrate … [privacy's] non-existence as a right'. The absence of a firm favourable precedent was thus not fatal to upholding a privacy right, though Cobb conceded that it should lead the courts to 'proceed with caution'.[63]

Justice Cobb buttressed his defensible, if borderline, legal argument with two other wider sources that he claimed justified a privacy right. First, Cobb looked to legal 'side lights', namely other areas of law that indirectly upheld a 'right to be let alone'. He recounted diverse examples from Roman law to common law nuisance, trespass, eavesdropping and protection against search and seizure. The latter represented 'instances where the common law had both tacitly and expressly recognized the right of an individual to repose and privacy'.[64] Second, Cobb noted that though the facts of the *Pavesich* dispute may have been novel, the principles at stake were not. Where there was an absence of precedent, Cobb stated 'the common law will judge according to the law of nature and the public good'.[65] In this way, Justice Cobb filled the precedential 'gap' that he had created with natural law.

[59] *Pavesich* (n 36) 213. Justice Cobb also quoted the dissenting Justice Gray in *Roberson* thus: the 'absence of exact precedent … upon the subject are of no material importance in awarding equitable relief' and the majority were 'unduly influenced by a failure to find precedents in analogous cases … which would precisely apply,' at 214.

[60] Including *Manola v Stevens* (1890) (unreported) and *Pollard* (n 1), both of which had been cited by Warren & Brandeis (n 10). To this Cobb added *Marks v Jaffa* 6 Misc 290, 292 (1893). *Pavesich* (n 36) 205–207.

[61] The following unfavourable authorities were reconciled as follows: *Schuyler v Curtis* (1895) 147 N.Y. 434 (deemed inconclusive on the existence of a privacy right during one's lifetime); *Corliss v E W Walker Co* (1894) 64 F. 280 and *Atkinson v Doherty* (n 11) (both deemed to have denied relief on the basis that the image used was of a deceased public figure); *Murray v Gast* (n 17) (deemed a correct finding that a privacy action could not be brought by a parent).

[62] *Pavesich* (n 36) 211–212, 213–217.

[63] ibid 193, 213.

[64] ibid 197–198. In taking this approach, he was following the argument put forward by Warren & Brandeis (n 10).

[65] *Pavesich* (n 36) 193–194.

A. A Natural Right to Privacy

Natural law looms large in *Pavesich*. To justify upholding the privacy right, Justice Cobb advanced a three-pronged argument based upon natural law, the constitution and regular law.[66] Cobb's upholding of the privacy right was (at least partly) based upon natural law in that it deemed privacy an eternal God-given right bestowed upon individuals. In particular, he drew closely on Lockean notions of social contract, natural right and property whose influence run strongly throughout the judgment.[67]

According to Cobb, there exist 'laws sometimes characterised as immutable because they are natural, and so just at all times, and in all places, that no authority can either change or abolish them', and he confirmed that privacy was one such right. Yet this grand claim had an arguably modest basis; it was a matter of instinct (specifically, the instinct of those with 'normal' intellect):

> The right of privacy has its foundation in the instincts of nature. *It is recognised intuitively* … Any person whose *intellect* is in a *normal condition* recognises at once that as to each individual member of society there are matters private and there are matters public so far as the individual is concerned. Each individual as instinctively resents any encroachment by the public upon his rights … *A right of privacy* in matters purely private *is therefore derived from natural law*.[68]

Drawing upon the essential features of Locke's social contract, Cobb claimed that this natural right of privacy was enjoyed by the individual in the lawless state of nature and was retained when they surrendered many – but not all – of their rights and liberties in exchange for the benefits of civil society.

Justice Cobb depicted the natural right of privacy as an element of two other absolute natural rights, namely personal security and liberty. Security encompassed uninterrupted enjoyment of life and body and played a fairly peripheral role in the judgment. But Cobb's linkage of privacy to liberty was a crucial aspect of his reasoning. He put forward a very wide conception of the natural right to liberty. It was not merely concerned with the absence of physical restraint, but embraced 'the power of locomotion, of changing situation, or moving one's person to whatsoever place one's own inclination may direct' (in modern parlance, freedom of movement) and 'the right of a man to be free in the enjoyment of the faculties with which he has been endowed by his Creator'.[69] Cobb propounded a conception of liberty as respect for individual autonomy

[66] Justice Cobb claimed the privacy right is 'derived from natural law, recognised by the principles of municipal law, and guaranteed … by the constitutions of the United States and the State of Georgia, in those provisions which declare that no person shall be deprived of liberty': ibid 197.

[67] Such influences have been widely noted. See, eg: Kent (n 4) 6–10.

[68] Emphasis added. *Pavesich* (n 36) 194.

[69] ibid 195.

over a range of life choices generally, and over the extent to which one engages with society in particular:

> Liberty includes the right to live as one will … One may desire to live a life of seclusion; another may desire to live a life of publicity; still another may wish to live a life of privacy as to certain matters and of publicity as to others. … Each is entitled a liberty of choice as to his manner of life.[70]

This assumed a close link between privacy and individual autonomy, a view shared by numerous modern commentators.[71] By respecting and encompassing a wide range of the individual's choices, liberty thus included both publicity ('The right of one to exhibit himself to the public at all proper times, in all proper places, and in a proper manner') *and* privacy ('The right to withdraw from the public gaze at such times as a person may see fit, when his presence in public is not demanded by any rule of law'). Liberty thus necessarily embraced privacy and Cobb emphasised this relationship by repeatedly referring to the 'liberty of privacy' across the judgment.[72] By employing this rhetorical device, he subtly linked privacy with a right that enjoyed greater pedigree and explicit recognition in the US Constitution.[73] Yet this link with liberty also led to the most controversial claim in the judgment, discussed in section VI, where Cobb likened the unauthorised use of Pavesich's image to 'slavery'.

The preceding natural law-based reasoning enabled Justice Cobb to downplay any appearance of undesirable judicial overreach by maintaining that the Court was not creating a new right, but simply finding and articulating a right that already existed.[74] This rationale was already coming to be condemned as a misleading fiction by select early forerunners to legal realism who argued, on the contrary, that judges *do* in fact make law.[75] The modern secular lawyer schooled in such debates (as well as Hume's guillotine and modern restatements of natural law) may read Justice Cobb's natural law reasoning with some justifiable circumspection. Cobb's exalted claims based upon 'instinct' and 'normal' intellect should be treated with caution as a textbook example of – if not 'nonsense on stilts' – then subjective judicial preferences clothed in grand universalist claims.[76] However, there have been spirited defences of this natural law aspect of the *Pavesich* judgment. First, Justice Cobb's approach must be viewed in its intellectual-cultural context. According to Peikoff, ethical

[70] ibid 196.

[71] A Westin identifies protecting autonomy as the first function of privacy: *Privacy & Freedom* (Ig Publishing, 1967). See also: J Rachels, 'Why Privacy is Important' (1975) 4(4) *Philosophy & Public Affairs* 323–333; C Bryant, 'Privacy, Privatisation and Self-Determination' in *Privacy* JB Young (ed), (Chichester, John Wiley, 1978) ch 3, 80.

[72] *Pavesich* (n 36) 196, 200, 201.

[73] The 14th Amendment to the US Constitution states 'nor shall any state deprive any person of life, liberty or property, without due process of law'.

[74] *Pavesich* (n 36) 201.

[75] See, eg, JC Gray, 'The Nature and Sources of the Law' (1909) in *American Legal Realism* (n 58) 36–38.

[76] See, eg, OW Holmes, 'Natural Law' (1918) 32(1) *Harvard Law Review* 40–44.

intuitionism was popular at the start of the twentieth century, and certain rights were widely accepted in the US as inalienable and self-evident.[77] Furthermore, references to natural law were not uncommon in Georgian judgments.[78] Against this background, Cobb's claims would have been intellectually respectable and uncontroversial. Indeed, for Peikoff it is precisely the Pavesich judgment's 'appeal to political and moral philosophy' that makes its contribution to privacy law so 'distinctive' and 'compelling'.[79] Furthermore, even shorn of its natural law grandeur, Allen argues that Cobb's account of privacy as a fundamental human need inherently linked to liberty is highly persuasive per se.[80]

B. The Influence of Lockean Property

This Lockean natural law core discussed above sets up what is, in my view, the most significant feature of the *Pavesich* judgment; its use of property. To be sure, similar notions of property were present and influential in other similar cases of the time, but Justice Cobb's systematic and detailed natural law reasoning articulated the privacy right's theoretical basis, especially its Lockean roots, more fully. In particular the judgment adopted a shifting and ambiguous use of the term 'property', applying it to the individual to create the 'self-ownership' upon which the privacy right was initially based.

Cobb's reasoning brought in earlier privacy cases where property notions had been employed, including *Corliss* where the court viewed the privacy in one's portrait as a property right akin to copyright as well as a personal right.[81] The influence of property notions in early privacy cases has been noted by select commentators. Post, for example, has drawn out such issues in Warren and Brandeis' seminal article, showing how the authors 'disentangled' privacy from existing property laws.[82] More specifically, Kent discusses the property notions in *Pavesich*, claiming that the judgment 'overflows with themes and language familiar to the law of property' and 'demonstrate[s] that privacy rights and property rights are similar creatures with similar philosophical and historical origins'.[83]

[77] A Peikoff, 'No Corn on This Cobb: Why Reductionists Should be All Ears for Pavesich' (2004) 42 *Brandeis Law Journal* 751, 787. See, eg, The Declaration of Independence (4 July 1776) which states: 'We hold these truths to be self-evident, that all men are created equal, that they are endowed by their Creator with certain unalienable Rights, that among these are Life, Liberty and the pursuit of Happiness.'

[78] Allen (n 19) 1198.

[79] Peikoff (n 77) 790, 791.

[80] Allen (n 19) 1212, 1215.

[81] *Pavesich* (n 36) 208–209.

[82] RC Post, 'Rereading Warren and Brandeis: Privacy, Property, and Appropriation' (1991) 41 *Case Western Reserve Law Review* 647, 648–649. See also: B Bratman, 'Brandeis & Warren's Right to Privacy & the Birth of the Right to Privacy' (2002) 69 *Tennessee Law Review* 623.

[83] Kent (n 4) 17, 21–22.

Two examples of property notions at work in Justice Cobb's judgment are worthy of particular attention. First, is his explicit endorsement and quotation of Justice Gray's dissent in *Roberson*, specifically a passage where Gray deemed the search for a property right 'unduly restrictive', before going on to claim:

> Property is not, necessarily, the thing itself which is owned; it is the right of the owner in relation to it. The right to be protected in one's possession of a thing, or in one's privileges, belonging to him as an individual … is property.[84]

This statement is a textbook illustration of how notions of property were changing around this time. Vandervelde argues that by the end of the nineteenth century understandings of 'property' had transformed from the traditional Blackstonian conception of absolute dominion over physical things to a de-physicalised understanding concerned with protecting value rather than 'things'. This newer approach was often justified by reference to natural law or public policy.[85] Justice Gray's comment adapted 'property' in this way, to construct it as an individual right in relation to a 'thing' *or* 'privileges', thus enabling it to potentially cover a new and wider range of circumstances; Cobb adopted this reasoning wholesale and justified it with reference to higher natural law.

A second related passage in the *Pavesich* judgment is also significant. Justice Cobb stated:

> The form and features of the plaintiffs are *his own*. The [defendant] … had no more authority to display them in public for the purpose of advertising … than they would have had to compel the plaintiff to place himself upon exhibition for this purpose.[86]

This is yet another aspect of the judgment in which Locke looms large, albeit implicitly. In claiming that Pavesich's appearance belonged to him Cobb was utilising established Lockean notions of individual self-ownership. A core premise of Locke's social contract was that each individual 'owned' himself. This was expressed at various points in his Second Treatise, but was encapsulated in the claim that 'every man has a "property" in his own "person". This nobody has a right to but himself.'[87] So, for Locke, the individual 'owns' his person and what his person does (its labour) and this is a natural right prior to the formation of civil society. Justice Cobb logically extended this reasoning; 'owning' his body

[84] *Pavesich* (n 36) 215.

[85] K Vandervelde, 'The New Property of the Nineteenth Century: The Development of the Modern Concept of Property (1980) 29 *Buffalo Law Review* 325, 328–335.

[86] Emphasis added. *Pavesich* (n 36) 217.

[87] J Locke, *Two Treatises of Government* (Cambridge, Cambridge University Press, 1989) Book II [27], [173]. Elsewhere, Locke writes: 'man (by being master of himself, and proprietor of his own person, and the actions and labour of it) had still in himself the great foundation of property', at [44].

also necessarily entailed 'owning' what that body looked like, its appearance. This rationale applied to such an extent that displaying Pavesich's image against his will was tantamount to physically displaying him to the public against his will, despite the fact that physical coercion would clearly be necessitated by the latter but not the former.

So, as *Pavesich* demonstrates, concepts of property were evolving and could include a Lockean-based right of ownership over one's physical person (and its appearance) upon which a privacy right could be based. A crucial aspect of the Lockean natural right to 'own' one's person is that it was universal; the right was enjoyed equally by all men in the state of nature.[88] MacPherson explains that this aspect of Locke's theory reflected traditional Christian notions of the moral equality and the equal natural rights of man.[89] Consistent with this, Justice Cobb confirmed the universal applicability of privacy, claiming it was a natural right 'which every man is entitled to enjoy, whether out of society or in it', and later stating 'Each *person* has a liberty of privacy.'[90] The notion of individual self-ownership reflected in equal rights universally held by all (use of male terminology notwithstanding) has a clear moral appeal and forms a core tenet of political liberalism. But were such claims all they appeared? Did the *Pavesich* reasoning – and the Lockean theory on which it was primarily based – live up to their stated ideals? It is to this question that discussion now turns.

VI. A UNIVERSAL NATURAL RIGHT?

For all its universal natural right rhetoric, the privacy propounded by the *Pavesich* Court was – in reality – a limited, culturally-specific right to be primarily enjoyed by wealthy middle-class white men, to the (silent) exclusion of other groups. This section demonstrates the gap between the formal stated ideal set out in *Pavesich* and the substantive real-life effect of privacy law more generally across less powerful social groups. Furthermore, it argues that this gulf between de jure and de facto privacy is entirely consistent with a similar rupture in the Lockean theory upon which it was based.

A. A Bourgeois Right?

The proposition that, at its inception, the privacy right was (at least in part) an expression of class-related interests is relatively uncontroversial. As has been

[88] ibid [3], [4].

[89] CB Macpherson, *The Political Theory of Possessive Individualism* (Oxford, Oxford University Press, 2011) 243–244.

[90] Emphasis added. *Pavesich* (n 36) 194, 200.

well-documented, Warren and Brandeis' elite social background, associated patrician values and even personal experiences with the press of the day clearly informed their articulation of the privacy 'problem' and their proposed solution of a privacy right.[91] Such genteel, middle-class concerns were articulated at select points in the *Pavesich* judgment, for example in the court's libel finding (outlined in section IV) that use of the plaintiff's photograph for payment would make him 'odious to every decent individual'. They are also evident in Justice Cobb's disdainful references to the defendant's 'mercenary' profit motive which reflect a suspicion about the market.[92] Elsewhere the court expressed passing concern that the plaintiff's photograph might end up hanging in a place of ill-repute such as – God forbid – 'the bar of the saloon-keeper' or 'the walls of a brothel'.[93] This brief yet telling remark is a strong indicator that the court viewed the interest at stake as (at least partly) maintaining a particular 'respectable' identity or reputation. Clearly, not all social groups would have such a standing to protect.

This gap between stated equal universal rights and substantive inequality also beset Locke's possessive individualism upon which the privacy right in *Pavesich* was based. Macpherson notes a tension in Locke's work between two conflicting visions of society; on one hand, the traditional Christian natural law values of the moral equality of all men (outlined above) and, on the other, a new market society comprised of those with real property (ie estates) and those without.[94] He shows that Locke managed to maintain equal, universal rights whilst justifying vastly unequal ownership of wealth via three related tactics. First, Locke employed subtle strategic shifts in the meaning of 'property', from wide (encompassing persons, lives, liberties and estates) to narrow (covering only estates).[95] Second, Locke projected the prevailing social assumptions of his day back into the nature of man, assuming that an individual owed nothing to society for their abilities or talents, nor formed part of a wider community.[96] Finally, Locke assumed that men were not just equal in natural rights, but in their capacity to manage their lives. Yet he also claimed there were differences in the rationality and industry of individuals so that estates would come to be justifiably held by the more willing and able. So, as Macpherson shows, Locke's theory was at heart, a defence of emerging capitalism and an attempt

[91] See the particularly critical take in: Barron (n 9). See also: A Gajda 'What if Samuel D Warren Hadn't Married A Senator's Daughter: Uncovering the Press Coverage That Led to the Right of Privacy' [2008] *Michigan State Law Review* 35.

[92] '[O]ne who, *merely* for advertising purposes and from *mercenary motives*, publishes the likeness of another without his consent … … '; 'the publication of one's picture without his consent by another as an advertisement, for the *mere* purpose of *increasing the profits and gains* of the advertiser, is an invasion of this right': Emphasis added. *Pavesich* (n 36) 219–220.

[93] ibid 218.

[94] Macpherson (n 89) 243–244.

[95] ibid 198, 220, 247–251.

[96] ibid 3, 197.

to maintain the rhetoric of the formal equality of all men whilst simultaneously justifying substantive inequality.[97] Relevant feminist and critical race literature confirms the presence of just such a gulf between the formal universal natural right to privacy articulated in *Pavesich* and the wider substantive inequality of privacy outside and beyond it.

B. A Patriarchal Right?

Privacy has long been a key target for feminist critique,[98] and numerous academics argue that the privacy right was gendered from its very inception.[99] For example, Allen notes privacy's 'origins in nineteenth century [gender] bias'. She argues that nineteenth-century notions of privacy were cast in distinctly masculine terms (solitude, retreat from the public realm) which did not account for women's experiences or privacy needs (eg, with respect to marital and reproductive autonomy, or household labour where 'Women had enjoyed few meaningful forms of personal privacy').[100] Furthermore, when it did directly concern women, the privacy advocated by Warren and Brandeis and set forth in early case law was influenced by prevailing paternalist attitudes that feminine modesty should be protected and 'the ideal of the cloistered lady'.[101] The patriarchal approach of the *Roberson* court has been widely noted and its latent ideals of femininity are evident in the language of the majority judgment.[102] Yet despite centring on a male plaintiff, the *Pavesich* case also supports the proposition that early privacy laws were inherently gendered.

Lake astutely points out that Pavesich is unusual because 'It was one of the very few cases at this time in which a man's image was used purely because it was pleasing to the eye.'[103] Most early photography-based image disputes concerned

[97] ibid 256, 257, 220–1, 247.

[98] A full account of such critiques is beyond the scope of this chapter, but for an overview of some such criticisms see: R Gavison, 'Feminism & the Public/Private Distinction' (1992) 45(1) *Stanford Law Review* 1–45.

[99] See, eg, Lake (n 16); SE Gallagher, 'Privacy & Conformity: Rethinking The Right Most Valued by Civilized Men' (2017) 33(1) *Touro Law Review* 159–175.

[100] Allen notes 'the problem of women's privacy within the home. That problem was the problem of too much of the wrong kinds of privacy – too much modesty, seclusion, reserve and compelled intimacy – and too little individual modes of personal privacy and autonomous, private choice.' A Allen and E Mack, 'How Privacy got its Gender' (1990) 10 *Northern Illinois University Law Review* 441–478, esp 477. See also: Gallagher (n 99).

[101] Allen and Mack (n 100) 457. Later in this piece the authors write 'Women appear in the Warren & Brandeis article as seduced wives and daughters', at 459.

[102] For example: 'she [the plaintiff] has been caused to suffer mental distress where others would have appreciated the compliment to their beauty implied in the selection of the picture for such purposes'. *Roberson* (n 2) 543.

[103] Lake (n 16) 70. Lake notes that the other 2 cases were: *Henry v Cherry* (n 13) and *Munden v Harris* (n 13).

women plaintiffs[104] as their images were more frequently used in advertising and by the media (objectification being, of course, another feminist concern). Where a man's image was used, it tended to be due to their public renown or achievements rather than their 'beautiful countenance'.[105] Commenting on the *Pavesich* case in 1905, *The Philadelphia Inquirer* drew parallels with *Roberson* and confirmed the plaintiff 'was a vigorous, good-looking young fellow'.[106] Yet Lake identifies crucial differences that distinguish Pavesich from the attractive female plaintiffs in other similar cases. The first crucial difference is, of course, outcome:

> In an area of law dominated and shaped by female plaintiffs, it is notable that the first superior court case to recognise a right to privacy at common law was brought by a man.[107]

The second crucial distinction of *Pavesich* lies in the language and reasoning employed by Justice Cobb. Here the Georgia Supreme Court moved away from privacy-as-protection-of-female-modesty as employed in *Roberson* and similar cases. Instead, as Lake argues, the Court adopted 'strikingly different' language to 'momentarily reconfigure the doctrine in masculine terms'. This is evidenced via Justice Cobb's linking of privacy to liberty (discussed earlier) so that Pavesich's claim became one of a natural right of autonomy over his life and actions rather than, eg, protection of his modesty.[108] So *Pavesich* shows the inherently gendered understandings that permeated privacy discourse from the outset in subtle but significant ways. It highlights the partial, selective nature of a supposedly 'universal' privacy right that remained blind to the many pressing privacy problems faced by countless women beyond the narrow issue of 'the circulating portrait'. Furthermore, it reveals the courts adopting culturally divergent modes of reasoning depending on whether the privacy was concerned with protecting a man's liberty or a woman's modesty.

C. A White Right?

Race also arises in *Pavesich*, most notably in Justice Cobb's controversial slavery analogy. In this passage, written only 40 years after slavery was abolished by the Thirteenth Amendment in 1865, Cobb stated:

> The knowledge that one's features and form are being used for … advertisements … brings … [one] to a realization that his liberty has been taken away from him

[104] *Pollard v Photographic Company* (n 1); *Manola v Stevens* (n 60); *Roberson* (n 2).

[105] The plaintiff's argument in *Roberson* ran: 'If the plaintiff has such a beautiful countenance that her photographic likeness is saleable in the markets, who is entitled to the proceeds of such sales?' Quoted in Lake (n 16) 58–65.

[106] *The Philadelphia Inquirer* (Philadelphia, Pennsylvania) 24 July 1905, 8.

[107] Lake (n 16) 4, 70, 74.

[108] ibid 14, 71–72.

> and … he can not be otherwise than conscious of the fact that he is, for the time being, under the control of another, that he is no longer free, and that he is in reality a slave without hope of freedom, held to service by a merciless master.[109]

This claim that unauthorised use of one's image is akin to slavery has been deemed 'remarkable'[110] and 'at once both offensive and appealing'.[111] Two initial points about this analogy should be noted. First, Justice Cobb's slavery claim is the correlative of his liberty-based framing of privacy. If privacy is understood as freedom to present oneself or retreat from the crowd as one chooses, such liberty is eradicated by unauthorised use of one's image because it takes the decision out of one's hands. Second, the slavery claim should be viewed in the light of Justice Cobb's family background. As section V outlined, Cobb's family had been active Confederates and slave-owners. Furthermore, his father and uncle authored well-known pro-slavery literature and Allen suggests he would have been exposed to such views in childhood. Yet, as we have seen, Cobb did not share his elder family members' views on slavery. Allen accepts that likening the cruelty and degradation of slavery to a relatively trivial misuse of an affluent subject's image is on one level 'hyperbolic and highly offensive'. But she nevertheless defends it as powerful, attention-grabbing rhetoric employed to protect a fundamentally important right that people need and value.[112]

Even so, the problematic nature of Justice Cobb's slavery analogy is cogently demonstrated by the selective and distorted way in which laws concerning privacy and identity were deployed in relation to race across this broad era. A particularly striking and egregious instance is *State v Mann* (1829) where the Supreme Court of North Carolina reversed the earlier conviction of a slave owner who had shot and wounded a slave woman on the basis that great 'danger' that would arise if the courts became involved in policing master-slave relations that enjoyed 'impunity by reason of [their] privacy'.[113] Elsewhere, Osucha draws out the racial elements in early privacy discourse which understood privacy as 'a distinctive property right and cultural privilege' concerned with maintaining white dignity and white femininity in particular.[114] She situates the bourgeoise concerns expressed by Warren, Brandeis and the *Roberson* dissenters against the backdrop of widespread racial stereotyping in the era's commercial visual culture. The concern to preserve the honorific value of (white) portraits such as Abigail Roberson's stands in stark contrast

[109] *Pavesich* (n 36) 220.

[110] J Kahn, 'Controlling Identity: Plessy, Privacy, and Racial Defamation' (2005) 54 *DePaul Law Review* 755, 758.

[111] Allen (n 19) 1209.

[112] ibid 1206, 1209–1210.

[113] *State v Mann* 13 N. C. 263 (1829).

[114] E Osucha, 'The Whiteness of Privacy: Race, Media, Law' (2009) 24(1) *Camera Obscura* 66–107, 72, 73, 97.

to the proliferation of 'grotesque' black caricatures in advertising and the mass media which consolidated racial difference, eg the famed 'Aunt Jemima' pancake mix trade mark based on Nancy Green, a servant and former slave.[115] Osucha terms this 'commodity racism', a phenomenon that lay beyond the interest of privacy discourse 'which was strictly concerned with representations of individuals, not types'. Yet this racially-loaded understanding of 'publicity as commodification' also influenced white anxieties about the circulating portrait.[116] Though Osucha does not cover *Pavesich*, she offers further grim context by which to view Justice Cobb's slavery analogy; beyond the obvious 'surface' claim about deprivation of liberty lie racial connotations about cultural-social status.

Khan also draws out the racial bias inherent in *Pavesich* by undertaking a comparison with racial defamation cases and *Plessy v Ferguson* (1896) where the US Supreme Court upheld racial segregation on railway carriages as constitutional.[117] Railway segregation laws empowered train conductors to determine whether passengers were 'white' or 'coloured' for the purposes of travel and Plessy, a mixed-race passenger, challenged his arrest for sitting in a white first-class carriage. Khan argues that despite their doctrinal differences, both *Pavesich* and *Plessy* were about controlling identity. The *Plessy* Court essentially approved the state's authority to categorise the race of individuals, and in doing so it denied black people the ability to control their own racial identity. Yet merely nine years later, 'Cobb forcefully invoked the specter of slavery' so that a white man could control *his* identity.[118] Khan thus draws out the racial undercurrents of Cobb's slavery analogy, thus:

> To deny Pavesich control of his image did not simply enslave his identity in some abstract sense, rather it relegated him to the status of a black person in society – someone who had no access to legal control over his own identity. In making a claim to control his identity, Pavesich was implicitly … 'performing whiteness'[119]

Yet, in a final potential twist to the tale, it is possible that Paolo Pavesich may have been Jewish.[120] Whether this was the case or not, as an immigrant in his exclusive line of work for socially elite clients there would have been professional advantages to Pavesich 'performing whiteness' and there is perhaps some evidence of this; he was occasionally referred to as the anglicised 'Paul' Pavesich, for example in his obituary and certain society pages.[121]

[115] ibid 75–76, 78–9, 86–91, 98.
[116] ibid 79–80, 82, 97.
[117] 163 US 537 (1896).
[118] Kahn (n 110) 759–760, 762–763, 768, 772, 776–777.
[119] ibid 781.
[120] Reports recount his daughter performing at a meeting of the Council of Jewish women in Atlanta: *The Atlanta Constitution* (Atlanta, Georgia) 30 January 1916, 3. But it should be noted that Judaism tends to be matrilineal, so it may be the case that Pavesich married a Jewish woman.
[121] *Atlanta Constitution* (n 21) 17; 1 December 1911, 6.

So as with gender, in terms of race the natural right to privacy was far from the 'universal' equal right it claimed to be. Again, it was selective; concerned with certain forms of the 'circulating portrait' whilst disregarding other more pernicious modes of image commodification. Furthermore, *Pavesich* was at odds with other legal doctrines that denied other groups the ability to control their identities. One may legitimately question whether the *Pavesich* judgment would have reached the same outcome or adopted the same liberty – and self-ownership-based reasoning had the plaintiff been black; Khan's account of *Plessy* and racial defamation cases suggests not. Such matters indicate that the content of the early privacy right reflected the power inequalities and implicit assumptions of the day, and that it was at least partly concerned with upholding the standing of 'respectable' white elites.

VII. RECEPTION AND LEGACY

Despite the preceding shortcomings and limitations of the privacy right set out in *Pavesich*, the judgment had a range of significant impacts. Most obviously, the *Pavesich* decision had direct consequences for the parties to the dispute, particularly the plaintiff himself. However, as this section explains, its impact extended far beyond the litigants, capturing the attention of the wider public and media of the day and, ultimately, creating a longer-term legal legacy.

Little is known of what happened to those most closely involved in the *Pavesich* dispute. Davis confirms that the Georgia Supreme Court's reversal of outcome would have normally led to a new trial at the City Court of Atlanta. Unfortunately, the case files from this period have been lost and Davis thus suggests one of two possible outcomes; either the trial was held and neither side appealed or, more likely, the parties settled out of court.[122] In any event, an intriguing newspaper story from July 1906 perhaps provides a clue as to the outcome of the dispute. It reported that Paulo Pavesich was back in Tampa for a few days, and claimed 'Prof Pavesich has not relinquished his ambition to own an orange grove in this section and may make a purchase on this visit.'[123] Coming just over a year after the successful judgment in his favour, was this purchase to be made with his settlement from the case? We do not know, but we do know that in the years following his case, Pavesich's fresco work continued; in 1909 he worked in Florida[124] and spent winters there, with *The Tampa Tribune* reporting on his rattle-snake hunting prowess.[125]

[122] Davis (n 19) 117–118.

[123] *The Tampa Tribune* (Tampa, Florida) 14 July 1906, 8.

[124] *Tampa Tribune* (Tampa, Florida) 27 January 1909, 4; (n 35) 3.

[125] Pavesich 'makes a speciality while visiting Florida of killing rattlesnakes, quite a number of which fell victim to his prowess last winter. He expects to break all past records before 'gentle

The wider public reception of *Pavesich* is better documented and the consensus, even among media commentators with strong interests in free expression, was generally supportive of the decision. Barbas writes that the case 'was celebrated nationally',[126] and a select summary of contemporary newspaper reports confirms this. *The New York Times* compared *Pavesich* favourably with the much-maligned *Roberson* case, writing that the Georgian Supreme Court had 'shown itself the more trustworthy organ of civilization' than the New York Court of Appeals. The paper continued that the Georgian Court's conclusion

> is that which most open-minded men, including a formidable part of the bench and bar, reached in the discussion [of Roberson, but] which the decision of our Court of Appeals [in that case], instead of closing, merely opened.[127]

The Philadelphia Inquirer made a similar comparison between *Roberson* and *Pavesich*, concluding on the latter:

> That's fair. It satisfies alike the dictates of reason and the sense of justice, for if one has no property right in one's own features how can there be any ownership whatever?[128]

Elsewhere, *The Atlanta Constitution*, the very newspaper where the disputed advert was printed, perhaps understandably, offered more neutral treatment. It provided only a basic factual account of the case (with no reference to its role in the dispute) under the headline 'Supreme Court Holds Pavesich Entitled to Damages'.[129] Finally, select academic law journals also provided some coverage of the decision. The *Michigan Law Review* provided a favourable summary of the legal arguments justifying a privacy right and praised the *Pavesich* Court for 'brush[ing] away the cobwebs of legal reasoning' that had hitherto obstructed recognition of 'this instinctively recognised right'.[130] Elsewhere, a case note in the *Harvard Law Review* afforded *Pavesich* cursory treatment, noting it was the first time a higher court had upheld a privacy right and contrasting its outcome

springtime' again puts in appearance': *The Tampa Tribune* (n 32) 3. Of that earlier trip, it was reported: 'Among other trophies of the hunt, … [Pavesich] brought to Tampa with him last night the rattles of a big rattle-snake, which came very near ending the career of the fresco artist. Prof Pavesich stepped directly over the snake, which immediately assumed its death-dealing coil. Hearing the rattle, the professor turned to see the big fellow striking at him. He emptied the contents of his gun into the snake, killing it instantly.' *The Tampa Tribune* (Tampa, Florida) 14 November 1906, 6.

[126] Barbas (n 3) 61.

[127] Author's addition. *The New York Times* (New York) 23 April 1905, 8.

[128] *Philadelphia Inquirer* (n 106) 8.

[129] *The Atlanta Constitution* (Atlanta, Georgia) 4 March 1905, 7.

[130] 'The Right of Privacy' (1905) 3 *Michigan Law Review* 559–563.

with the regrettable *Roberson*, before predicting (in somewhat understated terms) 'It seems probable … that [Pavesich] will have a following.'[131]

Beyond its initial reception, *Pavesich* did indeed 'have a following' and its enduring legal legacy arguably cements its place as a landmark privacy case. Following the decision, Justice Cobb wrote to Louis Brandeis, drawing the judgment to his attention and predicting that similar judgments would follow.[132] Justice Cobb's optimism was borne out by subsequent events. Though there remained isolated instances of courts in other states refusing to uphold a privacy right,[133] judicial and legislative support for such a right gained momentum in the years that followed. Peikoff claims *Pavesich* was 'indispensable in the drive to persuade the country's courts to adopt a common-law right to privacy'.[134] By the mid-twentieth century the courts across 24 American states had recognised a right of privacy, and three states had enacted privacy-protecting statutes.[135] The *Pavesich* decision has also occasionally been cited by the US Supreme Court,[136] most notably in *Griswold v Connecticut* by the dissenting justices Black and Stewart who, ironically, refused to find a privacy right in the US Constitution and accused the majority of giving constitutional status to a private tort.[137]

VIII. CONCLUSION

The impact of any individual case in isolation, including those in this volume, must not be overstated. Instead, when viewed in its wider social and historic context, we see that any case is necessarily an expression of pre-existing dominant political values or ideas, rather than simply a free-standing instigator of social change. As such *Pavesich* is just one piece of the privacy law jigsaw, but it is a crucial one, and not only because it laid the groundwork for privacy law's protection of the photographic subject which remains a live issue over a century later.[138] *Pavesich* also represents a privacy law landmark for the two related reasons argued in this chapter.

[131] 'Right of Privacy – Infringement – Unauthorized Use of Portrait for Advertising Purposes' (1905) 18 *Harvard Law Review*, 625. A further brief note in the *Harvard Law Review* (some two years later) afforded Pavesich somewhat more equivocal treatment, claiming 'this case turns the scale of American authority in what is probably the right direction'; 'Right of Privacy' (1907) 21 *Harvard Law Review*, 63.

[132] Kahn (n 110) 756–757. See also: Davis (n 19) 118.

[133] See, eg, *Henry v Cherry* (n 13).

[134] Peikoff (n 77) 757.

[135] Davis (n 19) 119.

[136] *Cox Broadcasting Corporation v Cohn* 420 U.S. 469 (1975); *Goldman v United States* 316 U.S. 129 (1942), cited by Murphy (dissenting).

[137] *Griswold v Connecticut* 381 U.S. 479 (1965).

[138] For a current discussion, see: R Moosavian, 'Stealing 'Souls'? Article 8 and Photographic Intrusion' (2018) 69(4) *Northern Ireland Legal Quarterly* 531–558.

First, *Pavesich* fully articulated the classical liberal Lockean model upon which the privacy right was founded and, in so doing, helps to expose the shared assumptions that underlie both. *Pavesich* adopted the terminology of 'property', but represented part of a shift away from traditional constructions of that term towards de-physicalised interpretations of it as an individual right in relation to a 'thing' (the body?) or 'privileges'. This shifting and ambiguous use of 'property' – also present in Locke's *Second Treatise* – enabled it to become a valuable judicial tool to respond to new developments in a rapidly-changing society; the formation of the privacy right is one notable example of this. Closely linked to this point, *Pavesich* entrenched and expanded Locke's notion of the possessive individual who (somehow) 'owned' their physical person as a form of property and, therefore 'owned' its appearance also. This enabled the court to find that unauthorised use of the plaintiff's image was a 'trespass' of sorts in the form of a privacy right violation.

Second, the *Pavesich* judgment was beset with latent (and sometimes not-so-latent) assumptions about gender, race and class that simultaneously undermined Justice Cobb's perfectionist depiction of a privacy right that is 'eternal', 'immutable' and 'just at all times and in all places'. The universal privacy right upheld by the *Pavesich* Court reflected 'intuitive' truths as discerned by 'normal intellects'. Yet these intellects – such as those of the Georgian Supreme Court bench and its like – were not a conduit to some higher eternal law, but unavoidably a product of their time, place and culture. The court could thus understand and recognise the concern that a 'respectable' man would feel were his photo to hang in a saloon, or be used to endorse a product (for payment or otherwise). It inevitably viewed privacy as a crucial aspect of a man's liberty, rather than focusing on (eg) his modesty or vulnerability. Finally, it could equate a relatively trivial misuse of a white man's image with the inhuman institution of slavery whilst elsewhere courts denied black litigants similar control over aspects of their identity. In this sense, the *Pavesich* privacy right was not universally or equally enjoyed despite Justice Cobb's grand claims to the contrary. Instead, this was a privacy that tended to respect, protect and reflect a white, male social elite.

Ultimately, the discussion of *Pavesich* in this chapter encourages us to consider the extent to which modern privacy law may still contain historic sediments of the ideas and assumptions set out in that case (and any resulting wider implications). Furthermore, it invites us to be attentive to the contemporary subconscious beliefs or blind spots that may continue to silently shape our current understandings of the privacy right.

'In my healthy and productive period of life I bought insurance in the New England Mutual Life Insurance Co., of Boston, Mass, and today my family is protected and I am drawing an annual dividend on my paid up policies.'

'When I had health, vigor and strength I felt the time would never come when I would need insurance. But I see my mistake. If I could recall my life I would buy one of the New England Mutual's 18-Pay Annual Dividend Policies.'

Figure A The Pavesich Advert

4

Whalen v Roe (1977)

RONALD J KROTOSZYNSKI, JR.

I. INTRODUCTION

THE STANDARD NARRATIVE about constitutional privacy law posits that the United States lacks comprehensive legal protections for personal information and generally fails to safeguard 'informational privacy'. It is certainly true that the US Constitution, unlike the European Charter of Fundamental Rights, does not include an express guarantee of informational privacy.[1] Nor does US constitutional law feature a constitutional privacy

[1] See EU Charter of Fundamental Rights, Art 8(1) ('Everyone has the right to the protection of personal data concerning him or her.'). By way of contrast, several US state constitutions do include express privacy guarantees and these guarantees extend to informational privacy. See, eg, Fla. Const. Art. I, § 23 (1968) ('Every natural person has the right to be let alone and free from governmental intrusion into the person's private life except as otherwise provided herein.'); Mont. Const. Art II, § 10 (1972) ('The right of individual privacy is essential to the well-being of a free society and shall not be infringed without the showing of a compelling state interest.'). The Montana constitutional right of privacy clearly encompasses informational privacy. See PA Cain, 'The Right to Privacy Under the Montana Constitution: Sex and Intimacy' (2003) 64 *Montana Law Review* 99, 104; see also *Missoulian v Bd. of Regents*, 207 Mont. 513, 675 P. 2d 962 (1984) (holding that the Montana State Constitution's privacy guarantee protects confidential employment records related to state government employees and protected confidential performance evaluations of an incumbent university president). Thus, the absence of an express privacy guarantee in the federal Constitution has not precluded the inclusion of such guarantees in state constitutions. Currently, 11 state constitutions include an express right of privacy. See E Buchanan, Note, 'Alaska's Explicit Right to Privacy Warrants Greater Protection of Alaskans' Personal Data' (2020) 37 *Alaska Law Review* 25, 30 & 30 fn 30 ('Demonstrating the importance of individuality and privacy to Alaskans, Alaska is only one of eleven states with an explicit right to privacy in its constitution.'); M Silverstein, 'Privacy Rights in State Constitutions: Models for Illinois?' [1989] *University of Illinoi Law Review* 215, 216 & 216 fn 14 (discussing the importance of express privacy protections in state constitutions and listing the ten states that provided an express right of privacy prior to New Hampshire adopting such a provision in 2018). For a general overview of how state constitutions can confer rights that the federal Constitution does not recognise, see WJ Brennan, Jr., 'State Constitutions and the Protection of Individual Rights' (1977) 90 *Harvard Law Review* 489. Justice Brennan argued that the expansion of human rights protections at the federal level 'must not be allowed to inhibit the independent protective force of state law – for without it, the full realization of our liberties cannot be guaranteed' and emphasised that 'State constitutions, too, are a font of individual liberties.' ibid 491.

doctrine anything like German law, which maintains a comprehensive right to 'informational self-determination' under the landmark *Census Case*.[2] In Germany, the right to informational self-determination is broad and deep and safeguards 'the right of the individual to determine for himself whether the state may divulge or use personal data'.[3] Even so, however, legal scholars who claim that the US lacks *any* meaningful constitutional protection of informational privacy are mistaken.[4]

In 1977, the Supreme Court announced in *Whalen v Roe*[5] that the Constitution prohibits the government from collecting, storing, and disseminating sensitive

[2] *Volkszählungsurteil* (*Census Act Case*), 65 BverfGE 1, 68–69 (15 December 1983), partially translated and reprinted in DP Kommers and RA Miller, *The Constitutional Jurisprudence of the Constitutional Republic of Germany,* 3rd edn (North Carolina, Duke University Press, 2012) 408–14 (providing a partial translation of the *Census Act Case* and discussing the concept of informational self-determination in German constitutional law); see N Jacoby, 'Redefining the Right to be Let Alone: Privacy Rights and the Constitutionality of Technical Surveillance Measures in Germany and the United States' (2007) 35 *Georgia Journal of International and Comparative Law* 433, 465 ('In the Census Act Case of 1983, the court recognized for the first time a right to informational self-determination that flowed from the general right to personality and human dignity under Articles 1 and 2(1) of the Basic Law.'); G Hornung and C Schnabel, 'Data Protection in Germany I: The Population Census Decision and the Right to Informational Self-Determination' (2009) 25 *Computer Law & Security Review* 84 (discussing the *Census Act Case* and subsequent jurisprudential developments related to the right of informational self-determination in the Federal Republic of Germany).

[3] *Census Act Case*, reprinted and translated in Kommers and Miller, above (n 2) 410; see S Simitis, 'Reviewing Privacy in an Information Society' (1987) 135 *University of Pennsylvania Law Review* 707, 734 (explaining that the *Census Act Case* holds that 'unrestricted access to personal data imperils virtually every constitutionally guaranteed right', positing that '[n]either freedom of speech nor freedom of association nor freedom of assembly can be fully exercised as long as it remains uncertain whether, under what circumstances, and for what purposes, personal information is collected and processed', and arguing that control over personal information 'determine[s] the choice between a democratic and an authoritarian society').

[4] See J Kang, 'Information Privacy in Cyberspace Transactions' (1998) 50 *Stanford Law Review* 1193, 1230 (positing that '[t]he collection of personal information in America by transacting parties is largely unregulated by law', observing that '[u]nlike certain European nations, the United States has no omnibus privacy law covering the private sector's processing of personal information', and characterising US law as 'featur[ing] a patchwork of rules that regulate different types of personal information in different ways, depending on how it is acquired, by whom, and how it will be used'): JP Kesan, CM Hayes and MN Bashir, 'Cloud Computing: Consumers, Privacy Preferences, and Market Efficiency' (2013) 70 *Washington and Lee Law Review* 341, 418–19 (observing that '[t]he United States and the European Union take very different theoretical approaches to privacy' and positing that '[t]he United States does not have sufficient privacy laws'); O Tene, 'The Second Wave of Global Privacy Protection: Privacy Law's Midlife Crisis: A Critical Assessment of the Second Wave of Global Privacy Law' (2013) 74 *Ohio State Law Journal* 1217, 1225 (asserting that 'information privacy is not a constitutionally protected right in the United States'). Most US legal scholars advance the more limited claim that the constitutional right to informational privacy is weak, amorphous, or both. See MD Fan, 'Constitutionalizing Informational Privacy by Assumption' (2012) 14 *University* of *Pennsylvania Journal of Constitutional Law* 953, 954 (observing that the in the US 'law struggles to define the metes and bounds of the claimed constitutional right'); S Skinner-Thompson, 'Outing Privacy' (2015) 110 *Northwestern University Law Review* 159, 161 ('Despite that this year marks the fiftieth anniversary of *Griswold v. Connecticut*, where the Supreme Court first acknowledged the right to decisional privacy, neither scholars nor the Court have definitively resolved these questions or outlined the contours of a workable right to constitutional informational privacy.')

[5] 429 U.S. 589 (1977).

personal information without a legitimate purpose.[6] Moreover, government programs that collect and store such personal information must include both procedural and substantive protections against unwarranted or unauthorised disclosures.[7] Writing for a unanimous Supreme Court, Justice John Paul Stevens opined that '[w]e are not unaware of the threat to privacy implicit in the accumulation of vast amounts of personal information in computerized data banks or other massive government files'[8] and cautioned that government information gathering and storage programs that failed to include 'security provisions' would likely violate the constitutional right of privacy.[9]

Some 34 years later, in *NASA v Nelson*, the Supreme Court broadly reaffirmed this approach. Invoking *Whalen*, the *Nelson* majority said that it would assume that 'the Constitution protects a privacy right' that safeguards confidential personal information from unwarranted or unauthorised public disclosure when considering a challenge to the federal government's employee background check program.[10] Although it is odd for the Supreme Court to assume a right without ever formally recognising its existence, the justices have taken this approach in other areas of constitutional privacy law – for example, the right of a mentally competent adult to refuse unwanted medical treatment rests on an assumed rather than announced constitutional right.[11] Most of the time, such assumptions usually turn out to reflect constitutional rules and lower federal and state courts typically treat the 'assumed' constitutional rights as legally binding legal rules.[12]

[6] See ibid at 598–604.

[7] ibid at 605–06.

[8] ibid at 605.

[9] See ibid at 605–06. It bears noting that contemporary private law, namely the law of torts, does not provide a reliable means of securing informational privacy against the government because, as a general matter, the government is immune from tort suits under the doctrine of sovereign immunity. See *FDIC v Meyer*, 510 U.S. 471, 475 (1994) ('Absent a waiver, sovereign immunity shields the Federal Government and its agencies from suit.'); *Bivens v Six Unknown Named Agents of the Federal Bureau of Narcotics*, 403 U.S. 388, 389-92 (1971) (finding an implied constitutional right of action for intentional constitutional torts against federal law enforcement agents, but solely in their personal capacities and not against the federal government itself); see generally DJ Solove and NM Richards, 'Prosser's Privacy Law: A Mixed Legacy' (2010) 98 *California Law Review* 1887, 1889 ('Today, the chorus of opinion is that the tort law privacy has been ineffective, particularly in remedying the burgeoning collection, use, and dissemination of personal information in the Information Age.')

[10] *NASA v Nelson*, 562 U.S. 134, 138 (2011). But *cf* ibid at 160 (Scalia, J., concurring) ('A federal constitutional right to 'informational privacy' does not exist.')

[11] See *Cruzan v Director, Mo. Dept. of Health*, 497 U.S. 261, 279 (1990) (observing that the constitutional right of privacy 'would embrace such a liberty interest [in refusing unwanted medical treatment]' and, consistent with this jurisprudential approach, 'assum[ing] that the United States Constitution would grant a competent person a constitutionally protected right to refuse lifesaving hydration and nutrition').

[12] This was certainly true with respect to *Cruzan*'s assumption that the right of privacy encompassed the right of a mentally competent adult to refuse unwanted medical treatment. See *Washington v Glucksberg*, 521 U.S. 702, 720 (1997) ('We have also assumed, and strongly suggested, that the Due Process Clause protects the traditional right to refuse unwanted life saving medical treatment.') Lower federal and state courts have little choice but to treat the Supreme Court's 'assumptions'

As this chapter will explain in greater detail, government programs that collect, store, and disseminate confidential personal information are constitutional in the US *only* if they feature a 'statutory or regulatory duty to avoid unwarranted disclosures'.[13] To be clear, the scope of this constitutional right of informational privacy is limited and in most instances, the government will prevail against objections to its efforts to collect and store personal information. Provided that the government can articulate a legitimate reason for collecting and storing the data, and the government's program includes substantive and procedural safeguards that protect against the unauthorised or unwarranted disclosure of confidential personal information, the government's data collection and retention program will not violate the constitutional right of informational privacy.[14] In sum, although it would be entirely fair and quite accurate to say that the constitutional right of informational privacy in the US is weak or limited, it would go too far to posit that no such right exists under the US Constitution.

One might also ask, given the obvious importance of informational privacy, why the Supreme Court has issued only two major decisions that address the existence of this right over the last half-century.[15] The answer is relatively simple: the federal courts have been able to avoid further developing a jurisprudence of constitutional informational privacy because, in the contemporary US, federal statutes more often than not protect against the unwarranted or unauthorised public release of confidential personal information that the government collects and stores. This is not to suggest that the statutory protections are ideal – far from it. Nevertheless, in most instances the federal courts will find that the statutory provisions that create data gathering and retention programs contain sufficient substantive and procedural safeguards to avoid running into constitutional difficulties under the 'assumed' constitutional right of informational privacy.

about the existence of privacy rights as requiring heightened scrutiny of laws and regulations that abridge or deny a privacy interest – whether that interest happens to implicate autonomy and control over one's body or the ability to control the collection, storage, and dissemination of confidential personal information.

[13] *Whalen*, 429 U.S. at 605.

[14] See below text and accompanying notes 48 to 82.

[15] I should note that a third privacy precedent exists but unlike *Whalen* and *Nelson*, the decision engages only tangentially with the constitutional right of informational privacy. See *Nixon v Administrator of General Servs.*, 433 U.S. 425, 457–58 (1977) (acknowledging a constitutional 'interest in avoiding disclosure' and 'undue dissemination of private materials'). Because the Supreme Court described President Richard M Nixon's interest in informational privacy as 'weaker' than that of the patients and physicians in *Whalen*, the decision's treatment of the interest is more cursory and less illuminating. See ibid at 458–59. In sum, *Whalen* rather than *Nixon* established the existence of a constitutional right of informational privacy as an aspect of a broader 'right of privacy' that arises from the Due Process Clauses of the Fifth and Fourteenth Amendments. See *Roe v Wade*, 410 U.S. 113, 152–56 (1973) (holding that a right of privacy exists as a fundamental liberty interest protected under the Due Process Clauses and that 'the right of personal privacy includes the abortion decision').

II. *WHALEN v ROE* AND THE CONSTITUTIONAL RIGHT TO INFORMATIONAL PRIVACY

The US Supreme Court has recognised, albeit on an 'assumed' basis, a constitutional interest in informational privacy. Moreover, the Supreme Court took this important step in 1977, six years before the Federal Constitutional Court, in Germany, issued its highly influential decision in the *Census Act Case*.[16] To be sure, the US iteration of a constitutional right of informational privacy is far less robust than its German cousin, the constitutional right of informational self-determination.

It would be an overstatement – and a big one – to posit that the constitutional right of privacy in the US is analogous to Germany's constitutional right of informational self-determination. Nevertheless, it would be equally incorrect to suggest that informational privacy has no constitutional moorings in the US. Instead, in the US, the right of informational privacy serves as a kind of background principle that requires government entities to exercise caution when collecting, storing, accessing, or disseminating sensitive personal data. Indeed, in many respects, the US version of the right to informational privacy requires the same sort of safeguards that the Court of Justice of the European Union required in its landmark *Digital Rights Ireland* decision.[17] Governments in the US, as in Europe, may collect, store, and access sensitive personal information – but *Whalen* makes clear that adequate substantive and procedural safeguards must be in place to ensure that malicious or even merely negligent disclosures of personal information do not occur.

However, before analysing and critiquing *Whalen*'s constitutional 'assumption' of a right of informational privacy, one must first consider the decision itself and the New York data collection program that gave rise to it. One should also keep in mind that *Whalen* arose at the very dawn of the computer age, when governments in the US and abroad were first establishing programs to collect, store, and access vast quantities of personal information. The *Whalen* litigation thus presented the federal courts with an early and important opportunity to

[16] *Volkszählungsurteil* (*Census Act Case*), 65 BverfGE 1, 68–69 (15 December 1983), partially translated and reprinted in DP Kommers and RA Miller, *The Constitutional Jurisprudence of the Constitutional Republic of Germany*, 3rd edn (North Carolina, Duke University Press, 2012) 408–11. Professor Robert G Schwartz, Jr. observes that '[t]he landmark Census Act decision established the constitutional right to "informational self-determination" (*informationelle Selbstbestimmung*).' RG Schwartz, Jr., 'Privacy in German Employment Law' (1992) 15 *Hastings International and Comparative Law Review* 135, 146. The German Federal Constitutional Court held that 'the Basic Law gives individuals the authority to decide for themselves the scope of exposure and the uses of their personal information' and the doctrine 'enshrine[s] the principle that citizens should be able to learn who knows what about them and to control how that information is used'. ibid.

[17] *Digital Rights Ireland Ltd v Minister for Communications, Marine, and Natural Resources*, joined Cases C-293/12 and C-594/12 EU:C:2014:238, [2015] QB 127 (decided 8 April 2014), available at curia.europa.eu/juris/document/document.jsf?text=&docid=150642&pageIndex= 0&doclang=en&mode=req&dir=&occ=first&part=1&cid=404289 [http://perma.cc/54C5- A8WL].

consider whether – and if so how – the Constitution restricts the government's ability to create vast databases of confidential personal information.

Facing a growing problem with the abuse of prescription pain killers, the New York State legislature enacted the New York State Controlled Substances Act of 1972 ('Act').[18] The Act created a regulatory program that required physicians prescribing opioids and other potentially addictive pain-killers, including 'cocaine, methadone, amphetamines, and methaqualone',[19] to record and report such prescriptions to the New York State Department of Health (DOH). It mandated that physicians prescribe these drugs on special triplicate forms; the forms required 'identification of the prescribing physician, the pharmacy that dispensed the drug, the drug and dosage, and the name, address, and age of the patient'.[20] The DOH prepared and distributed these special prescription forms to practicing physicians in New York.[21] Under the terms of the Act and its implementing regulations, the prescribing physician and pharmacist both retained a copy of the scrip, with the third copy to be filed with the DOH.[22]

The trial court found that the DOH received around 100,000 prescription forms per month – over 1 million of the forms per year. The DOH processed the forms by inputting the data on to magnetic computer tapes and retaining the original forms for a five-year period. After five years, the DOH destroyed the forms (as the state law required).[23] The DOH stored the computer tapes and forms in a secure room 'surrounded by a locked wire fence and protected by an alarm system'.[24] Both the forms and computer tapes were kept under lock and key and '[w]hen the tapes are used, the computer is run "off-line," which means that no terminal outside the computer room can read or record any information.'[25] The statute also prohibited public disclosure of the information and provided civil and criminal penalties for violations, including a fine of up to $2,000 and imprisonment for up to a year.[26] Access to the prescription data was limited to a defined subset of DOH employees. Within the first two years of the statute coming into force, the DOH had accessed the data only twice – incident to criminal investigations 'involving alleged overuse by specific patients'.[27]

[18] 1970 N.Y. Laws, c. 474.

[19] N.Y. Pub. Health Law § 3306.

[20] ibid at §§ 3334, 3338.

[21] ibid at § 3331; see *Whalen*, 429 U.S. at 593 n 9 (discussing the mandatory prescription form and the filing requirement with the DOH).

[22] N.Y. Pub. Health Law §§ 3331–3333, 3339.

[23] *Whalen*, 429 U.S. at 593 and 593 n. 11; see N.Y. Pub. Health Law § 3370 (requiring retention of the forms for five years and their subsequent destruction). The prescribing physician and pharmacist were also required to retain the forms for five years. *Whalen*, 429 U.S. at 593 n 11.

[24] *Whalen*, 429 U.S. at 594.

[25] ibid.

[26] N.Y. Pub. Health Law § 3371.

[27] *Whalen*, 429 U.S. at 595.

A group of physicians and patients initiated litigation in federal district court seeking to have the statute held unconstitutional on privacy grounds.[28] The three-judge district court enjoined enforcement of the law's data collection and storage provisions because these requirements impeded the 'doctor-patient relationship', which constituted an aspect of the constitutional right of privacy protected under the Due Process Clauses of the Fifth[29] and Fourteenth Amendments.[30] The three-judge district court also enjoined enforcement of the Act with respect to recording and storing the names of particular patients and their addresses. By the time the injunction issued, however, the record keeping rules and procedures had been in force for almost two years.

The Supreme Court reversed and held that New York could enforce the reporting and record keeping requirements of the Act.[31] The plaintiffs had failed to show that the procedural and substantive safeguards set forth in the statute were insufficient to guard against the misuse or unauthorised disclosure of confidential patient information.[32] Justice Stevens, writing for a unanimous bench, also rejected the plaintiffs' argument that the record keeping and storage requirements would unduly chill the willingness of patients 'to acquire and to use needed medication'.[33] The plaintiffs failed to offer persuasive evidence showing that a material risk existed that physicians and their patients would compromise patients' health care by avoiding the use of drugs subject to New York's reporting and record keeping rules.[34] In sum, the Supreme Court squarely and flatly rejected the privacy-based challenges to New York's data gathering and retention program for addictive prescription drugs.

[28] ibid at 595.

[29] U.S. Const. amend. V (providing that 'no person shall ... be deprived of life, liberty, or property, without due process of law').

[30] U.S. Const. amend. XIV, § 1 (providing that '[n]o State shall make or enforce any law which shall abridge the privileges or immunities of citizens of the United States; nor shall any State deprive any person of life, liberty, or property, without due process of law'). The Supreme Court recognised that the Due Process Clause of the Fourteenth Amendment protected a right of privacy in 1965, see *Griswold v Connecticut*, 381 U.S. 479, 481–86 (1965), and reaffirmed that holding in 1973 when holding that the right of privacy encompassed a right to reproductive autonomy, see *Roe v Wade*, 410 U.S. 113, 152–54 (1973). For a modern application of the right of privacy to protect sexual autonomy and self-determination, see *Lawrence v Texas*, 539 U.S. 558 (2003). In *Lawrence*, the Supreme Court invalidated a state criminal law proscribing sex between gay men and explained that the 'right to liberty under the Due Process Clause gives [gay men] the full right to engage in their conduct without intervention of the government'. *Lawrence*, 539 U.S. at 578; see *Planned Parenthood of Southeastern Pennsylvania v Casey*, 505 U.S. 833, 847 (1992) (Joint Opinion) ('It is a promise of the Constitution that there is a realm of personal liberty which the government may not enter.').

[31] *Whalen v Roe*, 429 U.S. 589, 600 (1977) (holding that '[w]e are persuaded, however, that the New York program does not, on its face, pose a sufficiently grievous threat' to justify its invalidation on substantive due process grounds).

[32] See ibid at 601 ('There is no support in the record, or in the experience of the two States that New York has emulated, for an assumption that the security provisions of the statute will be administered improperly.').

[33] ibid at 603.

[34] See ibid at 603–04.

If that was all that *Whalen* had to say on the subject of informational privacy, it would not be a particularly interesting case – and certainly would not merit inclusion in a book dedicated to landmark or seminal privacy cases. However, the Supreme Court felt it necessary to offer '[a] final word about issues we have not decided.'[35] This is the most interesting – and important – part of the *Whalen* decision.

Justice Stevens explained that the justices 'are not unaware of the threat to privacy implicit in the accumulation of vast amounts of personal information in computerized data banks or other massive government files'.[36] After describing the myriad government programs that involve the collection, retention, and accessing of confidential personal information, Stevens observed that '[t]he right to collect and use such data for public purposes is typically accompanied by a concomitant statutory or regulatory duty to avoid unwarranted disclosures.'[37] He then posited that this duty to avoid unwarranted disclosures 'arguably has its roots in the Constitution'.[38] Thus, substantive and procedural protections associated with the collection, storage, and use of confidential personal data are not discretionary; the government has a duty not to grant unauthorised access to this information or to disseminate it without good cause.

The New York law requiring reporting of prescriptions for potentially addictive drugs provided adequate substantive and procedural safeguards against the disclosure of a patient's identity. In light of this fact, it was not necessary for the Court to 'decide any questions which might be presented by the unwarranted disclosure of accumulated private data – whether intentional or unintentional – or by a system that did not contain comparable security provisions'.[39]

Justice William J Brennan, Jr., in a concurring opinion, would have gone even further than Justice Stevens's opinion for the Court, and squarely held that '[b]road dissemination by state officials of such information … would clearly implicate constitutionally protected privacy rights, and would presumably be justified only by compelling state interests.'[40] Justice Brennan was particularly concerned that the collection and storage of personal data on computer systems created a clear and present danger of unauthorised or unjustified disclosures of such information. As he stated his concern,

> [t]he central storage and easy accessibility of computerized data vastly increase the potential for abuse of that information, and I am not prepared to say that future developments will not demonstrate the necessity of some curb on such technology.[41]

[35] ibid at 605.
[36] ibid.
[37] ibid.
[38] ibid.
[39] ibid at 605–06.
[40] *Whalen v Roe*, 429 U.S. 589, 606 (1977) (Brennan, J., concurring).
[41] ibid at 607.

Despite these lingering concerns, however, Brennan could not 'say that the statute's provisions for computer storage, on their face, amount to a deprivation of constitutionally protected privacy interests, any more than the more traditional reporting provisions'.[42]

Whalen deserves more attention than it has received to date in the US. It effectively establishes that individuals possess a constitutional right of privacy in their personal data against the government. The majority opinion sustains the New York data collection and storage program, but sends up a clear 'constitutional flare'[43] – namely, a clear warning to the elected branches of both the federal and state governments that the government's collection, storage, and use of sensitive personal data implicates a constitutional limitation. Moreover, a constitutional line exists and, if crossed, would provoke a judicial intervention. This approach, sending up a 'flare', involves a reviewing court sustaining a government program but also warning that it implicates important constitutional values (in this instance, the right of privacy). It allows judges to avoid engaging in 'artful dodges to avoid hard questions' and instead 'require[s] federal judges to share openly concerns regarding the potential constitutional difficulties associated with particular policy choices'.[44]

Arguably, a dialectic approach of this sort could well serve important constitutional values. Moreover, the constitutional courts in other countries have adopted this dialectic approach as a means of enforcing entrenched human rights (most notably, the Supreme Court of Canada).[45] *Whalen* opens up a dialogue between the courts and the federal and state legislatures regarding the constitutional rules of the road for the government's collection, storage, and use of confidential personal data. This approach provides a clear warning before actually taking the step of invalidating a statute.[46] Thus, '[r]ather than intervening to block a constitutionally dubious first step by [New York's state legislature], the judiciary [offered] a candid warning which, if heeded, would avoid the constitutional difficulty' in the future.[47]

[42] ibid.

[43] See RJ Krotoszynski, Jr., 'Constitutional Flares: On Judges, Legislatures, and Dialog' (1998) 83 *Minnesota Law Review* 1, 5–9, 49–52 (arguing that courts and legislatures could engage in an ongoing dialogue that includes federal courts sending up 'constitutional flares' in their decisions that warn legislatures when a policy stays within constitutional boundaries but comes perilously close to transgressing the applicable constitutional limit).

[44] ibid at 49; see G Calabresi, *A Common Law for the Age of Statutes* (Cambridge, MA, Harvard University Press, 1982) (proposing that courts engage in an active and ongoing dialogue with legislatures about the need to 'update' statutes that have fallen into desuetude and therefore require revision).

[45] See RJ Krotoszynski, Jr., *Privacy Revisited: A Global Perspective on the Right to Be Left Alone* (New York, Oxford University Press, 2016) 50–52 and 52 n. 123 (describing and discussing the Supreme Court of Canada's dialectic model of engaging with Canada's federal Parliament regarding the scope and meaning of the right of privacy secured by Section 7 of the Canadian Charter of Rights and Freedoms).

[46] See Krotoszynski, above (n 43) 49.

[47] ibid.

In sum, when a government program involves the collection, storage, and accessing of sensitive personal data, the constitutional right of informational privacy imposes both substantive and procedural limits on the program. More specifically, such programs must advance an important government interest, include substantive restrictions on when and why the government may access the confidential personal data, and impose procedural safeguards to ensure that the government actually honours the statute's substantive restrictions in practice. Because New York's program for tracking prescriptions for potentially addictive drugs featured these mandatory design elements, it did not violate the constitutional right to informational privacy. On the other hand, however, a federal or state information gathering and storage program that lacked these design elements would face the prospect of judicial invalidation.

III. SUBSEQUENT JUDICIAL DEVELOPMENTS SURROUNDING THE RIGHT OF INFORMATIONAL PRIVACY IN THE FEDERAL COURTS

To be sure, *Whalen* constitutes something of a dog that did not bark; the decision's assumption of a constitutional interest in informational privacy lied fallow for literally decades at the Supreme Court level.[48] In 2011, the US Supreme Court effectively reaffirmed *Whalen*'s approach by once again assuming that the right of privacy, implicit in the concept of due process of law, safeguarded an individual's interest in informational privacy. In *NASA v Nelson*,[49] the Supreme Court reconsidered the dangers that the government's collection, storage, and use of confidential personal information could present. However, as in *Whalen*, the majority found that the government had established constitutionally adequate guardrails to prevent either the unwarranted or unauthorised public release of sensitive personal information.

Nelson involved background investigations into government-contractor employees working at the Jet Propulsion Laboratory (JPL), which 'is staffed exclusively by contract employees' at the California Institute of Technology (commonly known as 'Caltech'), in Pasadena, California.[50] Justice Samuel Alito, writing for the *Nelson* majority, explained that 'JPL is the lead NASA center for

[48] This may be an unduly pessimistic assessment. See SF Kreimer, 'Sunlight, Secrets, and Scarlet Letters: The Tension Between Privacy and Disclosure in Constitutional Law' (1991) 140 *University of Pennsylvania Law Review* 1, 120–21, 137–39 (describing and discussing lower court cases applying *Whalen*'s dicta and observing that these decisions reflect a balancing approach that weighs the importance of safeguarding the confidentiality of sensitive personal information against the government's need to collect, store, and review the personal information); see also SF Kreimer, 'The Right to Privacy in the Pennsylvania Constitution' (1993) 3 *Widener Journal of Public Law* 77, 79, n. 8 ('The lower federal courts have discerned from *Whalen* and a few other cases a federal right to the confidentiality of information regarding intimate activities that must be balanced against the magnitude of the government interest at stake.').

[49] 562 U.S. 134 (2011).

[50] ibid at 139.

deep-space robots and communications' and has taken primary responsibility for '[m]ost of this country's unmanned space missions.'[51]

After the 9/11 attacks, the federal government required standard background checks, known as 'National Agency Check with Inquiries (NACI)', for all 'contract employees with long-term access to federal facilities'.[52] Long-term employees of JPL, who were technically employed by Caltech rather than the federal government, objected to some of the questions relating to drug and alcohol use.[53] Responses provided incident to the NACI process are covered by the federal Privacy Act, which generally prohibits disclosure of the information without the subject's express consent.[54] Nevertheless, the JPL employees complained that the background check questions violated their 'constitutional right to informational privacy'.[55]

The lower federal courts split on the merits of the JPL employees' claim. The district court rejected the employees' informational privacy claim, but the US Court of Appeals for the Ninth Circuit reversed.[56] The Ninth Circuit explained that '[t]o justify actions infringing upon the right, the government must show that its use of the information would advance a legitimate state interest and that its actions are narrowly tailored to meet that interest.'[57] In a subsequent decision, it flatly reversed the district court's order permitting NASA to require the JPL employees to cooperate with the NACI background check process.[58] The panel held that the 'open-ended and highly private questions' were not 'narrowly tailored to any legitimate government interest'.[59]

The Supreme Court granted a write of certiorari and proceeded to review and reverse the Ninth Circuit's ruling. Justice Alito, citing *Whalen*, 'assume[d] for present purposes that the Government's challenged inquiries implicate a privacy interest of constitutional significance'.[60] Nevertheless, the majority held 'that, whatever the scope of this interest, it does not prevent the government from asking reasonable questions of the sort' associated with the NACI background check process.[61] The government, as an employer, has a legitimate and constitutional interest in assessing the suitability of a potential employee working with confidential government information.[62] The questions that the JPL

[51] ibid.

[52] ibid at 139–40.

[53] See ibid at 140–42.

[54] Privacy Act, 5 U.S.C. § 552a(b) (2018).

[55] *Nelson*, 562 U.S. at 142.

[56] *Nelson v NASA*, 506 F.3d 713, 715 (9th Cir. 2007) ('Because of the nature of the information subject to which the waiver applies, serious privacy concerns arise.').

[57] ibid.

[58] *Nelson v NASA*, 512 F.3d 1134, 1144–45 (9th Cir. 2008), *rev'd*, 562 U.S. 134 (2011).

[59] ibid at 1145.

[60] *Nelson*, 562 U.S. at 147.

[61] ibid at 147–48.

[62] See ibid at 149–50 (discussing the government's need for the information it sought and concluding that 'the Government has an interest in conducting basic employment background checks').

employees challenged 'consist[ed] of reasonable, employment-related inquiries that further the Government's interest in managing its internal operations'.[63] The Constitution does not require the government, when conducting employment-related background checks, 'to demonstrate that its questions are "necessary" or the least restrictive means of furthering its interests'.[64]

Justice Alito also rejected the employees' arguments that the Privacy Act provided insufficient protection against the unauthorised disclosure of the information, reasoning that the law provided adequate safeguards against both '*unwarranted* disclosures' and '*undue* disclosures' and that the Constitution's right of informational privacy does not require the government to provide 'an ironclad disclosure bar'.[65] The Constitution requires only reasonable protections against unauthorised disclosures. On these facts, 'the Government's inquiries do not violate a constitutional right to informational privacy'.[66]

Justice Antonin Scalia, joined by Justice Clarence Thomas, concurred in the result but dissented from the majority's decision to assume the existence of a constitutional right of informational privacy. In Scalia's view, '[a] federal constitutional right to "informational privacy" does not exist.'[67] He observed that '[l]ike many other desirable things not included in the Constitution, "informational privacy" seems like a good idea – wherefore the People have enacted laws at the federal level and in the States restricting government collection and use of information.'[68] Scalia's objections notwithstanding, a 7-2 majority of the Supreme Court reaffirmed *Whalen*'s dicta that the Constitution *does* in fact constrain the government's ability to collect, store, and disseminate an individual's sensitive personal information.

The lower federal and state courts have struggled to make sense of *Whalen* as glossed by *Nelson*. Most of the US Courts of Appeals have recognised a constitutional right of informational privacy,[69] and for those that have, the governing legal standards are unclear – with some circuits applying something like rationality review and others using intermediate scrutiny or even strict scrutiny.[70]

[63] ibid at 151.

[64] ibid at 153.

[65] ibid at 157 (emphasis in the original).

[66] ibid at 159.

[67] ibid at 160 (Scalia, J., concurring); see ibid at 169 (Thomas, J., concurring) ('I agree with Justice Scalia that the Constitution does not protect a right to informational privacy.').

[68] *Nelson*, 562 U.S. at 159–60 (Scalia, J., concurring).

[69] See Skinner-Thompson, above (n 4) 184 ('While the majority of circuits have concluded that a constitutional right to informational privacy does exist, the circuits are divided. Those circuits that do recognize the right have rarely enforced it.').

[70] ibid 184–89 (collecting and discussing cases from the lower federal courts regarding the constitutional right of informational privacy). Professors Solove and Richards, both well-regarded US legal scholars of privacy, explain that, in the tort context, '[t]he current privacy torts have struggled in recognizing more nuanced understandings of privacy in terms of levels of accessibility of information.' Solove and Richards, above (n 9) 1920. They emphasise that '[c]ombining disparate data together or taking inaccessible information and disseminating it much more widely are both significant incursions on privacy', ibid, but do not clearly generate tort liability under the contemporary tort-law right of privacy in the US. See ibid 1920–21.

Post-*Nelson*, the US Court of Appeals for the Eighth Circuit appears to have rejected the existence of a constitutional right of informational privacy.[71] The Tenth Circuit, by way of contrast, has held that its pre-*Nelson* precedents remain good law but that absent further doctrinal developments 'we do not know the doctrinal boundaries of the protection against government disclosure'.[72] The Tenth Circuit was merely deciding whether government officials who released a patient's cancer diagnosis enjoyed qualified immunity – which did not require the *Leiser* Court to rule on the scope of the right of informational privacy.[73] By way of contrast, however, the Sixth Circuit has clearly recognised a constitutional right of informational privacy – at least when the information relates to a fundamental right (such as sexual autonomy, free association, or freedom of conscience).[74] And, taking the same approach as the Sixth Circuit, the Seventh Circuit seems to have re-affirmed its pre-*Nelson* precedents that recognise a constitutional right of informational privacy.[75]

At least some legal scholars reject the contention that *Nelson* altered the legal rules of the road with respect to a constitutional right of informational privacy.[76] For example, Professor Larry Pittman claims that

> even with the confusion that *Nelson* caused with its attempt to weaken *Whalen*'s precedential value, substantially all of the thirteen circuit courts of appeals have rejected *Nelson*'s interpretation that *Whalen* establishes only an assumption of a constitutional right to informational privacy.[77]

[71] *Dillard v O'Kelley*, 961 F. 3d 1048, 1057 (8th Cir. 2020) (en banc) (Grasz, J., concurring) ('The constitutional right to informational privacy in the Eighth Circuit is dead.').

[72] *Leiser v Moore*, 903 F. 3d 1137, 1144 (10th Cir. 2018).

[73] See ibid 1144–45.

[74] *Lee v City of Columbus, Ohio*, 636 F. 3d 245, 259–260 and 260 n. 8 (6th Cir. 2011); see *Bloch v Ribar*, 156 F. 3d 673, 683–84 (6th Cir. 1998) ('Unlike many other circuits, this court has narrowly construed the holdings of *Whalen* and *Nixon* to extend the right to informational privacy only to interests that implicate a fundamental liberty interest.') Professor Skinner-Thompson seems to endorse stronger constitutional protection for 'intimate information' and 'information pertaining to political thought' – a position consistent with the Sixth Circuit's approach to the constitutional right of informational privacy. See Skinner-Thompson, above (n 4) 204–05, 211–12.

[75] *Chasensky v Walker*, 740 F. 3d 1088, 1096 (7th Cir, 2014) ('Indeed, it is true that "[t]he courts of appeals, including this court, have interpreted *Whalen* to recognize a constitutional right to the privacy of medical, sexual, financial, and perhaps other categories of highly personal information – information that most people are reluctant to disclose to strangers – and have held that the right is defeasible only upon proof of a strong public interest in access to or dissemination of the information."' (citing and quoting *Wolfe v Schaefer*, 619 F.3d 782, 785 (7th Cir. 2010)).

[76] LJ Pittman, 'The Elusive Constitutional Right to Informational Privacy' (2018) 19 *Nevada Law Journal* 135, 156–57 (arguing that 'the Court's analysis in *Whalen* and *Nixon*, and its reference to *Whalen* in the *Ferguson* opinion' support the legal conclusion 'that the Court has conclusively held that the liberty interest protection of the Fourteenth Amendment includes a constitutional right to informational privacy').

[77] ibid 160. Pittman adds that '[i]Instead of following *Nelson*, substantially all of the federal circuit courts of appeals presently cite *Whalen* as definitively establishing a constitutional right to informational privacy.' ibid 167–182.

He concedes that '[t]here is a division among the federal circuits regarding the specific standards used to evaluate informational privacy claims, with some circuit courts having more expansive standards for resolving the claims, and others having more narrow standards.'[78] This description seems unduly generous toward the rulings of certain circuits, including the D.C. Circuit and Eighth Circuit, which seem to have come very close to holding that no constitutional right of informational privacy exists. Pittman is correct, however, to posit that some circuits have retained their pre-*Nelson* precedents that hold such a right exists.[79]

In sum, *Nelson* appears to resolve any residual doubts about whether *Whalen*'s dicta established a constitutional right of informational privacy; the harder question is the precise scope of the right. Accordingly, in the US, neither the federal nor a state government may collect and freely disseminate sensitive personal information without observing any substantive or procedural limits. When the government collects, stores, and accesses sensitive personal information, it must have a legitimate reason for doing so. Moreover, the personal information that the government collects must be safeguarded from both intentional and negligent release to the public. Provided that the government has a legitimate reason for collecting personal information, stores the information securely, and reliably limits access to the information, the program will not violate the constitutional right of informational privacy.

For example, suppose that a state government opposed to the use of birth control collected information regarding prescriptions for birth control pills and regularly published the names, addresses, and phone numbers of women with current prescriptions for birth control pills[80] – or required physicians who provide abortions to send the state government the names, addresses, and phone numbers of their patients and then regularly publishes this information on a government-operated website. The federal courts, on the authority of *Whalen* and *Nelson*, would certainly invalidate such state laws.[81]

[78] ibid 167.

[79] See ibid 182.

[80] See *Griswold v Connecticut*, 381 U.S. 479, 480 (1965) (invalidating on privacy grounds a Connecticut state law that prohibited both the distribution of birth control and instruction on its use).

[81] See Fan, above (n 4) 956 (observing that a constitutional right of informational privacy 'has flourished by assumption over the decades' and noting that the lower federal and state courts have found violations 'in cases of alleged abuses of official power that register high on the outrage and creepiness emotional meter'). Fan notes that examples of cases where courts have found the constitutional line to have been crossed include 'law enforcement officials aggressively outing HIV-positive people and trying to get them fired or harming their familial relations and the ability of their children to attend school; or threatening to disclose a teenager's gay sexual orientation to his grandfather after arresting him for suspected underage drinking, causing him to commit suicide; or "gratuitously and unnecessarily" releasing humiliating details of a rape for no other purpose than to retaliate against the rape victim for criticizing an ineffectual investigation; or keeping a sex videotape featuring an extortion victim in a desk drawer and allegedly viewing it, inviting other officers to view it, and reproducing it for personal gratification rather than any public purpose.' ibid 956–57. But see Solove and Richards, above (n 9) 1922 (observing that 'courts have struggled to recognize harm from leaked or improperly disseminated data').

By way of contrast, the information New York collected and stored in *Whalen* directly related to efforts to control drug abuse facilitated by unscrupulous physicians and pharmacists; the background checks at issue in *Nelson* involved the potential risks that could arise from employing persons with criminal backgrounds or drug abuse problems. Neither program involved the gratuitous collection and dissemination of potentially embarrassing confidential personal information. Moreover, both programs limited access to the information, required the information to be stored securely, and imposed serious penalties for the unauthorised disclosure of a person's confidential information.

IV. STATUTORY PRIVACY PROTECTIONS IN THE UNITED STATES OFTEN WILL OBVIATE THE NEED FOR A JUDICIAL INTERVENTION TO SECURE THE RIGHT OF INFORMATIONAL PRIVACY

One might reasonably question the wisdom of leaving informational privacy up to Congress and the state legislatures to protect. For the most part, the federal courts have simply cautioned against the unthinking collection, storage, and release of sensitive personal information and have not – to date at least – found federal or state data collection programs to violate the right of informational privacy. This reticence to issue bold decisions enforcing the constitutional right to informational self-determination probably reflects, at least in part, the Supreme Court's failure to provide clear rules of the road delimiting the scope of the right.

As Professor Scott Skinner-Thompson accurately describes the current state of play, '[f]aced with this "doctrinal obscurity," the circuit courts continue to wrestle with constitutional informational privacy.'[82] Making a similar argument, Professor Fan expresses dismay at 'the approach of regulation by fog and assumption' because it 'has costs beyond even those Justice Scalia enumerated' that include 'the risk of chilling policy innovations by the political branches and an inability to, and an inconsistency in, separating out or even defining meritorious claims from the vast pool of chaff that should be rapidly sorted out at the threshold'.[83] The right of informational privacy in the US has been fuzzy and ill-defined since its inception in *Whalen*. But surely a poorly defined constitutional right is still a federal constitutional right?

In the US, federal judges have the last word on the meaning and requirements of the US Constitution.[84] However, the failure of the lower courts to

[82] Skinner-Thompson, above (n 4) 184.
[83] Fan, above (n 4) 957.
[84] See *Marbury v Madison*, 5 U.S. (1 Cranch) 137, 177 (1803) ('It is emphatically the province and duty of the judicial department to say what the law is. Those who apply the rule to particular cases, must of necessity expound and interpret that rule. If two laws conflict with each other, the

enforce *Whalen* and *Nelson* broadly – or even coherently – has left the scope of informational privacy largely in the hands of Congress and the state legislatures. Nevertheless, *Whalen* and *Nelson* still exert some constraining force. As Professor Margaret Hu has argued, *Whalen* established a right of informational privacy with constitutional roots[85] and '[w]hat *Nelson* did was enable precedent on informational privacy rights to survive – precedent that Justices Scalia and Thomas thought should be overruled.'[86] Legislators and bureaucrats alike know that when they create programs to collect, store, and access sensitive personal data, the programs are subject to constitutional attack if they fail to advance a sufficiently important government interest or lack essential procedural safeguards.

Whether or not because of the 'constitutional flares'[87] that the Supreme Court sent up in *Whalen* and *Nelson*, a general socio-legal expectation exists in the contemporary US that the government will handle sensitive personal information with care. Congress and state legislatures routinely include both substantive and procedural protections to safeguard informational privacy when adopting programs that collect and store confidential personal data.

Consider, for example, the Privacy Act of 1974, a generic federal law that protects personal information held by the federal government from unwarranted or unauthorised disclosure.[88] In relevant part, the Privacy Act provides that

> No agency shall disclose any record which is contained in a system of records by any means of communication to any person, or to another agency, except pursuant to a written request by, or with the prior written consent of, the individual to whom the record pertains.[89]

The law also guarantees that individuals will enjoy access to federal government records that pertain to them[90] and requires federal agencies to adopt security

courts must decide on the operation of each.') In point of fact, the proponents of ratification of the Constitution, in The Federalist Papers, made it clear that the federal courts, not Congress, would have the last word on the meaning of the Constitution. See *The Federalist* No 78, 464, 468 (James Madison) (Clinton Rossiter ed, 1961) (explaining that 'where the will of the legislature, declared in its statutes, stands in opposition to that of the people, declared in the Constitution, the judges ought to be governed by the latter rather than the former'). What is more, 'the prior act of a superior ought to be preferred to the subsequent act of an inferior and subordinate authority; and that accordingly, whenever a particular statute contravenes the Constitution, it will be the duty of the judicial tribunals to adhere to the latter and disregard the former'. ibid; see WW Van Alstyne, 'A Critical Guide to *Marbury v. Madison*' [1969] *Duke Law Journal* 1 (providing a detailed and thoughtful analysis of the Supreme Court's landmark *Marbury* decision and a defence of the necessity of judicial review to enforcement of a written constitution).

[85] M Hu, 'Big Data Blacklisting' (2015) 67 *Florida Law Review* 1735, 1796–98.

[86] ibid 1796.

[87] See Krotoszynski, above (n 43) 49–62 (discussing how courts and legislatures engage in an ongoing dialectic about constitutional norms and values and why this dialogue between the branches can help to better secure and maintain constitutional rights).

[88] Privacy Act of 1974, Pub. L. 93–579, 88 Stat. 1896 (codified at 5 U.S.C. § 552a (2018)).

[89] 5 U.S.C. § 552a(b) (2018).

[90] ibid at 552a(d)(1).

measures that will prevent unauthorised disclosures of confidential personal information.[91] Moreover, federal agencies that collect and store personal data must adopt and enforce regulations that set forth how they will comply with the Privacy Act.[92] Finally, the Privacy Act establishes both civil and criminal penalties for violations.[93] If a federal agency fully complies with the Privacy Act's requirements, it is unlikely to violate the constitutional right of informational privacy described in *Whalen* and *Nelson*.[94]

The same sort of situation arises in the context of procedural due process in federal agency adjudications subject to the Administrative Procedure Act (APA).[95] When the APA's rules for formal adjudications apply and an agency scrupulously follows them, virtually no chance exists of the proceedings failing to meet the requirements of the Fifth Amendment's Due Process Clause.[96] This, of course, does not mean that the Constitution is irrelevant to the fairness of agency procedures when agencies conduct quasi-adjudicative proceedings not governed by the APA; instead, it simply demonstrates that Congress often legislates against a backdrop of judicially-enforced constitutional constraints.[97]

Other federal laws protect informational privacy in the context of medical records,[98] financial records,[99] and educational records.[100] These laws apply to both private and government entities that collect, store, and access personal information and, like the Privacy Act, impose both substantive limits on the use of such information and procedural requirements to ensure that such information is stored securely – and provide civil and criminal penalties for violations.

[91] ibid at 552a(e)(10).

[92] ibid at 552a(f).

[93] ibid at 552a(g).

[94] Indeed, Justice Alito makes this very point in *Nelson*. See *NASA v Nelson*, 562 U.S. 134, 155–59 (2011). He noted that the JPL employees objecting to the background checks failed to provide 'any plausible scenario in which their information might be unduly disclosed' and concluded that '[i]n light of the protection provided by the Privacy Act's nondisclosure requirement' no violation of a 'constitutional right to informational privacy' existed. ibid at 158–59.

[95] 5 U.S.C. §§ 554, 556 and 557 (2018).

[96] See *Mathews v Eldridge*, 424 U.S. 319 (1976) (setting forth the requirements of procedural due process).

[97] See generally Hu, above (n 85) 1797 (arguing that the constitutional right of informational privacy is essential because it establishes 'a systemic-type remedy to address system-wide harms').

[98] The Health Insurance Portability and Accountability Act of 1996, Pub. L. 104–191, 110 Stat. 1936 (codified as amended in scattered sections of 18, 26, 29, and 42 U.S.C. (2018)). Commonly referred to as 'HIPPA', this federal law protects a patient's medical records from unauthorised disclosure and mandates that such records be stored securely. For a general overview of HIPPA, see J Hiller et al., 'Privacy and Security in the Implementation of Health Information Technology' (2011) 17 *Boston University Journal of Science & Technology Law* 1, 11–18.

[99] The Fair Credit Report Act of 1970, Pub. L. 91–508, 84 Stat. 1114 (codified at 15 U.S.C. §§ 1681–1681x (2018)).

[100] Family Educational Rights and Privacy Act of 1974 (FERPA), Pub. L. 93–380, 88 Stat. 571 (codified at 20 U.S.C. § 1232g (2018)).

Although the US does not have a national law that comprehensively protects all personal data, in the fashion of the EU's General Data Protection Regulation (GDPR),[101] these federal statutes nevertheless provide meaningful, albeit piecemeal, protection of privacy in some of the areas that would be most likely to trigger the constitutional right of informational privacy. As a consequence, most of the claims brought in the federal courts seeking to invoke *Whalen* and *Nelson* are marginal and often involve complaints involving unauthorised release of personal information due to the criminal acts of third parties (ie, the hacking of government-maintained databases that contain confidential personal information). Obviously, a federal agency, such as the Office of Personnel Management or the Internal Revenue Service, cannot be held strictly responsible for criminal acts that result in data breaches – despite the agencies taking reasonable measures to maintain the information securely.[102]

In sum, there is something of a chicken and egg question about the effect of *Whalen* and *Nelson* on the behaviour of government agencies that collect, store, and access sensitive personal data. Some of the most important federal privacy laws predate *Whalen* – this is true of the Fair Credit Reporting Act and the Privacy Act. However, the vigilance with which federal agencies enforce these laws surely reflects at least some concern about the possibility of federal court oversight of their efforts (under both the statutes themselves and the constitutional right of informational privacy). *Whalen* thus provides an important background consideration that helps to delimit and shape how the federal and state governments collect, store, and use personal information.

To be sure, the constitutional right of informational privacy in the US is a (very) pale shadow of the German right to informational self-determination. Moreover, in the US, an individual's control over personal data is far more circumscribed than in Europe under the GDPR and the European Charter. Even so, however, the US does recognise that the collection, storage, and use of sensitive personal data implicates constitutional values and, more specifically, a fundamental liberty interest in privacy.

[101] General Data Protection Regulation (GDPR), 2016/679 (EU). The GDPR came into force on 25 May 2018. For a general overview and discussion of the GDPR and its requirements, see *Google LLC v CNIL*, Case C-507/17, 24 September 2019 (Grand Chamber), available at curia.europa.eu/juris/document/document.jsf?docid=218105&doclang=EN.

[102] See *In Re U.S. Office of Personnel Management Data Security Breach Litigation*, 928 F. 3d 42, 72–74 (D.C. Cir. 2019). But *cf* Solove and Richards, above (n 9) 1922–23 ('Courts can readily understand the harm caused by disclosure of a naked photograph of a person but they struggle in locating a harm when non-embarrassing data is disclosed or leaked' and arguing that '[a] broader understanding of harm is needed' to address 'the extensive gathering, dissemination, and use of information by various businesses and organizations'). The D.C. Circuit explained that no precedents support a constitutional violation where the government itself failed to release the confidential personal information. *In Re U.S. Office of Personnel Management*, 928 F.3d at 73–74. One might imagine liability existing where a government agency's security protocols are so weak as to be negligent or reckless – on the other hand, the Privacy Act would create statutory liability for an agency's failure to properly safeguard personal data on such facts.

V. CONCLUSION

In *Whalen*, the US Supreme Court effectively recognised a constitutional right of informational privacy and, in *Nelson*, reaffirmed *Whalen*'s important dicta 34 years later. To be sure, the constitutional right of informational privacy in the US is not particularly strong or robust; it imposes a set of minimal obligations on the government to justify the collection, storage, and use of sensitive personal information with a legitimate reason; the government's collection and storage protocols must be sufficiently robust to prevent the information's misuse or inadvertent public disclosure; and, finally, the information must not be retained longer than necessary to accomplish the government's legitimate objectives. If a government agency heedlessly collected and then released sensitive personal information – such as medical records or internet surfing habits – the federal courts would almost certainly invoke *Whalen* and *Nelson* and invalidate the data collection program.

One might reasonably wonder why the federal courts have not found it necessary to squarely address the existence and scope of a constitutional right of informational privacy with greater frequency and clarity. In point of fact, lower court decisions do exist that impose stricter controls on the collection and dissemination of personal data.[103] A better explanation relates to the existence of federal statutes that safeguard personal data involving medical records, educational records, and financial records. Despite the absence of a comprehensive national data privacy law, the US maintains targeted statutory privacy protections that cover some of a person's most sensitive personal information. The Privacy Act also creates a general obligation on the part of federal government entities to adopt rules and procedures that secure personal data and prevent the unauthorised release of such information.

Thus, because statutory safeguards routinely accompany the creation of government programs to collect and store confidential personal information, the federal courts have not found it necessary to issue broad constitutional rulings that definitively address informational privacy as an aspect of substantive due process.[104] *Whalen*, however, plainly supports the claim that the US Constitution requires the government to protect confidential information when it establishes programs that collect, store, and facilitate access to such information.

[103] See Fan, above (n 4) 956–57. Professor Fan explains that '[i]n the lower courts, where the right has flourished by assumption over the decades … potential violations have been found[] most frequently in cases of alleged abuses of official power that register high on the outrage or creepiness emotional meter.' ibid 956.

[104] See JL Entrikin, 'Family Secrets and Relational Privacy: Protecting Not-So-Personal, Sensitive Information from Public Disclosure' (2020) 74 *University of Miami Law Review* 781, 851–52 (arguing that 'any federal right to information privacy is grounded in the Privacy Act, not the Constitution').

5

Kaye v Robertson (1990)

JACOB ROWBOTTOM*

I. INTRODUCTION

THE COURT OF Appeal's ruling in *Kaye v Robertson* is an unusual candidate for status as a landmark case.[1] The case did not raise any complex or novel issues of law. The judgments were relatively brief and did not break any new ground. The facts of the case were memorable but straightforward. The case is nonetheless notable because it illustrated what the law did not do at the time. The three judgments in the Court of Appeal made powerful statements about the absence of a right to privacy in the common law. The case also provided an example of a media intrusion at a key moment in the debates about press ethics in Britain. The significance of the case lies in its notoriety, marking a low point in the protection of privacy.[2]

This chapter will start by setting out the facts of the case and will then place the case in the context of the tabloid culture at the time. The years preceding *Kaye* saw a rise in intrusive styles of tabloid journalism that often focused on celebrities. By the late 1980s, the concerns about press intrusion were such that the introduction of privacy laws were on the political agenda. The chapter will explain how *Kaye* was significant in its contribution to that political debate. The chapter will then assess the legal significance of the decision, noting how it did not preclude the development of the common law to offer greater protection to privacy. Since 1990, the facts of the case have faded from public memory and the legal position stated in the case has been eroded. Three decades later, the case provides a point of reference from which to assess the subsequent developments, which will be considered in the final sections.

* Thanks to Peter Coe for comments on an earlier draft of this chapter.

[1] *Kaye v Robertson* [1991] FSR 62.

[2] In *Mills v News Group Newspapers* [2001] EMLR 41 at [22], Lawrence Collins J described the case as 'notorious'.

II. THE FACTS AND DECISION

The claimant, Gorden Kaye, was an actor best known for playing the lead character, René Artois, in the popular BBC television comedy *'Allo 'Allo!*.[3] The invasion of Kaye's privacy arose from an incident in January 1990, when the UK was struck by the 'Burns Day Storm', which was one of the most powerful wind storms in Europe.[4] The storm caused damage to buildings, tore down an estimated three million trees,[5] caused road accidents and disrupted power lines. In the UK, 47 people died as a result of the storm. Kaye came close to being an additional fatality. On 25 January 1990, Kaye was driving during a shopping trip in London and was caught in the storm. The wind tore a piece of wood from an advertising billboard, which smashed through Kaye's windscreen.[6] Kaye was struck on the head above the right eye, causing severe head and brain injuries. He was taken to hospital for brain surgery, placed on a life support machine for three days and was then taken into intensive care.

Given the high profile of the actor and the level of public affection for him, there was considerable concern for his well-being and significant media interest in the accident.[7] Steps were therefore taken to protect the claimant from intrusion. When he was moved into a private room in the hospital on 2 February, notices were placed on the entrance to the ward and on the door to his room asking visitors to see a member of staff before entering. A list of people permitted to visit the patient was also posted outside his room.

On 13 February, Ray Levine and Gazza Thompson, two journalists working for the *Sunday Sport*, gained access to the hospital and entered Kaye's room. They ignored the notices displayed on the ward and did not seek permission to gain access. Kaye (apparently) agreed to speak to them and did not object to photographs being taken of the flowers and cards in the room. Photographs were also taken of Kaye, showing the scars to his head. When hospital staff were alerted, they asked the journalists to leave. The request was not successful, and the journalists were subsequently removed by security. Kaye was in no fit condition to consent to the interview and had no recollection of the incident shortly afterwards.

The *Sunday Sport* planned to publish an article based on the interview and include some of the photographs taken. The claimant sought a pre-trial

[3] In 1988, its Christmas Day episode was the 8th most watched programme of the year (with an audience of 17.05 million), www.barb.co.uk/resources/tv-facts/tv-since-1981/1988/top10/. In 1986, its Christmas episode had an audience of 16.65 million, 'Christmas television viewing figures', *The Guardian*, 10 January 1986.

[4] www.metoffice.gov.uk/binaries/content/assets/metofficegovuk/pdf/weather/learn-about/uk-past-events/interesting/1990/burns-day-storm---25-january-1990---met-office.pdf.

[5] *The Times*, 30 January 2013.

[6] See, G Kaye and H Bonner, *René and Me* (London, Pan, 1990) 171–73.

[7] For example, the *Daily Mirror* on 26 January 1990 carried a full front page story on the incident, with the headline 'Pray For Rene' and featuring a photograph of the smashed windscreen.

injunction to restrain publication of the article. The injunction was initially granted by Potter J which prohibited the newspaper from publishing any of the photographs taken in the hospital and any of the statements taken from the claimant by the reporters. The injunction also prevented the newspaper from stating that the claimant had consented to the photographs or interview. The newspaper's appeal was heard by the Court of Appeal on 23 February. Following that hearing, the terms of the original injunction were replaced with a more limited order. Under the new injunction, the newspaper was restrained from publishing anything that could be reasonably understood to mean that Kaye had agreed to be interviewed and photographed. The injunction did not stop the publication of the information acquired through the intrusion. Following the Court of Appeal's decision, the *Sunday Sport* went ahead and published an article on 4 March 1990. The article featured pictures of Kaye in his hospital room and quotes taken from the journalists' unauthorised visit. To comply with the injunction, the article made clear that the actor had not consented to the photos or an interview.

III. THE CONTEXT: TABLOIDS, PRESS INTRUSION AND THE POLITICS OF REFORM

A. The Tabloids in the 1980s

Before assessing the legal and political significance of the case, it is important to place the Court of Appeal's decision in the context of the tabloid culture that had arisen during the 1980s and the role played by the defendant in that sector of the media. During this period, British tabloid journalism had been dominated by a rivalry between two daily titles, *The Sun* and the *Daily Mirror*. The two papers were owned by two rival media moguls, Rupert Murdoch (*The Sun*) and Robert Maxwell (*Mirror*). Both papers had large circulations, with *The Sun* having an average circulation in excess of 4 million and the *Mirror* in excess of 3 million. Of the two rivals, *The Sun* was famous for its brash headlines and editorials. The Sunday tabloid market was similarly dominated by the *News of the World* (the sister newspaper to *The Sun*, also owned by Murdoch), the *Sunday Mirror* and the *People* (both owned by Maxwell's company at the time). The Sunday tabloids became known for a style of journalism that gave increasing attention to the lives of celebrities and the royal family.[8]

The rivalry between the leading tabloids was just one part of the newspaper market. There were mid-market titles such as the *Daily Express* and *Daily Mail*, and broadsheet newspapers such as *The Times*, *The Daily Telegraph* and

[8] See A Bingham and M Conboy, *Tabloid Century: The Popular Press in Britain, 1896 to the Present* (Oxford University Press, 2015) 127–28.

The Guardian. The *Daily Star* provided a more downmarket tabloid. That title was launched in 1978 by the owner of the *Daily Express* to make full use of (and maximise the return on) its printing facilities. Even with such a range of titles, there was still space in the market for yet another, even more downmarket, tabloid. That space was filled by the *Sunday Sport*, which was published by the second defendant in *Kaye v Robertson*. The weekly newspaper was launched in 1986 by David Sullivan,[9] who had previously made his money from a chain of sex shops and by publishing adult magazines.[10] In September 1987, Drew Robertson, the first defendant in *Kaye*, was appointed editor of the *Sunday Sport*.[11]

The description of the *Sunday Sport* as a newspaper is something of a stretch, as the publication contained very little of what could be considered news.[12] The *Sunday Sport* was known for including many photographs of topless models, estimated in 1990 to be between 5–10 per cent of its content.[13] At the time, a considerable proportion of the paper consisted of advertisements for adult phone lines, pornographic videos and magazines.[14] The paper also became known for the publication of bizarre and sensational stories. Possibly its best known headline was 1988's 'World War 2 bomber found on Moon'.[15] Other headlines included 'Bus Found Buried at South Pole',[16] 'Statue of Elvis found on Mars',[17] 'Adolf Hitler was a Woman',[18] and 'Woman Gives Birth To 8lb Duck'.[19] With such headlines, the newspaper followed a tradition more closely associated with the *National Enquirer* in the US than any British newspaper.

The formula proved to be successful. In October 1988, the *Sunday Sport* had a weekly circulation of 589,000.[20] By the end of 1989, the circulation had fallen, but was still significant at just under 500,000.[21] In 1988, a Wednesday edition of the paper was launched and 1989 saw the launch of a further Friday edition, though the content of those weekday versions was a little more toned down than that of its Sunday counterpart.[22]

[9] Sullivan (who owned 50% of the shares in the publishing company) sought to cater for the 'bottom end of the market', Monopolies and Mergers Commission, *Mr David Sullivan and The Bristol Evening Post PLC: A report on the proposed transfer of a Controlling interest as defined in section 57(4) of the Fair Trading Act 1973* (1990) [4.36] (hereafter 'MMC').

[10] M Brown, 'Porn king plans Sunday paper' *The Guardian*, 21 January 1986.

[11] MMC (n 9) [4.70], having previously served as its deputy editor.

[12] ibid, [6.12].

[13] ibid, [2.9].

[14] ibid, estimating at around 30% of its content. See also *Kaye* (n 1).

[15] 24 April 1988. For various examples see 'A headline you can believe: The 'Sport' closes' *The Independent*, 23 October 2011.

[16] 12 February 1989.

[17] 1 October 1989.

[18] 31 July 1988.

[19] 30 June 1990.

[20] MMC (n 9) [2.21].

[21] ibid, [2.21].

[22] ibid, [2.8].

Given its position in the market, the *Daily Star* was thought to be concerned that a daily version of the *Sunday Sport* would impact on its own circulation.[23] In 1987, in what was seen as an attempt to pre-empt such competition in the dailies market, Sport Newspapers entered into a brief association with the *Daily Star*. Express Newspapers (which owned the *Star*) acquired a 24.8 per cent stake in the company owning the *Sunday Sport*.[24] Under the arrangement, the *Sunday Sport's* Mike Gabbert became the editor of the *Star*, which it was hoped would revive the daily newspaper's fortunes and even allow it to rival *The Sun* and *Mirror*.[25]

Under Gabbert's editorship, the *Star* was taken further downmarket. The paper's new editor promised at least two topless models each day.[26] In one notorious example from 7 September 1987, the front page of the *Star* featured a picture of a 15-year-old girl, with a headline announcing 'She's going topless in 34 days'. In *The Times*, Tony Blair referred to the article as an example of the 'crude exploitation of people' in the press and called for a 'statutory press body armed with real powers' to regulate newspapers.[27] By October 1987, Tesco withdrew all its advertising from the *Daily Star* on the basis that its content 'degrades women'.[28] Gabbert's editorship lasted only eight weeks, after which the shares in Sport Newspapers reverted back to the original owner and the link between the two papers ended. The *Star*'s association with Sport Newspapers was not a success.

The episode with the *Star* shows how the *Sunday Sport* occupied a distinct and unusual position in the newspaper market. The publication presented itself as a newspaper and was sold on newsagent shelves alongside other newspapers.[29] However, the title took some of the crudest and most sensational elements of tabloid culture and magnified them. The paper therefore remained on the periphery of the mainstream media, and its approach to journalism proved to be unsuitable even for its nearest potential rival, the *Daily Star*. The position of the newspaper presented a dilemma in relation to debates about press ethics: should the *Sunday Sport* be seen as a special case which says nothing about the media more generally, or was the content of the paper the logical conclusion of a tabloid market which relied on sex, sensationalism and low-cost stories to maximise sales?

[23] ibid, [4.25].

[24] ibid, [2.10].

[25] 'Star in battle for the bottom' *The Times*, 6 September 1987.

[26] ibid.

[27] T Blair, 'Licence to print anything' *The Times*, 13 October 1987.

[28] 'Nudes cost newspaper its adverts' *The Guardian* 3 October 1987.

[29] The Press Council had advised that the paper be placed on the higher shelves, see *The Independent* 11 February 1990, 'Sunday Sport faces porn ad curbs', *The Times*, 5 March 1991.

B. Press Intrusion – Acceptable in the 80s?

While some of the content in the *Sunday Sport* could be explained by the paper's distinctive character, the intrusion at the heart of *Kaye* was typical of the broader tabloid culture at the time. The media market described above generated a highly competitive environment in which newspapers had a strong incentive to get the stories that were mostly likely to maximise audiences and sales.[30] Details about people's sex lives and 'kiss and tell' stories were a regular feature in the tabloids. While these stories often referred to politicians and public figures, those lower down on the ladder of celebrity could also be the subject of such articles.[31] Tabloids would also publish stories about people who were not in the public eye, but who had unusual sex lives.[32] Sometimes careers were ruined as a result of the disclosures.[33] Such reporting still came with legal risks. In 1988, *The Sun* published allegations about Elton John, and later settled the following libel action for £1 million and a front-page apology.

Gorden Kaye himself had been the subject of media attention in relation to his private life. In January 1989, the *Mirror* ran a story with the frontpage headline 'My Rent Boy Secrets: 'Allo 'Allo star Rene confesses to the Mirror'.[34] In the article, the actor revealed to the public that he was gay and had used male prostitutes. The article stated that Kaye had decided to make the disclosure after he had been told a Sunday newspaper had been following him and were going to reveal the private information. The disclosure therefore did not amount to the voluntary courting of publicity, but was rather an attempt by the actor to get the facts out on his own terms before another tabloid published a more hostile article. Despite Kaye's fears, the article did not end his career with the BBC, and he continued in his roles for television and the theatre.

The tabloid intrusions were not limited to disclosures about sexual activities. The newspapers also published details of other areas of private life, such as a person's health, and featured stories about the victims of high-profile crimes and accidents. In 1986, *The Sun* published a photograph of the victim of what was

[30] D Calcutt, *Report of the Committee on Privacy and Related Matters* (Cm 1102, 1990) ('Calcutt Report') [4.8].

[31] For example, exposing the 'romps' of a popular ventriloquist, see discussion in J Felton, *Sunburn* (London, Sphere, 2020) 37.

[32] A 1978 *News of the World* story about a maths teacher who attended sex parties is one controversial example, as the subject of the article committed suicide. See P Burden, *News of the World? Fake Sheikhs and Royal Trappings* (London, Eye Books, 2008) 69, 'All the News That's Unfit to Print', *The Evening Standard*, 23 February 1994.

[33] TV presenter Frank Bough's time at the BBC ended following disclosures in 1988 that he had taken cocaine and worn ladies' underwear at parties. His TV career finally ended following further disclosures in 1992. See 'Unflappable yet flawed, Frank Bough deserved better than the BBC's cruel jokes', *The Telegraph* 26 October 2020.

[34] *Daily Mirror*, 21 January 1989. Strangely, the headline for the longer article on the inside pages of the *Mirror* referred to the 'Tormented tragic life of Rene', which was at odds with the sympathetic tone of the feature which portrayed a private, quiet and largely content person.

known as the 'Ealing vicarage rape attack', with a black line covering her eyes.[35] The Press Council censured *The Sun* for the publication and called for the law to offer greater protection for the anonymity of victims of such crimes.[36] Other stories were notable for the inclusion of gory images and details of accidents.[37] Several newspapers were criticised for publishing close-up photographs showing individuals suffering, and also of dead or dying victims at the Hillsborough disaster in April 1989.[38]

Aside from the content of such stories, infringements of privacy could result from the methods of gathering information. While the TV presenter Russell Harty was in intensive care at St James hospital in 1988, regular attempts were made to access information about his condition. A newspaper rented a flat opposite the ward, so that a photographer with a long lens camera could capture images of the celebrity inside the hospital.[39] Attempts were made to contact other patients, in the hope that they would provide information.[40] One reporter was said to have put on a doctor's white coat in order to get access to Harty's medical notes, claiming that the liver specialists needed to see them urgently.[41] Such incidents were similar to the intrusion suffered by Kaye and showed that such methods were more widely used by some parts of the press.[42]

C. The Last Chance Saloon

Given the various episodes involving the tabloid press, questions of press ethics and legal controls on newspapers moved on to the political agenda. In December 1988, the Conservative MP John Browne introduced a Private

[35] P Chippindale and C Horrie, *Stick It Up Your Punter!: the rise and fall of the Sun* (London, Faber, 2013) ch 16.

[36] 'Guilty: 5 papers blamed for vicarage rape case blunders', *Daily Mirror*, 6 March 1987, and 'Toughen law to protect rape victims, says Press Council', *The Times*, 6 March 1987. *The Guardian*, *The Times* and *Sunday Times* were also criticised. At the time, the Sexual Offences (Amendment) Act 1976 only provided for anonymity once a person had been 'accused' of the rape offence, which was defined under s 4(6). The law was further amended in the Criminal Justice Act 1988, s 158 to prohibit certain information being published after an 'allegation' had been made.

[37] This was sometimes referred to as 'yuck journalism'. See Chippindale and Horrie (n 35).

[38] 'Close-ups of dying Hillsborough victims "gross intrusion"', *The Times*, 31 July 1989. Since then, the *Sun* has been the focus of sustained criticism for its notorious article blaming the fans of Liverpool FC for the events.

[39] Chippindale and Horrie (n 35) ch 16.

[40] M Wainwright, 'The haunting of Harty', *The Guardian*, 27 June 1988. Chippindale and Horrie (n 35).

[41] Wainwright, ibid.

[42] In another example, Jonathan Aitken MP told the House of Commons that reporters from an unnamed tabloid had sought to access the intensive care unit of the captain of the Herald of Free Enterprise, HC Deb 27 January 1989, vol 145, col 1306.

Members' Bill that would make a publisher liable in tort law for publishing private information without the subject's consent.[43] A further Bill was introduced by the Labour MP Tony Worthington to create a legal right of reply for individuals to correct factual inaccuracies about themselves that had been published in the media.[44] Neither Bill received government support nor made it into law. However, the government responded to the political pressure by establishing an independent review into privacy and the media.[45] The reviewing body was set up in 1989 under the chairmanship of Sir David Calcutt and was called the Committee on Privacy and Related Matters (the 'Calcutt Committee'). By the end of 1989, the government had not endorsed any reform proposals, but the future of press regulation and the protection of privacy was up in the air. As the then Home Office Minister David Mellor famously said in December 1989, the press were 'drinking in the last chance saloon'.[46]

As the Calcutt Committee conducted its review, the newspaper industry engaged in a number of measures to show that it was already addressing the concerns about its conduct.[47] Some witnesses to the Committee argued that there had already been a 'change of climate' in which newspapers were 'more careful and more restrained', and that the worst forms of intrusion had already been curbed.[48] The Press Council published the findings of an internal review in December 1989 and introduced a number of reforms to its processes.[49] The Newspaper Publishers' Association produced a Code of Practice in November 1989.[50] Certain newspapers appointed an ombudsman to handle complaints.[51] The various steps aimed to at least give the impression of a new era of good behaviour and stronger press ethics, and diffuse any momentum towards new laws or regulations. The intrusion into Kaye's privacy during this period blew a significant hole in the façade.[52] For every time that the importance of press freedom was asserted to push back on demands for privacy laws, Kaye's case provided a powerful example of how press freedom could still be abused, even in the supposed new climate.

[43] Protection of Privacy HC Bill (1988–89). The Bill was based on an earlier Private Members' Bill introduced by William Cash MP.

[44] Right of Reply HC Bill, (1988–89). The Bill was based on an earlier Private Members' Bill introduced by Ann Clywd.

[45] HC Deb 21 April 1989, vol 151, col 595.

[46] 'Mellor lambasts popular press for morbid intrusion', *The Times*, 22 December 1989.

[47] 'The Calcutt Report: Blom-Cooper's attempts to promote reforms fail at self-regulation fail', *The Independent*, 22 June 1990.

[48] Calcutt Report (n 30) [13.17].

[49] ibid, [14.35].

[50] 'The Calcutt Report: Blom-Cooper's attempts to promote reforms fail at self-regulation fail', *The Independent*, 22 June 1990. See also Calcutt Report (n 30).

[51] ibid.

[52] There was already some scepticism about the claims of a new climate for press ethics, Calcutt Report (n 30) [13.19].

IV. THE REASONING IN THE COURT OF APPEAL

The discussion so far has shown how the facts of *Kaye v Robertson* arose at a sensitive time for questions of media ethics. The Court of Appeal provided its reasoned decision in March 1990, as the Calcutt Committee continued its review. The Court stated that there is no general right to privacy in the domestic law. As the substance of the claimant's case was based on other specific legal grounds, the judges could simply have focused on those doctrines. However, each judge made powerful statements that were critical of the lack of protection for privacy rights. In a brief paragraph at the start of his judgment, Glidewell J stated:

> It is well-known that in English law there is no right to privacy, and accordingly there is no right of action for breach of a person's privacy. The facts of the present case are a graphic illustration of the desirability of Parliament considering whether and in what circumstances statutory provision can be made to protect the privacy of individuals.[53]

Similarly, Bingham LJ described the absence of such protection as a 'failure of both the common law of England and statute'.[54] He also noted the strong merits for the legal protection of Kaye's privacy interest:

> If ever a person has a right to be let alone by strangers with no public interest to pursue, it must surely be when he lies in hospital recovering from brain surgery and in no more than partial command of his faculties.[55]

Both of these statements show the sympathy for Kaye and how the lack of an effective remedy created a lamentable gap in the law.

The judicial statements have to be understood in the political context. The judges did not want to pre-empt the Calcutt Committee by developing a privacy right, yet made a contribution to the political debate by showing the unsatisfactory state of the law. Following Glidewell J's call for Parliament to consider the matter, Bingham LJ expressed the hope that the Committee would address the gap:

> The problems of defining and limiting a tort of privacy are formidable, but the present case strengthens my hope that the review now in progress may prove fruitful.[56]

Leggatt LJ also stated that it was for Parliament to enact a change to the law and expressed the hope that 'the making good of this signal shortcoming in our law will not be long delayed'.[57] These brief statements were the most important

[53] *Kaye v Robertson* (n 1) 66.
[54] ibid, 70.
[55] ibid, 70.
[56] ibid, 70.
[57] ibid, 71.

parts of the ruling in *Kaye*, which signalled the need for legislative intervention to correct the deficiency in the law. The ruling did not justify the absence of a privacy right, but placed the ball in Parliament's court.

With no general right to privacy, Kaye's case was based on four other legal doctrines: libel, malicious falsehood, passing off and trespass to the person. Reading the case today, lawyers will be surprised to see that the claimant did not rely on breach of confidence (which will be discussed later). The reliance on the multiple grounds reflected the 'piecemeal' protection of privacy, in which various doctrines protect different aspects of a person's privacy. The case showed that even if those doctrines offered significant protection in the aggregate, there were various gaps between them which could leave privacy interests unprotected.

Glidewell J quickly rejected those parts of the application for a pre-trial injunction that were based on trespass to the person and passing off. The claim in libel had greater merit and was based on the fact that the proposed article implied that Kaye had consented to the interview. The argument followed the decision in *Tolley v Fry*, in which an advertisement featuring the name and caricature of an amateur golfer was capable of being defamatory in so far as it implied the golfer had agreed to and received payment for the advertisement.[58] While Kaye may have had good grounds in the substance of the claim, the court noted that pre-trial injunctions should be granted sparingly in defamation cases, and only in the clearest cases where a jury would find the matter to be libellous.[59] Glidewell J stated that a jury would 'probably' find for the claimant in libel, but found that such a conclusion was not inevitable.[60] As a result, the pre-trial injunction could not be upheld under defamation law.

Kaye had more success with the claim in malicious falsehood. Liability in that tort arises where the defendant maliciously publishes words about the claimant that are false and where special damage follows as a natural and direct result. Glidewell J found that these elements were established. The implication that Kaye had consented to the interview was clearly false. The requirement of malice was also satisfied, as it would have been clear to the journalists and editor that Kaye was in no position to consent to the interview. Even if there had been any doubt about that at the time of the interview, it was clear to the publisher from the evidence in the legal proceedings that there was no consent. The damage requirement was met as the publication deprived Kaye of the chance to sell an interview for its full value (as the unauthorised publication in the *Sunday Sport* would have reduced the value of an authorised interview). While the court noted that pre-trial injunctions should also be granted sparingly in relation to malicious falsehood, there was no equivalent to the requirement in libel that the

[58] *Tolley v Fry* [1931] AC 333.
[59] Glidewell J relied on *Coulson v Coulson* [1887] 3 TLR 46.
[60] *Kaye* (n 1) 67.

statement be defamatory. Instead, for a pre-trial injunction in malicious falsehood it was necessary to show only that the words were clearly false.

The Court of Appeal therefore concluded that Kaye's claim in malicious falsehood provided the basis for a more limited injunction, which prohibited the publisher from stating (expressly or impliedly) that Kaye had consented to the interview or to the photographs. The injunction did not prohibit the *Sunday Sport* from publishing an article using the information or photographs acquired, as long as it did not give such a misleading impression of consent.

V. THE AFTERMATH

A. The 'Showbiz Scoop of the Year'

With the more limited injunction in place, the *Sunday Sport* did not publish its initial proposed article. However, it published a revised version of the article on 4 March 1990 with the headline 'TV Star Rene … Photos He Tried To Ban'. The front page included a photograph of Kaye lying down with his eyes shut. The newspaper also had a feature spread over the centre pages of the paper, which included a full picture of the actor in his hospital bed in a dressing gown. The tone of the article was light hearted, with several references to the running jokes from the series *'Allo 'Allo*.[61] To avoid further legal action, the articles repeatedly made clear that Kaye did not consent to the photos or the 'interview'. With considerable chutzpah (given the previous legal proceedings), the newspaper claimed it was 'motivated simply by the overwhelming concern of the British public for the condition of their favourite comedy actor'. The articles presented the story as a way to reassure fans by showing the actor 'on the road to recovery' and 'relaxing in hospital'.

The newspaper described the story as 'the showbiz scoop of the year'. However, aside from the photographs, the article contained very little detail other than a description of his hospital room and some unilluminating quotes from the brief conversation with the actor. The content was therefore very different from the usual stories in the *Sunday Sport*. The front pages in the previous weeks had headlines including, 'I Lost 30 Stone in 21 Months and Lived',[62] 'Preacher Girl's Sex Secret',[63] 'I'm Gorby's Secret Sister!'[64] and 'Alien Baby Snatch'.[65] In the weeks that followed the Kaye article, the paper was back to its formula with headlines such as 'Sex Mad Satanist Stuffed Girl into Sunday Roast'.[66] By contrast, the article about Kaye was one of the less

[61] For example, the article claims the reporters presented the actor with a giant German sausage.
[62] 25 February 1990.
[63] 18 February 1990.
[64] 11 February 1990.
[65] 4 February 1990.
[66] 18 March 1990.

sensational front page stories published in the *Sunday Sport*. The story had no element of fantasy, no sex scandal, no extreme obesity or other topics favoured by the paper at the time. The article was simply about an actor who had been seriously injured and was recovering in hospital. On this occasion, the story in the *Sunday Sport* had a lot more in common with the types of intrusive reporting seen in the mainstream tabloid press. As noted earlier, the article about Kaye seemed to represent the problem of tabloid intrusion more generally and the newspaper's conduct did not merely reflect the peculiarities of the *Sunday Sport*.

B. The Politics of Reform after *Kaye*

The Calcutt Committee published its report in the summer of 1990 and was to some degree influenced by the events in *Kaye*.[67] The Committee included the Court of Appeal's judgment as an appendix to the report. The Committee stated that the case showed 'the limitations of peer group pressure' and demonstrated that assurances of good behaviour from the press would not be sufficient to address the concerns about press ethics.[68] One of the Committee's recommendations sought to address the type of intrusion suffered by Kaye by proposing that it should be a criminal offence to enter private property without the consent of the lawful occupant with intent to gain private information with a view to its publication.[69] The Committee also recommended that there should be a power to restrain the publication of information acquired through such intrusion.[70]

The government initially accepted the case for the new offences proposed by Calcutt.[71] However, John Major's government was re-elected with a smaller majority in 1992, and lacked the political capital to push through the necessary statutory measures.[72] By early 1994, the position of the government became more ambivalent towards the proposed offences, noting both arguments for and against.[73] The following year, the proposals were dropped.

[67] While the Committee claimed that its response was not based on the actions of a 'maverick newspaper', Munro viewed such a disclaimer with considerable suspicion, C Munro, 'Press Freedom – How the Beast was Tamed' (1991) 54 *Modern Law Review* 104, 105.

[68] Calcutt Report (n 30) [13.21].

[69] ibid, [6.33] A similar offence was also proposed for taking photos or recording a person's voice on private property with a view to publication.

[70] ibid, [6.38].

[71] David Waddington MP, HC Deb 21 June 1990, vol 174, col 1125; Peter Brooke MP, HC Deb 14 January 1993, vol 216, col 1068.

[72] A Bingham, '"Drinking in the Last Chance Saloon" The British press and the crisis of self-regulation, 1989–95' (2007) 13 *Media History* 79, 85, and Lord Justice Leveson, *An Inquiry into the Culture, Practices and Ethics of the Press: Report* (HC 780, 2012), 1253.

[73] See Leveson, ibid 1251. Bingham, ibid, notes that the change of heart came about due to concerns that the offence could lead to the disclosure of police and security service surveillance methods in open court, 88.

The Secretary of State for National Heritage told the House of Commons that the government had given the proposals 'the most painstaking consideration', but concluded 'that the difficulties of scope and definition of the proposed offences, and the necessary defences, are formidable'.[74] The government concluded that the offences would create more problems than they solved. In criticising the government's decision, the Opposition spokesman used the examples of Russell Harty and Gorden Kaye to show why legislation was necessary.[75] While the case had an impact on the political debate, it did not result in legislative change.

The Calcutt Committee also looked at a range of other issues relating to press ethics and concluded that a statutory right of reply and a privacy tort should not yet be introduced.[76] Instead, the Committee proposed an overhaul of press self-regulation, with the Press Council being disbanded and replaced with the Press Complaints Commission.[77] However, the Committee concluded that if the new system of press self-regulation proved to be ineffective, then it should be replaced with a system of statutory regulation.[78] Two years later, Calcutt reviewed the new system of press self-regulation and concluded in a second report that it was not working effectively, and therefore proposed the introduction of a statutory tribunal to handle complaints about the press. Among the various reasons for the negative assessment of the new self-regulatory system, Calcutt cited the 'contemptuous' attitude of the *Daily Sport* (the *Sunday Sport's* sister paper) towards the Press Complaints Commission, when it named the victim of a sexual assault.[79] The statutory system proposed in the second Calcutt Report was not implemented by the government either.[80]

The response to the Calcutt proposals shows that by the mid-1990s the political climate had changed and an already weakened government was not willing to engage in a political fight with the newspaper industry. In *Kaye*, the courts had left the issue of intrusion to Parliament, which in turn declined to enact new measures and left the matter to the newspaper industry. The decision in *Kaye* had given momentum towards proposals for stronger press regulation and the protection of privacy, but the political impact of the case proved to be short-lived.

[74] HC Deb 17 July 1995, vol 263 col 1325.

[75] Chris Smith MP, HC Deb 17 July 1995, vol 263, col 1326.

[76] Calcutt Report (n 30) [12.5].

[77] ibid, [14.38].

[78] ibid, ch 16.

[79] D Calcutt, *Review of Press Self-Regulation* (Cm 2135, 1993), [4.25–4.27] and [5.23], at the time of the incident a law restricting the naming of such victims had not been brought into force.

[80] The government also rejected calls for a civil remedy for breach of privacy, stating its preference newspaper self-regulation. Secretary of State for National Heritage, *The Government's Response to the House of Commons National Heritage Select Committee: Privacy and Media Intrusion* (Cm 2918, 1995).

VI. THE LEGAL LEGACY OF *KAYE V ROBERTSON*

A. The Common Law after *Kaye*

To assess the legal impact of the Court of Appeal's decision on privacy, it is important to consider exactly what the court ruled. The most obvious reading of *Kaye* is that the Court of Appeal confirmed that there is no general right to privacy in domestic law[81] and that any change in that position should be brought about by Parliament. However, even that basic reading of the case was challenged in *Douglas v Hello*, in which Sedley LJ argued that the court had simply adopted and shared counsel's assumption that there was no right of privacy and thereby did not determine the status of the right in the common law.[82] This more limited interpretation of the case was not shared by Buxton LJ in the Court of Appeal in *Wainwright*, who stated that when a court adopts and shares an assumption, 'that assumption then becomes part of its reasoning, whatever may have been the origin of the point'.[83] This latter reading of the case was followed by the House of Lords in *Wainwright*, which affirmed that there was no general privacy right in the common law.[84] Lord Hoffmann cited *Kaye* and noted that all three judges in the case were 'flat against a judicial power to declare the existence of a high-level right to privacy'.[85]

While Lord Hoffmann in *Wainwright* found that the common law did not recognise a 'high-level' general right, that did not stop the existing common law doctrines from being developed to give broader protection to privacy. That path was taken up by the court in the years following *Kaye*, and the equitable doctrine of confidence was expanded to cover private information. The shift allowed for a more flexible application of the law of confidence, so that a relationship was not always required between claimant and defendant, and an obligation could be inferred from the private nature of the information. Early on in the 1990s, the court in *Shelley* noted that this step was not precluded by *Kaye*, which was taken to be 'adverting solely to invasions of "privacy" as a possible branch of the law of tort and not to predations of confidential information which is primarily an equitable doctrine and a very different question'.[86] A series of cases, such as *Hellewell*[87] and

[81] *Khorasandjian v Bush* [1993] QB 727 at 744, and *Wainwright v Home Office* [2001] EWCA Civ 2081, [2002] QB 1334 Buxton LJ in the Court of Appeal, [99–102] and [111].

[82] *Douglas v Hello* [2001] QB 967, [113]. Support for such a view can also be taken from *R v Khan (Sultan)* [1997] AC 558 in 1996, in which Lord Nicholls treated the status of a more general privacy right in the domestic law as an unsettled question, stating that he would 'prefer to leave open for another occasion the important question whether the present, piecemeal protection of privacy has now developed to the extent that a more comprehensive principle can be seen to exist'.

[83] *Wainwright v Home Office* [2001] EWCA Civ 2081, [2002] QB 1334, [100].

[84] *Wainwright v Home Office* [2003] UKHL 53, [2004] 2 AC 406.

[85] ibid, [26].

[86] *Shelley Films Limited v Rex Features Limited* [1994] EMLR 134, 147.

[87] *Hellewell v Chief Constable* [1995] 1 WLR 804, 807.

Douglas v Hello,[88] continued down this path, and spurred by the Human Rights Act 1998, the courts gave privacy a more concrete foundation in Article 8 of the ECHR. The development of the law of confidence reached its destination in *Campbell v MGN*, in which the expanded version of breach of confidence was labelled 'misuse of private information'.[89]

While the subsequent evolution of the common law in relation to privacy is formally consistent with *Kaye* (for the reasons stated above), that development is in tension with some parts of the Court of Appeal's ruling. First, the reluctance of the court in *Kaye* to recognise a general privacy tort and the judges' emphasis on the need for Parliament to take the initiative signalled caution about an expansion in the protection of privacy being led by the courts. That caution may well have been the product of the political context, with the judges being aware of the Calcutt Committee's work. Later in the decade, as the issue of privacy and press ethics moved off the political agenda, the courts became more willing to take the initiative in developing the law.

The second point of tension is whether subsequent developments have in effect created the equivalent of a common law privacy right and thereby undermined the position stated in *Kaye* and *Wainwright*. While the *Campbell* tort was initially developed with reference to informational privacy, contemporary debates ask whether the current doctrines provide a foundation for a more general protection against intrusion.[90] Given these debates, the question of whether there is a general right to privacy in the common law remains unresolved, despite the clear judicial statements to the contrary. While formally there is no general tort, the core point that *Kaye* was cited for has been increasingly marginalised with the incremental growth of privacy protection.

B. Should Kaye have Relied on Breach of Confidence?

As noted earlier, it is striking that Kaye's lawyers did not rely on breach of confidence.[91] With the benefit of hindsight, the doctrine of confidence offered the most promising ground for an injunction for someone in Kaye's position. The decision not to rely on the doctrine may seem all the more surprising given that the expansion of the law of confidence was already underway prior to *Kaye*. In *Spycatcher*, Lord Goff had indicated that in some circumstances the recipient

[88] *Douglas v Hello* [2001] QB 967, [110]. Sedley LJ commented that this gradual expansion of confidence meant that 'we have reached a point at which it can be said with confidence that the law recognises and will appropriately protect a right of personal privacy'.

[89] *Campbell v MGN* [2004] UKHL 22, [2004] 2 AC 457.

[90] See N Moreham, 'Beyond Information: Physical Privacy in English Law' (2014) 73 *CLJ* 350 and P Wragg, 'Recognising a privacy-invasion tort: the conceptual unity of informational and intrusion claims' (2019) 78 *CLJ* 409.

[91] The point was made shortly after the *Kaye* decision by Scott J, 'Developments in the Law of Confidentiality' (1990) 5 *Denning Law Journal* 77.

of information may be under an obligation even where there was no prior relationship.[92] However, as Lord Phillips later noted, the significance of Lord Goff's words 'was not immediately appreciated'.[93] Even if the point was arguable at the time, it is fair to say that the expansion of the confidence doctrine had yet to gain the momentum seen later in the 1990s.[94] As a result, reliance on the doctrine may not have been such an obvious choice for Kaye's lawyers.

In any event, a claim based on breach of confidence may not have made much difference to Kaye's application for an injunction. The cautious tone of the three judgments in *Kaye* suggest that there was no appetite to embark on a significant expansion of the law. The decision was on an application for a pre-trial injunction and had to be decided in a tight time frame, for which there would have been limited scope to prepare and hear arguments on such a point. Given the desire not to pre-empt the Calcutt Committee, it is easy to see why the court would not have used the case as an opportunity to develop the law of confidence. While such an argument is speculative, it is to some degree reinforced by Lord Bingham's comment about the case in 1996, that 'a claim for breach of confidence could not have been successfully made, at any rate without doing impermissible violence to the principles upon which that cause of action is founded'.[95]

While it is not possible to know what would have happened had breach of confidence been relied upon by Kaye, it is clear that the law has since moved on. The tort of misuse of private information would now cover the facts of *Kaye*. In 2009, Sir David Eady acknowledged this change:

> So we have come, for good or for ill (and it is not for me to say which), a very long way in a short space of time. Gordon Kaye and Russell Harty would now obtain a remedy so easily that the newspapers would know that such conduct was out of bounds – without even having to ask a lawyer.[96]

Applying the test for misuse of private information, a person in a hospital would clearly have a reasonable expectation that journalists would not be able to publish information acquired by entering a ward without authorisation and by interviewing a person not capable of consenting. Several of the criteria for *Campbell* tort would be met in such circumstances, as the information is captured in a private space, involves medical information, is embarrassing for

[92] *AG v Guardian Newspapers (No 2)* [1990] 1 AC 109. Such circumstances would arise where the recipient ought to have known that the information was confidential. For example, a stranger that finds a person's lost diary could be in breach of confidence if he or she discloses its contents.

[93] *Douglas v Hello! Ltd* [2005] EWCA Civ 595, [61].

[94] Whether the expansion of confidence should have been foreseen at the time of *Kaye* is debatable. Scott (n 91) argues that the earlier case of *Francome v Mirror Group Newspapers* [1984] 1 WLR 892 could have been relied upon.

[95] T Bingham, 'Should there be a law to protect rights of personal privacy?' (1996) 5 *European Human Rights Law Review* 450, 457.

[96] Sir David Eady, Speech to The Intellectual Property Lawyers' Association, 18 February 2009 (published in House of Commons Culture Media and Sport Committee, *Press standards, privacy and libel*, Vol II (2010, HC362-II).

the subject and involves the use of photographs.[97] As a result, there would be a very good case for restraining the publication of such information.[98]

C. The Impact on the Views of Lawyers and Judges

The above analysis shows that while there is no general privacy tort, the outcome in *Kaye* no longer reflects the state of the law. The case serves as a reminder of how things were and how things have changed. Perhaps its biggest legal legacy lies in shaping the views and attitudes of lawyers. In a lecture in 1996, Bingham LJ (as he then was) described the case as one where the courts were 'unable to afford adequate relief to a plaintiff who plainly deserved it'.[99] As with his opinion in *Kaye*, he still expressed a preference for the change to come about through legislation. However, this time he added an important qualification: that if legislative action 'is not forthcoming' then it is 'almost inevitable that cases will arise in the courts in which the need to give relief is obvious and pressing; and when such cases do arise, I do not think the courts will be found wanting'.[100] The caution expressed in *Kaye* was therefore a temporary position, with a warning that Parliament was also in the last chance saloon.

While Lord Bingham was influential on human rights issues, he did not make a significant contribution in the leading cases on misuse of private information in the 2000s.[101] By contrast, Sir David Eady decided a number of cases that helped to shape the law on misuse of private information. While he was a barrister, he sat on the Calcutt Committee and would have thought carefully about press ethics at the time of the decision in *Kaye*. A profile of the judge in *The Times* reported that he had been strongly influenced by the 'gross intrusion' that went largely unremedied in *Kaye*.[102] The legal legacy of *Kaye* may well lie in influencing lawyers by showing the need for a gap in the law to remedied and by providing an illustration of a clear abuse of press freedom.

VII. THE PARTIES AFTER KAYE

In 1990, months after *Kaye* was decided, the owner of the *Sunday Sport* suffered a setback when the Monopolies and Mergers Commission blocked

[97] *Murray v Express Newspapers* [2008] EWCA Civ 446, [2009] Ch. 481.

[98] As noted earlier, the contemporary debate about the scope of privacy now revolves around whether the acquisition of such information amounts to a tort as a result of the intrusion, even where there is no publication.

[99] Bingham (n 95) 456.

[100] ibid 462.

[101] Lord Bingham did not sit on the appeal in *Campbell* and gave the briefest concurring opinions in *Wainwright* and *Re S* [2004] UKHL 47, [2005] 1 AC 593.

[102] F Gibb, 'Lawyer who used to act for the red-tops became judge who championed privacy' *The Times*, 25 July 2008.

a proposed transfer that would have given David Sullivan a 25 per cent shareholding in the *Bristol Evening Post*. In its report, the Commission examined the operations of the *Sunday Sport*, its content and its short-lived association with the *Daily Star*. In explaining its conclusion, the Commission identified 'various adverse effects on the public interest which we think would be likely to arise, and in particular the effects on the standing, character and content of the BEP newspapers'.[103] The decision in *Kaye* was not a major part of the Commission's reasoning, though it is likely that the bad publicity did not help. David Sullivan told the Commission that he considered the story at the centre of *Kaye* to be 'bad journalism' and that he would not have sent the reporters to get the story had he been the editor.[104] Similarly, the then editor of the *Sunday Sport*, Drew Robertson, told the Monopolies and Mergers Commission that it had been 'wrong for the reporters to have conducted themselves in the manner they did'.[105] Given the context of the Commission's enquiry, it is unsurprising that the newspaper's representatives sought to distance themselves from the episode.

The co-defendant in *Kaye*, Drew Robertson, left the paper in November 1990, reportedly after writing an article titled 'Bollocks to the Press Council'.[106] Ray Levine, one of the reporters who entered the Kaye's room, went on to work for other tabloids, including *The People* (where he worked on the story revealing the then minister David Mellor's affair) and the *News of the World*.[107] The bad publicity and disapproval of the episode did not hurt the *Sunday Sport*'s business and profits. In October 1991, Sport Newspapers launched a sister newspaper to the *Sunday Sport*, titled the *Daily Sport*. At the time of writing, there is still a Wednesday and Friday print edition of the *Sport*, and the *Sunday Sport* also continues its print edition.[108]

Gorden Kaye recovered after the accident and was back on the stage later in the same year. He also continued filming further episodes of *'Allo 'Allo*, with the final series broadcast in 1992. After that, he did not go on to similarly prominent roles in television, but continued with roles in the theatre.[109] Kaye died in January 2017 at the age of 75.

[103] MMC (n 9) [6.21].
[104] ibid, [4.41].
[105] ibid, [4.74].
[106] 'Drew Robertson, editor of Sunday Sport dismissed' *The Times*, 28 November 1990.
[107] 'Privacy law pending as the lessons of a super-snoop', *The Sunday Times*, 2 August 1992. See also G Johnson, *Hack: Phone Taps, Honey Traps and Celebs Papped – Life as a Tabloid Journo* (Simon and Schuster, 2012) ch 1.
[108] In 2011, following declining circulation, the print edition of the *Daily Sport* was discontinued.
[109] 'Gorden Kaye', *The Times*, 24 January 2017.

VIII. PRESS CULTURE AND REFORM REVISITED

In the decades since the Court of Appeal's decision, the law and media landscape have changed significantly. The development of misuse of private information has restrained the publication of certain types of 'kiss and tell' story.[110] As noted, Kaye would be likely to have a remedy on similar facts today. Moreover, the newspapers no longer enjoy the large print circulations seen in the late 1980s and 90s. The papers still have a wide reach through online distribution, but find themselves facing significant financial pressures and have to compete with the digital media for attention.[111]

Despite the changes, there has been considerable continuity in the lines of debate about press self-regulation. After the Calcutt Report, a pattern emerged in which reports would criticise the Press Complaints Commission (the body that replaced the Press Council), which would prompt further measures to tweak the system of self-regulation until further criticisms were made (and the process was then repeated). The regular pattern was interrupted by the Leveson Inquiry, which recommended a new system of 'independent self-regulation'.[112] However, the national newspapers have so far worked outside of the system based on the Leveson proposals and have successfully staved off significant legislative interventions. Writing in 2021, Leveson seems to have been a replay of Calcutt (albeit with a larger and higher profile inquiry) and periodically the newspapers continue to make claims about a new climate of press ethics (and have set up a new self-regulatory body).

Some of the problems highlighted by *Kaye* have not gone away either, despite the stronger legal protection for privacy. The coverage of the attack on the Manchester Arena in 2017 provides a notable example of the intrusive techniques still employed by the media to get information about the victims of serious crime and their families. According to the Kerslake Report, a worker at a hospital treating victims of the attack 'spoke of a note offering £2,000 for information being included in a tin of biscuits given to the staff.[113] The technique of an offer hidden in a gift is reminiscent of the methods used by reporters to acquire information about Russell Harty nearly three decades earlier.[114]

[110] *PJS v News Group Newspapers* [2016] UKSC 26, [2016] AC 1081 is one example.

[111] See discussion in F Cairncross, *A Sustainable Future for Journalism* (Department for Digital, Culture, Media and Sport, 2019) 25–26 and Ofcom, *News Consumption in the UK: 2020* (August 2020).

[112] Leveson (n 72).

[113] *The Kerslake Report: An independent review into the preparedness for, and emergency response to, the Manchester Arena attack on 22nd May 2017* (2018) at [2.32].

[114] Chippindale and Horrie (n 35) ch 16 refer to a journalist sending flowers concealing the newspaper's number and money to a patient in intensive care, in an attempt to acquire information on Harty.

The Kerslake Report also noted that a reporter had attempted to gain access to a person's home by 'ramming a foot in the doorway'.[115] Kerslake referred to two examples of impersonation, in which a person 'talked on the phone to someone saying they were a Bereavement Nurse' and another person described 'talking to someone who they felt sounded to be more like a journalist but who purported to be from the police'.[116] Such claims were reported by those affected and it is not known who engaged in such tactics or who such people were working for. However, the examples provide evidence that where there is a strong commercial incentive to acquire private information, some reporters are still willing to engage in highly intrusive methods at moments when people are vulnerable and in distress. Even if the law has changed and offers a remedy where such reporters can be identified, it is still not clear just how far the law deters intrusion.

IX. CONCLUSION

As a legal precedent, *Kaye v Robertson* is not a particularly important or interesting case and has had limited weight as an authority. The decision was an appeal from a decision granting a pre-trial injunction. The Court of Appeal's hearing took place 10 days after the reporters entered Kaye's hospital room, and the judges gave their initial decision on the day of that hearing.[117] Such a context meant that the Court of Appeal was not likely to break new legal ground. The case is notable for an expression of the limits of legal protection at the time. While the judges expressed regret at that state of affairs, the ruling reflects a position of restraint and a preference for legislative intervention. That restraint can also be understood with reference to the political context, with the judges knowing that the Calcutt Committee was soon to make recommendations to the government on press ethics.

That context gives the decision in *Kaye* its significance. The intrusion into Kaye's privacy stood as a byword for the excesses and abuses of the media in the height of the tabloid era. The newspaper had clearly crossed an ethical line. While the defendant newspaper was normally something of outlier, even among the tabloids at the time, on this occasion its intrusion seems to have been more typical of the tabloid press. The unsatisfactory resolution of Kaye's case made a powerful argument for a privacy law in the 1990s. Every time a person worried that privacy laws may curb a free press or restrict the criticism of public figures,

[115] *The Kerslake Report* (n 113) [2.34].
[116] ibid, [2.36].
[117] The fully reasoned decision of the court was delivered the following month.

the facts of *Kaye* would make a powerful counterargument. As has been shown, any momentum the case gave to legislative change was soon diffused in the political realities facing the government in the 1990s. While the case may have expressed a position of restraint, the unsatisfactory outcome of the case may have helped to spur changes in the common law. The unfairness to Kaye can now be cited to justify the subsequent legal developments and growth of privacy law in the following decades.

6

Australian Broadcasting Corporation v Lenah Game Meats Pty Ltd (2001)

DAVID ROLPH*

I. INTRODUCTION

HISTORICALLY, THE COMMON law did not recognise a right to privacy. In recent decades, this has begun to change across the Commonwealth. The first apex court this century to consider whether such a right should be recognised was the High Court of Australia in *Australian Broadcasting Corporation v Lenah Game Meats Pty Ltd.*[1] This decision superseded the earlier decision of the same Court in *Victoria Park Racing & Recreation Grounds Co Ltd v Taylor*,[2] which had been cited for the proposition that there was no right to privacy under Australian law. Yet the High Court's decision in *ABC v Lenah Game Meats* has not served as the impetus for the development of an Australian law of privacy. In the intervening decades, whilst a law of privacy has developed and consolidated in the UK and New Zealand, the protection of privacy under the common law of Australia remains comparatively underdeveloped.

This chapter examines *ABC v Lenah Game Meats* and its impact not only on Australian law but also on other legal systems as they developed their own forms of common law privacy protections, sometimes in application, sometimes by counterpoint. It grapples with the conundrum of why *ABC v Lenah Game Meats* has not led to the development of an Australian law of privacy and why the protection of privacy at common law remains moribund in Australia. It contrasts the lack of case law and legislative action with the large volume of law reform activity in Australia directed at the greater legal protection of privacy,

* The author would like to thank Olivia Ronan for her excellent research assistance. Any errors remain the author's own.

[1] *Australian Broadcasting Corporation v Lenah Game Meats Pty Ltd* (2001) 208 CLR 199 (hereafter '*ABC v Lenah Game Meats*').

[2] *Victoria Park Racing & Recreation Grounds Co Ltd v Taylor* (1937) 58 CLR 479 (hereafter '*Victoria Park Racing v Taylor*').

suggesting that an Australian law of privacy is dependent upon either the bringing of a proper test case or a change in legislative will, whichever comes first.

II. THE LAW IN AUSTRALIA PRIOR TO AUSTRALIAN BROADCASTING CORPORATION V LENAH GAME MEATS

To appreciate the status of *ABC v Lenah Game Meats* under Australian law, it is necessary to understand the landmark case it replaced. For more than six decades, the High Court of Australia's decision in *Victoria Park Racing v Taylor*[3] was cited as authority for the proposition that there was no common law right to privacy in Australia.[4] In this case, a racecourse operator sought an injunction to restrain a nearby resident from allowing his property to be used by a race-caller from a commercial radio station. The resident permitted an observation platform to be constructed on his property from which the race-caller could observe and commentate on the horse races being run at the racecourse. The alleged effect of the radio broadcasts was to drive down the number of people attending the racecourse in person, thereby causing its operator financial loss. The racecourse operator sought a perpetual injunction against the resident, the race-caller and the radio station.[5] The principal cause of action relied upon at first instance[6] and on appeal was private nuisance. Before the High Court, causes of action for copyright infringement[7] and a novel tort of unfair competition[8] were raised but readily dismissed.

By majority, the High Court held that the racecourse operator was not entitled to the injunctive relief it sought. Latham CJ held that there was no conduct by the defendants which interfered with the racecourse operator's use and enjoyment of its land.[9] His Honour could not identify any right that the defendants had infringed, stating:

> Any person is entitled to look over the plaintiff's fences and to see what goes on in the plaintiff's land. If the plaintiff desires to prevent this, the plaintiff can erect a higher fence … In my opinion the law cannot by an injunction in effect erect fences which the plaintiff is not prepared to provide.[10]

[3] *Victoria Park Racing v Taylor* (n 2). See generally J McKeough, 'Horses and the law: the enduring legacy of *Victoria Park Racing*' in A Kenyon (ed), *Landmarks in Australian Intellectual Property Law* (Cambridge, Cambridge University Press, 2011); M Richardson and M Trabksy, 'Radio and the Technology of the Common Law in 1930s Australia: *Victoria Park Racing v Taylor* Revisited' (2011) 20 *Griffith Law Review* 1020.

[4] See, eg, *Cruise v Southdown Press Pty Ltd* (1993) 26 IPR 125, 125 (Gray J); *Australian Consolidated Press Ltd v Ettingshausen* (CA(NSW), 13 October 1993) 26–27 (Kirby P); *GS v News Ltd* (1998) Aust Torts Reports ¶81–466, 64, 913–64,15 (Levine J).

[5] As to the facts and procedural history of this case, see *Victoria Park* (n 2) 492 (Latham CJ).

[6] *Victoria Park Racing & Recreation Grounds Co Ltd v Taylor* (1936) 37 SR(NSW) 322.

[7] *Victoria Park Racing v Taylor* (n 2) 497–98 (Latham CJ), 510–11 (Dixon J), 527 (McTiernan J).

[8] ibid, 509–10 (Dixon J).

[9] ibid, 493 (Latham CJ).

[10] ibid, 494 (Latham CJ).

Latham CJ found that no wrong was committed by looking over the plaintiff's fence or describing what could be seen by doing so.[11] His Honour rejected the argument that the fact that the defendants had created an artificial structure to permit them to overlook the racecourse had any impact on their liability.[12] Latham CJ expressly rejected the contention that the law of nuisance protected a right to privacy.[13]

Similarly, Dixon J, noting that the principal cause of action relied upon was private nuisance,[14] observed that '[t]he law fixes those rights' protected by this tort.[15] His Honour noted that the tort of private nuisance had never protected freedom from view or inspection as a right or an incident attached to the possession of land. This was the case whether the overlooking was achieved by natural or artificial means.[16] Dixon J accepted that this meant that a plaintiff was not entitled to enforce privacy on his or her own land.[17]

The other judge in the majority, McTiernan J, held that the overlooking of the racecourse was not actionable as an invasion of privacy.[18] His Honour emphasised that, to commit a private nuisance, there needed to be an infringement of a legal right protected by the tort.[19] McTiernan J could discern no such right.

Rich J dissented. Unlike Latham CJ, Rich J thought, in relation to the racecourse, that '[i]ts privacy or exclusiveness is guarded by suitable fences or gates'.[20] After citing Winfield's influential *Law Quarterly Review* article on privacy,[21] his Honour observed that there was no exhaustive definition of nuisance and the fact that there was no precedent for the instant case did not preclude the tort from expanding to deal with it.[22] Rich J considered that private nuisance was sufficiently flexible to adapt to changing circumstances.[23] Of particular importance to his Honour's reasoning was the defendants' non-natural use of the land.[24] Rich J emphasised that the right to view or observe adjacent land was never absolute.[25] His Honour suggested that the grant of an injunction may depend upon the motive of the defendant.[26]

[11] ibid.
[12] ibid, 494–95 (Latham CJ).
[13] ibid, 495–96 (Latham CJ), citing *Chandler v Thompson* (1811) 3 Camp 80, (1811) 170 ER 1312, *Turner v Spooner* (1861) 30 LJ Ch 301, 303 and *Tapling v Jones* (1865) 11 HLC 290, (1865) 11 ER 1344, 1350, 1352, 1353.
[14] ibid, 506 (Dixon J).
[15] ibid, 507 (Dixon J).
[16] ibid, 507–08 (Dixon J).
[17] ibid, 507 (Dixon J).
[18] ibid, 523 (McTiernan J).
[19] ibid, 524 (McTiernan J).
[20] ibid, 498 (Latham CJ).
[21] PH Winfield, 'Privacy' (1931) 47 *Law Quarterly Review* 23.
[22] *Victoria Park* (n 2) 500 (Rich J).
[23] ibid, 501 (Rich J).
[24] ibid, 501–03 (Rich J).
[25] ibid, 504 (Rich J).
[26] ibid, 504–05 (Rich J).

Evatt J also dissented. Like Rich J, Evatt J made a point at the outset of his judgment that the fence was 'sufficiently high to ensure privacy for all practical purposes'.[27] Also like Rich J, Evatt J emphasised that the tort of private nuisance was flexible and could adapt to address the artificial use to which the defendants put the land.[28] His Honour noted that the defendants submitted that there was no general right to privacy. Evatt J responded:

> That is true, but it carries the defendant no further, because it is not merely an interference with privacy which is here relied upon, and it is not the law that every interference with privacy must be lawful.[29]

For his Honour, the novelty of the issue was not an impediment to the grant of injunctive relief, given the novelty of the technology involved.[30] Like Rich J, Evatt J relied upon Winfield's work on privacy[31] and equally emphasised the importance of the defendants' motive to the question of relief.[32]

III. THE JUDGMENTS IN AUSTRALIAN BROADCASTING CORPORATION V LENAH GAME MEATS PTY LTD

Like the High Court authority it supplanted, *ABC v Lenah Game Meats* was centrally concerned with a corporation's attempt to identify a cause of action to support the grant of an injunction. Lenah Game Meats Pty Ltd is a game meat producer in Tasmania. It specialises in indigenous meat products, in particular wallaby and possum, as well as other game, such as venison, rabbit and hare. It not only purveys its meat within Tasmania and mainland Australia but also has an export business. Persons unknown trespassed onto Lenah Game Meats' premises and installed hidden cameras to film the processing of brush tail possums. They then handed the footage to Animal Liberation Ltd, which, in turn, handed the footage to the national broadcaster, the Australian Broadcasting Corporation (ABC). The ABC intended to broadcast part of the footage. Lenah Game Meats became aware of this intention and applied to the Supreme Court of Tasmania for an interim injunction.[33] In early May 1999, Underwood J refused to grant relief on the basis that the statement of claim did not disclose a cause of action against the ABC.

[27] ibid, 512 (Evatt J).
[28] ibid, 516–17 (Evatt J).
[29] ibid, 517 (Evatt J).
[30] ibid, 519 (Evatt J).
[31] ibid, 520 (Evatt J).
[32] ibid, 521 (Evatt J).
[33] As to the facts of this case, see *ABC v Lenah Game Meats* (n 1) 220–21 (Gleeson CJ), 233 (Gummow and Hayne JJ).

Lenah Game Meats appealed against Underwood J's decision. By majority (Wright and Evans JJ, Slicer J dissenting), the Full Court of the Supreme Court of Tasmania allowed the appeal. In his judgment, Wright J noted that there had been a series of decisions in Australia in which a media outlet trespassing on private property and, in the course of which, obtaining video footage, had been restrained from broadcasting the footage.[34] An injunction had been granted in those cases to restrain the use of what was styled 'the fruits of the trespass'. His Honour correctly observed that the ABC was not itself a trespasser in this case and that it would be straining legal principle to hold the ABC vicariously liable for the unknown trespasser's conduct. Thus, the line of authority whereby a trespassing media outlet could be restrained from broadcasting footage during the course of the trespass had no direct application. The central issue therefore was whether there was a cause of action available to Lenah Game Meats which could support the grant of injunctive relief. Lenah Game Meats conceded that it had no cause of action for defamation or breach of confidence. Instead, it made the novel submission that an injunction should be granted because it would be unconscionable for the ABC knowingly to use the fruits of the trespass.[35] Wright J was prepared to accept Lenah Game Meats' proposition that a court could grant an injunction, in the exercise of its auxiliary jurisdiction, to restrain the use of unlawfully obtained material, whether or not a cause of action could be found against the person so enjoined. However, his Honour suggested that Lenah Game Meats did have an arguable cause of action in negligence against the ABC.[36] The fact that the damage would be pure economic loss was no obstacle.[37] The reasoning in the judgment is somewhat difficult to follow. Wright J then reverted back to the grant of an injunction based on a general notion of unconscionability and suggested that the ABC had conceded that this was possible. Applying general equitable principles, his Honour held that there was a prima facie case and that the balance of convenience favoured the grant of the injunction.[38]

The other majority judgment was given by Evans J. His Honour noted that the court could grant an injunction in its auxiliary jurisdiction if there were a pre-existing cause of action. It could also grant an injunction in its exclusive jurisdiction, which need not depend upon a pre-existing cause of action.[39]

[34] *Lenah Game Meats Pty Ltd v Australian Broadcasting Corporation* (1999) 9 Tas R 355, 357–58 (Wright J), citing *Lincoln Hunt Australia Pty Ltd v Willesee* (1986) 4 NSWLR 457, *Emcorp Pty Ltd v Australian Broadcasting Corporation* [1988] 2 Qd R 169 and *Rinsale Pty Ltd v Australian Broadcasting Corporation* (1991) Aust Torts Reports ¶81–231.

[35] ibid, 358 (Wright J).

[36] ibid, 359 (Wright J).

[37] ibid, 360 (Wright J).

[38] ibid, 362–63 (Wright J).

[39] ibid, 385–86 (Evans J).

Evans J was satisfied that an injunction could be granted on the basis of unconscionability in the exclusive jurisdiction.[40]

Slicer J dissented. His Honour held that the failure to identify a cause of action was a sufficient basis to dismiss the appeal.[41]

The ABC obtained special leave to appeal to the High Court of Australia. A significant difficulty with the High Court's decision is the lack of a clear *ratio decidendi*. There are a number of discrete issues determined in the case, which are dealt with differently in the various judgments. The lack of clear guidance in the judgments of the High Court is one of the main reasons why the case has not provided the impetus for the development of some form of direct privacy protection at common law in Australia.

On the threshold issue of whether it was necessary for Lenah Game Meats to identify a right, at common law, in equity or under statute, in order to obtain an injunction, the majority of the High Court found that this was required[42] and rejected the notion that a generalised concept of unconscionability could support such relief.[43] Consequently, it was necessary to identify a cause of action against the ABC which would support an injunction.[44]

Lenah Game Meats did not allege any breach of statute,[45] so the right would have to arise either at common law or in equity.[46] On appeal, Lenah Game Meats sought to raise, for the first time, whether Australian law should be developed to recognise an enforceable right to privacy. It had expressly disavowed such an argument in the courts below. It was permitted to raise the issue on appeal for the first time because it involved only questions of law, so there was no procedural unfairness to the ABC.[47]

Gleeson CJ reasoned that the activities being filmed were not secret and were not confidential. His Honour pointed out that inspectors and other visitors regularly visited the abattoir and that the operations were licensed by a public authority tended against them being confidential.[48] The film did not embody any trade secret.[49] Gleeson CJ acknowledged that the broadcast may cause distress to viewers and loss of business to Lenah Game Meats but neither amounted to an actionable right in and of themselves.[50] His Honour accepted that the film embodied information about Lenah Game Meats' business but it

[40] ibid, 386–89 (Evans J).
[41] ibid, 365 (Slicer J).
[42] *ABC v Lenah Game Meats* (n 1) 218 (Gleeson CJ), 232 (Gaudron J), 241 (Gummow and Hayne JJ).
[43] ibid, 218–19 (Gleeson CJ), 244–45 (Gummow and Hayne JJ).
[44] ibid, 217–19 (Gleeson CJ), 240–41 (Gummow and Hayne JJ).
[45] ibid, 220 (Gleeson CJ), 232 (Gaudron J).
[46] ibid, 232 (Gaudron J).
[47] ibid, 238 (Gummow and Hayne JJ), 261–62 (Kirby J).
[48] ibid, 221 (Gleeson CJ).
[49] ibid, 222 (Gleeson CJ).
[50] ibid, 221 (Gleeson CJ).

was not confidential.[51] His Honour rejected the analogy suggested by Lenah Game Meats that information obtained during the course of a trespass should be treated in the same way as confidential information.[52] Even though there was no relationship of trust and confidence between Lenah Game Meats and the trespassers, an obligation may be imposed to restrain the publication of confidential information improperly or surreptitiously obtained. His Honour accepted that a photographic image improperly or surreptitiously obtained where what is depicted is private can constitute confidential information.[53] Gleeson CJ noted that Lenah Game Meats had invited the High Court to depart from *Victoria Park Racing v Taylor* and to declare that Australian law recognised a tort of invasion of privacy. In response, his Honour stated that '[i]f the activities were filmed were private, then the law of breach of confidence is adequate to cover the case.'[54] Gleeson CJ went on to record his view that '[t]he law should be more astute than in the past to identify and protect interests of a kind which fall within the concept of privacy.'[55] However, the imprecision of the concept of privacy and the tensions between privacy and free speech were reasons against declaring a new tort.[56]

Gleeson CJ then made the following observations, which have proved to be influential:

> There is no bright line which can be drawn between what is private and what is not. Use of the term 'public' is often a convenient method of contrast, but there is a large area in between what is necessarily public and what is necessarily private. An activity is not private simply because it is not done in public. It does not suffice to make an act private that, because it occurs on private property, it has such measure of protection from the public gaze as the characteristics of the property, the nature of the activity, the locality, and the disposition of the property owner combine to afford. Certain kinds of information about a person, such as information relating to health, personal relationships, or finances, may be easy to identify as private; as may certain kinds of activity, which a reasonable person, applying contemporary standards of morals and behaviour, would understand to be meant to be unobserved. The requirement that disclosure or observation of information or conduct would be highly offensive to a reasonable person of ordinary sensibilities is in many circumstances a useful practical test of what is private.[57]

His Honour considered it unnecessary to decide whether a corporation could invoke privacy. Gleeson CJ accepted that '[s]ome forms of corporate activity are

[51] ibid, 222–24 (Gleeson CJ).
[52] ibid, 222–23 (Gleeson CJ).
[53] ibid, 224 (Gleeson CJ), citing *Hellewell v Chief Constable of Derbyshire* [1995] 4 All ER 473, [1995] 1 WLR 804, 807 (Laws J).
[54] ibid, 225 (Gleeson CJ).
[55] ibid.
[56] ibid, 225–26 (Gleeson CJ).
[57] ibid, 226 (Gleeson CJ).

private' but equally suggested that 'the foundation of much of what is protected, where rights of privacy, as distinct from rights of property, are acknowledged, is human dignity', which would be 'incongruous' when applied to corporations.[58] In his Honour's view, though, even if the plaintiff were a natural person, it still could not obtain relief because the activities were not private.[59] Ultimately, Gleeson CJ found that Lenah Game Meats had failed to supply a ground upon which the illegality of the trespassers' conduct prevented the ABC from publishing the footage.[60]

In their joint judgment, with which Gaudron J agreed,[61] Gummow and Hayne JJ noted that Lenah Game Meats did not allege that the ABC was implicated in, or privy to, the trespass, nor did it allege that the ABC engaged in the tort of conspiracy.[62] Gummow and Hayne JJ suggested one possible way in which Lenah Game Meats may have been able to restrain the ABC from broadcasting the footage obtained in the course of the trespass. For the purposes of copyright law, the footage was a cinematograph film.[63] The ownership of it vests in the makers of the cinematograph film.[64] However, given that the cinematograph film was made in the course of a trespass, it may be unconscionable for the trespassers to be able to assert copyright. Although the trespassers are the legal owners of the copyright in the cinematograph film, it may be that they hold it on constructive trust for Lenah Game Meats. Knowing that the footage was obtained in the course of a trespass, it would be unconscionable for the ABC to receive and broadcast it in breach of that trust.[65] However, this argument had not been raised by Lenah Game Meats.[66]

Gummow and Hayne JJ turned to consider the status of *Victoria Park Racing v Taylor* under Australian law and its impact on the recognition of some form of cause of action for invasion of privacy. Their Honours stated clearly that:

> *Victoria Park* does not stand in the path of the development of such a cause of action.[67]

Gummow and Hayne JJ observed that, in *Victoria Park Racing v Taylor*, a corporate defendant sought an injunction principally on the basis of private nuisance. Their Honours stated that *Victoria Park Racing v Taylor* stood for the

[58] ibid.
[59] ibid, 226–27 (Gleeson CJ).
[60] ibid, 228, 230–31 (Gleeson CJ).
[61] ibid, 231 (Gaudron J).
[62] ibid, 234 (Gummow and Hayne JJ).
[63] *Copyright Act 1968* (Cth) s 90.
[64] ibid, s 98.
[65] *ABC v Lenah Game Meats* (n 1) 246 (Gummow and Hayne JJ).
[66] ibid, 247 (Gummow and Hayne JJ). For a subsequent, unsuccessful attempt to rely upon this process of reasoning in similar circumstances, see *Windridge Farm Pty Ltd v Grassi* (2011) 254 FLR 87, 104–07 (Hall J).
[67] *ABC v Lenah Game Meats* (n 1) 248 (Gummow and Hayne JJ).

proposition, perhaps paradoxically or counterintuitively, that private nuisance does not protect privacy but says nothing about whether Australian law more generally protects privacy.[68] Gummow and Hayne JJ derived two propositions from *Victoria Park Racing v Taylor*, which were relevant in the instant case. First, their Honours suggested that the 'preferable legal method' was 'the development and adaptation of recognised forms of action to meet new situations or circumstances' rather than to 'search for the ingredients of a generally expressed wrong'. Second, Gummow and Hayne JJ emphasised that privacy was understandably not central to the claims in *Victoria Park Racing v Taylor* because the plaintiff was a corporation and thus not one which might be expected to be able to assert such a right.[69]

Their Honours turned to consider the position under English[70] and US law,[71] focussing particularly on corporate privacy. Lenah Game Meats could not rely upon 'an emergent tort of invasion of privacy' to support injunctive relief because, in the view of Gummow and Hayne JJ, '[w]hatever development may take place in that field will be to the benefit of natural, not artificial, persons.'[72] Their Honours concluded their reasoning on this issue by emphasising that, in relation to individual privacy, nothing in the judgment should be taken as foreclosing any debate or indicating any particular outcome in the development of the common law.[73]

Kirby J held that establishing a cause of action was not necessary in order to obtain an interlocutory injunction.[74] His Honour further found that a general equitable notion of unconscionability would provide a sufficient basis for such relief.[75] Given this conclusion, it was strictly unnecessary for Kirby J to deal with the issue of a cause of action for invasion of privacy.[76] His Honour noted that the Australian Law Reform Commission, in its 1979 report, *Unfair Publication: Defamation and Privacy*, had recommended against the introduction of a general cause of action for invasion of privacy.[77] Kirby J characterised the issue of departing from *Victoria Park Racing v Taylor* as 'a difficult question' and postponed answering it.[78] His Honour did record, however, his doubt that a corporation had a right to privacy.[79]

[68] ibid, 249 (Gummow and Hayne JJ).
[69] ibid, 250 (Gummow and Hayne JJ).
[70] ibid, 250–52 (Gummow and Hayne JJ).
[71] ibid, 252–57 (Gummow and Hayne JJ).
[72] ibid, 258 (Gummow and Hayne JJ).
[73] ibid.
[74] ibid, 264–71 (Kirby J).
[75] ibid, 271–76 (Kirby J).
[76] ibid, 277 (Kirby J).
[77] ibid, 277. See Australian Law Reform Commission, *Unfair Publication: Defamation and Privacy* (Report No 11, 1979) [244]. At the time of the report, Kirby J was the President of the Australian Law Reform Commission.
[78] *ABC v Lenah Game Meats* (n 1) 278 (Kirby J).
[79] ibid, 279 (Kirby J).

Ultimately, although Kirby J found that the Supreme Court of Tasmania had the power to grant an interlocutory injunction without establishing a cause of action, his Honour held that the courts below had erred in the exercise of their discretion by failing to give sufficient weight to the implied freedom of political communication, derived from the text and structure of the Commonwealth Constitution.[80]

Like Kirby J, Callinan J found that Lenah Game Meats could obtain an interlocutory injunction against the ABC even without establishing a cause of action against it.[81] His Honour would, in any event, have grounded an interlocutory injunction on a general concept of unconscionability.[82] Unlike the other judges on appeal, Callinan J found that Lenah Game Meats' activities were 'private, albeit in a qualified sense', although his Honour did not make explicit the relevant qualification. Callinan J stated that Lenah Game Meats did not want to stop public discussion of its activities but rather public broadcast of the footage, as that would cause irreparable economic loss to its business.[83] His Honour rejected drawing a distinction between public and commercial broadcasters for the purposes of the appeal.[84] This led Callinan J into a disquisition on 'the circumstances prevailing today', specifically in relation to the Australian media environment. In doing so, his Honour traversed the emergence of infotainment, the proliferation of surveillance technologies, the concentration of media ownership and journalists' codes of ethics.[85]

Like Kirby J, it was strictly unnecessary for Callinan J to deal with whether Australian law should recognise a tort of invasion of privacy. Nevertheless, his Honour expressed some tentative views.[86] Callinan J observed that *Victoria Park Racing v Taylor* was 'a product of a different time'.[87] His Honour examined US, New Zealand and English law on privacy protection.[88] Unlike the other judges on appeal, Callinan J refused to rule out the possibility that a corporation might be able to assert a cause of action for invasion of privacy.[89] Callinan J concluded:

> that, having regard to current conditions in this country, and developments of the law in other common law jurisdictions, the time is ripe for consideration whether a tort of invasion of privacy should be recognised in this country, or whether the legislatures should be left to determine whether provisions for a remedy should be made for it.[90]

[80] ibid, 286 (Kirby J).
[81] ibid, 288 (Callinan J).
[82] ibid, 315–16 (Callinan J).
[83] ibid, 297 (Callinan J).
[84] ibid, 297–98 (Callinan J).
[85] ibid, 315–16 (Callinan J).
[86] ibid, 320 (Callinan J).
[87] ibid, 321 (Callinan J).
[88] ibid, 323–26 (Callinan J).
[89] ibid, 328 (Callinan J).
[90] ibid.

Callinan J was the only judge on appeal who would have granted the injunction to Lenah Game Meats.

IV. IMPACT ON THE DEVELOPMENT OF AUSTRALIAN LAW

Following the High Court's decision in *ABC v Lenah Game Meats*, one might have expected further litigation to test some of the suggestions in tantalising *dicta* in that case. In particular, one might have expected test cases brought by natural persons, to see whether some form of privacy protection might develop for their benefit, if not for corporations. Yet in the intervening two decades since *ABC v Lenah Game Meats*, there have only been two decisions, both of inferior courts, in which a cause of action for invasion of privacy has been recognised and damages awarded to the plaintiff.

In *Grosse v Purvis*,[91] the plaintiff, Alison Grosse, was the Mayor of Maroochy Shire in Queensland and the chair of the board of the Sunshine Coast Regional Group Apprentices Ltd. Through her chairing of that board, she met the defendant, Robert Purvis. The parties had a brief sexual relationship. Following the breakdown of that relationship, Purvis engaged in a course of conduct towards Grosse which she alleged resulted in her developing a psychiatric illness.[92] Grosse commenced proceedings against Purvis in the District Court of Queensland. The trial judge, Skoien DCJ, accepted that Purvis' overall conduct towards Grosse should be characterised as stalking.[93] Grosse pleaded a wide range of torts – private nuisance, trespass to land, assault, battery, negligence and the action on the case from the intentional infliction of harm[94] – arising from discrete incidents. In addition, she claimed damages for the novel torts of invasion of privacy and harassment.[95]

In relation to the tort of invasion of privacy, his Honour acknowledged that no previous case had found one. However, according to Skoien DCJ's reading of the judgments in *ABC v Lenah Game Meats*, there was clear support for the development of such a tort. His Honour then considered US, English and New Zealand privacy jurisprudence to inform the development of the tort. Skoien DCJ concluded that:

> It is a bold step to take, as it seems, the first step in this country to hold that there can be a civil action for damages based on the actionable right of an individual person to privacy. But I see it as a logical and desirable step. In my view there is such an actionable right.[96]

[91] *Grosse v Purvis* (2003) Aust Torts Reports ¶81–706.
[92] As to the facts of this case, see ibid, 64, 134–64, 136.
[93] ibid, 64, 183.
[94] *Wilkinson v Downton* [1897] 2 QB 57.
[95] *Grosse v Purvis* (n 91) 64, 133.
[96] ibid, 64, 187.

His Honour proceeded to identify the elements of the tort of invasion of privacy thus:

(a) a willed act by the defendant,
(b) which intrudes upon the privacy or seclusion of the plaintiff,
(c) in a manner which would be considered highly offensive to a reasonable person of ordinary sensibilities,
(d) and which causes the plaintiff detriment in the form of mental psychological or emotional harm or distress or which prevents or hinders the plaintiff from doing an act which she is lawfully entitled to do.[97]

Skoien DCJ expressly left open whether negligence would suffice as the fault standard for this tort. His Honour held that a public interest defence should be available for this tort but none could be established on the facts.[98] Having readily established liability for this novel tort, Skoien DCJ awarded Grosse $108,000 compensatory damages, $50,000 aggravated damages and $20,000 exemplary damages.[99]

The possibility of liability being imposed for negligent invasion of privacy was considered in *Doe v Australian Broadcasting Corporation.*[100] In this case, a woman was raped by her estranged husband. He was tried, convicted and imprisoned for that offence.[101] As the victim of a sexual offence, the woman was entitled by statute to the suppression of her identity.[102] Unfortunately, on the sentencing date, across three bulletins, ABC radio news directly or indirectly identified her.[103] The woman commenced proceedings against the ABC in the Victorian County Court, alleging breach of statutory duty, negligence, breach of confidence and invasion of privacy.[104] In dealing with the latter two causes of action, Judge Hampel stated that breach of confidence and invasion of privacy were intertwined.[105] Following on from Gleeson CJ's judgment in *ABC v Lenah Game Meats*, Judge Hampel found that it was no longer necessary for there to be a relationship between the parties importing an obligation of confidence, that it was sufficient that the information was self-evidently private or confidential.[106] Her Honour held that confidential information was information in respect of which a person had a reasonable expectation of privacy.[107] Judge Hampel readily found that Doe's identity as a victim of sexual assault was

[97] ibid.
[98] ibid.
[99] ibid, 64, 190–64, 191.
[100] *Doe v Australian Broadcasting Corporation* [2007] VCC 281 (hereafter '*Doe v ABC*').
[101] ibid, [1].
[102] *Judicial Proceedings Reports Act 1958* (Vic) s 4(1A).
[103] *Doe v ABC* (n 100) [3].
[104] ibid, [5].
[105] ibid, [148].
[106] ibid, [110]–[112].
[107] ibid, [116], citing *Campbell v MGN Ltd* [2004] UKHL 22, [2004] 2 AC 457.

confidential information.[108] Disclosure to family and close friends, police, prosecutors and medical practitioners was not inconsistent with that conclusion.[109]

Whilst inferior courts in Australia have been willing to develop a tort of invasion of privacy following *ABC v Lenah Game Meats*, superior courts have been more reticent about the effect of the High Court's decision. In *Kalaba v Commonwealth*, Heerey J stated that, following *ABC v Lenah Game Meats*, 'there is no tort of invasion of privacy in Australia'.[110] On appeal, the Full Court of the Federal Court of Australia upheld Heerey J's judgment.[111] In the New South Wales Court of Appeal in *John Fairfax Publications Pty Ltd v Hitchcock*, McColl JA stated that 'Australian common law does not recognise a tort of privacy, although some members of the High Court have tentatively acknowledged that such a tort may emerge, at least for individuals rather than corporations.'[112] Four years later, in the same court, Basten JA observed that '[t]he absence from the common law of an established tort of unjustified invasion of privacy has been noted on more than one occasion'[113] but suggested that *ABC v Lenah Game Meats* 'may well lay the basis for development of liability for unjustified intrusion on personal privacy, whether or not involving breach of confidence'.[114] In *Sands v State of South Australia*, a decision of the Supreme Court of South Australia, Kelly J opined that:

> The *ratio decidendi* of the decision in *Lenah* is that it would require a further development in the law to acknowledge the existence of a tort of privacy in Australia. In my view, the statements of the majority in *Lenah* do not support the suggestion that the High Court in *Lenah* held out any invitation to intermediate courts to develop the tort of privacy as an actionable wrong.[115]

In *Chan v Sellwood*, Davies J, sitting in the Supreme Court of New South Wales, stated that it was 'unclear' whether Australian law recognised a tort of invasion of privacy and suggested that *ABC v Lenah Game Meats* 'would not appear to preclude the emergence of such a tort'.[116] Returning to the issue more recently, his Honour observed that it was still unclear, almost a decade hence, whether Australian law would protect privacy through an extension and adaptation of breach of confidence or whether it would recognise a general tort of invasion

[108] ibid, [119].

[109] ibid, [122]–[123], [125]–[126], [132]–[134].

[110] *Kalaba v Commonwealth of Australia* [2004] FCA 763, [6].

[111] *Kalaba v Commonwealth of Australia* [2004] FCAFC 326, [8], [13] (Tamberlin, North and Dowsett JJ).

[112] *John Fairfax Publications Pty Ltd v Hitchcock* (2007) 70 NSWLR 484, 515, citing *ABC v Lenah Game Meats* (n 1) 258 [132] (Gummow and Hayne JJ), 328 [335] (Callinan J).

[113] *Maynes v Casey* [2011] NSWCA 156 [34] (Basten JA).

[114] ibid, [35] (Basten JA).

[115] *Sands v State of South Australia* [2013] SASC 44 [614].

[116] *Chan v Sellwood* [2009] NSWSC 1335 [37]. See also *Gee v Burger* [2009] NSWSC 149 [53]–[56] (McLaughin AsJ).

of privacy.[117] Davies J acknowledged that no Australian superior court had yet recognised such a tort.[118]

The highest appellate consideration of *ABC v Lenah Game Meats* and its effect on Australian privacy law was the decision of the Victorian Court of Appeal in *Giller v Procopets*.[119] The parties were in a de facto relationship which ended acrimoniously. In an attempt to rehabilitate their relationship, they resumed having sexual intercourse. The male defendant initially filmed their sexual encounters surreptitiously. The female plaintiff became aware of this but consented to the continued filming. Eventually, however, the relationship broke down irretrievably. Following that event, the defendant showed, or threatened to show, videos to various members of the plaintiff's family, friends and employer.[120] In proceedings brought in the Supreme Court of Victoria, seeking relief in relation to a number of aspects of their relationship, the plaintiff pleaded three causes of action arising from the videos, namely, breach of confidence, the intentional infliction of emotional distress and invasion of privacy.[121] The plaintiff was understandably distressed by the defendant's conduct but did not seek to prove that she had suffered any psychiatric injury as a result of it.[122]

At first instance, dealing with the claim for breach of confidence, Gillard J had little difficulty in finding that sexual activity between de facto partners constituted private information in the course of a relationship importing an obligation of confidence.[123] His Honour accepted that the unauthorised disclosure of the video constituted a breach of that obligation.[124] However, Gillard J concluded that general damages for distress could not be awarded for breach of confidence as it was an equitable cause of action.[125] The plaintiff's claim for the intentional infliction of harm, based on *Wilkinson v Downton*,[126] failed because she had not proved that she had suffered a recognised psychiatric injury. Mere distress was insufficient.[127] Gillard J dealt briefly with the claim for invasion of privacy, noting that, since *ABC v Lenah Game Meats*, it had been 'in a process of development' with 'a degree of encouragement' from the judgment of Gummow and Hayne JJ, but concluded that Australian law had not yet developed to recognise such a cause of action.[128] Consequently, his Honour found that a single wrong had been committed against the plaintiff in respect of the videos – breach of confidence – but that no relief was available.

[117] *Kostov v Nationwide News Pty Ltd (No 1)* [2018] NSWSC 1822 [64]–[66].
[118] ibid, [66] (Davies J).
[119] *Giller v Procopets* (2008) 24 VR 1.
[120] *Giller v Procopets* [2004] VSC 113 [9]–[10], [145].
[121] ibid, [18].
[122] ibid.
[123] ibid, [153], [156], citing *Argyll v Argyll* [1967] Ch 302 and *Stephens v Avery* [1988] Ch 449.
[124] ibid, [159].
[125] ibid, [165], [169]–[170].
[126] *Wilkinson v Downton* (n 94).
[127] *Giller v Procopets* [2004] VSC 113 (n 120) [175], [177], [185]–[286].
[128] ibid, [187]–[188].

On appeal, the Victorian Court of Appeal unanimously upheld the trial judge's finding as to liability for breach of confidence but found that his Honour had erred in refusing to grant relief. Neave JA (with whom Maxwell P agreed) held that damages were available for a breach of a purely equitable obligation, such as breach of confidence[129] and that the trial judge erred in finding otherwise.[130] In doing so, Neave JA reviewed English case law[131] but noted that these decisions were unclear as to the precise juridical basis for awarding damages for distress for breach of confidence, whether it was equitable compensation, damages under Lord Cairns' Act or on some other basis.[132] In her Honour's view, *ABC v Lenah Game Meats* supported the availability of damages for distress for breach of confidence because the favoured approach of the High Court in that case was 'strengthening the protection afforded to privacy interests by existing causes of action'.[133]

In his separate judgment, Ashley JA held that the plaintiff's only avenue for redress was breach of confidence, as mere distress was not a compensable injury for *Wilkinson v Downton* liability and 'a generalised tort of invasion of privacy is not yet recognised in Australia'.[134] His Honour held that, even though damages were not available at common law, they should be recoverable in equity.[135] Ashley JA also accepted that exemplary damages should not be available for an equitable cause of action like breach of confidence because equity was not a punitive jurisdiction[136] but that aggravated damages, being compensatory in purpose, were permissible.[137] Because a remedy was available for breach of confidence in the present case, there was, in Ashley JA's view, no need to develop a tort of invasion of privacy. In any event, his Honour noted that such a tort was not sanctioned by any superior court of record in Australia and faced 'substantial definitional problems'.[138]

The Victorian Court of Appeal's approach was followed by Mitchell J in the Supreme Court of Western Australia in *Wilson v Ferguson*.[139] In this case, the female plaintiff and the male defendant shared explicit images and videos of themselves with each other during the course of their de facto relationship.[140] As an act of revenge following the breakdown of their relationship, the defendant posted 16 photographs and two videos of the plaintiff to his Facebook page,

[129] *Giller v Procopets* (2008) 24 VR 1 (n 119) 94–95 (Neave JA).
[130] ibid, 96 (Neave JA).
[131] ibid, 97–99 (Neave JA), citing *Campbell v MGN Ltd* (n 107), *Douglas v Hello! Ltd (No 2)* [2005] EWCA Civ 595 (CA), [2006] QB 125 and *Cornelius v De Taranto* [2001] EMLR 12 (QB).
[132] ibid, 99–100 (Neave JA).
[133] ibid, 102 (Neave JA).
[134] ibid, 28 (Ashley JA).
[135] ibid, 31–32 (Ashley JA).
[136] ibid, 33 (Ashley JA), citing *Harris v Digital Pulse Pty Ltd* (2003) 56 NSWLR 298.
[137] ibid, 34 (Ashley JA).
[138] ibid, 35 (Ashley JA).
[139] *Wilson v Ferguson* [2015] WASC 15.
[140] ibid, [22]–[23].

making them available to approximately 300 Facebook friends.[141] The plaintiff brought a claim for breach of confidence. Mitchell J had little difficulty in finding liability. The intimate images had the necessary quality of confidence.[142] They were obtained in circumstances imposing an obligation of confidence on the defendant. In reaching this conclusion, his Honour relied heavily on the nature of the images in question being clearly private, thereby binding the conscience of the defendant, rather than the nature of the de facto relationship importing an obligation of confidence.[143] By posting the images on Facebook, the defendant misused the images, causing the plaintiff serious distress.[144] Mitchell J granted the plaintiff a permanent injunction against the defendant to prevent repetition of the conduct.[145] His Honour accepted that equitable compensation was available for breach of confidence[146] and, following *Giller v Procopets*, could be awarded for non-economic loss, including distress.[147] Dealing with *ABC v Lenah Game Meats*, Mitchell J stated that:

> prospective developments in the equitable doctrine of breach of confidence were contemplated by at least some of the members of the High Court in *Lenah Game Meats*.[148]

His Honour observed that the development of breach of confidence in *Giller v Procopets* was consistent with developments in English law, although noting that the domestic and European human rights obligation in that legal system had no counterpart in Australia.[149] Mitchell J was further fortified in his conclusion by technological advances, which, in his Honour's view, demonstrated the need for greater privacy protection under Australian law.[150] Mitchell J awarded the plaintiff $35,000 for non-economic loss, as well as $13,404 for economic loss.[151]

The tendency of superior courts in Australia is to favour the development of breach of confidence to provide greater protection for privacy.[152] Cases dealt

[141] ibid, [27]–[28].
[142] ibid, [56].
[143] ibid, [57]–[58].
[144] ibid, [59].
[145] ibid, [61]–[66].
[146] ibid, [68].
[147] ibid, [71]–[76].
[148] ibid, [76].
[149] ibid, [77].
[150] ibid, [78]–[81].
[151] ibid, [85].
[152] See, eg, *Seven Network (Operations) Ltd v Australian Broadcasting Corporation* [2007] NSWSC 1289 [8]; *Ogbonna v Qantas Airways Ltd* [2019] WASCA 146 [48] (Quinlan CJ, Murphy and Mitchell JJA). See also M Richardson, 'Whither Breach of Confidence: A Right of Privacy for Australia?' (2002) 26 *Melbourne University Law Review* 381, 392–93; Hon Justice I Callinan AC, 'Privacy, Confidence, Celebrity and Spectacle' (2007) 7 *Oxford University Commonwealth Law Journal* 1, 7; B McDonald, 'Tort's Role in Protecting Privacy: Current and Future Directions', in S Degeling, J Edelman and J Goudkamp (eds), *Torts in Commercial Law* (Sydney, Thomson Reuters, 2011) 75, 78; B McDonald, 'A Statutory Action for Breach of Privacy: Would it Make a (Beneficial) Difference?' (2013) 36 *Australian Bar Review* 241, 244–50.

with in the UK through misuse of private information continue to be dealt with by Australian courts through a straightforward application of breach of confidence, without the need to develop a law of privacy.[153] However, there are limitations to protecting privacy through an extension and adaptation of breach of confidence. Some are well-known and common to jurisdictions with a shared history of equity. Breach of confidence is concerned with information but there are ways of invading privacy which do not involve disclosure of confidential or private information. The recognition in some jurisdictions of a tort of intrusion upon seclusion demonstrates this.[154] More fundamentally, privacy and confidentiality, though often interchangeable terms, are not co-extensive or identical concepts.[155]

Beyond these common problems, there are some distinctive, additional factors in the Australian context. A more purist (or fundamentalist)[156] approach to equity prevails in Australia, particularly in New South Wales. In that jurisdiction, the Judicature Acts reforms were only introduced by the Supreme Court Act 1970 (NSW), almost a century after these reforms came into effect in English courts. Four of the judges who decided *ABC v Lenah Game Meats* were educated and practised in New South Wales when common law pleading prevailed. An influential text on equity, *Meagher, Gummow and Lehane's Equity Doctrines and Remedies*, has been influential in warning against 'fusion fallacy'. The idea is that the Judicature Acts did not fuse common law and equity into a single jurisdiction but were procedural and institutional reforms aimed at having a single court administering these distinct jurisdictions concurrently.[157] The persistence of this idea in Australia, curious to outsiders, helps explain why issues such as the insistence on referring to equitable compensation rather than damages as a remedy for breach of confidence, the concern as to the proper juridical basis for equitable compensation and whether compensation for mere distress is available in equity when damages for such harm would not be available at common law, concern Australian judges, as *Giller v Procopets* and *Wilson v Ferguson* demonstrate, in a way which is absent from English case law on misuse of private information.[158] Given the prevailing approach to equity in Australia, the prospect of the equitable cause of action for breach of confidence transforming into a free-standing tort of misuse of private information, as has occurred in

[153] See, eg, *Earl v Nationwide News Pty Ltd* [2013] NSWSC 839.

[154] See, eg, *C v Holland* [2012] 3 NZLR 672, 699 (Whata J); *Jones v Tsige* (2012) 108 OR (3d) 241, 260–62 (Sharpe JA).

[155] *Hosking v Runting* [2005] 1 NZLR 1, 16 (Gault and Blanchard JJ).

[156] See P Birks, 'Reviews and Notes: Meagher, Gummow and Lehane's Equity Doctrines and Remedies, 4th ed' (2004) 120 *Law Quarterly Review* 344, 347.

[157] JD Heydon, MJ Leeming and PG Turner, *Meagher, Gummow and Lehane's Equity Doctrines and Remedies*, 5th edn (Chatswood, LexisNexis Butterworths, 2013) [2–130]–[2–150].

[158] See, eg, McDonald (n 152) 63–68, 80 ('a smorgasbord approach to legal remedies is not one that has been accepted in Australia').

English law,[159] is remote. There is also a crucial difference between English and Australian approaches to breach of confidence. Whilst a public interest defence to breach of confidence was established under English law prior to the introduction of the Human Rights Act 1998 (UK),[160] such a defence has been consistently denied under Australian law. Rather, the narrower defence of iniquity has been preferred.[161] If breach of confidence is used as the vehicle for protecting privacy under Australian law, the combination of an ongoing commitment to doctrinal purity and the absence of a public interest defence, coupled with the absence of human rights protection, will mean that the resulting privacy law will vary markedly from the English law of privacy.

The High Court of Australia itself has returned to the issue of whether *ABC v Lenah Game Meats* has endorsed the development of an Australian law of privacy on a number of occasions. Although in *Batistatos v Roads and Traffic Authority of New South Wales*, Callinan J described his position in *ABC v Lenah Game Meats* that 'the time was ripe' for considering whether Australian law should recognise a cause of action for invasion of privacy was a dissenting one,[162] the High Court has, on more than one occasion, indicated its receptivity to such a development. Subsequently, in *Glencore International AG v Commissioner of Taxation*,[163] the High Court, in a unanimous judgment, refused an injunction sought by a group of companies to restrain the Commissioner of Taxation from using copies of the 'Paradise Papers'. To obtain the relief sought, the corporate group needed to identify a cause of action to support it. Their Honours noted that the corporate group did not seek to rely on breach of confidence, because the 'Paradise Papers' were in the public domain, and furthermore, did not 'seek to expand any area of the law such as any tort of

[159] *Vidal-Hall v Google Inc* [2015] EWCA Civ 311, [2016] QB 1003, 1024 (Lord Dyson MR and Sharp LJ). See also B McDonald and D Rolph, 'Remedial Consequences of the Classification of a Privacy Action: Dog or Wolf, Tort or Equity?' in JNE Varuhas and NE Moreham (eds), *Remedies for Breach of Privacy* (Oxford, Hart Publishing, 2018).

[160] *Initial Services Ltd v Putterill* [1968] 1 QB 396 (CA) 405–06 (Lord Denning MR); *Fraser v Evans* [1969] 1 QB 349 (CA) 362 (Lord Denning MR); *Beloff v Pressdram* [1973] 1 All ER 241 (QB) 260–61 (Ungoed-Thomas J); *Woodward v Hutchins* [1977] 2 All ER 751 (CA) 754 (Lord Denning MR); *Lion Laboratories Ltd v Evans* [1985] QB 526 (CA) 536 (Stephenson LJ), 548 (O'Connor LJ), 550 (Griffiths LJ); *X v Y* [1988] 2 All ER 648 (Fam) 658 (Rose J); *Attorney-General v Guardian Newspapers Ltd (No 2)* [1990] 1 AC 109 (HL) 268–69 (Lord Griffiths), 282–83 (Lord Goff of Chieveley).

[161] *Corrs Pavey Whiting & Byrne v Collector of Customs (Vic)* (1987) 14 FCR 434, 451–56 (Gummow J); *Smith Kline & French Laboratories (Aust) Ltd v Department of Community Services and Health* (1990) 22 FCR 73, 110–11 (Gummow J); *Sullivan v Sclanders* (2000) 77 SASR 419, 420 (Williams J), 426 (Gray J); *Australian Football League v The Age Co Ltd* (2006) 15 VR 419, 438–443 (Kellam J). See further Heydon, Leeming and Turner (n 157) [42–160]–[42–185]. For a recognition of the denial of a public interest defence to breach of confidence as a limitation on the efficacy of this cause of action as a vehicle for protecting privacy, see D Butler, 'Protecting personal privacy in Australia: Quo vadis?' (2016) 42 *Australian Bar Review* 107, 119–21.

[162] *Batistatos v Roads and Traffic Authority of New South Wales* (2006) 226 CLR 256, 319 (Callinan J). See also Callinan AC (n 152) 10 (describing the case for a tort of intrusion upon privacy as 'unanswerable') 19.

[163] *Glencore International AG v Commissioner of Taxation (Cth)* (2019) 265 CLR 646.

unjustified invasion of privacy'.[164] More recently, in *Smethurst v Commissioner of Police*,[165] the Australian Federal Police obtained and executed warrants to search a journalist's home, seeking evidence of a breach of the Crimes Act 1914 (Cth). The journalist, Annika Smethurst, had published an article in *The Sunday Telegraph* newspaper disclosing planned legislation to allow the Australian Signals Directorate to access data covertly not only of non-citizens but also of Australian citizens. During the execution of the warrants, the AFP took Smethurst's mobile phone and copied data from it onto their computer. Smethurst challenged the validity of the warrants and sought to restrain the AFP from using information obtained from her mobile phone.[166] The High Court of Australia found that one of the warrants was invalid.[167] The difficulty was that Smethurst disavowed reliance upon a range of causes of action to support relief, instead arguing that the breach of the statute itself gave rise to an entitlement to an injunction to restrain the AFP using the data they had unlawfully collected. The High Court noted that one of the causes of action Smethurst expressly refused to rely upon was invasion of privacy, involving a development of the law from *ABC v Lenah Game Meats*.[168] Notwithstanding this forensic position, Kiefel CJ, Bell and Keane JJ described privacy after *ABC v Lenah Game Meats* as 'a possible right'.[169] Their Honours went further, venturing that:

> Without determining whether the common law of tort may recognise a tort of privacy, it cannot be said that there is no prospect of a remedy, at least for the first plaintiff [Smethurst].[170]

Ultimately, because Smethurst failed to identify a basis for the injunction, the High Court refused relief.[171] The position adopted by Smethurst in relation to invasion of privacy is consistent with the view adopted by most media outlets in Australia, which is hostile to the recognition of some form of right to privacy. This was so even when a right to privacy would have assisted Smethurst obtain relief against a gross intrusion upon journalistic freedom by police in an attempt to identify a journalist's sources. On one view, this shows consistency in the opposition to a right to privacy. On another view, though, it represents a missed opportunity. If a right to privacy is to be recognised under Australian law, as may eventually happen, having a journalist as the plaintiff arguing for one would have allowed media interests to shape the resulting law of privacy.

[164] ibid, 655.

[165] *Smethurst v Commissioner of Police (Cth)* (2020) 376 ALR 575 (hereafter '*Smethurst*').

[166] As to the facts of this case, see ibid, 578–80 (Kiefel CJ, Bell and Keane JJ).

[167] ibid, 587 (Kiefel CJ, Bell and Keane JJ).

[168] ibid, 587–88 (Kiefel CJ, Bell and Keane JJ). See also Hon Justice P Keane, 'Too Much Information: Civilisation and the Problems of Privacy' (2020 Griffith Law School, Michael Whincop Memorial Lecture, Brisbane, 27 August 2020) 14–15 cdn.hcourt.gov.au/assets/publications/speeches/current-justices/keanej/keanej27Aug2020.pdf (accessed 27 June 2021).

[169] *Smethurst* (n 165) 596 (Kiefel CJ, Bell and Keane JJ).

[170] ibid, 597 (Kiefel CJ, Bell and Keane JJ).

[171] ibid, 599–600 (Kiefel CJ, Bell and Keane JJ), 616–17 (Nettle J), 624–25 (Gordon J).

Giving the Michael Whincop Memorial Lecture at Griffith Law School in August 2020, Justice Keane of the High Court of Australia observed that the '[t]he problems of privacy are problems of civilisation'.[172] His Honour noted that there was still no general right to privacy under Australian law[173] but noted that, in the intervening decades, there had been substantial technological changes, posing even greater challenges to privacy.[174] Keane J then turned to *ABC v Lenah Game Meats*, stating that the majority of the judges in that case were open to the development of the common law to protect privacy. His Honour observed that:

> Given the tenor of the reasons of the majority in *Lenah Game Meats*, it would not be surprising were the High Court now to accept a tort of invasion of privacy, along the lines of the US *Restatement*. But such a cause of action would probably be confined to cases of intention intrusion, physically or otherwise, upon the solitude or seclusion of an individual or his or her private affairs. In the case of the publicising of a matter concerning the private life of an individual, the conduct would be actionable if the matter publicised is of a kind that would be highly offensive to a reasonable person and is not of legitimate concern to the public.[175]

Keane J reaffirmed the view that any such cause of action for invasion of privacy would not be for the benefit of corporations because privacy was an aspect of human dignity.[176] The problem of the underdevelopment of an Australian law of privacy is evidently not an unwillingness at the highest appellate level. The causes lie elsewhere.

V. IMPACT ON THE DEVELOPMENT OF ENGLISH AND NEW ZEALAND PRIVACY LAW

The development of privacy law across the common law world has been stimulated in part due to the cross-fertilisation of ideas between jurisdictions. Thus, the impact of *ABC v Lenah Game Meats* is not limited to Australia. As well as being the leading Australian case on a common law right to privacy, *ABC v Lenah Game Meats* proved influential upon the development of English and New Zealand privacy law. It predated the UK case of *Campbell v MGN Ltd*[177] and the New Zealand case of *Hosking v Runting*.[178] Both of these significant appellate cases engaged with the reasoning in *ABC v Lenah Game Meats* but to different effect. In particular, the judgment of Gleeson CJ in *ABC v Lenah*

[172] Keane (n 168) 6.
[173] ibid 9.
[174] ibid 10.
[175] ibid 11 (citations omitted).
[176] ibid.
[177] *Campbell v MGN Ltd* (n 107).
[178] *Hosking v Runting* [2005] 1 NZLR 1.

Game Meats on what is private and the working formulation of the relevant test as being whether a matter is 'highly offensive to a reasonable person of ordinary sensibilities', itself derived from the American Law Institute's *Restatement (Second) of Torts*,[179] has been significant. In New Zealand law, these aspects of *ABC v Lenah Game Meats* in particular have thus far been endorsed, although its influence may become the subject of reconsideration, whereas in English law, the case has principally served as a counterpoint in the development of the cause of action for misuse of private information.

In the landmark New Zealand case, *Hosking v Runting*, Gault and Blanchard JJ endorsed Gleeson CJ's 'highly offensive' formulation as a test for invasion of privacy.[180] This has been repeatedly endorsed in subsequent cases.[181] However, there has been disagreement on this issue. In her dissenting judgment in *Television New Zealand Ltd v Rogers*, Elias CJ suggested that the court should reserve its position on the issue of whether the publicity given to private facts needed to be 'highly offensive'. Her Honour noted that such an approach had been doubted by the House of Lords in *Campbell v MGN Ltd*.[182] In recent decisions, this formulation of the test has been increasingly criticised.[183] Most recently, the New Zealand Court of Appeal in *Hyndman v Walker* were invited to remove the 'highly offensive' formulation from the test for invasion of privacy and to reformulate the requirements of the tort. Although their Honours expressed the view that the privacy tort warranted re-examination, they concluded that the instant case was not an appropriate vehicle for that, given that the claim would have failed even on the application of the more liberal test to the reasonable expectation of privacy under English law.[184] Whilst there have been changing views about the 'highly offensive' formulation for the test of invasion of privacy, Gleeson CJ's working test for what is private in *ABC v Lenah Game Meats* has been consistently approved of by New Zealand courts.[185]

In early English privacy decisions, Gleeson CJ's *dicta* in *ABC v Lenah Game Meats* on what is private and in particular his 'highly offensive' formulation of

[179] American Law Institute, *Restatement (Second of Torts* (1977) § 652B.

[180] *Hosking v Runting* (n 178) 35 (Gault and Blanchard JJ).

[181] See, eg, *Mafart v Television New Zealand Ltd* [2006] 3 NZLR 534, 546; *Hyndman v Walker* [2019] NZHC 2188 [90]–[92] (Thomas J); *Hyndman v Walker* [2021] NZCA 25 [33] (Miller J). The 'highly offensive' formulation as the test for what constitutes an invasion of privacy had been endorsed in earlier cases on the tort of public disclosure of private facts in New Zealand. See, eg, *Bradley v Wingnut Films* [1993] 1 NZLR 415, 424 (Gallen J); *P v D* [2000] 2 NZLR 591, 601 (Nicholson J).

[182] *Television New Zealand Ltd v Rogers* [2008] 2 NZLR 277, 290.

[183] See, eg, *Henderson v Walker* [2019] NZHC 2184 [203] (Thomas J) (describing this formulation of the test as 'controversial'); *Peters v Bennett* [2020] NZHC 761 [82] (Venning J).

[184] *Hyndman v Walker* (n 181) [2]–[3], [75]–[76] (Miller J).

[185] *Hosking v Runting* (n 178) 32 (Gault and Blanchard JJ) (describing it as 'helpful'); *Andrew v Television New Zealand Ltd* [2009] 1 NZLR 220, 227–28 (Allan J); *Faesenkloet v Jenkin* [2014] NZHC 1637 [31] (Asher J); *Driver v Radio New Zealand Ltd* [2019] NZHC 3275 [93] (Clark J); *Peters v Bennett* (n 183) [95] (Venning J).

the test were considered and applied.[186] This changed markedly after the House of Lords' decision in *Campbell v MGN Ltd*. In his speech, Lord Nicholls of Birkenhead observed that the 'highly offensive' formulation 'should be used with care' and 'could be a recipe for confusion'. This was because it suggested a stricter approach to what constitutes private information than a reasonable expectation of privacy and potentially introduced issues going to the proportionality of the intrusion into private life into that threshold question.[187] In his speech, Lord Hope of Craighead pointed out that, viewed in context, Gleeson CJ's *dicta* in *ABC v Lenah Game Meats* did not require recourse to the 'highly offensive' formulation where the information was obviously private. In such circumstances, whether the person had a reasonable expectation of privacy would be a sufficient test.[188] Baroness Hale of Richmond agreed with Lord Hope's characterisation of Gleeson CJ's *dicta* in *ABC v Lenah Game Meats*.[189] Her Ladyship preferred '[a]n objective reasonable test' to a 'highly offensive' formulation, on the basis that it was 'much simpler'.[190] In his speech, Lord Carswell stated that the resolution of the appeal did not require recourse to Gleeson CJ's *dicta* in *ABC v Lenah Game Meats*.[191]

Following the landmark House of Lords' judgment in *Campbell v MGN Ltd* with its affirmation of the reasonable expectation of privacy as the threshold issue, Gleeson CJ's *dicta* in *ABC v Lenah Game Meats* assumed less importance. Recently, an incidental reference by Lord Sumption to offensiveness as an aspect of the test derived from *Campbell v MGN Ltd*[192] was rejected as a misstatement of the effect of that House of Lords decision, the error possibly attributable to the consideration and rejection of Gleeson CJ's formulation in *ABC v Lenah Game Meats*.[193]

VI. RECOMMENDATIONS FOR PRIVACY LAW REFORM

Over the last 15 years, privacy has been the subject of intense interest to law reform bodies in Australia. Within that period, it has been the subject of two references to the Australian Law Reform Commission ('the ALRC'). In 2008, in its final report in the first inquiry, the ALRC recommended the introduction

[186] See, eg, *A v B plc* [2002] EWCA Civ 337, [2003] QB 195, 206 (Lord Woolf CJ); *Campbell v MGN Ltd* [2002] EWHC 499 (QB) [40] (Morland J); *Douglas v Hello! Ltd* [2003] EWHC 786 (Ch) [188]–[192] (Lindsay J); *Campbell v MGN Ltd* [2002] EWCA Civ 1373, [2003] QB 633, 659–60.

[187] *Campbell v MGN Ltd* (n 107) 466.

[188] ibid, 482–83.

[189] ibid, 496.

[190] ibid, 495.

[191] ibid, 504.

[192] *Khuja v Times Newspapers Ltd* [2017] UKSC 49, [2019] AC 161 [21].

[193] *Brake v Guy* [2021] EWHC 671 (Ch) [271] (HHJ Paul Mathews).

of a statutory cause of action for invasion of privacy.[194] In 2012, the then Commonwealth Attorney-General, Mark Dreyfus QC, gave the ALRC another reference on privacy, this time to formulate a statutory cause of action for serious invasions of privacy. Following a change of government and before the ALRC could release its final report, the new Commonwealth Attorney-General, Senator George Brandis, categorically ruled out introducing such a reform.[195]

The issue of privacy has also engaged the attention of State law reform bodies. In 2009, the New South Wales Law Reform Commission recommended the enactment of a general, open-textured statutory cause of action for invasion of privacy.[196] In 2010, the Victorian Law Reform Commission, in its final report on surveillance in public places, recommended the introduction of two specific statutory causes of action, one for misuse of private information, the other for intrusion upon seclusion.[197] In 2016, the South Australian Law Reform Institute recommended the introduction of a general statutory tort of invasion of privacy, covering bodily, territorial, information and communications privacy.[198]

Parliamentary committees, at a national and State level, have endorsed the enactment of a statutory cause of action for invasion of privacy. In its report on drones and their impact on air safety and privacy, the House of Representatives Standing Committee on Social Policy and Legal Affairs, a multi-party committee of the Commonwealth Parliament, made this recommendation in its unanimous report.[199] The Senate Standing Committee on Legal and Constitutional Affairs, in its report on the 'phenomenon colloquially referred to as "revenge porn"', recommended that the Commonwealth Government 'give further consideration to' the ALRC's proposal for a statutory cause of action for invasion of privacy.[200] The New South Wales Legislative Standing Committee on Law and Justice was given a reference to inquire into remedies for the serious invasion of privacy. In its final report, it recommended the introduction of a statutory cause of action for invasion of privacy, based on the ALRC's proposal.[201] Six months after the

[194] Australian Law Reform Commission, *For Your Information: Australian Privacy Law and Practice* (Report No 108, August 2008) Recommendations 74–1, 74–2, 74–3, 74–4, 74–5, 74–6, 74–7.

[195] C Merritt, 'Brandis rejects privacy tort call' *The Australian* (Sydney, 4 April 2014) 27.

[196] New South Wales Law Reform Commission, *Invasion of Privacy* (Report No 120, April 2009) Recommendation, App A.

[197] Victorian Law Reform Commission, *Surveillance in Public Places* (Final Report No 18, May 2010) Recommendations 22–38.

[198] South Australian Law Reform Institute, *A Statutory Tort for Invasion of Privacy* (Final Report No 4, March 2016) Recommendations 1–34.

[199] Parliament of the Commonwealth of Australia, House of Representatives, Standing Committee on Social Policy and Legal Affairs, *Eyes in the Sky: Inquiry into drones and the regulation of air safety and privacy* (July 2014) Recommendation 3.

[200] Senate Standing Committee on Legal and Constitutional Affairs, *Phenomenon colloquially referred to as 'revenge porn'* (Report, February 2016) Recommendation 6.

[201] New South Wales Legislative Council, Standing Committee on Law and Justice, *Remedies for the serious invasion of privacy in New South Wales* (Report No 57, March 2016) Recommendations 3, 4, 5, 6 and 7.

report was released, the then New South Wales Attorney-General, Gabrielle Upton MP, issued the government's response, ruling out the introduction of such a cause of action.

Other bodies beyond law reform commissions and parliamentary committees have recommended the introduction of a statutory cause of action for invasion of privacy. The Australian Human Rights Commission also proposed that the statutory cause of action should be implemented as part of its discussion paper into human rights and technology.[202] In its final report into digital platforms, the Australian Competition and Consumer Commission ('the ACCC') recommended that the statutory cause of action proposed by the ALRC should be enacted.[203] In its response to the ACCC's final report, the Federal Government merely noted the recommendation for the introduction of a statutory cause of action for invasion of privacy and supported further consideration of this initiative in a broader review of Australian privacy law.[204] Subsequently, the Commonwealth Attorney-General, the Hon Christian Porter MP, established a review of the Privacy Act 1988 (Cth), including, as foreshadowed, questions on whether a statutory cause of action for invasion of privacy should be introduced into Australian law.[205] The Privacy Act 1988 (Cth) is concerned with the collection and storage of personal information. At the time of writing, submissions to this legislative review were still being received. Writing about the legislative review in *The Sydney Morning Herald* newspaper, Professor Barbara McDonald of the University of Sydney, the commissioner who chaired the ALRC's 2014 inquiry into the statutory cause of action for serious invasions of privacy began her opinion piece:

> I suppose that if you asked the same question often enough, you might finally get the answer you wanted in the first place

and ended it:

> Perhaps it would save us all a lot of work and the taxpayers some expense if this time, the government told us the answers it wants.[206]

Notwithstanding the sustained interest of law reformers in introducing some general form of privacy protection into Australia, none of these recommendations has been implemented by legislators.

[202] Australian Human Rights Commission, *Human Rights and Technology* (Discussion Paper, December 2019) Proposal 4.

[203] Australian Competition and Consumer Commission, *Digital Platforms Inquiry* (Final Report, June 2019) Recommendation 19.

[204] Australian Government, *Regulating the digital age: Government Response and Implementation Roadmap for the Digital Platforms Inquiry* (2019) 19.

[205] Australian Government, Attorney-General's Department, *Privacy Act Review* (Issues Paper, October 2020) 2.

[206] B McDonald, 'No easy answers on how to best protect our privacy' *Sydney Morning Herald* (Sydney, 5 November 2020, 33.

VII. WHY HAS NO CAUSE OF ACTION FOR INVASION OF PRIVACY ARISEN UNDER AUSTRALIAN LAW YET?

There are a number of possible, interrelated and overlapping reasons why the prospect of some form of general law protection of privacy has not been realised in Australia in the following decades since *ABC v Lenah Game Meats*. The most obvious reason is that test cases to develop the law have not been brought in Australia. Without them, courts cannot develop a law of privacy. The absence of test cases is partly attributable to the courts' own equivocal and divergent positions on how Australian privacy law should develop. Indeed, this can be traced back to the judgments in *ABC v Lenah Game Meats* themselves. Legal practitioners are understandably loath to advise, and parties unwilling to risk, litigation where the law is so uncertain. What is notable about the cases in Australia which raise the possibility of a general law right to privacy is that they have been brought by private individuals. This contrasts markedly with the position in the UK, where the development of privacy law has been driven by supermodels,[207] musicians,[208] businessmen,[209] television presenters,[210] actors,[211] authors,[212] a lot of footballers[213] and even royalty.[214] The privacy law developed through cases involving claimants with a public profile can then be invoked by private individuals but the risky and expensive work has already been done. A rare instance of a well-resourced, high-profile plaintiff suing for invasion of privacy in Australia were the proceedings commenced by the richest woman in Australia, and, depending on the iron ore price, the richest woman in the world, Gina Rinehart. Rinehart sued over a docudrama, *House of Hancock*, which was broadcast on Channel Nine and portrayed her difficult relationship with her iron ore magnate father, Lang Hancock, and the maid-turned-stepmother, Rose. The case settled prior to trial, so made no law.[215] Without this kind of plaintiff, a general law of privacy is difficult to develop.

In Australia, high-profile, well-resourced plaintiffs also have another cause of action which they can rely upon, which they are familiar with and which may

[207] *Campbell v MGN Ltd* (n 107).

[208] *McKennitt v Ash* [2006] EWCA Civ 1714, [2008] QB 73; *Ntuli v Donald* [2010] EWCA Civ 1276, [2011] EMLR 10; *Weller v Associated Newspapers Ltd* [2015] EWCA Civ 1176, [2016] 1 WLR 1541.

[209] *Browne v Associated Newspapers Ltd* [2007] EWCA Civ 295, [2008] QB 103.

[210] *Theakston v MGN Ltd* [2002] EWHC 137 (QB), [2002] EMLR 22.

[211] *Douglas v Hello! Ltd* [2001] QB 967 (CA).

[212] *Murray v Express Newspapers Ltd* [2007] EWHC 1908 (Ch), [2008] EWCA Civ 446, [2009] Ch 481.

[213] *A v B plc* (n 186); *Terry v Persons Unknown* [2010] EWHC 119 (QB), [2010] EMLR 16; *CTB v News Group Newspapers Ltd* [2011] EWHC 1232 (QB); *Ferdinand v MGN Ltd* [2011] EWHC 2454 (QB).

[214] *HRH Prince of Wales v Associated Newspapers Ltd* [2006] EWCA Civ 1776, [2008] Ch 57; *Duchess of Sussex v Associated Newspapers Ltd* [2021] EWHC 273 (Ch), [2021] 4 WLR 35.

[215] See generally D Rolph, 'Mining for Drama: *House of Hancock*, Gina Rinehart and the Law' in M Arrow, J Baker and C Monagle (eds), *Small Screens: Essays on Contemporary Australian Television* (Clayton, Monash University Publishing, 2016).

obviate the need to develop a law of privacy: defamation. The self-perception of Australians may be that they are a laidback and easy-going people but this is somewhat belied by their ready recourse to defamation law. Australian defamation law still broadly favours plaintiffs. For instance, there is in force no statutory serious harm threshold and no public interest defence in Australia, their common law analogues also having failed to develop.[216] Given how few obstacles currently confront plaintiffs commencing defamation proceedings under Australian law, it is unsurprising that public figures can and do sue for defamation and are frequently successful. Such cases even make international headlines, as they did when actor, Rebel Wilson, was awarded $600,000 aggravated damages for stories in *Woman's Day* magazine suggesting that she had lied about her birth name, age and upbringing,[217] and when actor, Geoffrey Rush, was awarded $2.87 million damages, including aggravated damages and damages for economic loss, over a tabloid front page story published under the headline, 'KING LEER', which accused the Oscar winner of engaging in sexually inappropriate conduct onstage and in the rehearsal room during a Sydney Theatre Company production of the Shakespearean tragedy, *King Lear*.[218]

Cases which might otherwise be dealt with as privacy claims tend to be dealt with through defamation law in Australia. For instance, the tabloid newspaper, *The Sunday Telegraph*, published a front-page story, 'King of the Kastle', showing Daniel Johns, the lead singer of the Australian rock band, Silverchair, in the vicinity of a bondage and discipline venue, the Kastle, located in inner Sydney, and alleging that he was 'swagger[ing] out of a notorious bondage dungeon after a two-week bender'. The story contained a detailed account of Johns' alleged activities inside the club, including his alleged sexual proclivities, all attributed to unnamed sources. When Johns sued in the Supreme Court of Victoria, he did not claim for breach of confidence or invasion of privacy, only defamation. Johns denied that he had been in the venue, as did the venue's operator. Johns ultimately settled the proceedings for a reported $170,000, as well as his legal fees and a prominent apology.[219]

An earlier example of a high-profile plaintiff using defamation law indirectly to protect privacy was the case brought by rugby league footballer, Andrew Ettingshausen against *HQ* magazine. The magazine published a grainy black-and-white full-frontally naked photograph of Ettingshausen in the showers after an international representative match. Ettingshausen sued for defamation in the Supreme Court of New South Wales, the principal imputation being that

[216] At the time of writing, reforms to the national, uniform defamation laws, including a statutory serious harm threshold and a statutory public interest defence have been enacted, but not commenced, in New South Wales, South Australia and Victoria.

[217] *Bauer Media Pty Ltd v Wilson (No 2)* (2018) 56 VR 674.

[218] *Nationwide News Pty Ltd v Rush* (2020) 380 ALR 432.

[219] A Hornery, 'Musician Daniel Johns received six figure settlement from News Corp' *Sydney Morning Herald* (Sydney, 9 May 2020) 3.

he deliberately permitted a naked photograph of himself to be published in a widely circulated magazine. At trial, the jury awarded him $350,000 damages. On appeal, the New South Wales Court of Appeal set aside the jury verdict as manifestly excessive.[220] Kirby P (as his Honour then was) noted that Australian law did not recognise an enforceable right to privacy and observed that it was impermissible to award Ettingshausen damages for invasion of privacy per se.[221] Clarke JA opined that the jury may have awarded excessive damages for defamation because it was impermissibly 'expressing its outrage at the gross invasion of the respondent's privacy'.[222]

Yet the indirect protection of privacy through defamation law in Australia is unsurprising. There are *dicta* suggesting that privacy is a value or interest protected by defamation law.[223] Moreover, prior to the introduction of the national, uniform defamation laws in 2005, proof of substantial truth alone was not a complete defence to defamation in four of the eight jurisdictions within the Australian Federation. There was an additional element of public interest or public benefit.[224] In New South Wales, this had been a requirement continuously since the first defamation legislation was introduced in 1847.[225] Thus, in many Australian jurisdictions, defamation law operated as an indirect protection of privacy for a long time. It may have been hoped that the removal of the additional element of public interest or public benefit, after *ABC v Lenah Game Meats* was decided, may have stimulated the development of some direct form of privacy protection in Australia but this has clearly not occurred.[226]

Another possible reason that Australian law has not developed a general law right to privacy is the absence of a constitutional or statutory protection of human rights. Two states and one Territory in Australia have human rights legislation, which includes a right to privacy.[227] The presence of this human right has not, however, stimulated the development of privacy law in any of those jurisdictions. At a national level, Australia is unique amongst western liberal democracies in having no constitutional or statutory human rights protection. The enactment of the Human Rights Act 1998 (UK) was the impetus for the development of privacy law in that jurisdiction. In the absence of constitutional

[220] *Australian Consolidated Press Ltd v Ettingshausen* (CA (NSW), 13 October 1993) 4 (Gleeson CJ), 40 (Kirby P), 32 (Clarke JA).

[221] ibid, 14 (Kirby P).

[222] ibid, 32 (Clarke JA).

[223] See, eg, *John Fairfax Publications Pty Ltd v Hitchcock* (n 112) 515 (McColl JA).

[224] See Defamation Act 1974 (NSW) s 15(2)(b) (repealed); Defamation Act 1889 (Qld) s 15 (repealed); Defamation Act 1957 (Tas) s 15 (repealed); Civil Law (Wrongs) Act 2002 (ACT) s 127 (repealed).

[225] Slander and Libel Act 1847 (NSW) s 4 (repealed).

[226] D Rolph, 'Preparing for a Full-Scale Invasion? Truth, Privacy and Defamation' (2007) 25(3/4) *Communications Law Bulletin* 5.

[227] Human Rights Act 2004 (ACT) s 12; Charter of Human Rights and Responsibilities Act 2006 (Vic) s 13; Human Rights Act 2019 (Qld) s 25.

or statutory human rights protection, human rights have to be protected through the political process. As the position under Australian law demonstrates, it is often difficult to engage the attention of legislators.

There is another feature of the Australian legal landscape which a law of privacy has not developed. It is an aspect of judicial, rather than parliamentary, politics. In *Farah Constructions Pty Ltd v Say-Dee Pty Ltd*,[228] the High Court of Australia trenchantly criticised the New South Wales Court of Appeal for developing the law on an issue for which there was no binding High Court precedent. Their Honours held that intermediate appellate courts are bound to follow not only the *rationes* of High Court decisions but also seriously considered *dicta* contained in them.[229] The reluctance of superior courts below the High Court of Australia to embark upon an exercise of judicial creativity involved in the recognition of a new cause of action for invasion of privacy may be attributable in part to this command. The inhibition generated by this High Court decision should not be underestimated.

Finally, the media landscape in Australia may suggest a reason why a law of privacy has yet to develop. It has already been noted that most plaintiffs who try to plead an invasion of privacy are private individuals, rather than celebrities. Another feature of these cases is that the defendants are also overwhelmingly private individuals, rather than media outlets. *Doe v ABC* is an exception. This contrasts markedly to the way in which English privacy law developed, where high-profile plaintiffs brought proceedings, often seeking injunctive relief, against tabloid newspapers.

Australia does not have the tabloid newspaper market which the UK does. The competition between weekday and Sunday tabloid newspapers – the *Sun*, the *Mail*, the *Mirror*, the *Express* and the *Star* and previously and notoriously, the *News of the World* – has no parallel in Australia. As the Leveson Inquiry demonstrated, tabloid newspapers were, in significant measure, responsible for intrusions into the privacy of public figures which it uncovered.

The explanation for this is in part cultural: the continued publication of these newspapers, with the exception of the *News of the World*, which closed in response to the phone hacking scandal in June 2011, suggests that there remains a market segment for celebrity-based journalism amongst the newspaper reading public. By contrast, in Australia, weekly tabloid newspapers, like the *Truth*, and competing afternoon newspapers closed or amalgamated in the 1980s.

However, the differences are not merely cultural. More fundamentally, the differences in media landscapes between Australia and the UK are geographical and economic. The population of the UK is more than two and a half times that of Australia. Australia's population is spread over a vast geographical area.

[228] *Farah Constructions Pty Ltd v Say-Dee Pty Ltd* (2007) 230 CLR 89.
[229] ibid, 151–52.

By contrast, the UK is densely populated within a relatively small geographical area. Thus, it is economically viable in the UK to have multiple, competing national newspapers, in a way which it is not in Australia. There is a single national newspaper, the *Australian*, as well as a national business newspaper, the *Australian Financial Review*. More significant in Australia, though, are the newspapers of the State capital cities. Only Sydney and Melbourne have large enough populations to sustain a broadsheet and a tabloid newspaper – the *Sydney Morning Herald* and the *Daily Telegraph*, in Sydney, and the *Age* and the *Herald-Sun*, in Melbourne. All other State capital cities – Brisbane, Perth, Adelaide and Hobart – have only one daily newspaper, which has to serve both the serious and the tabloid ends of the market.

The smaller, geographically diffuse media market in Australia means that there is less incentive for media outlets to intrude upon celebrities' privacy. It is not in the commercial self-interest of media outlets to intrude upon the privacy of genuinely international celebrities, such as Cate Blanchett, Russell Crowe, Hugh Jackman or Nicole Kidman. Media outlets would want to maintain access to such stars in the future so would not risk alienating them through gratuitous intrusion upon privacy. For more local or minor celebrities, the commercial proposition is different. Here, the interdependence of media and celebrity interests becomes apparent in a smaller market like Australia. Many media outlets still want celebrity-based content, so it is not in their interest to be unduly intrusive upon celebrities' privacy. Equally, for local or minor celebrities, because there are fewer opportunities in a smaller, geographically dispersed market like Australia, there is a greater disincentive to sue for invasion of privacy and a greater incentive to commodify their privacy. There have been instances in Australia of minor celebrities working with paparazzi to stage 'candid' photographs and share in the proceeds of their sale to newspapers and magazines.[230] The commercial interests of media outlets and celebrities are more aligned in the Australian media market than in the UK. Media outlets get their celebrity-based content and celebrities get paid.

This is not to say that the Australian media never invade celebrities' privacy. It still occurs from time to time, and when it is litigated, it tends to be done through defamation, rather than a novel cause of action for invasion of privacy. Nevertheless, intrusions into celebrities' privacy has not been a staple part of Australian media culture in the way it has been for English tabloid newspapers. It is not only the differences in legal culture between Australia and the UK which help explain the divergent development of privacy law in these countries, but also the significant differences in media landscapes between these respective jurisdictions.

[230] J Marshall, 'Fake paps exposed', *Sunday Telegraph* (Sydney, 10 June 2012) 7; S O'Brien, 'Dirty secrets of the papped', *Herald-Sun* (Melbourne, 12 June 2012) 13.

VIII. CONCLUSION

General law protection of privacy in Australia is underdeveloped, in comparison to the UK, New Zealand and Canada. Twenty years after *ABC v Lenah Game Meats*, a cause of action for invasion of privacy under Australian law is still described as developing or emerging.[231] There remain unresolved questions about whether the development of a cause of action for invasion of privacy should be addressed by the legislature or the courts;[232] whether it should be achieved through an extension and adaptation of breach of confidence, through the recognition of a new tort or a *sui generis* cause of action; and whether it should be directed to the protection of privacy generally or limited to filling gaps in existing legal protections.[233] This process has not begun, significantly due to the lack of interest shown by legislators in this issue, the opposition of mainstream media outlets[234] and the lack of tests cases being brought before the courts. If courts are going to develop a law of privacy in Australia, they can only do so based on the cases brought before them. It took six decades for one landmark case, *Victoria Park Racing v Taylor*, which appeared to establish that there was no right to privacy at common law in Australia, to be supplanted by another landmark case, *ABC v Lenah Game Meats*, which seemed to suggest that there might be right to privacy (but not for corporations). It is to be hoped that it will not take as long for the prospect of some form of general privacy protection to be realised under Australian law.

[231] See, eg, *Moore-McQuillan v Work Cover Corporation* [2005] SASC 13 [18]; *Holloway v State of Tasmania* (2005) 15 Tas R 127, 138 (Evans J); *Hutchens v City of Holdfast Bay* (2007) 98 SASR 412, 417; *John Fairfax Publications Pty Ltd v Hitchcock* (n 112) 515 (McColl JA); *Chan v Sellwood* (n 116) [37]. For an example predating *ABC v Lenah Game Meats*, see *Church of Scientology Inc v Woodward* (1982) 154 CLR 25, 68 (Murphy J).

[232] J Caldwell, 'Protecting Privacy Post *Lenah*: Should the Courts Establish a New Tort or Develop Breach of Confidence?' (2003) 26 *University of New South Wales Law Journal* 90, 92.

[233] D Butler, 'A Tort of Invasion of Privacy in Australia?' (2005) 29 *Melbourne University Law Review* 339, 388; McDonald, 'Tort's Role in Protecting Privacy' (n 152) 65; McDonald, 'A statutory action for breach of privacy: Would it make a (beneficial) difference?' (n 152).

[234] See, eg, Free TV Australia, *Submission by Free TV Australia: Privacy Act Review* (December 2020) www.ag.gov.au/sites/default/files/2021-02/freetv-australia.PDF (accessed 27 June 2021) 3; GNM Australia Pty Ltd, *Response to the Attorney-General's review of the Privacy Act 1988* (December 2020) www.ag.gov.au/sites/default/files/2021-02/the-guardian-australia.PDF (accessed 27 June 2021) 16; Nine, *Nine's Submission in response to the Privacy Act Review Issues Paper* (10 December 2020) www.ag.gov.au/sites/default/files/2020-12/nine.PDF (accessed 27 June 2021) 6; SBS, *SBS Submission to the Australian Attorney-General's Department Privacy Act Review* (November 2020) www.sbs.com.au/aboutus/sites/sbs.com.au.aboutus/files/66_sbs_submission_-_privacy_act_review_final_4_dec_2020.pdf (accessed 27 June 2021) 2, 8.

7

A v B & C (2002)

N A MOREHAM*

I. INTRODUCTION

THE COURT OF Appeal decision in *A v B & C v MGN Ltd* (aka *Flitcroft v MGN Ltd*)[1] is one of a handful of cases which, early this century, kickstarted the transformation of the breach of confidence action from its traditional incarnation into the misuse of privacy tort that we know today. Decided just a year after the Court of Appeal had held that courts were obliged to develop the breach of confidence action consistently with the right to respect for private life in Article 8 of the European Convention on Human Rights 1950,[2] it gave important early guidance on how that development should take place. It set out the requirements of the extended breach of confidence action – fusing the concepts of confidence and privacy as it did so – and explained how the balance between Articles 8 and 10 should be determined in an injunction application. And it did all this in the context of what was to become the stock-in-trade of privacy cases – a kiss-and-tell tabloid story about the extramarital sexual activities of a public figure – decided against a backdrop of both intense legal interest in (and media resistance to) the likely impact of the Human Rights Act 1998 (HRA) on privacy protection in the common law. *A v B & C* was therefore decided at an important transition point in English law and represents a unique fusion of breach of confidence and modern privacy thinking.

* Thanks to Adam Speker KC of 5RB, London and Ass Prof Dean Knight and Prof Claudia Geiringer, both of Victoria University of Wellington for helpful comments on an earlier draft. Thanks also to Rita Shasha and Jess McPherson for copy-editing assistance. The usual disclaimers apply.

[1] *A v B & C* (aka *Flitcroft v MGN Ltd*) [2002] EWCA Civ 337.

[2] *Douglas v Hello!* [2001] 1 QB 967. Article 8 provides that: '1. Everyone has the right to respect for his private and family life, his home and his correspondence. 2. There shall be no interference by a public authority with the exercise of this right except such as is in accordance with the law and is necessary in a democratic society in the interests of national security, public safety or the economic well-being of the country, for the prevention of disorder or crime, for the protection of health or morals, or for the protection of the rights and freedoms of others.'

Reading *A v B & C* in this context helps us both to understand its reasoning and to assess its ongoing relevance. This chapter will examine the decision through this transition-focused lens. It starts by looking at how the test for establishing a breach of confidence/privacy was applied arguing that, although the Court had introduced the language of privacy to its formulation of the confidence test, its emphasis on the relationship between the parties in *A v B & C* and on both parties' right to tell their own story showed that traditional breach of confidence principles still prevailed. The second part of the chapter examines how the Court balanced privacy with freedom of expression interests. These sections highlight, in particular, the Court's generous interpretation of the freedom of expression interest and of the public interest in public figures' lives.

II. THE CONFIDENCE/PRIVACY TEST

A v B & C involved an unsuccessful attempt by a premiership footballer (later revealed to be Blackburn Rovers player, Garry Flitcroft) to obtain an interim injunction restraining a newspaper (B) from publishing a salaciously detailed kiss-and-tell by two women with whom he had had extramarital affairs (known in the judgment as C and D).[3] Lord Woolf CJ (speaking for the Court) began his disposal of the case by setting out how the principles of Articles 8 and 10 of the Convention should be incorporated into the requirements of breach of confidence in cases involving a breach of privacy claim.[4] Having confirmed that section 6 of the HRA required the Court, as a public authority, not to act in a way which was incompatible with those Convention rights,[5] Lord Woolf CJ explained that compatibility could be achieved by:

> absorbing the rights which Articles 8 and 10 protect into the long-established action for breach of confidence. This involves giving a new strength and breadth to the action so that it accommodates the requirements of those Articles.[6]

He said that privacy and freedom of expression interests needed to be balanced against each other and observed that both Articles 8 and 10 are qualified,

[3] C was a party to the litigation but D was not.

[4] *A v B & C* (n 1) at [4]. Article 10 provides: '1. Everyone has the right to freedom of expression. This right shall include freedom to hold opinions and to receive and impart information and ideas without interference by public authority and regardless of frontiers. This Article shall not prevent States from requiring the licensing of broadcasting, television or cinema enterprises. 2. The exercise of these freedoms, since it carries with it duties and responsibilities, may be subject to such formalities, conditions, restrictions or penalties as are prescribed by law and are necessary in a democratic society, in the interests of national security, territorial integrity or public safety, for the prevention of disorder or crime, for the protection of health or morals, for the protection of the reputation or rights of others, for preventing the disclosure of information received in confidence, or for maintaining the authority and impartiality of the judiciary.'

[5] *A v B & C* (n 1) at [4].

[6] ibid.

'expressly in a way which allows the interests under the other Article to be taken into account'.[7] Turning to when the privacy/confidence interest will be established, he explained that '[a] duty of confidence will arise whenever the party subject to the duty is in a situation where he either knows or ought to know that the other person can reasonably expect his privacy to be protected'.[8] Put another way:

> If there is an intrusion in a situation where a person can reasonably expect his privacy to be respected then that intrusion will be capable of giving rise to liability in an action for breach of confidence unless the intrusion can be justified.[9]

This is an early articulation of the 'reasonable expectation of privacy' test which has gone on to be the cornerstone of courts' protection of privacy in England and Wales. Its parameters have been discussed in dozens of cases since this decision and its meaning repeatedly refined in both case law and academic discussion[10] (perhaps belying Lord Woolf CJ's prediction that 'whether there exists a private interest worthy of protection will be obvious').[11] This is enough on its own to make *A v B & C* a 'landmark' decision. Of equal significance though, at least for present purposes, is the way both the formulation and application of the test in *A v B & C* reflects the unique transition point at which the case was decided.

A. The Importance of Relationship

The fusion of breach of confidence and privacy concepts in *A v B & C* is immediately apparent from the way the test for determining whether something was confidential/private was articulated. The fact that the Court explained how the claimant could establish 'a duty of *confidence*' by reference to 'reasonable expectations of *privacy*' reflects the elision of privacy and confidentiality which was taking place in the decision and in the development of privacy protection at the time it was decided.[12] Indeed, although the test for determining privacy/confidentiality had at its heart the concept of the reasonable expectation of privacy, the Court's determination of the existence of a privacy/confidence interest was principally grounded in breach of confidence. This manifested particularly in

[7] ibid, at [6].
[8] ibid, at [11(ix)].
[9] ibid, at [11(x)].
[10] See, eg, *Campbell v MGN Ltd* [2004] UKHL 22 (*Campbell (HL)*); *Murray v Big Pictures* [2008] EWCA Civ 446; *JR38* [2015] UKSC 42; NA Moreham 'Unpacking the Privacy Test' (2018) 134 *Law Quarterly Review* 652; NA Moreham and M Warby (eds), *Tugendhat & Christie: Law of Privacy and the Media*, 3rd edn (Oxford, Oxford University Press, 2016) [5.20]–[5.158]; and J Rowbottom *Media Law* (Oxford, Hart Publishing, 2018) 68–81.
[11] *A v B & C* (n 1) at [11(vii)].
[12] This fusion of the language of confidence and privacy when setting out the reasonable expectation of privacy test continued for some years after *A v B & C*. Eventually the label 'misuse of private information' took hold and the action was reconceived as a tort.

the Court's almost exclusive focus on the nature of the relationship between the parties when determining whether the claimant had a privacy interest which could be protected. Having said that the range of situations in which protection could be provided was extensive, Lord Woolf CJ said that whether there will be a duty of confidence 'which courts can protect, if it is right to do so, will depend on all the circumstances of the relationship between the parties at the time of the threatened or actual breach of the alleged duty of confidence'.[13]

He went on to disagree with the conclusion of the judge below that, in the context of 'modern sexual relations', protection should be accorded to information about the kind of relationships at issue in *A v B & C*; namely, in the case of C, a sexual relationship which lasted approximately two months, involved regular contact by phone and three meetings at her home or overnight in hotels and in D's case, an affair (which started when she performed as a lap dancer for him) involving regular communication and occasional meetings in hotel rooms or at her flat over the course of a year.[14] Lord Woolf CJ said that that there is a 'significant difference' between the confidentiality which attaches 'to what is intended to be a permanent relationship and … [this] category of relationships'.[15] He also approved of Ouseley J's observation in *Theakston v MGN Ltd* (which concerned the threatened disclosure of information about and photographs of a television presenter's visit to a brothel) that it was:

> impossible … to invest with the protection of confidentiality all acts of physical intimacy regardless of circumstances … whilst the degree of intimacy is a very relevant factor, it cannot be taken in isolation from the relationship within which the physical intimacy occurs and from the other circumstances particularly the location … Sexual relations within marriage at home would be at one end of the range or matrix of circumstances to be protected from most forms of disclosure; a one night stand with a recent acquaintance in a hotel bedroom might very well be protected from press publicity. A transitory engagement in a brothel is yet further away.[16]

All this makes sense once it is observed that the Court in *A v B & C* was still applying a paradigm under which personal information is protected because of the nature of the relationship in which it was confided (traditionally, relationships such as lawyer-client, doctor-patient, husband and wife).[17] Understanding

[13] *A v B & C* (n 1) at [11(ix)].

[14] ibid, at [43(ii)] (see also [14]–[16]). Lord Woolf CJ said that '[t]here was never any question so far as A is concerned of his leaving his wife for C or D' (*A v B & C* at [14]).

[15] *A v B & C* (n 1) at [43(ii)].

[16] *Theakston v MGN Ltd (Theakston)* [2002] EWHC 137 (QB) [59]–[60] cited in *A v B & C* (n 1) at [43(ii)]. For criticism of reliance on confidentiality principles in *A v B & C* see H Fenwick and G Phillipson *Media Freedom under the Human Rights Act* (Oxford, Oxford University Press, 2006) 734–738.

[17] See *A v B & C* (n 1) at [47] where Lord Woolf CJ concludes that the 'situation is one at the outer limits of *relationships* which require the protection of the law' (emphasis added). See also *Argyll v Argyll* [1967] Ch 302 (regarding the confidentiality of the marriage relationship) and more generally, F Gurry *Breach of Confidence* (Clarendon, Oxford University Press, 1984) Ch VII.

this paradigm also explains why the Court was, first, concerned about the duration and level of commitment in the relationships in *A v B & C* and second, felt that the relationships had failed to reach a sufficient level of formality or commitment to warrant protection.

This focus on the nature of the relationship between the parties in a kiss-and-tell case would now, of course, be regarded as too narrow. It has been made clear in numerous cases since *A v B & C*, that whether a person has a reasonable expectation of privacy depends on a broad range of factors. As the Court of Appeal said in *Murray v Express Newspapers Plc*:

> the question whether there is a reasonable expectation of privacy is a broad one, which takes account of all the circumstances of the case. They include the attributes of the claimant, the nature of the activity in which the claimant was engaged, the place at which it was happening, the nature and purpose of the intrusion, the absence of consent and whether it was known or could be inferred, the effect on the claimant and the circumstances in which and the purposes for which the information came into the hands of the publisher.[18]

In the kiss-and-tell context, the nature of the activity in question is particularly important with courts often stressing that sexual activity is a quintessential part of a person's private sphere. For example, in *Mosley*, Eady J held that as long as the participants are genuinely consenting adults and there is no question of exploiting the young or vulnerable, 'one is usually on safe ground in concluding that anyone indulging in sexual activity is entitled to a degree of privacy'.[19] Courts have also paid careful attention to the 'nature of the proposed intrusion' taking a particularly dim view of publications which contain detailed disclosures about a relationship and/or the sexual activity which took place in the course of it (as opposed to disclosures about the 'bare fact' of the relationship).[20] The negative effect of publicity on a claimant's children and other family members will also be considered when deciding whether to grant an injunction.[21]

As a result of this wider focus, a claimant could now expect to obtain an injunction to restrain publication of photographs or detailed descriptions of a sexual relationship in which he or she was involved even if it was of very short

[18] *Murray v Express Newspapers Plc* [2008] EWCA Civ 446 at [36].

[19] *Mosley v News Group Newspapers Ltd (Mosley)* [2008] EWHC 1777 (QB) at [98] and [100]. He cites *Dudgeon v United Kingdom* Series A no 45 (1982) 4 EHRR 149 at [60] in support of this proposition (*Mosley* at [100]). See also *PJS v News Group Newspapers Ltd (PJS)* [2016] UKSC 26 at [32].

[20] See, eg, *Ntuli v Donald* [2010] EWCA Civ 1276 at [18] and *Hutcheson v News Group Newspapers Ltd (Hutcheson (CA))* [2011] EWCA Civ 808 at [40]; and *Campbell (HL)* (n 10) at [60] (per Lord Hoffmann).

[21] See, eg, *ETK v News Group Newspapers Ltd* [2011] EWCA Civ 439 at [17]–[19]; *PJS* (n 19) at [72]–[78] (per Baroness Hale); *CTB* [2011] EWHC 1334 [3]. *Cf AAA v Associated Newspapers Ltd (AAA)* [2012] EWHC 2103 (QB) at [114].

duration.[22] *A v B & C* does remind us though that even in the modern misuse of private information action, relational context is important. In particular, courts will consider how openly the affair between the parties was conducted. Thus, in *Hutcheson v News Group Ltd*, Eady J said (in a decision that was upheld on appeal) that the court would need to take into account 'the extent to which the relationship in question has been conducted in secrecy'[23] and in *AAA v Associated Newspapers Ltd*, the claimant's previous lack of discretion when discussing the identity of the child's father undermined her claim for a reasonable expectation of privacy in respect of that same information.[24] Relationship, then, although no longer the central consideration, remains important.

B. The Women's Attitude to the Information

The Court's focus on breach of confidence and the relationship between the parties also led it to place significant weight on C and D's own attitude to the relationships in question; specifically, the fact that neither woman regarded the sexual encounters with the claimant as confidential. Lord Woolf CJ said that determining whether information is confidential is 'more difficult' in this situation:

> This is a material factor in situations where two people have shared a sexual relationship outside marriage. If one wishes to exercise his or her Article 10 rights that must impact on the other's right to maintain confidentiality. For example the information may relate, as in this case, to a situation where there is a sexual relationship between two parties and one of the parties informs the media about the relationship without the consent of the other party. Here the conflict between one party's right to privacy and the other party's right of freedom of expression is especially acute.[25]

This makes it more difficult for the claimant to establish confidentiality:

> although … we would not go so far as to say there can be no confidentiality where one party to a relationship does not want confidentiality, the fact that C and D chose to disclose their relationships to B [the newspaper] does affect A's right to protection of the information. For the position to be otherwise would not acknowledge C and D's own right to freedom of expression.[26]

[22] See, eg, *PJS* (n 19) above; *YXB v TNO* [2015] EWHC 826 (QB); *NPV v QEL and ZED* [2018] EWHC 703 (QB); and P Wragg 'The Benefits of Privacy-Invading Expression' (2013) 64 *Northern Ireland Legal Quarterly* 187, 190–192.

[23] *Hutcheson (formerly 'KGM') v News Group Newspapers Ltd MGN Ltd and Associated Newspapers Ltd (Hutcheson (HC))* [2010] EWHC 3145 (QB) at [21]. See also the interim injunction decision, *AMC and KLJ v News Group Newspapers Ltd* [2015] EWHC 2361 (QB) at [17] where the fact that the claimants were careful to keep the relationship a secret weighed in favour of a reasonable expectation of privacy in respect of it.

[24] *AAA* (n 21) at [115]–[116].

[25] *A v B & C* (n 1) at [11(xi)].

[26] ibid, at [43(iii)].

Lord Woolf CJ concluded that the relationships were not of the type which the court should be 'astute to protect when the other parties to … [them] do not want them to remain confidential'.[27]

This focus on the defendants' views on the confidentiality of the relationship is, again, consistent with the breach of confidence principles which were being applied in *A v B & C*. Since the Court's primary concern was with the nature of the relationships between the claimant and the two women (including their duration and level of commitment) it is understandable that it regarded the women's attitude to confidentiality as relevant. But as with the relationship between the parties generally, this consideration has received much less emphasis in subsequent kiss-and-tell cases. Courts have been unsympathetic to defendants who, on their assessment, were claiming that they wanted to tell their own story when they were in fact capitalising on their association with the claimant for their own gain. For example, in *McKennitt*, the Court of Appeal endorsed Eady J's conclusion that a tell-all book written by a former friend of folksinger, Loreena McKennitt, was not 'in any real sense about [the defendant] at all'.[28] Buxton LJ held that the defendant had 'no story to tell that was her own as opposed to being the first claimant's' and that even if she had, her interest in telling it needed to yield to the claimant's privacy interests.[29] Courts are even less sympathetic where the defendant is seeking to sell a salacious story to the media[30] and/or to blackmail the claimant.[31]

A v B & C reinforces the point, however, that even in the modern misuse of private information context there are limits on the extent to which one party to a sexual relationship can determine whether and on what terms the other party can speak about it. Courts have stressed that there is a difference between a desire to keep information about something to yourself and a *legally enforceable* right to prevent other people from disclosing it. As the Court of Appeal observed in *Hutcheson v News Group Newspapers Ltd*, '[t]here is an important distinction between the desire to keep information private and invoking the full panoply of the Court's jurisdiction in order to do so'.[32]

[27] ibid, at [45]. Buxton LJ endorsed this conclusion in *McKennitt v Ash* [2006] EWCA Civ 1714 at [30]. He said that the relationship between McKennitt (a well-known folk singer) and the defendant (her former friend and confidante) was 'miles away from the relationship between A and C and D … [That was] a relationship of casual sex. A could not have thought, and did not say, that when he picked the women up they realised that they were entering into a relationship of confidence with him' (ibid).

[28] *McKennitt v Ash* (n 27) at [31].

[29] *McKennitt v Ash* (n 27) at [51].

[30] See *Ntuli v Donald* (n 20) at [23].

[31] See, eg, *ASG v GSA (ASG)* [2009] EWCA Civ 1574 at [25]; *SOJ v JAO* [2019] EWHC 2569 (QB) at [43] and [45.4] and *NPV* (n 22) at [26].

[32] *Hutcheson (CA)* (n 20) at [48]. Eady J had also held that whilst it might be reasonable to treat information about the existence of an extramarital relationship discreetly, 'that is not the same as enforcing a right to keep it secret vis-à-vis the right of another to exercise freedom of speech by referring to it' (*Hutcheson (HC)* (n 23) at [36] (cited with approval in *SKA and PLM v CRH and persons unknown who have threatened to reveal private information about the claimants (SKA)* [2012] EWHC 766 (QB) at [68]–[70]).

i. Limited Disclosures

It is unsurprising, in light of that, that modern courts are reluctant to restrain *limited* disclosures about a relationship or sexual encounter, especially when the defendant was a party to it. First, in an approach reminiscent of the qualified privilege defence in defamation, courts have held that people are generally at liberty to pass on information about an extramarital relationship to someone with a particular interest in knowing about it. Thus, even if an injunction restraining broader publication is imposed, courts will not usually prevent communication of information about an extramarital relationship to the claimant's spouse or partner. For example, in *ASG v GSA*, the Court of Appeal said that the claimant was less likely to obtain an injunction at trial restraining a woman from telling the claimant's wife about the affair than from talking about it in the press.[33] As with the qualified privilege defence, the recipient's interest in receiving the information is central to this thinking.[34] In *TVK and BVP v ICM*, Warby J said that a person who finds out that a married individual has been unfaithful to his or her spouse 'may, in some circumstances, have every right to inform the wronged spouse, who may have a right to know that information'.[35] Similarly in *SKA and PLM v CRH*,[36] Tugendhat J held that the claimant did not have a reasonable expectation that his wife and grown-up children would not be told (this time by a third party) that he was having an extramarital relationship with the second claimant and that they were expecting twins. He said that the first family's interest in receiving the information also needed to be taken into account when balancing the claimant's rights with those of others. He emphasised the importance of individual freedom of expression,[37] and said that 'to tell a grown up child that his or her father aged in his 70s is, or is about to be, the father of twins, is speech of a high order of importance'.[38] He therefore declined to award an injunction to prevent the disclosure of that information even though the defendant was trying to blackmail the claimant.

It is suggested that cases recognising individuals' freedom to make these kinds of disclosures are consistent with social norms (at least in the absence

[33] *ASG* (n 31) at [25]. Although because the case involved attempted blackmail, the Court awarded a short interim injunction restraining any form of disclosure in any event (at [26]).

[34] See *Gatley on Libel and Slander*, 12th edn (London, Sweet & Maxwell, 2017) ch 14 (especially [14.1]). In *Peters v Attorney-General* [2021] NZCA 355, [2021] 3 NZLR 191 at [119], the New Zealand Court of Appeal held that there will be a defence to a limited disclosure of private material if 'the recipient(s) had a legitimate interest in receiving the information'. It said that development of that defence should be informed by the requirements of the qualified privilege defence in defamation, including the exception for bad faith disclosures (ibid at [120]).

[35] *TVK and BVP v ICM* [2016] EWHC 2810 (QB) at [18]. He suggests, however, that the way in which the informant discovered the information and his or her motivation for passing it on, might be relevant to the desirability of granting the injunction (ibid). In that case, no injunction was granted because of the unlawful way in which the defendant discovered the information (at [19]–[21]).

[36] *SKA* (n 32).

[37] *SKA* (n 32) at [88].

[38] *SKA* (n 32) at [77]. A permanent injunction was later granted in respect of any disclosure which went beyond the claimant's wife and family and of any information which revealed more than the bare fact of the relationship and the twins' existence (*SKA, PLM* and *CRH v Persons Unknown* [2012] EWHC 2236 (QB) especially at [22]).

of blackmail). Whilst people might respond in a range of ways to the discovery, say, that their friend's husband is having an affair, few would expect the law to stop them from passing the information on to the friend. This goes for the 'other woman/man' as well. It is notable that in *A v B & C* itself, C – feeling duped by the claimant – approached the claimant's family with information about the affair.[39] It is suggested that most people in her position would expect to be free to do so.

ii. Therapeutic Disclosures

Courts developing the misuse of private information action have also consistently recognised that an injunction imposed to stop one party to a relationship from talking about it in public should not prevent him or her from discussing it with people they are close to. For example, in *Ntuli v Donald*, the Court of Appeal stressed that an injunction restraining the appellant from talking about the affair she engaged in with the respondent did not extend to conversations with a family member or close friend.[40] The injunction in *CC v AB* also excluded disclosures made to health professionals and other support people. Explaining that the trial judge was unlikely to award an injunction restraining the defendant, a 'cuckolded' husband, from speaking to anyone about his wife's adulterous relationship with the claimant, he said that:

> It would not be proportionate … to prevent the defendant, for example discussing his wife's adultery with a close friend, or with members of the family, or (if he needed to do so) with a family doctor, counsellor or social worker, or with his lawyers.[41]

These exceptions protect important interests on the part of the defendant. Talking about significant life events with family, friends and/or health professionals is acknowledged to play a vital role in the preservation of both intimate relationships and health and well-being.[42] Preventing somebody from doing this would therefore be a serious interference with his or her self-expression and autonomy.[43] In recognition of this, the European Court of Human Rights (ECtHR) has held that the right to respect for private life includes 'the right to personal development, and the right to establish and develop relationships with other human beings and the outside world'.[44] It is therefore desirable that the therapeutic disclosures identified in *CC* should be protected. Indeed, wider disclosures – say, to a group therapy session or a WhatsApp friend group – should probably also be permissible.

[39] *A v B & C* (n 1) at [16].
[40] *Ntuli v Donald* (n 20) at [7].
[41] *CC v AB* [2006] EWHC 3083 (QB) at [35].
[42] See, eg, S Jourard 'Some Psychological Aspects of Privacy' (1966) 31 *Law & Contemporary Problems* 307; C Fried 'Privacy' (1968) 77 *Yale Law Journal* 475 and J Reiman 'Privacy, Intimacy and Personhood' (1977) 6 *Philosophy and Public Affairs* 26.
[43] For discussion of theorists' recognition of the individual benefits of expression, see Wragg (n 22) 192–194.
[44] *Pretty v United Kingdom* [2002] ECHR 427, (2002) 35 EHRR 1 at [61].

iii. Telling One's Own Story

That leaves the question of whether, in the modern misuse of private information context, the right to tell one's own story could ever justify dissemination of information about a sexual relationship to the public at large. Courts have acknowledged that sharing one's story with the world at large can be an important exercise of the dignity and autonomy which underpins both Articles 8 and 10. For example, in *Re Angela Roddy (a minor)*, Munby J varied an order preventing the media from publishing the story of a 16-year-old who had been taken into care and had her child put up for adoption when she was 12 years old. This was because:

> amongst the rights protected by Article 8 … is the right, as a human being, to share with others – and, if one so chooses, with the world at large – one's own story, the story of one's childhood, development and history … It is natural for us to want to talk to others about ourselves and about our lives. It is fundamental to our human condition, to our dignity as human beings, that we should be able to do so … Article 8 thus embraces both the right to maintain one's privacy and, if this is what one prefers … to share what would otherwise be private with others, indeed, with the world at large. So the right to communicate one's story to one's fellow beings is protected not merely by Article 10 but also by Article 8.[45]

This right to tell one's own story can potentially justify public disclosure of information which another person would like to keep private. In *Couderc and Hachette Filipacchi Associés v France*,[46] the Grand Chamber of the ECtHR held that the applicant magazine, *Paris Match*, was entitled to publish the story of a woman, Ms Coste, who had a son with Prince Albert of Monaco even though he wanted the information to remain private. The Court held that although the birth of the child is an event of 'an intimate nature' it does not come solely within the private sphere of the persons concerned by it: it 'also falls within the public sphere, since it is in principle accompanied by a public statement … and the establishment of a legal parent-child relationship'.[47] It continues:

> the purely family and private interest represented by a person's descent is supplemented by a public aspect, related to the social and legal structure of kinship. A news report about a birth cannot therefore be considered, in itself, as a disclosure concerning exclusively the details of the private life of others, intended merely to satisfy the public's curiosity.[48]

[45] *Re Angela Roddy (a minor)* [2003] EWHC 2927 (Fam) at [35]–[36]. See also *Rhodes v OPO and others* [2015] UKSC 32, [2016] AC 219 where the Supreme Court rejected a claim that the tort of intentional infliction of emotional harm should prevent a well-known classical musician from publishing a book about sexual abuse he suffered as a child because of the harm it could do to his psychologically vulnerable son. Baroness Hale and Lord Toulson held that the appellant had a 'legitimate interest' in telling his story to the world at large in the way in which he wished to tell it and that the public had a corresponding interest in hearing his story (ibid at [75]). See also ibid, [76]–[78].

[46] *Couderc and Hachette Filipacchi Associés v France (Couderc)* App no 40454/07 (ECtHR, 10 May 2015).

[47] *Couderc* (n 46) at [107].

[48] ibid, at [107]. The Court held that the information about the birth also had 'undeniable public-interest value – at least for the subjects of the Principality' because the child's father was heir to the throne in the Principality of Monaco (*Couderc* at [108]).

Further, although Ms Coste's individual free speech interests were not directly at play (because the claim was brought by the publishers), the Court still regarded them as relevant.[49] When considering the weight of the interest in favour of publication, it emphasised that the article was not just about the Prince's private life but also Ms Coste's private life and that of her son. The publication contained details about her pregnancy, her own feelings, the birth of her son, health problems suffered by the child, and their life together. The Court said that '[t]hese were elements relating to Ms Coste's private life, in respect of which she was certainly not bound to silence and was free to communicate'.[50] It continued that it 'cannot ignore the fact that the disputed article was a means of expression for the interviewee and her son'.[51] In other words, the claimant had a protected right to talk about her son's paternity, even in the media.

It is possible that, even without the question of royal succession at play, English courts would reach the same conclusion. The publicness of the parent-child relationship has been recognised by English courts on more than one occasion. For example, in *Hutcheson*, the Court of Appeal observed that there is an 'unavoidably public nature' to certain aspects of the life of the married claimant's second family,[52] ultimately allowing publication of information about it because it was in the public interest.[53] Tugendhat J also noted in *SKA and PLM v CRH*, that it was unlikely that the first claimant's paternity of the unborn twins could remain a secret. He said '[i]t is a normal part of life, and an exercise and freedom of expression' for people to talk about each other's lives: 'The birth of babies is a normal topic of such conversations, and there is no reason why it should not be.'[54] Whether that conclusion would extend to publication in the media (as opposed to the limited publication to SKA's first family) remains to be seen; it seems at least arguable that it could be.

Either way, cases like *Couderc* and *A v B & C* are important reminders that it is not always appropriate to prevent one party from speaking about his or her own experiences in a relationship just because the other party – usually the more powerful party – wants to keep the information private. Injunctions preventing limited disclosure to family and friends should almost never be imposed and, at least in the absence of blackmail, disclosures to interested parties should also usually be protected. Further, whilst *A v B & C* might now be regarded as too defendant-friendly, courts should be open to the possibility that there are some circumstances in which a person will be entitled to tell the world at large about a relationship to which he or she was a party even though the other party does not want them to.

[49] *Couderc* (n 46) at [129].
[50] *Couderc* (n 46) at [127].
[51] *Couderc* (n 46) at [127].
[52] *Hutcheson (CA)* (n 20) at [40] and [47(iv)].
[53] ibid, at [48].
[54] *SKA* (n 32) at [89].

III. BALANCING PRIVACY AND FREEDOM OF EXPRESSION

Lord Woolf CJ's conclusion on the first part of the claim in *A v B & C* was, therefore, that the 'degree of confidentiality to which A was entitled, notwithstanding that C and D did not wish their relationships with A to be confidential, was very modest'.[55] As a result, the situation was 'at the outer limits of relationships which require the protection of the law'.[56] That conclusion made it much easier for the defendants to show that they had a free speech interest which outweighed the claimant's right to confidence. Their job was made easier still by the generous weighting given to freedom of expression concerns in Lord Woolf CJ's balancing of Article 8 and 10 interests. Indeed – perhaps reflecting once more the transition point at which *A v B & C* was decided – the Court of Appeal's approach can be seen as the high watermark of free speech protection in the development of the English common law privacy action.

A. Is Freedom of Expression Conterminous with Public Interest in the Material?

Lord Woolf CJ began this part of the judgment by explaining that section 12 of the HRA reinforced the point (the importance of which had been recognised before its enactment) that once established, the privacy interest needed to be balanced against any countervailing interest in freedom of expression.[57] Reflecting his emphasis on the importance of the latter, Lord Woolf CJ held that, when considering freedom of expression, it is not enough simply to protect disclosures which the court regards as being in the public interest. Rather, he said:

> Any interference with the press has to be justified because it inevitably has some effect on the ability of the press to perform its role in society. This is the position irrespective of whether a particular publication is desirable in the public interest. The existence of a free press is in itself desirable and so any interference with it has to be justified.[58]

He went on to say that the fact that section 12(4) requires courts to have particular regard to whether it would be in the public interest for the material to be

[55] *A v B & C* (n 1) at [44].

[56] ibid, at [47].

[57] Section 12 provides that if the court is considering whether to grant relief which might affect the exercise of the Convention right to freedom of expression (s 12(1)) then it must have particular regard to the importance of that right and where the proceedings relate to 'journalistic, literary or artistic material' (or conduct connected with the same) then it should also have regard to the extent to which the material has or is about to become available to the public, is or would be in the public interest, and to any relevant privacy code (s 12(4)). If interim relief is being contemplated, the court must be satisfied that the claimant is 'likely' to establish that publication should not be allowed (s 12(3)).

[58] *A v B & C* (n 1) at [11(iv)].

published 'does not mean that the court is justified in interfering with the freedom of the press where there is no identifiable special public interest in any particular material being published'.[59] He said that such an approach would turn section 12(4) upside down: 'Regardless of the quality of the material which it is intended to publish prima facie the court should not interfere with its publication. Any interference with publication must be justified.'[60]

This approach was, however, superseded soon after. In *Campbell v MGN Ltd*, the House of Lords held that privacy and free speech interests weighed equally in the balance with neither taking precedence over the other. As Lord Hoffmann said:

> There is in my view no question of automatic priority. Nor is there a presumption in favour of one rather than the other. The question is rather the extent to which it is *necessary* to qualify the one right in order to protect the underlying value which is protected by the other. And the extent of the qualification must be proportionate to the need.[61]

Courts – both in *Campbell* and subsequent cases – have also held, contrary to what was said in *A v B & C*, that the weight of the defendant's freedom of expression interest will be conterminous with the public interest in the information or material in question. Lord Hoffmann said in *Campbell* that 'when press freedom comes into conflict with another interest protected by the law, the question is whether there is a sufficient public interest in that particular publication to justify curtailment of the conflicting right'.[62] Where there is no public interest in the information in question, then the freedom to disclose it 'weighs little in the balance against the privacy of personal information'.[63] This approach has been followed in numerous subsequent decisions. For example, in the Court of Appeal decision in *ETK*, 'the contribution the published information will make to a debate of general interest' was 'the decisive factor' in the balancing of Article 8 and Article 10.[64] And in *Browne*, the Court of Appeal said:

> at a trial balance will have to be struck between the claimant's rights under Article 8 and the newspaper's rights under Article 10. In the case of each of the pieces of information in dispute, the court must consider whether the justification in Article 10(2) is established … The question is sometimes said to be to ask where the public interest lies. It is a question of balance.[65]

[59] ibid, at [11(v)].

[60] ibid.

[61] *Campbell (HL)* (n 10) at [55] (original emphasis). See also [20] (Lord Nicholls) and [139]–[141] (Baroness Hale).

[62] *Campbell (HL)* (n 10) at [56].

[63] ibid. See also [22] (Lord Nicholls); [117] (Lord Hope) and [148]–[149] (Baroness Hale).

[64] *ETK v News Group Newspapers Ltd* (n 21) at [23]. See also *ZXC v Bloomberg (CA)* [2020] EWCA Civ 611, [2021] QB 28 at [106]. The Supreme Court in *ZXC* described it as 'a factor of particular importance' (*Bloomberg LP v ZXC (SC)* [2022] UKSC 5, [2022] AC 1158 at [62]).

[65] *Lord Browne of Madingley v Associated Newspapers Ltd (Browne)* [2007 EWCA Civ 295, [2008] QB 103 at [38]. See also *Associated Newspapers Ltd v HRH Prince of Wales* [2006] EWCA

This focus on the public's legitimate interest in receiving the information reflects the fact that, as Baroness Hale puts it in *Campbell*, Article 10 confers both a 'freedom to *receive* and impart information and ideas'.[66] When it comes to the dissemination of private information to the public at large, the defendant's freedom to impart private material is (subject to the points above about individual freedom of expression) almost always dependent on the court's assessment of the public's interest in *receiving* it.[67] Although, as *A v B & C* recognises, freedom of expression has an inherent value which extends beyond this, the circumstances in which that interest will prevail over the claimant's interest in privacy is now almost invariably determined by that assessment.

B. The Public Interest in Public Figures' Private Lives

Although the Court in *A v B & C* held that the degree of public interest in the information should not determine how the balance between free speech and privacy is struck, it did accept that if there *is* a public interest then the case for awarding an injunction will be weakened.[68] And, again, the Court took a generous approach to setting out what is in the public interest. Lord Woolf CJ said that although '[a] public figure is entitled to a private life', he or she:

> should recognise that because of his public position he must expect and accept that his actions will be more closely scrutinised by the media. Even trivial facts relating to a public figure can be of great interest to readers and other observers of the media. Conduct which in the case of a private individual would not be the appropriate subject of comment can be the proper subject of comment in the case of a public figure. The public figure may hold a position where higher standards of conduct can be rightly expected by the public. The public figure may be a role model whose conduct could well be emulated by others. He may set the fashion. The higher the profile of the individual concerned the more likely that this will be the position. Whether you have courted publicity or not you may be a legitimate subject of public attention.[69]

This expansive approach was grounded in a desire to support a thriving media culture. Lord Woolf CJ acknowledged that in many cases it might be 'overstating

Civ 1776, [2008] Ch 57 at [65]; *Hutcheson (CA)* (n 20) at [35]; and, in the breach of confidence context, *ABC and others v Telegraph Media Group Ltd* [2018] EWCA Civ 2329 at [22].

[66] *Campbell (HL)* (n 10) at [126] (emphasis added). See also *Couderc* (n 46) at [89].

[67] This is still the case in decisions which apply the ECtHR's approach of considering numerous factors at the second stage of the Articles 8 and 10 balancing (see, eg, *Axel Springer v Germany* [2012] ECHR 227, (2012) 55 EHRR 6). Even on this approach, domestic courts usually place particular emphasis on the requirement that the publication makes a contribution to a debate of general interest (see, eg, *Ali and Aslam v Channel 5 Broadcasting Ltd* [2019] EWCA Civ 677 at [87]–[89]; *ZXC v Bloomberg (CA)* (n 64) at [106]; and *Bloomberg v ZXC (SC)* (n 64) at [62]).

[68] *A v B & C* (n 1) at [11(viii)].

[69] ibid, at [11(xii)]. He went on to say that if you have courted public attention then you have even less ground to object to the intrusion which follows [(11(xii))].

the position' to say that there is a public interest in the information – '[i]t would be more accurate to say that the public have an understandable and so a legitimate interest in being told the information'.[70] He said that this can appropriately be taken into account when deciding on which side of the line a case falls but 'courts must not ignore the fact that if newspapers do not publish information which the public are interested in, there will be fewer newspapers published, which will not be in the public interest'.[71] The same is also true, he said, of other parts of the media.[72]

Courts were also reminded that they should not act as censors or arbiters of taste when weighing up competing privacy and freedom of expression interests. Lord Woolf CJ held that the fact that disclosure was more lurid than it needed to be or could be regarded as unattractive should not affect the result of an application if the information is otherwise not the proper subject of restraint.[73]

It is not surprising, in light of these statements of the law, that Lord Woolf CJ was loath to conclude that there was no public interest in the defendants' story about the affairs. He said:

> it is not self-evident that how a well-known premiership football player, who has a position of responsibility within his club, chooses to spend his time off the football field does not have a modicum of public interest. Footballers are role models for young people and undesirable behaviour on their part can set an unfortunate example. While [the judge below] was right to say on the evidence which was before him that A had not courted publicity, the fact is that someone holding his position was inevitably a figure in whom a section of the public and the media would be interested.[74]

This broad articulation of the public interest in a public figure's conduct has been criticised by both judges and commentators.[75] Although it is still sometimes acknowledged,[76] the importance of celebrity stories for newspapers' commercial viability now carries limited weight in the privacy/free speech balance. In his

[70] *A v B & C* (n 1) at [11(xii)].

[71] ibid.

[72] ibid.

[73] ibid, at [11(xiii)].

[74] ibid, at [43(vi)]. See also *Theakston* (n 16) at [69] where Ouseley J held that there was a public interest in the fact that the claimant had visited a brothel because, '[w]hilst he may not be presented as a role model, nonetheless the very nature of his job as a TV presenter of programmes for the younger viewer means that he will be seen as somebody whose lifestyle, publicised as it is, is one which does not attract moral opprobrium and would at least be generally harmless if followed'.

[75] See, eg, K Hughes 'The Public Figure Doctrine and the Right to Privacy' (2019) 78 *Cambridge Law Journal* 70, especially 90; G Phillipson, 'Press Freedom, the Public Interest and Privacy' in A Kenyon (ed), *Comparative Defamation and Privacy Law* (Cambridge, Cambridge University Press, 2016) 136; J Campbell 'The Origin and Development of the Right to Privacy' in A Koltay and P Wragg (eds), *The Origins and Development of the Right of Privacy* published in *Comparative Privacy and Defamation*(Cheltenham, Edward Elgar, 2020) 9, especially 19–20; *AMC and KLJ v News Group Newspapers Ltd* (n 23) at [19]–[20] and *McKennitt v Ash* (n 27) at [60]–[66].

[76] See, eg, *ETK* (n 21) at [13] and *Hutcheson (CA)* (n 20) at [34].

majority judgment in the Supreme Court case of *PJS*, Lord Mance said that the fact that information about the private sexual conduct of the claimant and his partner 'might interest the public and help sell newspapers or copy' was 'beside the point'.[77] He said, citing Lord Lester of Herne Hill, that it is essential that the commercial pressures of the news industry do not drive newspapers to violate proper standards of journalism.[78] He also approved of the ECtHR's observation in *Mosley v United Kingdom*, that:

> press reports concentrating on sensational and, at times lurid news, intended to titillate and entertain, which are aimed at satisfying the curiosity of a particular readership regarding aspects of a person's strictly private life … do[] not attract the robust protection of Article 10 afforded to the press. As a consequence, in such cases, freedom of expression requires a more narrow interpretation.[79]

Soon after *A v B & C* was decided, the Court of Appeal in *Campbell* also questioned the desirability of allowing the fact that somebody has been placed on a pedestal to be used as an excuse to criticise their private conduct. In a passage which was also adopted by the Court of Appeal in *McKennitt*, Lord Phillips MR said it is not 'necessarily … in the public interest that an individual who has been adopted as a role model, without seeking this distinction, should be demonstrated to have feet of clay'.[80]

As a result of all this, modern courts demand more from a defendant seeking to establish a public interest in a public figure's private life than general references to the role the person plays in society and/or the interest others have in knowing about his or her private life. In fact, the starting point is that there is no public interest in a person's private life simply because he or she is a public figure. As Lord Phillips MR held in *Campbell*, 'the fact that an individual has achieved prominence on the public stage does not mean that his private life can be laid bare by the media'.[81] Lord Mance in *PJS* also held that it was 'beside the point' that the appellant and his partner were the subjects of public and media attention in other contexts noting that if that were not the case 'the issue would hardly arise or come to court'.[82] Nor, he said, is there a public interest in private sexual encounters 'even though they involve adultery or more than one person at the same time'.[83] So the fact that a person holds a position which makes him or her more interesting to the public is not enough, on its own, to establish a public interest in his or her adulterous sexual activities.

[77] *PJS* (n 19) at [21].

[78] PJS (n 19) at [21] citing A Lester, *Five Ideas to Fight For: How Our Freedom is Under Threat and Why It Matters* (London, Oneworld Publications, 2016) 152.

[79] *PJS* (n 19) at [22] citing *Mosley v United Kingdom* App no 48009/08 (ECtHR, 10 May 2011) at [114].

[80] *Campbell v MGN Ltd* [2002] EWCA Civ 1373 at [41] (*Campbell (CA)*) (cited with approval in *McKennitt v Ash (CA))* at [63] and [65].

[81] *Campbell (CA)* (n 80) at [41].

[82] *PJS* (n 19) at [21].

[83] *PJS* (n 19) at [32].

i. The Continued Relevance of Being a Role Model

It is important to stress, however, that the role model argument in *A v B & C* does continue to have some relevance. Subsequent cases, including recent misuse of private information decisions, have confirmed that there will be a public interest in private information if the claimant holds a genuinely socially important role and the information suggests that he or she is failing to fulfil the obligations associated with it. As Baroness Hale explained in *Campbell*:

> The free exchange of information and ideas on matters relevant to the organisation of the economic, social and political life of the country is crucial to any democracy ... This includes revealing information about public figures, especially those in elective office, which would otherwise be private but is relevant to their participation in public life.[84]

She said this could even include information about an office holder's health: 'Sometimes there will be ... justifications for publishing, especially where the information is relevant to the capacity of a public figure to do the job.'[85] In *AAA*, these principles were applied to private information which revealed unattractive aspects of a political figure's character. Nicola Davies J held that publication of the fact that the claimant's father was a married politician (later revealed to be Boris Johnson) was in the public interest because the father had achieved 'a level of notoriety as a result of extramarital adulterous liaisons' and the claimant was alleged to be the second such child born as a result of such a liaison.[86] She said that, 'such information goes to the issue of recklessness on the part of the supposed father, relevant both to his private and professional character, in particular his fitness for public office'.[87]

Although these principles apply most obviously to elected office holders, they also extend to unelected powerbrokers. For example, the Court of Appeal in *Browne*, said that the defendant was justified in publishing the fact that the CEO of BP, Lord Browne of Madingley, had misused company information and resources by sharing confidential information about the company with his romantic partner and allowing him to use BP's personnel and equipment for his own purposes.[88] Likewise, in *Goodwin v NGN Ltd and VBN*, Tugendhat J held that if he had decided that Royal Bank of Scotland CEO, Fred Goodwin, had a reasonable expectation of privacy in respect of the fact that he was having an extramarital affair with a senior employee, then it would have been in the public interest to have a 'public discussion of the circumstances in which it is proper for a chief executive (or other person holding public office or exercising official

[84] *Campbell (HL)* (n 10) at [148].

[85] *Campbell (HL)* (n 10) at [157]. See also *Cooper v Turrell* [2011] EWHC 3269 (QB) at [44] where Tugendhat J stressed that illness had *not* affected the claimant's ability to perform his duties as a chief executive.

[86] *AAA* (n 21) at [118].

[87] ibid.

[88] *Browne* (n 65) at [51]–[53].

functions) should be able to carry on a sexual relationship with an employee in the same organisation'.[89]

Importantly for the potential ongoing relevance of *A v B & C*, this public interest in a lack of suitability for a role can also extend to high profile sportspeople, including footballers. In *Ferdinand v MGN Ltd*, the claimant's role as England football captain was central to the rejection of his damages claim for publication of information about an extramarital affair in which he engaged after publicly declaiming his former 'wild' image and claiming to be more mature and in a stable family relationship. Nicol J said:

> The claimant voluntarily assumed the role of England captain. It was a job that carried with it an expectation of high standards. In the views of many the captain was expected to maintain those standards off as well as on, the pitch.[90]

Having cited statements from the Sports Minister and prominent football leaders, he therefore held that Ferdinand was indeed a role model.[91] And because the affair (and the fact that he had tried to sneak the woman concerned into a hotel in breach of team rules) called into question the claimant's fitness 'to be the role model which was expected of England captain', the balance came down in favour of publication.[92] Similarly, in *Terry (formerly LNS) v Persons Unknown* Tugendhat J was unwilling to accept that there could be no social utility in the revelation of the fact that a high profile sportsman (later revealed to be England football captain, John Terry) was having an affair.[93] Although there are some questions about exactly how far this now extends (with some cases suggesting that it might only justify disclosures which are in some way connected with the claimant's sporting life),[94] footballers clearly can be 'role models' in whom others are legitimately interested.

So, the conclusion in *A v B & C* that there will be a public interest in the private activities of someone who is a 'role model' or 'sets the fashion' is still

[89] *Goodwin v NGN Ltd and VBN* [2011] EWHC 1437 (QB), [2011] EMLR 27 at [132]. See also [103] and *SOJ v JAO* [2019] EWHC 2569 (QB) at [32].

[90] *Ferdinand v MGN (Ferdinand)* [2011] EWHC 2454 (QB) at [89].

[91] *Ferdinand* (n 90) at [90].

[92] See *Ferdinand* (n 90) at [91]–[105] (especially [91]).

[93] *Terry (formerly LNS) v Persons Unknown* [2010] EWHC 119 (QB) at [97]–[104]. See also *McLaren v News Group Newspapers Ltd* [2012] EWHC 2466 (QB), [2012] EMLR 33 at [34] where Lindblom J held (declining an interim injunction restraining publication of information about an extra marital affair) that a former England football manager was a person of whom 'a higher standard of conduct' could be expected.

[94] See, eg, *Spelman v Express Newspapers Ltd* [2012] EWHC 355 (QB) at [72], in which Tugendhat J held that there was a public interest in the 'sporting life' of a 17 year old international rugby player and the effect that his sport was having upon him (the information in question was later revealed to be a drugs ban); and *AMC and KLJ v News Group Newspapers Ltd* (n 23) at [19]–[20] in which Elizabeth Laing J stressed that although sportspeople can be regarded as role models, 'any scrutiny of [the claimant's] conduct away from sport ought to bear a reasonable relationship with the fact that he is a sportsman'.

good law but only if the claimant genuinely does hold a significant public role and the disclosure at issue raises questions about his or her fitness for that role. Although this requirement can clearly be satisfied by a person with a significant role in the world of football – as it did in *Ferdinand* and *Terry* – it is unlikely that holding 'a senior role within his club' (as the claimant in *A v B & C* did) would now be enough to satisfy this requirement.

IV. CONCLUSION

Although the question of when it might be legitimate to reveal a public figure's extramarital affair remains a complex one, it is safe to say that it is unlikely that *A v B & C* would be decided in the same way today. Rather than focus on the transient nature of the relationship between the parties, a court considering whether a kiss-and-tell claimant had a reasonable expectation of privacy is more likely to emphasise the intimate nature of the sexual activities in question and the likely impact of the disclosures on the claimant's family and children. And when it comes to balancing privacy and freedom of expression, it seems unlikely that a court would see someone like Garry Flitcroft as enough of a role model to justify the privacy interference involved. The judgment does, however, contain important reminders that, even in the modern misuse of private information context, it is still important to consider the relational context in which information is disclosed and the individual freedom of expression of participants in the sexual relationship in question. And if someone really is a role model who is failing to live up to the expectations of his or her role, there will still be a public interest in information which reveals that.

So, some aspects of *A v B & C* have more ongoing relevance than others. This is understandable once the decision is seen as a creature of its time, ie, a period in which privacy law was finding its place within both the common law and society as a whole. To extend the landmark metaphor, *A v B & C* is perhaps best seen as a bridge between the relationship-focused breach of confidence action and the more broadly focused misuse of private information action we have today. So, whilst not all aspects of the Court's reasoning in *A v B & C* have endured, its significance in the development of the protection of privacy in England and Wales cannot be doubted.

V. POSTSCRIPT

For the media, *A v B & C* became something of a cause célèbre. The tabloid press – already resistant to the new privacy protections emerging in the courts – were determined to retain their freedom to publish salacious stories about celebrities and their sex lives. Once the injunction was lifted, coverage of the stories Garry Flitcroft had sought to suppress was therefore intense. The day after the injunction lapsed, for example, *The Mirror* devoted its entire front page to the words 'It's Garry Flitcroft'.[95]

Years later, Garry Flitcroft gave evidence to Sir Brian Leveson's 'Inquiry into the Culture, Practices and Ethics of the Press' on the nature and effect of this intense media interest on him and his family. Summarising this evidence, Sir Brian Leveson explained that:

> Between 20 and 25 journalists and photographers congregated outside Mr and Mrs Flitcroft's home. Other journalists went to the homes of other family members, including that of Mrs Flitcroft's father who was suffering from Parkinson's disease and found the episode extremely distressing. In the months that followed, Mrs Flitcroft was forced to stop taking her children to school to avoid journalists and photographers while on the school run. Mr and Mrs Flitcroft's marriage broke down. Mr Flitcroft said that, even today, his children suffer teasing and abuse in relation to the stories.[96]

Sir Brian Leveson doubted whether Mrs Flitcroft had, as one journalist had suggested to him, benefited from finding out about her husband's affair given that it had happened 'in the gaze of the tabloid press, hounded by photographers, and forced [her] to hide from public'.[97] The impact on Garry Flitcroft's father was also described as 'catastrophic':

> A long-term sufferer of depression, he found it very difficult to deal with the press coverage about his son. Having attended every football match since his son was aged seven, he stopped going to football matches to avoid the humiliation of listening to the chants and mockery from other fans. Mr Flitcroft believed that his failure to attend football matches after the publication of the story was a significant factor in the worsening of his depression, which tragically ended in his suicide in 2008.[98]

This evidence provides a valuable insight into what happens to claimants like Garry Flitcroft after a claim for an injunction is lost and more generally, into the harm that press intrusion and unwanted disclosures of personal information can cause. At the time that *A v B & C* was decided, discussion of those effects – either in case law or public discourse – was still limited. Few privacy cases had gone to trial and it was to be some years before a significant body of evidence emerged (from the Leveson Inquiry itself and cases like *Mosley* and *Gulati v MGN Ltd*) on the impact of privacy intrusions by the media.[99] As Sir Brian Leveson acknowledged in his Report, Garry Flitcroft's evidence brought home

[95] *The Mirror* 30 March 2002.

[96] Sir B Leveson, Vol II of *An Inquiry into the Culture, Practices and Ethics of the Press* (London, The Stationery Office, 2021) Part F at [2.33].

[97] ibid, at [2.36].

[98] ibid, at [2.34].

[99] *Mosley* (n 19) and *Gulati v MGN Ltd* [2015] EWHC 1482 (Ch). See also NA Moreham and Y Tinsley 'The Impact of Grief Journalism On its Subjects: Lessons From the Pike River Mining Disaster' [2019] *Journal of Media Law* 1.

that what might be a run-of-the-mill 'kiss and tell' to a newspaper will 'always be a big story to the subjects of the story and their families'.[100] None of this is to say that information about the sexual activities of public figures or other individuals should never be published; sometimes there will be a legitimate public interest in doing so. When deciding whether that is the case, however, the significant personal consequences of publication for both the subjects and their families should not be disregarded.

[100] Leveson (n 96) Part F at [2.36].

8

Campbell v Mirror Group Newspapers (2004)

GAVIN PHILLIPSON*

I. INTRODUCTION

OF ALL THE cases considered in this volume, the decision of the then House of Lords in *Campbell v Mirror Group Newspapers*[1] must be considered one of the most significant landmarks in the development of privacy law. To mark the ten-year anniversary of the decision, some of the papers from a conference on the subject were published in the *Journal of Media Law*.[2] In their Introduction to 'The *Campbell* Legacy', Tom Bennett and Daithí Mac Síthigh refer to the case as 'the most dramatic' development in media law since the HRA, a decision that is 'rightly regarded as seminal'.[3] *Campbell* indeed made a series of decisive advances in the development of English privacy law that were so strong and significant that the case effectively birthed a new tort – misuse of private information. As Bennett and Síthigh note, it also proved of major influence internationally:

> Courts in Canada and New Zealand have, whilst developing their own privacy torts, given substantial consideration to the *Campbell* model. Furthermore, the Australian Law Reform Commission recently recommended the adoption of a 'misuse of private information' tort, taking its preferred nomenclature directly from *Campbell*.[4]

Remarkably also, for a legal culture that has generally proved reluctant to do more than follow the caselaw of the European Court of Human Rights,[5] the

* Grateful thanks to the editors for their patience with this chapter and very helpful editorial comments.

[1] [2004] UKHL 22; [2004] 2 AC 457 (hereafter '*Campbell*').

[2] See the papers in (2015) 7(2) *Journal of Media Law*.

[3] ibid 152.

[4] ibid.

[5] See *R (Ullah) v Special Adjudicator* [2004] UKHL 26, [2004] 2 AC 323 and subsequent cases including *Moohan v Lord Advocate (Advocate General for Scotland intervening)* [2014] UKSC 67; [2015] AC 901 at para 105 and *R (on the application of AB (Appellant) v Secretary of State for Justice (Respondent)* [2021] UKSC 28, [2022] AC 487 at 54–59 stressing that courts should not provide 'more generous' rights than those enunciated by the Strasbourg Court.

decision was a very rare example of a domestic court anticipating Strasbourg on a point of major importance by finding that Article 8 did indeed require a cause of action between private parties for invasion of privacy – something by no means clear till then.

Thus *Campbell* – the biggest milestone in the development of a tort that fused common law development with human rights principles drawn from the ECHR – was remarkable in doing so by making major innovations at *both* these levels. Not only was effectively a new tort fashioned from elements of breach of confidence, but the human rights principles being used to drive that process were themselves taken forward well beyond the stage the Strasbourg Court itself had reached; moreover, *Campbell* did this, not only on the Article 8 issue, but on how, in such 'horizontal' disputes, the tension with Article 10 should be handled. As I will argue below, this is part of a broader tendency in the judgment – its 'big picture' approach. I will contend that, whereas the approach of the Court of Appeal in the case was dry, technocratic, unimaginative, and unsympathetic, the judgment of the House of Lords was a *transformation*, not just of the law, but in the recognition and exposition of the human rights and human values at stake.

Perhaps most importantly, *Campbell* was no mere flash in the pan: the momentous changes it made have firmly bedded down in the law since then and key aspects of the decision are still regularly cited and applied to this day. The broad and flexible 'reasonable expectation test' which emerged from the decision avoids bogging the law down in the unworkable 'categories' approach to privacy, whereby *only* personal information that falls into fixed, defined categories (health, sexuality, family life etc) can be protected.[6] Instead, in broadly following models of privacy that rest on the individual's 'informational autonomy',[7] or their desire not to have their personal information accessed against their wishes,[8] it has left the new tort open to develop organically and incrementally in classic common law fashion. Thus, the most recent major appellate decision handed down in 2022 – *ZXC v Bloomberg*[9] – used the *Campbell* test, as expounded and refined by subsequent cases,[10] to find a reasonable expectation of privacy in the fact of being under criminal investigation by the state, pre-charge.[11]

[6] For a persuasive critique of the 'categories' approach, see NA Moreham, 'Privacy in the Common Law' (2005) 121 *LQR* 628, 642–43.

[7] *Campbell*, Lord Hale, [134]; understandings of privacy as control over personal information have been put forward by several scholars including A Westin, *Privacy and Freedom* (London, The Bodley Head Ltd, 1970); R Wacks, *The Protection of Privacy* (London, Blackstone, 1980) 10–20.

[8] Moreham, n 6 above; her approach draws on R Gavison 'Privacy and the Limits of Law' (1980) 89(3) *Yale Law Journal* 421.

[9] *Bloomberg LP (Appellant) v ZXC (Respondent)* [2022] UKSC 5.

[10] Particularly *Murray v Express Newspapers plc* [2008] EWCA Civ 446, [2009] Ch 481 esp. [36].

[11] For an argument supporting this outcome, see R Craig and G Phillipson 'Privacy, Reputation and Anonymity Until Charge: *ZXC* goes to the Supreme Court' (2021) 13(2) *Journal of Media Law* 153–185 available open access: doi.org/10.1080/17577632.2021.2016211.

Finally, *Campbell* established a new approach to balancing privacy rights with freedom of speech, correcting several problems that had bedevilled the caselaw until then and establishing both the presumptive equality of the two rights and a sophisticated methodology for resolving the conflict between them in individual cases. It is fair to say, however, that this aspect of the decision – and its application in subsequent caselaw – has remained controversial; this chapter responds to a particularly important critique of this aspect both of *Campbell* and its legacy.[12]

The approach of this chapter is straightforward; after a brief reminder of the facts and key findings of the case in Part II, Part III will explore the remarkably different tone and approach of the House of Lords judgment, as contrasted with that of the Court of Appeal. Part IV will briefly survey the key developments made by Campbell, explaining their significance and how they have shaped the caselaw to this day. Finally, Part V will seek to answer the critique just mentioned.

II. *CAMPBELL:* THE FACTS AND FINDINGS

Given how well known the case is, only a brief description will be given. Naomi Campbell brought an action in breach of confidence[13] after the *Mirror* newspaper had published details of her treatment for drug addiction with Narcotics Anonymous (NA). Crucially, the coverage included surreptitiously-taken photographs of her leaving the clinic and hugging other clients, which made the location of the NA centre that Campbell had been attending clearly identifiable to anyone familiar with the area.[14] In the trial, the information in question was divided into five classes:

(1) the fact of Miss Campbell's drug addiction;
(2) the fact that she was receiving treatment;
(3) the fact that she was receiving treatment at Narcotics Anonymous;
(4) the details of the treatment – how long she had been attending meetings, how often she went, how she was treated within the sessions themselves, the extent of her commitment, and the nature of her entrance on the specific occasion; and
(5) the visual portrayal [through photographs] of her leaving a specific meeting with other addicts.[15]

[12] P Wragg 'Protecting Private Information of Public Interest: Campbell's Great Promise, unfulfilled' (2015) 7(2) *Journal of Media Law* 225.

[13] She also claimed for breaches of the Data Protection Act 1998 which were found to stand or fall with the main action in confidence: *Campbell*, [32] and [130].

[14] As Lord Nicholls found, *Campbell*, [5].

[15] ibid, [23].

The applicant had conceded that the *Mirror* was entitled to publish the information in categories (1) and (2) – the vital fact that she was a drug addict and was receiving treatment for her addiction. This was because it was accepted that the press was entitled to expose the falsity of her previous public statements that she did not take drugs and was not a drug addict. The dispute therefore centred around whether publishing the further details and the photographs (categories (3)–(5)) could attract liability. The Court of Appeal had found that the extra details in these categories simply gave colour and interest to a legitimate story.[16] This finding was overturned by the House of Lords on a three to two majority, Lord Hope, Lord Carswell and Lady Hale in the majority; Lord Nicholls and Lord Hoffmann in the minority.

The majority found that the additional material in categories (3)–(5) constituted particularly intrusive revelations, in which Campbell had a reasonable expectation of privacy, since information relating to health and therapeutic treatment was obviously private. It was held further that the revelations risked serious damage to the treatment that Campbell was undergoing, by destroying her belief in the confidentiality and anonymity of the process, thus risking a relapse in her struggles against drug addiction. While her expectation of privacy had to be balanced against the Article 10 rights of the *Mirror*, the majority found that these extra details made little or no contribution to the public interest and so were outweighed by Campbell's strong privacy interests in them. Although she was a famous public figure, this did not deprive her of her privacy rights in relation to categories (3)–(5). While there was a public interest in putting the record straight about her previous misleading statements that she did not use drugs, this did not extend to the additional intrusive details, including the photographs, to which she objected.

An important feature of the decision is that, although their Lordships divided on the application of the relevant principles to the facts, they largely agreed on key aspects of those new principles. As Lord Hoffmann put it:

> the importance of this case lies in the statements of general principle on the way in which the law should strike a balance between the right to privacy and the right to freedom of expression, on which the House is unanimous.[17]

Indeed, the dissents of Lords Nicholls and Hoffmann are probably as much cited in subsequent caselaw as the speeches of the majority. This unanimity on key points of principle may have helped give the decision much of its enduring power, despite some typical common-law style attempts, particularly by the majority judges, to present what was happening as merely an application of *existing* law.[18] These examples in the judgment of what Sedley LJ nicely

[16] [2002] EWCA Civ 1373, [2003] QB 633, 661 (hereafter *Campbell, CA*).

[17] ibid, [36].

[18] I analysed this tendency in detail in 'The Common Law, Privacy and the Convention', in H Fenwick, R Masterman and G Phillipson (eds), *Judicial Reasoning under the UK Human Rights Act* (Cambridge, CUP, 2007) 215–234 and so do not go over it here.

identifies as the 'perennial need' of the common law 'to appear not to be doing anything for the first time'[19] should not obscure the remarkable degree to which *Campbell* was, truly, transformative.

III. CONTRASTING THE JUDGMENTS OF THE HOUSE OF LORDS AND COURT OF APPEAL

When one reads the two judgments, two striking differences are immediately apparent. Essentially, the approach of the House of Lords – *including* the dissenters – is both principled and humanistic. That is, their Lordships recognised and expounded both the fundamental principles at stake *and* the human vulnerability and struggle at the centre of the case. In contrast, the Court of Appeal was brusque – the central breach of confidence claim is disposed of in only 16 pages – formalist, and insensitive both to the issues of principles engaged and the human condition of the claimant. These contrasts are pervasive.

A. The Judgment of the Court of Appeal

In doctrinal terms, the Court of Appeal's approach was dryly formalist; for example the Court refuses to see the photographs as of any significance: the relevant confidential *information* was conveyed by the text so the photos on their own added nothing.[20] In other words, while the photos *may* have caused Campbell distress, since the issue was purely to do with whether sufficiently sensitive *confidential facts* were revealed, that distress could not be slotted into any of the limbs of the cause of action the Court must consider and must therefore be disregarded. As for principle, there was no citation of any Article 8 caselaw and very little influence from the ECHR overall; indeed, the single case cited was on the Article 10 side (*Fressoz v France*).[21] In this specific matter, the case was typical of the trend reversed by the House of Lords. As this author noted at the time, a single decision of the Australian High Court – *Lenah Game Meats* – had been having 'far more influence on the development of confidence as a privacy remedy than any principles derived from Article 8'.[22]

So determined to be dryly objective was the Court that, when applying the then current 'high offensiveness' test, it revealingly declined to ask whether Naomi Campbell herself had found the publication of the details of her treatment and photo of her at the clinic offensive. Instead, it asked whether a

[19] *Douglas v Hello!* [2001] QB 967, 997.
[20] *Campbell (CA)*, [32–34].
[21] (2001) 31 EHRR 2.
[22] G Phillipson, 'Transforming breach of confidence? Towards a common law right of privacy under the Human Rights Act' (2003) 66(5) *MLR* 726, 731, citing n 70 below.

hypothetical 'reasonable reader' would have felt such offence, as if the purpose of privacy laws is not to protect the individual from intrusions into their private life but – as if it were a law on public decency – to stop *readers* from feeling offence:

> We do not consider that a reasonable person of ordinary sensibilities, on reading that Miss Campbell was a drug addict, would find it highly offensive, or even offensive that the Mirror also disclosed that she was attending meetings of Narcotics Anonymous. The reader might have found it offensive that what were obviously covert photographs had been taken of her, but that, of itself, is not relied upon as ground for legal complaint.[23]

The Court of Appeal judgment is also notable for its total lack of appreciation of the nature of the struggle against drug addiction that Naomi Campbell had been going through: the issues are seen largely through the lens of the newspaper editor. For example, the articles attacking Campbell published after she sent her letter before action to the *Mirror* are described simply as 'unsympathetic' by the Court, with no details given. In the House of Lords, Lord Nicholls (dissenting!) describes them as 'offensive and disparaging'[24] and as 'the subsequent mean-spirited attack, with its shabby reference to a chocolate soldier, made by the 'Mirror' on a person known to be peculiarly vulnerable'.[25] Even when adverting to the distress Naomi Campbell herself *may* have felt the tone remains decidedly un-empathic:

> We do not believe that it can have been easy in practice to separate the distress Miss Campbell felt at being identified as a drug addict, together with the distress she felt at the intrusion of the covert photographs, from any additional distress that she felt at the disclosure that she was attending meetings of Narcotics Anonymous. If that additional distress was, however, significant, we consider that Miss Campbell was, in that respect, over sensitive.[26]

Meanwhile, the publication of precisely the deeply intrusive details about which Campbell complained – where and how she was being treated, together with the photographs betraying its location to the world (thus inviting paparazzi to hang around the area) – are portrayed as an act of *sympathy* by the editor of the *Mirror:*

> Mr Morgan was making what had been accepted to have been proper disclosure of the discreditable fact that Miss Campbell was a drug addict. We think it harsh to criticise him for painting a somewhat fuller picture in order to show her in a sympathetic light.

The Court here seems to miss the point: it is not a disciplinary tribunal, so the issue does not concern 'criticising' a journalist or editor. The point was that the

[23] *Campbell* (CA), [54].
[24] *Campbell*, [9].
[25] ibid, [35].
[26] *Campbell, CA*, [55].

further details invaded Campbell's privacy far more than simply revealing her addiction and attempt to seek treatment. Moreover, the article could easily have been sympathetic in *tone*, without including the photos of Campbell outside – and details of her treatment at – Narcotics Anonymous to which she so objected.

A nice example of the Court's perspective is its argument that leaving out the intrusive details would have been 'unreal' and 'absurd':

> The primary information that had been conveyed to the appellants was that Miss Campbell was regularly attending Narcotics Anonymous. The fact that she was a drug addict was a secondary inference from this primary fact ... We find the suggestion that the Mirror should have published the secondary inference without publishing the primary fact from which this inference was drawn to be lacking in realism. What is it suggested that the Mirror should have published? 'Naomi Campbell is a drug addict. The Mirror has discovered that she is receiving treatment for her addiction'? Such a story, without any background detail to support it, would have bordered on the absurd.[27]

B. Judgment of the House of Lords

The treatment of the same case by the House of Lords forms an extraordinary contrast. On reading it, one is immediately struck by how the formalistic analysis of the Court of Appeal about duties of confidence, and what might, or might not, be offensive to readers, gives way in the House of Lords to the broad sweep of principle and a keen grasp of the human struggle at the heart of the case. Thus Lord Nicholls approaches the whole thing through the lens of privacy – whose importance is eloquently expressed at the outset as 'lying at the heart of liberty'.[28] Without worrying about the highly technical debate around 'horizontal effect', Lord Nicholls simply turns to applying 'the values underlying Arts 8 and 10'.[29] The point is not just the approach I have noted above, of using the Convention rights as the key framing and influence, in contrast to the Commonwealth-common law approach of the Court of Appeal, but what goes with it – the broad, normative approach of the House of Lords as compared to the narrow, doctrinal reasoning of the Court of Appeal. Even though Lord Nicholls found against Campbell, one can immediately note the difference between talk of offending readers by disclosing details and asking:

> did the further information relating to her attendance at Narcotics Anonymous meetings *retain its character of private information sufficiently to engage the protection afforded by article 8?* I doubt whether it did.[30]

[27] ibid, [62].
[28] *Campbell*, [12].
[29] ibid, [16]–[19].
[30] ibid, [25]–[26] (emphasis added).

We saw above how the appeal to those 'statements of general principle' on which the Lordships were agreed comes at the very start of Lord Hoffmann's speech.[31] One such crucial principle was that the law should now recognise private information not merely as something that may be subject to duties of confidentiality in certain specific circumstances but rather, per Lord Hoffmann, 'as something worth protecting as an aspect of human autonomy and dignity'.[32] This recognition is transformative:

> Instead of the cause of action being based upon the duty of good faith applicable to confidential personal information and trade secrets alike, it focuses upon the protection of human autonomy and dignity – the right to control the dissemination of information about one's private life and the right to the esteem and respect of other people.[33]

As we will see in Part V below, the same approach is evident in the way the House of Lords seeks a proper resolution of the competing Article 8 and 10 rights.

When it comes to the level of human concern and awareness of what they were dealing with, the contrast between how *all* their Lordships write and the desiccated language of the Court of Appeal is even stronger. Thus Lord Nicholls, even though he found against Campbell on the photos, as well as the other intrusive details, said:

> I say at once that I wholly understand why Miss Campbell felt she was being hounded by the 'Mirror'. I understand also that this could be deeply distressing, even damaging, to a person whose health was still fragile. But this is not the subject of complaint.[34]

Lord Hope in some ways took the most 'orthodox' approach to the case, but it is striking how eloquently he explains just why intrusion into treatment for drug addiction is so invasive and damaging:

> … there are few areas of the life of an individual that are more in need of protection on the grounds of privacy than the combating of addiction to drugs or to alcohol. It is hard to break the habit which has led to the addiction. It is all too easy to give up the struggle if efforts to do so are exposed to public scrutiny. The struggle, after all, is an intensely personal one. It involves a high degree of commitment and of self-criticism. The sense of shame that comes with it is one of the most powerful of all the tools that are used to break the habit. But shame increases the individual's vulnerability as the barriers that the habit has engendered are broken down. The smallest hint that the process is being watched by the public may be enough to persuade the individual to delay or curtail the treatment.[35]

[31] Above, text to n 17.
[32] ibid, [50].
[33] ibid, [51].
[34] *Campbell*, [30].
[35] ibid, [81].

And again, here focusing on why strict confidentiality is an essential aspect of the kind of group therapy used at NA:

> It is well known that persons who are addicted to the taking of illegal drugs or to alcohol can benefit from meetings at which they discuss and face up to their addiction. The private nature of these meetings encourages addicts to attend them in the belief that they can do so anonymously. The assurance of privacy is an essential part of the exercise. The therapy is at risk of being damaged if the duty of confidence which the participants owe to each other is breached by making details of the therapy.[36]

And Lord Hope, unlike the Court of Appeal, insists that the legal test must, as it were, stand imaginatively in the shoes of a drug addict: it is *this* person who needs to be considered, not some hypothetical reasonable reader:

> The context was that of a drug addict who was receiving treatment. It is her sensibilities that needed to be taken into account. Critical to this exercise was an assessment of whether disclosure of the details would be liable to disrupt her treatment. It does not require much imagination to appreciate the sense of unease that disclosure of these details would be liable to engender, especially when they were accompanied by a covertly taken photograph. The message that it conveyed was that somebody, somewhere, was following her, was well aware of what was going on and was prepared to disclose the facts to the media.[37]

The contrast with the 'quite unreal'[38] approach of the Court of Appeal is stark.

Baroness Hale's approach is similar. Indeed, she starts her judgment by sketching a caricature of the case – 'a prima donna celebrity against a celebrity-exploiting tabloid newspaper'[39] – precisely in order to explain why this easy, tempting picture seriously understates the importance of the case:

> Drug abuse can be seriously damaging to physical health; indeed it is sometimes life-threatening. It can also lead to a wide variety of recognised mental disorders (see The ICD-10 Classification of Mental and Behavioural Disorders, WHO 1992, F10 – F 19). Drug addiction needs treatment if it is to be overcome. Treatment is at several levels .... There is therapy aimed at tackling that underlying dependence, which may be combined with a transfer of the dependence from illegal drugs to legally prescribed substitutes. Then there is therapy aimed at maintaining and reinforcing the resolve to keep up the abstinence achieved and prevent relapse. This is vital. Anyone who has had anything to do with drug addiction knows how easy it is to relapse once returned to the temptations of the life in which it began and how necessary it is to try, try and try again to achieve success.[40]

Placed in this context, as Lady Hale argues, it is easy to see why the *Mirror's* story, far from being one about which Campbell had merely been 'over sensitive',

[36] ibid, [95].
[37] ibid, [98].
[38] ibid, [99] (Lord Hope).
[39] ibid, [143].
[40] ibid, [144].

as the Court of Appeal so brusquely put it,[41] was potentially deeply damaging. For as her Ladyship noted, the leaking of details from inside the clinic 'contributed to the sense of betrayal by someone close to [Campbell] of which she spoke, and which destroyed the value of Narcotics Anonymous as a safe haven for her'.[42] Meanwhile the picture showing the location of the clinic 'added to the potential harm, by making her think that she was being followed or betrayed, and deterring her from going back to the same place again'.[43] Then, in direct contrast to the Court of Appeal's imagined 'absurd' story, giving only the bare facts without the complained-of details and photographs,[44] Lady Hale points out that there was no necessity for these intrusive and destructive details:

> There was no need to do this. The editor accepted that even without the photographs, it would have been a front-page story. He had his basic information, and he had his quotes. There is no shortage of photographs with which to illustrate and brighten up a story about Naomi Campbell.[45]

Even the brief judgment of Lord Carswell portrays the case in human terms; the story, he said:

> revealed where the treatment was taking place and the text went into the frequency of her treatment. In this way it intruded into what had some of the characteristics of medical treatment and it tended to deter her from continuing the treatment which was in her interest and also to inhibit other persons attending the course from staying with it, when they might be concerned that their participation might become public knowledge.[46]

What is the significance of the contrast I have sought to draw out? I would characterise it as a vivid manifestation of how the whole approach of the House of Lords, as well as the actual decision, transformed this area of law. The notion of confidentiality – the basis on which the action was originally brought – is not a human rights principle. Governmental bodies of all kinds need to and do keep certain classes of information confidential, and the British government famously used the breach of confidence action to try to prevent publication of the whistleblowing book, *Spycatcher*, about illegal activities of the Security Services.[47] All large organisations, including corporations, generate confidential information and may wish to use breach of confidence to prevent or deter the release of commercially sensitive, valuable or damaging information.[48] Thus the point of

[41] Above, n 26.
[42] ibid, [153].
[43] ibid, [155].
[44] Above, text to n 27.
[45] *Campbell*, [156].
[46] ibid, [165].
[47] *Attorney-General v Guardian Newspapers Ltd (No 2)* [1990] 1 AC 109.
[48] *Shelley Films Limited v Rex Features Limited* [1994] EMLR 134; *Coco v AN Clark (Engineers) Limited* [1969] RPC 41; *Li Yau-wai v Genesis Films Ltd.* [1987] HKLR 711.

this Part has been to highlight how the move to thinking and speaking about the case as centring around the protection of *privacy* – a *human* right, that only natural persons can claim – naturally brought with it not only an engagement with the values underlying that claim, like dignity and autonomy, but also a keen awareness of the human cost of invasions of privacy. The next Part draws out the doctrinal innovations by which this transformation came about.

IV. CAMPBELL'S MULTIPLE INNOVATIONS

A. Transforming English Law: From Breach of Confidence to Misuse of Private Information

Breach of confidence had long been recognised[49] as the action most capable of filling the notorious gap in English law deplored by the Court of Appeal in *Kaye* v *Robertson*[50] – considered in this volume by Jacob Rowbottom.[51] Post the Human Rights Act, it was also seen as the likeliest common law route by which to satisfy the court's own duty to act compatibly with the ECHR rights under that Act.[52] As Lord Woolf famously observed in *A* v *B*:

> Under section 6 of the [Human Rights Act], the court, as a public authority, is required not to act 'in a way which is incompatible with a Convention right.' The court is able to achieve this by absorbing the rights which articles 8 and 10 protect into the long-established action for breach of confidence.[53]

I have dealt extensively elsewhere[54] with how both the findings in *Campbell* and the expansive dicta that accompanied them brought about the decisive transformation from even the extended and more flexible action in confidence seen in earlier cases, to reach the point at which Lord Nicholls could say 'The essence of the tort is better encapsulated now as misuse of private information.'[55] Hence only the briefest rehearsal is needed here, with a reminder that breach of confidence traditionally required, first, information with the quality of confidence and second, 'circumstances importing an obligation of confidence'[56] – previously,

[49] See H Fenwick and G Phillipson, 'Privacy and Confidence: A Re-Examination' (1996) 55(3) *CLJ* 447–455.

[50] [1991] FSR 62.

[51] See ch 5.

[52] Under s 6 (1) and (3) Human Rights Act 1998.

[53] [2002] EWCA Civ 337, [2002] 3 WLR 542, 546. The case is considered by Nicole Moreham in this volume: ch 7. The Court of Appeal in *Campbell* made the lesser finding that they were bound to 'have regard to' both Articles 8 and 10 in deciding such cases: [2003] QB 633, 658.

[54] 'The Right of Privacy in England and Strasbourg compared' in A Kenyon and M Richardson (eds), *New Directions in Privacy Law: International and Comparative Perspectives* (Cambridge, CUP, 2006) 184, 187–202. I draw on this briefly in the explanation that follows. See also H Fenwick and G Phillipson, *Media Freedom under the UK Human Rights Act* (Oxford, OUP, 2006) ch 14.

[55] *Campbell*, [14].

[56] *Coco v A N Clark (Engineers) Ltd* [1969] RPC 41.

an express agreement or established relationship of confidence, reduced more recently by the time of *Campbell*, to some objective indications that a given scene or piece of information was to be treated as confidential.[57] The crucial point in *Campbell* came from the fact that liability was imposed in respect of the photographs taken in the street outside NA: this was the first time that an English appellate court had imposed liability for use of personal information, in the absence of any circumstances imposing the obligation save for the private nature of the information itself. And since the first limb – the nature of the information – alone imposed the obligation, then the second limb of confidence simply fell away.[58]

As to the former first limb, this too underwent a decisive change: while the details of the treatment had been leaked from inside NA in an obvious and traditional breach of confidence, again the fact that liability was found for the photographs was crucial. It was because of this that *Campbell* logically entailed the final abandonment of the test for the first limb being based upon the *confidentiality* of the information, as opposed to its private or personal character. As Jonathan Morgan, arguing *against* developments in confidence to give greater protection to privacy,[59] had said, confidentiality and privacy 'are radically different qualities' and, in particular, 'much private information is not confidential'.[60] He cited the very fact that information 'in the public domain' cannot be protected under the law of confidence as evidence for this proposition, including specifically within that category, photographs of an individual in a public space. Thus, the fact that such information – photographs of Campbell in the street outside NA – *was* protected in the decision, established definitively that the Law Lords were now asking whether the information related to private life, *not* whether it was confidential. Well-known dicta by their Lordships, finding a breach of the claimant's 'right to privacy',[61] identifying the new 'touchstone' as being 'whether in respect of the disclosed facts the person … had a reasonable expectation of privacy',[62] or asking, 'whether the information that was disclosed was private and not public',[63] make the 'shift in the centre of gravity'[64] by the decision unmistakeable. What the Court of Appeal was shortly to call 'The action formerly known as breach of confidence'[65] had become one

[57] As in *Shelley Films v Rex Features Ltd* [1994] EMLR 134 *Creation Records Ltd v News Group Newspapers Ltd* [1997] EMLR 444 and in the *Douglas v Hello!* litigation: *Douglas v Hello! Ltd* [2001] QB 967; [2003] 3 All ER 996; [2006] QB 125.

[58] As acknowledged by Morgan: 'Privacy in the House of Lords – Again' (2004) 120 *LQR* 563, 563–6.

[59] J Morgan, 'Privacy, Confidence, and Horizontal Effect: "Hello" Trouble' (2003) 62 *CLJ* 444, 452.

[60] ibid.

[61] Lord Carswell, *Campbell*, [171].

[62] ibid, Lord Nicholls, [21].

[63] ibid, Lord Hope, [92].

[64] ibid, Lord Hoffmann, [51].

[65] *Douglas III* [2006] QB 125, [53]. See further on the shift from the equitable action in confidence to the new privacy tort, Phillipson, 'Supreme Court confirms suspects' privacy rights: the judgment

that protected simply against misuse of private information. This shift had been underway for some time, but *Campbell* took the final and decisive steps from what had become an extended and more flexible action in breach of confidence to the new privacy tort.

As is now well-known, that tort now has two stages: the first, reasonable expectation of privacy test, involves asking first whether 'the information [in question is] private in the sense that it is in principle protected by article 8?'[66] If so, all the relevant circumstances (non-exhaustively enumerated as 'the *Murray* factors')[67] will be examined to see whether they serve to strengthen or negate that in-principle protection. Thus, stage one – in making satisfaction of part of an English tort claim dependent upon an Article 8 issue – itself exemplifies the fusion between common law and ECHR that *Campbell* engineered. If the claimant succeeds at the first stage, the court then considers whether, at the second stage, their prima facie reasonable expectation of privacy must give way to the defendant's interest in freedom of expression, something that, as discussed below in Part V, generally turns on an assessment of the public interest in the disputed publication.

It is true that, as Moreham points out, their Lordships were far from unanimous on the 'reasonable expectation' test in *Campbell*. This was partly because of the tendency in the judgment, noted above,[68] adopted particularly by Lord Hope, of seeking to give a greater appearance of continuity with existing law than was actually merited. Thus two other approaches from previous cases appeared in the speech of Lord Hope and Moreham was critical of the judgment at the time for producing what she referred to as 'three alternative tests'.[69] That probably overstated the matter, however, especially as Lord Hope made clear that two of them were actually part of one test: his Lordship, citing the Australian case of *Australian Broadcasting Corporation v Lenah Game Meats*,[70] had referred to some kinds of information being 'obviously private' but that, if they were not, asking whether their revelation would be '"highly offensive to a reasonable person of ordinary sensibilities"' could be a useful practical step.[71] Moreover, it was perhaps a little mischievous of Moreham to suggest that Lord Hope was suggesting 'obviously private' as a *test* – and one that was at variance with the reasonable expectation approach. I read Lord Hope as simply observing that some kinds of information are easy to identify as private, an approach that – though he did not say so – in fact fits perfectly well within the broad reasonable expectation of privacy test. In any event, the overall logic of

clarified, two criticisms answered' (2022) *Journal of Media Law* https://doi.org/10.1080/17577632.2022.2139568.

[66] *McKennitt v Ash* [2006] EWCA Civ 1714, [2008] QB 73 at [11].

[67] Above, n 10.

[68] Above, text to nn 18–19.

[69] Above, n 6, 632–34.

[70] [2001] HCA 63.

[71] Moreham herself notes (n 6 above) that these two elements are part of the same test, citing Lord Hope in *Campbell*, [94]–[96].

Campbell's approach to using Article 8 principles ensured that the 'high offensiveness test', borrowed from Australia but with no mooring in Article 8, rapidly and rightly fell away: hence the reasonable expectation of privacy test decisively emerged as stage one of the new tort the decision birthed.

B. Interpreting Article 8 ECHR

As noted in the Introduction, *Campbell* was one of the rare English cases that actually anticipated Strasbourg in elucidating what that Court would call 'positive obligations' under Article 8 – here, the possible duty on the state to provide a remedy for intrusion into private life by private parties, in particular, the press. In domestic law, this of course is achieved via the courts' duties as public authorities to act compatibly with Articles 8 and 10 in developing and applying what, as we just saw, became the tort of misuse of private information. What was remarkable about *Campbell* is that, reading sections 2[72] and 6 HRA together, courts *generally* only give domestic effect to what the Strasbourg Court has found to be the requirements of Article 8. In *Campbell* however, the House of Lords broke genuinely new ground in the interpretation of what Article 8 required. As argued previously, it was by no means clear by the time the case reached the House of Lords, that Article 8 *required* states to furnish a remedy for individuals against non-state bodies for intrusion into private life: indeed the Strasbourg caselaw at the time was 'meagre, with no directly relevant successful applications'.[73] The seminal decision in *Von Hannover v Germany*[74], considered by Kirsty Hughes in this volume,[75] did give a definitive answer to that question – but not until *after* the House of Lords had decided *Campbell.* Thus, at the Strasbourg level, it was not clear that Article 8 actually required what the House of Lords so boldly used it to achieve in *Campbell.*

Meanwhile, at the level of domestic law, the much-debated conundrum of whether, under the HRA, courts could, should or must develop common law compatibly with the ECHR rights in cases where no public authority were involved was still unresolved, despite the confident dicta of Lord Woolf noted above.[76] Indeed, we noted above how minimal the impact of Article 8 had actually been in the caselaw prior to *Campbell.*[77] These two factors make the boldness with which their Lordships put Articles 8 and 10 to work in the judgment hugely

[72] The duty to have regard to the Strasbourg caselaw: for the caselaw on it, see above, n 5.

[73] G Phillipson and H Fenwick, 'Breach of Confidence as a Privacy Remedy in the Human Rights Act Era' (2000) 63(5) *MLR* 660, 664–667.

[74] (2005) 40 EHRR 1.

[75] See ch 9.

[76] Above, n 53.

[77] Above, text to n 22.

striking, even if *Campbell cannot* be said to have provided a clear resolution to the UK horizonal effect debate in general.[78]

V. THE CAMPBELL APPROACH TO BALANCING FREE SPEECH AND PRIVACY: A REPLY TO PAUL WRAGG

A. The Wragg Critique of *Campbell* and its Legacy

Amongst the papers published to mark the tenth anniversary of *Campbell*, one by Paul Wragg, one of the editors of this volume, praised the judgment as 'a momentous decision', an example of 'judicial activism [by which] British judges pioneer effective rights protection and influence European human rights law'.[79] However, Wragg argued that, despite the 'great promise' of the decision, it had a fatal flaw that had infected the whole of the subsequent case law. Given the importance of this criticism, this seems a fitting place to offer a partial response to it.

The essence of Wragg's argument is that *Campbell* – and the decision in *Re S*[80] in which Lord Steyn summarised the principles deriving from it – speak of using proportionality to balance Articles 8 and 10, firmly said by both judgments to be of *equal* importance. However, Wragg says, the reality is that this does not happen. This is partly because:

> …*Campbell* poses a question that it does not answer. If cases are to be determined by 'balancing' the respective claims then what is the unit of measurement by which the extent of public interest in expression is assessed?[81]

In the absence of guidance as to how to assess the importance of particular speech claims, he argues that, rather than undertaking a detailed analysis of whether such claims *outweigh* the privacy right of the claimant on the facts, there is 'usually little or no real comparison of the two'.[82] In fact, while courts consider not only the existence but the *gravity* of an invasion of privacy, 'when judges discuss the free speech claim, they do not measure its weight'.[83] Hence, at stage two, 'judges do not balance but, instead, apply [a] simple rule'. That is, 'either the privacy claim fails because there is a public interest in publication, or it succeeds because there is no such public interest'.[84]

[78] G Phillipson, 'Clarity Postponed: Horizontal Effect after Campbell and Re S' in n 18 above; N Bamforth 'Horizontal Effect of Human Rights in the UK and Canada' in I Loveland (ed), *British and Canadian Public Law in Comparative Perspective* (Oxford, Hart, 2022).

[79] Above, n 12, 225.

[80] *Re S* [2005] 1 AC 593, [17].

[81] Above, n 12, 226.

[82] ibid 227.

[83] ibid.

[84] ibid 226.

His conclusion then is that:

> Since privacy … can only succeed where public interest expression is not at stake, freedom of expression occupies a privileged position, rendering the prospective equality of the two rights largely redundant.[85]

In other words, instead of what is meant to be a complex and delicate analysis that resolves the conflict between the two rights in a principled way, courts apply a simple binary: once a reasonable expectation of privacy is found, if the speech is found to be of public interest, the press wins, if it is not, the claimant does. Not only does this fail to do what is promised, Wragg contends, but in practice, since privacy always loses to public interest speech, *Campbell*'s promise of presumptive equality between the two rights is also broken. Moreover, it is not just that *Campbell's* 'great promise' in this area that has not been fulfilled by subsequent cases, *Campbell* itself fails to live up to its own billing – because it does *not* 'demonstrate the proportionality exercise at work'.[86] These are serious criticisms indeed.

The first thing to say is that Wragg has put his finger on a really important point and a significant problem. He is quite right to say that, in the post-*Campbell* case law in general, the courts appear extremely reluctant to weigh up the claims of speech they find to have *some public interest* against the invasion of privacy the publication in question entails and decide which is more important and why. Thus, *as a matter of the post-Campbell caselaw*, Wragg is right to identify this as a problem, and one that, in some ways at least, appears still to privilege free speech over privacy, undermining the presumptive equality between the two that *Campbell* proclaimed.

Having made this important concession, I would however, give four reasons why I nevertheless consider Wragg's critique to be over-stated. First, *Campbell* did make an important advance in this regard, even if it does not go as far as Wragg would like. Second, *contra* Wragg, *Campbell does* show the proportionality analysis at work, at least to some extent. Third, it is not right to say that *Campbell* provides *no* answer to the question of how to weigh the two rights against each other: it does, albeit at quite a high level of generality. Wragg may want more detail and precision, but as I will argue, this may be asking more than is realistic. Finally, I suggest that, if we look behind what courts *say* they are doing, we may find that the reality is different and does not break the promise of *Campbell* in the way Wragg suggests. These points are taken in turn.

B. A Simple but Crucial Advance Made by *Campbell*

As just noted, one of Wragg's key claims is that *Campbell* fails to provide the necessary guidance to enable the speech side of the equation to be weighed or

[85] ibid.
[86] ibid 228.

evaluated. In response I would start by stressing that we need to keep distinct two different aspects of the balancing act that is performed. As I have previously put it:

> The satisfactory resolution of the potential conflict between Articles 8 and 10 must … be found at two levels. First there is the issue of the *structure* of the reasoning process by which the balancing act between the two rights should be undertaken. Second, there is the issue of *substance*: what principles should the court use to weigh the two rights against each other when carrying out this process?[87]

My argument here is that, in focusing on *Campbell's* shortcomings at the second level – of substance – Wragg does not give sufficient credit to the decision for the vital work it did at the first level of *structure*. I deal with the issue of substance below, in section D; for now, the point I wish to stress is that *Campbell* was *primarily* concerned with this first level: their Lordships, in setting out the new approach noted above, were seeking primarily to correct the structural imbalance between the two rights clearly apparent in much of the previous caselaw,[88] which manifested itself as a two-fold problem. The second of these is examined in section C below but the first is simple: while courts did make some attempt to evaluate the strength or otherwise of the Article 8 claim, this was not done *at all* for the speech side. The problem with this was that the consequent approach suffered from 'a structural imbalance' that prevented the fair resolution of the speech-privacy conflict.[89] I had thus argued before the House of Lords judgment that what was needed instead was for the *weight* of any Article 10 claim to be 'assessed by reference to the contribution that the publication in question makes to a debate of serious public concern' and recognition that 'where the speech makes no such contribution, it may readily be overridden by … Article 8'.[90]

It will be apparent that my concern here was thus the same as that of Wragg – judicial failure properly to weigh the speech side of the claim. My difference with Wragg is that I do not think he properly acknowledges that the issue requires consideration at the two levels enunciated above, and that *Campbell* did make an important advance in the first level. This is because it corrected

> the notable tendency … to treat the public interest in a story as wholly separate from the issue of the application of Article 10, taking the view that the latter is fully engaged even where the former is wholly absent.[91]

That tendency has at least been corrected – as Wragg notes, as a result of *Campbell* the courts do now enquire into whether or not the story – or distinct

[87] Above, n 54, 213.
[88] This structural imbalance had been critiqued by the author (above, n 22) – an article cited in *Campbell*, [17] that I understand was used by counsel in argument.
[89] Above, n 54, 214.
[90] ibid 216.
[91] ibid.

parts of it – do have any public interest value. This amounts to some attempt – even if a somewhat simplistic one – to do what the caselaw to date had not done and assess the *weight* of the Article 10 claim.[92]

It is important to stress that this was achieved only *because* all of their Lordships – including Lord Nicholls and Lord Hoffmann – rejected the notion of Article 10 having any presumptive priority over Article 8. Such priority had been assumed by courts in some previous judgments because judges had been following an approach, taken from Strasbourg, whereby a court deciding whether a given interference with free expression was necessary in a democratic society 'is faced not with a choice between two conflicting principles, but with a principle of freedom of expression that is subject to a number of exceptions which must be narrowly interpreted'.[93] The problem was that this approach was not designed to be used where the conflicting interest or 'exception' was itself another Convention right. When applied in such circumstances the result was that Article 8

> lost its Convention status as a fully-fledged right, becoming instead merely a narrowly interpreted exception to the right of freedom of expression. This in turn [produced] a striking asymmetry whereby the protection of the right to privacy would have to be justified as *necessary* in a democratic society, while the claims of free speech would be simply assumed.[94]

It was this tendency that led directly to the failure to ask whether there was any public interest value in the free speech claim: this was because the sole question being asked was whether the privacy claim was sufficiently weighty to justifying allowing it, exceptionally, to prevail against Article 10.

Hence the rejection by their Lordships of this effective downgrading of Article 8 by embracing instead the presumptive equality of the two rights was crucial. The dicta here are well known but clearest perhaps was Lord Hoffmann, in stressing that:

> There is in my view no question of automatic priority [of speech over privacy]. Nor is there a presumption in favour of one rather than the other. The question is rather the extent to which it is necessary to qualify the one right in order to protect the underlying value which is protected by the other. And the extent of the qualification must be proportionate to the need.[95]

Lord Hope took the same view, insisting that 'Neither article 8 nor article 10 has any pre-eminence over the other in the conduct of this exercise.'[96] Lady Hale

[92] Above, n 22, 756.
[93] ibid 749.
[94] Above, n 73, 686.
[95] *Campbell*, [55].
[96] ibid, [113].

agreed,[97] and in the subsequent House of Lords decision in that case, Lord Steyn, giving the unanimous opinion of the House, helpfully distilled the approach we have been discussing into four key principles which he said, 'clearly emerge[d] from the speeches' given in *Campbell*:

> First, neither article has as such precedence over the other. Secondly, where the values under the two articles are in conflict, an intense focus on the comparative importance of the specific rights being claimed in the individual case is necessary. Thirdly, the justifications for interfering with or restricting each right must be taken into account. Finally, the proportionality test must be applied to each.[98]

Thus, the judgment was emphatic in correcting the mistaken previous approach of either de jure or de facto treating freedom of expression as the primary right and privacy as a mere exception to it. This in turn meant that the court made at least some inquiry into the weight of the free speech claim. It did so by asking whether it engaged the public interest. Wragg of course complains that this leads to a binary enquiry – on which he is at least partly right; however, this critique should not be allowed to obscure this important, if basic advance. It is now so taken for granted that courts must enquire into the public interest value of a privacy-invading story that it is easy to forget that pre-*Campbell*, this often simply did not happen.

C. *Campbell* Does Use Proportionality – At Least Partially!

Here I respond to Wragg's claim that *Campbell* itself fails to carry out the proportionality exercise it advocates as the method for balancing the two rights. Here, while I concede that it did not do so fully, I contend that it did do so *to some extent*, because it corrected the second tendency I identified above as a structural flaw in the previous caselaw: the failure to deal with the level of intrusive detail in stories about private lives as a proportionality issue. This correction was a result of courts, from *Campbell* on, conducting the 'parallel analysis' outlined above, in which as their Lordships insist, *both parties* are required to justify the interference they propose to make with the other's right. This, inter alia, required judges to do something they had proved remarkably reluctant to do previously: ask whether the complained-of publication went further than was necessary in conveying the legitimate public interest elements of the story.

A well-known example of this tendency was the *A v B* case, considered by Moreham in chapter 7 – a good illustration precisely because much of the story went far beyond just revealing the affair between a premiership footballer and a lap dancer and instead was concerned with 'salacious descriptions of the sexual activity between the claimant and [two lap-dancers] intended for the

[97] ibid, [138] and [141].
[98] Above, n 80, [17].

prurient'.[99] The court treated this as a matter of 'taste' or editorial judgment, on which it should not intervene. However, this failed to take Article 8 seriously: doing so and hence employing a proportionality test would mean that 'interferences with it should be the minimum necessary to satisfy the other, competing right'. Under such an approach, the intimate details about sexual activity 'would have to be shown to be justifiable in terms of the value they added under Article 10'.[100]

My point here about *Campbell* is that it does take on this challenge: their Lordships accepted that it must be asked whether the level of intrusive detail contained in the publication in question went further then was necessary in carrying out the press's legitimate function of informing the public. As Lord Hope put it, 'Decisions about the publication of material that is private to the individual raise issues that are not simply about presentation and editing.'[101] Here he dealt squarely with the argument of the *Mirror* and the Court of Appeal that the decision to add the extra details about the Campbell situation – the fact that she was receiving treatment from NA, details of the therapy and the photos – lay within the legitimate discretionary choice of the journalists[102] – an idea enunciated in *Jersild v Denmark*[103] and *Fressoz v France*.[104] In the latter, quoted by the Court of Appeal in *Campbell*, the Strasbourg Court had said:

> It is not for this court, nor for the national courts for that matter, to substitute their own views for those of the press as to what technique of reporting should be adopted by journalists. In this context the court recalls that article 10 protects not only the substance of the ideas and information expressed, but also the form in which they are conveyed.[105]

The crucial point, however, as Lord Hope points out, is that neither of these Strasbourg cases involved a balance between Article 10 and another Convention right (Article 8). *Campbell*, however, did – and this transforms the nature of the appropriate legal analysis. Instead of extra details merely being a matter of taste or editorial discretion, each one the Mirror added constituted an additional and further invasion of Campbell's Article 8 rights.

The editor's argument in effect was that it was within the paper's sole discretion how much to infringe her Article 8 rights in order to make a good story. This, the Court of Appeal and – to an extent – the dissenters in *Campbell* accepted.[106] But a moment's thought shows that it cannot be right; it would

[99] Above n 53, 555F.
[100] Above, n 22, 753.
[101] *Campbell* 113.
[102] Above, n 27.
[103] (1994) 19 EHRR 1.
[104] (2001) 31 EHRR 28.
[105] Above, n 103, [31].
[106] Albeit Lord Hoffmann nuanced it by arguing that in light of her historic close and symbiotic relationship with the press, Campbell, in particular could not complain of the additional 'circumstantial detail': *Campbell*, [66].

in effect allow the balance struck between the two parties and their respective rights to be decided *by one of the parties themselves*, rather than an independent body – the court. Thus, the general statement from *Jersild cannot* simply be read across to a situation in which each additional detail further invaded someone's Article 8 rights. Recognising this, Lord Hope found:

> It is hard to see that there was any compelling need for the public to know the name of the organisation that she was attending for the therapy, or for the other details of it to be set out.[107]

This indeed was the whole basis for the finding in favour of Campbell by the majority: *because* the publication was examined in terms of the five classes described above,[108] the *Mirror* was required to *justify* the greater level of intrusion represented by the publication of the details of treatment and the photographs; and it was found that it had not discharged that burden. Moreover, the House of Lords made a real attempt to do what it said should be done – apply this proportionality approach to *both* parties. Thus, it was found that Campbell could not justify imposing liability for publishing the basic facts because of the legitimate public interest in them – something she had indeed conceded. *Both* sides therefore had to give some ground; the case turned upon working out a way of ensuring the minimum impairment of each person's rights. This retained a measure of both privacy *and* of free expression, rather than as in the Court of Appeal decision in *Campbell*, as well as in similar, pre-*Campbell* case law,[109] giving expression full rein, with the result that the competing privacy rights were wholly overridden.

Wragg would I think concede this point – that this aspect of the decision was an advance on simply asking whether a story *as a whole* was in the public interest, without breaking it down, as their Lordships did, to consider whether some particularly intrusive elements of it went further than necessary, given their lack of public interest. He is, however, right to say that there were elements of the proportionality balance that their Lordships did *not* really do – for example, explaining why exactly the right to reveal the basic facts of the story (the first two categories of information) overrode Campbell's privacy rights. Moreover, there is some potential inconsistency in the judgment between Baroness Hale's dicta that 'the possession and use of illegal drugs is a criminal offence and a matter of serious public concern' that the press must be free to reveal[110] and Lord Hoffmann's view below[111] that revealing a person's drug dependency would *not* generally be in the public interest. On closer inspection that apparent inconsistency can probably be resolved – Hale was stressing, as she said,

[107] ibid, [118].

[108] Above, n 15 and accompanying text.

[109] *A v B* (above n 53), *Theakston v MGN* [2002] EWHC 137 (QB), [2002] EMLR 22; *D* v *L* [2003] EWCA Civ 1169, [2004] EMLR 1.

[110] *Campbell*, [151].

[111] Below, text to n 118.

the importance of the press being free to 'expose the truth and put the record straight' about *Naomi Campbell's* previous false statements that she did *not* use drugs, while Lord Hoffmann was deliberately referring to the hypothetical position of 'an ordinary citizen' having their drug dependency revealed. But even if this is granted it remains the case that, as Wragg argues, their Lordships did not really attempt to explain *why* the importance of putting the record straight outweighed Campbell's privacy interests in relation to the first two categories of information about her drug addiction. I do think the concession by her Counsel that she was not disputing these revelations makes this omission forgivable. However, it does show that, while the decision, in breaking down the information into the five categories, *did* use a form of proportionality to resolve it, at another level it does still reveal the binary Wragg complains of: in relation to each category, it was found either to be of public interest or not, rather than being properly weighed and evaluated against the privacy interest.

I explain in section E below why I think this does not appear to happen in privacy cases but conclude this section by stressing again that even if only partially achieved, this was still the first time an English court had even *tried* to apply a dual proportionality test like this in a speech-privacy case. Even its partial success in doing so is, I believe, part of what makes it a landmark.

D. Does *Campbell* Show Us How to Weigh a Speech Claim?

I argued in section B above that *Campbell* did insist on the basic but vital point that courts must enquire into whether a given privacy-invading story serves the public interest or not. However, as noted above, Wragg complains that, beyond this simple point, the House of Lords failed to give guidance as to how the speech side of such cases is to be weighed or assessed – this being the level two issue of substance, noted above at p 175. In response I would argue that *Campbell* does provide *some* guidance on this point: it is simply not of the degree of precision Wragg would like,[112] and indeed uses principles to which he strongly objects. Despite the vagaries of its approach to assessing freedom of expression, I would argue that it is both broadly apparent in Strasbourg's Article 10 caselaw and both necessary and right. A full defence of this approach and argument against

[112] Wragg at one points sounds as if he is demanding the impossible when suggesting that the case should have provided a 'unit of measurement' for assessing the weight of the speech claim (n 12, 226): balancing is not, in this or similar areas of law, anything like as precise as that. In this regard the analogy of precise balancing *scales* that can determine with certainty and objectivity which interest is of more *weight* – as if the exercise were like determining physical mass – is misleading (see on this R Moosavian, 'A Just Balance or Just Imbalance: The Role of Metaphor in Misuse of Private Information' (2015) 7(2) *Journal of Media Law* 196). Much of the exercise is a form of practical moral reasoning – no precise 'weights' are available and reasonable minds can and will differ over the weights assigned and the outcome reached. It would be better and more honest in this regard to speak of 'evaluating' the weight of each right, rather than 'balancing' them.

the more comprehensive and categorical protection for free speech that Wragg supports (drawing largely on First Amendment writers and theorists) must await another day.[113] For now, we can simply note that *Campbell* does give us *some* conceptual tools for assessing the value of speech claims.

To do this, their Lordships drew on the so-called hierarchy of speech apparent in the Strasbourg jurisprudence: 'political expression, artistic expression and commercial expression', noting that the Court 'consistently attaches great importance to political expression and applies rather less rigorous principles to expression which is artistic and commercial'. Applying this approach, Lord Hope found that 'there were no political or democratic values at stake here, nor has any pressing social need been identified'.[114] Similarly Lord Nicholls acknowledged that, 'The need to be free to disseminate information regarding Miss Campbell's drug addiction is of a lower order than the need for freedom to disseminate information on some other subjects such as political information.'[115] Lady Hale also held that 'there are undoubtedly different types of speech' and that some of those 'are more deserving of protection in a democratic society than others'.[116] Applying this approach to *Campbell*'s case, her Ladyship found that:

> The political and social life of the community, and the intellectual, artistic or personal development of individuals, are not obviously assisted by poring over the intimate details of a fashion model's private life.[117]

Lord Hoffmann similarly emphatically accepted the use of underlying values as a way of balancing the two interests:

> Take the example … of the ordinary citizen whose attendance at NA is publicised in his local newspaper. The violation of the citizen's autonomy, dignity and self-esteem is plain and obvious. Do the civil and political values which underlie press freedom make it necessary to deny the citizen the right to protect such personal information? Not at all … there is no public interest whatever in publishing to the world the fact that the citizen has a drug dependency. The freedom to make such a statement weighs little in the balance against the privacy of personal information.[118]

These *dicta* show the welcome recognition by English courts in privacy cases that Article 10 does not engage a one-size-fits-all weight, and at least open

[113] I have sought to do the first of these, while arguing from free speech theories for more precise principles that could be used by courts to weigh free speech claims in particular instances, for example revelations about the private lives of politicians, in the *Media Freedom* book (above, n 54) 683–88 & 778–805.

[114] *Campbell*, [117].

[115] ibid, [29].

[116] ibid, [148].

[117] ibid, [148–9].

[118] ibid, [56].

the way to a principled resolution of clashes between expression interests and Article 8.

A recent example is *PJS*, in which, after extensively quoting from Strasbourg caselaw that repeatedly distinguishes genuine public interest journalism from 'tawdry' and 'sensationalist' gossip journalism, the Supreme Court concludes:

> it may be that the mere reporting of sexual encounters of someone like the claimant, however well known to the public, with a view to criticising them does not even fall within the concept of freedom of expression under article 10 at all. But, accepting that article 10 is not only engaged but capable in principle of protecting any form of expression, these cases clearly demonstrate that this type of expression is at the bottom end of the spectrum of importance (compared, for example, with freedom of political speech or a case of conduct bearing on the performance of a public office). For present purposes, any public interest in publishing such criticism must, in the absence of any other, legally recognised, public interest, be effectively disregarded in any balancing exercise and is incapable by itself of outweighing such article 8 privacy rights as the claimant enjoys.[119]

It is certainly true that this analysis – as in *Campbell* – takes place at a level of some generality. It also displays precisely the tendency of which Wragg complains: the Court expressly says that any public interest in such speech, rather than being *weighed* in the balancing act, must instead 'be disregarded' (though I would argue, rightly in this case). However, developing *detailed* principles by which speech claims can be evaluated and hence weighed is something that common law courts do incrementally over time. *Campbell* provided some basic principles: refining and fleshing those out to evaluate particular cases is something that courts should do progressively over time.[120] That is how the common law works.

E. Re-interpreting Judicial Practice

It will be apparent therefore that I would largely exonerate *Campbell* from the charge Wragg lays against it, although I would agree with him that its promise has been partly at least unfulfilled in this regard. That is because, as noted above, I agree that the courts seem markedly reluctant to weigh speech *of some admitted public interest* against a privacy intrusion and decide which is of more importance on the facts. *Why* the judges frame the matter this way is a matter of speculation, but I would suggest that a possible answer may be found by delving beneath the text of judgments to find what may be the sub-text.

[119] *PJS v News Group Newspapers Ltd* [2016] UKSC 26; [2016] AC 1081, 1097.
[120] Subject to my comments below at p 183 about what we can realistically expect of judges.

My suspicion is that the way judges *present* this matter may partly be because they are all too aware of the potentially negative 'optics' in this area. Judges are certainly aware that both the development of MPI, and particular cases in which privacy claimants win, are bitterly attacked by the press, often in highly immoderate tones. This is only to be expected, given that torts like MPI give people at least some ability to rein in the often unrestrained and unaccountable power of the mass media.[121] Were courts to do what Wragg – correctly, in a way insists on – and openly state that speech of some public interest can sometimes be outweighed by a privacy claim, they would be open to furious headlines, proclaiming: 'Judge-made privacy law stifles public interest journalism'. Hence my suggestion is, that when courts find that there is 'no' public interest in a given story (as Wragg complains) this should at least sometimes be read as meaning 'insufficient public interest to outweigh a privacy claim'. I suspect that quite often judges probably do privately consider that the speech in question has *some*, minor public interest value but that they choose to present it in their judgments as lacking *any*. If this is right, the issue may be less one of substance and more of presentation. Of course, even as presentation it is still unhelpful – it prevents a more transparent and clearly-articulate set of reasons for resolving the balance in particular cases, rhetorically reducing it to the simple binary of which Wragg complains. It is just that the rhetoric here may be disguising, rather than revealing, the actual judicial reasoning.

Finally, there may be a more practical reason why the courts do not give us more here: simple judicial awareness that the only way to engage in really nuanced and detailed weighting of speech and privacy interests would be to delve into the philosophical values underpinning each and assess how far they are at stake. This they are sometimes prepared to do – as *Campbell* and *PJS*[122] show – but only in a fairly rudimentary way. We may *want* courts to speak like philosopher-kings, but busy judges have a practical job to do, and generally prefer to leave philosophy to academics. Indeed, it is part of our role to try and formulate and then proffer these kinds of deeper, philosophical arguments to judges – and counsel, in the hope that they may be used to enrich judicial reasoning on these matters.

However, if I am right that courts, in practice, *are* prepared to allow speech of some minor public interest value to be overridden by stronger privacy claims, whatever they may say, they may still be upholding the presumptive equality of the two rights. That would mean they are fulfilling a key promise of *Campbell* after all.

[121] See further on this Rowbottom, ch 5 in this volume and his essay on the *Campbell* legacy collection referred to: 'A landmark at a turning point: Campbell and the use of privacy law to constrain media power' (2015) 7(2) *Journal of Media Law* 170–195.

[122] Above, n 119.

VI. CONCLUSION

The analysis above might have struck some readers as being under-critical – even adulatory – of the *Campbell* case. It is not meant to be, and I am not blind to its flaws. As noted above, while making bold use of horizontal effect, their Lordships took different approaches to it, and the judgment overall resoundingly failed to offer any authoritative general resolution of that vexed issue – though it should be noted that no other decision has either.[123] It is also true that the decision was a characteristic mix of the bold and the cautious, with elements in the reasoning that might have obscured or even partially confounded the transformation of the law it actually brought about.[124] Moreover, while finding parts of Wragg's – and Moreham's – critiques to be over-stated, I have acknowledged that other aspects of them are justified. I have, however, sought to set out a clear case for seeing the Houses of Lords' decision, especially when viewed in the context of the cases that had come before it, as a true landmark, a real turning point in the development of English privacy law. I have tried to show how it transformed not just the doctrine but the *language* in privacy cases: how viewing the case through a human rights lens unlocked the judicial capacity to see the situation it concerned in deeply human terms.

One final point may be apposite: as I finished writing this chapter, the Johnson Government introduced into Parliament, as a replacement for the Human Rights Act, the Bill of Rights Bill 2022, clause 4 of which instructed courts to give the importance of protecting free speech 'great weight'. By copy-editing stage in September 2022, the new Government under Liz Truss had abruptly withdrawn the Bill, but by proof stage in early November, Truss had been replaced by Sunak, and, as this book goes to press, it appears that the Bill, with its clause 4, will shortly resume its passage through Parliament. Whatever happens, the appearance of clause 4 remains of interest. As drafted, the extra weight for free speech would *not* have applied as against the state when it seeks to criminalise speech or restrict its exercise through various other means.[125] This striking drafting, when combined with various government statements[126] makes it obvious that one of the main targets of this provision was precisely the privacy tort birthed by *Campbell* that this chapter has considered. Specifically, clause 4 appeared to be squarely aimed at precisely the presumptive equality of speech and privacy rights that *Campbell* so importantly established. As such, the provision serves

[123] See above, n 78.

[124] As I have discussed fully elsewhere: above, n 18.

[125] See clause 4(3), which provides that the 'great weight' provision does not apply: (a) in criminal proceedings, or to assessing the compatibility of criminal laws with Art 10, (b) in traditional situations of breach of confidence like the *Spycatcher* litigation noted above, n 47, (c) in immigration or deportation situations, and (d) where national security is in play.

[126] See, eg' Raab to claim overhaul of human rights law will counter "political correctness"', *The Guardian*. 14 December 2021, available at www.theguardian.com/law/2021/dec/14/raab-to-claim-overhaul-human-rights-law-counter-political-correctness.

as the latest reminder that this principle of equality is constantly under bitter attack by elements of the press; that in turn, the remarkable power of the press over government means it is often in legislative peril too. Indeed, as Rowbottom's analysis of the politics of press intrusion in this volume reminds us, so cowed have successive governments been by the press's bitter hostility to the introduction of statutory privacy rights (or truly independent regulation) that it was left to the courts, using the general provisions of the Human Rights Act to finally craft a common law remedy for those whose private lives the press invade.[127] That they succeeded in doing so, where both parliament and government had failed, is perhaps the final reason why *Campbell* – the case that created the new tort – so richly deserves recognition as a landmark case in privacy law.

[127] See further on this 'Privacy and Breach of Confidence: The Clearest Case of Horizontal Effect?' in D Hoffman (ed), *The Impact of the UK Human Rights Act on Private Law* (Cambridge, CUP, 2011) 136–164.

9

Von Hannover v Germany (2004)

KIRSTY HUGHES

IT IS ALMOST 20 years since the European Court of Human Rights controversially declared that Germany had violated Article 8 ECHR by failing to protect Princess Caroline von Hannover from press intrusion into her private life.[1] This was the first time that the Strasbourg Court held that states have obligations in respect of press intrusion into privacy and that this extended to the publication of anodyne photographs of a public figure in a public place. This vastly expanded the ambit of Article 8 ECHR beyond what many previously thought imaginable.[2] It was, indeed, a landmark moment.

Much has happened since *Von Hannover* and this collection provides a valuable opportunity to consider its significance within the subsequent trajectory of the Article 8 ECHR privacy case law. This is particularly pertinent as whilst *Von Hannover* was groundbreaking; the Court's reasoning was cursory. Indeed, the dearth of judicial reasoning meant that scholars were left working with breadcrumbs in seeking to understand the ramifications of the case. In particular, it was queried whether Article 8 ECHR could be as wide-ranging as it appeared in *Von Hannover.* For example, it was questioned whether the publication of *any* photograph of any individual without their consent would trigger the application of the Convention right or alternatively whether Article 8 ECHR would be limited to situations in which photographs were obtained in a climate of paparazzi harassment.[3] Equally, it was unclear whether Article 8

[1] *Von Hannover v Germany* (2005) 40 EHRR 1.

[2] See, eg, I Leigh, 'Horizontal Rights, the Human Rights Act and Privacy: Lessons from the Commonwealth' (1999) 48(1) *International and Comparative Law Quarterly* 57, 72–74. See also discussion in H Fenwick and G Phillipson, *Media Freedom under the UK Human Rights Act* (Oxford, Oxford University Press, 2006) 667 in respect of how various scholars had assumed that Article 8 did not require any private law privacy remedy.

[3] Fenwick and Phillipson (n 2) 680–683, G Phillipson, 'The 'Right' of Privacy in England and Strasbourg Compared' in A Kenyon and M Richardson (eds), *New Dimensions in Privacy Law: International and Comparative Perspectives* (Cambridge, Cambridge University Press, 2006) 184–228, G Phillipson, 'The Common Law, Privacy and the Convention' in H Fenwick, G Phillipson and R Masterman (eds), *Judicial Reasoning under the UK Human Rights Act* (Cambridge, Cambridge University Press, 2007).

ECHR only applied to the *publication* of photographs or whether the right was also applicable at the point at which the photograph was *taken*.[4] Later case law has, however, confirmed that the parameters of Article 8 ECHR are in fact as broad as the Court first hinted in *Von Hannover*.[5]

Yet whilst the Court adopted a robust approach to the protection of privacy in *Von Hannover* it recalibrated its approach in several important respects in its subsequent Grand Chamber judgment in *Von Hannover (No.2)*.[6] First, it revisited its definition of a public figure and the relevance of that status to the convention rights in ways that arguably rendered the protection of a public figure's right to privacy less assured than it was in *Von Hannover*.[7] Second, it restricted its own role in determining the balance that should be struck between the competing convention rights, adopting a model of rights reasoning which accords a significantly wider margin of appreciation to states.[8] The impact of these developments suggests that two decades on we might be inclined to regard *Von Hannover* as the high-water mark of the European Court of Human Rights' role in *protecting* the privacy of public figures vis-a-vis the press.

Yet, whilst the Strasbourg Court has clearly limited its role and adopted a more complex stance on the privacy of public figures it has certainly not retreated on the *scope* of Article 8 ECHR. Indeed, what was remarkable about *Von Hannover*, and what remains significant to this day is the sheer breadth that the Court accorded to Article 8 ECHR. In so doing the Court embedded a concept of privacy in which it refused to delineate Article 8 ECHR along simplistic binary distinctions between public and private. This chapter argues that it is this dynamic conception of private life that is the real legacy of *Von Hannover*. Moreover, it suggests that is this conception of the right that has perhaps led the Court to recently return to engage in greater scrutiny than perhaps initially appeared following *Von Hannover (No.2)*.

This chapter explores these issues as follows. Section I considers the development of privacy theory and the move from binary conceptions to a social interaction perspective as a means of exploring the ramifications of the Court's approach in *Von Hannover*. Section II explores the evolution of state obligations in respect of privacy and the press culminating in the *Von Hannover* judgment. It considers the questions that were left unanswered by *Von Hannover*, initial reactions to *Von Hannover* and how the post-*Von Hannover* case law confirmed

[4] K Hughes, 'Photographs in Public Places and Privacy' (2009) 1(2) *Journal of Media Law* 159.

[5] See, eg, *Reklos and Davourlis v Greece* [2009] EMLR 16 and *Dupate v Latvia* (App no 18068/11) (2021) 72 EHRR 34 (19 November 2020) discussed further below.

[6] *Von Hannover (No.2) v Germany* (2012) 55 EHRR 15. See also *Axel Springer v Germany* (2012) 55 EHRR 6.

[7] K Hughes, 'The Public Figure Doctrine and the Right to Privacy' (2019) 78(1) *Cambridge Law Journal* 70, G Phillipson, 'Press Freedom, the Public Interest and Privacy' in A Kenyon (ed) *Comparative Defamation and Privacy Law* (Cambridge, Cambridge University Press, 2016).

[8] *Von Hannover (No.2)* (n 6), *Axel Springer* (n 6).

the scope of Article 8 ECHR vis-à-vis photography. Section III examines the Grand Chamber's subsequent retreat from *Von Hannover* in *Von Hannover (No.2)* and addresses the implications of this for public figures, the balancing criteria and the Court's role. It argues that *Von Hannover (No.2)* and the cases that immediately followed suggested that the Court had neutered its own role. Finally, section IV suggests that recent cases indicate a revival of the Court's role – one that is ultimately driven by the dynamic conception of privacy and the special protection of photographs that the Court first identified in *Von Hannover*. It also suggests that this conception of private life has paved the way for the development of other positive obligations in Article 8 ECHR, and the Court's approach to reconciling Articles 8 and 10 in contexts beyond privacy. Ultimately, it concludes that *Von Hannover* remains a landmark case.

I. PRIVACY THEORY AND THE RECOGNITION OF A SOCIAL INTERACTION CONCEPTION OF PRIVACY

Although Article 8 ECHR expressly includes a right to respect for private life there is no definition of that right in the Convention.[9] Given that the right is framed in terms of *private* life it might therefore have been expected that the Court would seek to determine the ambit of the right by relying upon a binary distinction between public and private life. The notion that the world can be separated into public and private spheres, such that privacy exists in the private realm but not in the public realm is one that obviously has a long history in political thought. It is also prevalent in theories of privacy, especially those that centre upon the identification of private places or private information as a means of establishing what is private and thus what is worthy of protection. Such models, as Helen Nissenbaum observes presume that 'it follows seamlessly that the concept and value of privacy corresponds with, or applies to, the sphere of the private alone'.[10]

One approach is to seek to identify what is private by adopting a spatial approach. Through this lens privacy is possible in private places but not in public places. The paradigmatic private place is the home; the place where one can, in theory, lock the door, close the curtains and shut out the rest of the world.[11] Yet it

[9] For analysis of the interests contained in the right to respect for private life see N Moreham, 'The Right to Respect for Private Life in the European Convention on Human Rights: A Re-examination' [2008] *European Human Rights Law Review* 44.

[10] H Nissenbaum, 'Protecting Privacy in an Information Age: The Problem of Privacy in Public' (1998) 17 *Law and Philosophy* 559, 568.

[11] There is, however, a vast body of scholarship that contests such utopian visions of the home, and highlights the dangers of rendering the home private and off-limits for state intervention, see A Allen, *Why Privacy Isn't Everything: Feminist Reflections on Personal Accountability* (Lanham, MD, Rowman & Littlefield Publishers, 2003).

is evident that few if any of us, are willing to leave all notions of privacy behind when we leave our homes. Consequently, a more nuanced approach recognises the need for privacy in what might traditionally have been cast as 'public places', and acknowledges that there are different types of experiences of privacy, many of which are not states of solitude or intimacy, but are in fact desired when we are interacting with many others.[12] Hence it is commonly accepted amongst privacy theorists that there is a need for some form of privacy in public.[13]

Another binary approach emerges from models that seek to focus upon the identification of private information as a means of identifying what is private.[14] Again, however, the difficulties that arise with this approach are well-documented. First, that we do not have universally shared views about what information is private. What you regard as private information may be rather different to what I regard as private information. Second, that whilst some of our desires for privacy may concern the protection of information, we may also object to intrusions such as surveillance, not because we are concerned about what information may be obtained about us, but rather because we object to the intrusion itself, regardless of whether any information at all is obtained.[15]

Thus, privacy theorists have long argued that experiences of privacy are more nuanced than binary public/private models suggest, in part because privacy is subjective in ways that render it difficult to delineate in such universal terms. A response to these conceptual difficulties has therefore been to suggest that it is impossible to formulate a single universally accepted definition of privacy. Hence we are warned that privacy is 'a concept in disarray', and that 'difficulty in articulating what privacy is and why it is important has often made privacy law ineffective and blind to the larger purposes it must serve'.[16] Scholars have cautioned, that defining privacy is a 'treacherous path', that '[b]elieving that one must define or provide an account of privacy before one can systematically address critical challenges can thwart further progress' and that attempts to

[12] A Westin, *Privacy and Freedom* (New York, Athenuem, 1967).

[13] N Moreham, 'Privacy in Public Places' [2006] *Cambridge Law Journal* 606, K Hughes, 'A Behavioural Understanding of Privacy and its Implications for Privacy Law' (2012) 75(5) *Modern Law Review* 806.

[14] R Wacks, 'The Poverty of Privacy' (1980) 96 *Law Quarterly Review* 73, R Wacks, *The Protection of Privacy* (London, Sweet and Maxwell, 1980), R Wacks, *Personal Information, Privacy and the Law* (Oxford, Clarendon Press, 1989), R Wacks, *Privacy and Press Freedom* (London, Blackstone Press, 1995), R Wacks, 'Why there will never be an English Common Law Privacy Tort' in A Kenyon and M Richardson (eds), *New Dimensions in Privacy Law: International and Comparative Law Perspectives* (Cambridge, Cambridge University Press, 2006).

[15] R Gavison, 'Privacy and the Limits of the Law' (1980) 89 *Yale Law Journal* 421, N Moreham, 'Privacy in the Common Law: A Doctrinal and Theoretical Analysis' (2005) 121 *Law Quarterly Review* 628, Hughes (n 13), P Wragg, 'Recognising a Privacy-Invasion Tort: The Conceptual Unity of Informational and Intrusion Claims' (2019) 78(2) *Cambridge Law Journal* 409.

[16] D Solove, *Understanding Privacy* (Cambridge, MA, Harvard University Press, 2008) 2.

maintain the various meanings 'while delineating a concept to support policy, moral judgment and technical design seems a hopeless ambition'.[17]

In many ways the Court's approach to private life in *Von Hannover* resonates with what has been developed in privacy scholarship as a broader social interaction understanding of privacy.[18] As we will see, the Court did not seek to define privacy, nor private life. Nor did it purport to delineate the scope of Article 8(1) ECHR by reference to a public/private divide. On the contrary, the vindication of a public figure's right to privacy in public was a clear rejection of a spatial model, whilst, the principles that the Court espoused were also indicative of a more dynamic conception of privacy. In particular, the Court's declaration that Article 8 ECHR includes 'a zone of interaction of a person with others, even in a public context' as well as a 'right to establish and develop relationships with other human beings'.[19] They embedded an approach to the right that recognises that privacy is a state of experience that is not restricted to the home or states of solitude but that persists throughout our interactions, including those that take place in public.[20] Of course, *Von Hannover* was not the first time that the Court had recognised privacy in public,[21] but by bringing these principles into play in this context the Court embedded a conception of the right which has endured, and which has had ramifications for the subsequent development of Article 8 ECHR, particularly when that right collides with Article 10 ECHR.[22]

II. *VON HANNOVER V GERMANY* – A LANDMARK JUDGMENT?

A. Article 8 ECHR Prior to *Von Hannover*

Having set the scene for considering *Von Hannover* within the broader framework of privacy theory, we also need to contemplate it within the evolution of Article 8 ECHR. Privacy scholars had certainly waited a long time for the European Court of Human Rights to confirm that Article 8 ECHR applied in respect of press intrusions into privacy as the Commission had first received an application all the way back in 1986 in *Winer v United Kingdom*.[23] On that

[17] H Nissenbaum, *Privacy in Context: technology, Policy and the Integrity of Social Life* (Palo Alto, Stanford University Press, 2010) 2. See also T Bennett, 'Triangulating Intrusion in Privacy Law' (2019) 39(4) *Oxford Journal of Legal Studies* 751.

[18] Hughes (n 13). See also analyses of physical privacy, Moreham (n 15), Gavison (n 15).

[19] *Von Hannover* (n.1) at [50].

[20] Westin (n 12).

[21] *X v Iceland* (App no 2525/65) (06 February 1967).

[22] See section IV below.

[23] *Winer v the United* Kingdom (App no 10871/84) Commission Dec. 10 July 1986, DR 48, 154. For discussion see G Phillipson and H Fenwick, 'Breach of Confidence as a Privacy Remedy in the Human Rights Act Era' (2000) 63(5) *Modern Law Review* 660–693.

occasion the Commission declined to determine the issue, but it hinted that Article 8 ECHR might be applicable stating that there is a question as 'to what extent the High Contracting Party must impose positive obligations on persons within its jurisdiction in order to ensure compliance with Article 8'.[24] Following that decision other cases, such as *Spencer v United Kingdom*[25] and *Peck v United Kingdom*,[26] also suggested that Article 8 ECHR might be applicable.[27] Nevertheless, there was no clear determination until *Von Hannover* and thus for a number of years it was unclear what position the Convention institutions would take in respect of Article 8 ECHR. Sadly, the catalyst for the recognition of the right to privacy in Article 8 ECHR was probably the tragic death of Diana, Princess of Wales during a paparazzi car chase in Paris in 1997. Indeed, it is questionable whether the Court would have taken quite the stance that it eventually took in *Von Hannover* if the case had not arrived in the aftermath of that tragedy. The death of Princess Diana shook the Council of Europe and the following year it published Resolution 1165 (1998) affirming 'the importance of every person's right to privacy' and declaring that 'the right to privacy afforded by Article 8 of the European Convention on Human Rights should not only protect an individual against interference by public authorities, but also against interference by private persons or institutions, including the mass media'.[28] After this it seemed that it would only be a matter of time until the issue would come before the European Court of Human Rights.

B. Von Hannover v Germany

The opportunity arose when Princess Caroline von Hannover applied to the Strasbourg Court in June 2000 with allegations of paparazzi harassment that were reminiscent of the experiences of Princess Diana. Princess Caroline lived in the south of France where privacy laws provided strong protection against the publication of photographs. Yet whilst those laws restricted publication of her image in France, this did not protect her from press intrusion as (just as Princess Diana experienced in Paris) the paparazzi pursued her in order to obtain photographs to sell to publishers in other jurisdictions. Consequently, since the early 1990s Princess Caroline had been engaged in challenging the publication of photographs in the tabloid press in Germany.[29]

[24] *Winer v the United Kingdom* (n 23).
[25] (App no 28851/95 28852/95) Commission Dec. 16 January 1998.
[26] (2003) 36 EHRR 41.
[27] For discussion see Phillipson and Fenwick (n 23).
[28] Council of Europe Parliamentary Assembly Resolution 1165 (1998) – Right to Privacy, 26 June 1998.
[29] *Von Hannover* (n 1) at [9].

Her arguments had initially been rejected by the Hamburg Regional Court which held that she had no applicable right to privacy in respect of photographs taken in public places.[30] It reasoned that for figures of contemporary society 'par excellence' (such as Princess Caroline) the right to protection of private life stops at their front door.[31] That stance was clearly premised upon the intersection of two sharp public/private distinctions, namely one in respect of public/private figures and one in respect of public/private places. The Hamburg Court of Appeal upheld that position.[32] Their approach was, however, later overturned by the Federal Court of Justice and the Federal Constitutional Court.[33] The higher courts adopted a more nuanced approach, albeit one that was ultimately premised upon the same binary distinctions. Those courts rejected the approach of the lower courts on the basis that even figures of contemporary society 'par excellence' are entitled to a right to respect for private life which is not simply limited to their home.[34] They then went on to redefine the boundaries of the right distinguishing between public places and secluded places. They determined that whilst figures of par excellence status could not rely on the right to privacy in public places they were entitled to privacy in secluded places.[35] In this regard it was held that a secluded place meant somewhere away from the public eye – where it was objectively clear to everyone that they wanted to be alone and where, confident of being away from prying eyes, they behaved in a given situation in a manner in which they would not behave in a public place.[36] Thus the Federal Court of Justice and Federal Constitutional Court perpetuated a model of privacy that was premised upon the intersection of binary distinctions between public and private places and public and private figures, albeit that the spatial boundaries were drawn differently.

Applying this recalibrated approach to the facts they determined that Princess Caroline was a public figure of par excellence status who was entitled to privacy in secluded places.[37] Accordingly, the Princess succeeded in arguing that some of the photographs should not be published. Nevertheless, this left her unprotected in public places, meaning that photographs of her engaged in activities such as shopping, skiing, canoeing and at a beach club were not restricted. It was those images that eventually formed the basis for her application to the European Court of Human Rights, which she lodged with the Court in June 2000. This was the first in a series of Strasbourg cases in respect of her right to privacy.

[30] ibid, at [19].
[31] ibid.
[32] ibid, at [20].
[33] ibid, at [22]–[38].
[34] ibid, at [23].
[35] ibid.
[36] ibid.
[37] ibid.

i. The Arguments Advanced before the Court

In *Von Hannover* Princess Caroline argued that she had spent more than ten years trying to establish her right to the protection of her private life in Germany.[38] She emphasised that whenever she left her house she was constantly hounded by paparazzi who followed her every movement, be it crossing the road, fetching her children from school, doing her shopping, out walking, engaging in sport or going on holiday.[39] She thus argued that the concept of a 'secluded place' was too narrow. She also argued that it was unworkable as it required her to establish that she had been in a secluded place. Consequently, she had to keep a permanent record of her every movement, whilst in respect of many of the photographs it was impossible to determine the exact time and place at which they had been taken.[40] She acknowledged that the press are protected under Article 10 ECHR as they play a vital role in a democratic society, but she denied that they were fulfilling such a role here as they were simply making huge profits from satisfying readers' voyeuristic tendencies.[41]

Germany sought to refute her arguments. It claimed that its legal framework contained sufficient safeguards and that its domestic courts had struck a fair balance between Princess Caroline's rights and freedom of the press. It also emphasised that a margin of appreciation should be accorded to states when balancing the competing rights.[42] Unsurprisingly, the press associations that acted as third-party interveners agreed that German law struck the right balance and that the Court should defer to that approach.[43]

ii. The Applicability of Article 8 ECHR and the Principles Identified by the Court

Given that this was the first occasion upon which the Court recognised positive obligations in this context it might have been anticipated that the Court would discuss at length the applicability of the Convention right. It might also have been anticipated that the Court would identify a trigger or set a threshold for the application of the positive obligations. The Court did not appear to do this. Instead, its reasoning as to the applicability of Article 8 ECHR was limited to the identification of the following points of principle.

(i) that the concept of private life extends to aspects relating to personal identity, such as a person's name or a person's picture;
(ii) private life includes a person's physical and psychological integrity;

[38] ibid, [44].
[39] ibid.
[40] ibid.
[41] ibid.
[42] ibid, at [45].
[43] ibid, at [46]–[47].

(iii) the guarantee afforded by Article 8 of the Convention is primarily intended to ensure the development, without outside interference, of the personality of each individual in his relations with other human beings;
(iv) there is therefore a zone of interaction of a person with others, even in a public context, which may fall within the scope of 'private life';
(v) in certain circumstances, a person has a 'legitimate expectation' of protection and respect for his or her private life;
(vi) as regards photos, with a view to defining the scope of the protection afforded by Article 8 against arbitrary interference by public authorities, the European Commission of Human Rights had regard to whether the photographs related to private or public matters and whether the material thus obtained was envisaged for a limited use or was likely to be made available to the general public.[44]

After stating these principles, the Court then simply concluded that in this case 'there is no doubt that the publication by various German magazines of photos of the applicant in her daily life either on her own or with other people falls within the scope of her private life'.[45] Consequently, whilst these few brief paragraphs dramatically expanded the ambit of Article 8 ECHR scholars were left scrambling to discern their ramifications.

Yet whilst the Court's reasoning was limited it was at least possible to determine the following. First, that the Court rejected a spatial approach to the Convention right that would entirely exclude privacy in public places. This was not the first time that the Court had recognised some form of privacy in public,[46] but it was a clear rejection of any argument that the press were free to photograph matters which take place in public.[47] This was significant as there had been earlier Commission case law which had suggested that photography in public was simply an unwanted form of social interaction that must be tolerated, rather than an invasion of privacy.[48] Moreover, the Court appeared to be open to a social interaction conception of privacy. This was implicit in its declaration that the right includes 'a zone of interaction of a person with others, even in a public context, which may fall within the scope of "private life".[49]

Second, that whilst the Court referred to a 'legitimate expectation' of protection there was no evidence that the Court adopted this as a threshold for determining whether the Convention right was applicable. The notion of a 'legitimate expectation' or as it is more commonly referred to 'reasonable expectation of privacy' is one that arises frequently in privacy law in various

[44] ibid, at [50]–52].
[45] ibid, at [53].
[46] See, eg, *Peck v United Kingdom* (n 26).
[47] Moreham (n 13).
[48] *Friedl v Austria* (App no 15225/89) 19 May 1994.
[49] *Von Hannover* (n 1) at [50].

jurisdictions, often providing the benchmark for determining whether there has been an interference with a right to privacy.[50] However, in *Von Hannover*, there was no analysis of whether Princess Caroline had a 'reasonable or legitimate expectation of privacy' and there was nothing to clearly indicate that this constituted a threshold test for determining the applicability of the Convention right. This is a stance that has persisted in subsequent case law, where the modus operandi of the Court has generally been to assume that Article 8 ECHR is applicable and then swiftly proceed to considering the balance that has been struck between Articles 8 and 10 ECHR. It is true that there are some hints in the case law that there is in fact a latent severity threshold[51] akin to that which has been developed in respect of other positive obligations under Article 8 ECHR,[52] but it is fair to say that the Court's analysis in the privacy cases centres upon the balancing criteria.

Beyond this it became much more difficult to discern the implications of the principles laid out by the Court. In particular, whilst it was evident that photographs are accorded a degree of special protection, the scope and nature of that protection was somewhat undefined. Consequently, scholars swiftly declared *Von Hannover* 'a radical extension of the court's jurisprudence'[53] and 'far-reaching'[54] with many lamenting 'the almost entire absence of justificatory reasoning' for this extension.[55] Indeed, one scholar suggested at the time that the judgment left 'the contours of the "private" wholly undefined'.[56] Given the various warnings that privacy scholars have advanced as to the perilous nature of seeking to define privacy some might argue that the absence of a definition of 'private' was itself no bad thing. Nevertheless, even those privacy scholars that had long campaigned for the recognition of a right to privacy against the press

[50] On the concept of a reasonable expectation of privacy in respect of privacy in public see Moreham (n 13), Hughes (n 13), E Barendt, 'A Reasonable Expectation of Privacy; A Coherent or Redundant Concept' in A Kenyon (ed), *Comparative Defamation and Privacy Law* (Cambridge, Cambridge University Press, 2016), N Moreham, 'Unpacking the Reasonable Expectation of Privacy Test' (2018) 134 *Law Quarterly Review* 651.

[51] In *Couderc and Hachette v France* (App no 40454/07) (Grand Chamber) 10 November 2015 the Grand Chamber emphasised as part of its articulation of the general principles the 'importance of assessing the seriousness of the intrusion into private life' at [87], but it is not clear whether this is intended to go to the applicability of Art 8 ECHR or whether it is directed to the balance that is struck between the competing rights. A case which more clearly indicates a severity threshold is *Vucina v Croatia* (App no 58955/13) 24 September 2019 at [31]. Yet whilst the Court decided in *Vucina* that the level of severity was not met and that Art 8 ECHR was not applicable this was after the Court considered the issues that it would consider in respect of the balancing exercise.

[52] For example, in the context of speech that affects reputation the expression must 'attain a certain level of seriousness', *Denisov v Ukraine* (App no 76639/11) 25 September 2018 at [112]–[114], whilst in the context of hate speech it must reach a 'certain level' also referred to as the 'threshold of severity' *Behar v Bulgaria* (App no 29335/13) 16 February 2021 at [67].

[53] Phillipson (n 3) 202.

[54] Moreham (n 13) 609.

[55] Fenwick and Phillipson (n 2) 672.

[56] MA Sanderson, 'Is Von Hannover v Germany a Step Backwards for the Substantive Analysis of Speech and Privacy Interests' (2004) 6 *European Human Rights Law Review* 631, 643.

were cautious about the way in which this was achieved in *Von Hannover*, in particular the opacity of the Court's reasoning, and the implications of this for the development of privacy rights.[57]

The first question raised by *Von Hannover* was whether all or only a subset of photographs fell within the scope of Article 8 ECHR. One possibility was that Article 8 ECHR was limited to photographs of 'private matters' in public places. This would make sense of the Court's reference to the Commission's reasoning in *Friedl v Austria* (1996) 21 EHRR 83. A distinction that would, of course, require future courts to determine what constitutes a public or a private activity.

Another way of interpreting the ambit of Article 8 ECHR was to limit its application to photographs obtained in a climate of harassment recognising that this was what was driving Princess Caroline's application. Writing shortly after *Von Hannover* Gavin Phillipson suggested that a harassment approach was preferable and more realistic given that the absolutist approach would require all contracting states to 'move to something like the French model of privacy'.[58] He also suggested that this was easier to reconcile with developments in the newly emerging English tort of misuse of private information, given that the House of Lords in *Campbell v MGN* did not seem to be open to such a radical approach to photographs in public.[59] An alternative view was offered by Nicole Moreham who argued that 'the English courts have shown a willingness to protect' privacy in public places and that 'the courts therefore seem well-equipped to deal with the challenge set down for them in *Von Hannover*'.[60] Twenty years later, whilst it is evident that Article 8 ECHR has not been restricted to harassment,[61] the potential gap between *Von Hannover* and *Campbell* is one that arguably has never been confronted by the domestic courts, except in the cases of children.[62]

A further point of uncertainty was whether the right was only applicable when the photographs were published, or whether it was also applicable at the point at which the photographs were taken.[63] Such a distinction would align with the Court's reference to *Freidl*, but it would also suggest that Article 8 ECHR is concerned with what is disseminated (ie the information that is disclosed) rather

[57] Fenwick and Phillipson (n 2) 672.

[58] Phillipson (n 3) 186.

[59] *Campbell v MGN* [2004] UKHL 22, Baroness Hale at [154]. For discussion see Phillipson (n 3) 186.

[60] Moreham (n 13).

[61] *Dupate v Latvia* (n 5).

[62] *Murray v Big Pictures Limited* [2008] EWCA Civ 446.

[63] For discussion on whether the right should be applicable in such contexts see Moreham (n 13) 634–635 in which she argues that taking a photograph in a public place 'should be legally actionable if the person photographed is involuntarily having an intimate or traumatic experience, is in a place where he or she reasonably believes he or she is imperceptible by others, or if the defendant has used technological devices to break through his or her self-presentation barriers'. On the development of Art 8 ECHR jurisprudence in respect of photography in public places see Hughes (n 4), R Moosavian, 'Stealing 'Souls'? Article 8 and Photographic Intrusion' (2018) 69(4) *Northern Ireland Legal Quarterly* 531.

than the intrusion into unwanted access to self that arises at the point at which the image is taken. Thus, this interpretation was difficult to square with the Court's recognition of a 'zone of interaction of a person with others, even in a public context, which may fall within the scope of "private life"'.

Consequently, these ambiguities meant that the principles said to underpin Article 8 ECHR were open to interpretation in ways that pointed towards different facets and potentially even different conceptions of privacy. In particular, whether privacy is concerned with the protection of private information, or whether it is also about restricting unwanted access to self. These conceptual points are critical for photography in public places given that photography may interfere with the privacy-related interests of the person photographed because of what it reveals (ie the information itself) and/or because the initial act of taking the photograph subjected the person photographed to unwanted access. Correspondingly identifying which conception of privacy underpinned the Convention right was relevant to determining at what point the right is applicable as well as determining the weight to be accorded to the right. Subsequent case law has established that the right is applicable at each stage in the life cycle of photography and that it does not just protect private information.[64] It has therefore confirmed that Article 8 ECHR is in fact as broad as the Court suggested in *Von Hannover*.

iii. Violation of Article 8 ECHR

Having held that Article 8 ECHR was applicable the Court then went on to consider the conflict of rights that this entailed between private life and freedom of expression. In respect of Article 10 ECHR, it emphasised that the press has an essential role in a 'democratic society' whilst also noting that the press must 'not overstep certain bounds, in particular in respect of the reputation and rights of others'.[65] In respect of Article 8 ECHR the Court identified two points of consideration. First, that these were 'images containing very personal or even intimate "information" about an individual';[66] a questionable interpretation of the nature of the photographs.[67] Second, that 'photos appearing in the tabloid press are often taken in a climate of continual harassment which induces in the person concerned a very strong sense of intrusion into their private life or even of persecution'.[68]

In evaluating the two competing rights, however, the Court declared that the 'decisive factor' is 'the contribution that the published photos and articles make

[64] *Dupate v Latvia* (n 5), *Hajovsky v Slovakia* (App no 7796/16) 1 July 2021 – discussion in section IV below.

[65] *Von Hannover* (n 1) at [58].

[66] ibid, at [59].

[67] ibid.

[68] ibid.

to a debate of general interest'. The Court then went on to consider whether the applicant's status affected the extent to which the publication contributed to a debate of general interest.[69] In this respect the Court declared that public figures status may affect whether the publication contributes to a debate of general interest, but that only those who exercise official functions are public figures.[70] Consequently, it held that as the Princess did not have official functions she was not a public figure.[71] Moreover, the Court held that as the sole purpose of the photographs was to satisfy readers' curiosities that the publications did not contribute to any debate of general interest to society.[72] For these reasons the Court concluded that the criteria on which the domestic courts had based their decisions did not adequately protect the applicant's private life.[73]

Scholars subsequently criticised the Court for: (i) substituting its own view of the balance to be struck between competing rights (hence affording no margin of appreciation to Germany); and (ii) for its narrow approach to public figures which ultimately equated the Princess (as someone who did not perform official functions) with an ordinary private citizen.[74]

III. VON HANNOVER (NO.2) – A RETREAT FROM VON HANNOVER

Given these criticisms it was perhaps unsurprising that the Court revisited its approach in *Von Hannover (No.2)*.[75] The background to the case was that following *Von Hannover (No.1)* the Princess and her husband had sought injunctions restraining further publication of three photographs that had been taken without their consent during skiing holidays in St Moritz between 2002 and 2004. The Federal Court of Justice and the Federal Constitutional Court sought to implement *Von Hannover* when striking the balance between the competing rights. They thus granted an injunction in respect of two photographs on the basis that they did not contribute to a debate of general interest, whilst refusing to issue an injunction in respect of another photograph. This photograph also depicted the applicants taking a walk during a skiing holiday in St Moritz, however, it was accompanied by an article reporting on, among other issues, Princess Caroline's father's poor health and the family's absence during this period. The German courts distinguished that publication on the basis that the reigning Prince's poor health was a subject of general interest and that the

[69] ibid, at [76].
[70] ibid.
[71] ibid.
[72] ibid, at [65].
[73] ibid, at [74].
[74] Fenwick and Phillipson (n 2) 673. For a critical take on the normative balance struck between privacy and freedom of expression see P Wragg, 'The Benefits of Privacy Invading Expression' (2013) 64(2) *Northern Ireland Legal Quarterly* 187.
[75] *Von Hannover (No.2)* (n 6).

press had been entitled to report on the manner in which his children reconciled their obligations of family solidarity with the legitimate needs of their private life, among which was the desire to go on holiday.

Following that judgment, the Princess applied to the Strasbourg Court once more. This time the case went to the Grand Chamber which took the opportunity to recalibrate its approach. There were three key points of difference which emerged between the Grand Chamber's approach and the earlier *Von Hannover* judgment. First, it expanded the range of balancing criteria that need to be considered in striking the balance between the convention rights. Second, it adopted a broader approach to the ambit of the public figure doctrine in ways that arguably rendered the protection of a public figure's right to privacy less assured than it was in *Von Hannover*. Third, that *Von Hannover (No.2)* saw the Strasbourg Court adopt a more nuanced and more deferential approach to the balance to be struck between privacy and freedom of expression, adopting a model of rights reasoning which accords a significantly wider margin of appreciation to states.[76] The impact of these developments suggests that two decades on we might regard *Von Hannover* as the high-water mark of the Court's role in *protecting* the privacy of public figures vis-a-vis the press.

On the first issue it will be recalled that in *Von Hannover* the decisive factor was whether the publication contributes to a debate of general interest. In *Von Hannover (No.2)* the Grand Chamber emphasised that this is an essential criterion, but then went on to identify the following further factors as relevant to the balancing exercise:

- How well known is the person concerned and what is the subject of the report?
- Prior conduct of the person concerned.
- Content, form and consequences of the publication.
- Circumstances in which the photographs were taken.[77]

This more holistic approach enables an evaluation of the implications for both rights, whereas the 'decisive factor' in *Von Hannover* had focused exclusively upon the impact on freedom of expression.

Yet by considering factors such as the applicant's status and conduct this rendered it more likely that public/private figure distinctions will be reintroduced at the balancing stage.[78] On this point the Grand Chamber, in contrast to the Chamber in *Von Hannover (No.1)*, held that irrespective of the question to what extent Princess Caroline assumed official functions on behalf of the

[76] ibid and *Axel Springer* (n 6).
[77] *Von Hannover (No.2)* (n 6) at [108]–[113].
[78] Hughes (n 7), Phillipson (n 7).

Principality of Monaco, it could not be claimed that the applicants, who were undeniably very well known, were ordinary private individuals. They had to be regarded as public figures.[79] Thus the second point of distinction was the Grand Chamber's broader approach to public figure status. Indeed, it is evident in the case law that has followed *Von Hannover (No.2)* that the Court has adopted an approach to the public figure doctrine that has significantly amended the stance that it took in *Von Hannover (No.1)*.[80] Weakening, but not denying that public figures have a right to privacy.

The third distinction was that the Grand Chamber stated in *Von Hannover (No.2)* that where the balancing exercise has been undertaken by the national authorities in conformity with those criteria that it will require strong reasons to substitute its view for that of the domestic courts.[81] This was a retreat from the more interventionist approach that had been severely criticised in *Von Hannover.*

Applying all of this to the facts the Grand Chamber held that the domestic courts' characterisation of Prince Rainier's illness as an event of contemporary society could not be considered unreasonable and that the domestic courts had carefully balanced the publishing companies' right to freedom of expression against the applicants' right to respect for their private life. In those circumstances, and regard being had to the margin of appreciation enjoyed by the national courts when balancing competing interests, the domestic courts had not failed to comply with their positive obligations under Article 8.

The balancing criteria developed in *Von Hannover (No.2)* dominated the Court's reasoning in later cases. Certainly, the Court's analysis in cases such as *Ruusunen v Finland* and *Lillo-Stenberg v Norway*[82] suggested it was reluctant to intervene provided that the contracting state has applied the *Von Hannover (No.2)* balancing criteria, even if this seemed to lead to inconsistent results.[83] This restrained approach is certainly not unique to the right to privacy. Indeed, in other aspects of the Article 8 ECHR case law, such as immigration, the Court has also set out various criteria and then indicated that it needs strong reasons to intervene where either sufficient safeguards are met or where domestic courts have taken into consideration the criteria developed in the Court's jurisprudence.[84] Nevertheless, *Von Hannover (No.2)* suggested that the level of protection accorded to privacy may have fallen by some margin from the Court's approach in *Von Hannover.*[85]

[79] *Von Hannover (No.2)* (n 6) at [120].
[80] Hughes (n 7).
[81] *Von Hannover (No.2)* (n 6) at [107].
[82] *Ruusunen v Finland* (73579/10); *Lillo-Stenberg v Norway* [2014] 1 WLUK 268.
[83] K Hughes and N Richards, 'The Atlantic Divide on Privacy and Free Speech' in A Kenyon (ed), *Comparative Defamation and Privacy law* (Cambridge, Cambridge University Press, 2016).
[84] For example, we see a similar approach in immigration case law: *Ndidi v United Kingdom* (App no 41215/14) 14 September 2107, *Unuane v United Kingdom* (App no 80343/17) 24 November 2020.
[85] Hughes and Richards (n 82), Phillipson (n 7).

IV. AN ENHANCED ROLE FOR THE COURT?

Yet whilst there is no doubt that the Court has retreated from the role that it accorded itself in *Von Hannover*, recent cases indicate that the Court has perhaps retained a more active role than may first have appeared in the aftermath of *Von Hannover (No.2)*. Certainly, a willingness to critically examine domestic courts' application of the balancing criteria was evident in *Couderc and Hachette v France*.[86] On that occasion the Grand Chamber examined in considerable detail each of the balancing criteria before concluding that France had violated Article 10 ECHR.[87] Although this was in the context of upholding freedom of expression, it nevertheless suggested a willingness for the Court to engage in a closer degree of scrutiny than had initially been evident after *Von Hannover (No.2)*. Indeed, there were indications that the Court was not only considering whether the domestic courts had considered the matter, but in fact coming to its own view on some of the issues.

Since then there have been a number of other cases in which the Court has found violations of Article 8 ECHR by subjecting the reasoning of domestic courts to a greater degree of scrutiny. The Court has thus found a violation of Article 8 ECHR in *Dupate v Latvia*,[88] *Bogomolova v Russia*,[89] *Hajovsky v Slovakia*[90] and *IVT v Romania*.[91] Although in many of these cases the Court has indicated that the domestic courts have not engaged sufficiently with the balancing criteria, these cases also demonstrate that the Court has not reneged from the broad approach to privacy that it first affirmed in *Von Hannover*. In particular the Court affirmed in *Dupate* that privacy in public is not limited to situations of harassment;[92] whilst in *Hajovsky* it emphasised that privacy is not simply concerned with the protection of personal information, that it is concerned with intrusion, and that prior disclosure does not negate the right to privacy.[93] This was an important rejection of the waiver argument that some had argued was introduced in *Von Hannover (No.2)*, as such it provides important protection for privacy.[94]

Moreover, these cases also suggest that the Court is continuing to develop the state's positive obligations through its identification of necessary safeguards, albeit that in many respects these developments perhaps prompt more questions than they answer. In this regard the Court has hinted that in cases where an image is obtained surreptitiously that masking may be a necessary safeguard.

[86] *Couderc and Hachette v France* (n 51).
[87] ibid, at [74].
[88] *Dupate v Latvia* (n 5).
[89] *Bogomolova v Russia* (App no 13812/09) 20 June 2017.
[90] *Hajovsky v Slovakia* (App no 7796/16) 1 July 2021.
[91] *IVT v Romania* (App no 35582/15) 1 March 2022.
[92] *Dupate v Latvia* (n 5) at [72].
[93] *Hajovsky v Slovakia* (n 89) at [48].
[94] Phillipson (n 7), see also R Moosavian, 'Hájovský v. Slovakia, Further Guidance On Rights-Balancing and Photographs' *Inforrm*, 28 July 2021.

This issue arose in *Hajovsky* where it was suggested that the surreptitious nature of the recording should 'have alerted the journalist and the newspaper publisher to the need to use that material with caution and not to disseminate it without masking or blurring the applicant's face'.[95]

The case law also indicates that the Court regards consent as an important safeguard, at least in the context of children.[96] Certainly, it has been evident since *Reklos* that parental consent may be necessary prior to the taking of a child's photograph.[97] The Court also affirmed in *Bogomolova* that even if the photograph had initially been taken with consent, that consent remains an essential safeguard prior to publication.[98] It thus appears that domestic courts should consider whether consent has been given at each stage and if they do not consider this then this will itself violate Article 8 ECHR.

The absence of consent was also at the heart of *IVT v Romania*, a case that concerned the broadcasting of a television interview with a child, without parental consent. It is important to acknowledge that in *IVT* consent formed part of the domestic legal framework, but that consent had not in fact been sought from IVT's parents. Nevertheless, the Court did not approach this as a case in which the state had failed to act in accordance within its legal framework. On the contrary, it took the opportunity to emphasise that states have a 'positive obligation to take into account the particular vulnerability of young persons'.[99] It thus declared that 'prior parental consent had to be considered as a safeguard for the protection of the applicant's image, rather than as a mere formal requirement'.[100] Moreover, it stated that special legal safeguards are required in respect of children given that 'disclosure of information concerning their identity could jeopardise the child's dignity and well-being even more severely than in the case of adult persons, given their greater vulnerability'.[101] Consequently states have positive obligations to ensure that there are special legal safeguards in place to protect those that are vulnerable, in order to protect dignity and well-being.

This connection with 'dignity and well-being' brings me to the final point that I want to make in reflecting upon the legacy of *Von Hannover*, namely that the recognition of positive obligations in the context of privacy has arguably influenced the Court in developing its Article 8 ECHR case law in other contexts. In particular, it is interesting to observe the development of state obligations in respect of hate speech under Article 8 ECHR and the ways in which

[95] *Hajovsky v Slovakia* (n 89) at [49].

[96] *Bogomolova v Russia* (n 88) at [56]. More generally see J Gligorijevic, 'Children's Privacy: The Role of Parental Control and Consent' (2019) 19 *Human Rights Law Review* 201.

[97] *Reklos and Davourlis v Greece* (n 5) at [43]. Hughes (n 4).

[98] *Bogomolova v Russia* (n 88).

[99] *IVT v Romania* (n 90) at [46].

[100] ibid, at [54].

[101] ibid, at [59].

the Court has sought to draw upon the same framework for resolving cases involving competing Article 8 and 10 rights.

It has long been evident in both the Article 10 ECHR and Article 17 ECHR jurisprudence that states can justify criminalising hate speech. Yet whilst those expressing hate speech could seek to rely on Article 10 ECHR in order to argue that the state had violated their right to freedom of expression, it is only recently that the Court has developed positive obligations in respect of protection of the victims of hate speech under the auspices of Article 8 ECHR. Here there are indications that the way in which the Court construed Article 8 ECHR in *Von Hannover* has influenced the way in which the Court articulates the values which underpin Article 8 ECHR in order to justify imposing positive obligations. For example, in the recent landmark case of *Behar and Gutman v Bulgaria* the Court cited the 'zone of interaction' from *Von Hannover* in determining that 'negative public statements about a social group can be seen as affecting the "private life" of individual members of that group to the point of triggering the application of Article 8'.[102] Whilst the Court's approach to resolving the conflict between Articles 8 and 10 also mirrors the approach that has developed in the post-*Von Hannover* case law. Thus, demonstrating the extent to which *Von Hannover* triggered a far broader process of judicial development in respect of the interface between these two rights and the Court's role in resolving such conflicts.

V. CONCLUSION

It is evident that in the years that have followed *Von Hannover* that it was not the last word from the Court on the right to privacy, in particular the Court has had to revisit the concept of a public figure, the balancing criteria and its own role in this analysis. Does this mean that *Von Hannover* is not a landmark case in the development of the Article 8 ECHR right to privacy? In contemplating this it is worth thinking about what it means to call something a 'landmark'. The word 'landmark' brings to my mind images such as a lighthouse beaming across the water or Neil Armstrong firmly staking the United States' flag on the moon. For me these images capture not only the visual and symbolic nature of landmarks, but also their spatial attributes. In particular, the way in which landmarks take ownership of the surrounding environment, reconfiguring it, imposing structure, order or direction. Another way of thinking about 'landmarks' is in the context of a 'landmark moment', this brings to the fore their temporal role in demarcating distinct periods or pinpointing a turning point in history. Bringing these spatial and temporal perspectives together we

[102] *Behar and Gutman v Bulgaria* (n 52) at [54]–[55].

might therefore say that a landmark case is that which: (i) provides a turning point in legal history; (ii) identifies the boundaries of an area of law or legal concept; and/or (iii) sets out principles which direct future cases. Applying this to *Von Hannover* I suggest that it is a landmark case in each of these senses. It was the first case in which the Court held that a state had positive obligations in respect of press intrusions into privacy and found a violation of those obligations. It established the wide ambit of Article 8 ECHR, and in so doing it set out the principles that has shaped not only future press intrusion cases, but other aspects of Article 8 ECHR as well.

10

Douglas v Hello! Ltd (2005)

TANYA APLIN AND JUDITH SKILLEN

I. INTRODUCTION

DOUGLAS V HELLO! Ltd (No 3)[1] is, of course, only one of the several decisions spawned during the litigation between the Douglases, *OK!* magazine and *Hello!* magazine, nevertheless, we consider it a 'landmark' decision in the English landscape of privacy protection for two main reasons. The first is that it genuinely straddles the notions of privacy and confidentiality and in so doing demonstrates that these actions are awkward companions. The Court of Appeal indicated its disgruntlement that privacy protection was situated within the equitable action for breach of confidence, while at the same time it looked to delineate points of divergence, such as in relation to the publication of photographs. This arguably contributed to the later reformulation of an independent tort of misuse of private information. The court also accepted that privacy protection and commercialisation of confidential personal information are compatible and indeed allowed for twin-track claims of privacy intrusion and traditional breach of confidence, which in turn gave a third party (*OK!*) a basis on which to claim. While a parallel case to *Douglas (No 3)* has not occurred, it has recently been confirmed that motivations for keeping information private can legitimately extend to 'controlling' one's public image.[2] The second reason for the landmark status of the case is that it gestured at key challenges for the development of privacy protection in the sphere of remedies. The law of privacy in England and Wales was in a transitional stage at the time of *Douglas (No 3)*. Personal privacy protection was still rather awkwardly being framed in the equitable doctrine of breach of confidence, and the tort of misuse of private information was in embryonic form. Therefore, as the law of privacy was undergoing some growing pains at the time of *Douglas (No 3)*, it

[1] *Douglas v Hello! Ltd (No 3)* [2005] EWCA Civ 595; [2006] QB 125 ('*Douglas (No 3)*').

[2] *Duchess of Sussex v Associated Newspapers Ltd* [2021] EWHC 273 (Ch) [102] ('*Sussex*'), upheld on appeal: *Duchess of Sussex v Associated Newspapers Ltd* [2021] EWCA Civ 1810; [2022] 4 WLR 81 ('*Sussex* (CA)').

is unsurprising to see the court grappling with questions of potential remedies in the context of personal privacy. While *Douglas (No 3)* did not resolve these matters – such as, the possibility of negotiating damages – it marked out what would become the terrain for later debate.

We examine *Douglas (No 3)* in several sections to illustrate its landmark status. We begin in section II with an overview of the decision, before turning in section III to assess how the court grappled with the independence or otherwise of privacy protection. In section IV, the privileged approach to photographs is discussed before moving to consider in section V how controlling one's image interfaced with privacy protection. Section VI analyses the wide-ranging remedial issues raised during the litigation.

II. THE LITIGATION

The extensive litigation brought by the Douglases and *OK!* against *Hello!* spanned several years. It arose when surreptitious and unauthorised photographs taken at the wedding between Michael Douglas and Catherine Zeta-Jones were sold to *Hello!* magazine. *Hello!* sought to publish these in advance of *OK!* magazine's exclusive coverage of the event (for which *OK!* had paid the Douglases £1 million). The claimants were initially granted an ex parte interim injunction restraining publication, which was later discharged by the Court of Appeal in *Douglas (No 1)* (the details of which are discussed later in section VI).[3] At trial, Lindsay J found in favour of the Douglases and *OK!* on the basis of an actionable breach of confidence.[4] The Court of Appeal dismissed *Hello!*'s appeal against the Douglases but allowed the appeal against *OK!*.[5] *OK!* successfully appealed to the House of Lords, which restored the order of Lindsay J.[6]

Given the focus of this chapter, further details about the second Court of Appeal decision will be provided. Lord Phillips MR, who delivered the judgment of the court,[7] offered a helpful summary of the liability issues to be decided:

> The issues in relation to the Douglases' claim are as follows. (Disregarding the effect of the OK! contract) did the law of confidence protect information about the wedding as being private information? If so, did the OK! contract destroy that protection? Did the law of confidence protect the Douglases' commercial interest in the information about their wedding?
>
> The issues in relation to OK!'s claim are as follows. Did the OK! contract have the effect of extending to OK! the protection of the law of confidence in respect of the

[3] *Douglas v Hello! Ltd (No 1)* [2000] EWCA Civ 353; [2001] QB 967 ('*Douglas (No 1)*').
[4] *Douglas v Hello! Ltd* [2003] EWHC 786 (Ch); [2003] EMLR 31 ('*Douglas* (Ch D)').
[5] *Douglas (No 3)* (n 1).
[6] Reported as *OBG Ltd v Allan* [2007] UKHL 21; [2008] 1 AC 1 ('*Douglas* (HL)').
[7] To which Clarke and Neuberger LJJ contributed.

> information about the wedding? If so was that protection lost when OK! published the authorised photographs?[8]

The Court of Appeal (after referring inter alia to *Campbell v MGN Ltd*[9]) held that 'in so far as private information is concerned, we are required to adopt, as the vehicle for performing such duty as falls on the courts in relation to Convention rights, the cause of action formerly described as breach of confidence'.[10] Rather than asking whether the information was confidential, the court noted that it had to ask whether the information was 'private'.[11] It held that applying the test in *Campbell* the photographs of the Douglases wedding 'plainly portrayed aspects of the Douglases' private life'.[12]

The court then went on to consider whether the Douglases' contract with *OK!*, in which approved photographs would be published, affected their claim for protection of privacy under the English law of confidence.[13] The qualitatively different nature of information conveyed via photographs, rather than via verbal description, was emphasised.[14] However, the court observed that:

> To the extent that an individual authorises photographs taken on a private occasion to be made public, the potential for distress at the publication of other, unauthorised, photographs, taken on the same occasion, will be reduced.[15]

This was said to be relevant in terms of damages, as opposed to whether a privacy claim existed and the court described the award of damages for distress as 'a very modest sum'.[16] Thus, the Court of Appeal held that the first and second claimants' Article 8 ECHR right was engaged and that commercialisation of their privacy interest did not affect liability, but rather only the damages to be awarded.

The Court of Appeal recognised that the award of damages for the labour and expense of editing the photographs that were to be provided to *OK!* was a head of damage that related to the Douglases' commercial exploitation of their wedding and had nothing to do with interference with their private life.[17] Unlike Lindsay J at first instance, the Court of Appeal saw that: '[r]ecognition of the right of a celebrity to make money out of publicising private information about himself, including his photographs on a private occasion, breaks new

[8] *Douglas (No 3)* (n 1) [43]–[44].
[9] *Campbell v MGN Ltd* [2004] UKHL 22; [2004] AC 457 ('*Campbell*').
[10] *Douglas (No 3)* (n 1) [53].
[11] ibid, [83].
[12] ibid, [95].
[13] ibid, [107].
[14] ibid, [105].
[15] ibid, [107].
[16] ibid, [107], [110].
[17] ibid, [111].

ground.'[18] However, the court was not opposed to this development as a matter of principle:

> We can see no reason in principle why equity should not protect the opportunity to profit from confidential information about oneself in the same circumstances that it protects the opportunity to profit from confidential information in the nature of a trade secret.[19]

The Court of Appeal, however, overturned Lindsay J's decision vis-à-vis *OK!* magazine. The court stated that Lindsay J had (incorrectly) 'treated the information about the wedding as if it were property when he referred to its benefit being "shared between and … enforceable by co-owners or by a successor in title"'.[20] Further, the court observed that any transfer of a right to use photographs was no more than an exclusive licence to exploit commercially approved photographs, as opposed to any photographic information about the wedding.[21] In relation to the unauthorised photographs, it was only the Douglases 'who had the right to protect this area of privacy or confidentiality'.[22] *OK!* subsequently appealed successfully to the House of Lords on this issue. The Court of Appeal also held in obiter that the virtually simultaneous publication of the approved and unauthorised photographs (which occurred because *OK!* was trying to mitigate its damage) did not have the effect of destroying any rights of confidentiality held by *OK!*.[23]

Although this section has recounted the facts as they related to *OK!*'s claim, this chapter will focus only on the Douglases claims because they straddled privacy and breach of confidence, whereas *OK!*'s claim did not.

III. BREACH OF CONFIDENCE VERSUS MISUSE OF PRIVATE INFORMATION

The *Douglas* litigation occurred either side of the House of Lords' decision in *Campbell v MGN Ltd*.[24] The decision of the Court of Appeal in *Douglas (No 1)* to discharge the interim injunction which had been granted to the claimants came before *Campbell* and was the 'first detailed analysis of the impact of the Human Rights Act 1998 on the protection of privacy afforded by English law and, in particular, the law of confidence'.[25] The second Court of Appeal decision in *Douglas (No 3)* was heard after *Campbell*; however, it appears that the

[18] ibid, [113].
[19] ibid, [113].
[20] ibid, [128].
[21] ibid, [132], [134].
[22] ibid, [136].
[23] ibid, [140].
[24] *Campbell* (n 9). See ch 8 of this collection by G Phillipson for a discussion of this case.
[25] *Douglas (No 3)* (n 1) [63].

significance of *Campbell* in establishing an informational privacy tort was not immediately apparent.[26] This much is clear from Lord Phillips MR's judgment, in which he appeared to regard Lord Nicholls' terminology of misuse of private information in *Campbell* as more of a semantic development, as opposed to heralding a cause of action distinct from breach of confidence. Lord Phillips MR referred to Lord Nicholls' terminology of misuse of private information, but only as a passing reference,[27] and also noted Lord Nicholls' reference to Lord Woolf CJ's dicta in *A v B plc*,[28] which described English law as 'absorbing the rights which articles 8 and 10 protect into the long-established action for breach of confidence'.[29] Similarly, Lord Phillips MR cited Lady Hale's speech in *Campbell*, noting that her Ladyship 'said that the Human Rights Act 1998 did not create any new cause of action between private persons'.[30]

In articulating the legal principles relevant to the Douglases' claim, the Court of Appeal therefore identified breach of confidence, as opposed to a tort of misuse of private information, as the cause of action for advancing personal privacy claims. Lord Phillips MR observed that 'full, direct horizontal effect', initially advocated by Professor Sir William Wade, had not been adopted by the House of Lords in *Wainwright v Home Office* or *Campbell*.[31] Instead, it was the court's duty to 'develop the action for breach of confidence in such a manner as will give effect to both article 8 and article 10 rights', paying heed to Strasbourg jurisprudence,[32] adopting, in effect, a position of (some kind of) indirect horizontal effect.[33] But the court's dissatisfaction with this approach was remarked upon by Lord Phillips MR: '[w]e cannot pretend that we find it satisfactory to be required to shoehorn within the cause of action of breach of confidence claims for publication of unauthorised photographs of a private occasion'.[10] Indeed, Lord Phillips MR commented obiter that one consequence of 'shoehorning' the claim in this way was that, for the purposes of choice of law, the Douglases' claim 'does not fall to be treated as a tort under English law: see *Kitechnology BV v Unicor GmbH Plastmaschinen* [1995] FSR 765, para 40 …'.[34]

The Court of Appeal clearly felt constrained to continue to locate privacy protection within the action for breach of confidence. Yet, on appeal to the

[26] It is interesting to note that Lord Phillips MR made a similar observation about the impact of another significant case to the law of privacy, *Attorney-General v Guardian Newspapers (No 2)* [1990] 1 AC 109. In *Douglas (No 3)* (n 1) at [61] his Lordship notes '[t]he potential that Lord Goff's analysis had for protecting private information that was not recorded in a document was not immediately appreciated'.

[27] *Douglas (No 3)* (n 1) [51] and [77].

[28] *A v B plc* [2002] EWCA Civ 337; [2003] QB 195 [4].

[29] *Douglas (No 3)* (n 1) [51].

[30] ibid, [52].

[31] ibid, [50]. *Wainwright v Home Office* [2003] UKHL 53; [2004] 2 AC 406 and *Campbell* (n 9).

[32] ibid, [53].

[33] J Morgan, 'Privacy in the House of Lords, Again' (2004) 120 *Law Quarterly Review* 563, 565.

[34] *Douglas (No 3)* (n 1) [96].

House of Lords in *Douglas v Hello!*, Lord Nicholls reiterated his characterisation in *Campbell*, indeed in somewhat firmer terms:

> As the law has developed breach of confidence, or misuse of confidential information, *now covers two distinct causes of action, protecting two different interests: privacy, and secret ('confidential') information*. It is important to keep these two distinct.[35]

In assessing *OK!*'s appeal, Lord Nicholls made clear that confidentiality, and not privacy (which was limited only to the Douglases), was the relevant cause of action. Lord Hoffmann (in the majority) agreed with this approach. Privacy was a distinct issue, restricted to the Douglases, whereas commercially confidential information was at stake when it came to *OK!*'s interests.[36] While their Lordships still connected privacy protection to the action for breach of confidence, there was clearly a recognition of it now having twin, distinct branches. This approach acknowledged the indirect, horizontal effect of the Human Rights Act 1998 but at the same time created the space to develop privacy protection independently of the requirements of 'old fashioned' breach of confidence.

Treating 'privacy' and 'confidentiality' as twin branches stemming from breach of confidence was maintained in *Mosley v NGN Ltd*[37] with Eady J finding that the claim was 'partly founded, as in *McKennitt v Ash*' upon 'old-fashioned' breach of confidence, and also unauthorised disclosure of private information.[38] As such, Eady J considered both whether Article 8 was engaged and whether a duty of confidence was owed. He concluded that, in light of Strasbourg jurisprudence it was 'fairly obvious' that Article 8 was engaged.[39] Further, he held that the participant who surreptitiously filmed the sex party owed a duty of confidence to the claimant because of the nature of the relationship, and that 'an "old fashioned breach of confidence"' had been committed.[40] Moreover, Eady J examined, to some extent, the basis of this 'expanded' cause of action and whether it was a tort, for the purposes of assessing available remedies. He observed that the Court of Appeal in *Douglas (No 3)* had suggested the expanded action was *not* a tort[41] and further that the same court had not interpreted Lord Nicholls' comments in *Campbell* as signalling that 'infringements of privacy should now be regarded as an independent tort uncluttered by any limitations deriving from its equitable origins'.[42]

In the later Court of Appeal decision, *Tchenguiz v Imerman*,[43] the court commented that following *Campbell* 'there is now a tort of misuse of private

[35] *Douglas* (HL) (n 6) [255] (emphasis added).
[36] ibid, [118].
[37] *Mosley v NGN Ltd* [2008] EWHC 1777 (QB); [2008] EMLR 20 ('*Mosley*').
[38] ibid, [4]–[6].
[39] ibid, [104].
[40] ibid, [108].
[41] ibid, [181].
[42] ibid, [182].
[43] *Tchenguiz v Imerman* [2010] EWCA Civ 908; [2011] 2 WLR 592.

information' and, citing *Douglas (No 3)*, that 'a claim based on misuse of private information has been "shoehorned" into the law of confidence'.[44] The court also indicated that '[a]s Lord Phillips MR's observation suggests, there are dangers in conflating the developing law of privacy under article 8 and the traditional law of confidence'.[45] The court further observed that 'privacy is still classified as part of the confidentiality *genus*'[46] and called for the somewhat contradictory goal of developing the law consistently and coherently 'in both privacy and "old fashioned confidence" cases, even if they sometimes may have different features'.[47]

In the light of these decisions after *Douglas (No 3)* it is therefore somewhat surprising that a later Court of Appeal decided to sever the 'privacy' branch entirely from the trunk of breach of confidence. In *Google v Vidal-Hall* the Court of Appeal had to consider the nature of privacy protection, for the purposes of whether service could be made out of the jurisdiction.[48] The court indicated that this was a case where 'classification' made a difference.[49] If privacy protection was tortious, service was possible. If it was grounded in the equitable action for breach of confidence, then it would not be possible, according to the authority of *Kitechnology BV v Unicor GmbH Plastmaschinen*.[50] The court held that it was clear that 'there are now two separate and distinct actions: an action for breach of confidence; and one for misuse of private information'.[51] In reaching that conclusion, the court relied on Lord Nicholls' comments obiter in *Douglas v Hello!* as supporting the fact that '[a]ctions for breach of confidence and actions for misuse of private information rest on different legal foundations'.[52] As well, the court noted that the Court of Appeal in *Douglas (No 3)* had 'clearly regarded assimilating a claim to protect privacy rights with a claim for breach of confidence as unsatisfactory' and 'was hesitant about not categorising the claim as a tort'.[53] (The court also stated that the question of whether misuse of private information was a tort for the purposes of applicable law did not directly arise in *Douglas (No 3)*).[54] The Court of Appeal in *Vidal-Hall* thus concluded that misuse of private information *was* a tort without any equitable characteristics for the purposes of service out of the jurisdiction and, as such, *Kitechnology* was not applicable since it concerned an action for breach of confidence.[55]

[44] ibid, [65].
[45] ibid, [66].
[46] ibid, [67].
[47] ibid, [67].
[48] *Google Inc v Vidal-Hall* [2015] EWCA Civ 311; [2016] QB 1003 ('*Vidal-Hall*').
[49] ibid, [17].
[50] *Kitechnology BV v Unicor GmbH Plastmaschinen* [1995] FSR 765.
[51] *Vidal-Hall* (n 48) [21].
[52] ibid, [25].
[53] ibid, [41].
[54] ibid, [39].
[55] ibid, [43], [50]–[51].

This characterisation was not seen as creating a new cause of action but 'simply [giving] the correct legal label to one that already exists'.[56] The *Vidal-Hall* decision also apparently applied more broadly than the issue of service out of the jurisdiction because the court commented obiter: '[w]e are conscious of the fact that there may be broader implications from our conclusions, for example as to remedies, limitation and vicarious liability … such points will need to be considered as and when they arise.'[57]

This untethering of privacy protection from breach of confidence and its judicial recognition as a tort of misuse of private information was entrenched by the 2016 Supreme Court decision in *PJS v NGN Ltd*.[58] In this case, an interim injunction to restrain publication of details of an extramarital affair of a well-known entertainer was upheld by a majority of the court (Lord Toulson dissenting), even though details had been published in magazines in the US, Canada, and Scotland and on various websites. Lord Mance (with whom the other members of the court agreed) referred, on several occasions, to 'tortious invasion of privacy rights' in his decision[59] and overturned the Court of Appeal's decision to discharge the injunction, in part because the court 'did not give due weight to the qualitative difference in intrusiveness and distress likely to be involved in what is now proposed by way of unrestricted publication by the English media'.[60] Lord Neuberger (with whom the other members of the court also agreed), referred to the claimants' Article 8 or privacy claim[61] and was at pains to distinguish the different nature of this claim from one based on confidentiality. He noted that if the claimants' case 'was simply based on confidentiality (or secrecy) … it would have substantial difficulties' because of the degree of publication of the story outside of the UK.[62] However, claims based on 'privacy and family life do not depend on confidentiality (or secrecy) alone'[63] and intrusion into PJS and his family's private lives would continue to occur if the interim injunction was not granted to the claimants.[64]

Thus, the 'shoehorning' of privacy protection within breach of confidence complained of by the Court of Appeal in *Douglas (No 3)* has not ultimately transpired. Subsequent courts, including at the most senior appellate level, have felt able to develop protection for privacy interests without the constraints of 'old fashioned' breach of confidence, to the point that the action is now seen as a distinct tort[65] and one that arguably embraces informational as well as intrusion

[56] ibid, [51].
[57] ibid, [51].
[58] *PJS v NGN Ltd* [2016] UKSC 26; [2016] AC 1081 ('*PJS*').
[59] ibid, [32], [33], [44].
[60] ibid, [35].
[61] ibid, [51], [58], [68].
[62] ibid, [57].
[63] ibid, [58].
[64] ibid, [65], [68].
[65] Eg, see *Sussex* (n 2) [29] (Warby J): '[d]omestic law gives effect to this framework [Human Rights Act 1998] through the tort of misuse of private information'; approved in *Sussex* (CA) (n 2)

interests.[66] The Court of Appeal's explicit frustration with situating privacy protection within breach of confidence is what resonated in subsequent judicial decisions, to the point that appellate courts were inspired, after almost a decade, to separate out the equitable action from a distinct tort.

IV. PRIVACY INTERESTS IN PHOTOGRAPHS

The Court of Appeal's decision in *Douglas (No 3)* was significant also for its focus on privacy in photographs. Lord Phillips MR remarked that '[o]nce intimate personal information about a celebrity's private life has been widely published it may serve no useful purpose to prohibit further publication. The same will not necessarily be true of photographs'.[67] He pointed to 'a further important potential distinction between the law relating to private information and that relating to other types of confidential information'.[68] This was that widespread publication of photographs would not destroy the privacy interest. Rather, repeated publication could cause a 'fresh intrusion of privacy when each additional viewer sees the photograph and even when one who has seen a previous publication of the photograph is confronted by a fresh publication of it'.[69] This seemed linked to the qualitatively different nature of photographs which do 'more than convey information' and enable 'the viewer to focus on intimate personal detail'.[70]

This aspect of the court's decision was in keeping with earlier decisions, which it cited, namely, *Theakston*, *Peck*, *Von Hannover (No 1)* and *Campbell*, where photographs were treated as qualitatively different. In *Theakston v MGN Ltd*,[71] Ouseley J refused to grant an interim injunction against publication of the fact and details of the claimant's visit to a brothel on the basis that the information lacked confidentiality,[72] but did grant an injunction to restrain publication of photographs of the claimant in the brothel on the grounds that the unauthorised photographs would 'constitute an intrusion into his private and personal life and would do so in a peculiarly humiliating and damaging way'.[73] In *Peck*

[33] (Vos MR). See also *The Racing Partnership Ltd v Sports Information Services Ltd* [2020] EWCA Civ 1300; [2021] Ch 233 [70] (Arnold LJ).

66 On the tort of misuse of private information embracing informational and intrusion interests see: P Wragg, 'Recognising a privacy-invasion tort: the conceptual unity of informational and intrusion claims' (2019) 78 *Cambridge Law Journal* 409. For a contrasting view see: N Moreham, 'Beyond Information: Physical Privacy in English Law' [2014] *Cambridge Law Journal* 350.

67 *Douglas (No 3)* (n 1) [105].

68 ibid.

69 ibid, [105].

70 ibid, [105].

71 *Theakston v MGN Ltd* [2002] EWHC 137 (QB); [2002] EMLR 22.

72 ibid, [61]–[64].

73 ibid, [78].

v UK[74] the ECtHR had found that CCTV footage of the applicant following a suicide attempt that was disseminated by the media was a violation of the applicant's Article 8 right. This was despite the fact the applicant was in a public street because, in effect, the footage 'far exceeded any exposure to a passer-by or to security observation'.[75] In *Von Hannover v Germany (No 1)*,[76] the applicant sought to establish that publishing photographs of her going about her daily business was a violation of her Article 8 ECHR right. The court accepted that Article 8 conferred on states both negative and positive obligations[77] and the claimant's right had been infringed. Although she was a public figure, her private activities were not relevant to any public or official functions[78] and the photographs did not contribute to any debate of general interest to society.[79] The Strasbourg Court also had regard to the fact that such photos were often taken 'in a climate of continual harassment that induces in the persons concerned a very strong sense of intrusion into their private life'.[80] Finally, two of their Lordships in *Campbell* placed 'particular weight on the intrusive nature of the photographs'.[81] Lord Hope observed that the photographs 'were taken deliberately, in secret and with a view to their publication in conjunction with the article'.[82] While Lady Hale indicated that the photographs showed the claimant 'coming either to or from the NA meeting … [and] showed the place where the meeting was taking place'.[83]

In cases immediately following *Douglas (No 3)*, first instance courts placed emphasis on photographs, but only if the photographs themselves revealed something 'obviously private'. Take, for example, the interim injunction application in *John v Associated Newspaper Ltd*.[84] In *John*, the claimant objected to publication of a photograph of him on the street outside his home, dressed casually. Eady J cited *Douglas (No 3)* in passing and concluded that the photograph was not 'private' because it did not contain private information (such as health or personal relationships or attempted suicide as in *Peck*) but was 'much more akin to "popping out for a pint of milk"'.[85] Further, referring to *Von Hannover (No 1)*, Eady J noted that the photograph was not taken, it seems, in a climate of harassment.[86] As such, the application for an injunction was denied.

[74] *Peck v United Kingdom* (2003) 36 EHRR 41.
[75] ibid, [62].
[76] *Von Hannover v Germany (No 1)* (2005) 40 EHRR 1 ('*Von Hannover (No 1)*').
[77] ibid, [57].
[78] ibid, [63]–[64], [76].
[79] ibid, [65].
[80] ibid, [59]. See also [68].
[81] *Douglas (No 3)* (n 1) [88].
[82] *Campbell* (n 9) [123].
[83] ibid, [155].
[84] *John v Associated Newspapers Ltd* [2006] EWHC 1611 (QB); [2006] EMLR 27 ('*John*'). See also *Mahmood v Galloway* [2006] EWHC 1286 (QB); [2006] EMLR 26.
[85] *John* (n 84) [15].
[86] ibid.

Thus, in the immediate wake of *Douglas (No 3)* photographs were only treated as qualitatively different *if* they contained information that was private, in the sense of being embarrassing or intimate in some way. Yet, later cases post *Douglas (No 3)*, in the context of children, pushed against this apparent barrier. In *Murray v Express Newspapers*, where photographs had been taken on a public street of JK Rowling's child, the Court of Appeal observed that it was arguable that such routine acts could attract a reasonable expectation of privacy, depending on the circumstances.[87] In *Weller v Associated Newspapers Ltd*[88] the Court of Appeal upheld the first instance decision that publication of photographs of Paul Weller's children (aged 10 months and 16 at the time) taken during a 'family day out' was a misuse of private information. In considering whether the claimants had a reasonable expectation of privacy in the unpixellated images of their faces that were published, the court reiterated that, while the same broad approach must be adopted for adults and children, there were considerations pertinent to children 'which may mean that in a particular case a child has a reasonable expectation of privacy where an adult does not'.[89] The court concluded that the claimants had a reasonable expectation of privacy. Although the photographs were taken in a public location, it was a private family outing and no consent had been given to being photographed. The critical factor, however, was that there were children, identified by surname, who had not courted publicity and nor had their parents (who were in the public arena). There was also evidence of negative impact on the teenage child.[90] Finally, there is the decision in *AAA v Associated Newspapers Ltd*[91] where several articles were published speculating as the paternity of the claimant. The allegation was that the father of the claimant was a well-known elected politician who had engaged in an adulterous affair. The articles also featured a photograph of the claimant (a young baby) that had been taken while she was in a public place (and without the knowledge or consent of the claimant's mother). Apparently, the photographs had been included in the articles in order to illustrate the family resemblance between the claimant and alleged father. At first instance, Nicola Davies J held that publication of the photograph was actionable. She stated:

> The articles provided sufficient information: no more was required, particularly when the same involved the image of a young child photographed and published without the parent's consent.[92]

[87] *Murray v Express Newspapers* [2008] EWCA Civ 446; [2009] Ch 481 [55].
[88] *Weller v Associated Newspapers Ltd* [2015] EWCA Civ 1176; [2016] 1 WLR 1541 ('*Weller* (CA)').
[89] ibid, [29] (Lord Dyson MR with whom Tomlinson and Bean LJJ agreed). See also *In the matter of an application by JR38 for Judicial Review (Northern Ireland)* [2015] UKSC 42; [2016] AC 1131 [95] (Lord Toulson) and [113] (Lord Clarke) (Lord Hodge in agreement with both justices).
[90] *Weller* (CA) (n 88) [59]–[66] (Lord Dyson MR with whom Tomlinson and Bean LJJ agreed).
[91] *AAA v Associated Newspapers Ltd* [2012] EWHC 2103 (QB); [2013] EMLR 2 ('*AAA*').
[92] ibid, [122].

In relation to the information contained in the articles, however, the judge held that the claimant's Article 8 right was diluted by the behaviour of her mother and outweighed by the public interest 'in the supposed father and in particular the recklessness, relevant to his character and fitness for public office'.[93] Subsequent articles were not actionable because the information as to alleged paternity was now in the public domain.[94] On appeal, the Court of Appeal upheld the first instance decision.[95]

Douglas (No 3) arguably signalled the way for the approaches taken in *Murray, Weller* and *AAA*.[96] While the wedding was not a 'routine' act and was not held in public, there is an intimation that taking photographs of people enjoying their private sphere is enough to warrant an intrusion. In particular, Lord Phillips MR commented on the nub of the complaint:

> The objection to the publication of unauthorised photographs taken on a private occasion is not simply that the images that they disclose convey secret information, or impressions that are unflattering. It is that they disclose information that is private. The offence is caused because what the claimant could reasonably expect would remain private has been made public. The intrusion into the private domain is, of itself, objectionable.[97]

What is interesting about the above paragraph is that it is not the embarrassing nature of the photographs that is problematic. Rather, it is the expectation that this private occasion would remain private – the 'intrusion into the private domain' itself. While *Murray, Weller* and *AAA* involved acts in public places – whereas the location of the wedding was not 'public' because of restrictions on guests – the emphasis on the privacy interest in *Douglas (No 3)* – a wedding being part of one's private life – arguably helped pave the way for the courts to consider 'private life' more broadly and to focus on the intrusion into that private life rather than insisting on photographs that were obviously embarrassing or intimate in nature. In *Murray*, for example, it was argued – based on *Douglas (No 3)* – that photographs are inherently invasive and that this was a family outing. In *Weller*, Lord Dyson MR (delivering the leading judgment, with Tomlinson and Bean LJJ in agreement) observed that Lord Phillips MR in *Douglas (No 3)* had said, 'that photographs were a 'particularly intrusive'

[93] ibid, [119].

[94] ibid, [120]. Note Nicola Davies J at [76] stated the claimant had accepted what the Court of Appeal held in *Douglas (No 3)* at [105] that '[o]nce intimate personal information about a celebrity's private life has been widely published it may serve no useful purpose to prohibit further publication'.

[95] *AAA v Associated Newspapers Ltd* [2013] EWCA Civ 554.

[96] As, arguably, did *Reklos and Davourlis v Greece* App no1234/05, Judgment 15 January 2009 [40]: 'A person's image constitutes one of the chief attributes of his or her personality, as it reveals the person's unique characteristics and distinctions the person from his or her peers. The right to the protection of one's image is thus one of the essential components of personal development and presupposes the right to control the use of that image.'

[97] *Douglas (No 3)* (n 1) [107] (emphasis supplied).

violation of one's privacy',[98] again with an emphasis on this being an outing with the family. Lord Dyson MR went on to note that '[w]here a child has a famous parent, this security and safety concern is arguably heightened even further'.[99] In *AAA*, the photographs of the claimant were innocuous but in the context of allegations about the claimant's paternity were held to be intrusive.

Another way in which the law has developed since *Douglas (No 3)* is that repeated privacy intrusions are imaginable not only for photographs, but for private information generally. In *PJS*, Lord Toulson (dissenting) observed that 'the court needs to be very cautious about granting an injunction preventing publication of what is widely known' and that the position for photographs indicated in *Douglas (No 3)* was because photographs were qualitatively different.[100] However, as discussed above, a majority of the Supreme Court held that unrestricted, widespread publication of private information (even if already circulated to some extent) was able to be restrained by injunction. In *PJS* the potential for privacy intrusion moved to embracing *any* private information and the degree of pre-existing circulation did not negate that intrusion from occurring, even in the absence of photographs.

V. IMAGE CONTROL

Arguably the most fascinating aspect of *Douglas (No 3)* is how the privacy interests at stake intertwined with the Douglases' desire to maintain control of their image and the way in which that was dealt with *both* as a privacy claim and as one that was purely about controlling commercially valuable confidential information. The Douglases had sought to control their image by licensing *OK!* to publish authorised photographs of their wedding.[101] An issue was whether the intention to publish authorised photographs affected the Douglases' privacy claim in relation to the unauthorised photographs. On this point, the Court of Appeal held:

> To the extent that an individual authorises photographs taken on a private occasion to be made public, the potential for distress at the publication of other, unauthorised, photographs, taken on the same occasion, will be reduced. This will be very relevant when considering the amount of any damages. *The agreement that authorised photographs can be published will not, however, provide a defence to a claim, brought under the law of confidence, for the publication of unauthorised photographs.*

[98] *Weller* (CA) (n 88) [37].
[99] ibid.
[100] *PJS* (n 58) [88].
[101] *Douglas (No 3)* (n 1) [108]: 'This conclusion endorses that reached by Sedley LJ, who held at the interlocutory stage [2001] QB 967, para 140, that the Douglases "were careful by their contract to retain a right of veto over publication of OK!'s photographs in order to maintain the kind of image which is professionally and no doubt also personally important to them. This element of privacy remained theirs and Hello!'s photographs violated it."'

> It follows that we do not accept Mr Price's submission that the effect of the OK! contract precluded the Douglases' right to contend that their wedding was a private occasion and, as such, protected by the law of confidence.[102]

The court went on to find that not only were damages for mental distress payable,[103] but a perpetual injunction against publication of unauthorised photographs was granted.[104]

The role of a claimant's intention to publish private information resurfaced many years later in *Duchess of Sussex v Associated Newspapers Ltd*[105] and we can see the influence of *Douglas (No 3)* in the court's reasoning. The claimant in this case brought an action, alleging misuse of private information and infringement of copyright, in relation to the defendant's publication in the *Mail on Sunday* and *MailOnline* of large parts of a five-page letter that she had sent to her father. The defendant argued that the claimant's alleged intention to publicise her letter (in a book, 18 months later) meant that she had no reasonable expectation of privacy. Warby J at first instance rejected this argument and, in so doing, observed that *Douglas (No 3)* 'does indicate that an intention to publish may be "very relevant' to damages", but the court held that "the fact that authorised photographs can be published will not provide a defence …"'.[106] Warby J, also relying on *Douglas (No 3)*, gave short shrift to the defendant's argument that the claimant was looking to control her public image and this somehow diminished her privacy right. He explained:

> On this point, *Douglas (No 3)* is instructive. At [109], the Court agreed that the Douglases were entitled to complain about the unauthorised photographs infringed [sic] their privacy 'on the ground that these detracted from the favourable picture presented by the authorised photographs and caused consequent distress.' It is true that the unauthorised photographs did not convey exactly the same information as those the Douglases had authorised, but the point remains valid. If (which she emphatically denies) the claimant provided the Letter or information about it to the Authors with a view to publication, or wrote it with a view to later publicity, she might have exposed herself to claims that she had libelled her father or infringed his other rights, but she would have been well within her rights, so far as her own privacy is concerned.[107]

[102] *Douglas (No 3)* (n 1) [107] (emphasis supplied).

[103] ibid, [109]: 'We agree that the Douglases were entitled to complain about the unauthorised photographs as infringing their privacy on the ground that these detracted from the favourable picture presented by the authorised photographs and caused consequent distress.'

[104] For critique of the grant of a perpetual injunction see C Michalos, 'Douglas v Hello: The Final Frontier' (2007) 18(7) *Entertainment Law Review* 241, 245–246.

[105] *Sussex*. The decision of Warby J in *Sussex* was upheld by the Court of Appeal in *Sussex* (CA) (n 2). While the Court of Appeal did not expressly approve of the passages excerpted from Warby J's judgment in the next paragraph, the court also did not disapprove of those statements.

[106] ibid, [93].

[107] ibid, [102].

Thus, the position in *Douglas (No 3)* about controlling one's privacy in order to control one's image has endured. This is perhaps no surprise if one sees the essence of exercising autonomy over one's information as the decision if, when and how to share private activities or information. However, the tension between privacy and 'image control' is one that continues to cause concern. It arose in *Douglas (No 3)* because the Douglases were able also to commercialise the photographs of their wedding through the exclusive licence to *OK!*. The Court of Appeal in *Douglas (No 3)* held that it was possible to protect confidential information about oneself *as a trade secret*:

> Where an individual ('the owner') has at his disposal information which he has created or which is private or personal and to which he can properly deny access to third parties, and he reasonably intends to profit commercially by using or publishing that information, then a third party who is, or ought to be, aware of these matters and who has knowingly obtained the information without authority, will be in breach of duty if he uses or publishes the information to the detriment of the owner.[108]

A troubling aspect of this principle is that it is difficult to apply. More specifically, the fact that the 'owner' must reasonably intend to profit commercially from using or publishing the information is uncertain. What will determine whether the intention to profit is reasonable or not? Will it be the existence of a market for that information? If so, then the requirement of 'reasonableness' seems superfluous. Or is it a narrower basis, namely, that a person is selling the information to better protect their privacy, which is what the claimants argued in *Douglas (No 3)*? Further, there is possible slippage into a right of publicity. For there to be a right of publicity, at least in the US sense, a person needs to *own* their image and thus be entitled to realise that commercial value by assigning or licensing it.[109] Admittedly, the Court of Appeal stressed that the term 'owner' was being used loosely and it did not designate the information as property, capable of ownership and transferral.[110] But if we accept, in principle, that persons are entitled to protect the commercialisation of private information, as well as their privacy interest, an argument about the right to control one's image, in a proprietary sense, may seem less of a logical leap and become more readily accepted.

[108] *Douglas (No 3)* (n 1) [118].

[109] P Jaffey, 'Rights of privacy, confidentiality, and publicity, and related rights' in P Torremans (ed), *Copyright and Human Rights* (Zuidpoolsingel, Kluwer Law International, 2004) 157–181, 173–174. Contrast the notion in a civil law setting which tends to characterise publicity protection as a subset of personality rights: see G Black, *Publicity Rights and Image: Exploitation and Legal Control* (Oxford, Hart, 2011) 16–19; H Beverley-Smith, A Ohly and A Lucas-Schloetter, *Privacy, Property and Personality: Civil Law Perspectives on Commercial Appropriation* (Cambridge, CUP, 2005) chs 4 and 5; and F Hofman, 'The right to publicity in German and English Law' [2010] *Intellectual Property Quarterly* 325.

[110] *Douglas (No 3)* (n 1) [119].

However, it is important to note that, unlike Lindsay J and the Court of Appeal, Lord Hoffmann in the House of Lords did not view this as an instance of commercialisation of private information. Instead, his view was that:

> The information in this case was capable of being protected, not because it concerned the Douglases' image any more than because it concerned their private life, but simply because it was information of commercial value over which the Douglases had sufficient control to enable them to impose an obligation of confidence.[111]

In other words, Lord Hoffmann was not interested in why the information had commercial value (which, naturally, was because it related to the Douglases wedding), but rather the *fact* that it was commercially valuable. This meant he was not interested in applying the various caveats that the Court of Appeal had suggested about 'reasonably intending to profit commercially'. This apparently leaves us in a situation where the same information is classified as private *and* commercial and this duality to the character of the information may seem odd.

One explanation is that the tort of misuse of private information evolving, and eventually severing itself, from breach of confidence did not negate or eclipse the existence of confidential (personal) information under the 'traditional' action. Another explanation is that this duality is possible because privacy protects the decision/s to share information about oneself but, once this choice is made, the information is able to take on a commercial or exploitable character. Yet there remains an oddity about treating personal information as a trade secret. While this might be a technically plausible argument to make[112] under the EU Trade Secrets Directive,[113] there is also literature to suggest that commercial or trade secrets do not (and should not) encompass commercially valuable private information.[114] Thus, the issue, as it relates to individuals, might be better conceived as one of *privacy* only and issues of intended publication or publication (including for commercial value) seen through the prism of Articles 8 and 10 ECHR and remedies. The difficulty with this approach, however, is that third party interests, such as that of *OK!*'s, would be left only to contract.

[111] *Douglas* (HL) (n 6) [124].

[112] See T Aplin, 'A Critical Evaluation of the Proposed Trade Secrets Directive' (2014) *Intellectual Property Quarterly* 257, 261–263.

[113] [2016] OJ L157/1. Implemented in the UK by the Trade Secrets (Enforcement, etc) Regulations 2018 (Regulations) SI 2018/597. For a discussion see T Aplin and R Arnold, 'UK implementation of the Trade Secrets Directive' in J Schvosbo, T Minssen and T Riis, *The Harmonisation and Protection of Trade Secrets in the EU – An Appraisal of the EU Directive* (Edward Elgar, 2020), ch 5, 65–85.

[114] See N de Sousa, 'What exactly is a trade secret under the proposed directive?' (2014) 9 *Journal of Intellectual Property Law and Practice* 923 and J Lapousterle et al, 'What protection for trade secrets in the European Union? A comment on the Directive proposal' (2016) *European Intellectual Property Review* 255, 257 arguing that 'the protection of trade secrets must … preserve its roots in the sphere of business life'.

VI. REMEDIES

A. Compensatory Damages

Lindsay J awarded the Douglases a total of £14,600,[115] a sum which was upheld by the Court of Appeal in *Douglas (No 3)*. By way of an initial observation, Lindsay J spoke of awarding 'damages' to the Douglases as opposed to equitable compensation. However, the precise underlying nature of the monetary award – whether equitable compensation or common law damages – was not explored in any depth by the judge.[116] Similarly, neither the Court of Appeal nor the House of Lords examined the question of whether equitable compensation or common law damages were being awarded. It may be that the question of the underlying nature of the award was thought to be of more conceptual than practical importance given that the House of Lords in *Target Holdings v Redferns* held that the basic principles underlying damages at common law and equitable compensation are the same.[117] However, it is clear that were the Douglases to bring their case today and plead misuse of private information, damages would be awarded at common law in light of misuse of private information being recognised as a tort in *Google v Vidal-Hall*.[118]

The Douglases' total sum consisted of nominal damages under the Data Protection Act 1998 ('DPA') (£50 each), as well as an award of £7,000 for loss incurred by the Douglases in bringing forward the preparation, provision and approval of the authorised photographs. The *Douglas* litigation is notable for being one of the few instances in which pecuniary losses were claimed in a privacy case.[119] Instead, when compensation is sought for misuse of private information, it is typically for non-pecuniary loss in the form of distress and injury to feelings. This head of damage also featured in the *Douglas* litigation. The Douglases were awarded £3,750 each in respect of distress caused by breach of their privacy. As noted above, in section II, this low sum for distress is in part due to the Douglases having commercialised their privacy interests in their wedding. However, this modest amount awarded for distress is, in general, emblematic of quantum awarded in early privacy cases. For example, Naomi

[115] *Douglas v Hello!* [2003] EWHC 2629 (Ch); [2004] EMLR 2 [56]–[58] ('*Douglas quantum*').

[116] However, in an earlier decision on liability, the judge spoke of 'damages or equitable compensation' in relation to the claimants' breach of confidence claim: *Douglas* (Ch D) (n 4) [193], [203], [273]. That the judge then spoke of 'damages' in the decision on quantum *may* indicate that the award was at common law, but this is inconclusive.

[117] *Target Holdings v Redferns* [1996] AC 421, 432 (Lord Browne-Wilkinson).

[118] *Vidal-Hall* (n 48).

[119] Another example being the £750 awarded in *Cornelius v De Taranto* [2001] EMLR 12 (QB) ('*De Taranto*') in respect of costs incurred by the claimant in trying to retrieve copies of medico-legal report retained in NHS records. A recent case which saw significant pecuniary losses awarded (£33,000) is *Sicri v Associated Newspapers Ltd* [2020] EWHC 3541; [2021] 4 WLR 9 (QB).

Campbell received £2,500 for distress caused by the publication of photographs of her taken outside a Narcotics Anonymous meeting (as well as a further £1,000 in aggravated damages).[120] Lady Archer received £2,500 for distress caused by a former employee's breach of confidence in disclosing her personal information to a newspaper, which eventually resulted in newspaper publications.[121] In that case, Jackson J held that '[g]eneral damages for injury to feelings should be kept to a modest level and should be proportionate to the injury suffered. Such awards should be well below the level of general damages for serious physical or psychiatric injury'.[122] Similarly, in *McKennitt v Ash* the claimant, a Canadian singer-songwriter, was awarded £5,000 for injured feelings and distress caused by the publication of her private and confidential information in a book written by a former friend and colleague.[123] In another relatively early privacy case, *Applause Store Productions Ltd v Raphael*, the claimant received £2,000 where the defendant published defamatory and private information about, inter alia, the claimant's sexual preferences on Facebook.[124] *Applause Store* provides a useful insight into how, at the time the case was decided in 2008, courts perceived the role of compensatory damages as limited to compensating distress or injury to feelings. The judge summarised the principles relating to compensation for breaches of privacy in the following terms: '[i]t is reasonably clear that damages in cases of misuse of private information are awarded to compensate the claimant for the hurt feelings and distress caused by the misuse of their information … Typically, such damages have been modest'.[125]

It is worthwhile remembering that, when the *Douglas* litigation began, non-pecuniary losses as a head of damages in breach of confidence cases had not long been recognised. The first case to award such damages was *Cornelius v De Taranto*, decided in 2000.[126] *Cornelius* saw £3,000 awarded to the claimant for distress caused by the defendant's disclosure of a medico-legal report, containing confidential information, to the claimant's GP. Morland J, cognisant of the novelty of the remedy awarded to the claimant, also held that 'damages must be modest' in such cases.[127] However, in the years since the *Douglas* litigation, there has been somewhat of an upward trend in compensation awarded to claimants for infringements of their right to privacy. A greater willingness on the part of judges to award higher sums of compensation was noted by Tugenhadt J in *Spelman v Express Newspapers*:

> If a remedy in damages is to be an effective remedy, then the amount that the court may award must not be subject to too severe a limitation. Recent settlements in the

[120] *Campbell v MGN Ltd* [2002] EWHC 499; [2002] EMLR 30 (QB).
[121] *Lady Archer v Williams* [2003] EWHC 1670 (QB); [2003] EMLR 38 ('*Archer*').
[122] ibid, [76].
[123] *McKennitt v Ash* [2005] EWHC 3003 (QB); [2006] EMLR 10.
[124] *Applause Store Productions Ltd v Raphael* [2008] EWHC 1781 (QB) ('*Applause Store*').
[125] ibid, [81].
[126] *De Taranto* (n 119).
[127] ibid, [80].

> much publicised phone hacking cases have been reported to be in sums far exceeding what in the past might have been thought to be available to be awarded by the courts. The sums awarded in the early cases such as *Campbell* were very low. But it can no longer be assumed that damages at those levels are the limit of the court's powers.[128]

Significantly, in concert with higher sums of compensation, another significant development has emerged in remedies jurisprudence since *Douglas (No 3)*: a novel head of damage for breach of the right itself. This head of damage was explicitly recognised in 2015 in *Gulati v MGN Ltd*,[129] but arguably damages of this sort had been awarded in a number of cases prior to *Gulati*. A notable case is *Mosley v NGN Ltd*, which saw the claimant awarded £60,000 for the defendant's publication of articles, photographs (both in print and online) and video footage (online) of the claimant's participation at a sadomasochistic sex party.[130] The sum awarded in *Mosley* was significantly larger than compensation awarded in previous privacy cases. The high sum may potentially be explained by orthodox compensatory principles in that the breach of privacy caused severe adverse consequences for Mosley. Undoubtedly in *Mosley*, there was a particularly egregious breach of privacy which caused the claimant acute distress. Eady J in *Mosley* recognised this, noting that '[t]he scale of distress and indignity in this case is difficult to comprehend. It is probably unprecedented'.[131] Both Eady J and the European Court of Human Rights (ECtHR) said that Mosley was 'hardly exaggerating' when he said 'that his life was ruined'.[132] However, Eady J did not seem to decide quantum on distress alone as it was held that:

> Apart from distress, there is another factor which probably has to be taken into account of a less tangible nature. It is accepted in recent jurisprudence that a legitimate consideration is that of *vindication to mark the infringement of a right*: see e.g. *Ashley v Chief Constable of Sussex* [2008] 2 WLR 975 at [21]–[22] and *Chester v Afshar* [2005] 1 AC 134 at [87]. Again, it should be stressed that this is different from vindication of reputation (long recognised as a proper factor in the award of libel damages). It is *simply to mark the fact that either the state or a relevant individual has taken away or undermined the right of another* – in this case taken away a person's dignity and struck at the core of his personality. It is a relevant factor, but the underlying policy is to ensure that an infringed right is met with "an adequate remedy".[133]

Thus, in *Mosley* there is support for damages to mark the infringement of a right, separate from (and potentially in addition to) any consequences suffered by the breach of privacy. This head of damages is sometimes called vindicatory damages, substitutive damages or normative damages – though the labels may change, the essence remains the same.

[128] *Spelman v Express Newspapers* [2012] EWHC 355 (QB) [114].

[129] *Gulati v MGN Ltd* [2015] EWHC 1482 (Ch); [2016] FSR 12 ('*Gulati*'). Upheld by the Court of Appeal: [2015] EWCA Civ 1291; [2017] QB 149.

[130] *Mosley* (n 37).

[131] ibid, [216].

[132] ibid, [236]. *Mosley v UK* [2012] EMLR 1 [28].

[133] *Mosley* (n 37) [216] (emphases added).

In *Lumba v Secretary of State for the Home Department*, the approach of Eady J in *Mosley* was viewed as endorsing vindicatory damages for the infringement of privacy.[134] However, at least formally, the head of vindicatory damages in privacy cases was short-lived as a majority of the Supreme Court in *Lumba* rejected vindicatory damages as a head of damages in English tort law.[135] However, despite *Lumba*, vindicatory damages seem to have persisted informally in privacy cases after *Mosley*. For example, the awards of £15,000 to the infant in *AAA*[136] and £2,500 each to the infant twins in *Weller*[137] cannot reflect distress or injury to feelings since the claimants were too young to have experienced this loss.

In *Gulati v MGN Ltd* Mann J expressly awarded, and formally recognised, substantive damages 'to reflect infringements of the right itself', irrespective of and in addition to damages which compensated distress and injury to feelings caused by the breaches of privacy in the litigation.[138] Mann J's approach to damages was upheld by the Court of Appeal.[139] Whilst Mann J did award substantive damages for the breach of the right itself in *Gulati*, the ambit of the decision is still unclear. Mann J did not suggest that such damages ought to be awarded in *every* case, and no concrete guidance was given as to when awarding damages for breach of the right itself will be appropriate:

> While the law is used to awarding damages for injured feelings, there is no reason in principle, in my view, why it should not also make an award to reflect infringements of the right itself, *if the situation warrants it*... If one has lost "the right to control the dissemination of information about one's private life" then I fail to see why that, of itself, should not attract a degree of compensation, *in an appropriate case*... Distress will often be the consequence of the infringement to such a degree as to subsume any potential separate award for the infringement itself; *but where appropriate* the stated values [of autonomy and dignity] ought of themselves to be protectable with an award of damages.[140]

That damages for loss of control of private information can be awarded has been confirmed by numerous cases since *Gulati*,[141] but it has not always been clear whether the quantum arrived at by the court includes a separate award for this type of loss. Take for example Arnold J's award of £10,000 to each claimant

[134] *Lumba v Secretary of State for the Home Department* [2011] UKSC 12; [2012] 1 AC 245 [99] (Lord Dyson).

[135] For example, see Lord Dyson (in the majority) at [100]–[101].

[136] *AAA* (n 91) [121], [127].

[137] *Weller v Associated Newspapers Ltd* [2014] EWHC 1163 (QB); [2014] EMLR 24. Compare these sums to the £5,000 awarded to the 16-year-old claimant who did experience injury to feelings caused by the publication: [168].

[138] *Gulati* (n 129) [111]. For details of the facts of *Gulati*, see ch 13 of this collection by J Hartshorne.

[139] *Gulati v MGN Ltd* [2015] EWCA Civ 1291; [2017] QB 149.

[140] *Gulati* (n 129) [111] (emphases added).

[141] Including, inter alia, *TLT v Secretary of State for the Home Department* [2016] EWHC 2217 (QB) [17]; *Richard v BBC* [2018] EWHC 1837 (Ch); [2019] Ch 169 [350]; *Brake v Guy* [2021] EWHC 671 (Ch) [290]; *Reid v Price* [2020] EWHC 594 (QB) [51].

in *Ali v Channel 5 Broadcasting Ltd* for misuse of private information.[142] *Ali* saw the claimants, a husband and wife, being filmed as they were evicted from their rental home after falling into arrears. Footage of the eviction was then broadcast by Channel 5 on a television programme. It is not altogether clear what role, if any, that damages for the breach itself played in *Ali*. While the judge recognised that 'compensation for the misuse of private information' may be awarded 'even if it does not cause distress' following *Gulati*,[143] not much else was said about the head of damages recognised in *Gulati*.[144] Considering that the footage was watched by 9.65 million viewers at the time of trial, and that the footage was of a sensitive nature depicting the claimants 'at their lowest ebb',[145] the sum may be explicable by distress alone. By contrast, *ST (A Child) v L Primary School* is a recent example where damages for breach of the right itself were clearly awarded.[146] In *ST*, liability arose when the head-teacher of the defendant school sent a letter to parents of all year five pupils which contained information about the behaviour of the claimant, a pupil who had Down's syndrome. The pupil was unaware that letter had been sent to her class-mates, and therefore suffered no distress in light of the breach of her privacy. For this reason, the judge declined to award damages under the DPA 1998: it could not be said that 'damage' (as required under section 13 of the Act) was suffered by the claimant.[147] However, the judge did award the child £1,500 for misuse of her private information, an award which can only be explained as damages for breach of the right itself in light of the judge's findings on distress.[148] Because of the uncertain scope of *Gulati* it cannot be said with certainty that, were the Douglases to bring their case today, the quantum of their damages would greatly increase, though one might expect an uplift of some kind.

B. Negotiating Damages

Both the first instance judge and the Court of Appeal rejected the Douglases' claim for negotiating damages (which are sometimes referred to as licence fee damages, user fee damages, *Wrotham Park* damages or restitutionary damages; we adopt the term negotiating damages to reflect the approach of the UK Supreme Court in *Morris-Garner v One Step (Support) Ltd*).[149] After much

[142] *Ali v Channel 5 Broadcasting Ltd* [2018] EWHC 298 (Ch); [2018] EMLR 17.
[143] ibid, [212].
[144] ibid, [215]–[220].
[145] ibid, [148].
[146] *ST (A Child) v L Primary School* [2020] EWHC 1046 (QB), [2020] ELR 555 ('*ST*').
[147] ibid, [110].
[148] ibid, [114] (Deputy Master Hill QC): 'In my view this sum is appropriate to reflect the *sending of the letter in itself*' (emphasis added).
[149] *Morris-Garner v One Step (Support) Ltd* [2018] UKSC 20; [2019] AC 649 ('*One Step*').

judicial and academic debate over the nature and purpose of such damages, in *One Step* the Supreme Court held that negotiating damages were compensatory in nature. However, such damages were also said to compensate loss of an unconventional kind, namely where the claimant has lost their right to control use of a valuable asset.[150] As Andrew Burrows (now Lord Burrows) notes,[151] Lord Reed's analysis can be viewed as endorsing Sharpe and Waddams' analysis of negotiating damages as 'loss of opportunity to bargain' for use of the asset in question.[152] The most common method of assessing the quantum of negotiating damages is for the court to conduct a hypothetical negotiation 'between a willing (buyer) … and a willing seller' of licence to use the asset or property in question, both assumed to be acting reasonably.[153] As the court conceives of this as a purely hypothetical bargain, the 'fact that one or both parties would in practice have refused to make a deal is therefore to be ignored'.[154] Negotiating damages have been awarded in cases involving intellectual property,[155] and for breaches of confidence in a commercial context,[156] though such damages have not yet been formally recognised in the context of personal information.[157]

Lindsay J refused the Douglases' claim for negotiating damages on the basis that the notional fee would be less than the award of conventional compensatory damages; this meant the judge did not have to resolve the issue of law as to availability of negotiating damages for breaches of privacy in general.[158] The Douglases' appealed this point before the Court of Appeal, in an attempt to receive higher quantum. Similar to Lindsay J, the Court of Appeal did not fully grasp the nettle and address the issue of whether negotiating damages can *ever* be available for breaches of privacy. Rather, the court refused negotiating damages

[150] ibid, [30] (Lord Reed).

[151] A Burrows, *Remedies for Torts, Breach of Contract, and Equitable Wrongs*, 4th edn (Oxford, OUP, 2019) 324.

[152] R Sharpe and S Waddams, 'Damages for Lost Opportunity to Bargain' (1982) 2 *Oxford Journal of Legal Studies* 290.

[153] *Pell Frischmann Engineering Ltd v Bow Valley Iran Ltd* [2009] UKPC 45; [2011] 1 WLR 2370 [49] ('*Pell Frischmann*').

[154] ibid. However, the fictional nature of the exercise has drawn some judicial criticism. See, eg, Leggatt J in *Marathon Asset Management LLP v Seddon* [2017] EWHC 300 (Comm); [2017] FSR 36 [189]. Lord Reed in *One Step* (n 149) [75] also noted how the 'artificiality of the exercise can be a further problem … the premise of the hypothetical negotiation – that a reasonable person in the claimant's position would have been willing to release the defendant from the obligation in return for a fee – breaks down in a situation where any reasonable person in the claimant's position would have been unwilling to grant a release'.

[155] For example, see *Pell Frischmann* (n 153) [48]: negotiating damages are available 'for patent infringement and breaches of other intellectual property rights of a proprietary character'.

[156] For example, see *Vercoe v Rutland Fund Management Ltd* [2010] EWHC 424 (Ch); [2010] Bus LR D141.

[157] Though it has been suggested by J Edelman et al (eds), *McGregor on Damages*, 21st edn (London, Sweet & Maxwell, 2020) 47-013 that *Gulati* may be understood as awarding negotiating damages for the personal information. This interpretation of *Gulati* was rejected by Warby J in *Lloyd v Google LLC* [2018] EWHC 2599 (QB); [2019] EMLR 4 [81].

[158] *Douglas quantum* (n 115) [64].

on the facts. However, many of the court's reasons for refusing to award negotiating damages in *Douglas (No 3)* seem applicable to most privacy cases. There was said to be 'obvious problems' with awarding damages on the basis of a hypothetical bargain.[159] The first issue identified by the court is that negotiating damages fails to capture the gist of the claimant's privacy claim: their 'upset and affront at an invasion of privacy, not the loss of opportunity to earn money'.[160] Second, the 'unreality of the fictional negotiation' in the Douglases' case was said to be 'palpable'.[161] This reason will be particularly pertinent in the majority of privacy cases where a claimant will not want the information to be published or accessed *at all*. When compared with a case where the claimant would *never* be prepared to sell their information, the Douglases might have had a stronger case than most given that they were prepared to commercialise their private information. Finally, and particular to the unusual facts of *Douglas (No 3)*, the court explained how 'having sold the exclusive right to publish photographs of the reception to OK!, the Douglases would not have been in a position to grant a licence to Hello!'; as such it was said that the Douglases might have been unjustly enriched by an award of negotiating damages since they already sold their information to *OK!* for £1 million and would not be required to account to *OK!* for negotiating damages if awarded.[162]

Whilst the Court of Appeal's decision in *Douglas (No 3)* provides the most sustained analysis of the possibility of awarding negotiating damages for breaches of privacy to date, the view against awarding such damages may not hold before a court today following recent obiter dicta from the Supreme Court in *Lloyd v Google LLC*.[163] *Lloyd* involved a representative claim, backed by a litigation funder, under the DPA 1998 on behalf of millions of iPhone users who had their internet activity secretly tracked by Google for several months in late 2011 and early 2012, with their data then collected and sold.[164] Due to the representative nature of the claim, Mr Lloyd could not claim compensation for each affected iPhone user if such compensation had to be individually assessed (and this, the court speculated, perhaps explained why a concurrent claim in misuse of private information was not also brought).[165] Instead, mirroring the head of damage recognised in *Gulati*, Mr Lloyd sought to claim damages for 'loss of control' of data; this head, argued Mr Lloyd, represented the infringement of data protection rights and did not need to be quantified on an individualised basis, but instead could be awarded on a uniform per capita basis. A sum of £750

[159] *Douglas (No 3)* (n 1) [246].
[160] ibid.
[161] ibid.
[162] ibid, [247].
[163] *Lloyd v Google LLC* [2021] UKSC 50 ('*Lloyd* (UKSC)').
[164] For a summary of the case, see J Skillen, 'Damage in the Supreme Court' (2022) 81 *Cambridge Law Journal* 14.
[165] *Lloyd* (UKSC) (n 163) [106].

each was suggested in Mr Lloyd's letter of claim, which would have amounted to an overall award of £3 billion to the eligible class of iPhone users. The central issue under the DPA 1998 was whether loss of control of data could constitute 'damage'. A unanimous Supreme Court held that it could not: on a proper interpretation, section 13 required proof of material damage or distress. This same logic meant that the court also rejected the availability of negotiating damages under the DPA 1998. However, the court expressed misgivings as to *Douglas (No 3)* on the potential for negotiating damages for the tort of misuse of private information. Lord Leggatt, providing the sole judgment of the court, stated:

> The view has sometimes been expressed that asserting privacy in information is inconsistent, or at least in tension, with treating such information as a commercial asset: see *eg Douglas v Hello! Ltd (No 3)* [2005] EWCA Civ 595 … But once the basis of the right to privacy is understood to be protection of a person's freedom to choose and right to control whether and when others have access to his or her private affairs, I think that any tension largely disappears.[166]

Rather, the Supreme Court in *Lloyd* thought that a claim in misuse of private information based on a similar fact-pattern 'would naturally lend itself to an award of user damages'.[167] The court did not go so far as to expressly say that *Gulati* itself awarded a form of negotiating damages to the claimants, but there appears to be some linkage between the heads of damage in the court's reasoning when it stated that the 'decision in *Gulati* shows that damages may be awarded for the misuse of private information itself on the basis that, apart from any material damage or distress that it may cause, it prevents the claimant from exercising his or her right to control the use of the information'.[168] There appears therefore to be little water between the court's conception of the aims of negotiating damages for breaches of privacy in *Lloyd* and the damages awarded in *Gulati*.

Before leaving monetary relief and turning to injunctions, it is worthwhile noting that *Hello!* did not make a profit on their publication of the unauthorised photographs, which meant that an account of profits was not open to the Douglases as an avenue for more a more substantial monetary award; this will likely partially explain why negotiating damages were pursued.[169] Moreover, the Court of Appeal indicated the Douglases would have succeeded in claiming account of profits.[170] However, account of profits has yet to be awarded for misuse of private information, despite dicta in *Douglas (No 3)* and, more latterly, by the Supreme Court in *PJS*.[171]

[166] ibid, [142].
[167] ibid, [141].
[168] ibid.
[169] *Douglas (No 3)* (n 1) [248].
[170] ibid.
[171] *PJS* (n 58) [42] (Lord Mance).

C. Injunctions

The claimants initially sought injunctive relief. On 20 November 2000, an ex parte interim injunction was granted by Buckley J; the injunction was continued by Hunt J the following day after a hearing at which *Hello!* was also represented. However, on 23 November 2000, the injunction was discharged by the Court of Appeal consisting of Brooke, Sedley and Keene LJJ (*Douglas (No 1)*).[172] In *Douglas (No 3)* the claimants only sought damages; however, the Court of Appeal doubted the correctness of the decision in *Douglas (No 1)* to lift the interim injunction. Lord Phillips MR stated: 'in light of the law as it can now be seen to be, that decision was wrong and the interlocutory injunction should have in fact been upheld'.[173] It was said that, in *Douglas (No 1)*, the court gave insufficient weight to two factors. The first factor was the 'strength of the Douglases' claim for an injunction', and it was suggested that a different outcome may have been reached had the decisions of *Campbell v MGN* and *Von Hannover (No 1)* been before the court.[174] The strength of the Douglases' claim appeared to be twofold: that the publication of the unauthorised photographs would infringe their privacy, and the lack of a strong countervailing public interest which might justify such an infringement.[175] The second factor was 'the likely level of damages which the Douglases' would recover' were the injunction to be refused and later liability in confidence (or privacy) to be found. As already discussed in this section, the Douglases' damages were in the end a 'relatively small sum'.[176]

Though *Douglas (No 1)* was said to be decided incorrectly, the court's analysis of the meaning of section 12 of Human Rights Act 1998 ('HRA') in that case has not been doubted. Section 12 HRA is engaged in any case where 'a court is considering whether to grant any relief which, if granted, might affect the Convention right of freedom of expression'.[177] In particular, sections 12(4) and 12(3) applied on the facts. Under section 12(4):

> The court must have particular regard to the importance of the Convention right to freedom of expression and, where the proceedings relate to material which the respondent claims, or which appears to the court, to be journalistic, literary or artistic material (or to conduct connected with such material), to—
>
> (a) the extent to which—
>
> (i) the material has, or is about to, become available to the public; or
>
> (ii) it is, or would be, in the public interest for the material to be published;
>
> (b) any relevant privacy code.

[172] *Douglas (No 1)* (n 3).
[173] *Douglas (No 3)* (n 1) [251].
[174] ibid, [253].
[175] ibid.
[176] ibid, [255].
[177] Human Rights Act 1998, s 12(1).

On its face this provision might suggest that Article 10 ECHR, the right to freedom of expression, is given priority or importance over other Convention rights, such as Article 8 ECHR, the right to privacy. The court emphatically rejected such an interpretation: neither the right to privacy nor the right to freedom of expression have priority over another. Central to the court's reasoning was the qualified nature of the right to freedom of expression 'in favour of the reputation and rights of others and the protection of information in confidence. In other words, you cannot have particular regard to article 10 without having equally particular regard at the very least to article 8'.[178] Thus, the court's interpretation of section 12(4) HRA gave further protection to the right of privacy in English law by ensuring that privacy interests are, prima facie, placed on an equal footing to the right to freedom of expression.

As we shall see, the court's analysis of section 12(4) had influenced its interpretation of the meaning of section 12(3). Section 12(3) concerns prior restraint, and it amends the general position as regards interim injunctions under English law. It reads:

> No such relief is to be granted so as to restrain publication before trial unless the court is satisfied that the applicant is likely to establish that publication should not be allowed.

Before considering how section 12(3) HRA signals a departure from the general principles on interim injunctions, we must first lay out these general principles. The general approach was set out by Lord Diplock in *American Cyanamid v Ethicon Ltd.*[179] First, a claimant must establish that there is a 'serious question to be tried', or in other words, 'that the claim is not frivolous or vexatious'.[180] Second, the claimant must then show that the 'balance of convenience' favours the granting of an interim injunction.[181] In *American Cyanamid*, the House of Lords rejected the judge's and the Court of Appeal's approach of requiring the claimants to make out a 'prima facie case' in order to be granted an interim injunction. Lord Diplock reasoned that, in effect, requiring a prima facie case was to try the substantive issues of the case without the court having the benefit of the full evidence and cross-examination.[182] Instead, the House of Lords reminded courts of the purpose of an interim injunction, which is 'to protect the [claimant] against injury by violation of his right for which he could not be adequately compensated in damages' were the claimant to be successful at trial.[183] That aim would be 'stultified' were courts to only award interim

[178] *Douglas (No 1)* (n 3) [133] (Sedley LJ).
[179] *American Cyanamid v Ethicon Ltd* [1975] AC 396.
[180] ibid, 407.
[181] ibid, 408.
[182] ibid, 404.
[183] ibid, 406.

injunctions were the claimant's chances to be evaluated as greater than fifty percent; therefore, the intended effect of *American Cyanamid* was to ensure that claimants had an easier time of securing an interim injunction than the 'prima face' case approach which had been adopted by the lower courts.[184]

In *Douglas (No 1)*, the Court of Appeal recognised that section 12(3) HRA constituted a legislative departure from the *American Cyanamid* principles in the context of confidence (and now privacy) claims. The court was unanimous in its view that 'likely' should be interpreted to mean that a claimant must be 'more likely than not' to succeed, thereby creating a more onerous initial threshold for claimants compared to *American Cyanamid*. Sedley LJ stated that the effect of section 12(3) was to require '*probability* of success at trial. The gauging of this probability, by virtue of section 12(4), will have to take into account the full range of relevant Convention rights'.[185] Keene LJ elaborated that gauging the probability of success at trial:

> requires the court to look at the merits of the case and not merely to apply the *American Cyanamid* test. Thus the court has to look ahead to the ultimate stage and to be satisfied that the scales are likely to come down in the applicant's favour. That does not conflict with the Convention, since it is merely requiring the court to apply its mind to how one right is to be balanced, on the merits against another right, without building in additional weight on one side.[186]

Therefore, because section 12(4) HRA was read to place Convention rights on an equal footing, without giving primacy to freedom of expression, under section 12(3) neither privacy nor freedom of expression is given initial priority in the assessment of the merits of the case.

In *Douglas (No 1)* the court indicated that the claimants would surmount the initial threshold of likely success at trial,[187] but nevertheless exercised its residual discretion to discharge the interim injunction. Since the claimants had sold their private information to *OK!*, the court was of the view that damages would suffice to protect what was now essentially a commercial asset.[188] As discussed above, in *Douglas (No 3)* the Court of Appeal disagreed with the court's *application* of the principles governing interim injunctions in *Douglas (No 1)*, but not the principles themselves. Furthermore, in *Cream Holdings Ltd v Banerjee*, the House of Lords endorsed the interpretation of section 12(3) in *Douglas (No 1)* (although *Douglas (No 1)* was not cited in the sole reasoned speech of Lord Nicholls). As put by his Lordship:

> Section 12(3) makes the likelihood of success at the trial an essential element in the court's consideration of whether to make an interim order ... As to what degree

[184] ibid.
[185] *Douglas (No 1)* (n 3) [134] (emphasis added).
[186] ibid, [150].
[187] ibid, [96] (Brooke LJ); [144] (Sedley LJ); [171] (Keene LJ).
[188] ibid, [97]–[101] (Brooke LJ); [144] (Sedley LJ); [171] (Keene LJ).

> of likelihood makes the prospects of success 'sufficiently favourable', the general approach should be that courts will be exceedingly slow to make interim restraint orders where the applicant has not satisfied the court he will probably ('more likely than not') succeed at the trial.[189]

Thus, the *Douglas* litigation encompasses a significant early decision on what is now the received effect of section 12 HRA on cases concerning confidence and privacy.

VII. CONCLUSION

While at the time of *Douglas v Hello!* there was contemporaneous commentary on aspects of the litigation,[190] this chapter has engaged in a wide-ranging analysis of *Douglas (No 3)*, situating its relevance in relation to English privacy jurisprudence pre and post the decision and evaluating its significance to the development of the tort of misuse of private information. As we have seen, the *Douglas* litigation and particularly the Court of Appeal's judgment in *Douglas (No 3)* involved a rich seam of issues that were important to the budding protection of privacy under English law at the time. This chapter has traced the contours of those issues and the imprint of *Douglas (No 3)* on present day privacy protection. In some instances that imprint is clearly discernible, such as the espousing of interim injunction principles under section 12(3) HRA and the recognition that an intention to commercialise private information does not destroy one's entitlement to privacy protection, although it may affect the available remedy. In other ways, the influence has been more subtle, such as criticising the 'shoe-horning' of privacy into breach of confidence, which arguably contributed to the actions being de-coupled over time such that the tort of misuse of private information has been recognised and developed independently. The approach in *Douglas (No 3)* to photographs of the Douglases' wedding also signalled that privacy is not just about preventing the disclosure of embarrassing or intimate information, but also a protection against intrusion into private life. Yet in another way the influence of *Douglas (No 3)* has faded almost

[189] *Cream Holdings Ltd v Banerjee* [2004] UKHL 44; [2005] 1 AC 253 [22] (Lord Nicholls).

[190] See, eg, J Hull, 'Property rights in secrets – Douglas v Hello! in the Court of Appeal' (2005) 27 *European Intellectual Property Review* 379; C Michalos, 'Image Rights and Privacy: after Douglas v Hello' (2005) 27 *European Intellectual Property Review* 384; J Morgan, 'Hello! Again: Privacy and Breach of Confidence' (2005) 64 *Cambridge Law Journal* 549; and R Mulheron, 'A Potential Framework for Privacy? A Reply to Hello!' (2006) 69 *Modern Law Review* 679. Subsequent commentary has considered *Douglas (No 3)* as part of the privacy jurisprudence, but without the same detailed focus as this chapter: see, eg, T Aplin, 'The Future of Breach of Confidence and the Protection of Privacy' (2007) 7 *Oxford University Commonwealth Law Journal* 137; I Callinan, 'Privacy, Confidence, Celebrity and Spectacle' (2007) 7 *Oxford University Commonwealth Law Journal* 1; and P Giliker, 'English Tort Law and the 'Tort' of Breach of Confidence' (2014) 1 *Juridical Review* 15.

entirely – we are thinking here of the modest award of damages for distress. Finally, *Douglas (No 3)* illustrates that some of the difficult issues it grappled with remain unresolved and contentious to this day, namely, the availability of negotiating damages and account of profits for misuse of private information and the extent to which commercialised private information should be treated, in parallel to a privacy claim, as confidential information or a trade secret.

11

Jones v Tsige (2012)

DAVID MANGAN

I. INTRODUCTION

THE MEASURED APPROACH in *Jones v Tsige*[1] to establishing an intentional tort of intrusion upon seclusion speaks to the common law's general hesitation with recognising private law privacy claims. The treatment of *Jones* by Canadian courts recalls why law pertaining to privacy has lingered with modest development for a remarkably long time.

Samuel Warren and Louis Brandeis' often-quoted 1890 article offered the retrospectively optimistic prognostication that the development of privacy was 'inevitable'.[2] Some instruction must be taken from the long-established arguments surrounding privacy in private law and the recognition of only particularised instances of privacy protection. Like other jurisdictions treated in this collection, Canada has moved lethargically and in a piecemeal manner. At common law, privacy has been protected incidentally through intentional torts. Along the way, the Supreme Court of Canada has made some distinctions.[3] A few provinces have passed statutes that offer some level of protection in certain instances. Although precedent-setting, *Jones* continued the pattern of protecting privacy in discrete instances. To the legal issue '[d]oes Ontario law recognize a right to bring a civil action for damages for the invasion of personal privacy?',[4] the Court responded with a deliberate, incremental step: 'it is appropriate for this court to confirm the existence of a right of action for intrusion upon seclusion.'[5]

The Ontario Court of Appeal's 2012 decision in *Jones* (written by Robert Sharpe JA) has increased the number of claims regarding a compensable right of privacy. And yet, anticipation of further development since then has been

[1] *Jones v Tsige* 2012 ONCA 32.
[2] S Warren and L Brandeis, 'The Right to Privacy' (1890) 4 *Harvard Law Journal* 193, 195.
[3] *R v Dyment*, [1988] 2 SCR 417 being one example.
[4] *Jones* (n 1) [1].
[5] *Jones* (n 1) [65].

equivocal, some endorsement[6] and some reticence.[7] This outcome is not due to the court in *Jones*.

Jones is a landmark decision, but not as an orthodox precedent. Although the decision has prompted much academic and judicial discussion of privacy and tort, it has not resulted in significant development in the area. Still, there should be an appreciation for the decision's direct engagement with Canadian common law's tentativeness with setting a general tort of invasion of privacy. Compared to other jurisdictions,[8] Canada has remained deliberative as it continues to consider following a path from *Jones*. Nevertheless, *Jones* is the 'incremental step'[9] the Court of Appeal intended it to be. The following pages critically consider the bases for this ruling: its evaluation of the influence of technology on society; its assessment of Canadian private sector privacy legislation; and its appraisal of the common law to that point in time. The chapter also elaborates upon the decision's muted (in comparison to other landmark cases) influence on development of privacy and tort. Despite this, *Jones* remains an important and significant decision in the fledgling development of tort and privacy in Canada because the Court of Appeal addressed this lethargy and still set a good, measured foundation for privacy law's future development. *Jones* is a signpost in a line of advances in the private law of Canadian privacy that has yet to be established.

II. THE FACTS

Jones' facts were straightforward for a case on privacy. Sandra Jones and Winnie Tsige worked at one of Canada's large banks, the Bank of Montreal (BMO). As would be common at such an employer, these two individuals did not know each other. They were drawn together, however, by Ms Tsige's romantic relationship with Ms Jones' ex-husband. Ms Tsige exhibited remarkable diligence in regularly checking Ms Jones' financial records, at least 174 times over a four-year period. The information BMO held to which Ms Tsige had access included transaction details and personal information such as Jones' date of birth, her marital status, and her home address. Ms Tsige did not record or distribute this information. It is unclear how, but Ms Jones suspected Ms Tsige was accessing her account, and she made a formal complaint to her employer. *Jones* may be distinct from other decisions in this volume because Ms Tsige admitted her wrongdoing (though not conceding tort liability) when she was confronted by BMO. Her accessing

[6] Such as the Federal Court of Appeal interpreting *Jones* as opening the door to a common law actionable tort in privacy: *Canada v John Doe* 2016 FCA 191.

[7] See *Owsianik v Equifax Canada Co*. 2021 ONSC 4112.

[8] Consider the discussions prompted by *Douglas v Hello!* [2005] EWCA Civ 595 and *Campbell v Mirror Group Newspapers* [2004] 2 AC 457 in the UK.

[9] *Jones* (n 1) [65].

Jones' personal banking information was beyond her work-related duties and, in fact, it was contrary to the Bank's Code of Business Conduct and Ethics. Ms Jones was 'very upset by the intrusion ... [but] suffered no public embarrassment or harm to her health'.[10] Ms Tsige attributed the persistent attention to Ms Jones' finances to her own financial dispute with Ms Jones' ex-husband. Ms Tsige explained to BMO at that time and asserted in response to Jones' action that 'she was involved in a financial dispute with the appellant's former husband and accessed the accounts to confirm whether he was paying child support to the appellant'.[11] Ms Tsige was apologetic, 'contrite and embarrassed'.[12] BMO disciplined Ms Tsige by suspending her for one week without pay, and denying her a bonus.

III. THE DECISION

The decision considered here was an appeal of a dismissed motion for summary judgment put forward by Jones in her claim against Tsige (consisting of the tort of invasion of privacy, and breach of fiduciary obligation).[13] Tsige also brought a motion for summary judgment to dismiss the case. Having failed in the initial stage, Jones was ultimately successful in her appeal.

A. Motion for Summary Judgment

In the motion, Jones sought general, punitive, and exemplary damages, as well as a permanent injunction against Tsige. As argued by Tsige, the court dismissed Jones' motion on the basis of the absence of a tort of privacy; concluding the decision of the Ontario Court of Appeal in *Euteneier v Lee*[14] was 'dispositive of the question as to whether the tort of invasion of privacy exists at common law'.[15] In *Euteneier*, the plaintiff sued the police after they strip searched her and subsequently left her bound and unclothed in a cell visible to passers-by for around 20 minutes. As the plaintiff conceded, the Court found that 'there is no 'free-standing' right to dignity or privacy under the *Charter* or at common law.'[16]

[10] ibid, [90].
[11] ibid, [5].
[12] ibid, [6].
[13] *Jones v Tsige* 2011 ONSC 1475.
[14] *Euteneier v Lee* (2005) 77 O.R. (3d) 621 (C.A.), leave to appeal to the Supreme Court of Canada refused, [2005] SCCA No 516.
[15] *Jones*, 2011 (n 13) [45]–[55].
[16] *Euteneier* (n 14) [62]–[63].

Jones could have made a complaint to the federal Privacy Commissioner which is a body applying federal law since the matter arose in the banking context.[17] The Personal Information Protection and Electronic Documents Act (PIPEDA)[18] had been the applicable law which provided a route for complaint, but did not afford a civil cause of action. Mister Justice Whitaker ruled a complaint to the Privacy Commissioner was available to Jones and would have provided her with some form of remedy, thereby negating Jones' contention that failing to recognise a tort of invasion of privacy left her without a remedy. He also found that privacy disputes were not a 'legal vacuum' which let 'wrongs to go unrighted'.[19] He concluded that the state of privacy at common law did not require '"judge-made" rights and obligations' because existing statutory schemes were 'carefully nuanced and designed to balance practical concerns and needs in an industry-specific fashion'.[20] The 2011 decision in *Jones* represented an orthodox approach to privacy claims: discussing the assorted pleadings that had been made, their varied success, and finally concluding that the law was not settled in this area.[21]

For his part, Sharpe JA's extra-judicial contention (made well after *Jones*) that the tendency to focus on appellate-level decisions as law-making 'underestimates the significant law-making powers of trial judges'.[22] His remarks offer more than passing interest for this discussion of *Jones*, as well as other decisions in this collection.[23]

B. The Court of Appeal's Decision

The issue before the Ontario Court of Appeal was whether the motion judge erred by dismissing Jones' claim for damages on the ground that Ontario law does not recognise the tort of invasion of privacy?[24] *Jones* applied the tort of intrusion upon seclusion to the facts before it; noting the action's origins as one of William Prosser's four privacy torts set out in his 'seminal'[25] 1960 article[26] as well as the adoption of these torts by the American Law Institute in

[17] Pursuant to the Constitution Act 1867, 30 & 31 Victoria, c. 3 (U.K.), s 91, banking falls under the authority of the federal government.

[18] SC 2000, c.5.

[19] *Jones* 2011 (n 13) [53].

[20] ibid, [56].

[21] ibid, [52].

[22] RJ Sharpe, *Good Judgment: Making Judicial Decisions* (Toronto, University of Toronto Press, 2018) 94; see further his discussion 94–97. Since he offered further and later commentary on *Jones v Tsige*, there will be frequent reference to this book.

[23] *Gulati v Mirror Group Newspapers* [2015] EWHC 1482 (Ch) is one example.

[24] *Jones* (n 1) [1]. A second issue was put to the court regarding costs. Since the motion judge's decision was set aside, the Court of Appeal deemed it unnecessary to treat this issue.

[25] Sharpe (n 22) 196.

[26] W Prosser, 'Privacy' (1960) 48 *California Law Rev* 383.

the *Restatement (Second) of Torts*.[27] The facts of the case exemplified a 'new threat to personal privacy'.[28] The court concluded: 'In my view, it is appropriate for this court to confirm the existence of a right of action for intrusion upon seclusion. Recognition of such a cause of action would amount to an incremental step that is consistent with the role of this court to develop the common law in a manner consistent with the changing needs of society.'[29]

The 'incremental step' was faithfully observed. The court did not explore, let alone recognise, a general right to sue for invasion of privacy due to a 'fear'[30] that a 'cause of action of any wider breadth would not only over-reach what is necessary to resolve this case, but could also amount to an unmanageable legal proposition that would, as Prosser warned, breed confusion and uncertainty'.[31] Nevertheless, the *Jones* Court of Appeal suggested this 'incremental step' would be one along a path of a more varied discussion of the common law's protection of an individual's privacy interests. As it was not appealed to the Supreme Court of Canada, this decision did not have the benefit of further appellate treatment. The Supreme Court of Canada referred to this decision well after *Jones*' release;[32] suggesting some praise for the Court of Appeal's reasoning.[33]

In the following subsections, the bases for the Court of Appeal's decision will be examined. Extra-judicially, Sharpe JA wrote of the reasons for the decision as including: 'the time had come to change the law';[34] 'there was a gradually evolving acceptance of claims for breach of privacy';[35] and 'the individual's privacy interest was a fundamental value underlying several traditional and existing claims or causes of action'.[36] The following pages will consider these aspects commencing with the way in which the decision considered the 'social conditions'[37] prevailing at the time. Then, as the *Jones* court had done, attention moves to relevant legislation, first, and the common law, second, leading up to the 2012 ruling.

i. *Privacy's Quasi-Constitutional Status*

In Canada, privacy has been established through section 8 of the Charter of Rights and Freedoms[38] (protection from unlawful search and seizure) which has

[27] *Restatement (Second) of Torts* (St Paul, MN, American Law Institute, 1977, updated 2010).

[28] Sharpe (n 22) 194. He connected the 21st century capacities for storage and access of personal information to the technological challenges to intrusions upon privacy criticised by Warren & Brandeis in 1890.

[29] *Jones* (n 1) [65].

[30] Sharpe (n 22) 197.

[31] *Jones* (n 1) [21].

[32] *Nevsun Resources Ltd. v Araya* 2020 SCC 5.

[33] '*Jones v. Tsige* provides a rare and instructive example of where a proposed new nominate tort was found by a court to have passed this test ….': ibid [243].

[34] Sharpe (n 22) 188.

[35] ibid 191.

[36] ibid 194.

[37] ibid 194.

[38] Enacted as Sch B to the Canada Act 1982, 1982, c. 11 (UK).

been applicable to criminal law matters; more so, than it has in private law.[39] Part of the challenge for private law has been the indirect manner in which privacy has been recognised. While the Charter explicitly identifies, for example, freedom of speech (section 2(b) of the Charter), a 'right to privacy' has been read into the Charter.[40] In 1984, the Supreme Court recognised the 'right to be let alone by other people' in *Hunter v Southam Inc.*[41] and that this right was independent of any right of trespass on the person or property. In 1987, the Supreme Court set out Canadian courts' inherent jurisdiction to develop the common law as the basis for the development of private law 'in a manner consistent with the fundamental values enshrined in the Constitution'.[42] In 1988, Canada's highest Court also recognised the 1972 Canadian Task Force on Privacy and Computers' three zones of privacy[43] as being protected by the Charter.[44] In the 1995 defamation case of *Hill v Church of Scientology of Toronto*,[45] Cory J situated protection of reputation within 'the right to privacy':

> reputation is intimately related to the right to privacy which has been accorded constitutional protection. … The publication of defamatory comments constitutes an invasion of the individual's personal privacy and is an affront to that person's dignity. The protection of a person's reputation is indeed worthy of protection in our democratic society and must be carefully balanced against the equally important right of freedom of expression.[46]

[39] Patients in a psychiatric institution who were strip searched had their class action certified where the causes of action included a claim for intrusion upon seclusion as well as breach of s 8 of the Charter (an atypical claim amongst class proceedings involving intrusion upon seclusion): *Murray v Capital District Health Authority* 2015 NSSC 61, affirmed 2017 NSCA 28.

[40] This is similar to other jurisdictions such as the EU with the European Convention on Human Rights, Art 8. The US Supreme Court, in *Griswold v Connecticut* 381 US 479 (1965), recognised a right to privacy in the US Constitution, even though there is no explicit reference to a right to privacy. Since the US Supreme Court's decision in *Dobbs v Jackson Women's Health Organization* 597 US ____ (2022), *Griswold* has come into question. Other jurisdictions do explicitly recognise a right to privacy such as the South African Constitution, s 14. In Canada, the Québec Charter of Human Rights and Freedoms, c.C-12, ss 4 & 5 contains a right to privacy. See also, *Aubry v Éditions Vice-Versa Inc.*, [1998] 1 SCR 591, where the Supreme Court of Canada confirmed the right to one's image as an element of the right to privacy under s 5 of the Québec Charter. Québec law will not be considered further here.

[41] *Hunter v Southam Inc.* [1984] 2 SCR 145, 159. The reading is helped by s 26 of the Charter.

[42] *Retail, Wholesale & Department Store Union, Local 580 v Dolphin Delivery* (1987) 33 DLR (4th) 174, 199.

[43] Department of Communications and Department of Justice, *Privacy and Computers: A Report of a Task Force* (Ottawa, Information Canada, 1972) 12–13.

[44] *R v Dyment* [1988] 2 SCR 417, with Mr Justice La Forest identifying overlap amongst these zones (429–430) within the context of s 8 of the Charter. The Court has continued to draw from privacy literature. It adopted Westin's (AF Westin, *Privacy and Freedom* (New York, Atheneum, 1967) 7) definition of informational privacy in *R v Tessling* 2004 SCC 67, [23].

[45] *Hill v Church of Scientology of Toronto* [1995] 2 SCR 1130.

[46] *Hill* (n 45) [121]. Despite the term not being used in the Charter, privacy still 'underlies many of the guarantees in ss. 2 and 7–15' of the Charter: R Solomon, M McInnes, E Chamberlain and S Pitel, *Cases and Materials on the Law of Torts*, 10th edn (Toronto, Carswell, 2019) 117. The use of 'dignity' is another area for further engagement by the court. For an elaboration in Canadian private law, see HJ Glasbeek, 'Outraged Dignity – Do We Need a New Tort?' (1968) 6 *Alberta Law Review* 77.

Although the Charter applies directly to the public sector (section 32), 'the common law must be interpreted in light of *Charter* values'.[47] This discussion of privacy has not been extensively elaborated upon by the Supreme Court.[48] The Supreme Court of Canada has written periodically of privacy's importance and has classified it as having quasi-constitutional status.[49] In *R v Jarvis*,[50] the Supreme Court of Canada set out a non-exhaustive list of considerations in evaluating whether an observed person had a reasonable expectation of privacy. As it stands, indirect recognition of a right to privacy obscures understanding of its place within Charter values.[51] The absence of clarity regarding privacy in private law allows the concept of protecting a right of privacy to languish. Coincidentally, the unbridled deployment of the term 'right to privacy' in law has additionally tempered 'the prospect of its own protection'.[52]

ii. Technology and Privacy in Society

Noting the starting point of Warren and Brandeis' 1890 article,[53] the *Jones* court outlined how the law confronted the particular challenges posed by technological innovations:

> For over one hundred years, technological change has motivated the legal protection of the individual's right to privacy. In modern times, the pace of technological change has accelerated exponentially. … The internet and digital technology have brought an enormous change in the way we communicate and in our capacity to capture, store and retrieve information. As the facts of this case indicate, routinely kept electronic data bases render our most personal financial information vulnerable. Sensitive information as to our health is similarly available, as are records of the books we have borrowed or bought, the movies we have rented or downloaded, where

[47] *Hill* (n 45) [65]. Cory J elaborated further ([97]): 'It must be remembered that the *Charter* 'challenge' in a case involving private litigants does not allege the violation of a *Charter* right. It addresses a conflict between principles. … *Charter* values, framed in general terms, should be weighed against the principles which underlie the common law. The *Charter* values will then provide the guidelines for any modification to the common law which the court feels is necessary.'

[48] There has been further development in the case law regarding s 8 of the Charter (search and seizure) where the focus is on criminal law. These decisions have informed privacy in private law, as noted in *Jones* (n 1) [41]–[42]. For further discussion see, LM Austin, 'Getting Past Privacy?: Surveillance, the Charter, and the Rule of Law' (2012) 27 *Canadian Journal of Law & Society* 381–398.

[49] As it was described in *Douez v Facebook, Inc.* 2017 SCC 33, [59].

[50] *R v Jarvis* 2019 SCC 10, [29].

[51] For a critical assessment of this case law, see LE Weinrib and EJ Weinrib, 'Constitutional Values and Private Law in Canada' in D Friedmann and D Barak-Erez (eds), *Human Rights in Private Law* (Oxford, Hart Publishing, 2001) 43–72. Relying upon EJ Weinrib, *The Idea of Private Law* (Cambridge, Mass., Harvard University Press, 1995), the authors pursue a corrective justice perspective on the place of constitutional values within private law.

[52] R Wacks, 'The Poverty of "Privacy"' (1980) 96 *Law Quarterly Review* 73, 89.

[53] Cooley wrote in his treatise on torts, two years earlier, of a right 'to be let alone': TM Cooley, *A Treatise on the Law of Torts or the Wrongs which Arise Independent of Contract*, 2nd edn (Chicago, Callaghan & Company, 1888) 29.

> we have shopped, where we have travelled, and the nature of our communications by cell phone, e-mail or text message.[54]

Sharpe JA saw a particular role for the common law: 'It is within the capacity of the common law to evolve to respond to the problem posed by the routine collection and aggregation of highly personal information that is readily accessible in electronic form.'[55]

Though *Jones* alluded to it, further treatment of the idea that privacy addresses freedom to be separate from others in some form would have aided the decision. Privacy is a part of freedom.[56] While people are social, privacy represents a limitation to the extent of social interaction. We do not interact with others at all points each day. If the concept of privacy entails exclusion (selectively sharing information or removing information from public access), then freedom accompanies this choice; the choice as to what or who is excluded.[57] This information or these spaces, however, are not impregnable because others can intrude upon them. *Jones* enters here, but it does not extend beyond an entitlement to keep private information that has already been secluded. *Jones* is about intrusion into an already cordoned off area (private banking information).

iii. Legislative Protection for Privacy

The passage of legislation in the years leading up to *Jones* additionally led the court to find that a common law action was appropriate. Each of British Columbia[58] Manitoba,[59] Newfoundland and Labrador[60] and Saskatchewan[61] have legislation explicitly providing for a tort based upon violation of another person's privacy.[62] Federal legislation,[63] classified as quasi-constitutional,[64]

[54] *Jones* (n 1) [67].

[55] ibid, [68].

[56] *R v O'Connor* [1995] 4 SCR 411, [113]. Two decades later D Solove contended that reputation and freedom are interlinked: *The Future of Reputation* (New Haven, Yale University Press, 2007).

[57] D Mangan, 'Situating Canadian defamation and privacy law in comparative context' in A Koltay and P Wragg (eds), *Research Handbook on Comparative Privacy and Defamation Law* (Cheltenham, Edward Elgar, 2020) 373–374.

[58] Privacy Act, R.S.B.C. 1996 c.373, s 1(1). The Supreme Court of Canada discussed this legislation (particularly s 4) in the context of a forum selection clause (contained in an online consumer contract of adhesion) in *Douez v Facebook Inc.* 2017 SCC 33. Class action proceedings based upon a combination of the privacy torts in provinces with statutory actions have been certified in *Douez v Facebook* 2022 BCSC 914. Class action proceedings using these statutory actions as well as the common law intrusion upon seclusion claim in the remaining jurisdictions have also been certified in *Severs v Hyp3R Inc.* 2021 BCSC 226.

[59] Privacy Act, C.C.S.M. c.P125, s 2. Under this Act, it was determined that only an individual's personal information was protected and not that of a corporation: *Dowd v Skip the Dishes Restaurant Services Inc.* 2019 MBQB 63, [71], aff'd (on other grounds) 2020 MBQB 155.

[60] Privacy Act, R.S.N.L. 1990, c.P-22, s 3.

[61] Privacy Act, R.S.S. 1978, c.P-24, s 2.

[62] These acts are broadly similar. For further detailed treatment of them, see B von Tigerstrom, *Information & Privacy Law in Canada* (Toronto, Irwin Law, 2020) 71ff.

[63] The Acts apply to the public sector (Privacy Act, R.S.C. 1985, c.P-21) and private sector (Personal Information Protection and Electronic Documents Act, S.C. 2000, c.5).

[64] As the Supreme Court identified the federal Privacy Act R.S.C., 1985, c. P-21in *Lavigne v Canada (Office of the Commissioner of Official Languages)* 2002 SCC 53, [24]–[25].

remains in existence, though its impact is limited to federally-regulated areas. The identified provincial statutes are similar in content insofar as they each provide for a limited right of action where the defendant acted wilfully[65] and without claim of right.[66] This similarity grounded the expansion of a class action proceeding that started in British Columbia to include Facebook users resident in each of these provinces.[67] These statutes earned the following assessment in *Jones*: 'no provincial legislation provides a precise definition of what constitutes an invasion of privacy. The courts in provinces with a statutory tort are left with more or less the same task as courts in provinces without such statutes.'[68]

The *Jones* Court of Appeal ruled that a common law action was not precluded by statute.[69] Plaintiffs have a choice of venues. The federal legislation, the PIPEDA,[70] took an 'institutional'[71] approach to privacy, which was distinct from the situation in *Jones* of 'private rights of action between individuals'.[72] Private law redress was not restricted to the PIPEDA complaint for three reasons: Jones would have been forced to raise a complaint against her own employer and not Tsige; Tsige acted in violation of her employer's policy; damages were not among the penalties available to Jones under PIPEDA.[73]

Whether legislation precluded a common law action was again considered after *Jones* in *Hopkins v Kay*[74] where the plaintiffs brought a class action for intrusion upon seclusion. The defendant sought to dismiss the claim by asserting that Ontario's Personal Health Information Protection Act 2004 (PHIPA)[75] barred the common law action. Justice Sharpe again authored the unanimous decision of the court which ruled that PHIPA did not prohibit a common law claim. Comparing the requirements of the statute and the common law action, Sharpe JA determined that the 'elements of the common law cause of action are, on balance, more difficult to establish than a breach of *PHIPA*'.[76]

[65] Except for Manitoba which states that a violation arises when a person has acted 'substantially, unreasonably, and without claim of right'.

[66] See, eg, Privacy Act, R.S.N.L. 1990, c.P-22, s 3(2).

[67] *Douez v Facebook Inc.* 2019 BCSC 715. In *Douez v Facebook* 2022 BCSC 914, the court determined that the BC court has jurisdiction to hear and decide claims under the Manitoba and Newfoundland and Labrador statutes.

[68] *Jones* (n 1) [54].

[69] *Chandra v CBC* 2015 ONSC 5303 followed this reasoning.

[70] S.C. 2000, c.5.

[71] Sharpe (n 22) 198.

[72] *Jones* (n 1) [51].

[73] ibid, [50]. The British Columbia Court of Appeal in a later decision agreed with this statement, pointing to PIPEDA's 'very limited focus on private law redress': *Tucci v Peoples Trust Company* 2020 BCCA 246, [30].

[74] *Hopkins v Kay* 2015 ONCA 112.

[75] S.O. 2004, c. 3, Sch A.

[76] *Hopkins* (n 74) [52].

Since *Jones*, there have been other statutes which carry on the trend of creating discrete actions for particular situations.[77] Of particular interest, in November 2020 the Canadian Government announced an intention to amend PIPEDA. With its draft version of the Digital Charter Implementation Act 2022, the government intended to strengthen private sector privacy law in Canada.[78] Amongst the steps to be taken, the government will repeal PIPEDA and replace it with the Electronic Documents Act (which will consist of the current relevant portions of PIPEDA excluding personal information protection provisions). The Office of the Privacy Commissioner of Canada will be given the power to levy penalties of up to five per cent of global revenues. The Personal Information and Data Protection Tribunal Act would be created and the tribunal, amongst other items, would play an enforcement role in the proposed Consumer Privacy Protection Act. As well, it would decide whether to impose the administrative penalties recommended by the Privacy Commissioner.

iv. 'Invasion of Privacy' as a Common Law Claim

Prior to *Jones*, Canadian common law had only set out a patchy range of discussions about a common law tort protecting privacy interests. Common law protection for privacy had been largely found in situations that were adjacent to privacy such as breach of confidence, defamation, breach of copyright, nuisance,[79] or in particular settings. Canadian courts seemed innately drawn to tort as the location of a privacy action, if there was one. To a certain extent, Sharpe JA attempted to draw out why tort was the place for privacy. Again, though, it is important to underscore that he drew from the common law only for the action for intrusion upon seclusion.[80]

a. The Common Law Tort of Intrusion Upon Seclusion

The *Jones* court commenced its analysis with a generous reading of privacy protection at common law: 'Technological change poses a novel threat to a right of privacy that has been protected for hundreds of years by the common law under various guises and that, since 1982 and the Charter, has been recognized as a right that is integral to our social and political order.'[81] Canadian common law had accepted that a 'right' to privacy was a point of discussion.

[77] For example, Protecting Canadians from Online Crime Act S.C. 2014, c.31 which created s 162.1 of the Criminal Code R.S.C. 1985, c.C-46, as amended; The Intimate Image Protection Act CCSM c. I87; Intimate Images and Cyber-protection Act, S.N.S. 2017, c. 7; Protecting Victims of Non-Consensual Distribution of Intimate Images Act, S.A. 2017, C.P-26.9.

[78] Innovation, Science and Economic Development Canada, 'Bill Summary: Digital Charter Implementation Act, 2022' (date modified: 16 June 2022) www.ic.gc.ca/eic/site/062.nsf/eng/00120.html.

[79] *Jones* (n 1) [15].

[80] ibid [33].

[81] ibid [68].

Sharpe JA determined that the trajectory of these cases led towards recognition of an action for privacy. One of the earliest decisions referenced in *Jones* was the 1976 judgment of the Alberta Court of Appeal in *Motherwell v Motherwell*,[82] 'a case involving harassing telephone calls'.[83] This court approached the matter as 'a new category' of private nuisance, 'invasion of privacy by abuse of the telephone system'.[84]

While Sharpe JA drew from *Motherwell*, he glossed over how this decision addressed the claim of invasion of privacy with regards to telephone communications. Clement JA actualised the common law's 'continuing ability to serve the changing and expanding needs of our present society'.[85] Rejecting the argument that the common law's 'heroic age' had been replaced by a sense of 'certainty and security in the law',[86] the court focused on the application of principles instead of depending upon authorities.[87] These principles were found applicable to the case before the court. Clement JA described the telephone in words that may be familiar today if applied to computers, the internet, and mobile devices: 'the telephone system is so much the part of the daily life of society that many look on it as a necessity. Its use is certainly taken as a right at least in a social sense'.[88] Far from a new technology in 1970s Canada, it would be atypical if a resident did not have a telephone. Still, the telephone system 'virtually makes neighbours not only of persons close at hand, but those in distant places, other cities, other countries'.[89] In *Motherwell*, this medium had been deployed in an abusive, invasive manner that constituted a private nuisance as the persistent telephone calls interfered with the family's use and enjoyment of their home. Moreover, Clement JA interpreted provincial legislation (The Alberta Government Telephones Act) as reinforcing the public interest in the proper use of the telephone system. Privacy as a cause of action needed to be grounded within another action, here the tort of private nuisance; itself a comment on the treatment of privacy interests at common law.[90] *Motherwell* accurately

[82] *Motherwell v Motherwell* (1976), 73 DLR (3d) 62 (Alta. S.C. (A.D.)).

[83] *Jones* (n 1) [33]. The tort of harassment, however, has not been recognised in Canada: *Merrifield v Canada (Attorney General)* 2019 ONCA 205, leave to appeal to the Supreme Court of Canada refused (19 September 2019).

[84] *Motherwell* (n 82) [26].

[85] *Motherwell* (n 82) [13].

[86] These are phrases Clement JA quoted from Lord Reid's decision in *Dorset Yacht Club v Home Office* [1970] AC 1004, 1026–1027. This passage was adopted by Spence J in *O'Rourke et al v Schacht* [1976] 1 SCR 53. *Motherwell* relied upon English and Canadian decisions, but did not reference American law or scholarship.

[87] Again the court relied upon Lord Reid's comments: 'In later years there has been a steady trend towards regarding the law of negligence as depending on principle so that, when a new point emerges, one should ask not whether it is covered by authority but whether recognised principles apply to it.' Though related to negligence, the *Motherwell* court wrote of the wider application of the statement beyond this tort.

[88] *Motherwell* (n 82) [27].

[89] ibid, [27].

[90] An early 21st century example is *Tran v Financial Debt Recovery Ltd.* (2000), 193 DLR (4th) 168 (S.C.J.) (reversed on other grounds, [2001] OJ No 4103 (Div. Ct.)).

highlighted what had been viewed as an intersection between privacy and other actions.[91] It may be surprising that invasion of privacy continues to be claimed in situations of nuisance.[92]

Of the referenced cases that were closer in time to the 2012 decision in *Jones*, some garnered specific mention. The *Jones* court described *Somwar v McDonald's Restaurants of Canada Ltd.*[93] as 'perhaps the most coherent definitive pronouncement in Ontario of the existence of a common law tort of invasion of privacy corresponding to the intrusion upon seclusion category.'[94] The *Somwar* court merely refused to strike out the plaintiff's claim of damages for invasion of privacy. Still, Sharpe JA drew attention to a lengthy passage in Stinson J's decision: 'the time has come to recognize invasion of privacy as a tort in its own right'.[95] Two years later (2008), another Ontario court followed *Somwar* identifying the case as a 'strong endorsement for the development of a common law remedy consistent with Charter values'.[96] Another decision cited in *Jones*, *Dyne Holdings Ltd. v Royal Insurance Co. of Canada*,[97] refused to strike out a claim that 'arguably amounted to an invasion akin to the category of intrusion upon seclusion'.[98]

Although the *Jones* court determined the overall trajectory was towards recognition of privacy interests, there were decisions suggesting another path. In a 1986 ruling, the Manitoba Court of Appeal wrote: 'It would appear that at common law the tort of violation of privacy in regard to disclosure of private information has not been recognized in Canada. Neither counsel has supplied us with a case indicating that this tort has been recognized. Counsel for defendants states simply that the tort has not been recognized.'[99] The plaintiff's claim of invasion of privacy against the defendant (for recording her in a change room at an ultrasound appointment) was not put to the jury by a 2003 Ontario Court because it found that 'insofar as a common law tort of invasion of privacy was recognized in Canada, it did not extend to these facts'.[100]

As is well-known, despite rulings such as those noted in the last paragraph, *Jones* confirmed the existence of a right of action for intrusion upon seclusion,[101]

[91] On this point of overlap with other actions, see *Roth v Roth* (1991), 4 O.R. (3d) 740 ((Gen. Div.)).

[92] See *Johnson v Cline* 2017 ONSC 3916, [113], aff'd *Cline v Drummond* 2019 ONCA 188, leave to appeal to the Supreme Court of Canada refused (25 July 2019).

[93] (2005), 79 O.R. (3d) 172 (S.C.).

[94] *Jones* (n 1) [30].

[95] *Somwar* [29], [31]; cited in *Jones* (n 1) [31].

[96] *Nitsopoulos v Wong* (2008), 298 DLR (4th) 265 (Ont.S.C.), [22].

[97] *Jones, Dyne Holdings Ltd. v Royal Insurance Co. of Canada* (1996), 135 DLR (4th) 142 (P.E.I.C.A.), leave to appeal to the Supreme Court of Canada refused, [1996] SCCA No 344.

[98] *Jones* (n 1) [34].

[99] *Bingo Enterprises Ltd v Plaxton* (1986), 26 DLR (4th) 604 (Man.C.A.), 608 per Monnin CJM. A similar finding was made by Twaddle JA (612).

[100] *T.W. v Seo*, [2003] OTC 940 (S.C.J.), [22] (varied on other grounds at (2005), 256 DLR (4th) 1 (C.A.))

[101] *Jones* (n 1) [65].

with Sharpe JA adopting the definition found in the American Law Institute's *Restatement*: 'One who intentionally intrudes, physically or otherwise, upon the seclusion of another or his private affairs or concerns, is subject to liability to the other for invasion of his privacy, if the invasion would be highly offensive to a reasonable person.'[102] The key features of this tort are: 'the defendant's conduct must be intentional' [including being reckless];[103] the defendant 'invaded, without lawful justification, the plaintiff's private affairs or concerns'; 'a reasonable person would regard the invasion as highly offensive causing distress, humiliation or anguish'.[104] The plaintiff is not required to demonstrate 'proof of harm to a recognized economic interest'. Damages would be 'measured by a modest conventional sum' because of the 'intangible nature of the interest protected'.[105] Claims for intrusion upon seclusion were limited to situations of 'deliberate and significant invasions of personal privacy.'[106] Sharpe JA added a further limiting description to the tort by identifying examples of these significant invasions: 'such as one's financial or health records, sexual practices and orientation, employment, diary or private correspondence that, viewed objectively on the reasonable person standard, can be described as highly offensive.[107] The court classified these intrusions as 'highly offensive' without much discussion. It may be argued that accessing a financial database (as in *Jones*) to view the aforementioned information constitutes highly offensive conduct. Accessing of personal health records was found to constitute the subject matter for a claim in intrusion upon seclusion, as discussed earlier in *Hopkins v Kay*.[108] However, the absence of further treatment of this list remains unfortunate. With online profile platforms such as LinkedIn, employment history may be of more debatable inclusion in this list. Presumably, the list was not exhaustive given the careful discussion of the court's 'incremental step'; to avoid an 'unmanageable legal proposition [that could] breed confusion and uncertainty'.[109] A further point for consideration is Sharpe JA's identification of 'competing claims', namely freedom of expression and freedom of the press.[110] Perhaps fortuitously, a competing freedom of expression claim was not an issue in *Jones*.

Jones, finally, contains an elaboration on how the court arrived at the sum of $10,000 in general damages for Ms Jones's claim. In so doing, it incorporated the 'considerations in awarding damages' from Manitoba's Privacy Act,

[102] ibid, [19].

[103] The Ontario Court of Appeal, in *Demme v Healthcare Insurance Reciprocal of Canada*, 2022 ONCA 503, discussed recklessness as being very close to intentional conduct. The extent to which reckless conduct may fall within this tort remains to be canvassed.

[104] ibid, [71].

[105] ibid, [71].

[106] ibid, [72].

[107] ibid, [72].

[108] *Hopkins v Kay* 2015 ONCA 112.

[109] *Jones* (n 1) [21] and reiterated in Sharpe (n 22) 197.

[110] On the collection of private information for journalistic purposes where intrusion upon seclusion may be claimed see the obiter in *Chandra v CBC* 2015 ONSC 5305, [59].

section 4(2).[111] The absence of a requirement for proof of loss for intrusion upon seclusion is a key facet of characterising the action overall. As there was no pecuniary loss, damages were 'symbolic' because they 'vindicate rights or symbolize recognition of their infringement'.[112] This explanation of the purpose of damages recalls that intrusion upon seclusion is an intentional tort where (general) damages may vindicate the fact of a right having been infringed.

b. Reception of Intrusion Upon Seclusion by Canadian Courts

Jones has been the source of a significant volume of varied academic commentary. It has been praised[113] and criticised.[114] It has been used to explore an intrusion tort in English law.[115] *Jones* remains a case that earns citation in articles on privacy law around the world.[116] There remain valuable discussions to be had along these lines, such as the influence of American and English law and scholarship on the direction of privacy law in Canada.[117]

This section evaluates the treatment of *Jones* (specifically the tort of intrusion upon seclusion) by Canadian courts. While *Jones* has been applied by Canadian courts,[118] caution has emerged from the cases discussed below. The equivocal response to *Jones* may be attributable to the fact that the Supreme Court of Canada has yet to speak authoritatively on a privacy tort action. This situation recalls an earlier assessment of the much broader concept of invasion of privacy which was described by an Ontario court as 'an inceptive, if not ephemeral, legal concept, primarily operating to extend the margins of the existing tort doctrine'.[119] The present analysis, however, should not detract from *Jones*' notable contribution to the law's engagement of privacy; though it was intended to

[111] *Jones* (n 1) [87].

[112] ibid, [75]. Here, Sharpe JA relied upon Professor Stephen Waddams' work in the area: S Waddams, *The Law of Damages*, loose-leaf edn (Toronto, Canada Law Book, 2011) [10.50].

[113] TDC Bennett, 'Privacy, Corrective Justice, and Incrementalism: Legal Imagination and the Recognition of a Privacy Tort in Ontario' (2013) 59 *McGill Law Journal* 49.

[114] CDL Hunt, 'Privacy in the Common Law: A Critical Appraisal of the Ontario Court of Appeal's Decision in *Jones v Tsige*' (2012) 37 *Queen's Law Journal* 665. Moreham assessed the highly offensive requirement in the New Zealand context, NA Moreham, 'Abandoning the "High Offensiveness" Privacy Test' (2018) 4 *Canadian Journal of Comparative and Contemporary Law* 161.

[115] J Hartshorne, 'The Need for an Intrusion upon Seclusion Privacy Tort within English Law' (2017) 46 *Common Law World Review* 287; TDC Bennett, 'Triangulating Intrusion in Privacy Law' (2019) 39 *Oxford Journal of Legal Studies* 751.

[116] See, eg, NA Moreham, 'Beyond Information: Physical Privacy in English Law' (2014) 73 *Cambridge Law Journal* 350.

[117] See, eg, S Beswick and W Fotherby, 'The Divergent Paths of Commonwealth Privacy Torts', as well as, C Hunt, 'Reasonable Expectations of Privacy in Canadian Tort Law' both in MI Hall (ed), *The Canadian Law of Obligations: Private Law for the 21st Century and Beyond* (Toronto, Lexis Nexis, 2018).

[118] Awarding $7,500 in damages (plus costs), it was followed in a case with similar facts: *McIntosh v Legal Aid Ontario* 2014 ONSC 6136. See also, *Von Maltzahn v Koopernaes* 2018 NSSC 192.

[119] *Ontario (Attorney General) v Dieleman* (1994), 117 DLR (4th) 449 (Ont. Gen. Div.), [568].

be an incremental step. As suggested at the start of this chapter, the wary treatment of *Jones* by Canadian courts is emblematic of privacy at common law as it continues its hesitant engagement of this subject matter.

Of the more negative assessments, the arguments against recognising a tort of intrusion upon seclusion, let alone a more general privacy action, centred around the absence of an authoritative judicial statement recognising any such claim. Intrusion upon seclusion (and more general attempts at a privacy action) have been characterised as 'pseudotorts' which were 'a matter of debate' by the late scholar of Canadian obligations law Gerald Fridman.[120] While some may require nothing less than a Supreme Court of Canada decision on the matter, Sharpe JA clearly did not share this opinion.[121]

Jones has been applied often by first instance courts. Garnering a small damages award ($1,500), it has been followed on occasions where personal information (such as a flight schedule) was accessed by a fellow employee and shared.[122] Regularly, there have been a number of dismissed strike out motions (frequently class actions) relating to claims for intrusion upon seclusion which give some restrained support to the tort.[123] In one of the more assertive decisions, the Federal Court of Appeal interpreted *Jones* as opening the door to a common law actionable tort in privacy (limited to intrusion upon seclusion); though it found in this instance that the pleadings were not supported by material facts.[124] On an appeal of an application for class action certification including a claim for intrusion upon seclusion, the Nova Scotia Court of Appeal allowed the certification of the claim to go forward. It employed careful wording in its ruling to the effect that *Jones* had not been appealed and that in two decisions of the Nova Scotia Supreme Court,[125] the intrusion upon seclusion tort 'ha[d] been twice acknowledged'.[126] In the same year an Ontario court described intrusion upon seclusion as 'just evolving. Its scope and content have not yet been fully determined'.[127] There has also been a refusal to strike out a claim made by close

[120] GHL Fridman, *Torts: A Guide for the Perplexed* (Toronto, Lexis Nexis, 2017), 35. For discussion of Fridman's criticism, see D Mangan, 'Perplexing Platforms for Tort' (2019) 93 *Supreme Court Law Review* (2d) 177.

[121] Discussed above, Sharpe JA lamented the underestimation of trial judges' law-making powers: Sharpe (n 22) 94.

[122] *Stevens v Walsh* 2016 ONSC 2418. The fact the defendant could access the flight schedule as a fellow employee did not excuse the intrusion on the basis of lawful justification. Similar reasoning was applied in *Leung v Shanks* 2013 ONSC 4943.

[123] Amongst other examples noted here, see also the class action certification in *Hynes v Western Regional Integrated Health Authority* 2014 NLTD(G) 137.

[124] *Canada v John Doe* 2016 FCA 191, [52]–[53]. The court, obiter, also wrote of the tort of 'unreasonable publicity given to the other's private life'.

[125] *Trout Point Lodge Ltd. v Handshoe* 2012 NSSC 245, [55]; *Doucette v Nova Scotia* 2016 NSSC 25, [172].

[126] *Capital District Health Authority v Murray* 2017 NSCA 28, [95].

[127] *Bennett v Lenovo* 2017 ONSC 1082, [23]. The comments were made in the context of rejecting a strike out motion for this tort.

family members of a 'victim' of a breach of privacy.[128] Similar to concerns in English law regarding privacy actions,[129] there has also been unease that intrusion upon seclusion may be used as an end-run around an unsuccessful libel claim.[130]

Some of the decisions that have applied *Jones* have developed elements of the action since 2012. *Stewart v Demme*[131] considered the duration of an intrusion upon seclusion with regards to establishing a claim. Ms Demme, a nurse at a health centre, fleetingly accessed patient medical files in order to determine if she could pilfer Percocet pills from them. Outdoing Ms Tsige's steadfastness over a four-year period, Ms Demme continued her search through patient records for approximately a decade, illegally accumulating 23,932 pills.[132] In this motion for a claim in intrusion upon seclusion, the first instance court certified the class action, writing: 'The intrusion – the loss of control – is its own harm.'[133] On appeal, the Divisional Court overturned the decision to certify because 'the information accessed was limited and the access was fleeting and incidental to the medication theft. Ms Demme was not "after" the information, nor did she retain it or share it with anyone else.'[134]

The types of conduct constituting an intrusion upon seclusion have been another point for consideration. In *Broutzas v Rouge Valley Health System*,[135] the plaintiffs' certification motion for a class action claiming intrusion upon seclusion was dismissed because disclosure of contact information was neither information about private affairs, nor highly offensive.[136] Accessing of personal information by parents in 'panic and vulnerability' was not highly offensive to a reasonable person.[137]

The availability of intrusion upon seclusion at common law in the province of British Columbia, which has its own statutory action, has been in question since *Jones*. British Columbia's Privacy Act,[138] section 1, provides for a tort action in privacy. It has been asserted that a common law action for privacy

[128] *Grant v Winnipeg Regional Health Authority et al.* 2015 MBCA 44, [127].

[129] *Terry v Persons Unknown (Rev 1)* [2010] EWHC 119.

[130] *Vachon v Canada Revenue Agency* 2015 ONSC 6096.

[131] *Stewart v Demme* 2022 ONSC 1790 (Div.Ct.).

[132] The access Stewart had as a nurse did not justify her accessing of the files, thereby rendering it a lawful justification. A claim for breach of privacy (pursuant to *Jones*) against a regulatory body was struck out where publication of a disciplinary record pursuant to statutory authority was a lawful justification: *Singh-Boutilier v Ontario College of Social Workers and Social Service Workers* 2015 ONSC 5297, [55]–[56].

[133] *Stewart v Demme* 2020 ONSC 83, [68].

[134] *Stewart* (n 131), [3].

[135] *Broutzas v Rouge Valley Health System* 2018 ONSC 6315.

[136] ibid, [152].

[137] *Baldwin v Morningstar* 2019 ONSC 1276. A credit report was not viewed as intruding into private affairs where the information was publicly available: *Powell v Shirley* 2016 ONSC 3577. See also *Larizza v Royal Bank of Canada* 2017 ONSC 6140, aff'd 2018 ONCA 632.

[138] R.S.B.C. 1996, c 373.

(including intrusion upon seclusion) could not proceed in British Columbia.[139] This position came into question in 2020 with the British Columbia Court of Appeal in *Tucci v Peoples Trust Company*[140] offering an opening for further treatment of the matter: 'In my view, the time may well have come for this Court to revisit its jurisprudence on the tort of breach of privacy.'[141] *Tucci* questioned the authorities that had been relied upon to that point (which pre-dated *Jones*). The court pointed out that the Court of Appeal in *Hung v Gardiner*[142] 'found it unnecessary to address the issue of whether a common law tort of breach of privacy exists'.[143] In *Mohl v University of British Columbia*,[144] the Court of Appeal's decision regarding the common law claim for breach of privacy was limited to the conclusion that no reasonable claim was disclosed based upon the facts. Although the *Mohl* court had written that there was 'no common-law claim for breach of privacy',[145] the *Tucci* court noted some misgivings about the breadth of this statement.[146] With *Tucci*, the question of a common law action for intrusion upon seclusion (drawing from *Jones*) has simply come back to the starting point.

It may be that *Jones*' restrained impact is attributable, in part, to the absence of a clear notion of privacy protection at common law. The opinion remains that a general right of privacy should not be set out,[147] and that in Canada there is no common law tort of breach of privacy.[148] *Jones* does not venture beyond the specific facts in that case. Instead, it continues the purpose-driven approach to privacy: 'Conceptualizing privacy is about understanding and attempting to solve certain problems.'[149] Technological innovations, though, suggest the need for a more thorough outline of how the law may protect privacy. There must be engagement in law with an overarching idea of privacy, coupled with an elaboration on what is being protected in law.[150] That we seem little further along

[139] See, eg, *Facilities Subsector Bargaining Assn. v B.C.N.U.* 2009 BCSC 1562; *Ari v Insurance Corporation of British Columbia* 2013 BCSC 1308; *Tucci v Peoples Trust Company* 2017 BCSC 1525, [151]–[155].

[140] *Tucci v Peoples Trust Company* 2020 BCCA 246.

[141] ibid, [55].

[142] *Hung v Gardiner* 2003 BCCA 257.

[143] *Tucci* (n 140) [57].

[144] *Mohl v University of British Columbia* 2009 BCCA 249, leave to appeal to the Supreme Court of Canada refused [2009] SCCA No 340.

[145] ibid, [13].

[146] *Tucci* (n 140) [62]. The *Tucci* court explicitly rejected the court of first instance's notion of 'federal common law' (*Tucci v Peoples Trust Company* 2017 BCSC 1525, [151]–[155] and a privacy claim being limited to that area.

[147] One example is *Wainwright v Home Office* [2003] UKHL 53.

[148] *Pinder v Canada (Minister of the Environment)* 2015 FC 1376, [107], aff'd on other grounds, 2016 FCA 317; *Al-Ghamdi v Alberta* 2017 ABQB 684, [160], aff'd 2020 ABCA 81. The Federal Court in *Pinder* specifically noted there is no common law tort aside from that set out by provincial statutes.

[149] D Solove, 'Conceptualizing Privacy' (2002) 90 *California Law Review* 1078, 1129.

[150] D Mangan, 'Situating Canadian defamation and privacy law in comparative context' in A Koltay and P Wragg (eds), *Research Handbook on Comparative Privacy and Defamation Law* (Cheltenham, Edward Elgar, 2020) 379.

from 1890 in determining what is meant by privacy than a 'right to be let alone' should be a source of consternation. Further factors in the limited development of *Jones* include some courts blurring any distinction by giving an impression of equivalence,[151] as well as continued reticence due to the action's relative youth.[152]

With intrusion upon seclusion being one of the few recognised privacy torts in Canadian common law, *Jones* has been relied upon by many plaintiffs. Plaintiffs' counsels continue to compel further consideration in Canadian courts by attempting to expand intrusion upon seclusion. Pleadings have included 'invasion of privacy based on the tort of intrusion upon seclusion'.[153]

Class actions for data breaches have been one example.[154] *Jones* has been claimed when defendants have allegedly handled/stored the plaintiffs' personal data improperly. Many claims have centred on third party intrusions,[155] (hacks) of databases maintained by defendants.[156] The viability of intrusion upon seclusion as claimed in the situation of data breaches due to a database hack has been in question. In *Owsianik v Equifax Canada Co.*,[157] the Divisional Court of Ontario reinforced its limitation as an intentional tort:

> The tort of intrusion upon seclusion was defined authoritatively only nine years ago. It has nothing to do with a database defendant. It need not even involve databases. It has to do with humiliation and emotional harm suffered by a personal intrusion into private affairs, for which there is no other remedy because the loss cannot be readily quantified in monetary terms. I agree that Sharpe J.A.'s definition of the tort is not necessarily the last word, but to extend liability to a person who does not intrude, but who fails to prevent the intrusion of another, in the face of Sharpe J.A.'s advertence

[151] 'In *Jones* the Court made an award based on the tort of invasion of privacy, or intrusion upon seclusion': *Marson v Nova Scotia* 2017 NSCA 17, [27]. See also *Patel v Steth* 2016 ONSC 6964, [104] where a husband surreptitiously set up a camera to record his wife in the bedroom and bathroom. Claims involving the recording of individuals in intimate settings are likely to increase according to the authors of one leading Canadian tort casebook: R Solomon, M McInnes, E Chamberlain and S Pitel, *Cases and Materials on the Law of Torts*, 10th edn (Toronto, Carswell, 2019) 115.

[152] 'The tort of intrusion upon seclusion was defined authoritatively only nine years ago': *Owsianik v Equifax Canada Co.* 2021 ONSC 4112, [54].

[153] See, eg, *Del Giudice v Thompson* 2020 ONSC 2676. The intrusion upon seclusion claim was dismissed in *Del Giudice v Thompson* 2021 ONSC 5379, [137], based upon the binding authority of the Divisional Court in *Owsianik v Equifax Canada Co.* 2021 ONSC 4112.

[154] There have been cases for certification of class actions on this point. See, eg, *Simpson v Facebook*, 2021 ONSC 968 (stemming from the notorious Cambridge Analytica scandal) where the court refused to certify the class proceeding. See also, *Setoguchi v Uber B.V.* 2021 ABQB 18, [72].

[155] In *Kaplan v Casino Rama Services Inc.* 2019 ONSC 2025, [28]–[29], the court dismissed a certification of a class action motion, but held that there was a cause of action for intrusion upon seclusion disclosed by the pleadings where a hacker breached the defendant's database. This decision was questioned by a majority of the Divisional Court in *Owsianik v Equifax Canada Co.* 2021 ONSC 4112, [56].

[156] Defendants are likely to be large businesses, organisations, or public entities. See *Drew v Walmart Canada Inc.* 2017 ONSC 3308, [7]–[8] which was settled without further remarks on the claim.

[157] *Owsianik v Equifax Canada Co.* 2021 ONSC 4112 (Div.Ct). In her dissent, Justice Sachs contended, amongst other points, that 'from a policy perspective, Sharpe J. A. was clearly driven by

> to the danger of opening the floodgates, would, in my view, be more than an incremental change in the common law.
>
> … But no one says that Equifax intruded, and that is the central element of the tort. The intrusion need not be intentional; it can be reckless. But it still has to be an intrusion. It is the intrusion that has to be intentional or reckless and the intrusion that has to be highly offensive. Otherwise the tort assigns liability for a completely different category of conduct, a category that is adequately controlled by the tort of negligence.[158]

Owsianik binds lower courts: 'an intrusion upon seclusion claim cannot apply to a hacker attack'.[159] Negligence may not be an alternative in this instance because it requires proof of harm and does not provide compensatory damages for 'upset, disgust, anxiety, agitation or other mental states that fall short of injury'.[160] *Jones* very much was the incremental step that Sharpe JA intended.[161] As a later composition of the Ontario Court of Appeal wrote: 'The tort of intrusion upon seclusion protects private information from unauthorized prying eyes.'[162] *Jones* is a formidable starting point for a wider discussion of privacy claims in private law. However, it does not purport to (nor should it) be the extent of this discourse. With this in mind, the next section examines whether *Jones* has opened a path for the remaining of Prosser's privacy torts.

c. Prosser's Remaining Privacy Torts at Common Law

With his opinion in *Jones*, it may be debated whether Sharpe JA brought the remaining of Prosser's privacy torts (and the *Restatement*'s articulation) within the ambit of Canadian common law.[163] He intended to leave the remaining categories of privacy torts set out by Prosser to be decided by later courts when appropriate.[164] Still, in *Jones*, he casually alluded to a particular direction on the matter when he determined there were prior decisions which could be

the need for the common law to be able to develop to protect the threats posed to privacy presented by the "routine collection and aggregation of highly personal information that is readily accessible in electronic form."'

[158] ibid [54]–[55].

[159] *Obodo v Trans Union of Canada, Inc.* 2021 ONSC 7297, [22]; *Del Giudice v Thompson* 2021 ONSC 5379, [137]; *Winder v Marriott International, Inc.* 2022 ONSC 390, [7].

[160] *Mustapha v Culligan of Canada Ltd.* 2008 SCC 27, [9]. In relation to certification of a negligence claim for improper access to medical information, the court in *Stewart v Demme* 2020 ONSC 83 declined to certify this claim in a class proceeding, citing this passage from the Supreme Court of Canada.

[161] *Jones* (n 1) [65]; Sharpe (n 22) 197.

[162] *Wakeling v Desjardins General Insurance* 2021 ONCA 672, [20]. See also *Owsianik v Equifax Canada Co.* 2021 ONSC 4112, [20]: 'the Court of Appeal deliberately defined the elements of that tort narrowly so that the only people who can be held liable for the tort are defendants who intentionally and illegally intrude to access the private information, not defendants who collect and store that information'.

[163] *Jones* recognised these torts in Ontario: *Del Guidice v Thompson* 2021 ONSC 5379, [131].

[164] Sharpe (n 22) 197.

categorised within Prosser's tort catalogue. By 2019, Ontario courts had recognised all of Prosser's privacy torts.

Public Disclosure of Embarrassing Private Facts

As expressed in the *Restatement (Second) of Torts*, the essence of the tort is that personal information of the plaintiff has been made public without the plaintiff's consent. Two further aspects are required: the private information publicised would be highly offensive to a reasonable person and the release of this information is not of legitimate public concern.[165] The means by which this information was obtained may itself be the subject matter of another action such as intrusion upon seclusion or breach of confidence. The claim may also stand alone. The fact of public disclosure means that unwanted attention has been brought upon the innocent party. The Federal Court of Appeal did not dismiss this claim when it was made in *Canada v John Doe*.[166] In 2016, an Ontario court in *Jane Doe 464533 v N.D.*[167] recognised this tort where the defendant had published a sexually explicit video of the plaintiff on the internet, without her consent or knowledge. The video was made at the persistent urging of the defendant. The court found for the plaintiff on each of her claims (breach of confidence, infliction of mental distress, invasion of privacy by which the court focused intrusion upon seclusion as set out in the *Restatement*[168]). No person appeared for the defendant in this case; but, the summary judgment was subsequently set aside.[169]

The action was recognised by another Ontario court in *Jane Doe 72511 v M. (N.)*.[170] This court applied the general discussion in *Jones* about privacy as well as the particular discussion of this tort in the first decision in *Jane Doe 464533 v N.D.* In *Jane Doe 72511*, in addition to N.M.'s violent physical abuse of the plaintiff (which his parents, the last two defendants, witnessed and failed to address in any way), the defendant also published a sexually explicit video of the plaintiff on a pornography website (which he admitted was 'revenge for Jane calling the police'[171]). The latter act is the focus here as it was the subject of a claim in public disclosure of private facts.[172] While the video had been removed

[165] These criteria were identified in *ES v Shillington* 2021 ABQB 739 when the court recognised this right of action.

[166] *Canada v John Doe* 2016 FCA 191. The claim was dismissed by the court because it was unsupported by any material facts. The claim for intrusion upon seclusion was dismissed for the same reason.

[167] *Jane Doe 464533 v N.D.*2016 ONSC 541.

[168] ibid, [41]. The court slightly modified it at [46].

[169] *Doe v.N.D.*, 2016 ONSC 4920. An appeal of this decision was rejected: *Jane Doe 464533 v N.D.*, 2017 ONSC 127.

[170] *Jane Doe 72511 v M. (N.)* 2018 ONSC 6607, [86]–[101].

[171] ibid [5].

[172] The privacy action in both of these *Jane Doe* cases dealt with 'revenge porn'. This terminology has been viewed as problematic: C McGlynn, E Rackley and R Houghton, 'Beyond "Revenge Porn": The Continuum of Image-Based Sexual Abuse' (2017) 25 *Feminist Legal Studies* 25. Note the *Jane Doe 72511* ([122]ff.) court's basis for using the phrase.

by the administrator, it had been viewed 60,000 times. The *Jane Doe 72511* court adopted the *Jane Doe 464533* court's slight amendment to the *Restatement*'s text (the court's addition is underlined): 'One who gives publicity to a matter concerning the private life of another is subject to liability to the other for invasion of the other's privacy, if the matter publicized <u>or the act of the publication</u> (a) would be highly offensive to a reasonable person, and (b) is not of legitimate concern to the public.'[173] To establish liability for this action, the plaintiff must prove: '(a) the defendant publicized an aspect of the plaintiff's private life; (b) the plaintiff did not consent to the publication; (c) the matter publicized or its publication would be highly offensive to a reasonable person; and (d) the publication was not of legitimate concern to the public.'[174] The court was satisfied the plaintiff made out these points[175] and awarded the plaintiff $50,000 in general, $25,000 in aggravated, and $25,000 in punitive damages. The court departed from the damages parameters set out in *Jones* because 'the breach of the plaintiff's privacy rights in a case like this are much more serious than in an action for intrusion on seclusion'.[176]

As has arisen in other cases, the intrusion upon seclusion action was cast within the context of a tort for invasion of privacy in the Nova Scotia case of *Racki v Racki*.[177] Stemming from an acrimonious divorce, an ex-husband self-published a book in which 'he disclosed Ms Racki had been addicted to sleeping pills and attempted suicide twice'.[178] *Jones* was the starting point for the court's deliberation on whether to recognise a right of action for public disclosure of private facts of another;[179] which it did, awarding $18,000 in general damages.

Publicity Placing a Person in False Light

This tort 'consists of publicity that places the plaintiff in a false light in the public eye';[180] whether it attributed a poor piece of writing to a famous author (as was the example of Lord Byron used by Prosser) or pertained to the unlicensed use of a photo of an individual to promote a product. The emphasis is on the unwarranted attention regarding one's reputation/name.

Prior to *Jones*, a Manitoba court ruled there was 'no foundation whatever for claiming from the primeval mud of the common law in force in Manitoba' the existence of a tort of false light invasion of privacy.[181] *Yenovkian v Gulian*[182]

[173] *Jane Doe 72511* (n 170) [97]–[98].
[174] ibid, [99].
[175] ibid, [100].
[176] ibid, [131]. See also ibid, [122]–[143].
[177] *Racki v Racki* 2021 NSSC 46. The court in *ES v Shillington* 2021 ABQB 739 drew from this decision, as well as *Jane Doe 464533* and *Jane Doe 72511*.
[178] ibid, [2].
[179] ibid, [26].
[180] Prosser (n 26) 398.
[181] *Parasiuk v Canadian Newspapers Company Limited* [1998] 2 WWR 737 (Man. Q.B.), 738.
[182] *Yenovkian v Gulian* 2019 ONSC 7279.

recognised the tort of publicity placing a person in a false light by drawing from the decision in *Jones*. The court adopted the action as set out in the *Restatement*.[183] Identified in both the *Restatement* and *Yenovkian*, the publicity in question may be defamatory, but defamation is not required as part of this claim. Rather, the plaintiff may establish 'that a reasonable person would find it highly offensive to be publicly misrepresented as they have been. The wrong is in publicly representing someone, not as worse than they are, but as other than they are. The value at stake is respect for a person's privacy right to control the way they present themselves to the world.'[184] The action also overlaps somewhat with the aforementioned tort of public disclosure of private facts. The difference between the actions has been found to be:

> ... public disclosure of private facts involves true statements, while 'false light' publicity involves false or misleading claims. (Two further elements also distinguish the two causes of action: 'false light' invasion of privacy requires that the defendant know or be reckless to the falsity of the information, while public disclosure of private facts involves a requirement that there be no legitimate public concern justifying the disclosure.)[185]

The court was concerned that failing to recognise the tort of publicity placing a person in a false light would result in a defendant avoiding liability for 'invasion of privacy simply because the statements they have made about another person are false'.[186] In this case, the ex-husband continued to post videos online about his ex-wife and her family, alleging amongst other false claims, that she was a kidnapper, abused their children, drugged the children, forged documents, and defrauded governments.[187] The ex-husband was also found liable for public disclosure of private facts for the statements he made in these videos which were true.[188] Adopting the discussion of damages in *Jane Doe 72511*, the court awarded damages for invasion of privacy in the amount of $100,000[189] (punitive damages of $150,000 were awarded for the entirety of the claims[190]).[191]

Appropriation of Personality

Finally, there is appropriation of personality (specifically of an aspect of the plaintiff's identity). It is usually committed with some form of gain in mind.

[183] ibid, [170]–[171].
[184] ibid, [171].
[185] ibid, [172].
[186] ibid, [173].
[187] ibid, [175].
[188] ibid, [183].
[189] ibid, [186]–[193].
[190] ibid, [194]–[202].
[191] In *Candelora v Fraser* 2020 NSSC 177, aff'd 2021 NSCA 49, the court found that the discussion of the conduct and damages under Nova Scotia's Intimate Images and Cyber-Protection Act S.N.S. 2017, c.7, ss 5, 8, were similar in this case to that found in *Yenovkian* (n 182) [160]–[193].

While Prosser contended there was no matter of intrusion here, it is suggested that this is indeed a matter of intrusion into reputation: appropriating an individual's identity for financial gain (because that identity facilitated it) or for purposes of sullying that individual's reputation. This tort seems to have more of a proprietary element.[192] Sharpe JA noted that the Ontario Court of Appeal had recognised the tort of wrongful appropriation of personality in *Krouse v Chrysler Canada Ltd.*[193] (where the Ontario Court of Appeal protected the commercial use of an individual's name (including his likeness, voice and reputation)) as an example of Prosser's torts applied in Canadian law.[194] Sharpe JA also considered *Athans v Canadian Adventure Camps Ltd.*[195] to have been a successful claim for appropriation of personality insofar as the defendant had used a photograph of the plaintiff (an expert water-skier) in advertisements.[196] Another Ontario court added to the understanding of appropriation of personality. In *Gould Estate v Stoddart Publishing Co.*,[197] a book on the Canadian pianist Glenn Gould was published in 1995 based upon 1956 interviews and photographs by Jock Carroll. The estate's lawsuit for appropriation of personality was dismissed because Gould was the subject of the work (and he was not commercially exploited or used in some manner to garner interest in the book itself (the 'sales vs subject distinction')) and also due to public interest in Glenn Gould. Since *Jones*, the court in *Chandra v CBC*[198] did not preclude the possibility of a claim in appropriation of personality.

A case that has been the subject of many decisions so far is *Douez v Facebook*.[199] The plaintiffs in this certified class action allege a violation of section 3(2) of BC's Privacy Act, 'unauthorized use of name or portrait of another'. The case may be better known for the Supreme Court of Canada's rejection of Facebook's argument that the forum selection clause in the terms of use specified California as the governing law.[200] The class of plaintiffs was subsequently expanded to include Facebook users resident in Manitoba, Newfoundland and Labrador, and Saskatchewan (provinces with similar privacy legislation).[201]

192 Robert Post saw reputation as a type of property where an individual builds up her reputation through hard work: R Post, 'The Social Foundations of Defamation Law: Reputation and the Constitution' (1986) 74 *California Law Review* 691.

193 *Krouse v Chrysler Canada Ltd.* (1970), 1 O.R. (2d) 225.

194 *Jones* (n 1) [28].

195 *Athans v Canadian Adventure Camps Ltd.* (1977), 17 O.R. (2d) 425 (H.C.J.)

196 *Jones* did not exhaustively canvass Canadian case law on this point. Courts in other provinces have also recognised this tort (though neither Prosser nor the *Restatement* are mentioned), such as *Poirier v Wal-Mart Canada Corp.* 2006 BCSC 1138.

197 *Gould Estate v Stoddart Publishing* Co. (1996), 30 O.R. (3d) 520 (Gen.Div.), affirmed (1998), 39 O.R. (3d) 545 (C.A.), leave to appeal to the SCC refused [1998] SCCA 373.

198 *Chandra v CBC* 2015 ONSC 5303, [43]–[44].

199 *Douez v Facebook* 2018 BCCA 186.

200 *Douez v Facebook Inc.* 2017 SCC 33.

201 *Douez v Facebook Inc.* 2019 BCSC 715.

IV. CONCLUSION

Jones is a dichotomy. This decision has been cited positively by other common law courts[202] and academics. And yet, the force of its ruling may only be starting to take effect in Canada. It may be surprising to read about the tentative steps taken after *Jones v Tsige*. This hesitation seems to repeat the approach in place since the nineteenth century: a long deliberative process towards discussing the concept of privacy in law, without necessarily committing to anything expanding beyond particular factual circumstances. There should be some level of frustration that this sluggish pace continues even with the impetus provided by rapid innovations in information technology. A more concerted effort to engage with these influences on the private law of privacy would be to the common law's benefit.

There should be some appreciation for Sharpe JA's measured entry into privacy. Recall that Raymond Wacks, in 1980, argued that '"Privacy" has grown into a large and unwieldy concept.'[203] With the internet affirming the point retrospectively, Wacks contended that the law should focus on the 'nucleus of the right to privacy, the protection of personal information'.[204] Arguably, Sharpe JA has adopted this approach. As noted above, *Jones* fits within the confines of intentional torts and while this classification takes an incremental step, it is also a step on a path that could be closed off. Even in the aforementioned discussion of the other privacy torts outlined in the *Restatement*, intention remains a key element. *Jones* was intended to be an incremental step down a much longer road than the intentional torts.

The inherently unwieldy nature of the concept of privacy[205] remains a formidable barrier to further development. Consider the following statement from one Canadian tort textbook: 'In view of the alternative remedies available, is a separate tort of "invasion of privacy" necessary? It is arguable that it is not. … It is more desirable to have the different aspects of privacy protection dealt with in separate torts which more clearly can focus on the principles at hand.'[206] The seeming preference amongst the legal community to adopt particularised actions as a next step in recognising privacy interests hampers efforts to grapple with the concept of privacy. While specific actions may be the next steps taken, they should be undertaken commensurately with a broader discussion of the protection of privacy at common law. Finally, although *Jones* correctly speaks to the perils of centralised databases of personal information with myriad ways in which they may be accessed, privacy was not limited to personal information when Warren and Brandeis wrote of it in 1890.

[202] See, eg, *C v Holland* [2012] 3 NZLR 672.

[203] R Wacks, 'The Poverty of 'Privacy' (1980) 96 *Law Quarterly Review* 73, 89.

[204] A Monti and R Wacks, *Protecting Personal Information: The Right to Privacy Reconsidered* (Oxford, Hart, 2019) 126.

[205] Wacks is not the sole author to point this out. Russell Brown, before he was elevated to the Supreme Court of Canada, also identified the various understandings of privacy: R Brown, 'Rethinking Privacy: Exclusivity, Private Relation and Tort Law' (2006) 43 *Alberta Law Review* 589.

[206] L Klar and C Jefferies, *Tort Law*, 6th edn (Toronto, Thomson Reuters, 2018) 104.

12

Google Spain, Google Inc. v Agencia Española de Protección de Datos (2014)

DAVID ERDOS

On 13 May 2014, a Grand Chamber of the Court of Justice of the European Union (CJEU) ruled that a Spanish individual Mr Costeja was entitled to require Google to assess his claim for the delisting of his personal data from a name-based search under both the rights to erasure and objection set out under the EU Data Protection Directive (DPD) 95/46.[1] Mr Costeja did not need to show any concrete prejudice and his rights would 'as a rule'[2] override Google's interest and even the interest of the general public in receiving information in this way. *Google Spain, Google Inc. v Agencia Española de Protección de Datos (AEPD), Mario Costeja González* (hereinafter *Google Spain*) was understood by both its detractors and supporters as an unequivocal assertion of the role of data protection in governing the public dissemination of personal data in a new digital context. Certainly, it was doctrinally striking that Google Search was found to have at least some controller responsibilities in EU data protection law and, even more so, that the Court proceeded on the basis that potentially far-reaching national derogations for journalistic (or cognate) expression could have no application. Practically, it has also led to many more Data Protection Authorities (DPAs) playing a high-profile role in relation to the online dissemination of personal data.

At the same time, this judgment is considerably more complex and challenging than appears at first sight. Whilst confirming a search engine's controller responsibilities, it also limited them to, if not simply ex post action on name searches, then at least only to intervention when its activities 'significantly,

[1] Directive 95/46/EC of the European Parliament and of the Council of 24 October 1995 on the protection of individuals with regard to the processing of personal data and on the free movement of such data.

[2] *Google Spain, Google Inc. v Agencia Española de Protección de Datos (AEPD), Mario Costeja González*, C-131/12, EU:C:2014:317, para 99.

and additionally' affected data subject rights and 'within the framework of its responsibilities, powers and capabilities'.[3] Its relationship with a contextual approach is also complex since it acknowledged the need for specific balancing in particular cases and, whilst pointedly unreferenced in the judgment itself, the CJEU in 2019 confirmed that this must take into account freedom of information (a sub-right of freedom of expression) and be applied to even the apparently peremptory sensitive data regime.[4] Whilst clearly applying data protection to an entity primarily based in California, *Google Spain*'s territorial holdings were also somewhat ambiguous and a later CJEU judgment in 2019 held that Google was *not* generally obliged to de-index material globally as opposed to when providing services within Europe itself.[5] It is also striking how many related questions within this area remain rather open including, for example, what responsibilities other so-called 'intermediary' publishers, such as social networking sites, have.

What *Google Spain* did clearly confirm is that EU data protection, as now instantiated in the General Data Protection Regulation (GDPR),[6] is a vital part of the landscape where issues of privacy, reputation, rehabilitation and freedom of expression intersect. It is, therefore, a landmark case, as it stands as the most significant CJEU case of the DPD period and so a veritable pinnacle of EU data protection. Nevertheless, much of that pinnacle, and also the wider panorama, remain shrouded in clouds and mist. The task of charting this complex topography and ensuring that both natural and legal persons are able to securely traverse within it remains a formidable ongoing challenge.

I. FACTS AND BACKGROUND

Google Spain originated from the claim which Mr Costeja González, a Spanish national resident in Spain, lodged in February 2010[7] against Google through its subsidiary Google Spain. He requested that it ensure that two announcements including his personal data published in the *La Vanguardia* newspaper in 1998 no longer appeared in any search which included his name. These announcements had been placed by order of the Spanish Ministry of Labour and Social

[3] ibid, para 38.

[4] *GC et. al. v Commission Nationale de l'Informatique et des Libertés*, C-136/17, EU:C:2019:773, para 46.

[5] *Google LLC v Commission Nationale de l'Informatique et des Libertés*, C-507/17, EU:C:2019:772, para 33. *Google Spain*, C-131/12, para 70.

[6] Regulation (EU) 2016/679 of the European Parliament and of the Council of 27 April 2016 on the protection of natural persons with regard to the processing of personal data and on the free movement of such data, and repealing Directive 95/46/EC (General Data Protection Regulation).

[7] *Google Spain, Google Inc. v Agencia Española de Protección de Datos (AEPD), Mario Costeja González*, C-131/12, EU:C:2013:424, Opinion of AG Jääkinen, para 19. Mr Costeja also made direct claims against the website publisher which were not accepted by the Spanish DPA and were not further pursued. See *Google Spain*, C-131/12, paras 15–16.

Affairs and related to a 'real-estate auction connected with attachment proceedings for the recovery of social security debts'.[8] Whilst not disputing that these matters related to him, Mr Costeja stated that the proceedings had been 'fully resolved for a number of years' and that reference to them was therefore 'entirely irrelevant'.[9] Google rejected the claim and Mr Costeja therefore proceeded to lodge a complaint with the Spanish DPA, the Agencia Española de Protección de Datos, which in July 2010 upheld it and ordered Google to take 'the measures necessary to withdraw the data from their index and to render future access to them impossible'.[10] Google resisted this and, citing a 'profound chilling effect on free expression', appealed to the Spanish Audiencia Nacional (National High Court).[11] After hearing preliminary arguments, in February 2012 that Court lodged a series of legal questions before the CJEU through the preliminary reference procedure, which ultimately led to the *Google Spain* judgment.

Although *Google Spain* appeared focused on a single individual case, it was umbilically tied to a far wider legal and regulatory context. Since 2007 the Spanish DPA had been issuing determinations requiring search engines to delist material[12] which, at least in relation to Google, had systematically been appealed. Indeed, by the time of the *Google Spain* reference in February 2012, more than 100 such appeals were pending before the Audiencia and by the time the CJEU gave its judgment this had risen to 217.[13] Also in 2007, the Spanish regulator published an overarching statement on search engines which not only examined search engines' extensive back-end profiling of users but also established the basis for the DPA's action as regards the public listing of third-party content.[14] This statement also fed into a common Article 29 Working Party Opinion of European Economic Area (EEA)[15] DPA's on search engines, published in 2008. This Opinion largely focused on back-end processing and was rather more equivocal about the responsibilities of internet search engines when listing public domain content, stating that:

> [t]he principle of proportionality requires that to the extent that a search engine provider acts purely as an intermediary, it should not be considered to be the

[8] *Google Spain*, C-131/12, para 14.

[9] ibid, para 15.

[10] *Google Spain*, C-131/12, Opinion of AG Jääkinen, para 22.

[11] 'Google fights Spanish privacy order in court', *BBC News*, www.bbc.co.uk/news/technology-12239674.

[12] See A Rallo, *The Right to be Forgotten on the Internet: Google v Spain* (EPIC, 2018) 47–96.

[13] M Peguera, 'In the Aftermath of *Google Spain*: How the "Right to be Forgotten" is Being Shaped by Courts and the Data Protection Authority' (2015) 23 *International Journal of Law and Information Technology* 325, 326.

[14] Agencia Española de Protección de Datos, *Statement on Internet Search Engines* (2007), web.archive.org/web/20100323135023/http://www.agpd.es/portalwebAGPD/canaldocumentacion/recomendaciones/common/pdfs/declaracion_aepd_buscadores_en.pdf, 6–7.

[15] EU secondary legislation on data protection in this area has extended throughout, not only the EU, but also to three associated states, namely Iceland, Norway and Liechtenstein, which together make up the European Economic Area (EEA). As a result, non-EU EEA states have been represented (though in a non-voting capacity) on the Article 29 Working Party and now on the European Data Protection Board.

> principal controller with regard to the content related processing of personal data that is taking place. In this case the principal controllers of personal data are the information providers. The formal, legal and practical control the search engine has over the personal data involved is usually limited to the possibility of removing data from its servers. With regard to the removal of personal data from their index and search results, search engines have sufficient control to consider them as controllers (either alone or jointly with others) in those cases, but the extent to which an obligation to remove or block personal data exists, may depend on the general tort law and liability regulations of the particular Member State.[16]

These regulatory developments also helped catalyse the explicit inclusion of 'right to be forgotten' language in the initial text for the GDPR released in January 2012[17] and, in fact, the European Commission's submission in the *Google Spain* case itself ultimately agreed with the great majority of the Spanish DPA's position.

Although it is sometimes misleadingly claimed that *Google Spain* was 'the case that gave birth to the "right to be forgotten"',[18] the themes with which it grappled have much deeper and wider roots within (at least European) data protection. Indeed, as early as the mid-1980s the head of the Norwegian DPA stated that it was crucial to address 'to what extent it is possible to give persons fair and necessary access to what personal information is reported about them through the data banks of press information, and how far is there a chance that wrong and misleading information could be corrected and adjusted in ways that prevent harm occurring'.[19] Meanwhile, in 2001, the French DPA issued a *deliberation* which argued that in light of developing online realities the '*droit à l'oubli*' (or 'right to be forgotten') pointed to the need in most circumstances for criminal and other jurisprudential information to be anonymised prior to its publication on the internet.[20] Nevertheless, it is striking that it was not until the late 2000s that data protection turned unequivocally to focus on the responsibilities of internet search engines themselves when disseminating data. As will be explored in this chapter, this reticence can be related to at least three issues: (i) the ability to conceptualise a search engine, not only as a publisher of personal data, but also as an intermediary; (ii) the realisation that its dissemination activities are quite different, not only to traditional journalism, but also

[16] Article 29 Working Party, *Opinion 1/2008 on Data Protection Issues Related to Search Engines* (2008) 14.

[17] Proposal for a Regulation of the European Parliament and of the Council on the Protection for Individuals with regard to the Processing of Personal Data and on the Free Movement of such Data (General Data Protection Regulation) COM (2012)11 final, recitals 53 and 54 and Article 17.

[18] D Kaye, *Speech Police: The Global Struggle to Govern the Internet* (Columbia Global Reports, 2019) 34.

[19] H Seip, 'The Individual in the Age of Telematics', *Transnational Data Report* (1984) 363.

[20] France, Commission nationale de l'informatique et des libertes, *Délibération no 01-057 du 29 novembre 2001 portant recommandation sur la diffusion de donne'es personnelles sur internet par les banques de données de jurisprudence*, web.archive.org/web/20130614052958/https:/www.cnil.fr/documentation/deliberations/deliberation/delib/17/.

back-end processing; and finally (iii) the reality that almost all relevant providers, including most notably the hugely dominant Google service, have their principal base outside the EU/EEA in the US. As will be seen, *Google Spain* has shone considerable new light on all these issues whilst continuing to leave many questions unresolved.

II. THE IMMEDIATE AND DIRECT AFTERMATH OF *GOOGLE SPAIN*

Before turning to look in earnest at these specific issues, it is important to emphasise that *Google Spain*'s core holdings, notably that search engines were obliged to consider claims for at least the name-based delisting of personal data under the rights to erasure and object within EU data protection, have exerted significant direct practical effect since 2014. Later that year, EEA DPAs collectively issued common guidelines indicating how they intended to interpret and police these requirements, including a list of indicative criteria for evaluating when a delisting claim would be justified.[21] In 2020, the European Data Protection Board updated the first part of these guidelines in light of the GDPR.[22] Moreover, since 2014, Google has received over 1.3 million requests for the delisting of personal data relating to over five million uniform resource locators (URLs). Approximately 49 per cent of these URLs have been removed at least from certain searches within the EEA, and also Switzerland.[23] The focus on Google is intentional since, perhaps unsurprisingly given it has over 90 per cent of the market share of searches in Europe,[24] almost all of the direct outcomes of the ruling have related to this one actor. By way of contrast, Microsoft Bing, the next most popular general search engine in Europe, indicated that by December 2021 it had received just less than 50,000 requests relating to approximately 170,000 URLs, although its removal rate of around 47 per cent was almost identical to that of Google's.[25]

[21] Article 29 Working Party, *Guidelines on the Implementation of the Court of Justice of the European Union Judgment on 'Google Spain and Inc v Agencia Española de Protección de Datos and Costeja González'. C-131/12* (2014), ec.europa.eu/newsroom/article29/item-detail.cfm?item_id=667236.

[22] European Data Protection Board, *Guidelines 5/2019 on the Criteria of the Right to be Forgotten in the search engine cases under the GDPR (part 1) – version adopted after public consultation* (2020), edpb.europa.eu/our-work-tools/our-documents/ohjeet/guidelines-52019-criteria-right-be-forgotten-search-engines_en.

[23] Google, *Transparency Report: Request to Delist Content under European Privacy Law* (n.d.), transparencyreport.google.com/eu-privacy/overview?hl=en (accessed 21 September 2022). It remains unclear why Switzerland, which is not itself subject to EU secondary legislation on data protection, has been treated by Google (and also Microsoft Bing) as falling squarely within the CJEU ruling.

[24] 'Search Engine Market Share in 2020', (Oberlo) www.oberlo.co.uk/statistics/search-engine-market-share.

[25] See Microsoft, 'Content Removal Requests Report "Right to be Forgotten" Requests', www.microsoft.com/en-us/corporate-responsibility/right-to-be-forgotten-removal-requests-report/. Alongside the EEA and Switzerland this report also details material delisted under Russian law.

From the start, *Google Spain* was greeted by both supporters and detractors as an unambiguous assertion of data protection's role in governing the dissemination of personal data online. Thus, the outgoing Vice-President of the European Commission, Viviane Reding, stated that it was a 'clear victory for the protection of personal data of Europeans', demonstrating that 'data belongs to the individual, not to the company',[26] whilst Wikipedia founder Jimmy Wales described it as 'one of the most wide-sweeping internet censorship rulings I've ever seen'.[27] These individuals were correct to recognise the great significance of this case. Nevertheless, and as will be explored below, the judgment incorporated many complexities which are not captured in these bold pronouncements.

III. AN INTERNET SEARCH ENGINE AS CONTROLLER 2.0?

The most central data protection issue brought to the CJEU in *Google Spain* concerned whether an internet search engine had data protection 'controller' responsibilities when indexing personal data. Whilst sometimes the beneficiary of wide-ranging exemptions to safeguard journalistic and cognate freedom of expression[28] (and potentially even outside EU data protection law entirely if based overseas[29]), it had never been in doubt that the original website determined the 'purposes and means of the processing' and thereby acted as a 'controller'[30] when publishing personal data.[31] In contrast, although a search engine could be conceptualised as an autonomous analyser and distributor of information, it could also be seen as a mere 'intermediary' between the original publisher of material and the end user. The EU's e-commerce framework, Directive 2000/31, had not explicitly included an intermediary shield for these services[32] and this entire code was in any case stated to be without prejudice to 'questions' covered by the EU data protection laws.[33] However, in Spain, local domestic

These have been discounted in the figures just cited. The global impact of the *Google Spain* judgment is considered in the last substantive section of this chapter.

[26] V Reding, 'Today's Court Judgment is a clear victory for the protection of personal data of Europeans!' (*Facebook*, 13 May 2014), www.facebook.com/permalink.php?story_fbid=304206613078842&id=291423897690447.

[27] D Lee, 'Google ruling 'astonishing', says Wikipedia founder Wales' (*BBC News*, 14 May 2014), /www.bbc.co.uk/news/technology-27407017.

[28] DPD, Art 9.

[29] *Google Spain*, C-131/12, para 84.

[30] See DPD, Art 2(d) and now GDPR, Art 4(7).

[31] For a precise holding on this point see *Bodil Lindqvist*, C-101/01, EU:C:2003:596.

[32] Instead, it had only made a commitment to re-examine this at a later date. See Directive 2000/31/EC of the European Parliament and of the Council of 8 June 2000 on certain legal aspects of information society services, in particular electronic commerce, in the Internal Market ('Directive on electronic commerce'), Art 21(2).

[33] The DPD, in turn, made no mention of e-Commerce Directive 2000/31. In contrast, Art 2(4) of the GDPR now itself states that it 'shall be without prejudice to the application of Directive 2000/31/EC, in particular the liability rules of intermediary service providers in Articles 12 to 15 of that Directive'. The relationship between these frameworks remains a site of contestation and confusion.

intermediary law did grant search engines a shield from liability prior to notice and did not clearly exclude data protection duties from this. This led the Spanish DPA to look to the interface between these two frameworks in order to establish a balance between liberty and responsibility here.[34] Given the nature of pan-EU law and its transposition in most Member States, that possibility was not open to most EEA DPAs. Instead, the Article 29 Working Party's 2008 Opinion drew on the broader principle of proportionality in order to argue an internet search engine (which obeyed website exclusion protocols and any requests to ensure its cache reflected current content) would only be a 'controller' when considering the removal of personal data from its index.[35] It further muddied the waters by stating that the extent of any obligation to act could depend on 'the general tort law'[36] in each of the Member States. This confusing landscape was one factor justifying a widespread reticence to engage. Indeed, the former head of the Spanish DPA, Artemi Lombarte, tellingly stated in 2015 that 'the Spanish agency had not allies in this struggle – any allies. That is the truth.'[37] This reticence was highlighted by Advocate General Jääkinen's Opinion in *Google Spain* itself, issued in June 2013, which urged rejection of the Spanish DPA's claims:

> In my view the internet search engine service provider cannot in law or in fact fulfil the obligations of controller … in relation to the personal data on source web pages hosted on third-party servers. Therefore a reasonable interpretation of the Directive requires that the service provider is not generally considered as having that position.
>
> An opposite opinion would entail internet search engines being incompatible with EU law, a conclusion I would find absurd. Specifically, if internet search engine service providers were considered as controllers of the personal data on third-party source web pages and if on any of these pages there would be 'special categories of data' referred to in Article 8 of the Directive (e.g. personal data revealing political opinions or religious beliefs or data concerning the health or sex life or individuals), the activity of the internet search engine would automatically become illegal, when the stringent conditions laid down in that article for the processing of such data are not met.[38]

Seen in this broader context, therefore, the CJEU's holding that search engine indexing did entail controller responsibilities was of seminal significance for

[34] Agencia Española de Protección de Datos, *Statement on Internet Search Engines* (2007) 7.

[35] Article 29 Working Party, *Opinion 1/2008 on Data Protection Issues Related to Search Engines* (2008), ec.europa.eu/justice/article-29/documentation/opinion-recommendation/files/2008/wp148_en.pdf, 14.

[36] ibid.

[37] Centre for European Legal Studies, *EU Internet Regulation After Google Spain* (2015), www.cels.law.cam.ac.uk/sites/www.law.cam.ac.uk/files/images/www.cels.law.cam.ac.uk/documents/google_spain_conference_report_-_16.12.2015.pdf, 13.

[38] *Google Spain*, C-131/12, Opinion of AG Jääkinen, paras 89–90. Technically, Jääkinen did accept that a search engine was a controller of the index itself but argued that (unless the service failed to respect a website exclusion code or a request by the website to update content) this should somehow be shorn from the actual content which the index was linking to (and, in fact, processing) and so raised no legal problem (at para 98). The Opinion also did not address the clear fact that the index would itself include special data, for example, data linking a particular individual to a specific disease and that this would presumptively require a special legal basis for processing.

internet regulation. It was particularly notable that the Court did not limit the status of controller only to ex post removal as the Article 29 Working Party had suggested. Nor was there any indication that a search engine would necessarily benefit from the intermediary shields set out in Directive 2000/31 or in Spanish national law. Instead, the Court held that in deciding of its own volition to index personal data the search engine was clearly determining 'the purposes of means of that activity' and so fell indubitably within the four corners of the 'controller' definition.[39] It mattered neither that the personal data had 'already been published on the internet'[40] nor that the search engine carried out 'the same operations in respect of other types of information and does not distinguish between the latter and the personal data'.[41]

The Court also stressed that a 'broad definition' of the concept of 'controller' was necessary in order to achieve the law's objective of ensuring 'effective and complete protection of data subjects'.[42] At the same time, however, it significantly but rather cryptically constrained the controller responsibilities which search engines had, stating in a crucial paragraph that:

> Inasmuch as the activity of a search is therefore liable to affect significantly, and additionally compared with that of the publishers of websites, the fundamental rights to privacy and to the protection of personal data, the operator of the search engine as the person determining the purposes and means of that activity must ensure, within the framework of its responsibilities, powers and capabilities, that the activity meets the requirements of Directive 95/46 in order that the guarantees laid down by the directive may have full effect and that effective and complete protection of data subjects, in particular of their right to privacy, may actually be achieved.[43]

A serious criticism of the judgment is that the grounding of these twin restrictions – significant and additional affect and acting within the context of responsibilities, powers and capabilities – remained unspecified. Such explicit justification was particularly necessary since these limitations do not mirror the legislative structure of EU data protection itself and are also in clear tension with the effective and complete protection of individuals, which was also emphasised in the same paragraph. Nevertheless, the Court failed to accept Google's claim that rights had to be curtailed here under 'the principle of proportionality',[44] or even to recognise that data protection restrictions interfered (albeit possibly justifiably) with freedom of expression, including, more particularly, the right to impart and receive information.

Perhaps unsurprisingly, given that this was the precise claim brought before the Court in *Google Spain*, Google and other search engines narrowly interpreted the ruling as only obliging them to consider claims for an ex post delisting

[39] *Google Spain*, C-131/12, para 33.
[40] ibid, para 29.
[41] ibid, para 28.
[42] ibid, para 34.
[43] ibid, para 38.
[44] ibid, para 63.

of personal data, only in relation to particularised URLs and only in relation to searches including a data subject's name. However, the restrictions enunciated by the Court itself were not as precisely defined and in principle were considerably more limited. Thus, it should be clear that indexing by reference to other widely used identifiers such as images or a job position may also significantly and additionally impact on an individual's data protection rights. Moreover, albeit only in restricted circumstances, such impact could even result from searching on terms which do not include any identifier. An example would be a search combining a reference to a small hamlet and a highly stigmatic allegation (for example, being a 'child sex offender') which brought up totally false allegations that an identified person within that neighbourhood was responsible for such offences. It is also far from self-evident that a search engine's 'responsibilities, powers and capabilities' are always only limited to acting ex post on specific URLs. Under EU data protection law itself, the starting point would ordinarily be that a controller is responsible to ensure the legality of its processing ex ante and on an ongoing basis. However, it is clear that such full responsibilities would make a principally automated search engine impossible. Determining how much search engines should be required to alter these ways of working to ensure data protection standards are achieved requires a difficult normative trade-off between the value of those protections and the rights and interests furthered by search engines. Nevertheless, even a fairly conservative assessment of a search engine's powers and capabilities could easily point to wider duties. For example, all the major search engines possess PhotoDNA technology which enables them to ensure that images which have already been analysed as manifestly illegal are not relisted. Deployment of this technology could be of considerable use, for example, to victims of ongoing and manifest revenge pornography but would require a search engine going beyond acting on specific URLs with all the hassle and delays that may entail for the data subject. It might even be argued that if a search engine is put repeatedly on notice about this sort of manifestly illegal material appearing on discrete websites then it might have the power and capability to limit the indexing of this site or engage in some ex-ante screening of this clearly circumscribed content.

At a practical level, the outcome of *Google Spain* has tended to be determined by Google itself and in the rather narrow way already specified. Indeed, the Article 29 Working Party's Guidelines in 2014 appeared to endorse Google's early restriction of any outcome here[45] to ex post delisting 'on the basis of a person's name'[46] after having been provided with 'specific URLs'.[47]

[45] See A Kuczerawy and J Ausloos, 'From notice-and-takedown to notice-and-delist: implementing Google Spain' (2015) 14 *Coloumbia Technical Law Journal* 14 219, 226–7.

[46] Article 29 Working Party, *Guidelines* (2014) 6. The Guidelines did, however, recognise 'pseudonyms and nicknames' as relevant search terms so long as the data subject could 'establish that they are linked to his/her real identity' (ibid, 6).

[47] ibid, 7. Nevertheless, the Guidelines did stress that individuals should be able to choose how to lodge their requests rather than necessarily using a search engine's sui generis form.

Nevertheless, especially after the transition to the GDPR, at least some regulators have interpreted the law more strictly. For example, in 2019 the Italian DPA mandated delisting of personal data against a search on the basis of an individual's job title, finding that the right to objection within the GDPR also extended to this kind of claim.[48] Meanwhile, new Guidelines finalised by the European Data Protection Board in 2020 stated that the right to delist 'is *mainly* based on [a] data subject's name' and, albeit whilst flagging up only the example of where a search engine had failed to respect a website's exclusion protocol, even emphasised that '[i]n some exceptional cases, they will need to carry out actual and full erasure in their indexes or caches'.[49] The recent CJEU Grand Chamber judgment of *GC et. al. v CNIL* similarly described a search on an individual's name as only a 'particular' example of where indexing would be liable to significantly affect data subjects.[50] At the same time, it confirmed that the sensitive data rules could only apply to search engine indexing by reason of some such significant referencing 'and thus via a verification, under the supervision of the competent national authorities, on the basis of a request by the data subject'.[51] Nevertheless, as regards general data protection principles such as relevance and non-excessiveness, the Court found that a search engine had more wide-ranging responsibilities than simply considering whether or not to delist. More specifically, in examining the processing of links to old information related to criminal proceedings, it held that even where a claim for delisting would not be justified a search engine was:

> in any event, at the latest on occasion of the request for de-referencing, to adjust the list of results in such a way that the overall picture it gives the internet user reflects the current legal position, which means in particular that links to web pages containing information on that point must appear in first place on the list.[52]

In sum, it is now clear that a search engine must consider a range of options when put on notice about a potential data protection problem arising from indexing. Furthermore, the reference to 'at the latest on the occasion of the request for de-referencing' suggests that there might be certain exceptional circumstances, for example potentially in the revenge pornography site example above, where a search engine may have certain fully ex ante obligations. It is nevertheless very apparent that many of the issues concerning search engine responsibilities which arose in the *Google Spain* judgment remain concerningly unclear and contested.

Another issue connected to this aspect of *Google Spain* is how it might relate to the broader landscape of active intermediary services beyond search engines.

[48] Italy, Garante per la Protezione dei Dati Personali, *Provvedimento del 20 giugno 2019 [9124401]*, www.garanteprivacy.it/home/docweb/-/docweb-display/docweb/9124401.

[49] European Data Protection Board, *Guidelines 5/2019 (Part 1) Version 2.0* (2020) 5 (emphasis added).

[50] *GC et. al. v CNIL*, C-136/17, para 46.

[51] ibid, para 47.

[52] ibid, para 79.

These services include social networking, video-sharing and potentially also some blogging or micro-blogging platforms. At least strongly moderated platforms could be understood to exercise such over-arching control of personal data on their services as to make many, if not all, of the limitations set out in *Google Spain* inapplicable. Conversely, it could be argued that any processing here would have a closer relationship with an original publisher and so it should generally only be this actor who should be held responsible for any problems of legality which arise. There is jurisprudence within EEA Member States which has found that many of these services do have some controller obligations although, reflecting their often more passive nature which is more akin to a 'processor'[53] rather than a 'controller', case law is conflicted on this question as regards blogging services.[54] Nevertheless, the relationship between these judgments and *Google Spain* remains unclear and, in the absence of unequivocal pan-European regulatory guidance, most of even the clearly active platforms have not implemented specific data protection policies and procedures related to the dissemination of personal data on their sites. The Article 29 Working Party's 2014 Guidelines did state that whilst *Google Spain* was 'specifically addressed to generalist search engines' this did 'not mean that it cannot be applied to other intermediaries' but rather that '[t]he rights may be exercised whenever the conditions established in the ruling are met'.[55] However, this point was not further developed. It is hoped that the European Data Protection Board will address these lacunae in the future, not least as it now has a specific GDPR obligation to 'issue guidelines, recommendations, and best practices on procedures for erasing links, copies or replications of personal data from publicly available communication services'.[56]

IV. SEARCH ENGINE INDEXING NOT JOURNALISTIC OR SIMILAR

Another striking aspect of *Google Spain* is that it clearly determined that search engine indexing could not be understood to be processing 'solely for journalistic purposes' (or, by implication, 'artistic or literary expression')[57] and therefore benefit from the far-reaching substantive, regulatory and remedial limitations for these special expressive activities which are established principally at national level.[58] Alongside many other factors, this finding was relevant to the CJEU's

[53] For the formal definition of this passive and reactive operator see GDPR, Art 4(8) and formerly DPD, Art 2(e).

[54] See generally D Erdos, 'Intermediary Publishers and European Data Protection: Delimiting the Ambit of Responsibility for Third-Party Rights through a Synthetic Interpretation of the EU Acquis' (2018) 26 *International Journal of Law and Information Technology* 189, 195–6.

[55] Article 29 Working Party, *Guidelines* (2014) 8.

[56] GDPR, Art 70(1)(d).

[57] DPD, Art 9.

[58] *Google Spain*, C-131/12, para 85. Whilst the English translation of this paragraph somewhat tentatively stated that it did 'not appear to be the case' that such processing could fall within this

holding that a data subject lodging a delisting claim could not be required 'to obtain first or in parallel the erasure of the information relating to them from the publishers of websites'.[59] However, its import was much more far-reaching and fundamental. Moreover, there is no reason to think that this finding has shifted as a result of the GDPR expanding these special expressive shields to include 'academic' expression and confining the requirement that processing be 'solely' for these special purposes to a recital.[60] Indeed, in *GC et. al. v CNIL*, another CJEU Grand Chamber found no role for the special expression regime when issuing binding determinations as to the relationship between search engine indexing and many specific substantive data protection provisions under both the DPD and the GDPR.

Although search engine indexing falls outside of the particularly permissive regime established for special expression, it remains vital to establish particular interpretations and even outright limitations on substantive data protection which are contextually rooted in the specific nature of this activity. Often the required analysis will necessitate a broad balancing of legal considerations pointing to the protection of the data subject and those favouring the continued spread of personal data. Indeed, this was signalled, albeit in restrained terms, in *Google Spain* itself. In sum, the Court stated that 'in light of the potential seriousness' of the type of processing at issue:

> it is clear that it cannot be justified by merely the economic interest which the operator of such an engine has in that processing. However, inasmuch as the removal of links from the list of results could, depending on the information at issue, have effects upon the legitimate interest of internet users potentially interested in having access to that information, in situations such as that at issue in the main proceedings a fair balance should be sought in particular between that interest and the data subject's fundamental rights under Articles 7 and 8 of the [EU] Charter. Whilst it is true that the data subject's rights protected by those articles also override, as a general rule, that interest of internet users, that balance may however depend, in specific cases, on the nature of the information in question and its sensitivity for the data subject's private life and on the interests of the public in having that information, an interest which may vary, in particular, according to the role played by the data subject in public life.[61]

The Court was rightly criticised for failing to acknowledge that data protection in this area clearly impacts on the enjoyment of a fundamental right, namely freedom of expression, including more specifically the right to receive and

definition, the authoritative Spanish text much more emphatically stated that '*no es el caso*' ('it is not the case').

[59] ibid, para 84. The other factors were that the website might be based entirely overseas, that the personal data in question could easily be replicated on other sites and that the legal basis and test for processing may be different in these two cases.

[60] See GDPR, Art 85(2) and recital 153.

[61] *Google Spain*, C 131/12, para 81.

impart information.[62] However, similar claims that the presumptive weighting established in favour of data protection conflicted with the theoretically equal value of (qualified) rights such as data protection and freedom of expression[63] were less well judged. Rather than being asserted as an a priori axiom, this presumption was grounded in a specific analysis of the potential for name-based search engine indexing, the activity being particularly considered, to potentially seriously interfere with an individual's data subject rights. This serious interference arose from such processing enabling:

> any internet user to obtain through the list of results a structure overview of the information related to that individual relating to that individual that can be found on the internet – information which potentially concerns a vast number of aspects of his private life and which, without the search engine, could not have been interconnected or could have been only with great difficulty – and thereby establish a more or less detailed profile of him.[64]

It is notable that, whilst explicitly acknowledging that at least the right to receive information was indeed engaged in these cases,[65] the CJEU in *GC et. al. v CNIL* reaffirmed this presumptive weighting and its particular rationale.[66] It should also be noted that potentiality is also distinct from a demonstration of individual concrete prejudice which *Google Spain* confirmed was not necessary to demonstrate when making a claim here.[67]

Whilst this presumptive weighting may not pose the serious problems which some have feared, ensuring a contextual application of EU data protection which takes into account broader forms of freedom of expression such as those furthered by search engine indexing remains a complex and underexplored challenge. Difficulties arise especially from the reality that, outside the special expressive framework, a good number of data protection's default substantive provisions would in principle apply without any particular limitation. Moreover, whilst some of these provisions, including most of the data protection principles, are relatively open textured, others appear much more bright-lined and peremptory. The clearest example of this is the regime for specified special categories of data such as health, political opinions and religious or philosophical beliefs data which, at least absent waiver from the data subject, is generally subject to a processing prohibition under both the GDPR[68] and formally the DPD.[69] An even stricter default applies for purely private sector

[62] See, eg, S Kulk and F Borgesius, 'Google Spain v González: did the court forget about freedom of expression' (2014) 5 *European Journal of Risk Regulation* 389.
[63] ibid 397.
[64] *Google Spain*, C-131/12, para 80.
[65] See *GC et. al. v CNIL* (n 50) para 75.
[66] ibid, para 53.
[67] *Google Spain*, C-131/12, para 96.
[68] GDPR, Art 9.
[69] DPD, Art 8(1)-(3).

processing of criminal-related data.[70] Grounding themselves in one plausible reading of *Google Spain*, a number of data subjects including (at least former) public figures and ex-criminals sought to rely on this prohibition in order to peremptorily require a delisting of this data. This issue was ultimately directly considered by the CJEU in *GC et al v CNIL* which held that a general[71] prohibition on processing did apply here but that a search engine could rely directly on the derogatory possibilities set out within the special data rules for use by Member States (and, under the GDPR, the EU itself).[72] It was stated that such reliance could only apply where the processing was found to be 'strictly necessary for protecting the freedom of information of internet users potentially interested in accessing that web page by means of such a search, a right protected by Article 11 of the [EU] Charter' and that the search engine must act 'in compliance with the conditions laid down in those provisions'.[73] The Court similarly held that, subject to a rearrangement of the results as a whole, a search engine could continue to process what would otherwise be outdated and irrelevant data using the same clauses and subject to the same tests.[74] The apparently general invocation of the special data derogation is puzzling since not only is a separate derogatory test set out for criminal-related data[75] but, aside from these specific cases, the broad test for substantive derogation is actually established in the general restrictions clause of Article 23 of the GDPR and formerly Article 13 of the DPD. Moreover, not only did *Google Spain* itself acknowledge the potential impact of the latter Article[76] but the new wording of Article 23 helps explain why principles such as data relevance always retain a role here through, for example, requiring a consideration of the results as a whole. In sum, Article 23 clearly provides that the data protection principles themselves can only be derogated from 'in so far as its provisions correspond to the rights and obligations provided for' in detailed data protection rules set out elsewhere in the instrument. The structure of this clause also justifies the Article 29 Working Party's and now the European Data Protection Board's insistence that a search engine's own handling of data subject claims upholds core data protection standards, which they have correctly interpreted as being incompatible with Google's comprehensive and unsafeguarded notification of original publishers

[70] GDPR, Art 10 and previously DPD, Art 8(5). Outside of control of official authority, the new GDPR wording rules out any 'comprehensive register of criminal convictions' and otherwise requires that 'processing is authorised by Union or Member State law providing for appropriate safeguards for the rights and freedoms of data subjects'.

[71] The Court's finding as regards criminal-related data is somewhat more complex since it found that the GDPR's general allowance for processing 'authorised by Union or Member State law providing for appropriate safeguards for the rights and freedoms of data subject' (GDPR, Art 10) may (for unclear reasons given that it is obviously an additional processing activity) justify search engine indexing 'where the information in question has been disclosed to the public by the public authorities in compliance with the applicable national law' (*GC et al v CNIL* (n 50) para 73).

[72] See GDPR, Art 9(2)(g) and formally DPD, Art 8(4).

[73] *GC et al v CNIL* (n 50) para 66.

[74] ibid, para 75.

[75] See GDPR, Art 10 and formally DPD, Art 8(5).

[76] *Google Spain*, C-131/12, para 71.

(or webmasters) when delisting data. Unfortunately, despite several years of effort, regulatory attempts to secure effective guarantees protecting the position of the data subject remain ongoing.[77]

It is clear that most of the aforementioned derogatory clauses presume that limitation will result from concrete legislation which itself sets out a specifically crafted balance. However, in the unfortunate general absence of this, it is extremely valuable that the CJEU has now confirmed that these clauses are essentially self-executing where this is manifestly necessary to vindicate a fundamental right. That is particularly justifiable under the GDPR since it now concretely obliges Member States to 'by law reconcile the right to the protection of personal data pursuant to this Regulation with the right to freedom of expression and information' even outside of special expression.[78] Although no explicit additional vires are set out in the clause, it is also likely to need to be directly invoked in order to justify some departures from the discipline provisions set out especially in chapter four of the GDPR so long as these maintain the essence of the substantive balance which are provided for in the other derogatory clauses. It might additionally be possible to invoke this provision in order to find some (albeit retrospective and very loose) legislative grounding for the scope-based limitations set out in *Google Spain* itself which were analysed in the previous section.

Notwithstanding the many conceptual conundrums which remain here, a significant body of regulatory guidance and regulatory and court jurisprudence has emerged which attempts to establish a contextual interpretation of data protection in this area. One important starting point is the non-exhaustive list of specific criteria published as the second part of the Article 29 Working Party Guidelines in 2014. These Guidelines sought to interpret the data protection principles and legal grounds for processing through the prism of more consolidated legal thinking, including from the European Court of Human Rights, on the tension between freedom of expression and at least privacy if not associated and emergent digital personality rights. The European Data Protection Board has signalled that it intends to update these criteria in the light of subsequent experiences through adding a second part to Guidelines which have already been released and finalised.[79] However, at least at first instance, the application of data protection law lies in the hands of search engines themselves and, more specifically, almost always Google. It has been argued that this is 'deeply flawed because it leaves important decisions about freedom of expression in the hands of an unaccountable private company with strong financial incentives to err on the side of censorship'.[80] Certainly the often contestable nature of

[77] For a detailed analysis of this issue see D Erdos, 'Disclosure, Explosure and the 'Right to be Forgotten' after *Google Spain*: Interrogating Google Search's Webmaster, End User and Lumen Notification Practices', (2020) 38 *Computer Law and Security Review*.

[78] GDPR, Art 85(1).

[79] European Data Protection Board, *Guidelines 5/2019 (Part 1) Version 2.0* (2020).

[80] R Post, 'Data Privacy and Dignitary Privacy: Google Spain, the Right to be Forgotten, and the Construction of the Public Sphere' (2018) 67 *Duke Law Journal* 1059, 1067. For similar concerns

these evaluations does raise many challenges and, so long as such communications can be properly safeguarded, it may be important in complex cases for a search engine to consult not only with the data subject but also with the original webmaster.[81] However, it is far from clear that an operator such as Google has a general tendency on err on the side of data protection here. To the contrary, Google Search's entire business model rests on a mission to 'organise the world's information and make it universally accessible and useful'[82] which points more to an incentive to resist rather than permit any restriction on the dissemination of personal data. Proper consideration of the case submitted by data subjects, which as noted above may sometimes also justify webmaster consultation, can be resource intensive and so may simply be avoided. Published output by regulators provide some anecdotal indications that these theoretical dangers may have emerged in practice. For example, the 2017 Annual Report of the Irish Data Protection Commissioner pointedly criticised an (unnamed) search engine for its response to a specific deindexing request, finding that it had apparently 'not properly examine[d] the complaint, but simply took the approach of assuming that because the complainant had previously been employed in a public role that the information in question was automatically in the public interest' and 'had assumed, without apparently even checking the factual background, that the complainant had been convicted of the criminal charges [detailed in the contested search result]'.[83] From the perspective of data subjects, therefore, it may be of more concern that only a small minority of claims[84] are appealed to DPAs, let alone the courts.

V. THE GEOGRAPHICAL REACH OF *GOOGLE SPAIN*

One of the most significant impediments to any attempt to regulate search engine indexing under EU data protection arose from these services being overwhelmingly provided by operators, including most notably Google Inc. (now Google LLC), which are principally based, not within the EU, but in the US. This raised controversy as to whether the EU law was even applicable and,

expressed from a more proceduralist standpoint see D Keller, 'The Right Tools: Europe's Intermediary Liability Laws and the EU 2016 General Data Protection Regulation' (2018) 33 *Berkeley Technology Law Journal* 287.

[81] See Kuczerawy and Ausloos (n 45) 238–241.

[82] See Google, *About* (n.d.), about.google/.

[83] Irish Data Protection Commissioner, *Annual Report 2017*, www.dataprotection.ie/sites/default/files/uploads/2018-11/Annual%20Report%202017.pdf, 19.

[84] Evidence from the first three years of Google Spain's implementation in the UK suggested that only around 1-1.5% of delisting claims rejected by Google were subsequently analysed by the UK DPA (the Information Commissioner's Office). See D Erdos, 'Unlikely to be Forgotten: Assessing the Implementation of Google Spain in the UK Three Years On' (*Blog Droit Européen*, 29 May 2017), blogdroiteuropeen.com/2017/05/29/unlikely-to-be-forgotten-assessing-the-implementation-of-google-spain-in-the-uk-three-years-on-by-david-erdos/.

if so, whether and how it could be practically enforced. It was, therefore, of profound significance that the CJEU in *Google Spain* followed Advocate General Jääkinen's Opinion in holding that Spanish and therefore EU data protection law did apply as a result of their being an 'inextricable lin[k]'[85] between Google Inc and Google Spain, an advertising subsidiary which was without doubt established on Spanish territory. According to the Court, this link arose 'since the activities relating the advertising space constitute the means of rendering the search engine at issue economically profitable and that engine is, at the same time, the means enabling those activities to be performed'.[86]

Notwithstanding its critical importance, this holding left open many issues concerning both the personal and territorial reach of the law. First, since Mr Costeja was 'a Spanish national resident in Spain',[87] the question of whether an individual who lacked such a close geographical connection to Europe could claim these rights was not addressed. Second, the judgment was also opaque as to whether this inextricable connection required a search engine to comply with EU law across all its service or rather only when this was sufficiently linked to the EU (or, in this case, Spain) and, if so, what linkage would be sufficient. Turning to the first issue, the Article 29 Working Party 2014 Guidelines held that:

> Article 8 of the EU Charter, which the ruling explicitly refers in a number of paragraphs, to, recognizes the right to data protection to 'everyone' [*sic*]. In practice, DPAs will focus on claims where there is a clear link between the data subject and the EU, for instance where the data subject is a citizen or resident of an EU Member State.[88]

Even at a strictly legal level, it is unlikely that claims against Google Search will be valid from any and all natural persons irrespective of 'nationality or residence'.[89] Nevertheless, the precise connection to the EU/EEA which must be present remains highly contested.[90] Turning to the second issue, Google (as was its usual practice in relation to local legal requirements) initially limited any compliance to national versions of its services (eg, google.es and google.fr). However, drawing on *Google Spain*'s requirement for 'effective and complete protection' of data subjects and emphasising the need to ensure that 'EU law cannot be easily circumvented' the Article 29 Working Party held that:

> limiting de-listing to EU domains on the grounds that users tend to access search engines via their national domains cannot be considered a sufficient means to satisfactorily guarantee the rights of data subjects according to the judgment. In practice,

[85] *Google Spain*, C-131/12 para 56.
[86] ibid, para 56.
[87] ibid, para 14.
[88] Article 29 Working Party, *Guidelines* (2014) 8.
[89] DPD, recital 2; GDPR, recital 2.
[90] In *Hegglin v Persons Unknown and Google* [2014] EWHC 2808 (QB) the England and Wales High Court allowed the issuing of a legal claim on Google Inc. out of jurisdiction despite the individual in question being a 'resident in Hong Kong' (at [1]) and not showing himself to be a UK (or EU) citizen. Hegglin had, however, previously been resident in London and continued to have a house and carry out substantial business in the UK.

> this means that in any case de-listing should also be effective on all relevant domains, including .com.[91]

Some EU DPAs, including even the Spanish,[92] interpreted this to require only that Google ensure through geo-location technology that no 'direct' access was possible from within the EU to any non-redacted version of the service including through the .com domain. In early 2016, Google agreed to adopt a version of that approach using internet protocol (IP) address information.[93] However, a number of other DPAs took the view that any remedy had to be effective worldwide and in March 2016 the French DPA used its powers under the DPD to fine Google €100,000 for its failure to ensure this.[94] Google appealed and on 19 July 2017 the French Conseil d'État referred the core legal questions to the CJEU. Citing principally the GDPR rather than the DPD, *Google LLC v Commission Nationale de l'Informatique et des Libertés* held that Google should generally only be required to adopt measures which had 'the effect of preventing or, at the very least seriously discouraging internet users in the Member States from gaining access to the [redacted] links'.[95] Whether Google's current IP approach would satisfy this threshold was not determined. The Court also held that the powerful effect of global online networks could in principle justify EU data protection law having a truly extra-territorial reach[96] but that other considerations including international comity and divergent understandings of fundamental rights pointed against mandating the French DPA's more extensive position. Nevertheless, it did find that national DPAs and courts were empowered in concrete cases to engage in a case-by-case balancing exercise between data protection and freedom of expression 'in light of national standards of protection of fundamental rights' and to order full global delisting 'where appropriate'.[97] The continued complex and partial answers to both these geographical questions arise from Google Inc/LCC not itself being an EU company. Indeed, if a search engine was exclusively based in Europe then the focus within EU data protection on ensuring universal protection would appear to indubitably mandate a fully global result for all data subjects worldwide. Explaining and exploring why this is not the case for Google has as much to do with public international law as it does with EU data protection itself.

An increasing awareness of the geographical limits of *Google Spain's* direct effect leads naturally to a consideration of the broader indirect influence of

[91] Article 29 Working Party, *Guidelines* (2014) 9.

[92] See M Peguera, 'The Application of the Right to be Forgotten in Spain' (*ISP Liability Blog*, 3 July 2017) ispliability.wordpress.com/2017/07/03/the-application-of-the-right-to-be-forgotten-in-spain/.

[93] F Lardinois, 'Google now uses Geolocation to hide 'Right to be Forgotten' from its Search Results' (*Tech Crunch*, 4 March 2016), techcrunch.com/2016/03/04/google-now-uses-geolocation-to-hide-right-to-be-forgotten-links-from-its-search-results/?guccounter=1.

[94] *Google LLC v Commission Nationale de l'Informatique et des Libertés*, C-507/17, para 33.

[95] ibid, para 70.

[96] ibid, para 57.

[97] ibid, para 72.

this seminal judgment. It has been shown that the essential statutory underpinnings for such influence are widely present including in the great majority of G20 jurisdictions.[98] Further analysis demonstrates that to date around half of the G20 states with established data protection legislation have supported a right to some ex post control for individuals over the online dissemination of their personal data.[99] *Google Spain* may well have exerted some galvanising impact here. This judgment was also positively cited by the European Court of Human Rights in the Grand Chamber case of *Delfi AS v Estonia* which held that the imposition on a news comment site of liability for extreme defamatory content even prior to notice did not violate freedom of expression.[100] Concrete attempts to apply data protection to general search engine indexing have been more limited. However, Russia enacted sui generis statute which (notwithstanding the severe rule of law issues in that jurisdiction) displayed formal similarity to that of the *Google Spain* judgment in 2015,[101] the Turkish DPA adopted a general decision in June 2020 which set down almost precisely the same approach as the Article 29 Working Party's 2014 Guidelines (even as regards the detailed delisting criteria),[102] and Canadian DPA efforts to definitely establish a right to search engine delisting in that country have been continuing since 2018.[103] This right also looks certain to continue in the UK even with the end of the Brexit transition period. In sum, whilst there are clear signs of *Google Spain* exerting impact beyond the EU/EEA's shores, such impact remains highly fragmentary and the barriers to a wide application of data protection to search engine indexing remain formidable.

VI. CONCLUSIONS

Google Spain should be seen as the most significant decision handed down by the CJEU under the DPD. Its subject matter pitted data protection against

[98] D Erdos and K Garstka, 'The 'Right to be Forgotten' Online Within G20 Statutory Data Protection Frameworks' (2020) 10 *International Data Privacy Law* 294. See also G Voss and C Castets-Renard, 'Proposal for an International Taxonomy on the Various Forms of the Right to Be Forgotten: A Study on the Convergence of Norms' (2015) 14 *Columbia Technology Law Journal* 281.

[99] D Erdos, 'The 'Right to be Forgotten' beyond the EU: An Analysis of Wider G20 Regulatory Action and Potential Next Steps' (2021) 13 *Journal of Media Law* 1. See also F Werro (ed), *The Right to be Forgotten: A Comparative Study of the Emergent Right's Evolution and Application in Europe, the Americas, and Asia* (Cham, Springer, 2019).

[100] *Delfi AS v Estonia* (2015) ECtHR 64669/09, (2016) 62 EHRR 6.

[101] See Federal Law of 13 July 2015 N 264-FZ 'On Amendments to the Federal Law "On Information, Information Technologies and Information Protection"'.

[102] Kişisel Verileri Koruma Kurumu, *Kişilerin Ad ve Soyadı ile Arama Motorları Üzerinden Yapılan Aramalarda Çıkan Sonuçların İndeksten Çıkarılmasına Yönelik Talepler ile ilgili olarak Kişisel Verileri Koruma Kurulunun 23/06/2020 Tarihli ve 2020/481 Sayılı Kararı* (2020), www.kvkk.gov.tr/Icerik/6776/2020-481.

[103] Office of the Privacy Commissioner of Canada, *Privacy Commissioner seeks Federal Court Determination on Key Issues for Canadians' Online Reputation* (10 October 2018), www.priv.gc.ca/en/opc-news/news-and-announcements/2018/an_181010/.

freedom of expression, territorial dilemmas and intermediary shield concerns. In nevertheless holding that Google Search had EU data controller responsibilities and fell outside of journalistic and other special expression, it clearly constitutes a pinnacle of the EU data protection landscape. Indeed, Zuboff has claimed that:

> The Court of Justice's decision, so often reduced to the legal and technical considerations related to the deletion or de-linking of personal data, was in fact a key inflection point at which democracy began to claw back rights to the future tense from the powerful forces of a new surveillance capitalism determined to claim unilateral authority over the digital future.[104]

Despite this, by ruling that a search engine only needed to act when it 'significantly, and additionally' affected data subject rights and only 'within the framework of its responsibilities, powers and capabilities',[105] the judgment curtailed the most logical (and far-reaching) application of EU data protection. Moreover, although strangely not acknowledging the tension with freedom of expression, the Court recognised the need for a contextual understanding of the law. Finally, whilst clearly applying EU data protection to Google, the precise geographical reach of the law remained undetermined. In sum, the pinnacle clearly had limits but many of those limits were shrouded in the clouds.

Seven years on, the clouds have lifted to reveal more of the basic contours of this edifice. In particular, the CJEU has recognised that freedom of expression (in the form of its sub-right freedom of information) is engaged in these cases, that a strict but contextual approach must be taken even to the sensitive data regime, and that Google only needs to secure a result within the EU/EEA itself unless (on the basis of national standards) a DPA or court specifically rules otherwise. Nevertheless, many other aspects including specification of the precise scope of a search engine's responsibilities remain rather shrouded. Not unrelatedly, mist continues to surround much of the broader landscape including the relationship between EU data protection and the dissemination activities of other active intermediary services such as social networking sites and video-sharing platforms. Notwithstanding the very real remedy it has offered many data subjects, Zuboff may therefore be right that *Google Spain* represents more of a new turning point than an ending in and of itself. Undoubtedly, this crucial judgment will be returned to again and again when seeking to address the many and perhaps increasing number of challenges which present themselves.

[104] S Zuboff, *The Age of Surveillance Capitalism: The Fight for a Human Future at the New Frontier of Power* (London, Profile Books, 2019) 59.

[105] *Google Spain*, C-131/12, para 38.

13

Gulati v Mirror Group Newspapers (2015)

JOHN HARTSHORNE

I. INTRODUCTION

IN THE PERIOD following the implementation of the Human Rights Act 1998 (HRA 1998), the judiciary succeeded in developing an action for misuse of private information (MOPI) out of the established equitable action for breach of confidence. A feature that played something of a 'Cinderella' role in some of the landmark decisions during this period was the question of the basis upon which damages may be awarded for a violation of informational privacy, and how to quantify such awards. This was certainly the position until the fine judgment of Eady J in *Mosley v News Group Newspapers Ltd*[1] (2008) but, as will be explained in this chapter, the approach to damages in this decision was subsequently questioned by the Supreme Court.[2] The decision of Mann J in *Gulati v Mirror Group Newspapers Ltd*[3] in 2015 (upheld on appeal later that year)[4] addressed this deficit, because in what has been described as a 'magisterial'[5] judgment, spanning some 712 paragraphs (and delivered less than two months after close of the hearing), Mann J sought to identify the heads of loss for which compensatory damages may be awarded in a claim for MOPI, and offered guidance upon the quantification of such awards. It is suggested that *Gulati* merits inclusion in this volume about landmark cases in privacy law, for three principal reasons. First, the decision established that a violation of privacy in itself should be recognised as a basis upon which compensatory damages may be awarded, irrespective of whether any injury to feelings might have flowed from the violation. In this respect the decision offered significant confirmation that autonomy, and dignity and standing, are vital facets of the

[1] *Mosley v News Group Newspapers Ltd* [2008] EWHC 1777 (QB), [2008] EMLR 20.

[2] R *(Lumba) v Secretary of State for the Home Department* [2011] UKSC 12, [2012] 1 AC 245.

[3] *Gulati v Mirror Group Newspapers Ltd* [2015] EWHC 1482 (Ch), [2016] FSR 12.

[4] [2015] EWCA Civ 1291, [2017] QB 149.

[5] JNE Varuhas, 'Varieties of Damages for Breach of Privacy' in JNE Varuhas and NA Moreham (eds), *Remedies for Breach of Privacy* (Oxford, Hart Publishing, 2018) 71.

right to informational privacy, which should be recognised and enforced by the law. Second, the decision offered important guidance upon the quantification of compensatory damages, confirming that, in appropriate circumstances, an aggregated approach would be possible where there had been multiple violations of privacy; this may, as in *Gulati*, lead to a substantial final award of damages. Finally, *Gulati* is significant for reasons going beyond those relating to damages, because it recognised that a claim for MOPI is still possible even where the wrongly acquired private information has not been published. In this regard *Gulati* showed that a claim for MOPI may now be pressed into action to address violations which in other jurisdictions are currently remedied using the tort of 'intrusion upon seclusion or solitude'.

II. THE LEGAL LANDSCAPE PRIOR TO *GULATI*

Prior to the decision in *Gulati* there had been relatively few privacy claims where damages had been sought. This was perhaps unsurprising, since with private information a primary concern is to retain control over it: the focus in the majority of MOPI claims therefore tended to be upon attempts to prevent others from disclosing the private information. Once 'the cat is out of the bag', as Eady J put it in *Mosley*,[6] the pursuit of a legal claim for damages carries the twin risks of incurring significant legal costs, and having further attention drawn to private matters through a potentially headline grabbing public trial. These factors offered a strong incentive to settle any claim brought; from a defendant's perspective a settlement could also avoid harmful attention being drawn to the methods they might have used to acquire the information.[7] One obstacle that appeared to have already been removed in the development of a privacy remedy was the question of whether, in principle, non-pecuniary compensatory damages could be awarded at all. In *Attorney General v Guardian Newspapers Ltd (No 2)* (1988) Lord Goff had stated that 'the remedy of damages … in cases of breach of confidence is now available, despite the equitable nature of the wrong, through a beneficent interpretation of the Chancery Amendment Act 1858 (Lord Cairns' Act)'.[8] This was taken further in 2000 in *Cornelius v De Taranto*,[9] where Morland J held that he was entitled to award damages for the

[6] *Mosley* (n 1) [209].

[7] For example, the £700,000 settlement in 2008 between Gordon Taylor, the then chief executive of the Professional Footballers' Association, and News Group Newspapers, owners of the *News of the World* newspaper, in his claim against the newspaper for phone hacking. NGN's motivations for wishing to settle the claim at the time are now obvious. See the Leveson Report: *An inquiry into the culture, practices and ethics of the press: report* volume 1 (HC 779 2012–13) 344–45.

[8] *Attorney General v Guardian Newspapers Ltd (No 2)* [1990] 1 AC 109, 286. An interpretation which, according to Stevens, 'cannot be correct': R Stevens, 'Damages for Wrongdoing in the Absence of Loss' in Varuhas and Moreham (n 5) 120.

[9] *Cornelius v De Taranto* [2001] EMLR 12, a claim for breach of a contractual duty of confidence.

mental distress and injury to feelings caused by the breach of confidence, as otherwise 'hollow protection'[10] would be afforded to the right to respect for private life. It also became established that an award for injury to feelings could be bolstered by additionally awarding aggravated damages, as shown in 2002 in *Campbell v MGN Ltd*.[11]

In *Mosley* Eady J conducted a broader examination of the basis upon which general compensatory damages may be awarded in privacy based claims, which acknowledged that this developing area of the law was concerned to protect such matters as personal dignity, autonomy and integrity: this meant that it was 'reasonable to suppose that damages for such an infringement may include distress, hurt feelings and loss of dignity'.[12] However, in a significant judgment, Eady J took matters further by suggesting that another factor which probably had to be taken into account was 'vindication to mark the infringement of a right';[13] in other words, the marking of the fact that the defendant had taken away or undermined the rights of the claimant and struck at the core of their personality. Eady J qualified his remarks by emphasising that, 'the underlying policy is to ensure that an infringed right is met with "an adequate remedy". If other factors mean that significant damages are to be awarded, in any event, the element of vindication does not need to be reflected in an even higher award.'[14] Any prospect that infringements of privacy rights could be remedied by awards of a vindicatory nature was, however, soon quashed by the Supreme Court in the false imprisonment decision in *R (Lumba) v Secretary of State for the Home Department* (2011), where Lord Dyson JSC saw 'no justification for letting such an unruly horse loose on our law'.[15] Nevertheless, in *AAA v Associated Newspapers Ltd*[16] (2012) and *Weller v Associated Newspapers Ltd*[17] (2015), decided after *R (Lumba)*, damages were awarded for the wrongful publication of photographs of infants, none of whom had suffered any distress or embarrassment; the basis for the awards in these decisions therefore needed to be properly accounted for.[18]

[10] ibid, [66].

[11] *Campbell v MGN Ltd* [2002] EWHC 499 (QB), [2002] EMLR 30.

[12] *Mosley* (n 1) [216].

[13] ibid.

[14] ibid.

[15] *R (Lumba)* (n 2) [101]. See also Lord Collins JSC [237], Lord Kerr JSC [256] and Lord Phillips PSC [335].

[16] *AAA v Associated Newspapers Ltd* [2012] EWHC 2103 (QB), [2013] EMLR 2.

[17] *Weller v Associated Newspapers Ltd* [2014] EWHC 1163 (QB), [2014] EMLR 24.

[18] In the *AAA* case Nicola Davies J cited with approval the passage in Eady J's judgment in *Mosley* where, according to the Supreme Court in *R (Lumba)*, vindicatory damages were being propounded, and it is possible that this played a role in the award in *AAA*, as evidenced by her Ladyship's comment that the award should 'serve as notice, both as to the present and the future, as to how seriously the court regards infringement of a child's rights'. (n 16, [127]). In *Weller* the damages were not awarded on a vindicatory basis because Dingemans J acknowledged, following *R (Lumba)*, that these could not be awarded for MOPI (ibid, [190]).

A notable feature of the awards made in the early privacy cases was their modesty, which contrasted starkly with the traditionally much more generous approach seen in defamation cases.[19] In *Campbell*,[20] for example, only £2,500 in compensatory damages was awarded for the injury to the claimant's feelings following wrongful publication of details of her treatment for drug addiction.[21] The findings on liability were reversed on appeal, but in a further appeal to the House of Lords the majority of their Lordships reinstated the award without passing any comment upon its size. Prior to *Gulati* the largest award, £60,000, was made in *Mosley* for the 'unprecedented'[22] distress and indignity that the claimant, the President of Formula 1 motor racing, had been caused to suffer following the revelation by the *News of the World* that he had been clandestinely engaging in sado-masochistic activities with dominatrices. In *Spelman v Express Newspapers* (2012) Tugendhat J, with some foresight, expressed the view that the 'sums awarded in the early cases such as *Campbell* were very low. But it can no longer be assumed that damages at those levels are the limit of the court's powers.'[23] At the time that cases such as *Campbell* and *Mosley* were being heard, what was publicly unknown was that certain journalists employed by the newspapers involved in those cases were systematically listening to voicemail messages left in the mobile phone inboxes of a large number of prominent individuals (a practice which became known as 'phone hacking'). The exposure of these activities several years after their fruits had been published in the offending newspapers, would result in a surge of claims for damages for MOPI. This offered an opportunity for the basis upon which compensatory damages may be awarded in a MOPI claim, and their size, to be reviewed in the *Gulati* litigation.

III. THE *GULATI* LITIGATION

A. The Factual Backdrop to the Litigation

The litigation arose out of a dark period in the history of the British press.[24] From the late 2000s it was claimed (most prominently by the *Guardian* newspaper)

[19] For a discussion of this issue see J Hartshorne, 'The Value of Privacy' [2010] *Journal of Media Law* 67.

[20] *Campbell* (trial) (n 11).

[21] Of course, the claim was not just about the money, and the precedent that Naomi Campbell's claim would eventually set in the House of Lords was worth far more than the damages awarded. Her success would also benefit generations of future celebrities.

[22] *Mosley* (n 1) [216].

[23] *Spelman v Express Newspapers* [2012] EWHC 355 (QB) [114]. The size of compensatory damages awards did seem to be on an upwards trend following *Mosley*, as seen in cases such as *Cooper v Turrell* [2011] EWHC 3269 (QB) (£30,000), and *AAA* (n 16) (£15,000).

[24] For an (sometimes unsettling) account of activities that were allegedly occurring within sections of the British press during the 1990s onwards, see N Davies, *Hack Attack: How the truth caught up with Rupert Murdoch* (London, Vintage Books, 2014).

that journalists at the *News of the World* newspaper had been hacking the voicemail messages of prominent individuals, in order to acquire private information for use in newspaper stories.[25] In 2011 it was further reported that journalists at the *News of the World* had intercepted voicemail messages left on the mobile phone of a schoolgirl who had gone missing, Milly Dowler, and who was later found to have been murdered.[26] This revelation resulted in a public and political outcry, which culminated in the *News of the World* being swiftly closed down by its owning company, and the then Prime Minister, David Cameron, establishing an independent public inquiry into the culture, practices and ethics of the press, to be chaired by Lord Justice Leveson.[27] Subsequent police investigations also led to the criminal convictions of several of those involved in hacking.[28] The three newspapers that became the subject of the *Gulati* litigation, the *Daily Mirror*, *Sunday Mirror* and *The People* (which each belonged to the Mirror Group of newspapers) had, as Mann J saw the position in *Gulati*, 'firmly and publicly denied knowledge of any phone hacking activities at any of its titles. Various executives and employees told the Leveson Inquiry that it did not happen, at least on their respective watches.'[29] Civil claims for MOPI were nevertheless brought against Mirror Group Newspapers Ltd (MGN) by a number of individuals who strongly believed, on the basis of circumstantial evidence, that MGN journalists had hacked messages left on their phones (or hacked messages that they had left on the phones of others), or used other illicit information gathering techniques against them. At first these claims were resisted by the defendant,[30] but in a change of direction it subsequently admitted liability (although not the extent of any illicit activity) and sent letters of apology to the claimants, as well as publicly apologising in its titles (albeit not on the front pages).[31]

The decision in *Gulati* related to eight cases brought before the High Court as part of managed litigation in which a large number of similar claims had been instigated,[32] the aim of the hearing being to ascertain the damages payable

[25] N Davies, 'Revealed: Murdoch's £1m bill for hiding dirty tricks' *The Guardian* (London, 9 July 2009) 1. As the *Guardian* article explains, in 2007 a *News of the World* journalist, Clive Goodman, and a private investigator he had commissioned, Glenn Mulcaire, were convicted for hacking into the voicemails of members of staff to the royal family. At the time the actions of Clive Goodman were dismissed by the *News of the World* as those of 'one rogue reporter'.

[26] N Davies and A Hill, '*News of the World* hacked Milly Dowler's phone during police hunt' *The Guardian* (London, 5 July 2011) 1.

[27] HC Deb 13 July 2011, vol 531, cols 311–312. The report was published in November 2012, see *An inquiry into the culture, practices and ethics of the press: report* vols 1–4 (HC 779 2012–13).

[28] 'Phone hacking: CPS calls end to prosecutions' (BBC News, 11 December 2015) www.bbc.co.uk/news/uk-35070715.

[29] *Gulati* (n 3) [19]. For examples, refer to evidence given to the Leveson Inquiry by witnesses from the newspapers and the Trinity Mirror group on 16 January 2012 (transcripts of evidence available at the *National Archives* website: webarchive.nationalarchives.gov.uk/20140122144906/http://www.levesoninquiry.org.uk/).

[30] See, eg, [2013] EWHC 3392 (Ch).

[31] See, eg, 'Phone hacking: We're sorry' *Daily Mirror* (London, 13 February 2015) 2.

[32] The Court of Appeal judgment in the case recorded 70 cases pending and 50 other letters of claim received: *Gulati* appeal (n 4) [2].

in the eight cases, so as to offer some guidance as to the damages payable in the other (and any future) claims. The eight claimants consisted of individuals in the public eye, and individuals associated with those in the public eye. The claims fell into three main categories – wrongfully listening to private or confidential information left for or by the claimants; wrongfully obtaining private information via private investigators; and the publication of stories based on that information. One of the claimants was Alan Yentob, who during the period of the hacking had occupied senior positions at the BBC. His claim differed from those of the others, since it was not alleged that the hacking of his phone had led to the publication of articles about him. Instead, it was likely that his phone had been hacked primarily to acquire private information about other individuals who were the subject of messages left on his phone.

The accounts provided in the judgment should cause anyone who questions the merits of legal protection for privacy to revisit their doubts. Expressions such as 'horror', 'distaste', 'distress' and 'distrust' ran throughout the claims. In the case of Alan Yentob, it was found that his phone had been hacked at least twice a day, and often several times a day, for a substantial part of a period of about seven years. He felt 'violated on a truly massive scale',[33] as if someone had been able to search through his personal belongings. In the case of the actor Shane Roche, he became so confounded by the stories that kept appearing about him that he had his house swept for listening devices, and assumed that a fellow actor had been leaking information about him to the press, leading to a five year rift between them. In the case of the actor and businesswoman Sadie Frost, her exasperation over continual press revelations about her private life drove her into wanting those close to her to enter into confidentiality agreements, including her mother, sisters, and brother. In the case of the footballer Paul Gascoigne, his sense that he was being spied upon meant that in group therapy sessions he was reluctant to open himself up, through fear that what he said would be reported to the press. Many of the claimants were frequently bewildered when they discovered photographers waiting for them as they arrived at various venues, including treatment clinics. The accounts resonate with the plot of the movie *The Truman Show*, where the lead character, played by Jim Carrey, lives in a world where, unknown to him, he is the star of a television show, subject to constant surveillance. The facts of the claims offered a stark illustration of the adverse consequences that can flow from the deprivation of autonomy and control over private information. Phone hacking is a particularly intrusive invasion of privacy because, as Mann J noted, many aspects of a person's personal, medical and professional life may to a very significant degree be laid bare in the voicemail messages that are left for them.[34]

[33] *Gulati* (n 3) [247].
[34] ibid, [32].

B. The Principal Issue in the Case: The Correct Approach to Damages for MOPI

i. Heads of Compensation

Despite the defendant's concessions on liability, Mann J was still required to make findings on the extent of the wrongdoing. Having considered the evidence (and applying the principle in *Armory v Delamirie*[35] which allows evidential inferences to be drawn where one party to litigation has lost or destroyed information) Mann J found that the phone hacking at the defendant's titles was 'widespread, institutionalised and long standing'.[36] There was a fundamental disagreement between the parties as to what it was that compensation could and should be awarded for in a claim for MOPI. No claims were pursued for exemplary or restitutionary damages. The claimants' case was that compensation could be awarded for several elements. First, compensation for the loss of privacy and autonomy resulting from the hacking or other illicit activity such as 'blagging' (obtaining information from the person holding it by deception), and the publication of the information. Second, compensation for injury to feelings (distress). Finally, compensation for damage or affront to dignity or standing. In contrast, the defendant averred that all that could be compensated for was the injury to feelings flowing from the infringement of privacy. The claimants were therefore seeking to establish that a loss of privacy in itself could amount to a head of compensable damage. The implications of this disagreement were most acute in the claim by Alan Yentob who, despite experiencing hurt feelings at learning of the extent of the hacking in his case, had not been forced to witness the revelation of details of his private life across the pages of mass circulation newspapers.

In addressing this dispute, Mann J commenced by noting that the values, or interests, which a privacy right was intended to create had been previously identified in the leading authority of *Campbell* as being the protection of human autonomy and dignity.[37] From this he was able to extrapolate as follows:

> Those values (or interests) are not confined to protection from distress, and it is not in my view apparent why distress (or some similar emotion), which would admittedly be a likely consequence of an invasion of privacy, should be the only touchstone for damages. While the law is used to awarding damages for injured feelings, there is no reason in principle, in my view, why it should not also make an award to reflect infringements of the right itself, if the situation warrants it. The fact that the loss is not scientifically calculable is no more a bar to recovering damages for 'loss of personal autonomy' or damage to standing than it is to damages for distress. If one has lost 'the right to control the dissemination of information about one's private life'

[35] *Armory v Delamirie* (1722) 1 Strange 505.

[36] *Gulati* (n 3) [209].

[37] Citing from the judgments of Lord Hoffmann and Baroness Hale in *Campbell* [2004] UKHL 22, [2004] 2 AC 457 at [50]–[51] and [134] respectively.

> then I fail to see why that, of itself, should not attract a degree of compensation, in an appropriate case. A right has been infringed, and loss of a kind recognised by the court as wrongful has been caused. It would seem to me to be contrary to principle not to recognise that as a potential route to damages.[38]

In arriving at the position that damages could be awarded for an infringement of privacy per se, Mann J was mindful of guidance from decisions of the European Court of Human Rights (ECtHR) such as *Armonienė v Lithuania*[39] that Article 8 must be interpreted to offer rights that are 'practical and effective' rather than 'theoretical or illusory'. From this he concluded that 'a regime in which damages were confined to damages for distress would render the rights (to a degree) "illusory" (to use the word used by the ECHR) and would, to a degree, fail to provide an effective remedy'.[40] Mann J further reinforced his view by citing the decisions in *AAA* and *Weller*, where damages were awarded to claimants who had experienced no apparent distress or injury to feelings (in the case of *AAA* a substantial award of £15,000 had been considered appropriate). Reference was also made to the decision of the ECtHR in *Halford v United Kingdom*,[41] where the court had awarded £10,000 for interception of the applicant's phone calls, despite there being no evidence to suggest that any of the distress she had suffered was attributable to the interceptions.

A potential obstacle to the claimants' position was the fallout from the decision in *Mosley* where, as noted earlier, Eady J had also adopted an approach acknowledging the possibility that damages could be awarded for a violation of privacy in itself, but which had subsequently been doubted by the Supreme Court in *R (Lumba)* as being tantamount to the recognition of vindicatory damages. Mann J was, however, undeterred, explaining that the specific point under consideration was not raised in argument in *Mosley*, and that, furthermore, there were indications in Eady J's language which suggested that compensatory (as opposed to vindicatory) damages were being awarded for something more than just the injury to feelings in that case. He nevertheless expressed his conclusions on this point with care:

> This conclusion is not to reintroduce vindicatory damages by the back door. I treat as being ruled out for these purposes the sort of damages referred to by *Lumba* and *Weller*. What is still open is to allow for compensation to be given for the act of misuse itself, where appropriate. I do not see in principle why that should not be allowed, and good reasons why it should be. If one assumes for the moment that what each claimant alleges to have happened has happened, the defendant will have helped itself, over an extended period of time, to large amounts of personal and private information and treated it as its own to deal with as it thought fit. There is an infringment of a right which is sustained and serious. While it is not measurable in money terms, that is not necessarily a bar to compensation (distress is not measurable in that

[38] *Gulati* (n 3) [111].
[39] *Armonienė v Lithuania* (2009) 48 EHRR 53.
[40] *Gulati* (n 3) [113].
[41] *Halford v United Kingdom* (1997) 24 EHRR 523.

way either). Damages awarded to reflect the infringement are not vindicatory in the sense of *Lumba*. They are truly compensatory.[42]

In approaching how the heads of recovery for MOPI should be compensated, an important point stressed by Mann J was that distress would often be the consequence of the infringement to such a degree as to subsume any potential separate award for the infringement itself. Thus it would not in all cases be necessary, or appropriate, to consider separating the misuse from the distress, since the infringement and its consequences may be too wrapped up; however, 'where appropriate the stated values ought of themselves to be protectable with an award of damages'.[43] It is worthy of note that Mann J acknowledged later on in his judgment that a sum may also be awarded, if appropriate, to compensate for 'damage to dignity or standing, so far as that is meaningful in this context and is not already within the distress element'.[44] In other words, 'damage to dignity or standing' arising through an infringement could attract compensation in the same way that 'loss of control' (violation of autonomy) could, these being core values or interests that a privacy right was intended to protect.

ii. Quantum of Compensation

The claims in *Gulati* arose out of a truly exceptional set of circumstances. The sizes of the final awards were attributable to the fact that it was agreed that each invasion of privacy (ie each occasion on which a phone had been hacked or information obtained using illicit means, and each time a story was published disclosing private information) gave rise to a separate cause of action. The principles Mann J applied in assessing the damages were summarised in principle (vi) at paragraph 229 of the judgment: 'The appropriate compensation will depend on the nature of the information, its significance as private information, and the effect on the victim of its disclosure.' He said that in calculating the awards in a case such as this, where there had been so many individual invasions over such an extended period, it was a matter for the judgment and discretion of the court whether 'a wrapped up approach, or a divided up approach'[45] was merited. Mann J preferred the latter of these courses, as if the general hacking (the substantial hacking which had been found to have occurred but which could not be linked to a subsequent publication) was not treated separately from the effect of the articles, 'its real impact may be lost'.[46] Accordingly, for the 'general hacking', which all the claimants had been victims of, a 'starting point' of £10,000 was selected for each year of serious levels of hacking, adjusted in each claim to take account of various factors, such as the nature of the

[42] *Gulati* (n 3) [132].
[43] ibid, [111].
[44] ibid, [168].
[45] ibid, [154].
[46] ibid, [155].

information likely to have been acquired. It was instructive to see how, in overall terms, Mann J's rulings on the heads of compensable recovery, the principles to be applied in determining quantum, and the 'divided up approach', were then translated into the damages finally awarded to the individual claimants.

The section of Mann J's judgment detailing the individual awards was lengthy, running to 469 paragraphs. In an impressively finely grained analysis, Mann J considered each claim, and within each claim he examined the extent of the hacking/blagging that had occurred, the content of any identified newspaper stories alleged to have arisen from this, and the impact of the infringements upon each claimant. For present purposes, only one of the claims will be used to illustrate this process, that involving the actress and businesswoman Sadie Frost. Twenty-nine published articles were identified that could be attributed to hacking/blagging. A separate amount was allocated to most of these articles, with the awards ranging in size from £750 (for a story about a holiday with a boyfriend and family members) to £25,000 (for stories about intimate marital difficulties and serious health matters). For the 'general hacking' that had occurred over the relevant period, £37,500 was awarded, along with £10,000 to reflect the general activities of private investigators (blagging). A sum of £30,000 was also awarded to reflect the overall effect of the defendant's activities, which had led to a sustained period of distress that was continuing to manifest itself at trial. Combining these amounts resulted in a final compensation award of £260,250, the largest combined privacy award to date, and far in excess of the £30,000 originally proposed by the defendant. This may be contrasted with the award of £85,000 to Alan Yentob, where no identifiable publications had ensued from the hacking.

C. The Court of Appeal Ruling in *Gulati*

The defendant appealed Mann J's ruling on four grounds: that damages could only be awarded for injury to feelings and not for the fact of the violation itself; that the global awards in the separate claims were disproportionate compared with the scale of damages awarded for personal injuries; that the awards were disproportionate compared with awards made by the ECtHR for breaches of privacy; and that Mann J had erred in that there was double counting in his assessment of damages. The appeal was heard by Arden, Rafferty, and Kitchin LJJ, with a single judgment being delivered by Arden LJ. The appeal was dismissed on each ground, with Arden LJ paying tribute to Mann J's 'careful and comprehensive judgment'.[47] The most pertinent ground of appeal was that relating to the heads of compensable recovery. Here the defendant argued that because MOPI was a tort, compensation could only be awarded for loss; it was

[47] *Gulati* appeal (n 4) [2].

submitted that to compensate for the breach itself (beyond nominal damages) would turn the law of damages on its head, since the claimant did not suffer loss merely because their right had been infringed. This argument was robustly rejected by Arden LJ, who, with an eye to avoiding falling into the trap of being accused of recognising a head of vindicatory damages, stated that: 'The essential principle is that, by misusing their private information, MGN deprived the claimants of their right to control the use of private information … The claimants are entitled to be compensated for that loss of control of information as well as for any distress.'[48] Accordingly: 'In the present context, the damages are an award to compensate for the loss or diminution of a right to control formerly private information and for the distress that the claimants could justifiably have felt because their private information had been exploited, and are assessed by reference to that loss.'[49] Violation of the right to privacy in itself could, therefore, in Arden LJ's opinion, establish a head of 'loss' for which compensation may be awarded. Permission to appeal against the Court of Appeal's decision was refused by the Supreme Court in 2016, on the basis that the application raised no arguable point of law.[50]

IV. SUBSEQUENT IMPACT OF *GULATI* UPON THE LAW

At the time of writing, it has only been six years since the judgments in *Gulati*, so this has inevitably limited the opportunities for *Gulati* to have an impact upon the subsequent development of the law. It is probably fair to say that, from a damages perspective, the impact of *Gulati* in the reported MOPI judgments has been a relatively low key one so far.[51] However, this assessment should be qualified by two considerations. First, it must be recalled that the events giving rise to the claims in *Gulati* were extraordinary. Subsequent cases have tended to be concerned with 'one off' violations (thus instantly removing the potential for large awards to be generated based upon multiple violations),[52] where it was more appropriate for the court to subsume the infringement and distress damages into a single award,[53] thereby masking the effects of the most

[48] ibid, [45].

[49] ibid, [48].

[50] UKSC 2016/0016 (23 March 2016).

[51] See, eg, *Reid v Price* [2020] EWHC 594 (QB) where, despite acknowledging that damages could be awarded for loss of control, Warby J predominantly referred to *Mosley* in identifying the principles to be applied in assessing damages. In *JQL v NTP* [2020] EWHC 1349 (QB) decided two months later, Lewis J also looked elsewhere in his search for principles, stating: 'The current approach to damages in privacy claims was summarised by Warby J succinctly in *Reid v Price*' ([154]).

[52] See, eg, *Burrell v Clifford* [2016] EWHC 578 (Ch) where £5,000 was awarded by Richard Spearman QC for a one-off disclosure of the claimant's letter to a limited number of people, which did not reveal innermost secrets, and where the contents had already been published by the claimant in a book by the time he learned of the disclosure.

[53] See, eg, *TLT v Secretary of State for the Home Department* [2016] EWHC 2217 (QB), [2016] Info TLR 373, £2,500 – £12,500 awarded for combined distress and loss of control of information.

radical aspect of the decision in *Gulati*. Second, it is likely that *Gulati* has had its greatest impact in those MOPI cases that have been resolved in an invisible way outside of the reported judgments, both as part of the managed litigation against MGN itself and in the many other clams that will have been brought for various alleged invasions of privacy since 2015. Indeed, it should not be forgotten that the very aim of the hearing in *Gulati* was to guide the quantum payable in the other claims against MGN.[54]

A good example of a decision where *Gulati* seemed to have little visible impact in the awarding of compensatory damages was *Ali v Channel 5 Broadcast Ltd*[55] (2018), where the misuse of private information consisted of the claimants being filmed, without consent and prior notice, by a television production company whilst they were being evicted from their property, with the footage later being broadcast by the defendant in a television series watched by 9.65 million viewers. The claim was complicated by the fact that parts of the eviction were also filmed by the landlord's son, accompanied by some accusatory comments from him, which were then posted on social media and later viewed by members of the claimants' local community. Arnold J awarded £10,000 in compensatory damages to each claimant,[56] and in assessing these seemed to pay greatest regard to the distress suffered by the claimants, noting that some of this would have been caused by the fact of the lawful eviction in itself, and also by the subsequent social media postings. Subsuming the infringement/distress heads into a single award made it difficult, however, to discern what contribution might have been represented by the fact of the infringement itself, and this leaves the decision vulnerable to the challenge that it overlooked the significant loss of *dignity* (a core privacy value) that arose through the broadcasting of the claimants' misfortune to so many viewers.[57] The Court of Appeal rejected an appeal against quantum (albeit acknowledging that other judges might well have reached a higher figure in the overall assessment of damages), being satisfied that the figure was not perverse.[58] Nevertheless, the decision in *Ali* sits uneasily with earlier cases such as *AAA*,[59] where, as previously explained, £15,000 was deemed appropriate to compensate for the publication of photographs of the infant claimant, even though she appeared to have suffered no distress or indignity in consequence.

The largest general damages award since *Gulati* (indeed the largest non-aggregated award to date in a MOPI claim) was made in another case decided

[54] *Gulati* (n 3) [2].

[55] *Ali v Channel 5 Broadcast Ltd* [2018] EWHC 298 (Ch), [2018] EMLR 17.

[56] An instructive case with which to compare *Ali* is *Bull v Desporte* [2019] EWHC 1650 (QB) where the defendant published a book revealing highly sensitive information, such as a description of the claimant's sex life, causing considerable distress to the claimant. However, the book had only garnered around 100 sales. Julian Knowles J also awarded £10,000.

[57] Dignity being one of the interests that Mann J in *Gulati* stressed was protected by the creation of a privacy right.

[58] [2019] EWCA Civ 677.

[59] *AAA* (n 16).

by Mann J, *Richard v British Broadcasting Corporation*[60] (2018). Here £190,000 was awarded to the singer Sir Cliff Richard OBE for the wrongful broadcasting of information relating to a police investigation into an allegation of an historical sexual offence (no charges were ever brought). The record size of the award did not seem to be attributable to any galvanising influence of *Gulati*, but was instead undoubtedly the product of a ruling in *Richard* which was as radical as that in *Gulati*. According to Mann J: 'Damages can and should be awarded for distress, damage to health, invasion of Sir Cliff's privacy (or depriving him of the right to control the use of his private information), and damage to his dignity, status and *reputation*.'[61] Subsequent decisions of the High Court have, however, questioned whether it would be appropriate for the defences available to a defendant in a defamation claim to be outflanked through allowing damages for reputation to be sought in a claim for MOPI.[62] Mann J's recognition in *Gulati* that 'dignity and standing' represented core interests or values that a privacy right was intended to protect, and for which compensation may be awarded, may prove to be significant in offering a route out of this legal quagmire, a point which seems to have been implicitly acknowledged in the post-*Richard* decisions which have considered this issue.[63] For example, in *Sicri v Associated Newspapers Ltd* (2020) Warby J said that whereas he would not take into account any impact upon the claimant's reputation in assessing damages, 'this is a different matter from the impact of the article on the claimant's dignity, or standing, and distress resulting from that. The distinction may be difficult to draw in practice, but it is real.'[64] With respect, the distinction may be better expressed as one of 'real difficulty', and the most subtle of knives may be required to separate 'dignity and standing' from 'reputation'. This is an issue sorely in need of attention from an appellate court.[65]

The confirmation in *Gulati* that compensatory damages could be awarded for an infringement of privacy in itself, suggested that MOPI was a tort actionable per se, although this was simultaneously contradicted by Mann J's assertion that such damages may be awarded 'where appropriate'.[66] In *NT1 and NT2 v Google llc*[67] (2018) no damages were awarded following the finding that there

[60] *Richard v British Broadcasting Corporation* [2018] EWHC 1837 (Ch), [2019] Ch 169.

[61] ibid, [350] (emphasis supplied).

[62] *ZXC v Bloomberg LP* [2019] EWHC 970 (QB), [2019] EMLR 20 (upheld on appeals, but no appeal was made against quantum: [2020] EWCA Civ 611, [2020] 3 WLR 838; [2022] UKSC 5, [2022] 2 WLR 424) and *Sicri v Associated Newspapers* [2020] EWHC 3541 (QB).

[63] *ZXC* (QB) (ibid) [151], [155].

[64] *Sicri* (n 62) [170].

[65] In *ZXC* although there was no appeal against quantum, the Supreme Court nevertheless said that: 'We have reservations about the extent to which quantification of damages for the tort of misuse of private information should be affected by the approach adopted in cases of defamation, but it is not appropriate to address this in this judgment.' (n 62) [79] (joint judgment of Lord Hamblen and Lord Stephens JJSC).

[66] *Gulati* (n 3) [132]. In contrast, Mann J also said in respect of hacking, 'there ought to be some compensation for this invasion per se' (*Gulati* (n 3) [169]). See also JNE Varuhas, *Damages and Human Rights* (London, Bloomsbury Publishing, 2016) 27.

[67] *NT1 and NT2 v Google llc* [2018] EWHC 799 (QB), [2019] QB 344.

had been a misuse of private information in the claim brought by NT2. The claim was primarily concerned with an internet search engine delisting request under the Data Protection Act 1998 (DPA 1998), and despite finding in NT2's favour on the DPA 1998 claim, no damages were awarded by Warby J under section 13 of this Act, as it was found that Google had not failed to take 'such care as in all the circumstances was reasonably required' to comply with the relevant provisions. Warby J concluded that for similar reasons no damages were payable in the successful MOPI claim either. Warby J showed his hand on this issue later that year in the DPA 1998 claim in *Lloyd v Google llc*[68] (2018), where he was required to consider whether a loss of control over personal data constituted 'damage' for the purposes of section 13. Rejecting the argument that, on the basis of *Gulati*, this inexorably followed, Warby J explained that on his reading of *Gulati* neither Mann J nor the Court of Appeal had held that damages *must* be awarded for the infringement of the right, in and of, itself; instead, the issue was whether the defendant's conduct had deprived the claimant of all or most of the *value* of their privacy right. This interpretation of *Gulati* was rejected when *Lloyd* went up to the Court of Appeal.[69] On a further appeal to the Supreme Court (2021), Lord Leggatt JSC, delivering the judgment of the court, said that MOPI, 'like other torts for which damages may be awarded without proof of material damage or distress, is a tort involving strict liability for deliberate acts, not a tort based on a want of care'.[70] This eliding of MOPI with torts such as battery further indicated that MOPI may indeed be a tort actionable per se, thus bringing into question the decision not to award damages in *NT1 and NT2*. However, Lord Leggatt JSC's categorisation of MOPI as a tort involving strict liability for deliberate acts was unsupported by a full analysis of this issue and made no reference to statements in *Campbell* indicating that the defendant's knowledge may indeed be a relevant factor to a finding of liability.[71] Uncertainty therefore remains over whether damages may be awarded as of right in a claim for MOPI. The Supreme Court confirmed in *Lloyd* that damages for loss of control over personal data may not be sought in a claim under the DPA, with damages only being available for any material damage and/or distress caused by the data breach. Had the outcome been otherwise, the decision in *Gulati* would have had its greatest subsequent impact in mass DPA claims such as the one attempted in *Lloyd*, where in excess of 4 million iPhone users could have become eligible to receive compensation.

V. *GULATI*: AN ASSESSMENT

The decision in *Gulati* made a landmark contribution to the law through its recognition that compensatory damages could be awarded for a violation of

[68] *Lloyd v Google llc* [2018] EWHC 2599 (QB), [2019] 1 WLR 1265.
[69] [2019] EWCA Civ 1599, [2020] QB 747.
[70] [2021] UKSC 50, [2021] 3 WLR 1268 [133].
[71] See, eg, Baroness Hale at [134] (*Campbell* (HL) n 37).

privacy in itself. In the previous section it was observed that in the reported MOPI claims this aspect of the decision has not had a visibly dramatic impact upon the law to date, although any impacts might have been masked by the subsumed approach taken towards the infringement and distress elements in the quantification of damages. As also noted in the previous section, in the field of compensation for reputational harm caused by a misuse of private information, the decision in *Gulati* may yet have further highly significant contributions to make. It is interesting to observe how through his reasoning Mann J essentially managed to reinstate the position that had been initially established by Eady J in *Mosley*, with Mann J's aim being to ensure that, as Eady J had put the matter, 'an infringed right is met with "an adequate remedy"'.[72] Indeed, as Mann J indicated, and contrary to what Lord Dyson JSC appeared to assume in *R (Lumba)*, it is likely that Eady J was advocating for a compensatory approach that achieved vindication, as opposed to one sanctioning awards of vindicatory damages. In this respect *Gulati* might have brought about an important correction, and restatement, of the law, rather than a development of it.

The broader impact of *Gulati* must also be acknowledged. It has helped to bring greater clarity to the purpose of the MOPI tort, confirming that it consists of a right to have one's privacy respected, in order to ensure protection for human autonomy and dignity. Most significantly, through its confirmation that damages may be awarded for a violation of privacy in itself, *Gulati* signals the law's recognition of the importance of this right, and its commitment to the protection of privacy. If in a claim such as Alan Yentob's compensation had only been available for the distress he had suffered, he would have been rightly justified in questioning the worth of the developments that had occurred since *Campbell*. It would also have sent out the most terrible signal to sections of the media that prolonged and substantial invasions of privacy were cheap at the price. As Mann J acutely appreciated, if the right is worth protecting in law through the grant of a non-disclosure order, it must surely also be worthy of a meaningful remedy in law where it is violated.[73] The decision also elevates the significance of the concepts of autonomy and dignity as underpinning values within the tort of MOPI.[74]

In assessing the contribution of *Gulati* to the development of the law, it would be remiss not to acknowledge that, at a conceptual level, the decision also brings certain difficulties with it. Moreham argues that the focus on autonomy and dignity in cases such as *Gulati* gives welcome recognition to the fact that if there is a violation, there is harm suffered, even if it is harm to intangible interests; she suggests that seeing privacy damages as compensation for harm suffered fits comfortably with the conventional rationale for private law damages.[75] As we have seen, Arden LJ in the *Gulati* appeal also located a violation of privacy

[72] *Mosley* (n 1) [216].
[73] *Gulati* (n 3) [111].
[74] See NA Moreham, 'Compensating for Loss of Dignity and Autonomy' in Varuhas and Moreham (n 5).
[75] ibid, 133.

within a detriment model, referring to the 'loss or diminution of a right to control formerly private information' arising from a violation.[76] However, these approaches struggle to account for two decisions that were fundamental to Mann J's reasoning, *AAA* and *Weller*. In neither of these cases were the infant claimants realistically in a position to exercise control over information about themselves, nor did the photographs cause any perceptible harm to their dignity. Yet if one strips away the loss of control and loss of dignity justifications for these awards, it becomes difficult to discern what the justification for them actually was. If it was argued that *AAA* and *Weller* belonged in a class of their own where the infants' interests were subrogated to those of the parents', this would then rob them of their significance as building blocks in Mann J's argument. Moreham explains that disseminating information about an infant could foreclose choices that would have been available to them on maturity, thereby resulting in a form of loss of control.[77] This is a reasonable response, and the point being made here is not intended to denounce that autonomy and dignity may have a crucial role to play in justifying awards of damages in privacy claims; but what it does serve to highlight is that some finessing is still required for why a violation of privacy in itself may be deserving of compensation.[78] Warby J in *Reid v Price* (2020) provided the reminder that: 'Compensation for the tortious disclosure of personal information should aim to restore the claimant to the position he would have occupied but for the tort.'[79] In all cases some account is therefore required for why the defendant's actions have left the claimant in a detrimental position.

The authors of *McGregor* suggest that the awards in *Gulati* should be understood as 'user damages' or 'licence fee damages.' They say that:

> The basis for the award is best understood as the value of the opportunity to use information … It is elementary justice that the defendant should have to pay the reasonable price for that opportunity or benefit, in addition to an award for the distress to the claimant.[80]

In *Lloyd* Warby J responded to this analysis in the following terms: 'This is not how the awards were explained by the court in *Gulati's* case at first instance … or on appeal … As will be apparent, I do not agree with the analysis.'[81] That the awards in *Gulati* should not be viewed as ones for user damages is also now patent

[76] *Gulati* appeal (n 4) [48].

[77] Moreham (n 74) 140.

[78] The reality is probably that an infant's rights are protected by the courts because the ECtHR has ruled that images of children published without consent engage Art 8 (see, eg, *Reklos v Greece* [2009] EMLR 16). However, the reasoning used in these cases, referring to image rights, would at present be unpalatable to the English courts as a basis upon which to award damages.

[79] *Reid* (n 51) [50].

[80] J Edelman, J Varuhas and S Colton (eds), *McGregor on Damages*, 21st edn (London, Sweet & Maxwell, 2020) para 47-013.

[81] *Lloyd* (QB) (n 68) [81].

from the Supreme Court's decision in *Lloyd*.[82] Reconceptualising the decision in *Gulati* in the way suggested in *McGregor* would bring difficulties with it. If we take the case of Alan Yentob, much of the information acquired from his voicemail did not relate to him personally, and he could not therefore have bargained for the purchase of it; yet accessing his voicemail to retrieve this information was still a wrong for which a remedy was required. Nevertheless, 'loss of control' also seems like an instinctively inappropriate description for what occurred in Alan Yentob's claim, and for the 'general hacking' that occurred in the other claims. The activity of hacking seems closer to what in other jurisdictions would be dealt with using torts of intrusion upon seclusion or solitude or *into private affairs*.[83] This again suggests that some further refinement is required from the courts, both as to the scope of the right, and as to the nature of the detriment arising in these situations.

The relationship between wrongs and remedies in privacy claims was subjected to a valuable analysis by Descheemaeker, who cautioned that: 'The law of privacy should not … be allowed to harbour logics which throw the rest of the law into disarray.'[84] Yet one is left wondering whether the root of the difficulties present in this area lies in the fact that the MOPI action is essentially a sui generis claim forged out of a desire to offer protection to a right contained in an international human rights instrument, but which has nevertheless been forced into the straightjacket of a 'tort' for reasons of domestic necessity.[85] Tilbury observes that 'privacy seems best regarded, conceptually, as simply a part of the law of human rights'.[86] If there was a more open acknowledgment by the courts that, given the genesis of the tort, an approach is required which fuses elements of the common law and considerations arising under ECtHR jurisprudence,[87] this may then allow for a more considered appraisal of the crux

[82] For further discussion of gain-based remedies, see K Barnett, 'Gain-Based Relief for Breach of Privacy' in Moreham and Varuhas (n 5).

[83] For discussion of this issue see NA Moreham, 'Liability for Listening: Why Phone Hacking is an Actionable Breach of Privacy' [2015] *Journal of Media* Law 155.

[84] E Descheemaeker, 'The Harms of Privacy' [2015] *Journal of Media Law* 278, 296. See also E Descheemaeker, 'Claimant-Focused Damages in the Law of Privacy' in Moreham and Varuhas (n 5).

[85] See, eg, *Shaw v Kovac* [2017] EWCA Civ 1028, [2017] 1 WLR 4773 where, in the context of a claim in negligence for damages for loss of autonomy, Davis LJ observed ([53]): 'It … may be debated whether actions framed in breach of privacy have possibly something of a special status in this regard.'

[86] M Tilbury, 'Privacy: Common Law or Human Right?' in N Witzleb and others (eds), *Emerging Challenges in Privacy Law* (Cambridge, Cambridge University Press, 2014) 178.

[87] There have been several references in the cases to courts being obliged to incorporate ECtHR and ECHR thinking into the domestic tort as a result of ss 6(1) and (3) HRA 1998. See, eg, Baroness Hale in *Campbell* (n 37) [132]: 'if there is a relevant cause of action applicable, the court as a public authority must act compatibly with both parties' Convention rights'. If one combines statements such as these with statements such as the following by Buxton LJ in *McKennitt v Ash* ([2006] EWCA Civ 1714, [2008] QB 73), 'in order to find the rules of the English law of breach of confidence we now have to look in the jurisprudence of articles 8 and 10. Those articles are now not merely of persuasive or parallel effect but … are the very content of the domestic tort that the English court has to enforce', then what we are left with is a situation where the courts may have to, justifiably, carve out special damages rules for the MOPI tort.

of the matter identified by Eady J in *Mosley* and Mann J in *Gulati*, which is that 'the underlying policy is to ensure that an infringed right is met with "an adequate remedy"'.[88] Given the uncertainty lingering over these issues it was surprising (and disappointing) that the Supreme Court was unpersuaded that an appeal from *Gulati* would raise an arguable point of law.

Moving away from the issue of damages, it needs to be noted that *Gulati* has the potential to make a further highly significant contribution towards the legal development of protection for privacy, through its apparent acknowledgment that a claim for MOPI may be brought in respect of private information which was wrongly acquired, yet never published.[89] This can be seen from the success of Alan Yentob's claim, and in the awards for the 'general hacking' in the other claims. Admittedly, the defendant conceded liability in respect of the hacking, and therefore Mann J did not need to make a finding of liability on this issue, but it is inconceivable that neither he, nor Arden LJ on appeal, would not have commented adversely on this concession had it been wrong in law. The fact that this concession was instead correct in law would seem to be supported by the earlier decision of the Court of Appeal in *Imerman v Tchenguiz*, where in a claim for breach of confidence it was said by Lord Neuberger MR that 'intentionally obtaining such information, secretly and knowing that the claimant reasonably expects it to be private, is itself a breach of confidence'.[90] Significantly Lord Neuberger MR also said that, 'the law should be developed and applied consistently and coherently in both privacy and "old fashioned confidence" cases, even if they sometimes may have different features'.[91]

This aspect of the *Gulati* litigation is important for several reasons. First, it confirms that MOPI is available to redress the myriad ways in which organisations and individuals may seek to exploit our use of electronic devices to acquire information about us for their own personal gain, whether this be commercial or voyeuristic in nature. Second, it arguably gives the green light for utilising MOPI to remedy those situations which in other jurisdictions are addressed using torts of intrusion into seclusion or solitude or into private affairs.[92] Admittedly, on the surface, the intrusion torts are concerned with violations of physical privacy,[93] but an intrusion upon private spaces, or into private affairs, is usually undertaken with a view to *finding something out*, and therefore, following *Gulati*, the

[88] *Mosley* (n 1) [216].

[89] The same point seems to arise implicitly from *Vidal-Hall v Google* [2015] EWCA Civ 311, [2016] QB 1003, but *Gulati* offers a much stronger indication that MOPI claims are possible in the absence of publication.

[90] *Imerman v Tchenguiz* [2010] EWCA Civ 908, [2011] 2 WLR 592 [68].

[91] ibid, [67].

[92] This issue is explored more fully by the present author elsewhere, see J Hartshorne, 'The Need for an Intrusion upon Seclusion Privacy Tort within English Law' [2017] *Common Law World Review* 287.

[93] For discussion of development of a remedy for physical intrusion see Moreham (n 83) and NA Moreham, 'Beyond Information: Physical Privacy in English Law' [2014] *Cambridge Law Journal* 350.

MOPI tort appears to be available as a remedy for intrusions where the purpose was to learn something about the claimant, at least until English law has sufficiently evolved so as to recognise claims for physical intrusions,[94] for example through utilising the reasoning that has been advanced by Wragg.[95] The point needs noting once more, however, that even though the MOPI tort may now apply where information has been acquired through intrusive activity such as hacking, 'loss of control' may not always be the most appropriate account for what has occurred, or appropriate basis upon which to award compensatory damages.

The availability of a MOPI claim in an intrusion context can be demonstrated through examining the cases which established intrusion type torts in Ontario and New Zealand respectively. In *Jones v Tsige*[96] the intrusion took the form of the plaintiff's personal banking records being accessed by a fellow employee at the bank where she was employed, and in *C v Holland*[97] it took the form of the defendant secretly filming the plaintiff whilst she was showering. Both of the plaintiffs in these cases would, it appears, now be able to seek a remedy using MOPI if these events occurred in England, because in both cases the defendants would have been seeking to acquire private information concerning the plaintiffs, for their own personal misuse, in circumstances where the plaintiffs would have clearly possessed a reasonable expectation of privacy. In the case of the plaintiff in *C v Holland* in particular, the MOPI tort is now sufficiently developed, following *Gulati*, to remedy the violation of autonomy, and the indignity, that the defendant's actions engendered in her.

VI. CONCLUSION

The decision in *Gulati* brings a full circle to the developments set in motion by the House of Lords in *Campbell*. Whereas their Lordships in *Campbell* were able to provide justifications for the recognition of a cause of action centred upon protection of privacy, grounded in the values of autonomy and dignity, *Gulati* has confirmed that a remedy in damages may be available where these values in themselves are diminished. In the absence of a damages remedy for a violation of these interests, the foundations of the tort of MOPI would be weak. This confirms the accolade that *Gulati* is a landmark case. Nevertheless, as noted earlier, the decision in *Gulati* arguably represents the commencement

94 There have been references to the concept of intrusion within the MOPI caselaw, but it is arguable that this has been in the context that media attention can be intrusive and distressing, rather than confirming that an intrusion into a private space is now actionable. See discussion of this point in Hartshorne (n 92) 295.

95 P Wragg, 'Recognising a Privacy-Invasion Tort: The Conceptual Unity of Informational and Intrusion Claims' [2019] *Cambridge Law Journal* 409.

96 *Jones v Tsige* (2012) ONCA 32 (Ontario Court of Appeal).

97 *C v Holland* [2012] NZHC 2155 (New Zealand High Court).

of a process that will need to be completed by later decisions, given that uncertainty remains over how awards in certain categories of case may be justified. *Gulati* should also prove to be a landmark case in advancing the legal protection for privacy where information is misused without publication. It will help to further dismantle the ruling of the House of Lords in *Wainwright v Home Office*[98] that there is no tort of privacy known to English law.

[98] *Wainwright v Home Office* [2003] UKHL 53, [2003] 3 WLR 1137.

14

PJS v News Group Newspapers Ltd (2016)

THOMAS DC BENNETT*

I. INTRODUCTION

THERE IS A scene in the 1997 comedy film, *Bean*, where Peter MacNicol's exasperated American, David, finally orders the hapless Mr Bean simply to stay put and 'do nothing', because 'if you do nothing, nothing can go wrong'. If the UK Supreme Court could ever be said to have pulled a lesson straight from the movies, then perhaps this is one that inspired its approach – to one particular issue, at least – in the 2016 case of *PJS v News Group Newspapers Ltd.*[1]

PJS is a case that achieves 'landmark' status – and thus its place in this collection – not by the substance of its judgment, but rather by the position that it occupies on the timeline along which the doctrine of 'misuse of private information' (MPI) has, since 2004, been developing. Its place on that timeline is indisputably significant; it is only the third MPI case to reach the UK's highest court. Having reached the Supreme Court, however, the case becomes far more noteworthy for what it did not say than for what it did.

The broader doctrinal context here is important. Put simply, the doctrine of MPI has developed in a rather haphazard and undeniably murky fashion. There are a number of reasons for this, to which we shall turn (briefly) in section II. But the upshot is that the doctrine contains a number of loose threads – matters upon which it fails to provide either clear guidance for litigants or clear rationalisations for the turns it has taken. I have identified some of these loose threads in earlier work.[2] One of these – the one that forms the focus of this chapter's

* I am grateful to the editors for their comments on an earlier draft, and to Christine Beuermann and Jamie Glister for helpful conversations on some of the themes in this chapter.

[1] *PJS News Group Newspapers Ltd* [2016] UKSC 26, [2016] 1 AC 1081.

[2] TDC Bennett, 'Judicial Activism and the Nature of "Misuse of Private Information"' (2018) 23(2) *Communications Law* 74.

analysis – is in respect of something I have previously termed the 'third party interests' (TPI) doctrine.[3] In short, the TPI doctrine is the emergent rule that the interests of third parties, who are neither claimant nor defendant, nor routinely represented, are relevant to (and may play a decisive role in determining) the courts' decision-making process within an MPI claim. The oddity of the TPI doctrine comes from the challenge it poses for the traditionally bilateral structure of tort claims – something that contributed to its rather unexpected emergence at the start of the last decade. It may be possible to rationalise the TPI doctrine in a coherent fashion – indeed it would be helpful if the courts would do so. But the lower courts have not (having offered two entirely unrelated justifications for the doctrine in apparent ignorance of each other). Thus, when it became apparent not only that a third MPI case was heading for the Supreme Court, but one in which the interests of third parties had been found relevant by the lower courts, a tantalising prospect appeared; perhaps – finally – the Court would rationalise the TPI doctrine and bring an end to the uncertainty surrounding it.

Alas, faced with the opportunity to do this, the Supreme Court instead did … nothing. Or rather it did nothing of any great significance. Obviously, it resolved the case to the satisfaction of one party (the claimant) and the dissatisfaction of the other. And it affirmed the notion that privacy injunctions may be issued even where the information is no longer confidential, so long as the injunction could still do some good.[4] And it gave the tabloid press a good slapping for having advanced a spurious public interest argument in its defence, seemingly in a bid to discourage future defendants from trying the same thing.[5] This was all very entertaining, if not particularly novel. But the bigger matter of serious conceptual significance – explaining the basis for the TPI doctrine – went unaddressed. The *real* question that this leaves us with, and which needs now to be answered, is *why* the Court so assiduously avoided dealing with these matters when the opportunity to do so was presented so clearly to it. For if we can get to grips with that, we will understand better that which makes *PJS* a landmark

[3] See TDC Bennett, 'Privacy, Third Parties and Judicial Method: *Wainwright*'s Legacy of Uncertainty' (2015) 7(2) *Journal of Media Law* 251, and 'The Relevance and Importance of Third Party Interests in Privacy Cases' (2011) 127 *LQR* 531.

[4] P Wragg, 'Privacy and the Emergent Intrusion Doctrine' (2017) 9(1) *Journal of Media Law* 14.

[5] *PJS* does make useful contributions to the development of MPI doctrine in some areas. It lays down a clear marker in its rejection of the argument that there is any public interest in the information (that the claimant engaged in a three-way sexual encounter) – an argument that is regularly raised by media outlets as a defence in privacy claims (at [24]–[25]). It also makes clear that different considerations apply in a privacy case than in a case based on confidentiality. Whilst in a confidentiality case, injunctive relief would be denied once the information no longer had the 'necessary quality of confidence' about it (*Coco v AN Clark (Engineers) Ltd* [1968] FSR 415, *PJS* (n 1) [32]–[35]) in a privacy (MPI) case, injunctive relief may still be granted where it can make some positive impact for the claimant and (perhaps or relevant third parties (such as their family). It is not, however, clear whether the Supreme Court envisages that injunctive relief could be granted in a situation where the claimant themselves would see no particular benefit from it, but where third parties – such as the claimant's children – might.

case – this absence of a voice in circumstances where we might have expected something of substance to have been said.

That is what I set out to do in this chapter. And I shall say at the outset that I have a theory. My theory is that the Court found itself faced with a situation in which the various ways in which it could have resolved the conceptual conundrum of the TPI doctrine each presented unpalatable options.[6] None of these were appealing. Faced with this situation, the Court preferred to do nothing – perhaps in the belief that, if it said nothing on the matter, it would at least not make a bad situation worse; 'if you do nothing, nothing can go wrong'. I cannot prove this theory conclusively. We may never know for certain what motivated these judges to sidestep this particular issue in this particular case, just as we may never know for certain why *any* judge rules as they do in *any* case – least of all when they are silent on the matter. But I can present the evidence and advance the theory as a plausible explanation of it. The evidence includes the uncertainty within the TPI doctrine in the lower courts, and sketches of various unappealing ways in which the doctrine might be rationalised. In this way, I can demonstrate that my theory is at least a plausible explanation for what might otherwise, and far less charitably, be considered the Supreme Court's abject failure to clear the murk surrounding the TPI doctrine.

II. TORT LAW AND MPI

Tort law is generally considered to have a fundamentally bilateral structure. That is, claims in tort feature a claimant and a defendant, and that is it; nobody else is normally a party to the proceedings.[7] For some, this bilateralism is a necessary condition of tort's primary focus on achieving corrective justice.[8] But even those who dispute the claim of corrective justice to hold primacy in tort law would generally accept that, as a matter of empirical reality, tort claims have historically adopted a bilateral structure. Observation is not, of course, a guarantee of permanency. There may be good reasons why tort law should adopt a different structure, either generally or in specific types of case. What is clear, however, is that this structure persists as a general rule, and that any departure from it is currently exceptional.

[6] I am going to assume – perhaps charitably – that the Court did not simply fail to appreciate the importance of resolving the issues surrounding the TPI doctrine and let it go without giving it a second thought.

[7] Of course, there may be multiple defendants. The key is the relationship between the parties – it is always one of claimant/defendant, wronged/wrongdoer.

[8] The best-known exponent of the notion that tort law is – and, in his view, can only be – structured bilaterally is the formalist scholar EJ Weinrib. For Weinrib, this is a necessary correlative of tort law being informed by a commitment to securing corrective justice. See *The Idea of Private Law* (Oxford, OUP, 1995).

The bilateral structure gives courts a framework within which, in the course of determining a dispute, they can consider and take seriously the interests of both parties. The flip-side of this structure is that the interests of other parties – those beyond claimant and defendant – are excluded. Whilst broad policy considerations that go beyond the interests of the parties do feature in tort judgments (particularly in negligence cases), they are interests of a fundamentally different order from those of particular individuals who might be affected by the outcome of a particular case. Consider, for example, a simple negligence case arising from a traffic accident. The injured claimant seeks compensation from the defendant negligent driver. No doubt the claimant's family would benefit from the award of compensation, whilst the defendant's family might well suffer. But these interests are not considered relevant by the courts to the determination of the claim – and with good reason. For it would shift tort's focus away from the relationship between claimant and defendant that arose as a result of their interaction (and, in corrective justice terms, from the defendant's wrongful infliction of harm upon the claimant) and towards a potentially wide-ranging series of inquiries into the impact that finding the defendant liable might have upon third parties. Ultimately, this might well result in a party with a family having stronger grounds either to insist upon or to avoid liability than a party who has no dependents. Perhaps some would say this would be a preferable way to go about attributing liability and awarding compensation.[9] But it is not the way that English tort law has traditionally gone about its business.

When the cause of action that has come to be known as 'misuse of private information' first emerged in the case of *Campbell*, it adopted a bilateral structure. In this way, it found itself in alignment with other torts and also with the equitable doctrine of confidence – a doctrine that exercised a profound influence over MPI's development.[10] This laid the groundwork for the doctrine to be treated as a tort, even when it was unclear that it was properly regarded as being of the tort *genus*.[11]

However, the development of a discrete doctrine within MPI that I call the 'third party interests' doctrine has introduced a significant methodological challenge to this bilateral normalcy. The TPI doctrine enables (and perhaps requires) courts to have regard to the significant interests of individuals who are

[9] See arguments made by some of the fictive judges in AC Hutchinson and D Morgan, 'The Canengusian Connection' (1984) 22(1) *Osgoode Hall Law Journal* 69.

[10] There is a general consensus amongst scholars and practitioners in the privacy field that the action for MPI is related to the older equitable doctrine of confidence. (See, eg, R Moosavian, 'Charting the Journey from Confidence to the New Methodology' (2012) 34(5) *European Intellectual Property Review* 324. However, there has been no detailed explanation of the nature of that relationship. This has given rise to some significant ambiguities, including on the most basic question of whether MPI can persuasively and/or coherently be said to be tortious rather than equitable (or something else entirely). I examine this thorny problem in Bennett (n 2).

[11] *Vidal-Hall v Google Inc* [2014] EWHC 13 (QB), [2014] WLR 4155, and *Vidal-Hall v Google Inc* [2015] EWCA Civ 311, [2016] QB 1003. For an argument that *Vidal-Hall* does not resolve the issue adequately, see Bennett (n 2).

not themselves parties to the proceedings (that is, they are neither claimant nor defendant) when adjudicating an MPI claim (whether at trial or at an interlocutory stage). The interests of these third parties, moreover, can prove determinative of the claim (for instance, where the interests of claimant and defendant roughly cancel each other out, the interests of third parties can become dispositive). When the High Court (in 2014) and Court of Appeal (in 2015) finally confirmed that MPI *is* a tort (albeit those rulings have significant analytical deficiencies), the shape of MPI – its no longer strictly bilateral structure – was conspicuous by its absence from those courts' analyses.[12]

Thus, from MPI's first appearance in English law, the situation was that we had no clear idea whether this emergent cause of action was tortious, equitable or – quite possibly – something else entirely. Its apparently bilateral structure gave it the appearance of a private law doctrine. But that structure was then undermined by the emergence of the TPI doctrine within MPI. So far, so confusing. And the picture quickly became even murkier. For the TPI doctrine emerges in the case law not from a single line of authority, but from two *differently reasoned* lines of authority, each decided apparently in ignorance of the other.[13]

PJS was unlikely ever to solve the Really Big Questions about MPI, such as whether the cause of action can persuasively be said to be tortious, equitable, or something else. But it did represent an opportunity to resolve the lasting murkiness of the TPI doctrine. Quite simply, the Supreme Court had an opportunity to tidy up the mess that had been created by the lower courts' use of these two competing lines of authority to explain and justify the doctrine's existence. Taking that opportunity would have entailed doing one of three things: deciding either that one line of authority was correct and stating clearly that the other was no longer good law, deciding that neither was correct and elaborating a third rationale for the doctrine, or simply abolishing the TPI doctrine altogether. As we shall see, however, in the end the Supreme Court did none of these things. It merely affirmed the relevance of third party interests in MPI without even acknowledging the mangled heap of doctrinal justifications that lay beneath it, let alone trying to sort it out.

At this point, it is necessary to delve in a little more detail into the messiness of the doctrine as elaborated by the lower courts, by examining these two competing lines of authority.

III. THIRD PARTY INTERESTS: THE COMPETING LINES OF AUTHORITY

There are two lines of authority in which the interests of third parties have been accorded relevance and importance in MPI cases by the courts. These lines of authority give rise to what I have termed the 'third party interests' doctrine,

[12] *Vidal-Hall*, ibid.

[13] I have detailed this in Bennett, 'Privacy' (n 3).

although it might be more accurate currently to speak of two distinct doctrines, such are the differences in reasoning between these two lines. Before we can critique the Supreme Court's failure in *PJS* to address the problems arising from these authorities, we must first bring them into focus.

The first line begins in the case of *Ambrosiadou v Coward*,[14] though its reasoning does not emerge until the subsequent decision (by the same judge) in *CDE v Mirror Group Newspapers Ltd*.[15] The second line, meanwhile, originates in *K v News Group Newspapers Ltd*.[16] At no point, prior to the *PJS* litigation, do these two lines meet one another; they have, it seems clear, developed entirely in ignorance of one another. It will be helpful at this point to outline the two lines of authority and the reasoning that features in each of them.

A. Ambrosiadou/CDE

The core feature of the *Ambrosiadou/CDE* line of authority is its bald reliance on Article 8 ECHR as justification for the relevance and importance of the third party's interests. In *Ambrosiadou v Coward*,[17] Eady J held that the privacy interests of the claimant's son were relevant to his decision to grant injunctive relief prohibiting the publication of the claimant's private information, despite the son not being a party to the proceedings. (The information did, in part, relate to the son, though he was not a named claimant.) The only basis that Eady J identified for taking the son's interests into account was the son's Article 8 ECHR right to private life. No other authority was identified. The formal difficulty with this approach is simple; the ECHR is not directly effective in 'horizontal' cases (those between private parties and not involving the state) in English law. Rather it is *indirectly* effective – it operates *through* existing domestic legal mechanisms (often common law doctrines).[18] Thus, in order to provide formal authority for

[14] *Ambrosiadou v Coward* [2010] EWHC 1794, [2010] 2 FLR 1775.

[15] *CDE v Mirror Group Newspapers Ltd* [2010] EWHC 3308 (QB), [2011] 1 FLR 1524. The judgment in *CDE* (which follows the approach in *Ambrosiadou*) was itself followed in *TSE v News Group Newspapers Ltd* [2011] EWHC 1308 (QB) and the interests of the claimant's children (as third parties) were taken into account.

[16] *K v News Group Newspapers Ltd* [2011] EWCA Civ 439, [2011] 1 WLR 1827.

[17] *Ambrosiadou* (n 14).

[18] The debate on which model of horizontal effect would apply to the HRA mainly took place in academic circles from the late 1990s to the mid-2000s, and revolved around notions of 'direct' and 'indirect' horizontal effect (both terms borrowed from European Union law). Later, the debate morphed into one considering which *type* of indirect horizontality would dominate. Key contributions to this debate include: M Hunt, 'The "horizontal effect" of the Human Rights Act' [1998] *PL* 423; R Buxton, 'The Human Rights Act and Private Law' (2000) 116 *LQR* 48; HRW Wade, 'Horizons of Horizontality' (2000) 116 *LQR* 217; A Lester and D Pannick, 'The Impact of the Human Rights Act on Private Law: The Knight's Move' (2000) 116 *LQR* 380; N Bamforth, 'The True "Horizontal Effect" of the Human Rights Act 1998' (2001) 117 *LQR* 34; D Beyleveld and S Pattinson, 'Horizontal Applicability and Horizontal Effect' (2002) 118 *LQR* 623; J Morgan, 'Privacy, Confidence and Horizontal Effect: "Hello" Trouble' [2003] *CLJ* 444; M Du Plessis and

Article 8's influence in this area, domestic authority ought to be cited. As an isolated incident, this case would probably not have caused much consternation. But it turned out not to be isolated.

Five months later, Eady J was again at the centre of matters in *CDE v Mirror Group Newspapers Ltd.*[19] In *CDE*, he again issued injunctive relief (in respect of private information about the claimant) and again identified the interests of third parties as relevant to his decision to do so. In this instance, the third parties were the claimants' child and also the family of the second defendant (the woman with whom the first claimant had, allegedly, had an extra-marital affair). These third party interests militated in favour of granting the injunction.

Once more, Article 8 takes centre-stage. This time, however, Eady J cites two decisions of the UK Supreme Court as authority for the proposition that third party interests should be taken into account, calling – rather uncomfortably, given the very limited amount of authority he cites in support of it – this principle (that they should be taken into account) 'well established'. These two cases are *AP v Secretary of State for the Home Department*[20] and *Donald v Ntuli.*[21] Neither, however, convince as authority for the proposition for which Eady J cites them. *AP* was a case involving 'control orders' – orders that placed restrictions on the freedoms of suspected terrorists. It was a public law case – a judicial review – in which a decision in respect of such an order, made by the Secretary of State, was challenged on human rights grounds. Eady J cites (in *CDE*) a passage from Lord Rodgers' judgment in *AP* which is itself a verbatim quote from an earlier judgment of the same Lord Rodgers in *In re Guardian.*[22] *In re Guardian* was also a public law case involving the judicial review of the decision of a public official on the ground that the decision was incompatible with the claimant's Convention rights and therefore in breach of the statutory prohibition, under section 6 Human Rights Act 1998, on public officials acting incompatibly with Convention rights.

There is a crucial difference between these sorts of cases (involving judicial review of decisions made in breach of section 6) and private law claims. The difference is that in a section 6 case, the defendant public official or public body is under a statutory duty – the section 6 duty – to take into account, when making decisions in their capacity as a public official/body, the Convention rights of *anyone who might be affected by those decisions*. Public officials are

J Ford, 'Developing the Common Law Progressively – Horizontality, the Human Rights Act and the South African Experience' [2004] *European Human Rights Law Report* 286. Later contributions of note include N Moreham, 'Privacy and Horizontality: Relegating the Common Law' (2007) 123 *LQR* 373; G Phillipson, 'Clarity Postponed: Horizontal Effect after Campbell' in H Fenwick, G Phillipson and R Masterman (eds), *Judicial Reasoning under the UK Human Rights Act* (Cambridge, CUP, 2007); G Phillipson and A Williams, 'Horizontal Effect and the Constitutional Constraint' (2011) 74(6) *MLR* 878.

[19] *CDE* (n 15).

[20] [2010] UKSC 24, [2011] 2 AC 1.

[21] *Donald v Ntuli* [2010] EWCA Civ 1276, [2011] 1 WLR 294.

[22] *In re Guardian News and Media Ltd* [2010] UKSC 1, [2010] 2 AC 697.

under a statutory duty to conduct a trawl for potentially affected Convention rights in order to ensure that the decisions they make are not incompatible with *anybody's* fundamental rights. By contrast, defendants in private law claims are not required, in the ordinary course of things, to conduct a trawl for potentially affected rights. The obligations placed on defendants by private law are generally quite tightly limited to a narrow class of potential claimants (for example, by concepts such as duty and remoteness in negligence and contract law, or by the fiduciary relationship in equity), and these obligations do not generally extend beyond those potential claimants. Keeping this state of affairs firmly in place is one of the effects of the indirect horizontal effect of the Human Rights Act.[23] If, instead, the Act had created obligations on all private law defendants to consider the potential impact of their actions on the Convention rights of *any and all* persons, this would be a hallmark of *direct*, rather than indirect, horizontality. The point here is that *AP cannot* provide convincing authority for the proposition that the Convention rights of third parties are relevant in private law because it was not a private law case, and because there is a very specific, statutory-based rationale for the principle that *AP* references *in its own context* that is fundamentally inapplicable in private law.

The other case cited by Eady J in *CDE* as authority for the TPI doctrine is *Donald v Ntuli*. This was a Court of Appeal decision upholding a decision to award a so-called 'super-injunction' in an MPI claim. The judge who had imposed the injunction at first instance had done so after taking into account the interests of the claimants' children. The Court of Appeal labelled the judge's decision in this respect 'proper', though it itself cites no authority explaining the basis of that propriety. Nor does any authority appear in the original first instance decision in *Donald v Ntuli*. Eady J cites, in *CDE*, the line in the Court of Appeal's *Donald* judgment where it says that the first instance judge had 'proper' regard to the interests of the third parties. And who was this first instance judge? With almost comical circularity, it was Eady J.

Eady J's reasoning in *CDE* for saying that the TPI doctrine is 'well established' is thus wholly unconvincing. It amounts simply to this: 1) in public law cases, public officials are statutorily obliged to consider the Convention rights of potentially affected persons and private law defendants ought to be too, even though this would cut entirely against the principle of indirect horizontality and the basic bilateral structure of private law; and 2) there is a case where the Court of Appeal said without explanation that it was 'proper' to do something that Eady J had himself done at first instance without explanation. Nothing about any of this convinces.

[23] There was a time, in the early years of the HRA era, when this direct mode of horizontality was considered a possible interpretation of the Act's effect. In the years since, however, consensus has firmly built up around indirect horizontality. It is now well-established that the HRA has indirect, rather than direct, horizontal effect. See n 18, above.

B. *K v NGN*

In an entirely separate development, in which no mention whatsoever is made of *Ambrosiadou* or *Donald* or *CDE*, nor of *AP* or *In re Guardian*, the Court of Appeal in *K v News Group Newspapers Ltd* recognised that the interests of third parties were relevant and significant to a claim for injunctive relief in MPI.[24] It did so on a more detailed, entirely different and yet still formally unconvincing basis. Since it was handed down, *K* has proven to be the instigator of a longer line of authority than *Ambrosiadou/CDE*.[25]

The core feature of the *K* case's basis for its version of the TPI doctrine is its focus on the 'best interests of the child' – a test in substance lifted from the Children Act 1989 and applied here for the first time in a private law privacy case. The claimant in *K* is a married man well-known in the entertainment industry. K had engaged in an adulterous affair with a work colleague, X. X had subsequently lost her job. The defendant newspaper planned to expose the affair, under the guise of a public interest story about a woman losing her job because of her relationship with a male co-worker. Neither K, nor his wife, nor X wanted the story published. The claim comes before the Court of Appeal a matter of hours after the initial claim for injunctive relief had been rejected in an *ex tempore* judgment given by the first instance judge in the middle of the night. Lord Justice Ward gives the only judgment, with which Laws and Moore-Bick LJJ agree. The Court of Appeal grants the injunction, after taking into account the interests of the claimant's children which militate against allowing publication of the information.[26]

A striking feature of the judgment is the significance placed by Ward LJ on the fact that the third parties in this case are children. He is concerned by the 'ordeal of playground ridicule … that would inevitably follow publicity'.[27] He asserts that 'the playground is a cruel place where the bullies feed on personal discomfort and embarrassment'.[28] He accords this sort of harm 'particular weight', despite it being assumed rather than actually evidenced in the proceedings.

In terms of authority, Ward LJ relies upon three cases (and two subtly different legal justifications) to support his assertion that the children's interests are relevant. The first is *Beoku-Betts v Secretary of State for the Home Department*.[29]

[24] *K* (n 16).

[25] The judgment in *K* has been followed on several occasions, although not all are MPI cases. Those which are MPI cases are: *Rocknroll v News Group Newspapers Ltd* [2013] EWHC 24 (Ch), *EF v AB* [2015] IRLR 619 (in which the third party was an adult), and *Bull v Desporte* [2019] EWHC 1650 (QB) (in which 'great weight' [113] was given to the interests of the claimant's children as third parties).

[26] This is despite the fact that the claimant did not pray in aid his children's interests at any point during the proceedings. I am indebted to Hugh Tomlinson QC, who acted for the claimant, for this insight.

[27] *K* (n 16) [17].

[28] ibid.

[29] *Beoku-Betts v Secretary of State for the Home Department* [2008] UKHL 39, [2009] AC 115.

He cites the passage in *Beoku-Betts* where Baroness Hale commented, in a short judgment, that

> [t]he right to respect for family life of one necessarily encompasses the right to respect for the family life of others, normally a spouse or minor children, with whom that family life is enjoyed.[30]

Despite paying lip-service to the fact that *Beoku-Betts* took place in 'another context',[31] Ward LJ has nonetheless fallen into the same difficulty as Eady J by citing it as authority for the TPI doctrine. For *Beoku-Betts* is another public law case – a judicial review – revolving around a decision by a public official (the Home Secretary) and its compatibility with section 6 HRA. For the same reasons discussed in the context of the *CDE* case, this sort of authority is of a fundamentally different nature to a private law case.

Ward LJ also presents a subtly different, secondary line of justification for his decision to consider the interests of third parties. This is the argument that the court must consider 'the best interests of the child', and as such it calls to mind that well-established statutory principle of family law.[32] He cites ECtHR authority for the broad proposition that, as a matter of consensus in international law, 'in all decisions concerning children, their best interests must be paramount'.[33] He also cites, from domestic precedent, the House of Lords' decision in *ZH (Tanzania) v Secretary of State for the Home Department*.[34] In that case, the Supreme Court held that the adverse effect upon the child of a non-citizen parent against whom deportation proceedings were being brought, when that child would inevitably have to leave with the parent if she were deported, must be taken into account.

Ward LJ states that the 'universal' principle that the court should act in the child's best interests 'cannot be ignored' in such a matter as the instant case (*K*).[35] He takes inspiration from Lord Kerr, who, in *ZH*, stated that

> in reaching decisions that will affect a child, a primacy of importance must be accorded to his or her best interests. This … is a factor … that must rank higher than any other. … Where the best interests of the child clearly favour a certain course, that course should be followed, unless countervailing reasons of considerable force displace them.[36]

[30] ibid, [4].

[31] *K* (n 16) [17].

[32] One issue relating to this 'best interests of the child' approach which remains unresolved is one we encountered earlier, namely how it is that the court came to determine that the children's interests were even relevant. However, we need not repeat our analysis of that issue here.

[33] *Neulinger v Switzerland* (2010) 28 BHRC 706 [135]. *Neulinger* concerned the potential return of a child to Israel, wherefrom he had been removed unlawfully by his mother in breach of an Israeli court order. Ward LJ (*K* at [18]) refers to the second principle of the United Nations Declaration of the Rights of the Child 1959, Art 3(1) of the Convention of the Rights of the Child 1989 (UNCRC) and Art 24 of the European Union's Charter of Fundamental Rights.

[34] *ZH (Tanzania) v Secretary of State for the Home Department* [2011] UKSC 4, [2011] 2 AC 166.

[35] *K* (n 16) [19].

[36] *ZH* (n 34) [46].

However, Ward LJ is not prepared simply to adopt this guidance without qualifying it. For

> … the interests of children do not automatically take precedence over the Convention rights of others. … The force of the public interest will be highly material, and the interests of affected children cannot be treated as a trump card.[37]

To a private lawyer, the appearance of the 'best interests of the child' principle is as unexpected as it is perplexing. Many thousands of private law cases – in negligence, nuisance, contract, breach of fiduciary duty and many other doctrines – will inevitably have some impact upon a child who is not a party to the proceedings. But there has been hitherto no suggestion that the court may, ought to or must engage in a 'best interests' analysis in those cases. All of a sudden, however, the Court of Appeal in *K* is declaring this to be not only appropriate but necessary. Our perplexed private lawyer's immediate concern is one of breadth. How widely applicable is this test? What are the limits of the relationship between the parties and the affected child within which the test is triggered? The judgment in *K* not only fails to answer these questions, it fails even to recognise their importance. Ward LJ simply proceeds on the basis that the need to conduct this test, as well as its ambit, is obvious and uncontroversial. In so doing, *K* contributes significantly to a confusing emergent picture of the TPI doctrine.

Neither *CDE* nor *K* adequately explain *why* third party interests warrant (let alone require) consideration in MPI cases as a matter of formal law. Moreover, since there is no cross-referencing between the two formulations of this doctrine, and since the core foundations of each are significantly different, we are left with a thoroughly confusing conundrum. We are left to wonder which of these rationales, if either, is the formally 'correct' rationale for the TPI doctrine. This is a conundrum that the Supreme Court could have resolved in *PJS*. It is a matter of lasting frustration that, presented with this opportunity, it did not take it. In the next section, we turn – at last – to *PJS* itself, to examine the extent of the Court's silence in respect of the TPI doctrine.

IV. *PJS*

PJS was a claim in MPI brought by a well-known, married individual in the entertainment industry.[38] The claimant, who had an open marriage with his spouse, engaged in a three-way sexual encounter with two other individuals. These individuals subsequently sought to sell their story to media outlets in the UK and the US. Some details of the encounter, including the claimant's identity, were published in outlets in the US. However, the High Court awarded the

[37] *K* (n 16) [19].
[38] *PJS* (n 1).

claimant injunctive relief to prohibit their publication in England and Wales. After the information became widely accessible online, the Court of Appeal discharged the injunction on the basis that the information it sought to protect was no longer confidential. The claimant appealed to the Supreme Court which reinstated the injunction on the basis that it could still do some good by limiting the extent of the intrusion that would occur into the claimant and his family's private life in the UK. In coming to that conclusion, the Supreme Court took into account the likely impact of publication, and the benefits of injunctive relief, on the claimant's children – third parties to the litigation.

The Supreme Court's treatment of the TPI issue is threadbare. Of the 93 paragraphs produced by the Court, spread across four judgments, only eight even mentioned the claimant's children. Of these eight paragraphs, only two contained any reference to authority that might support the TPI doctrine. And these two paragraphs (one in Lord Mance's judgment, the other in Lady Hale's) hint at different doctrinal justifications. Lord Mance, at paragraph 36, hints at a *K*-style analysis, drawing on the 'best interests of the child' test and citing four domestic authorities in which the courts have applied that test, all four of which are public law cases concerning either deportation or extradition.[39]

Lady Hale's judgment is just seven paragraphs long, of which three are redacted entirely in order to protect the claimant's identity. In those which remain, Lady Hale focuses not on the 'best interests' approach but instead on a more direct application of the children's Article 8 ECHR rights, in a manner reminiscent of Eady J's *CDE* approach. She gives two reasons for her conclusion that the children's interests 'deserve closer attention that they have so far received in this case'.[40] The first is a bare and unexplained assertion that the children have significant Article 8 interests of their own, separate from those of their parents. This reason is reminiscent of Eady J's approach in *Ambrosiadou*. It is entirely correct, as a matter of formal law, to point out that the children have such interests and that they are separately enforceable from those of their parents – plenty of authority could have been cited in support of such an assertion.[41] What is problematic about this assertion is the lack of justification for the court considering the children's interests in an ostensibly bilateral dispute between their parents and a publisher. Put simply, the *importance* of the children's interests is not in dispute, but their *relevance* in these proceedings is.

Lady Hale's second reason for taking into account the interests of the children is taken from section 12(4)(b) of the Human Rights Act, which requires a

[39] The authorities cited are: *ZH* (n 34, also cited in *K*), *BH v Lord Advocate* [2012] UKSC 24, 2012 SC (UKSC) 308 (cited in *PJS* as *H v Lord Advocate*), *H (H) v Deputy Prosecutor of the Italian Republic (Genoa)* [2012] UKSC 25, [2013] 1 AC 338, and *Zoumbas v Secretary of State for the Home Department* [2013] UKSC 74, [2013] 1 WLR 3690. All four involve challenges to orders either for deportation or extradition.

[40] *PJS* (n 1) [72].

[41] See, eg, *Murray v Express Newspapers Ltd* [2008] EWCA Civ 446, [2009] Ch 481, *Reklos v Greece* [2009] ECHR 200, [2009] EMLR 16, *AAA v Associated Newspapers Ltd* [2012] EWHC 2103 (QB), [2013] EMLR 2.

court considering imposing injunctive relief in circumstances where freedom of expression might, as a result, be curtailed, must 'have regard' to 'any relevant privacy code'. She, like Lord Mance, identifies the Independent Press Standards Organisation (IPSO) code as such a code. This code provides that 'editors must demonstrate an exceptional public interest to over-ride the normally paramount interests of [children under 16]'.[42] Lady Hale then goes on to say, without further reference to legal authority, that for a court to discharge this statutory obligation satisfactorily, it will need to consider evidence pertaining to the actual or likely impact of publication on the children, and that this will need to take place at trial.[43] Only then will it be possible to determine whether the children's interests (added to the claimant's) outweigh the defendant's interest in freedom of expression. This is a rather baffling conclusion to reach in this particular case, given that Lady Hale is adamant (as are her fellow Supreme Court justices) that there is 'no public interest in the legal sense in the publication of this information'.[44] If there is no arguable public interest in the publication of the information, it is unclear why evidence of the impact on the children would be needed, since presumably the claimant's own privacy interests – even if they were only minimal (which they are not in this case) – would suffice to defeat the defendant's public interest argument.

In the course of giving her second reason for considering the interests of the children, Lady Hale has essentially elevated the code of the press regulator (to which the defendant publisher had *voluntarily* signed up) to the level of law. In an area of doctrine that is marked by its freewheeling uncertainty, it is quite remarkable for a judge in our highest court to treat the IPSO code not only as a de facto legal standard, but as *the only* applicable de facto legal standard relating to third party interests. For only those defendants who have signed up to a 'relevant privacy code' will be bound by its provisions. This creates a potential imbalance between cases featuring commercial media bodies as defendants and cases featuring other sorts of defendants; whilst third parties will have emphasis placed on their interests in the former, this particular basis for doing so will be entirely absent in the latter. This is enormously problematic, because (quite apart from the IPSO code's internal deficiencies and the fact it was not the product of any form of either democratic (ie parliamentary) or considered judicial decision-making) the IPSO code quite obviously cannot form a *generally applicable* basis for legal doctrine in this field. Section 12(4)(b), therefore, cannot provide a *complete* rationale for the existence of the TPI doctrine; at best, it bolsters the case for considering third party interests in those cases where the defendant is a commercial entity that is signed up to a relevant code.

[42] *Editors' Code of Practice* (IPSO 2016), available at www.ipso.co.uk/media/1058/a4-editors-code-2016.pdf (accessed 1 January 2021).
[43] *PJS* (n 1) [73].
[44] ibid, [78].

This, then, is the sum total of the Supreme Court's input on the TPI doctrine in *PJS*. The Court has vaguely affirmed the doctrine, gently hinting at three different rationales for it (one of which is, as we have seen, incomplete) without indicating which (if any) of them is preferable or why. Its analysis of the matter is so lacking in development that the picture remains wholly unclear. Indeed, Lady Hale's introduction of a new, possible (but incomplete) rationale – section 12(4)(b) coupled with the IPSO code – muddies the already murky waters in this area still further.

Having explored what little the Supreme Court had to say on the TPI doctrine in *PJS*, it is now time to introduce my theory as to why it said so little. It seems obvious that a coherent rationalisation of the TPI doctrine would be desirable. For the more-or-less automatic assumption of most lawyers is that coherent rationalisation of doctrine is usually, if not always, desirable.[45] But when we pause to consider the ways in which the Court might actually have rationalised the TPI doctrine, we uncover a whole new set of problems. Put simply, there seems to be no obvious, coherent way to rationalise the doctrine that does not either create new problems, or exacerbate existing ones, for the law. In other words, whilst the Supreme Court may attract criticism for failing to clarify the TPI doctrine, perhaps this failure is forgivable (or at least understandable) because it found itself faced with a situation in which there were no good options. In order to explain and evidence the plausibility of this theory, in the next section I sketch out some of the ways in which the TPI doctrine could have been rationalised (or, in the case of the last option, abolished). As we shall see, none of these options are particularly appealing.

V. RATIONALISING THE TPI DOCTRINE: THE CHOICES

A. The 'Best Interests of the Child' Approach

Two approaches have already gathered some judicial support in the cases we have canvassed. We will deal with these before discussing others. The first is the 'best interests of the child' approach adopted by Ward LJ in *K* and mentioned briefly by Lady Justice Hale in *PJS*. The roots of this approach lie in Article 3 of the UN Convention on the Rights of the Child (UNCRC), which obliges courts to regard as a 'primary consideration' the best interests of the child in any legal case 'concerning children'.

There are three issues which make adopting this approach difficult, which may explain why the Supreme Court did not endorse it. The first is that, as an

[45] See, eg, W Lucy, 'Access to Justice and the Rule of Law' (2020) 40 *OJLS* 377, 384–389, arguing that coherence, amongst other desiderata associated with Lon Fuller, constitute the basis of the rule of law. (See further Lon L Fuller, *The Morality of Law*, revised edn (New haven, Yale University Press, 1969) ch 2.)

instrument of international law, Article 3 of the UNCRC is not directly effective in domestic law. Like any instrument of international law, unless statutorily incorporated into domestic law, it provides only persuasive rather than formally binding authority. Whereas there are areas in which the 'best interests' test has been incorporated by statute into English and Welsh law (most famously in the Children Act 1989), it has not been incorporated broadly into every domestic legal field. Indeed, Parliament may be thought to have taken the deliberate view that its incorporation should be limited to those fields for which it has incorporated the provision in legislation. The problem here is not so much with the courts choosing to deploy the 'best interests' test in MPI cases involving third party children, but with the courts choosing not to deploy it in other areas. We have seen children's interests litigated without the courts recognising the primary importance of acting in those children's 'best interests' in a range of tort cases, including in nuisance,[46] negligence,[47] the *Wilkinson* tort,[48] and also in MPI cases where the child is themselves the claimant, rather than a third party.[49] The 'best interests' test might seem like an easy justification for considering third party interests in MPI, but logically it must not only justify but compel their consideration in all other types of legal claim where the interests of third party children would be affected by the outcome. For some, this would quickly lead to an unpalatable level of judicial activism, as the range of relevant interests that would need to be considered in private law claims would expand. This would also inevitably bring increased cost to the proceedings, which would require more evidence of the impact on third party children to be taken, increasing the length of hearings and trials and generally increasing the administrative burden on an already overburdened legal system.

The second issue re-engages some of the concerns mentioned immediately above. For the courts would need to determine which legal actions 'concern children' for the purposes of triggering the 'best interests' test. It is unclear where the line should be drawn in terms of cases that 'concern children' and cases that do not. Intuitively, it seems entirely plain that if a litigant has responsibility for the care of children, those children are likely to be affected – at least to some degree – by the outcome, and indeed quite probably by the very process of the litigant being involved in, the litigation. But, to the best of my knowledge, nobody has ever seriously suggested in court that a claimant in a negligence case should be able to boost their chances of having the defendant found liable

[46] *Dobson v Thames Water Utilities Ltd* [2009] EWCA Civ 28, [2009] 3 All ER 319.

[47] *Perry & Anor v Harris (A Minor)* [2008] EWCA Civ 907, [2009] 1 WLR 19, also *O v A* [2014] EWCA Civ 1277, [2015] EMLR 4.

[48] *Wilkinson v Downton* [1897] 2 QB 57. The *Wilkinson* tort was revived by the Supreme Court in *O v A* [2015] UKSC 32, [2016] AC 219, wherein it was relabelled the tort of wilful infringement of personal safety.

[49] For example: *Murray* (n 41), *AAA v Associated Newspapers Ltd* [2013] EWCA Civ 554, [2013] WLR (D) 189, *O v A* (n 47), *Weller v Associated Newspapers Ltd* [2014] EWHC 1163 (QB), [2014] EMLR 24 and [2015] EWCA Civ 1176, [2016] 1 WLR 1541.

simply because such a finding would benefit their child. Yet the presence of the TPI doctrine in MPI effectively achieves just this, by the courts' admission that the child's interests could tip (and have tipped) the balance in favour of the claimant when all other matters are equal.[50] Thus, in the interests of coherence, the courts would need to find a way to determine and rationalise the outer limits of the phrase 'concerning children', which could prove tricky.

Third, the other glaring problem with the 'best interests' approach is that Article 3 of the UNCRC *only* applies to children. If the third parties to the litigation whose interests would be adversely affected by publication of the private information are aged 18 or over, then this approach would not justify taking their interests into account at all. In *K*, whilst the children's interests militated against publication, so did the interests of the claimant's wife and the woman with whom he had had his extra-marital affair. Likewise in *CDE*, Eady J considered the interests of an adult third party as well as those of children,[51] as did Slade J (following the *K* line of authority) in *EF*.[52] So the courts, if they relied solely on the 'best interests of the child' approach, would need to acknowledge that this would not justify considering the interests of adult third parties.[53] This would not rationalise the entirety of the TPI doctrine as it currently stands; it would limit its applicability and thus significantly alter it. It would create a situation in which the interests of a stoical seventeen-year-old would automatically be considered in an MPI case brought by the parent, but the interests of a suicidal nineteen-year-old would not. It would not give the courts the formal flexibility to consider the interests of adult third parties which, though they might ordinarily not be thought to be so severely affected as children, might in some circumstances be so.

B. The Article 8 ECHR Approach – (More) Direct Horizontality

The second approach the courts could take would be the other that features in the cases to date. This is the approach whereby Article 8 of the ECHR provides direct justification for considering the rights of third parties, much as it does in judicial reviews of deportation decisions (which, as we have seen, provide the bulk of the authorities relied on by those courts that have deployed this approach in MPI cases).

The problem with this approach is that which we identified in *CDE* and *K* – namely that it fails to recognise the difference between vertical and horizontal

[50] See *K* (n 16) [19]–[23].

[51] See *CDE* (n 15) [6].

[52] *EF* (n 25).

[53] It may be, of course, that the courts would prefer to limit the TPI doctrine to children. In *Terry v Persons Unknown* [2010] EWHC 119 (QB), [2010] EMLR 16, for example, Tugendhat J opined that adult third parties should normally attend court and give evidence if their interests are to be considered. This would, however, constitute a departure from the key cases (*K* and *CDE*) in this field.

human rights cases and thus undermines the basic premise, which is today widely accepted, that the Human Rights Act 1998 gives direct vertical effect, but *indirect* horizontal effect, to the ECHR. There simply is no formal justification for doing this, unless the courts are prepared to overturn nearly two decades of broad consensus on the nature of the HRA's horizontal effect and re-open the argument made by William Wade that the HRA would and should give *direct* horizontal effect to the ECHR.[54] With Wade's preferred approach having been roundly rejected by both the courts and much of the academy, this would be remarkable to say the least.[55] Moreover, it would seriously challenge the shape of MPI doctrine which has been labelled a tort but which, if it was the result of direct rather than indirect horizontality, would not need to be a tort at all.[56]

Re-opening the debate on horizontal effect would, of course, have a profound impact on private law in the UK. As Gavin Phillipson once dramatically put it, direct horizontality would 'threaten whole swathes of the common law with replacement by private HRA actions'.[57] This might not necessarily be a bad thing in itself, but it would be unpalatable to many. This is because it would involve a radical reshaping of the domestic legal landscape, and also because it would render that re-moulded landscape vulnerable to a rather chaotic situation in the event of the HRA being repealed and/or the UK withdrawing from the ECHR (both of which have been mooted by the UK's governing Conservative party in recent years). Put simply, neither those who see the ECHR as a malign influence on British sovereignty nor those who see it as an underused instrument of salvation would find this approach comfortable.

C. The Equitable Approach

The remaining approaches to rationalising the TPI doctrine in MPI have not made any overt appearance in any MPI cases. They are sketched out here for, to the best of my knowledge, the first time. This third approach would justify considering third party interests on straightforwardly equitable principles governing injunctive relief.

Injunctive relief is the most common remedy in MPI cases. This is because most MPI cases have their main hearing at the interlocutory stage, with very few thereafter proceeding to trial. The reason for this is simple. If the claimant succeeds in obtaining interim injunctive relief, the information usually quickly loses its newsworthiness and the defendant (who is oftentimes a media

[54] Wade (n 18).

[55] See n 18.

[56] A cause of action arising directly out of the HRA would be sui generis, and would not need to fit into any existing category of legal action.

[57] G Phillipson, 'Clarity postponed: Horizontal Effect after *Campbell* and *Re. S*', in H Fenwick, R Masterman and G Phillipson (eds), *Judicial Reasoning under the UK Human Rights Act* (Cambridge, CUP, 2007) 152.

organisation) is likely to abandon its defence of the claim. This is boosted by the test in section 12 HRA, which effectively prevents the court from granting interim relief unless it is satisfied that the claimant is more likely than not to obtain permanent injunctive relief at trial. If, on the other hand, the attempt to obtain interim injunctive relief fails, then the information will swiftly be published, leaving the claimant with no privacy left to protect. Whilst a claim could still proceed to trial seeking damages only, such cases are rare – probably at least in part because the trial would revitalise public interest[58] in the information several months down the line, which the claimant may wish to avoid.

The availability of injunctive relief in MPI cases is one of the remaining links between that doctrine and its predecessor,[59] the equitable doctrine of confidentiality. Injunctive relief is a discretionary remedy available in circumstances where damages would not be adequate. Violations of privacy or confidence are classic circumstances where damages are unlikely to be adequate. As an exercise of discretion, the court has broad latitude over the factors it considers when deciding whether or not to grant injunctive relief (whether interim or permanent), and so is at liberty to consider the interests of third parties as part of that exercise. At first glance, this seems like a potentially viable rationalisation of the TPI doctrine. But it, too, is fraught with difficulty.

First, it would not properly reflect what the courts have actually been doing. In the third party cases, the courts have not separated their findings on liability and remedy in the way this approach would suggest. That is, the courts have not first decided that the defendant must be liable to the claimant *without* considering the interests of third parties, and then imposed a particular remedy (injunctive relief) *after* considering the interests of third parties. Rather, consideration of third party interests has demonstrably been undertaken *as part of* the 'new methodology' – the two-stage test for *liability* in MPI cases.[60] The third party interests come into play at stage 2 (the multi-factorial balancing exercise known as the 'ultimate balancing test'[61]), which is a necessary component of establishing liability. Put simply, if the claimant's interests, which may be bolstered by

[58] In the non-legal sense of being interesting to the public.

[59] I have argued elsewhere that the conclusions reached by the High Court and Court of Appeal in *Vidal-Hall* that MPI is tortious (and not equitable) are unconvincing (see Bennett (n 2)). Since neither the courts nor mainstream scholarship has managed to convincingly explain the interrelationship between MPI and the older doctrine of confidence, it is uncomfortable – and quite possibly inaccurate – to describe equitable confidence as MPI's 'predecessor'. I do so here only in the interests of simplifying the analysis, not as an endorsement of the description.

[60] For clarity: at stage one, the court determines whether the claimant has a 'reasonable expectation of privacy' in respect of the information that is the subject of the complaint. If such a reasonable expectation is established, the court proceeds to stage two, at which point it conducts a multi-factorial balancing exercise to determine whether the claimant's privacy rights outweigh the defendant's rights to freedom of expression and/or any public interest in receiving (via publication) the information. See *Campbell v Mirror Group Newspapers Ltd* [2004] UKHL 22, [2004] 2 AC 457, *Murray* (n 41), *Re S (A Child)* [2004] UKHL 47, [2005] 1 AC 593 and *Mosley v News Group Newspapers Ltd* [2008] EWHC 1777 (QB), [2008] EMLR 20.

[61] *Re S* (ibid) [17].

the interests of third parties, do not outweigh the defendant's interests (which may be bolstered by, or indeed entirely superseded by public interest in publication of the information) at this stage, the claim simply fails on its merits. So the approach described in this subsection – regarding third party interests as relevant because of the injunctive nature of the relief sought – simply does not reflect the process that the courts are following in these cases.

This is not the only problem with this approach. Let us postulate that the first objection could be overcome, and equitable considerations built simultaneously into the tests for liability and the award of a particular remedy. If this were to happen, the doctrine of MPI would have *at its core* an equitable exercise of discretion. This would put the doctrine in significant tension with recent judicial pronouncements that MPI is tortious and not equitable.[62] It might be argued that these recent judicial pronouncements are incorrect, and that MPI is best categorised as neither tortious nor equitable but as some (hitherto poorly-explained) hybrid tortious-cum-equitable action with a methodology rooted in European-style human rights jurisprudence (the 'ultimate balancing test'). But thus far no serious effort has been devoted to conceptualising MPI in that fashion, either in academic scholarship or courts' judgments. So it seems clear that, at this point at least, English and Welsh courts would be unlikely to find this option attractive.

D. The 'Family Unit' Approach

At this point, we reach options that represent more radical departures from the courts' established practices. The mere fact of this makes their adoption less likely, for they would require a departure from the close adherence to precedent that is characteristic of the 'narrow incrementalism' that is more instinctively appealing to British judges than its less doctrine-bound (but still principle-based) 'wide' variant.[63] Departing significantly from established practices is something that judges who incline to modes of judging that bear the hallmarks of legal formalism – which is most obviously on display in those places where judges openly appeal to the importance of 'legal certainty'[64] – are likely to eschew.

[62] See *Vidal-Hall v Google Inc* (HC and CA). See also Bennett (n 2).

[63] The terms 'narrow incrementalism' and 'wide incrementalism' were coined by L Dolding and R Mullender in 'Tort Law, Incrementalism, and the House of Lords' (1996) 47(1) *Northern Ireland Legal Quarterly* 12. I have examined their relevance to analysis of the development of MPI in Bennett (n 2) and 'Privacy' (n 3).

[64] See, eg, Lord Hoffmann's judgment in *Wainwright v Home Office* [2003] UKHL 53, [2004] 2 AC 406, and Baroness Hale's judgment in *Campbell* (n60), in which both judges appeal to the importance of legal certainty as justification for refusing to introduce significant doctrinal development (in the form of the recognition of a novel cause of action). More recently, the Court of Appeal made a similar appeal to legal certainty as its justification for refusing to countenance the imposition of a duty of care in negligence on a parent planning to publish autobiographical material that could have an adverse impact on their autistic child in *O v A* (n 47) [57].

Nonetheless, since it may be possible to pursue these approaches by adopting a 'wide' incrementalist mode of judging (which would be just as constitutionally legitimate as its narrow variant, in terms of being a legitimate exercise of judicial power), it is worth considering these more 'activist' possibilities.[65]

One of these is to reframe the privacy claim at the heart of MPI as a claim brought not by an individual simply on behalf of themselves, but as one instead brought on behalf of the claimant's entire family unit. This would involve significantly reconceptualising not only the nature of the privacy interest at the heart of the claim, but also the traditionally bilateral nature of private law claims in England and Wales. For the scope of the claim's potential reach would be determined (not entirely, but in significant part) by the size of the claimant's family unit.

Under existing MPI methodology (as best we are able to understand it, given the ambiguities we explored in section III), third party interests are not considered at stage one (when the court determines the reasonable expectation of privacy issue) but come into play at stage two (when the court conducts the 'ultimate balancing test'). But if the privacy claim at the heart of MPI is reframed as a claim of and relating to the claimant's family unit, then in the interests of coherence, the interests of the entire family unit must be relevant at *both* stages. Thus, when determining whether the claim discloses a reasonable expectation of privacy, the court would need to consider whether the family unit *as a whole* has a reasonable expectation of privacy in respect of the information.

The impact that this could have on the disposal of claims would be significant. Consider the (entirely hypothetical, obviously) example of a high-profile politician holding high public office who has fathered a number of children with different women, some as the result of extra-marital liaisons. Suppose that a journalist uncovers evidence that, despite recently marrying his current partner, this politician has fathered yet another child with another woman so recently that he must have done so during his current relationship. The journalist may well seek to publish this information, arguing that there is public interest in the character of this political figure.

Under standard MPI methodology at present, the court would first determine whether the politician has a reasonable expectation of privacy in respect of this information. It might well determine that he does not, or that his reasonable expectation is significantly reduced owing to his status as a public figure. If the latter is the case, the court would then proceed to stage two and *only at that point* would it consider the interests of his various children and partners when determining whether the public interest in his extra-curricular activities outweighs the harm that publishing the information would cause to his (and, as an incidental matter, their) private life.

[65] On the potential for 'wide incrementalism' to justify early developments in the TPI doctrine, see Bennett, 'Privacy' (n 3).

However, under the 'family unit' approach we are considering here, the court would consider the claimant's entire family unit together at stage one. Rather than dealing with a single, obviously high-profile individual, the court would be dealing with a family unit that includes one high-profile individual but which also includes a substantial number of people, including young children who are not public figures and who, prima facie, must be regarded as any other private figure.[66] *As a unit*, the family's claim would likely be stronger at stage one. This extra strength will improve the chances of the claim surviving the defendant's public interest-based arguments at stage two and thus may dramatically affect the claim's prospect of success.

The biggest conceptual impact that a reworking of the MPI doctrine in this manner would have would be to shift its focus from being on an *informational* right (to privacy) to a right based more broadly on the integrity and wellbeing of the family unit. Such a move would, however, be deeply controversial, for a number of reasons. First, there is no obvious precedent for such a claim in English and Welsh law. Second, it would not deal with the challenge that the TPI doctrine has posed for the traditionally bilateral structure of private law so much as simply abandon that structure *for this particular type of claim*. Third, it would cohere poorly with at least one significant decision in MPI in recent years – the conclusion (of both the High Court and the Court of Appeal) in *O v A* that an individual who is not themselves the subject of the information, but whose psychological integrity would be harmed by its publication, simply has no standing to bring a claim in MPI.[67] If this approach were to be adopted, *O v A* would surely have to be regarded as wrongly decided on this point. This would lead to a fourth objection – that the upending of *O v A*'s prohibition on non-subjects bringing MPI claims could well open the floodgates. In theory, *any* member of the family unit could be the instigator of the claim because the true claimant is not an individual but the family unit itself. This in turn leads to a fifth objection – that it is wholly unclear where the line will be drawn in terms of the relevance of the interests of third parties (who would, of course, at this point no longer be third parties but simply members of the claimant unit). I have used the term 'family unit' simply as a reflection of the fact that in most of the TPI cases, the third parties involved have been members of the claimant's family. But in the twenty-first century, the whole notion of what constitutes a 'family unit' has been significantly expanded. Certainly, it goes beyond the nuclear family, and would surely incorporate foster children, step-children/parents, the children that unmarried adults have had with previous partners, and may include house-mates, carers, and others who live in a relationship of dependency with one another. As a sixth objection, none of this would cohere well with the remainder of tort doctrine, which would remain untouched by such a reconceptualisation in MPI and thus would remain resolutely bilateral and individualistic.

[66] *Murray* (n 41).
[67] *O v A* (n 47) and in the High Court at [2014] EWHC 2468 (QB), [2015] All ER (D) 23 (Jun).

The sheer scale and complexity of the changes that such an approach would entail, and the obviously large number of potential objections – even in a brief sketch such as this – would make this an unpalatable choice. Unless enacted (presumably statutorily) as part of a broader package of similar reforms to private law, it is highly unlikely that such a reworking would be undertaken at common law.

E. The Incidental Family (or the 'It's the Claimant's Family Interest, Really') Approach

A variant on the previous approach should also be briefly mentioned, lest my failure to do so become the basis for an objection to my analysis. This would be an approach that justifies considering the interests of the claimant's family only incidentally, as evidence of the harm done to the claimant's private life. Under this approach, the claim would – as in the previous approach – be a broad one in respect of interference with private and family life, but the claimant would only be bringing the claim in respect of herself (and not her family). Should embarrassing private information about the claimant be published, so the argument would go, her relationship with her family members (the third parties) might be damaged.[68] And so evidence of the impact of publication upon those family members becomes relevant in order to establish the factual basis of the claimant's claim.

In addition to triggering most of the concerns identified by the previous approach, this approach would also be rather convoluted and procedurally would make little sense. For in order to protect the relationship between the claimant and her family members, her family members would have to be kept unaware of the embarrassing information. But they may also have to give evidence in respect of its impact upon them; at the very least, evidence of its impact upon them will need to be presented from *somewhere*.[69] These two things are not easily compatible. In practice, this approach would ensure that third party interests would, in many cases, have to be evidenced without the direct testimony of the third parties themselves, which would likely reduce the impact those interests would have on the court's decision-making.

[68] See *Rocknroll v News Group Newspapers Ltd* (n 25).

[69] It is not clear, from the judgments in *PJS*, whether third parties would ever be expected to give evidence personally. Lady Hale is ambiguous on this point at [73]–[74]. What is clear is that Lady Hale expects the court to rule on the basis of *some* evidence, though from where this might be obtained is a matter open to interpretation. It might be that the courts continue in the vein of *K*, in which Ward LJ effectively (though not describing it as such) inferred the potential for harm to the claimant's children from playground bullies, presumably from a combination of the breadth of the intended publication, the nature of the allegations and the fact that the children were of school age.

F. The 'Assumption of Responsibility' Approach

The final approach that might rationalise the TPI doctrine that I will consider here is of an even more 'left field' variety. It would involve drawing on the notion of 'assumption of responsibility' – a concept which justifies the imposition of liability in other parts of tort law – to justify holding the defendant prima facie liable for harm caused to the third parties.

It is now well-established in negligence law that a person who assumes responsibility for the interests of another may be held liable for a negligent failure to secure those interests, in circumstances where no liability would have accrued if there had been no such assumption of responsibility. For example, if I see a child standing in the middle of the road, I am generally under no legal obligation to rescue the child from on-coming traffic. But if I have assumed responsibility for the child – perhaps by agreeing to 'watch' the child while its parent attends to a parking meter – my failure to act will now attract liability.

The interests of third parties in MPI could perhaps be secured in an analogous way. If a defendant (for example, a print media outlet) seeks to publish private information about a claimant, and that defendant has actual or constructive notice that there are third parties who might be adversely affected by publication, then it might be said – by virtue of 'voluntarily' publishing the piece – to have assumed responsibility for their wellbeing.[70] If publication occurs, this approach morphs into one where the third parties become claimants in their own right: if this publication actually results in harm, then the defendant may be liable in damages not just to the subject of the information but also to the affect third parties. But at the interlocutory stage, where most MPI claims live and die, the publication would merely be intended (rather than actual), and the third parties would simply be third parties. The claimant would argue that, by voluntarily acquiring and intending to publish the information in circumstances where an adverse effect upon known third parties is objectively likely, the defendant has assumed responsibility for their wellbeing, and may therefore be enjoined from publication if there is evidence of this likely adverse effect.

There are, however, significant reasons to think that the courts would find this approach, too, unpalatable. First, it would explicitly, rather than tacitly, make defendants responsible for considering the well-being of parties beyond the subject of the information. This would raise coherence issues – for if defendants are responsible for third parties in MPI cases, it is unclear why they should not also be in other torts such as defamation. Second, there are – as Donal Nolan has pointed out – definitional problems with the assumption of responsibility doctrine.[71] Both the terms 'assumption' and 'responsibility' lack clear

[70] This would, of course, be a highly controversial argument, and one that is unlikely to survive the objections to it – particularly the third one identified below.

[71] D Nolan, 'Assumption of Responsibility: Four Questions' (2019) 72(1) *Current Legal Problems* 123.

definition in the case law. And even though Nolan himself has made a forceful argument as to the best way in which both terms may be coherently understood, it remains impossible to reconcile all of the existing case law on the doctrine with his preferred understandings – indicating that this remains an area of live controversy. Whether judges in MPI cases would be open to drawing this controversy into the field of MPI is doubtful.

The third and perhaps most serious problem posed by this approach is the lack of either explicit or implicit agreement by the defendant to undertake the task of looking out for either the claimant's or the third parties' well-being. Unlike in the example featuring a child in the road whom I have agreed to watch out for, most MPI defendants are media organisations pursuing journalistic activity for their own and their readers' benefit, not for the claimant or affected third parties. So, the courts would have to extend the doctrine of assumption of responsibility into new territory in order that mere *awareness* of the presence of third parties who might adversely be affected by publication would trigger the duty to ensure reasonable care is taken for their wellbeing. This would be a highly significant development in negligent law, with potentially far-reaching consequences. As such, it is something the courts are likely to eschew at present.

Fourth, even if the courts were minded to pursue such a significant extension of the law, this approach would still run into a practical problem. The problem is that the assumption of responsibility approach would not protect third parties of whom the defendant was not and could not reasonably have been aware. This would leave a gap in protection for any such third parties, although it might be thought that, overall, this strikes a defensible balance (since imposing liability on defendants for causing harm to individuals of whom they had no actual or constructive knowledge might produce considerable chilling effects).

Fifth, there is a particularly acute problem of coherence emanating from the *O v A* case. In *O v A*, the Supreme Court held that only the subject of the private information has standing to bring an MPI claim. The assumption of responsibility approach would be in tension with this (at least at trial for damages), since it would ultimately make those who are not the subject of the information the claimants. No lower court could issue a ruling so obviously in tension with *O v A*, and so the matter would require intervention from the Supreme Court – and we have seen, in *PJS*, that Court's reluctance to engage with these issues. There would also be a less problematic tension with the High Court and Court of Appeal judgments in *O v A*, which ruled out claims in negligence against the defendant. Since the assumption of responsibility doctrine emerged from negligence law, it might be thought that the Court of Appeal's firm denial (albeit not supported by any cited authority) that there could be no duty of care imposed upon parents in respect of decisions pertaining to their child's upbringing (including the autobiographical publication of potentially distressing facts about a parent) should also be taken to rule out the imposition of such a duty as a result of the assumption of responsibility doctrine. However, since assumption of responsibility appears not to have been expressly argued (it is certainly not mentioned in the judgments), this is perhaps less immediately problematic.

G. Abolish the TPI Doctrine

The final option we will consider here is the simple abolition of the TPI doctrine. Rather than attempting to rationalise it – and inevitably encountering the difficulties outlined above – the courts could simply abolish it, and declare that only the interests of the parties are relevant in determining a claim in MPI. The attractiveness of this option lies in its provision of a simple solution to the problems with the competing lines of authority in this area identified in section III. However, there are reasons to conclude that the courts would find this option, too, unpalatable.

These reasons derive from the obvious keenness of the courts to consider the interests of third parties. It is quite clear from the competing lines of authority that, despite obvious doctrinal difficulties with them, the courts have nonetheless been keen that the interests of third parties should form part of their decision-making. This is in all likelihood a reflection of the normative appeal of finding novel ways to protect children from being adversely affected by publicity given to their parents' actions. This has been thematic in MPI cases for several years. Even before the TPI doctrine emerged, claims were creatively pleaded; in some, the children acted as the claimants, since they were more likely to succeed – particularly where the parents were public figures but the children were not.[72]

It is also clear, from the judgments in *PJS*, that whilst the Supreme Court is reluctant to rationalise the doctrine, it is keen to see it remain – and perhaps even flourish – as a component of MPI. The Court's endorsement of the doctrine may be bare and intellectually unhelpful, but it is nonetheless a powerful indicator that the Court regards the TPI doctrine as a normatively desirable part of tort law. It thus seems highly unlikely that the Court would perform the abrupt about-turn necessary to abolish it.

VI. CONCLUSION

The third party interests doctrine in MPI is a mess. It is conceptually incoherent, lacks a clear formal basis, and causes the entire cause of action for MPI to stick out in tort law like a proverbial sore thumb. It is easy to criticise the Supreme Court for failing, in *PJS*, to deal with this situation. But it is more useful to try to understand why it so failed. It is possible, of course, that the Court simply did not apprehend the degree of the challenges that the TPI doctrine poses for English and Welsh law, and that, having failed to appreciate its significance, it saw no

[72] *Murray* and *Weller* (both n 49).

reason to address it. But it may also be the case that the Court realised that it had no good options. For whilst it is possible to rationalise the TPI doctrine, doing so involves making hard choices. Each of the options considered in this chapter – albeit necessarily briefly – appear to have some unappealing features. Whichever path is taken will involve trade-offs between competing interests.

No doubt a compelling normative argument could be made for the adoption of one or more of the approaches outlined in this chapter. And indeed there may well be others that I have not thought of – the list is unlikely to be exhaustive – that might also be the subject of a persuasive argument in favour of adoption. But it is apparent that none will satisfy everyone, and some would cause more consternation than others.

PJS is a landmark case in English and Welsh privacy law. But it is a landmark for a rather ignominious reason. It is the case in which the UK's highest court could have taken a stance on an important issue of live controversy and conceptual confusion, but in which it did not do so. This failure may be forgivable. But the problems associated with the TPI doctrine will not go away. And some day, they will need to be reckoned with.

Index

Act to prevent the unauthorised use of the name on pictures of any person for the purposes of trade, An (US, 1903), 32
action in privacy in British Columbia, 252–3 (case law)
addictive drugs prescriptions, patient's identity protected, 72–3
***American Cyanamid* principles,** 233
appropriation (US), 32–3
  name or likeness, of, 33
Article 8 ECHR:
  Article 10 ECHR, balance with, 149, 175–6, 178–9
  Campbell case, interpreted in, 163
  discussion of, 187–8 (case law)
  interpretation of, 172–3
  invasion of privacy, 160
  no priority over Article 10, 176–7
  privacy tort, 171
  right to private life under, 15, 99, 137, 146, 194–5
  telling one's own story, 146
  TPI, justification of, and, 306–8 (case law)
  Von Hannover case, prior to, 191–2
  vertical and horizontal human rights cases, differences between not recognised, 316–17
  violations in, 202 (case law)
Article 10 ECHR:
  Article 8 ECHR and, 175–6, 176–7, 178–9
  confidentiality and, 142
  debate of general interest and, 149–50
  freedom of expression under, 182
Article 29 Working Party Guidelines (2014) on data protection, 275
assumption of responsibility doctrine, 323–5
  courts' approach to, 323–5
  defendant's requirement to look out for, claimant or third party, 324
  subjects of information can be claimants, 324–5
  third parties, lack of support for, 324
Australian:
  courts, breach of contract considered in, 122–3
  legislation, disclosure of to press, 125 (case law)
Australian Broadcasting Corporation (ABC), negligence action against, 111 (case law)
Australian Law Reform Commission (ALRC) and privacy law reform, 128–30
Australian privacy law:
  English and New Zealand privacy law, impact on, 126–8
  reform of, 128–30

balancing criteria:
  courts' approach to post-*Von Hannover* (2), 201
  domestic courts, in, 202
  underlying interests, use of, 181–2
'best interests of the child', 309–11 (case law), 314–16
  PJS case, in, 312–13
Bill of Rights Bill 2022, clause 4 and protection of free speech, 184–5
breach of confidence, 207–8 (case law)
  Australian courts' treatment of, 122–3
  breach of privacy cases involving, 138–9
  Douglas v Hello! Ltd, in, 211–12
  English and Australian approaches to, 124
  filming sexual intercourse, 120–1 (case law)
  head of damages as non-pecuniary losses, 224–5
  'instantaneous' photography and, 13
  MOPI and, 169–71, 213–14
  photographic cases, in, 9–10
  photographic sitters' rights and, 9–10
  photographs and images cited in cases, 10–11
  photography, application to, 15–17
  professional photographers' use of photos, 10–11
  protection of privacy, and instantaneous photography, 13–14
  reliance on, 100–1
  sharing explicit images and videos, 121–2 (case law)
breach of contract and photography, 7–9

breach of privacy cases included in breach of confidence cases, 138–9
British Columbia Privacy Act 1996, 252, 259

Calcutt Committee (1989), 92
new offences suggested by, 96–7
press ethics and self-regulation suggested by, 97
publication and proposals of (1990), 96–7
Campbell, Naomi, drug addiction:
CA judgment, 163–5
HL judgment, 165–9
treatment, *Mirror*'s publication of details, 161–3
celebrity and media interests (Australia), 135
children:
legal actions concerning, 315–16
photographing, 202–3 (case law)
television interviews with, 203 (case law)
third parties, as, 309–10 (case law)
circuit courts' (US) failure to enforce constitutional informational privacy, 79–80
class action certification, application for, 251
Cobb, Justice Andrew Jackson, *Pavesich* judgment, 47–8
common law:
claim, invasion of privacy as, 246–56
damages at, 223
development of, and human rights and values, 160
no right of privacy in, 98
common law privacy right, 99
US state Supreme Court upholds, 40
compensation:
calculation of, 289–90
individual awards, calculation of, 290
MOPI, for, 287–90
privacy cases, for, 223–4
reputational harm, for, 295
compensatory damages, 223–7
filming of claimants, for, 292
confidential:
information, photographic image as, 113 (case law)
relationship and contractual relationship, 14–15
confidentiality:
Article 10 rights for, 142
human rights principle, is not, 168
sexual encounters, in, women's views on, 142–3
confidentiality/privacy:
relationship between parties, and, 139–40
test, 138–47
constitutional right of informational privacy, 77–8
circuit courts' failure to enforce, 79–80
examples of, 78–9
contractual relationship and confidential relationship, 14–15
control orders, 307 (case law)
'controller' defined, 268
Court of Appeal:
Campbell judgment, 163–5
Gulati ruling, 290–1
right to privacy, statements on, 93–4
courts:
assumption of responsibility doctrine, approach to, 323–5
balancing criteria post-*Von Hannover (2)*, approach to, 201
consideration of public interest against privacy intrusion, 182–3

Daily Star **(newspaper),** 89
damages:
common law, at, 223
compensatory *see* compensatory damages
head of *see* head of damages
human autonomy and dignity, protection of, 287–8
infringement of privacy, for, 283, 288
MOPI, for, 226–7, 284–6
negotiating *see* negotiating damages
no award after internet search engine delisting, 293–4
nominal, 223
right, infringement of, for, 226–7
'user damages', 296–7
vindicatory *see* vindicatory damages
damages awards:
claim for MOPI, 294
Jones case, in, 249–50
privacy claims and, 282–3
data:
breaches, class action for (Canada), 254–5 (case law)
dissemination, internet search engines' responsibilities, 264–5
'loss of control' of, negotiating damages for, 229–30

data protection:
Article 29 Working Party Guidelines on, 275
Authorities (DPAs), 261
European Data Protection Board on, 275
Google Spain case's effect on, 278–9
guidance and regulation for, 275–6
internet search engines' 'controller' responsibilities, 266
proportionality and, 268
debate of general interest, 200
Article 10 (ECHR) and, 149–50
photographs' role in, 198–9
skiing holiday photos, 199–200
defamation cases, awards compared with privacy cases awards, 284
defamation law:
Australia, in, 132–5
HQ magazine, action against, 132–3
protection of law of privacy through, 132–5
delisting:
material from search engines, 263–4
personal data, guidelines for, 265, 270
derogatory clauses and GDPR, 275
detective cameras, 6
Diana, Princess of Wales, death of, 192
disclosure of contact information (Canada), dismissal of motion, 252 (case law)
disclosure of information:
sexual relationship or encounter, about, 144–5
therapeutic and private information, action on, 145
unwarranted and undue, 76
doctrine of confidence, 99–100
private information, expanded to cover, 98–9

elected office holders as role models, 153–4
emotional distress, filming sexual intercourse, 120–1 (case law)
English privacy law, Australian privacy law's impact on, 127–8
equal universal rights and substantive inequality, 54–5
equity considered in Australia, 123–4 (case law)
European Data Protection Board on data protection, 275

Facebook, unauthorised use of name or portrait, 259
family unit approach:
claimant's family incidental interests, 322
MOPI cases, in, 320–1
federal government, personal information held by protected, 80–1
fiduciary obligation, breach of, summary judgment motion, 239–40
financial records, illegal checking of, 238–9 (case law)
first instance courts (Canada), application of *Jones* case in, 251–2
Flitcroft, Garry, 155–7
Leveson Inquiry evidence, 156
Franklin Mills poster, consequences of publication, 19–20
free speech:
Bill of Rights Bill 2022 clause 4 protection of, 184–5
interests and privacy, 142, 149, 150–1
freedom of expression, 231–2
Article 10, under, 182
interference with the press and, 148
privacy and, 139, 151
public interest, conterminous with, 148–50
respect for private life and, 201
freedom of speech balanced with privacy rights, 161

General Data Protection Regulation (GDPR), 82, 262
derogatory clauses and, 275
Georgia Supreme Court:
Pavesich appeal to, 45–6
Pavesich judgment delivered, 40–2
Google Inc, location of operators, consequences of, 276–7
***Google Spain*:**
active intermediary services, control of, 270–1
removal of personal data, 265

harassment, 117–18 (case law)
climate of, photos obtained in, 197
harm, reputational, compensation for, 295
Harty, Russell, 91
hate speech, criminalisation of 204
head of damages:
breach of right, for, 225
non-pecuniary losses as, in breach of confidence cases, 224–5
***Hello!* magazine, publication of unauthorised photographs,** 208–9
'high offensiveness' test, 163–4
***HQ* magazine, defamation action against,** 132–3

human:
autonomy and dignity, infringement of, damages for, 287–8
concern and awareness, HL consideration of, 166–7
human rights:
Australia, lack of in, 133–4
confidential personal data, storage of and, 73–4
principle, confidentiality is not, 168
values, and, common law development and, 160
vertical and horizontal cases, Article 8's failure to distinguish between, 316–17
Human Rights Act, section 12 test, interim or permanent relief, 318

image control, 219–22
privacy claim and, 219–20
Independent Press Standards Organisation (IPSO) code, 313 (case law)
individual:
autonomy and privacy, 50
self-ownership (Lockean), 52–3
inequality, substantive, and equal universal rights, 54–5
information:
acquisition of and MOPI, 298–9
confidential, 222
informational privacy, 69–70
constitutional *see* constitutional informational privacy
federal laws for, 81–2
NASA v Nelson case, 74–9
violation of and MOPI, 281–2
informational self-determination, 69
infringement of privacy:
damages for, 288
information-gathering methods, 91
vindicatory damages for, 266
injunctions:
discharge and reinstatement of (TPI), 311–12
Douglas cases, in, 231–4
interim *see* interim injunctions
interlocutory, establishment of cause of action and, 115–16
pre-trial, and libel claim, 94
injunctive relief:
private information for, 307 (case law)
remedy for MOPI cases, 317–18

instantaneous photography:
breach of confidence and, 13
protection of privacy and, 13–14
interim injunctions, 232–3
discharge of, 233–4
granting, identifying cause of action for, 110–17 (case law)
interim relief, HRA section 12 test prevents granting of, 318
internet search engines:
controller's role and power over removing personal data (Spanish), 266–9
delisting, no damages award after, 293–4
dissemination of data, responsibility for, 264–5
intermediary role in information distribution, 266
'interpretation' and Victorian technology, 2–5
intrusion:
drug addiction treatment, in, 166
Gordon Kaye, suffered by, 96, 97, 104
MOPI claim and, 299
personal privacy, into, 119, 128, 139, 172, 182
press, 192
tabloid press (UK), 90–1, 92
intrusion upon seclusion (US tort), 33, 246–50
British Columbia, in, 252–3 (case law)
Canada, in, 254–5 (case law)
Canadian courts' interpretation of *Jones* case, 250–5
concept of, 248–9
right of action for, 241
invasion of privacy, 34, 117–18 (case law), 119–20 (case law)
Article 8 ECHR and, 160
Australia, in, 126, 134
common law claim, as, 246–56
false light, 257–8 (case law)
filming sexual intercourse, 120–1 (case law)
Gordon Kaye, of, 86–7
McDonald's Restaurants of Canada Ltd case, in, 248
negligent, 118–19 (case law)
summary judgment, motion for, 239–40
Irish Data Protection Commissioner, 2017 Annual Report, 276

Jet Propulsion Laboratory (JPL), 74–5 (case law)
journalism, public interest, distinguished from gossip journalism, 182
judicial precedents, reading of (nineteenth century), 3–4

Kaye, Gorden, 90
invasion of privacy, 86–7 (case law)
malicious falsehood, claim for, 94–5
Kerslake Report (2018), 103–4
King of the Kastle proceedings, 132

law and media, changes in, 103–4
law of privacy:
defamation and, 132–5
development of (Australia), 124–6
lack of test cases for, 131
Law of Torts (US), First and Second Restatements, 32, 33
legal:
interpretation, consequences of, 3–4
parent-child relationship, establishment of, 146–7
Leveson Inquiry (2021), 103
Garry Flitcroft's evidence to, 156
libel claims:
Pavesich's upheld, 46–7
pre-trial injunctions and, 94
libel (New York, 1900), 25–6
liberty and privacy rights, 49–50
Lockean natural rights, development of, 40

Mackenzie, Sir Morrell, right of privacy invaded, 24–5
malicious falsehood, Kaye's claim for, 94–5
media:
interest, consequences of, 156–7
tabloid market (Australia), 134–5
media and celebrity interests (Australia), 135
medical files, illegal access to (Canada), 252 (case law)
medication theft (Canada), 252 (case law)
Microsoft Bing, removal of personal data, 265
misappropriation (US), 32
misuse of private information (MOPI), 207–8, (case law), 212–13, 220, 281–2
acquisition of information and, 298–9
'assumption of responsibility' doctrine, 323–5
breach of confidence and, 169–71, 213–14
claim and intrusion, 299
claim for, damages award as right, 294
damages for, 226–7, 284–6
family unit approach, cases in, 320–1
heads of compensation, 287–90
information privacy, violation of, 281–2
injunctive relief is remedy for, 317–18
judgments, *Gulati's* impact on, 291–2
liability for deliberate act, 294
respect for privacy under, 295
tort, confirmed as, 303–5
misuse of private information (MOPI) action, 142
telling one's own story, 146–7
therapeutic disclosure, 145
misuse of private information (MOPI) cases:
judges' approach to, 319–20
liability two-stage test for, 318–19
'modern sexual relations', relationship of parties considered, 140–1

National Agency Check with Inquiries (NACI), 75–6
natural right to privacy, *Pavesich* judgment, in, 49–51
negligence, cause of action in, against ABC, 111 (case law)
negotiating damages, 227–30
compensatory nature of, 227–8
'loss of control' of data, for, 229–30
privacy cases, for, 228–9
Neighbors, The (art photographs), 34–7
court trials, 36–7
privacy action over, 36–7
Svenson's photographic methods, 35–6
New York Court of Appeals, right to privacy, judgment on, 29–31
New York courts, Restatement torts rejected by, 34
New York State Controlled Substances Act 1972, 70
unconstitutionality of, 71
New York State, reporting and record-keeping requirements of, 71
New Zealand privacy law, Australian privacy law's impact on, 126–7
Newspaper Publishers' Association Code of Practice 1989, 92
newspapers and right to privacy, 22

***OK!* magazine, publication of photographs in,** 209–10

'Paradise Papers' (Australia), 124–5 (case law)
parent-child relationship, disclosure of, 147
paternity claims, photographic proof of, 217–18
***Pavesich* judgment,** 47–53
natural law aspects, 50–1
racial bias in, 58
slavery analogy, 56–8

Pavesich, Paulo:
appeal to Georgia Supreme Court, 45–6
artistic career, 42–4
case details (1904), 45
legal legacy of case, 61
media comment on case, 60–1
post-trial consequences, 59
privacy action over use of image, 44
personal data:
delisting, guidelines for, 269, 270
individuals' right of privacy against the government, 73
removal of from *Google Spain*, 262–3 (case law)
storage of and human rights, 73–4
Personal Health Information Protection Act 2004 (PHIPA) (Ontario), 245
personal information:
legal protection for (US), 65–8
Personal Information Privacy and Electronic Documents Act (PIPEDA) (2000) 240, 245, 246
US government duty to protect, 72
personal privacy, invasion of, 237–8
personal security and privacy rights, 49–50
personality, appropriation of, 258–9 (case law)
phone hacking, 248–6 (case law)
photographic:
sitters' rights and breach of confidence, 9–10
technology, development of, 40
photographic images:
confidential information, can be, 113
misuse of, 40
photographs:
climate of harassment, obtained in, 197
debate of general interest, role in, 198–9
OK! magazine, publication of in, 209–10
paternity claims, proof of, 217–18
privacy interests in, 215–19
privacy intrusion, are proof of, 218–19 (case law)
private information in, 216–17
'private matters' in public places, limited to, 197
publication of, injunctions against, 141–2, 215–16
skiing holiday in St Moritz, taken on, 199–20
'time of publication or taking of' 197–8
unauthorised published in *Hello!* magazine, 208–9
photography:
application of law to, 4–5
breach of confidence applied to, 10–11 (case law), 15–17
breach of contract and, 7–9
children, of, 202–3 (case law)
'instantaneous' *see* instantaneous photography
privacy and, 4–5
private sitters' rights and, 7–9
right to privacy and, 6
pre-trial injunction and libel claim, 94
prescription painkillers and informational privacy, 70
press:
ethics and self-regulation, Calcutt Committee, suggested by, 97
freedom, lawyers' opinions on, 101
interference with and freedom of expression, 148
intrusion (UK), 90–1
Princess Caroline von Hannover, paparazzi harassment of, 192–3
privacy:
case law, 187–8
common law, no right to in, 98, 108–10
concept of, 190–1
corporate, 113–15 (case law)
enforceable right to, 112
free speech and, 142, 149, 150–1
freedom of expression and, 138–9, 151
individual autonomy and, 50
invasion of *see* invasion of privacy
law reform and ALRC, 128–30
legislation, 244–6
natural right to (*Pavesich* judgment), 49–51
photography and, 4–5, 215–19
protection of via defamation, 132–5
public spaces, excluded in, 195
reasonable expectation of test, 139
society in, 243–4
theory, generally, 189–90
violation and disclosure of private information, 248 (case law)
Privacy Act 1974 (US), 80–1
Privacy Act 1988 (Australia), 130
privacy cases:
awards compared with defamation cases awards, 284
compensation in, 223–4
negotiating damages in, 228–9

privacy claims:
claimant's family, initially brought by, 320–1
damages awards and, 282–3
failure of, 41–2
image control and, 219–20
Pavesich's upheld, 46–7
wrongs and remedies of, relationship between, 297–8
privacy intrusion, 207–8 (case law)
courts' consideration of against public interest, 182–3
photographs are proof of, 218–19 (case law)
privacy rights:
class aspects of, 53–4
freedom of speech, balanced with, 161
gender, race, class and, 55–6, 62
infringement of and damages, 283, 288
liberty and, 49–50
personal security and, 49–50
US Constitution, under, 67
Von Hannover case, in, 196–7
privacy tort:
Canada, in, 253–4
law, 12–13
stages of (Article 8 ECHR), 171
private:
banking information, intrusion into, 244
law claims and section 6 cases, differences between, 307–8
matters, photographs of in public places, 197
nuisance (Australia), 108–10 (case law)
property, trespassing on, 111 (case law)
sitters' rights in photography, 7–9
private information:
commercialisation of, 221–2
concept of, 190
control of, 295–6
disclosure of and privacy violation, 248 (case law)
doctrine of confidence expanded to cover, 98–9
injunctive relief issues, 307 (case law)
misuse of *see* misuse of private information
photographs, in, 216–17
prohibition of publication of, 306–7 (case law)
publication of, legislation against, 91–2
recognition of, 166
voicemail messages, obtained from, 284–6
private life:
Article 8 ECHR, interpretation of under, 194–5
respect for and freedom of expression, 201
Von Hannover case, in, 191, 194
property:
notions (Lockean), 51–2
Pavesich, interpreted in, 62
proportionality:
A v B & C case, in, 177–8
Campbell case, in, 177, 179
data protection and, 268
Prosser's privacy torts, 255–9
protection of privacy, 244–6, 298–9
caution over expansion of, 99
instantaneous photography and, 13–14
nineteenth century, in, 1
professional photographers' use of photographs and, 10–11
public:
places, privacy excluded in, 195
private and, distinction between, 200–1
public disclosure:
establishment of liability for, 257
private facts, of, 256–7
public figures:
private lives, public scrutiny of, 151–2
role models, as, 153
public interest:
Campbell case, in, 179
courts' consideration of against privacy intrusion, 182–3
freedom of expression, conterminous with, 148–50
judges' approach to, 150–1
publication of lectures and breach of confidence on trust, 10
Publicity Given to Private Life (US tort), 33
Publicity Placing Person in False Light (US tort), 33

race-course fences (Australia), 108–10 (case law)
racial bias in *Pavesich* judgment, 58
reading:
legal interpretation of, 3–4
self-reflexive practice of, 3–4
'reasonable expectation test', 160
HL consideration of, 71–2
'reasonable or legitimate expectation of privacy', 195–6
relationship of parties in 'modern sexual relations', 140–1
Resolution 1165 (Council of Europe, 1995), 192

Restatement torts (US), New York courts' rejection of, 34
Richard, Sir Cliff OBE, damages award, 292–3
right of privacy:
- Australian case law, 108–10
- CA statements on, 93–4
- definition, 33
- informational (MOPI), 321–2
- invasion of (1900), 20 (case law)
- none in common law, 98
- Sir Morrell Mackenzie's invaded, 24–5

'right to be forgotten', 264
right to privacy, 21, 22–3
- appeals against *Roberson* case (1900), 27–9
- arguments for in *Roberson* case (1900), 26–7
- Article 8 ECHR and, 15, 99, 137, 146
- establishment of, 22–3
- individual's in personal data against the government (US), 73
- New York Court of Appeal's judgment (1900), 29–31
- New York courts' approach to, 37–8
- newspapers and, 22
- nineteenth century case law, 1–2
- opposition to (Australia), 125 (case law)
- photography and, 6
- quasi-constitutional status of, 241–3 (case law)
- US, in, 23–4
- Warren and Brandeis's article (1890), 12–14, 20–1
- women's images, of, 23

right to talk, protected, 146–7
rights:
- breach of and head of damages, 225
- infringement of, damages awarded for, 226–7

role models, 153–5
- sports players as, 154

search engine indexing, 270, 271–2, 273
- legal and data protection considerations, 272–4

search engines:
- delisting material from, 263–4
- geographical range of, 277–8
- responsibility of, 270
- 'secluded place', interpretation of, 194

section 6 cases and private law claims, differences between, 307–8
sexual encounters and relationships:
- disclosure of information about, 144–5
- women's views on confidentiality, 142–3

sexual intercourse filming, emotional distress after, 120–1
slavery analogy, *Pavesich* judgment, in, 56–8
society, privacy and technology in, 243–4
special data derogation, 274–5
speech:
- claims, 180–1
- hierarchy, *Campbell* case, in, 181
- privacy case, 'putting the record straight', 179–80

sports players as role models, 154
***'Spycatcher'* case (1990),** 15–17
***Sunday Sport* (newspaper),** 88–9
- 1990 Gordon Kaye article, 95–6
- post-Kaye developments, 101–2

Svenson, Arne (art photographer), 34–7

tabloid:
- culture (1980's) (UK), 87–9
- intrusion, 90–1
- papers (UK), examples of, 87–8

technological advances and right to privacy, 22
technology in society, 243–4
telephone calls, harassing, 247–8 (case law)
third parties:
- assumption of responsibility doctrine, lack of support for, 234
- children as, 309–10 (case law)

'third party interests' doctrine (TPI), 302, 304–5, 308 (case law)
- abolition of, courts' reasons against, 325
- 'best interests of the child', focus on, 309–11 (case law)
- injunction discharged and reinstated, 311–12
- justification of, 306–8
- lines of authority, 305–6
- *PJS* case, in, 311–14

tort law, bilateralism of, 303–4

unconscionability concept, 111, 112, 115, 116
underlying interests used in balancing interests, 181–2

United Nations Convention on the Rights of the Child (UNCRC) Article 3, 314–15, 316
  adults interests not covered, 316
United States Constitution, privacy right under, 67

vindicatory damages, 288–9
  infringement of privacy, for, 226
voicemail messages, private information obtained from, 284–6

Warren, Samuel, personal interest in desire for privacy, 21–2
women's images and right to privacy, 23
Wragg, Paul, *Campbell* case, critique of, 173–4
writing, self-reflexive practice of, 3–4

Printed in the USA
CPSIA information can be obtained
at www.ICGtesting.com
LVHW021520021124
795463LV00003B/122

9 781509 940769